Lecture Notes in Computer Science 6787

Commenced Publication in 1973
Founding and Former Series Editors:
Gerhard Goos, Juris Hartmanis, and Jan

Joseph A. Konstan   Ricardo Conejo
José L. Marzo   Nuria Oliver (Eds.)

User Modeling, Adaption, and Personalization

19th International Conference, UMAP 2011
Girona, Spain, July 11-15, 2011
Proceedings

 Springer

Volume Editors

Joseph A. Konstan
University of Minnesota
Department of Computer Science and Engineering
4-192 Keller Hall, Minneapolis, MN 55455, USA
E-mail: konstan@cs.umn.edu

Ricardo Conejo
Universidad de Málaga, E.T.S. Ing. Informatica
Boulevard Lois Pasteur, 35, Malaga 29071, Spain
E-mail: conejo@lcc.uma.es

José L. Marzo
University of Girona, EPS Edifici P-IV (D.208)
Campus de Montilivi, Girona 17071, Spain
E-mail: joselius.marzo@udg.edu

Nuria Oliver
Telefonica R& D, Via Augusta, 177
Barcelona 08021, Catalonia, Spain
E-mail: nuriao@tid.es

ISSN 0302-9743   e-ISSN 1611-3349
ISBN 978-3-642-22361-7   e-ISBN 978-3-642-22362-4
DOI 10.1007/978-3-642-22362-4
Springer Heidelberg Dordrecht London New York

Library of Congress Control Number: 2011930852

CR Subject Classification (1998): H.3, I.2, H.4, H.5, C.2, I.4

LNCS Sublibrary: SL 3 – Information Systems and Application, incl. Internet/Web
and HCI

Typesetting: Camera-ready by author, data conversion by Scientific Publishing Services, Chennai, India

Printed on acid-free paper

Springer is part of Springer Science+Business Media (www.springer.com)

Preface

The 19th International Conference on User Modeling, Adaptation and Personalization (UMAP 2011) took place in Girona, Spain, during July 11–15, 2011. It was the third annual conference under the UMAP title, which resulted from the merger in 2009 of the successful biannual User Modeling (UM) and Adaptive Hypermedia (AH) conference series. Over 700 researchers from 45 countries were involved in creating the technical program, either as authors or as reviewers.

The Research Paper Track of the conference was chaired by Joseph A. Konstan from the University of Minnesota, USA, and Ricardo Conejo from the Universidad de Málaga, Spain. They were assisted by an international Program Committee of 80 leading figures in the AH and UM communities as well as highly promising younger researchers. Papers in the Research Paper Track were reviewed by three or more reviewers, with disagreements resolved through discussion among the reviewers, and the summary opinion reported in a meta review. The conference solicited Long Research Papers of up to 12 pages in length, which represent original reports of substantive new research. In addition, the conference solicited Short Research Papers of up to 6 pages in length, whose merit was assessed more in terms of originality and importance than maturity and technical validation. The Research Paper Track received 164 submissions, with 122 in the long and 42 in the short paper category. Of these, 27 long and 6 short papers were accepted, resulting in an acceptance rate of 22.13% for long papers, 14.29% for short papers, and 20.12% overall. Many authors of rejected papers were encouraged to revise their work and to resubmit it to conference workshops or to the Poster and Demo Tracks of the conference.

The Industry Paper Track was chaired by Enrique Frias-Martinez, from Telefonica Research in Spain, and Marc Torrens, from Strands Labs in Spain. This track covered innovative commercial implementations or applications of UMAP technologies, and experience in applying recent research advances in practice. Submissions to this track were reviewed by a separate Industry Paper Committee with 14 leading industry researchers and practitioners. Of 8 submissions that were received, 3 were accepted.

The conference also included a Doctoral Consortium, a forum for PhD students to get feedback and advice from a Doctoral Consortium Committee of 17 leading UMAP researchers. The Doctoral Consortium was chaired by Julita Vassileva from the University of Saskatchewan, Canada, and Liliana Ardissono, Universitá degli Studi di Torino, Italy. This track received 27 submissions of which 15 were accepted.

The traditional Poster and Demo Session of the conference was chaired by Slivia Baldiris, Universitat de Girona, Spain, and Nicola Henze, University of Hannover, Germany, and Fabian Abel, Delft University of Technology, The Netherlands. As of the time of writing, the late submission deadline is still 2 months away, and hence the number of acceptances is still unknown. We expect that this session will again have featured dozens of lively posters and system demonstrations. Summaries of these presentations will be published in online adjunct proceedings.

The UMAP 2011 program also included Workshops and Tutorials that were selected by Chairs Tsvi Kuflik, University of Haifa, Israel, and Liliana Ardissono, Universitá degli Studi di Torino, Italy. The following tutorials were offered:

- Personalization, Persuasion, and Everything In-between, taught by Shlomo Berkovsky and Jill Freyne
- Designing Adaptive Social Applications, taught by Julita Vassileva and Jie Zhang
- Designing and Evaluating New-Generation User Modeling, taught by Frederica Cena and Cristina Gena

And the following workshops were organized:

- SASWeb: Semantic Adaptive Social Web, chaired by Frederica Cena, Antonina Dattolo, Ernesto William De Luca, Pasquale Lops, Till Plumbaum and Julita Vassileva
- PALE: Personalization Approaches in Learning Environments, chaired by Alexander Nussbaumer, Diana Pérez-Marin, Effie Law, Jesus G. Boticario, Milos Kravcik, Noboru Matsuda, Olga C. Santos and Susan Bull
- DEMRA: Decision Making and Recommendation Acceptance Issues in Recommender Systems, chaired by Francesco Ricci, Giovanni Semeraro, Marco de Gemmis and Pasquale Lops
- AUM: Augmenting User Models with Real-World Experiences to Enhance Personalization and Adaptation, chaired by Fabian Abel, Vania Dimitrova, Eelco Herder and Geert-Jan Houbert
- UMMS: User Models for Motivational Systems: The Affective and the Rational Routes to Persuasion, chaired by Floriana Grasso, Jaap Ham and Judith Masthoff
- TRUM: Trust, Reputation and User Modeling, chaired by Julita Vassileva and Jie Zhang
- ASTC: Adaptive Support for Team Collaboration, chaired by Alexandros Paramythis, Lydia Lau, Stavros Demetriadis, Manolis Tzagarakis and Styliani Kleanthouse
- UMADR: User Modeling and Adaptation for Daily Routines: Providing Assistance to People with Special and Specific Needs, chaired by Estefania Martin, Pablo A. Haya and Rosa M. Carro

Finally, the conference also featured two invited talks. The invited speakers were:

- Ricardo Baeza-Yates, Yahoo! Research, on the topic: "User Engagement: A Scientific Challenge"
- Paul Resnick, University of Michigan, on the topic: "Does Personalization Lead to Echo Chambers?"

In addition to all the contributors mentioned, we would also like to thank the Local Arrangements Chair Ramon Fabregat from the University of Girona, Spain, and the Publicity Chair Eelco Herder from L3S Research Center in Germany. We deeply acknowledge the conscientious work of the Program Committee members and the additional reviewers, who are listed on the next pages. The conference would not have been possible without the work of many "invisible" helpers. We also gratefully acknowledge our sponsors who helped us with funding and organizational expertise: User Modeling Inc., ACM SIGART, SIGCHI and SIGIR, the Chen Family Foundation, Microsoft Research, the U.S. National Science Foundation, Springer, Telefonica de España, and the University of Girona. Finally, we want to acknowledge the use of EasyChair for the management of the review process and the preparation of the proceedings, and the help of its administrator Andrei Voronkov in implementing system enhancements that this conference had commissioned.

April 2011

Joseph A. Konstan
Ricardo Conejo
Jose L. Marzo
Nuria Oliver

Organization

UMAP 2011 was organized by the Institute of Informatics and Applications, Universitat de Girona, Spain, in cooperation in cooperation with User Modeling Inc., ACM/SIGIR, ACM/SIGCHI and ACM/SIGART. The conference took place during July 11–15, 2011 at Centre Cultural la Mercè, City Hall of Girona, Spain.

Organizing Committee

General Co-chairs

Jose L. Marzo	University of Girona, Spain
Nuria Oliver	Telefonica Research, Spain

Program Co-chairs

Joseph A. Konstan	University of Minnesota, USA
Ricardo Conejo	Universidad de Málaga, Spain

Industry Track Co-chairs

Enrique Frias-Martinez	Telefonica Research, Spain
Marc Torrens	Strands Labs, Spain

Workshop and Tutorial Co-chairs

Tsvi Kuflik	University of Haifa, Israel
Liliana Ardissono	Università degli Studi di Torino, Italy

Doctoral Consortium Co-chairs

Julita Vassileva	University of Saskatchewan, Canada
Peter Brusilovsky	University of Pittsburgh, USA

Demo and Poster Co-chairs

Silvia Baldiris	Universitat de Girona, Spain
Nicole Henze	University of Hannover, Germany
Fabian Abel	Delft University of Technology, The Netherlands

Local Arrangements Chair

Ramon Fabregat	University of Girona, Spain

Publicity Chair

Eelco Herder	L3S Research Center, Germany

Research Track Program Committee

Kenro Aihara	National Institute of Informatics, Japan
Sarabjot Anand	University of Warwick, UK
Liliana Ardissono	Università di Torino, Italy
Lora Aroyo	University of Amsterdam, The Netherlands
Helen Ashman	University of South Australia
Ryan Baker	Carnegie Mellon University, USA
Mathias Bauer	Mineway GmbH, Germany
Joseph Beck	Worcester Polytechnic Institute, USA
Shlomo Berkovsky	CSIRO, Australia
Maria Bieliková	Slovak University of Technology, Slovakia
Peter Brusilovsky	University of Pittsburgh, USA
Robin Burke	DePaul University, USA
Sandra Carberry	University of Delaware, USA
Rosa Carro	Universidad Autonoma de Madrid, Spain
David Chin	University of Hawaii, USA
Cristina Conati	University of British Columbia, Canada
Owen Conlan	University of Dublin, Ireland
Albert Corbett	Carnegie Mellon University, USA
Dan Cosley	Cornell University, USA
Alexandra Cristea	University of Warwick, UK
Hugh Davis	University of Southampton, UK
Paul De Bra	Eindhoven University of Technology, The Netherlands
Vania Dimitrova	University of Leeds, UK
Peter Dolog	Aalborg University, Denmark
Ben Du Boulay	University of Sussex, UK
Enrique Frias-Martinez	Telefonica Research, Spain
Eduardo Guzman	Universidad de Málaga, Spain
Neil Heffernan	Worcester Polytechnic Institute
Nicola Henze	University of Hannover, Germany
Eelco Herder	L3S Research Center, Hannover, Germany
Haym Hirsh	National Science Foundation
Ulrich Hoppe	University Duisburg-Essen, Germany
Geert-Jan Houben	Delft University of Technology, The Netherlands
Dietmar Jannach	Dortmund University of Technology, Germany
Lewis Johnson	Alelo, Inc., USA
Judy Kay	University of Sydney, Australia
Alfred Kobsa	University of California, Irvine, USA
Birgitta Konig-Ries	University of Karlsruhe, Germany
Tsvi Kuflik	University of Haifa, Israel
Paul Lamere	Sun Laboratories, UK
James Lester	North Carolina State University, USA
Henry Lieberman	MIT, USA
Frank Linton	The MITRE Corporation, USA

Paul Maglio	IBM Research Center, USA
Brent Martin	University of Canterbury, New Zealand
Judith Masthoff	University of Aberdeen, UK
Mark Maybury	MITRE, USA
Gordon McCalla	University of Saskatchewan, Canada
Lorraine McGinty	UCD Dublin, Ireland
Alessandro Micarelli	Roma Tre University, Italy
Eva Millan	Universidad de Málaga, Spain
Bamshad Mobasher	DePaul University, USA
Yoichi Motomura	National Institute of Advanced Industrial Science and Technology, Japan
Michael O'Mahony	UCD Dublin, Ireland
Jose Luis Perez de la Cruz	Málaga University, Spain
Francesco Ricci	Free University of Bolzan-Bolzano, Italy
John Riedl	University of Minnesota, USA
Jesús González Boticario	UNED, Spain
Cristobal Romero	University of Cordoba, Spain
Lloyd Rutledge	Open Universiteit Nederland, The Netherlands
Melike Sah	Trinity College, Dublin, Ireland
Olga Santos	UNED, Spain
Daniel Schwabe	Pontifícia Universidade Católica do Rio de Janeiro, Brazil
Frank Shipman	Texas A&M University, USA
Carlo Tasso	University of Udine, Italy
Loren Terveen	University of Minnesota, USA
Julita Vassileva	University of Saskatchewan, Canada
Vincent Wade	Trinity College Dublin, Ireland
Gerhard Weber	HCI Research Group, Germany
Massimo Zancanaro	Bruno Kessler Foundation, Italy
Diego Zapata-Rivera	ETS, USA

Industry Track Program Committee

Mauro Barbieri	Philips Research, The Netherlands
Mathias Bauer	Mineway, Germany
Vanessa Frias-Martinez	Telefonica Research, Madrid, Spain
Werner Geyer	IBM Research, Cambridge, MA, USA
Gustavo Gonzalez-Sanchez	Mediapro R&D, Spain
Maxim Gurevich	Yahoo Research, USA
Ido Guy	IBM Research, Haifa, Israel
Heath Hohwald	Telefonica Research, Madrid, Spain
Jose Iria	IBM Research, Zurich, Switzerland
Ashish Kapoor	Microsoft Research, Redmond, USA

George Magoulas   Birkbeck College, London, UK
Bhaskar Mehta   Google, Zurich, Switzerland
David R. Millen   IBM Research, Cambridge, USA
Qiankun Zhao   Audience Touch, Beijing, China

Doctoral Consortium Committee

Sarabjot Anand   University of Warwick, UK
Shlomo Berkovsky   CSIRO, Australia
Mária Bieliková   Slovak University of Technology, Slovakia
Peter Brusilovsky   University of Pittsburgh, USA
Susan Bull   University of Birmingham, UK
Robin Burke   DePaul University, USA
Federica Cena   Universitá degli Studi di Torino, Italy
David Chin   University of Hawaii, USA
Alexandra Cristea   University of Warwick, UK
Antonina Dattolo   Università di Udine, Italy
Vania Dimitrova   University of Leeds, UK
Peter Dolog   Aalborg University, Denmark
Benedict Du Boulay   University of Sussex, UK
Cristina Gena   Università di Torino, Italy
Floriana Grasso   University of Liverpool, UK
Jim Greer   University of Saskatchewan, Canada
Eelco Herder   L3S Research Center, Hannover, Germany
Indratmo Indratmo   Grant MacEwan University, Canada
Dietmar Jannach   Dortmund University of Technology, Germany
Judith Masthoff   University of Aberdeen, UK
Cecile Paris   CSIRO, Australia
Liana Razmerita   Copenhagen Business School, Denmark
Katharina Reinecke   University of Zurich, Switzerland
Marcus Specht   University of The Netherlands
Julita Vassileva   University of Saskatchewan, Canada
Stephan Weibelzahl   National College of Ireland

Additional Reviewers

Fabian Abel   Delft University of Technology, The Netherlands
Mohd Anwar   University of Saskatchewan, Canada
Michal Barla   Slovak University of Technology, Slovakia
Claudio Biancalana   University of Rome III, Italy
Kristy Elizabeth Boyer   North Caroline State University, USA
Janez Brank   J. Stefan Institute, Slovenia
Christopher Brooks   University of Saskatchewan, Canada
Stefano Burigat   University of Udine, Italy
Fabio Buttussi   University of Udine, Italy
Alberto Cabas Vidani   University of Udine, Italy

Table of Contents

Full Research Papers

Short Research Papers

Long Industry Papers

Doctoral Consortium Papers

Analyzing User Modeling on Twitter for Personalized News Recommendations

Fabian Abel, Qi Gao, Geert-Jan Houben, and Ke Tao

Web Information Systems, Delft University of Technology
Mekelweg 4, 2628 Delft, the Netherlands
{f.abel,q.gao,g.j.p.m.houben,k.tao}@tudelft.nl

Abstract. How can micro-blogging activities on Twitter be leveraged for user modeling and personalization? In this paper we investigate this question and introduce a framework for user modeling on Twitter which enriches the semantics of Twitter messages (tweets) and identifies topics and entities (e.g. persons, events, products) mentioned in tweets. We analyze how strategies for constructing hashtag-based, entity-based or topic-based user profiles benefit from semantic enrichment and explore the temporal dynamics of those profiles. We further measure and compare the performance of the user modeling strategies in context of a personalized news recommendation system. Our results reveal how semantic enrichment enhances the variety and quality of the generated user profiles. Further, we see how the different user modeling strategies impact personalization and discover that the consideration of temporal profile patterns can improve recommendation quality.

Keywords: user modeling, twitter, semantics, personalization.

1 Introduction

With more than 190 million users and more than 65 million postings per day, Twitter is today the most prominent micro-blogging service available on the Web[1]. People publish short messages (tweets) about their everyday activities on Twitter and lately researchers investigate feasibility of applications such as trend analysis [1] or Twitter-based early warning systems [2]. Most research initiatives study network structures and properties of the Twitter network [3,4]. Yet, little research has been done on understanding the semantics of individual Twitter activities and inferring user interests from these activities. As tweets are limited to 140 characters, making sense of individual tweets and exploiting tweets for user modeling are non-trivial problems.

In this paper we study how to leverage Twitter activities for user modeling and evaluate the quality of user models in the context of recommending news articles. We develop a framework that enriches the semantics of individual Twitter activities and allows for the construction of different types of semantic

---

[1] http://techcrunch.com/2010/06/08/twitter-190-million-users/

Joseph A. Konstan et al. (Eds.): UMAP 2011, LNCS 6787, pp. 1–12, 2011.

user profiles. The characteristics of these user profiles are influenced by different design dimensions and design alternatives. To better understand how those factors impact the characteristics and quality of the resulting user profiles, we conduct an in-depth analysis on a large Twitter dataset of more than 2 million tweets and answer research questions such as the following: how does the semantic enrichment impact the characteristics and quality of Twitter-based profiles (see Section 4.2)? How do (different types of) profiles evolve over time? Are there any characteristic temporal patterns (see Section 4.3)? How do the different user modeling strategies impact personalization (personalized news article recommendations) and does the consideration of temporal patterns improve the accuracy of the recommendations (see Section 5)?

Before studying the above research questions in Section 4-5, we will summarize related work in Section 2 and introduce the design dimensions of Twitter-based user modeling as well as our Twitter user modeling framework in Section 3.

2   Related Work

With the launch of Twitter in 2007, micro-blogging became highly popular and researchers started to investigate Twitter's information propagation patterns [3] or analyzed structures of the Twitter network to identify influential users [4]. Dong et al. [5] exploit Twitter to detect and rank fresh URLs that have possibly not been indexed by Web search engines yet. Lately, Chen et al. conducted a study on recommending URLs posted in Twitter messages and compare strategies for selecting and ranking URLs by exploiting the social network of a user as well as the general popularity of the URLs in Twitter [6]. Chen et al. do not investigate user modeling in detail, but represent Twitter messages of a user by means of a bag of words. In this paper we go beyond such representations and analyze different types of profiles like entity-based or hashtag-based profiles.

Laniado and Mika introduce metrics to describe the characteristics of hashtags – keywords starting with "#" – such as frequency, specificity or stability over time [7]. Huang et al. further characterize the temporal dynamics of hashtags via statistical measures such as standard deviation and discover that some hashtags are used widely for a few days but then disappear quickly [8]. Recent research on collaborative filtering showed that the consideration of such temporal dynamics impacts recommendation quality significantly [9]. However, the impact of temporal characteristics of Twitter-based user profiles on recommendation performance has not been researched yet.

Neither hashtag-based nor bag-of-words representation explicitly specify the semantics of tweets. To better understand the semantics of Twitter messages published during scientific conferences, Rowe et al. [10] map tweets to conference talks and exploit metadata of the corresponding research papers to enrich the semantics of tweets. Rowe et al. mention user profiling as one of the applications that might benefit from such semantics, but do not further investigate user modeling on Twitter. In this paper we close this gap and present the first large-scale study on user modeling based on Twitter activities and moreover explore how different user models impact the accuracy of recommending news articles.

Table 1. Design space of Twitter-based user modeling strategies

design dimension	design alternatives (discussed in this paper)
profile type	(i) hashtag-based, (ii) topic-based or (iii) entity-based
enrichment	(i) tweet-only-based enrichment or (ii) linkage and exploitation of external news articles (propagating entities/topics)
temporal constraints	(i) specific time period(s), (ii) temporal patterns (*weekend, night,* etc.) or (iii) no constraints

3   Twitter-Based User Modeling

The user modeling strategies proposed and discussed in this paper vary in three design dimensions: (i) the type of profiles created by the strategies, (ii) the data sources exploited to further enrich the Twitter-based profiles and (iii) temporal constraints that are considered when constructing the profiles (see Table 1). The generic model for profiles representing users is specified in Definition 1.

Definition 1 (User Profile). *The profile of a user $u \in U$ is a set of weighted concepts where with respect to the given user u for a concept $c \in C$ its weight $w(u, c)$ is computed by a certain function w.*

$$P(u) = \{(c, w(u, c)) | c \in C, u \in U\}$$

Here, C and U denote the set of concepts and users respectively.

In particular, following Table 1 we analyze three *types* of profiles that differ with respect to the type of concepts C: entity-, topic- and hashtag-based profiles – denoted by $P_E(u)$, $P_T(u)$ and $P_H(u)$ respectively. We apply occurrence frequency as weighting scheme $w(u, c)$, which means that the weight of a concept is determined by the number of Twitter activities in which user u refers to concept c. For example, in a hashtag-based profile $w(u, \#technology) = 5$ means that u published five Twitter messages that mention "#technology". We further normalize user profiles so that the sum of all weights in a profile is equal to 1: $\sum_{c_i \in C} w(u, c_i) = 1$. With $\boldsymbol{p}(u)$ we refer to $P(u)$ in its vector space model representation, where the value of the i-th dimension refers to $w(u, c_i)$.

The user modeling strategies we analyze in this paper exploit Twitter messages posted by a user u to construct the corresponding profile $P(u)$. When constructing entity- and topic-based user profiles, we also investigate the impact of further *enrichment* based on the exploitation of external data sources (see Table 1). In particular, we allow for enrichment with entities and topics extracted from news articles that are linked with Twitter messages (news-based enrichment). In previous work [11] we presented strategies for selecting appropriate news articles for enriching users' Twitter activities.

A third dimension we investigate in the context of Twitter-based user modeling is given by *temporal constraints* that are considered when constructing the profiles (see Table 1). First, we study the nature of user profiles created within specific time periods. For example, we compare profiles constructed by exploiting the complete (long-term) user history with profiles that are based only on Twitter messages published within a certain week (short-term). Second, we examine certain time frames for creating the profiles. For example, we explore the differences between user profiles created on the weekends with those created during the week to detect temporal patterns that might help to improve personalization within certain time frames.

By selecting and combining the different design dimensions and alternatives we obtain a variety of different user modeling strategies that will be analyzed and evaluated in this paper.

3.1   Twitter-Based User Modeling Framework

We implemented the profiling strategies as a Twitter-based user modeling framework that is available via the supporting website of this paper [12]. Our framework features three main components:

1. **Semantic Enrichment.** Given the content of Twitter messages we extract entities and topics to better understand the semantics of Twitter activities. Therefore we utilize OpenCalais[2], which allows for the detection and identification of 39 different types of entities such as persons, events, products or music groups and moreover provides unique URIs for identified entities as well as for the topics so that the meaning of such concepts is well defined.
2. **Linkage.** We implemented several strategies that link tweets with external Web resources and news articles in particular. Entities and topics extracted from the articles are then propagated to the linked tweets. In [11] we showed that for tweets which do not contain any hyperlink the linking strategies identify related news articles with an accuracy of 70-80%.
3. **User Modeling.** Based on the semantic enrichment and the linkage with external news articles, our framework provides methods for generating hashtag-based, entity-based, and topic-based profiles that might adhere to specific temporal constraints (see above).

4   Analysis of Twitter-Based User Profiles

To understand how the different user modeling design choices influence the characteristics of the generated user profiles, we applied our framework to conduct an in-depth analysis on a large Twitter dataset. The main research questions to be answered in this analysis can be summarized as follows.

1. How do the different user modeling strategies impact the *characteristics* of Twitter-based user profiles?
2. Which *temporal characteristics* do Twitter-based user profiles feature?

---

[2] http://www.opencalais.com

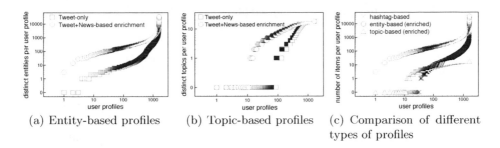

(a) Entity-based profiles   (b) Topic-based profiles   (c) Comparison of different types of profiles

Fig. 1. Comparison between different user modeling strategies with tweet-only-based or news-based enrichment

4.1 Data Collection and Data Set Characteristics

Over a period of more than two months we crawled Twitter information streams of more than 20,000 users. Together, these people published more than 10 million tweets. To allow for linkage of tweets with news articles we also monitored more than 60 RSS feeds of prominent news media such as BBC, CNN or New York Times and aggregated the content of 77,544 news articles. The number of Twitter messages posted per user follows a power-law distribution. The majority of users published less than 100 messages during our observation period while only a small fraction of users wrote more than 10,000 Twitter messages and one user produced even slightly more than 20,000 tweets (no spam). As we were interested in analyzing also temporal characteristics of the user profiles, we created a sample of 1619 users, who contributed at least 20 tweets in total and at least one tweet in each month of our observation period. This sample dataset contained 2,316,204 tweets in total.

We processed each Twitter message and each news article via the semantic enrichment component of our user modeling framework to identify topics and entities mentioned in the the tweets and articles (see Section 3.1). Further, we applied two different linking strategies and connected 458,566 Twitter messages with news articles of which 98,189 relations were explicitly given in the tweets by URLs that pointed to the corresponding news article. The remaining 360,377 relations were obtained by comparing the entities that were mentioned in both news articles and tweets as well as by comparing the timestamps. In previous work we showed that this method correlates news and tweets with an accuracy of more than 70% [11]. Our hypothesis is that – regardless whether this enrichment method might introduce a certain degree of noise – it impacts the quality of user modeling and personalization positively.

4.2 Structural Analysis of Twitter-Based Profiles

To validate our hypothesis and explore how the exploitation of linked external sources influences the characteristics of the profiles generated by the different user modeling strategies, we analyzed the corresponding profiles of the 1619 users from our sample. In Figure 1 we plot the number of distinct (types of) concepts in the topic- and entity-based profiles and show how this number is influenced by the additional news-based enrichment.

For both types of profiles the enrichment with entities and topics obtained from linked news articles results in a higher number of distinct concepts per profile (see Fig. 1(a) and 1(b)). Topic-based profiles abstract much stronger from the concrete Twitter activities than entity-based profiles. In our analysis we utilized the OpenCalais taxonomy consisting of 18 topics such as politics, entertainment or culture. The tweet-only-based user modeling strategy, which exploits merely the semantics attached to tweets, fails to create profiles for nearly 100 users (6.2%, topic-based) as for these users none of the tweets can be categorized into a topic. By enriching the tweets with topics inferred from the linked news articles we better understand the semantics of Twitter messages and succeed in creating more valuable topic-based profiles for 99.4% of the users.

Further, the number of profile facets, i.e. the type of entities (e.g. person, location or event) that occur in the entity-based profiles, increases with the news-based semantic enrichment. While more than 400 twitter-based profiles (more than 25%) feature less than 10 profile facets and often miss entities such as movies or products a user is concerned with, the news-based enrichment detects a greater variety of entity types. For more than 99% of the entity-based profiles enriched via news articles, the number of distinct profile facets is higher than 10.

A comparison of the entity- and topic-based user modeling strategies with the hashtag-based strategy (see Fig. 1(c)) shows that the variety of entity-based profiles is much higher than the one of hashtag-based profiles. While the entity-based strategy succeeds to create profiles for all users in our dataset, the hashtag-based approach fails for approximately 90 users (5.5%) as the corresponding people neither made use of hashtags nor re-tweeted messages that contain hashtags. Entity-based as well as topic-based profiles moreover make the semantics more explicit than hashtag-based profiles. Each entity and topic has a URI which defines the meaning of the entity and topic respectively.

The advantages of well-defined semantics as exposed by the topic- and entity-based profiles also depend on the application context, in which these profiles are used. The results of the quantitative analysis depicted in Fig. 1 show that entity- and topic-based strategies allow for higher coverage regarding the number of users, for whom profiles can be generated, than the hashtag-based strategy. Further, semantic enrichment by exploiting news articles (implicitly) linked with tweets increases the number of entities and topics available in the profiles significantly and improves the variety of the profiles (the number of profile facets).

4.3   Temporal Analysis of Twitter-Based Profiles

In the temporal analysis we investigate (1) how the different types of user profiles evolve over time and (2) which temporal patterns occur in the profiles. Regarding temporal patterns we, for example, examine whether profiles generated on the weekends differ from those generated during the week. Similar

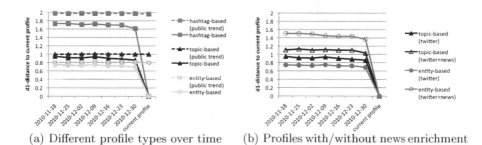

(a) Different profile types over time   (b) Profiles with/without news enrichment

Fig. 2. Temporal evolution of user profiles: average d_1-distance of current individual user profiles with corresponding profiles in the past

to the click-behavior analysis by Liu et al. [13], we apply the so-called d_1-*distance* for measuring the difference between profiles in vector representation: $d_1(\boldsymbol{p_x}(u), \boldsymbol{p_y}(u)) = \sum_i |p_{x,i} - p_{y,i}|$.

The higher $d_1(\boldsymbol{p_x}(u), \boldsymbol{p_y}(u)) \in [0..2]$ the higher the difference of the two profiles $\boldsymbol{p_x}(u)$ and $\boldsymbol{p_y}(u)$ and if two profiles are the same then $d_1(\boldsymbol{p_x}(u), \boldsymbol{p_y}(u)) = 0$. Figure 2 depicts the evolution of profiles over time. It shows the average d_1-distance of the current user profiles with the profiles of the same users created based on Twitter activities performed in a certain week in the past. As suggested in [13], we also plotted the distance of the current user-specific profile with the *public trend* (see Fig. 2(a)), i.e. the average profile of the corresponding weeks.

For the three different profile types we observe that the d_1-distance slightly decreases over time. For example, the difference of current profiles (first week of January 2011) with the corresponding profiles generated at the beginning of our observation period (in the week around 18th November 2010) is the highest while the distance of current profiles with profiles computed one week before (30th December 2010) is the lowest. It is interesting to see that the distance of the current profiles with the public trend (i) is present for all types of profiles and (ii) is rather constant over time. This suggests (i) a certain degree of individualism in Twitter and (ii) reveals that the people in our sample follow different trends rather than being influenced by the same trends.

Hashtag-based profiles exhibit the strongest changes over time as the average d_1-distance to the current profile is constantly higher than for the topic- and entity-based profiles. Figure 2(b) discloses that entity-based profiles change stronger over time than topic-based profiles when news-based enrichment is enabled. When merely analyzing Twitter messages one would come to a different (possibly wrong) conclusion (see Fig. 2(a)).

Figure 3 illustrates temporal patterns we detected when analyzing the individual user profiles. In particular, we investigate how profiles created on the weekends differ from profiles (of the same user) created during the week. For topic-based profiles generated solely based on Twitter messages, it seems that for some users the weekend and weekday profiles differ just slightly while for 24.9% of the users the d_1-distance of the weekend and weekday profile is maximal (2 is the maximum possible value, see Fig. 3(a)). The news-based enrichment reveals

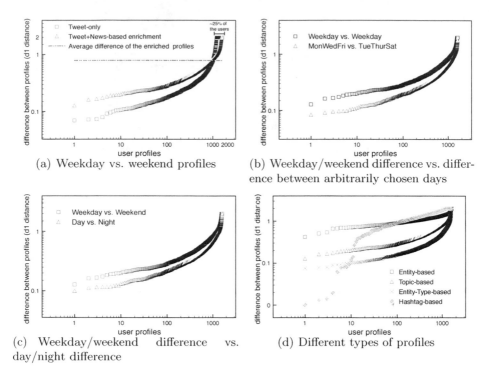

(a) Weekday vs. weekend profiles

(b) Weekday/weekend difference vs. difference between arbitrarily chosen days

(c) Weekday/weekend   difference   vs. day/night difference

(d) Different types of profiles

Fig. 3. Temporal patterns: comparison between weekend and weekday profiles by means of d_1-distance ((a)-(c): topic-based profiles)

however that the difference of weekend and weekday profiles is a rather common phenomenon: the curve draws nearer to the average difference (see dotted line); there are less extrema, i.e. users for whom the d_1-difference is either very low or very high. Hence, it rather seems that the tweets alone are not sufficient to get a clear understanding of the users concerns and interests.

Fig. 3(b) further supports the hypothesis that weekend profiles differ significantly from weekday profiles. The corresponding distances $d_1(\boldsymbol{p}_{weekend}(u)$, $\boldsymbol{p}_{weekday}(u))$ are consistently higher than the differences of profiles generated on arbitrarily chosen days during the week. This *weekend pattern* is more significant than differences between topic-based profiles generated based on Twitter messages that are either posted during the evening (6pm-3am) or during the day (9am-5pm) as shown in Fig. 3(c). Hence, the individual topic drift – i.e. change of topics individual users are concerned with – between day and evening/night seems to be smaller than between weekdays and weekends.

The weekend pattern is coherent over the different types of profiles. Different profile types however imply different drift of interests or concerns between weekend and weekdays (see Fig. 3(d)). Hashtag-based and entity-based profiles change most while the types of entities people refer to (persons, products, etc.)

do not differ that strongly. When zooming into the individual entity-based profiles we see that entities related to leisure time and entertainment become more important on the weekends.

The temporal analysis thus revealed two important observations. First, user profiles change over time: the older a profile the more it differs from the current profile of the user. The actual profile distance varies between the different types of profiles. Second, weekend profiles differ significantly from weekday profiles.

5   Exploitation of User Profiles for Personalized News Recommendations

In this section, we investigate the impact of the different user modeling strategies on recommending news articles:

1. To which degree are the profiles created by the different user modeling strategies appropriate for recommending news?
2. Can the identified (temporal) patterns be applied to improve recommendation accuracy?

5.1   News Recommender System and Evaluation Methodology

Recommending news articles is a non-trivial task as the news items, which are going to be recommended, are *new* by its very nature, which makes it difficult to apply collaborative filtering methods, but rather calls for content-based or hybrid approaches [13]. Our main goal is to analyze and compare the applicability of the different user modeling strategies in the context of news recommendations. We do not aim to optimize recommendation quality, but are interested in comparing the quality achieved by the same recommendation algorithm when inputting different types of user profiles. Therefore we apply a lightweight content-based algorithm that recommends items according to their cosine similarity with a given user profile. We thus cast the recommendation problem into a search and ranking problem where the given user profile, which is constructed by a specific user modeling strategy, is interpreted as query.

Definition 2 (Recommendation Algorithm). *Given a user profile vector $p(u)$ and a set of candidate news items $N = \{p(n_1), ..., p(n_n)\}$, which are represented via profiles using the same vector representation, the recommendation algorithm ranks the candidate items according to their cosine similarity to $p(u)$.*

Given the Twitter and news media dataset described in Section 4.1, we considered the last week of our observation period as the time frame for computing recommendations. The ground truth of news articles, which we consider as *relevant* for a specific user u, is obtained via the Twitter messages (including retweets) posted by u in this week that explicitly link to a news article published by BBC, CNN or New York Times. We thereby identified, on average, 5.5 relevant news articles for each of the 1619 users from our sample. For less than 10% of the

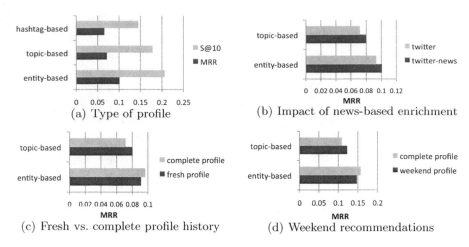

Fig. 4. Results of news recommendation experiment

users we found more than 20 relevant articles. The candidate set of news articles, which were published within the recommendation time frame, contained 5529 items. We then applied the different user modeling strategies together with the above algorithm (see Def. 2) and set of candidate items to compute news recommendations for each user. The user modeling strategies were only allowed to exploit tweets published before the recommendation period. The quality of the recommendations was measured by means of *MRR* (Mean Reciprocal Rank), which indicates at which rank the first item relevant to the user occurs on average, and *S@k* (Success at rank k), which stands for the mean probability that a relevant item occurs within the top k of the ranking. In particular, we will focus on S@10 as our recommendation system will list 10 recommended news articles to a user. We tested statistical significance of our results with a two-tailed t-Test where the significance level was set to $\alpha = 0.01$ unless otherwise noted.

5.2   Results

The results of the news recommendation experiment are summarized in Fig. 4 and validate findings of our analysis presented in Section 4. Entity-based user modeling (with news-based enrichment), which produces according to the quantitative analysis (see Fig. 1) the most valuable profiles, allowed for the best recommendation quality and performed significantly better than hashtag-based user modeling (see Fig. 4(a)). Topic-based user modeling also performed better than the hashtag-based strategy – regarding S@10 the performance difference is significant. Since the topic-based strategy models user interests within a space of 18 different topics (e.g., politics or sports), it further required much less run-time and memory for computing user profiles and recommendations than the hashtag- and entity-based strategies, for which we limited dimensions to the 10,0000 most prominent hashtags and entities respectively.

Further enrichment of topic- and entity-based profiles with topics and entities extracted from linked news articles, which results in profiles that feature more facets and information about users' concerns (cf. Section 4.2), also results in a higher recommendation quality (see Fig. 4(b)). Exploiting both tweets and linked news articles for creating user profiles improves MRR significantly ($\alpha = 0.05$). In Section 4.3 we observed that user profiles change over time and that recent profile information approximates future profiles slightly better than old profile information. We thus compared strategies that exploited just recent Twitter activities (two weeks before the recommendation period) with the strategies that exploit the entire user history (see Fig. 4(c)). For the topic-based strategy we see that *fresh* user profiles are more applicable for recommending news articles than profiles that were built based on the entire user history. However, entity-based user modeling enables better recommendation quality when the complete user history is applied. Results of additional experiments [12] suggest that this is due to the number of distinct entities that occur in entity-based profiles (cf. Fig. 1): long-term profiles seem to refine preferences regarding entities (e.g. persons or events) better than short-term profiles.

In Section 4.3 we further observed the so-called *weekend pattern*, i.e. user profiles created based on Twitter messages published on the weekends significantly differ from profiles created during the week. To examine the impact of this pattern on the accuracy of the recommendations we focused on recommending news articles during the weekend and compared the performance of user profiles created just by exploiting weekend activities with profiles created based on the complete set of Twitter activities (see Fig. 4(d)). Similarly to Fig. 4(c) we see again that the entity-based strategy performs better when exploiting the entire user history while the topic-based strategy benefits from considering the weekend pattern. For the topic-based strategy recommendation quality with respect to MRR improves significantly when profiles from the weekend are applied to make recommendations during the weekend.

6   Conclusions

In this paper we developed a user modeling framework for Twitter and investigated how the different design alternatives influence the characteristics of the generated user profiles. Given a large dataset consisting of more than 2 million tweets we created user profiles and revealed several advantages of semantic entity- and topic-based user modeling strategies, which exploit the full functionality of our framework, over hashtag-based user modeling. We saw that further enrichment with semantics extracted from news articles, which we correlated with the users' Twitter activities, enhanced the variety of the constructed profiles and improved accuracy of news article recommendations significantly.

Further, we analyzed the temporal dynamics of the different types of profiles. We observed how profiles change over time and discovered temporal patterns such as characteristic differences between weekend and weekday profiles. We also showed that the consideration of such temporal characteristics is beneficial to recommending news articles when dealing with topic-based profiles while for entity-based profiles we achieve better performance when incorporating the entire user history. In future work, we will further research the temporal specifics of entity-based profiles. First results [12] suggest that users refer to certain types of entities (e.g., persons) more consistently over time than to others (e.g., movies or events).

Acknowledgements. This work is partially sponsored by the EU FP7 project ImREAL (http://imreal-project.eu).

References

1. Lerman, K., Ghosh, R.: Information contagion: an empirical study of spread of news on Digg and Twitter social networks. In: Cohen, Gosling (eds.) Proc. of 4th Int. Conf. on Weblogs and Social Media (ICWSM). AAAI Press, Menlo Park (2010)
2. Sakaki, T., Okazaki, M., Matsuo, Y.: Earthquake shakes Twitter users: real-time event detection by social sensors. In: Rappa, et al. (eds.) Proc. of 19th Int. Conf. on World Wide Web (WWW), pp. 851–860. ACM, New York (2010)
3. Kwak, H., Lee, C., Park, H., Moon, S.: What is Twitter, a social network or a news media? In: Rappa, et al. (eds.) Proc. of 19th Int. Conf. on World Wide Web (WWW), pp. 591–600. ACM, New York (2010)
4. Weng, J., Lim, E.P., Jiang, J., He, Q.: TwitterRank: Finding topic-sensitive influential Twitterers. In: Davison, et al. (eds.) Proc. of 3rd Int. Conf. on Web Search and Web Data Mining (WSDM), pp. 261–270. ACM, New York (2010)
5. Dong, A., Zhang, R., Kolari, P., Bai, J., Diaz, F., Chang, Y., Zheng, Z., Zha, H.: Time is of the essence: improving recency ranking using twitter data. In: Rappa, et al. (eds.) Proc. of 19th Int. Conf. on World Wide Web (WWW), pp. 331–340. ACM, New York (2010)
6. Chen, J., Nairn, R., Nelson, L., Bernstein, M., Chi, E.: Short and tweet: experiments on recommending content from information streams. In: Mynatt, et al. (eds.) Proc. of 28th Int. Conf. on Human factors in Computing Systems (CHI), pp. 1185–1194. ACM, New York (2010)
7. Laniado, D., Mika, P.: Making sense of Twitter. In: Patel-Schneider, P.F., Pan, Y., Hitzler, P., Mika, P., Zhang, L., Pan, J.Z., Horrocks, I., Glimm, B. (eds.) ISWC 2010, Part I. LNCS, vol. 6496, pp. 470–485. Springer, Heidelberg (2010)
8. Huang, J., Thornton, K.M., Efthimiadis, E.N.: Conversational Tagging in Twitter. In: Chignell, M.H., Toms, E. (eds.) Proc. of 21st Conf. on Hypertext and Hypermedia (HT), pp. 173–178. ACM, New York (2010)
9. Koren, Y.: Collaborative filtering with temporal dynamics. In: Elder, et al. (eds.) Proc. of 15th Int. Conf. on Knowledge Discovery and Data Mining (KDD), pp. 447–456. ACM, Paris (2009)
10. Rowe, M., Stankovic, M., Laublet, P.: Mapping Tweets to Conference Talks: A Goldmine for Semantics. In: Passant, et al. (eds.) Workshop on Social Data on the Web (SDoW), Co-located with ISWC 2010, Shanghai, China, vol. 664, CEUR-WS.org (2010)
11. Abel, F., Gao, Q., Houben, G.J., Tao, K.: Semantic Enrichment of Twitter Posts for User Profile Construction on the Social Web. In: Antoniou, et al. (eds.) Extended Semantic Web Conference (ESWC), Springer, Heraklion (2011)
12. Abel, F., Gao, Q., Houben, G.J., Tao, K.: Supporting website: code, datasets and additional findings (2011), http://wis.ewi.tudelft.nl/umap2011/
13. Liu, J., Dolan, P., Pedersen, E.R.: Personalized news recommendation based on click behavior. In: Rich, et al. (eds.) Proc. of 14th Int. Conf. on Intelligent User Interfaces (IUI), pp. 31–40. ACM, New York (2010)

Ensembling Predictions of Student Knowledge within Intelligent Tutoring Systems

Ryan S.J.d. Baker[1], Zachary A. Pardos[2], Sujith M. Gowda[1],
Bahador B. Nooraei[2], and Neil T. Heffernan[2]

[1] Department of Social Science and Policy Studies, Worcester Polytechnic Institute,
100 Institute Road, Worcester, MA 01609 USA
rsbaker@wpi.edu, sujithmg@wpi.edu
[2] Department of Computer Science, Worcester Polytechnic Institute,
100 Institute Road, Worcester, MA 01609 USA
{zpardos,bahador,nth}@wpi.edu

Abstract. Over the last decades, there have been a rich variety of approaches towards modeling student knowledge and skill within interactive learning environments. There have recently been several empirical comparisons as to which types of student models are better at predicting future performance, both within and outside of the interactive learning environment. However, these comparisons have produced contradictory results. Within this paper, we examine whether ensemble methods, which integrate multiple models, can produce prediction results comparable to or better than the best of nine student modeling frameworks, taken individually. We ensemble model predictions within a Cognitive Tutor for Genetics, at the level of predicting knowledge action-by-action within the tutor. We evaluate the predictions in terms of future performance within the tutor and on a paper post-test. Within this data set, we do not find evidence that ensembles of models are significantly better. Ensembles of models perform comparably to or slightly better than the best individual models, at predicting future performance within the tutor software. However, the ensembles of models perform marginally significantly worse than the best individual models, at predicting post-test performance.

Keywords: student modeling, ensemble methods, Bayesian Knowledge-Tracing, Performance Factors Analysis, Cognitive Tutor.

1   Introduction

Over the last decades, there have been a rich variety of approaches towards modeling student knowledge and skill within interactive learning environments, from Overlay Models, to Bayes Nets, to Bayesian Knowledge Tracing [6], to models based on Item-Response Theory such as Performance Factors Analysis (PFA) [cf. 13]. Multiple variants within each of these paradigms have also been created – for instance, within Bayesian Knowledge Tracing (BKT), BKT models can be fit using curve-fitting [6], expectation maximization (EM) [cf. 4, 9], dirichlet priors on EM [14], grid search/brute force [cf. 2, 10], and BKT has been extended with contextualization of

Joseph A. Konstan et al. (Eds.): UMAP 2011, LNCS 6787, pp. 13–24, 2011.
© Springer-Verlag Berlin Heidelberg 2011

guess and slip [cf. 1, 2] and student priors [9, 10]. Student models have been compared in several fashions, both within and across paradigms, including both theoretical comparisons [1, 3, 15] and empirical comparisons at predicting future student performance [1, 2, 7, 13], as a proxy for the models' ability to infer latent student knowledge/skills. These empirical comparisons have typically demonstrated that there are significant differences between different modeling approaches, an important finding, as increased model accuracy can improve optimization of how much practice each student receives [6]. However, different comparisons have in many cases produced contradictory findings. For instance, Pavlik and colleagues [13] found that Performance Factors Analysis predicts future student performance within the tutoring software better than Bayesian Knowledge Tracing, whether BKT is fit using expectation maximization or brute force, and that brute force performs comparably to or better than expectation maximization. By contrast, Gong et al. [7] found that BKT fit with expectation maximization performed equally to PFA and better than BKT fit with brute force. In other comparisons, Baker, Corbett, & Aleven [1] found that BKT fit with expectation maximization performed worse than BKT fit with curve-fitting, which in turn performed worse than BKT fit with brute force [2]. These comparisons have often differed in multiple fashions, including the data set used, and the type (or presence) of cross-validation, possibly explaining these differences in results. However, thus far it has been unclear which modeling approach is "best" at predicting future student performance.

Within this paper, we ask whether the paradigm of asking which modeling approach is "best" is a fruitful approach at all. An alternative is to use all of the paradigms at the same time, rather than trying to isolate a single best approach. One popular approach for doing so is ensemble selection [16], where multiple models are selected in a stepwise fashion and integrated into a single predictor using weighted averaging or voting. Up until the recent KDD2010 student modeling competition [11, 18], ensemble methods had not used in student modeling for intelligent tutoring systems. In this paper, we take a set of potential student knowledge/performance models and ensemble them, including approaches well-known within the student modeling community [e.g. 7, 16] and approaches tried during the recent KDD2010 student modeling competition [cf. 11, 18]. Rather than selecting from a very large set of potential models [e.g. 16], a popular approach to ensemble selection, we ensemble existing models of student knowledge, in order to specifically investigate whether combining several current approaches to student knowledge modeling is better than using the best of the current approaches, by itself. We examine the predictive power of ensemble models and original models, under cross-validation.

2   Student Models Used

2.1 Bayesian Knowledge-Tracing

Corbett & Anderson's [6] Bayesian Knowledge Tracing model is one of the most popular methods for estimating students' knowledge. It underlies the Cognitive Mastery Learning algorithm used in Cognitive Tutors for Algebra, Geometry, Genetics, and other domains [8].

The canonical Bayesian Knowledge Tracing (BKT) model assumes a two-state learning model: for each skill/knowledge component the student is either in the learned state or the unlearned state. At each opportunity to apply that skill, regardless of their performance, the student may make the transition from the unlearned to the learned state with *learning* probability $P(T)$. The probability of a student going from the learned state to the unlearned state (i.e. forgetting a skill) is fixed at zero. A student who knows a skill can either give a correct performance, or *slip* and give an incorrect answer with probability $P(S)$. Similarly, a student who does not know the skill may *guess* the correct response with probability $P(G)$. The model has another parameter, $P(L_0)$, which is the probability of a student knowing the skill from the start. After each opportunity to apply the rule, the system updates its estimate of student's knowledge state, $P(L_n)$, using the evidence from the current action's correctness and the probability of learning. The equations are as follows:

$$P(L_{n-1}|Correct_n) = \frac{P(L_{n-1})*(1-P(S))}{P(L_{n-1})*(1-P(S))+ (1-P(L_{n-1}))*(P(G))} \tag{1}$$

$$P(L_{n-1}|Incorrect_n) = \frac{P(L_{n-1})*P(S)}{P(L_{n-1})*P(S)+ (1-P(L_{n-1}))*(1-P(G))} \tag{2}$$

$$P(L_n|Action_n) = P(L_{n-1}|Action_n) + \big((1 - P(L_{n-1}|Action_n)) * P(T)\big) \tag{3}$$

The four parameters of BKT, $(P(L_0), P(T), P(S)$, and $P(G))$, are learned from existing data, historically using curve-fitting [6], but more recently using expectation maximization (*BKT-EM*) [5] or brute force/grid search (*BKT-BF*) [cf. 2, 10]. Within this paper we use BKT-EM and BKT-BF as two different models in this study. Within BKT-BF, for each of the 4 parameters all potential values at a grain-size of 0.01 are tried across all the students (for e.g.: 0.01 0.01 0.01 0.01, 0.01 0.01 0.01 0.02, 0.01 0.01 0.01 0.03...... 0.99 0.99 0.3 0.1). The sum of squared residuals (SSR) is minimized. For *BKT-BF*, the values for Guess and Slip are bounded in order to avoid the "model degeneracy" problems that arise when performance parameter estimates rise above 0.5 [1]. For *BKT-EM* the parameters were unbounded and initial parameters were set to a $P(G)$ of 0.14, $P(S)$ of 0.09, $P(L_0)$ of 0.50, and $P(T)$ of 0.14, a set of parameters previously found to be the average parameter values across all skills in modeling work conducted within a different tutoring system.

In addition, we include three other variants on BKT. The first variant changes the data set used during fitting. BKT parameters are typically fit to all available students' performance data for a skill. It has been argued that if fitting is conducted using only the most recent student performance data, more accurate future performance prediction can be achieved than when fitting the model with all of the data [11]. In this study, we included a BKT model trained only on a maximum of the 15 most recent student responses on the current skill, *BKT-Less Data*.

The second variant, the *BKT-CGS* (Contextual Guess and Slip) model, is an extension of BKT [1]. In this approach, Guess and Slip probabilities are no longer estimated for each skill; instead, they are computed each time a student attempts to answer a new problem step, based on machine-learned models of guess and slip response properties in context (for instance, longer responses and help requests are less likely to be slips). The same approach as in [1] is used to create the model, where 1) a four-parameter BKT model is obtained (in this case *BKT-BF*), 2) the four-parameter model is used to generate labels of the probability of slipping and guessing for each action within the data set, 3) machine learning is used to fit models predicting these labels, 4) the machine-learned models of guess and slip are substituted into Bayesian Knowledge Tracing in lieu of skill-by-skill labels for guess and slip, and finally 5) parameters for *P(T)* and $P(L_0)$ are fit.

Recent research has suggested that the average Contextual Slip values from this model, combined in linear regression with standard BKT, improves prediction of post-test performance compared to BKT alone [2]. Hence, we include average *Contextual Slip* so far as an additional potential model.

The third BKT variant, the *BKT-PPS* (Prior Per Student) model [9], breaks from the standard BKT assumption that each student has the same incoming knowledge, $P(L_0)$. This individualization is accomplished by modifying the prior parameter for each student with the addition of a single node and arc to the standard BKT model. The model can be simplified to only model two different student knowledge priors, a high and a low prior. No pre-test needs to be administered to determine which prior the student belongs to; instead their first response is used. If a student answers their first question of the skill incorrectly they are assumed to be in the low prior group. If they answer correctly, they assumed to be in the high prior group. The prior of each group can be learned or it can be set *ad-hoc*. The intuition behind the *ad-hoc* high prior, conditioned upon first response, is that it should be roughly 1 minus the probability of guess. Similarly, the low prior should be equivalent to the probability of slip. Using PPS with a low prior value of 0.10 and a high value of 0.85 has been shown to lead to improved accuracy at predicting student performance [11].

2.2 Tabling

A very simple baseline approach to predicting a student's performance, given his or her past performance data, is to check what percentage of students with that same pattern of performance gave correct answer to the next question. That is the key idea behind the student performance prediction model called *Tabling* [17].

In the training phase, a table is constructed for each skill: each row in that table represents a possible pattern of student performance in n most recent data points. For $n = 3$ (which is the table size used in this study), we have 8 rows: $000, 001, 010, 011, 100, 101, 110, 111$. (0 and 1 representing incorrect and correct responses respectively) For each of those patterns we calculate the percentage of correct responses immediately following the pattern. For example, if we have 47 students that answered 4 questions in a row correctly (111 1), and 3 students that after answering 3 correct responses, failed on the 4th one, the value calculated for row 111 is going to be 0.94 (47/(47+3)). When predicting a student's performance, this method simply looks up the row corresponding to the 3 preceding performance data, and uses the percentage value as its prediction.

2.3 Performance Factors Analysis

Performance Factors Analysis (PFA) [12, 13] is a logistic regression model, an elaboration of the Rasch model from Item Response Theory. PFA predicts student correctness based on the student's number of prior failures F on that skill (weighted by a parameter ρ fit for each skill) and the student's number of prior successes S on that skill (weighted by a parameter γ fit for each skill). An overall difficulty parameter β is also fit for each skill [13] or each item [12] – in this paper we use the variant of PFA that fits β for each skill. The PFA equation is:

$$m(i, j \in KCs, s, f) = \beta_j + \sum(\gamma_j S_{ij} + \rho_j F_{ij}) \tag{4}$$

2.4 CFAR

CFAR, which stands for "Correct First Attempt Rate", is an extremely simple algorithm for predicting student knowledge and future performance, utilized by the winners of the educational data KDD Cup in 2010 [18]. The prediction of student performance on a given skill is the student's average correctness on that skill, up until the current point.

3 Genetics Dataset

The dataset contains the results of in-tutor performance data of 76 students on 9 different skills, with data from a total of 23,706 student actions (entering an answer or requesting help). This data was taken from a Cognitive Tutor for Genetics [5]. This tutor consists of 19 modules that support problem solving across a wide range of topics in genetics (Mendelian transmission, pedigree analysis, gene mapping, gene regulation and population genetics). Various subsets of the 19 modules have been piloted at 15 universities in North America.

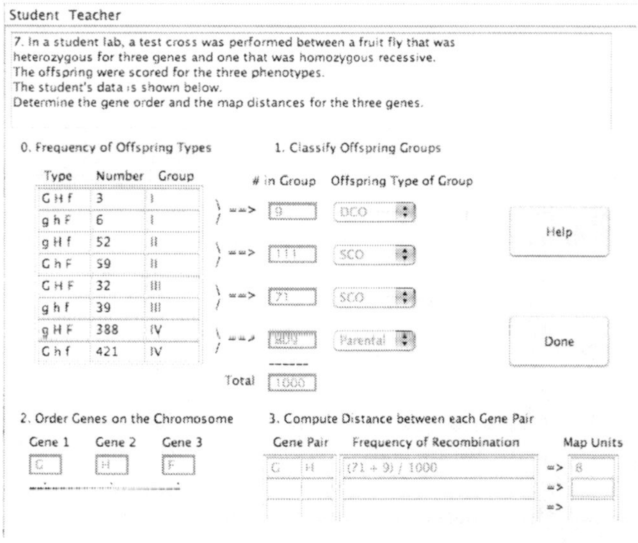

Fig. 1. The Three-Factor Cross lesson of the Genetics Cognitive Tutor

This data set is drawn from a Cognitive Tutor lesson on three-factor cross, shown in Figure 1. In three factor-cross problems, two organisms are bred together, and then the patterns of phenotypes and genotypes on a chromosome are studied. In particular, the interactions between three genes on the same chromosome are studied. During meiosis, segments of the chromosome can "cross over", going from one paired chromosome to the other, resulting in a different phenotype in the offspring than if the crossover did not occur. Within this tutor lesson, the student identifies, within the interface, the order and distance between the genes on the chromosome, by looking at the relative frequency of each pattern of phenotypes in the offspring. The student also categorizes each phenotype in terms of whether it represents the same genotype as the parents (e.g. no crossovers during meiosis), whether it represents a single crossover during meiosis, or whether it represents two crossovers during meiosis.

In this study, 76 undergraduates enrolled in a genetics course at Carnegie Mellon University used the three-factor cross module as an assignment conducted in two lab sessions lasting an hour apiece. The 76 students completed a total of 23,706 problem solving attempts across 11,582 problem steps in the tutor. On average, each student completed 152 problem steps (SD=50). In the first session, students were split into four groups with a 2x2 design; half of students spent half their time in the first session self-explaining worked examples; half of students spent half their time in a forward modeling activity. Within this paper, we focus solely on behavior logged within the problem-solving activities, and we collapse across the original four conditions.

The problem-solving pre-test and post-test consisted of two problems (counterbalanced across tests), each consisting of 11 steps involving 7 of the 9 skills in the Three-Factor Cross tutor lesson, with two skills applied twice in each problem and one skill applied three times. The average performance on the pre-test was 0.33, with a standard deviation of 0.2. The average performance on the post-test was 0.83, with a standard deviation of 0.19. This provides evidence for substantial learning within the tutor, with an average pre-post gain of 0.50.

4   Evaluation of Models

4.1   In-Tutor Performance of Models, at Student Level

To evaluate each of the student models mentioned in section 2, we conducted 5-fold cross-validation, at the student level. By cross-validating at the student level rather than the action level, we can have greater confidence that the resultant models will generalize to new groups of students. The variable fit to and predicted was whether each student first attempt on a problem step was Correct or Not Correct. We used A' as the goodness metric since it is a suitable metric to be used when predicted variable is binary and the predictions are numerical (predictions of knowledge for each model). To facilitate statistical comparison of A' without violating statistical independence, A' values were calculated for each student separately and then averaged across students (see [2] for more detail on this statistical method).

The performance of each model is given in Table 1. As can be seen, the best single model was BKT-PPS (A'=0.7029), with the second-best single model BKT-BF (A'=0.6969) and the third-best single model BKT-EM (A'=0.6957). None of these three BKT models was significantly different than each other (the difference closest to significance was between BKT-PPS and BKT-BF, Z=0.11, p=0.91). Interestingly, in light of previous results [e.g. 16], each of these three models was significantly better than PFA (A'= 0.6629) (the least significant difference was between BKT-PPS and PFA, Z=3.21, p=0.01). The worst single model was BKT-CGS (A'=0.4857), and the second-worst single model was CFAR (A'=0.5705).

Table 1. A' values averaged across students for each of the models

Model	Average A'
BKT-PPS	0.7029
Ensemble: linear regression without feature selection (BKT-PPS, BKT-EM, Contextual Slip)	0.7028
Ensemble: linear regression without feature selection (BKT-PPS, BKT-EM)	0.6973
BKT-BF	0.6969
BKT-EM	0.6957
Ensemble: linear regression without feature selection	0.6945
Ensemble: stepwise linear regression	0.6943
Ensemble: logistic regression without feature selection	0.6854
BKT-LessData (maximum 15 data points per student, per skill)	0.6839
PFA	0.6629
Tabling	0.6476
Contextual Slip	0.6149
CFAR	0.5705
BKT-CGS	0.4857

These models' predictions were ensembled using three algorithms: linear regression without feature selection (e.g. including all models), stepwise linear regression (e.g. starting with an empty model, and repeatedly adding the model that most improves fit, until no model significantly improves fit), and logistic regression without feature selection (e.g. including all models). When using stepwise regression, we discovered that for each fold, the first three models added to the ensemble were BKT-PPS, BKT-EM, and Contextual Slip. In order to test these features alone, we turned off feature selection and tried linear regression ensembling using only these three features, and linear regression ensembling using only BKT-PPS and BKT-EM (the first two models added). Interestingly, these restricted ensembles appeared to result in better A' than the full-model ensembles, although the difference was not statistically significant (comparing the 3-model linear regression vs. the full linear regression without feature selection – the best of the full-model ensembles – gives Z=0.87, p=0.39).

The ensembling models appeared to perform worse than BKT-PPS, the best single model. However, the difference between BKT-PPS and the worst ensembling model, logistic regression, was not statistically significant, Z=0.90, p=0.37.

In conclusion, contrary to the original hypothesis, ensembling of multiple student models using regression does not appear to improve ability to predict student performance, when considered at the level of predicting student correctness in the tutor, cross-validated at the student level.

4.2   In-Tutor Performance of Models at Action Level

In the KDD Cup, a well-known Data Mining and Knowledge Discovery competition, the prediction ability of different models is compared based on how well each model predicts each first attempt at each problem step in the data set, instead of averaging within students and then across students. This is a more straightforward approach, although it has multiple limitations: it is less powerful for identifying individual students' learning, less usable in statistical analyses (analyses conducted at this level violate statistical independence assumptions [cf. 2]), and may bias in favor of predicting students who contribute more data. Note that we do not re-fit the models in this section; we simply re-analyze the models with a different goodness metric. When we do so, we obtain the results shown in Table 2.

For this estimation method, ensembling appears to generally perform better than single models, although the difference between the best ensembling method and best single model is quite small (A'=0.7451 versus A'=0.7348). (Note that statistical results are not given, because conducting known statistical tests for A' at this level violates independence assumptions [cf. 2]). This finding suggests that how data is organized can make a difference in findings on goodness. However, once again, ensembling does not appear to make a substantial difference in predictive power.

Table 2. A' computed at the action level for each of the models

Model	A' (calculated for the whole dataset)
Ensemble: linear regression without feature selection (BKT-PPS, BKT-EM, Contextual Slip)	0.7451
Ensemble: linear regression without feature selection	0.7428
Ensemble: stepwise linear regression	0.7423
Ensemble: logistic regression without feature selection	0.7359
Ensemble: linear regression without feature selection (BKT-PPS, BKT-EM)	0.7348
BKT-EM	0.7348
BKT-BF	0.7330
BKT-PPS	0.7310
PFA	0.7277
BKT-LessData (maximum 15 data points per student, per skill)	0.7220
CFAR	0.6723
Tabling	0.6712
Contextual Slip	0.6396
BKT-CGS	0.4917

4.3 Models Predicting Post-Test

Another possible level where ensembling may be beneficial is at predicting the post-test; for example, if individual models over-fit to specific details of in-tutor behavior, a multiple-model ensemble may avoid this over-fit. In predicting the post-test, we account for the number of times each skill will be utilized on the test (assuming perfect performance). Of the eight skills in the tutor lesson, one is not exercised on the test, and is eliminated from post-test prediction. Of the remaining seven skills, four are exercised once, two are exercised twice and one is exercised three times, in each of the two posttest problems. These first two skills are each counted twice and the latter skill three times in our attempts to predict the post-test. We utilize this approach in all attempts to predict the post-test in this paper. We use Pearson's correlation as the goodness metric since the model estimates and the post-test scores are both numerical. Correlation between each model and the post-test is given in Table 3.

From the table we can see that BKT-LessData does better than all other individual models and ensemble models and achieves a correlation of 0.565 to the post-test. BKT-EM and BKT-BF perform only slightly worse than BKT-LessData, respectively achieving correlations of 0.552 and 0.548. Next, the ensemble involving just BKT-PPS and BKT-EM achieves a correlation of 0.54. The difference between BKT-LessData (the best individual model) and the best ensemble was marginally statistically significant, $t(69)=1.87$, $p=0.07$, for a two-tailed test of the significance of the difference between correlations for the same sample. At the bottom of the pack are BKT-CGS and Contextual Slip.

Table 3. Correlations between model predictions and post-test

Model	Correlation to post-test
BKT-LessData (maximum 15 data points per student, per skill)	0.565
BKT-EM	0.552
BKT-BF	0.548
Ensemble: linear regression without feature selection (BKT-PPS, BKT-EM)	0.540
CFAR	0.533
BKT-PPS	0.499
Ensemble: logistic regression without feature selection	0.480
Ensemble: linear regression without feature selection (BKT-PPS, BKT-EM, Contextual Slip)	0.438
Ensemble: linear regression without feature selection	0.342
PFA	0.324
Tabling	0.272
Ensemble: stepwise linear regression	0.254
Contextual Slip	0.057
BKT-CGS	-0.237

5 Discussion and Conclusions

Within this paper, we have compared several different models for tracking student knowledge within intelligent tutoring systems, as well as some simple approaches for ensembling multiple student models at the action level. We have compared these models in terms of their power to predict student behavior in the tutor (cross-validated) and on a paper post-test. Contrary to our original hypothesis, ensembling at the action level did not result in unambiguously better predictive power across analyses than the best of the models taken individually. Ensembling appeared slightly better for flat (e.g. ignoring student) assessment of within-tutor behavior, but was equivalent to a variant of Bayesian Knowledge Tracing (BKT-PPS) for student-level cross-validation of within-tutor behavior, and marginally or non-significantly worse than other variants of Bayesian Knowledge Tracing for predicting the post-test.

One possible explanation for the lack of a positive finding for ensembling is that the models may have been (overall) too similar for ensembling to function well. Another possible explanation is that the differing number of problem steps per student may have caused the current ensembling method to over-fit to students contributing larger amounts of data. Thirdly, it may be that the overall data set was too small for ensembling to perform effectively, suggesting that attempts to replicate these results should be conducted on larger data sets, in order to test this possibility.

A second interesting finding was the overall strong performance of Bayesian Knowledge Tracing variants for all comparisons, with relatively little difference between different ways of fitting the classic BKT model (BKT-EM and BKT-BF) or a recent variant, BKT-PPS. More recent approaches (e.g. PFA, CFAR, Tabling) performed substantially worse than BKT variants on all comparisons. In the case of PFA, these findings contradict other recent research [7, 13] which found that PFA performed better than BKT. However, as in that previous research, the differences between PFA and BKT were relatively small, suggesting that either of these approaches (or for that matter, most variants of BKT) are acceptable methods for student modeling. It may be of greater value for future student modeling research to attempt to investigate the question of *when* and *why* different student model frameworks have greater predictive power, rather than attempting to answer which framework is best overall.

Interestingly, among BKT variants, BKT-CGS performed quite poorly. One possible explanation is that this data set had relatively little data and relatively few skills, compared to the data sets previously studied with this method [e.g. 1], another potential reason why it may make sense to study whether these results replicate within a larger data set. BKT-CGS has previously performed poorly on other data sets from this same tutor [2], perhaps for the same reason. However, the low predictive power of average contextual slip for the post-test does not contradict the finding in [2] that average contextual slip plus BKT predicts the post-test better than BKT alone; in that research, these two models were combined at the post-test level rather than within the tutor. In general, average contextual slip was a productive component of ensembling models (as the third feature selected in each fold) despite its poor individual performance, suggesting it may be a useful future component of student models.

Overall, this paper suggests that Bayesian Knowledge-Tracing remains a highly-effective approach for predicting student knowledge. Our first attempts to utilize ensembling did not perform substantially better than BKT overall; however, it may be that other methods of ensembling will in the future prove more effective.

Acknowledgements. This research was supported by the National Science Foundation via grant "Empirical Research: Emerging Research: Robust and Efficient Learning: Modeling and Remediating Students' Domain Knowledge", award number DRL0910188, and by a "Graduates in K-12 Education" (GK-12) Fellowship, award number DGE0742503. We would like to thank Albert Corbett for providing the data set used in this paper, and for comments and suggestions.

References

1. Baker, R.S.J.d., Corbett, A.T., Aleven, V.: More Accurate Student Modeling through Contextual Estimation of Slip and Guess Probabilities in Bayesian Knowledge Tracing. In: Woolf, B.P., Aïmeur, E., Nkambou, R., Lajoie, S. (eds.) ITS 2008. LNCS, vol. 5091, pp. 406–415. Springer, Heidelberg (2008)
2. Baker, R.S.J.d., Corbett, A.T., Gowda, S.M., Wagner, A.Z., MacLaren, B.A., Kauffman, L.R., Mitchell, A.P., Giguere, S.: Contextual Slip and Prediction of Student Performance after Use of an Intelligent Tutor. In: De Bra, P., Kobsa, A., Chin, D. (eds.) UMAP 2010. LNCS, vol. 6075, pp. 52–63. Springer, Heidelberg (2010)
3. Brusilovsky, P., Millán, E.: User models for adaptive hypermedia and adaptive educational systems. In: Brusilovsky, P., Kobsa, A., Nejdl, W. (eds.) Adaptive Web 2007. LNCS, vol. 4321, pp. 3–53. Springer, Heidelberg (2007)
4. Chang, K.-m., Beck, J.E., Mostow, J., Corbett, A.T.: A bayes net toolkit for student modeling in intelligent tutoring systems. In: Ikeda, M., Ashley, K.D., Chan, T.-W. (eds.) ITS 2006. LNCS, vol. 4053, pp. 104–113. Springer, Heidelberg (2006)
5. Corbett, A., Kauffman, L., Maclaren, B., Wagner, A., Jones, E.: A Cognitive Tutor for Genetics Problem Solving: Learning Gains and Student Modeling. Journal of Educational Computing Research 42, 219–239 (2010)
6. Corbett, A.T., Anderson, J.R.: Knowledge Tracing: Modeling the Acquisition of Procedural Knowledge. User Modeling and User-Adapted Interaction 4, 253–278 (1995)
7. Gong, Y., Beck, J.E., Heffernan, N.T.: Comparing Knowledge Tracing and Performance Factor Analysis by Using Multiple Model Fitting Procedures. In: Aleven, V., Kay, J., Mostow, J. (eds.) ITS 2010. LNCS, vol. 6094, pp. 35–44. Springer, Heidelberg (2010)
8. Koedinger, K.R., Corbett, A.T.: Cognitive tutors: Technology bringing learning science to the classroom. In: Sawyer, K. (ed.) The Cambridge Handbook of the Learning Sciences, pp. 61 78. Cambridge University Press, New York (2006)
9. Pardos, Z.A., Heffernan, N.T.: Modeling Individualization in a Bayesian Networks Implementation of Knowledge Tracing. In: De Bra, P., Kobsa, A., Chin, D. (eds.) UMAP 2010. LNCS, vol. 6075, pp. 255–266. Springer, Heidelberg (2010)
10. Pardos, Z.A., Heffernan, N.T.: Navigating the parameter space of Bayesian Knowledge Tracing models: Visualizations of the convergence of the Expectation Maximization algorithm. In: Proceedings of the 3rd International Conference on Educational Data Mining, pp. 161–170 (2010)

11. Pardos, Z.A., Heffernan, N.T.: Using HMMs and bagged decision trees to leverage rich features of user and skill from an intelligent tutoring system dataset. To appear in Journal of Machine Learning Research W & CP
12. Pavlik, P.I., Cen, H., Koedinger, K.R.: Learning Factors Transfer Analysis: Using Learning Curve Analysis to Automatically Generate Domain Models. In: Proceedings of the 2nd International Conference on Educational Data Mining, pp. 121–130 (2009)
13. Pavlik, P.I., Cen, H., Koedinger, K.R.: Performance Factors Analysis – A New Alternative to Knowledge Tracing. In: Proceedings of the 14th International Conference on Artificial Intelligence in Education, pp. 531–538 (2009), Version of paper used is online at http://eric.ed.gov/PDFS/ED506305.pdf (retrieved January 26, 2011); This version has minor differences from the printed version of this paper
14. Rai, D., Gong, Y., Beck, J.E.: Using Dirichlet priors to improve model parameter plausibility. In: Proceedings of the 2nd International Conference on Educational Data Mining, Cordoba, Spain, pp. 141–148 (2009)
15. Reye, J.: Student modeling based on belief networks. International Journal of Artificial Intelligence in Education 14, 1–33 (2004)
16. Caruana, R., Niculescu-Mizil, A.: Ensemble selection from libraries of models. In: Proceedings of the 21st International Conference on Machine Learning, ICML 2004 (2004)
17. Wang, Q.Y., Pardos, Z.A., Heffernan, N.T.: Fold Tabling Method: A New Alternative and Complement to Knowledge Tracing (manuscript under review)
18. Yu, H.-F., Lo, H.-Y., Hsieh, H.-P., Lou, J.-K., McKenzie, T.G., Chou, J.-W., et al.: Feature Engineering and Classifier Ensemble for KDD Cup 2010. In: Proceedings of the KDD Cup 2010 Workshop, pp. 1–16 (2010)

Creating Personalized Digital Human Models of Perception for Visual Analytics

Mike Bennett[1] and Aaron Quigley[2]

[1] SCIEN, Department of Psychology, Jordan Hall, Building 01-420,
Stanford University, CA 94305, United States
mikemb@stanford.edu
[2] SACHI, School of Computer Science, North Haugh,
University of St Andrews, KY16 9SX, UK
aquigley@cs.st-andrews.ac.uk

Abstract. Our bodies shape our experience of the world, and our bodies influence what we design. How important are the physical differences between people? Can we model the physiological differences and use the models to adapt and personalize designs, user interfaces and artifacts? Within many disciplines Digital Human Models and Standard Observer Models are widely used and have proven to be very useful for modeling users and simulating humans. In this paper, we create personalized digital human models of perception (Individual Observer Models), particularly focused on how humans see. Individual Observer Models capture how our bodies shape our perceptions. Individual Observer Models are useful for adapting and personalizing user interfaces and artifacts to suit individual users' bodies and perceptions. We introduce and demonstrate an Individual Observer Model of human eyesight, which we use to simulate 3600 biologically valid human eyes. An evaluation of the simulated eyes finds that they *see* eye charts the same as humans. Also demonstrated is the Individual Observer Model successfully making predictions about how easy or hard it is to see visual information and visual designs. The ability to predict and adapt visual information to maximize how effective it is is an important problem in visual design and analytics.

Keywords: virtual humans, physiology modeling, computational user model, individual differences, human vision, digital human model.

1 Introduction

Our bodies shape our experience of the world, and our bodies influence what we design. For example clothes are not designed for people with three arms because designers implicitly model standard human physiology. Yet, human bodies differ, some people are born with small bodies, others with bodies that see colors differently (colorblindness). How important are these physical differences between people? Can we model the physiological differences and use the models to adapt and personalize designs, user interfaces and artifacts?

Joseph A. Konstan et al. (Eds.): UMAP 2011, LNCS 6787, pp. 25–37, 2011.

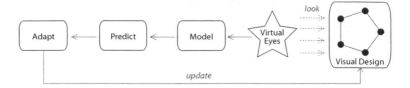

Fig. 1. To adapt a visualization or visual design we use Individual Observer Models of eyesight. The models integrate with predictors, which feed into adaption techniques for improving the layout and presentation of visualizations and visual designs.

Many domains, such as medicine, health, sports science, and car safety are creating digital human models [7]. These digital human models are very useful for identifying and evaluating the strengths and weakness in prototype artifacts and novel tools. Initially, the majority of the digital human models were primarily concerned with modeling humans' physical bodies and biomechanics [3]. Recently, there has been a move to richer and multifaceted digital human models, which are capable of modeling many aspects of being human, including modeling aspects of cognition, simulating affect (emotion) [12], modeling group and social dynamics, and simulating aesthetics and taste [6]. Numerous challenges and research opportunities exist for creating and integrating biomechanical models with cognitive and perceptual models [10,16,7].

In this work, we create personalized digital human models of perception, particularly focused on how humans see (Figure 1). With digital human models of eyesight a visual design can be evaluated to establish what parts of a design are easy or difficult to see. For example when viewing an information visualization on a wall sized display from far away, how small can the visual features of the information visualization be before they are impossible to clearly and easily see?

Individual differences in human bodies often cause differences in how humans perceive and experience the world, e.g. colorblindness. Introduced in this paper are *Individual Observer Models*, which are user models of individual bodies and perceptions. Individual Observer Models capture how our bodies shape our perceptions. Individual Observer Models are useful for adapting and personalizing user interfaces to suit individual users' bodies and perceptions.

We introduce and demonstrate an Individual Observer Model of human eyesight, which we use to simulate 3600 different biologically valid human eyes. An evaluation of the simulated eyes finds that they *see* eye charts the same as humans. Also demonstrated is the Individual Observer Model successfully making predictions about how easy or hard it is to see visual information. The ability to predict and adapt visual information to maximize how effective it is is an important problem in visual design and analytics.

2   Modeling and Creating Individual Virtual Eyes

To build the Individual Observer Model of human eyesight we create a simplified optical model of how the human eye works. The model has parameters for

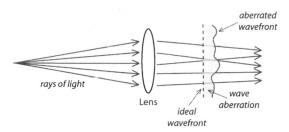

Fig. 2. Example of ideal and aberrated wavefronts generated by rays of light travelling through an optical system (eye)

controlling the amount of individual differences in eyesight. The eyesight model is built on research from vision science [14], optometry [13] and ophthalmology [9]. Fortunately, modeling individual differences in eyesight is extensively studied in optometry and ophthalmology research [4,21,8,13].

Building models of human eyesight is challenging, both technically and because many questions remain unsolved about how human vision works. In order to build a useful human vision model, we limit how much of human vision we model. Specifically, we focus on modeling how light travels through the human eye. Individual differences between peoples' eyes are accounted for by modeling individual differences in the physical structure of human eyes.

Depending on the physical structure of eyes, some peoples' eyes are very good at focusing light on the back of the eye, while in other cases the eyes are bad at focusing light. This difference in how well the eye does or does not focus light is due to the amount of aberrations in the eyes. People with eyes that have high amounts of aberrations usually have worse eyesight than those with low amounts of eye aberrations. Nobody has aberration free eyesight, but there are normal amounts and types of aberrations.

Differences in the amount of eye aberrations has a large impact on how easily people can or cannot see visual information. In particular, modeling eye aberrations is good for predicting the amount of visual detail people can see. The ability to see visual detail is called visual acuity. Good visual acuity commonly implies low amounts of eye aberrations, or that an eye has been corrected to reduce the impact of the aberrations. Correction is done either with eye glasses, or with various kinds of eye surgery. Visual acuity is known to significantly differ between people. In some cases this difference is genetic in origin, in other cases it is due to age related changes, and other times it is due to medical issues [21].

The ability to model individual human eyes gives us the ability to measure how individual eyes transform visual information. We can take a visual design, pass it through a virtual eye, then capture the visual design as it is seen at the back of the virtual eye.

2.1   Modeling the Flaws and Aberrations in a Human Eye

In this and the following subsections we briefly describe our model of the human eye and how it works. Background on the particular approach we adopt for modeling eye aberrations can be found in Krueger et al.'s work on human vision [9]. Far more vision science detail and background on our approach to modeling individual eyes and human vision can be found in [1].

Our eye model accounts for how rays of light travel through the human eye. Looking at Figure 2 you can see that multiple rays of light are entering a lens (eye). After the rays of light pass through the lens they are not aligned with each other, and in some cases mistakenly cross. In a perfect eye the rays of light are focused on a single spot (fovea), while in an aberrated eye the light rays are imperfectly focused. Depending on the location at which a ray of light passes through the lens, it will get aberrated in different ways and by different amounts. In order to model how different parts of the lens affect light rays, we use wavefronts. Wavefronts describe how numerous light rays simultaneously behave over many points of a lens [9]. A wavefront is perpendicular to the light ray paths.

For example, in Figure 2 we have an ideal wavefront and an aberrated wavefront. The ideal wavefront is the dotted line, and it represents all the light rays emerging from the lens in parallel. Unfortunately, all the light rays are not parallel so the wavefront is distorted and aberrated. Wavefronts are widely used by ophthalmologists when planning eye surgery to correct human vision, such as LASIK eye surgery [9].

2.2 Simulating Individual Differences in Eyesight

Wavefronts enable us to model individual eyes, because we can create and simulate wavefronts (W_{eye}), then use the wavefronts to transform a visual design into what is seen at the back of the human eye. Provided in Equation 1 is the wavefront aberration function for modeling wavefronts. For details on using Zernike Polynomials to model human eyes see [1,18,20,19,9].

The important thing to realize from the wavefront function equation is that the Zernike coefficients (C_n^m) weigh the Zernike modes (Z_n^m). Each Zernike mode (roughly) corresponds to a particular type of aberration commonly found in the human eye, such as astigmatism, defocus or coma. Each Zernike coefficient

Equation 1. Wavefront aberration function as weighted sum of Zernike Polynomials [20].

$$W_{eye}(p,\theta) = \sum_{n,m} C_n^m Z_n^m(p,\theta) \qquad (1)$$

where

C_n^m is Zernike coefficient in microns μm
Z_n^m is double indexed Zernike mode (see [19])

and

p is normalized pupil radius
θ is azimuthal component from 0 to 2π radians

describes how much of each particular kind of aberration occurs. When you sum up all the aberrations you end up with a virtual wavefont (W_{eye}) that describes how light is altered as it passes through the human eye.

To simulate the wavefront of an individual's eye, we sum the first fourteen aberrations (Zernike modes) and for each aberration set the amount of aberration (Zernike coefficient) by randomly picking a value from within the normal range for that type of aberration.

Elsewhere [20], it has been established what the normal values and ranges of each Zernike coefficient is. This was achieved by measuring and analysing over 2560 wavefronts of healthy human eyes [18]. We use the first fourteen aberrations as it has also been previously established that they matter the most. Provided in [1] on page 86 Table 3.2 are the ranges of Zernike coefficients we use.

2.3 Simulating What Is Seen at the Back of an Eye

Once we have a virtual eye wavefront (W_{eye}), we use the virtual eye (W_{eye}) to transform the original design into the design as seen by the back of the human eye. In order to transform the original design, we convert the W_{eye} to an image convolution kernel (widely used in image filtering), and then apply the image kernel to the original design. The resulting image is the design as it is seen at the back of the eye.

Shown in Figure 3 are examples of how a photograph of a pair of shoes on grass is seen by three different eyes. The amount of individual differences between the eyes is small. A limitation of our current eye simulation is that it is restricted to grayscale images. This restriction exists because in vision science it is not yet known what the normal aberration amounts for color eyesight are.

2.4 Predicting What Users Can or Cannot See

To predict what a user can or cannot see, we use the virtual eyes in a predictor (Figure 1). The predictor quantifies how differently individual eyes see the same visual information. Quantifying the impact of individual differences in eyesight enables us to improve the layout and presentation of visual information, by adapting it to suit individual eyes and groups of eyes.

The predictor works by *looking* at the original visual design through a virtual eye, then it compares the original design against the design as seen at the back of the eye. The difference between the original design and the perceived design gives a measure of how individual differences in peoples' eyesight impacts upon the perception of visual information.

Fig. 3. Example of how three different simulated eyes see a photograph of shoes on grass. First photograph is the original version.

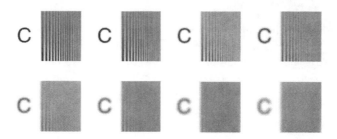

Fig. 4. Examples of how increasing amounts of aberration effects two different visual patterns. On the left is the letter C, while on the right is a pattern of alternating bars. Amount of aberration increasing from left to right, top to bottom.

In this work *Perceptual Stability For Visual Acuity* ($PERS_{va}$) [1] is used to measure the differences between the original and perceived design. $PERS_{va}$ is a space-scale approach to image analysis, which uses an information theoretic measure of image content. Further details on the vision science motivation and equations for $PERS_{va}$ can be found elsewhere [1].

When used, $PERS_{va}$ gives a single value score, which indicates how differently the original and perceived design look. A high $PERS_{va}$ score indicates that the visual design changes a lot and is harder to see due to passing through an aberrated eye, while a low score indicates that the visual design is easier to see and does not change much due to the aberrations.

For example, if the same virtual eye *looks* at the two visual patterns as shown in Figure 4. For the virtual eye, the C pattern has a lower $PERS_{va}$ score than the alternating bars, which indicates that the aberrations in the eye effect the perception of the alternating bars more than the perception of the C.

3 Evaluation

In order to evaluate the Individual Observer Model of human eyesight, we test whether the virtual eyes *see* the same as human eyesight. To establish whether the virtual eyes see the same as human observers, we generate 3600 different biologically valid eyes. Each of the 3600 virtual eyes looks at various visual patterns, such as eye charts. If the virtual eyes are valid, then they should agree with human judgements about what parts of the eye charts are easy or hard to see.

For example, shown in Figure 5 is an eye chart that is commonly used to measure how well people can or cannot see. It is known that a person looking at the eye chart will find letters at the top of the chart easier to see than at the bottom of the chart. Figure 8 shows how 300 virtual eyes judge what parts of the eye chart are easier or harder to see (the red text is the normalized $PERS_{va}$ scores). The top of the eye chart is white, indicating it is seen easiest, while the bottom of the eye chart is black, indicating it is the hardest part of the eye chart to see.

3.1   Eye Charts Are Gold Standard Measure of Human Eyesight

When creating models and simulations of human perception a significant challenge is figuring out how to test whether the simulation agrees with human judgements. For testing the virtual eyes it would be easy to create a stimulus, and then test how well the virtual eyes perceive the stimulus. Unfortunately, that could easily lead to cases where the eye model and simulation are optimized for properties of the stimulus. An additional concern is it is known that subtle variants in a stimulus can lead to significant differences in human perception. An important criteria for testing digital human models of human perception is: *Before testing a virtual human with a stimulus, the perceptual properities of the stimulus need to be well understood and established for humans.*

For testing the digital human models of eyesight we use three different eye charts, which test different aspects of human vision. The creation and validation of eye charts is a sub-field in optometry and vision science. Designing eye charts that do not have any subtle perceptual flaws is tricky, as subtle flaws do lead to incorrect evaluations of peoples' eyesight.

We tested the Individual Observer Model of eyesight with the three different eye charts shown in Figure 5, 6 & 7. These eye charts test different related facets of human vision that are known to effect peoples' ability to see visual information. Even though the range of visual features on the eye charts is limited (varying letters, size, contrast & lines), it is well established that human performance on these eye charts is a good predictor of human performance at many visual tasks [13,8].

The chart in Figure 5 is called the ETDRS Chart [5] and it tests how well people can see increasingly smaller letters. People can see the top of the chart easier than the bottom. Shown in Figure 6 is the Pelli-Robson Contrast Sensitivity Chart [15], which shows increasingly harder to see letters, where letter hardness increases from left to right going downwards. The letters become harder to see because of reduced contrast between letter color and background color. Figure 7 shows the Campbell-Robson Contrast Sensitivity Chart [2], which tests the combination of varying size and contrast. When looking at the Campbell-Robson Chart observers see the visual detail in the region on the right of the chart. As the observers' visual acuity increases or decreases the size and position of the region they can see detail in either moves up (better vision) or down (worse vision) and gets bigger (better vision) or smaller (worse vision).

3.2   Results of Evaluation of 3600 Virtual Eyes

Each eye chart is independently used as a stimulus, and each eye chart is divided into a range of equal sized regions. Depending on how each eye chart is used to test human vision, we expect that the predictor ($PERS_{va}$) correctly identifies what regions are easier to see when compared to other regions within the same eye chart.

For the evaluation 3600 virtual eyes viewed the eye charts and the resulting $PERS_{va}$ scores were averaged for all the eyes. If the virtual eyes are effective, then they should agree with human judgements for the eye charts.

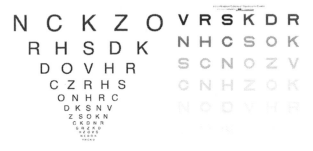

Fig. 5. ETDRS Eye Chart

Fig. 6. Pelli-Robson Contrast Sensitivity Chart

Fig. 7. Campbell-Robson Contrast Sensitivity Chart

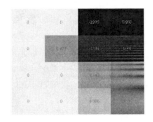

Fig. 8. Heatmap of ET-DRS eye chart when divided into 1 by 4 regions

Fig. 9. Heatmap of Pelli-Robson eye chart when divided into 2 by 2 regions

Fig. 10. Heatmap of Campbell-Robson chart when divided into 4 by 4 regions

For the eye charts we find that the predictions of what the virtual eyes see agrees with what humans see. Results are shown in Figure 8 to Figure 13. These figures show how the predictor scores (normalized $PERS_{va}$) compare between regions. When a region is colored white, it is the easiest to see (lowest normalised $PERS_{va}$ score), black indicates the hardest to see (highest $PERS_{va}$ score) and grayscale indicates intermediate hardness / $PERS_{va}$ score.

ETDRS Chart. In Figure 8 we see that the top of the eye chart is white, indicating it is seen easiest, while the bottom of the eye chart is black, indicating it is the hardest part of the eye chart to see. These results are correct.

Are the results due to how the eye chart is divided into 1 by 4 regions? That is addressed by also analysing the eye chart divided into 1 by 2 (Figure 11) and 1 by 3 regions. The results are also in agreement with human vision. That is the virtual eyes find top of the eye chart easier to see, with it becoming increasingly harder to see visual information towards the bottom of the eye chart.

Pelli-Robson Chart. We find that the virtual eyes see the Pelli-Robson Chart correctly. Shown in Figure 9 are the results, when the eye chart is divided into 2 by 2 regions. The eye chart gets harder to see from left to right going downwards,

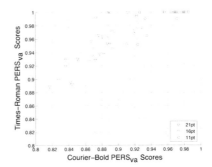

Fig. 11. Heatmap of ETDRS chart divided into 1 by 2 regions

Fig. 12. Heatmap of Pelli-Robson chart divided into 2 by 1 regions

Fig. 13. Heatmap of Campbell-Robson chart when divided into 2 by 2 regions

Fig. 14. Virtual eye comparison of font styles & sizes. Shown is mean & standard deviation of $PERS_{va}$ scores.

Fig. 15. Scatterplot showing how each virtual eye sees each font & font size. Each data point is a virtual eye.

where the lower right corner of the chart is the hardest to see. When the eye chart is divided into 2 by 1 (Figure 12) and 2 by 3 regions the results are also in agreement with human vision.

Campbell-Robson Chart. An especially interesting result is how the virtual eyes see the Campbell-Robson Chart. It is especially interesting because the eye chart does not use letters, rather it uses a more visually complex pattern. Our virtual eye models do see the Campbell-Robson Chart correctly.

When the chart is divided into 4 by 4 regions, results shown in Figure 10, we find the top right of the chart is hardest to see, while the lower right is easiest to see. Nothing is seen on the left side of the chart, as we would expect from human judgements. When the chart is divided into 1 by 2, 1 by 3, 1 by 4, 2 by 2 (Figure 13) and 3 by 3 the virtual eyes are in agreement with how humans see.

4   Demonstration: Looking at Fonts and InfoVis Graphs

Briefly, we describe two examples of the virtual eyes evaluating how easy it is to see different text font styles and different visual styles of graphs. Many fonts

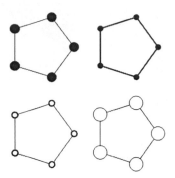

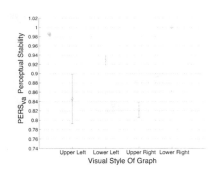

Fig. 16. Four different ways to draw the same simple graph. Nodes and lines vary.

Fig. 17. Comparison of graphs, mean & std of $PERS_{va}$ scores for graphs in Figure 16

styles are often used in visual designs, but it is usually unclear whether one font style is easier to see than another. Especially interesting is whether a particular font style is best for one individual, while a different font style is best for another person. An equivalent challenge for visual analytics and information visualization is correctly designing the visual style line or graph node so that it is easy to see.

Comparing Font Styles. Two different font styles are compared, at three different font sizes. Twenty virtual eyes looked at a paragraph of text drawn with the different fonts and at the different sizes. The first font style is Courier-Bold (CB) font, the second font is Times-Roman (TR), and the 3 font sizes are 11pt, 16pt and 21pt.

Shown in Figure 14 are the results of the twenty virtual eyes looking at the fonts. Based on the $PERS_{va}$ scores, the virtual eyes predict that the Courier-Bold point size 21 (CB 21pt) is the easiest font to see, while the hardest font to see is Times-Roman 11pt (TR 11pt). In Figure 15 we can check how easily the same eye sees CB versus TR fonts. For example, in Fig 15 the lower left blue triangle indicates a specific virtual eye had a $PERS_{va}$ score of approximately 0.815 for the CB 21pt font, while the same eye had a $PERS_{va}$ score of 0.89 for the TR 21pt font.

Particularly noteworthy is that these results are in agreement with the work of Mansfield et al [11], who evaluated how legible human subjects find the CB versus TR fonts. Figure 19 shows how each individual eyes see each font, these individual differences are discussed in the Discussion section.

Comparing Graph Styles. Shown in Figure 16 are the four different simple graphs that twenty virtual eyes looked at. The results shown in Figure 17 indicate that the upper left and upper right graphs are the easiest to see.

Interestingly in Figure 17 the upper left graph has a wider standard deviation, which indicates that due to the differences between the virtual eyes there is more

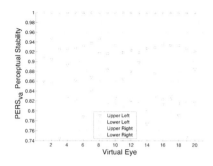 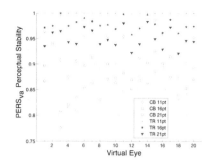

Fig. 18. Distribution of $PERS_{va}$ for each virtual eye for each graph style

Fig. 19. Distribution of $PERS_{va}$ score for each virtual eye for each font style & size

variability between people in how the upper left graph is seen when compared to the upper right graph. Figure 18 shows how each individual eye sees each graph, which is discussed below.

5   Discussion and Conclusions

In the Introduction we asked *Can we model the (users) physiological differences and use the models to adapt and personalize designs, user interfaces and artifacts?* In this work we have successfully addressed that question. By showing how to model individual physiological differences in eyesight, then demonstrating using the models (along with $PERS_{va}$) to evaluate a set of visual designs. After which, the best scoring visual design for a user's eyesight is identified and can be shown to a user, i.e. personalizing the visual design by picking from a set of competing visual designs.

Also posed in the Introduction was the related question *How important are these physical differences between people?* Or framing it another way, are there benefits by personalizing based on individual differences in users' physiology? The results in Figure 18 & 19 establishes that the individual differences between people do matter, though the extend to which they matter depends on the visual design. For some visual designs the physical differences between people matter more, for other designs they matter less. For an example of when the physical differences do matter - in Figure 18 most of the virtual eyes find it easiest to see the Upper Right graph (green circle) in Figure 16, while some of the eyes find it easier to see the Upper Left graph (blue triangle). In Figure 19 we find that the physical differences between individual eyes matter less, as all the virtual eyes agree that the Courier-Bold 21pt (red circle) is easiest to see.

An interesting limitation of this work is that our eye model is of low-level early stage vision - predominately concerned with modeling the optics of the human eyeball. There are other differences in human vision which may be worth modeling, e.g. light receptor density and distribution, perception of motion, optical flow, visual crowding [17].

There are also many opportunities for creating Individual Observer Models for various modalities of human experience, e.g. taste, smell, touch. Though creating Individual Observer Models is challenging because they require quantifying the relationship between a sensation and the perception of the sensation. While also requiring the creation of physiologically valid models of human bodies, and requiring that the Individual Observer Models model individual differences in physical function of the human body. Based on previous user modeling research, there are various user models that quantify the perception of designs and artifacts, so there may be opportunities to tie existing models of perception to individual physiological models of users.

Acknowledgements. This research was made possible with support from University College Dublin, SICSA - Scottish Informatics and Computer Science Alliance, Stanford Center for Image Systems Engineering, and Microsoft.

References

1. Bennett, M.: Designing For An Individual's Eyes: Human-Computer Interaction, Vision And Individual Differences. PhD thesis, College of Engineering, Mathematical And Physical Sciences, University College Dublin, Ireland (2009)
2. Campbell, F.W., Robson, J.G.: Application of fourier analysis to the visibility of gratings. Journal of Physiology 197, 551–566 (1968)
3. Chaffin, D.B.: Digtal human models for workspace design. Reviews of Human Factors and Ergonomics 4, 44–74 (2008)
4. Dong, L.M., Hawkins, B.S., Marsh, M.J.: Consistency between visual acuity scores obtained at different distances. Archives of Ophthalmology 120, 1523–1533 (2002)
5. Ferris, F., Kassoff, A., Bresnick, G., Bailey, I.: New visual acuity charts for clinical research. American Journal of Ophthalmology 94, 91–96 (1982)
6. Freyne, J., Berkovsky, S.: Recommending food: Reasoning on recipes and ingredients. In: De Bra, P., Kobsa, A., Chin, D. (eds.) UMAP 2010. LNCS, vol. 6075, pp. 381–386. Springer, Heidelberg (2010)
7. Fuller, H., Reed, M., Liu, Y.: Integrating physical and cognitive human models to represent driving behavior. In: Proceedings of Human Factors and Ergonomics Society 54th Annual Meeting, pp. 1042–1046 (2010)
8. Ginsburg, A., Evans, D., Sekuler, R., Harp, S.: Contrast sensitivity predicts pilots' performance in aircraft simulators. American Journal of Optometry and Physiological Optics 59, 105–108 (1982)
9. Krueger, R.R., Applegate, R.A., MacRae, S.M.: Wavefront Customized Visual Correction: The Quest for Super Vision II (2004)
10. Liu, Y., Feyen, R., Tsimhoni, O.: Queueing network-model human processor (qn-mhp): A computational architecture for multitask performance in human-machine systems. ACM Transactions on Computer-Human Interaction 13(1), 37–70 (2006)
11. Mansfield, J., Legge, G., Bane, M.: Psychophysics of reading: Xv. font effects in normal and low vision. Journal of Investigative Ophthalmology and Visual Science 37(8), 1492–1501 (1996)
12. Marsella, S.: Modeling emotion and its expression in virtual humans. In: De Bra, P., Kobsa, A., Chin, D. (eds.) UMAP 2010. LNCS, vol. 6075, pp. 1–2. Springer, Heidelberg (2010)

13. Norton, T.T., Corliss, D.A., Bailey, J.E.: The Psychophysical Measurement of Visual Function (2002)
14. Palmer, S.E.: Vision Science: Photons to Phenomenlogy (1999)
15. Pelli, D.G., Robson, J.G., Wilkins, A.J.: The design of a new letter chart for measuring contrast sensitivity. Clinical Vision Sciences 2(3), 187–199 (1988)
16. Reed, M., Faraway, J., Chaffin, D.B., Martin, B.J.: The humosim ergonomics framework: A new approach to digital human simulation for ergonomic analysis. In: Digital Human Modeling for Design and Engineering Conference, SAE Technical Papers Series (2006)
17. Rosenholtz, R., Li, Y., Mansfield, J., Jin, Z.: Feature congestion: A measure of display clutter. In: Proceedings of SIGCHI, pp. 761–770 (2005)
18. Salmon, T.O., van de Pol, C.: Normal-eye zernike coefficients and root-mean-square wavefront errors. Journal of Cataract Refractive Surgery 32, 2064–2074 (2006)
19. Thibos, L.N., Applegate, R.A., Schwiegerling, J.T., Webb, R., Members, V.S.T.: Standards for reporting the optical aberrations of eyes. Vision Science and its Applications, 232–244 (February 2000)
20. Thibos, L.N., Bradley, A., Hong, X.: A statistical model of the aberration structure of normal, well-corrected eyes. Journal of Ophthalmic and Physiological Optics 22, 427–433 (2002)
21. West, S.K., Muñoz, B., Rubin, G.S., Schein, O.D., Bandeen-Roche, K., Zeger, S., German, P.S., Fried, L.P.: Function and visual impairment in a population based study of older adults. Journal of Investigative Ophthalmology and Visual Science 38(1), 72–82 (1997)

Coping with Poor Advice from Peers in Peer-Based Intelligent Tutoring: The Case of Avoiding Bad Annotations of Learning Objects

John Champaign[1], Jie Zhang[2], and Robin Cohen[1]

[1] 200 University Ave W; Waterloo, Ontario N2L 3G1 Canada
[2] School of Computer Engineering Block N4 #02c-110
Nanyang Avenue Singapore 639798
{jchampai,rcohen}@uwaterloo.ca
zhangj@ntu.edu.sg

Abstract. In this paper, we examine a challenge that arises in the application of peer-based tutoring: coping with inappropriate advice from peers. We examine an environment where students are presented with those learning objects predicted to improve their learning (on the basis of the success of previous, like-minded students) but where peers can additionally inject annotations. To avoid presenting annotations that would detract from student learning (e.g. those found confusing by other students) we integrate trust modeling, to detect over time the reputation of the annotation (as voted by previous students) and the reputability of the annotator. We empirically demonstrate, through simulation, that even when the environment is populated with a large number of poor annotations, our algorithm for directing the learning of the students is effective, confirming the value of our proposed approach for student modeling. In addition, the research introduces a valuable integration of trust modeling into educational applications.

1 Introduction

In this paper we explore a challenge that arises when peers are involved, in the environment of intelligent tutoring systems: coping with advice that may detract from a student's learning. Our approach is situated in a scenario where the learning objects[1] presented to a student are, first of all, determined on the basis of the benefits in learning derived by similar students (involving a process of pre- and post-tests to perform assessments). In addition, however, we allow students to leave annotations of those learning objects. Our challenge then becomes to determine which annotations to present to each new student and in particular to be able to cope when there are a large number of annotations which are, in fact, best not to show, to ensure effective student learning.

---

[1] A learning object can be a video, chapter from a book, quiz or anything else a student could interact with on a computer and possibly learn from as described in [1].

Joseph A. Konstan et al. (Eds.): UMAP 2011, LNCS 6787, pp. 38–49, 2011.
© Springer-Verlag Berlin Heidelberg 2011

Our work is thus situated in the user modeling application area of intelligent e-learning and, in particular, in the context of peer-based intelligent tutoring. We seek to enhance student learning as the primary focus of the user modeling that we perform. Our user modeling in fact integrates a) a modeling of the learning achieved by the students, their current level of knowledge and their similarity to other students and b) a modeling of the trustworthiness of the students, as annotators.

The decision of which annotations to ultimately show to each new student is derived, in part, on the basis of votes for and against, registered with each annotation, by previous students. In this respect our research relates as well to the general topic of recommender systems (in a style of collaborative filtering). In the Discussion section we reflect briefly on how our work compares to that specific user modeling subtopic.

We ground the presentation of our research and our results very specifically in the context of coping with possible "bad" advice from peers. And we maintain a specific focus on the setting of annotated learning objects. From here, we reflect more generally on advice for the design of peer-based intelligent tutoring systems, in comparison with other researchers in the field, emphasizing the kind of student modeling that is valuable to be performing. We also conclude with a view towards future research. Included in our final discussion is also a reflection on the trust modeling that we perform for our particular application and suggestions for future adjustments. As such, we present as well a few observations on the value of trust modeling for peer-based educational applications.

2   Overview of Model Directing Student Learning

In this section, we present an overview of our current model for reasoning about which learning objects and which annotations to present to a new student, based on a) the previous learning of similar students b) the votes for annotations offered by students with a similar rating behaviour c) a modeling of the annotation's reputation, based, in part, on a modeling of the overall reputation of the annotator. The user modeling that is involved in this model is therefore a combination of student modeling (to enable effective student learning), similarity of peers (but grounded, in part, in their educational similarity) and trust modeling of students as annotators.

Step 1: Selecting a learning object
We begin with a repository of learning objects that have previously been assembled to deliver educational value to students. From here, we attach over time the experiences of peers in order to select the appropriate learning object for each new student. This process respects what McCalla has referred to as the "ecological approach" to e-learning [1]. The learning object selected for a student is the one with the highest predicted benefit, where each learning object l's benefit to active student s is calculated as [2]:

$$p[s, l] = \kappa \sum_{j=1}^{n} w(s, j)v(j, l) \qquad (1)$$

where v is the value of l to any student j previously exposed to it (which we measure by mapping onto a scale from 0 to 1 the increases or decreases in letter grade post-test assessment compared to pre-test assessment), w is the similarity between active student s and previous student j (measured by comparing current letter grade assessments of achievement levels) and κ is a normalizing factor currently set to $\frac{1}{n}$

Step 2: Allow annotations of learning objects and votes on those annotations

As students are presented with learning objects, each is allowed to optionally attach an annotation which may be shown to a new student. Once annotations are shown to students, they register a thumbs up or a thumbs down rating.

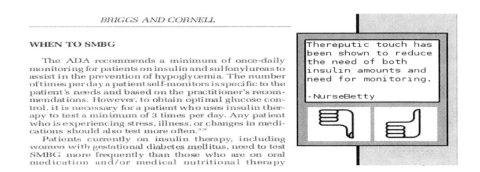

Fig. 1. Example of a low-quality annotation, adapted from [3]

The learning object presented in Figure 1 is for tutoring caregivers in the context of home healthcare (an application area in which we currently projecting our research [4]). The specific topic featured in this example is the management of insulin for patients with diabetes. This annotation recommends therapeutic touch (a holistic treatment that has been scientifically debunked, but remains popular with nurse practitioners). It would detract from learning if presented and should be shown to as few students as possible.

Consider now that: *In an ITS devoted to training homecare and hospice nurses, one section of the material discusses diet and how it is important to maintain proper nutrition, even for terminal patients who often have cravings for foods that will do them harm. One nurse, Alex, posts an annotation saying how in his experience often compassion takes higher precedence than strictly prolonging every minute of the patient's life, and provides details about how he has discussed this with the patients, their families and his supervisor.*

This annotation may receive many thumbs up ratings from caregivers who can relate to its advice. Since it is a real world example of how the material was applied, and it introduces higher reasoning beyond the standard instruction, that turns out to be a very worthwhile annotation to show to other students.

Some annotations may be effective for certain students but not for others. Consider now: *A section on techniques for use with patients recovering from eye surgery in a home healthcare environment has some specific, step-by-step techniques for tasks such as washing out the eye with disinfected water. A nurse, Riley, posts an advanced, detailed comment about the anatomy of the eye, the parts that are commonly damaged, a link to a medical textbook providing additional details and how this information is often of interest to recovering patients. The remedial students struggling with the basic materials find this annotation overwhelming and consistently give the annotation bad ratings, while advanced students find this an engaging comment that enhances the material for them and give it a good rating.*

Since our approach reasons about the similarity of students, over time, this annotation will be shown to advanced students, but not to students struggling with the material.

Some annotations might appear to be undesirable but in fact do lead to educational benefit and should therefore be shown. We present an example below. *An annotation is left in a basic science section of the material arguing against an assertion in the text about temperatures saying that in some conditions boiling water freezes faster than cooler water. This immediately prompts negative ratings and follow-up annotations denouncing the original annotator to be advocating pseudo-science. In fact, this is upheld in science (referred to as the Mpemba effect). A student adds an annotation urging others to follow a link to additional information and follow-up annotations confirm that the value of the original comment that was attached..*

While, at first glance, the original annotation appeared to be detracting, in fact it embodied and led to a deeper, more sophisticated understanding of the material. Our approach focuses on the value to learning derived from annotations and thus supports the presentation of this annotation.

Step 3: Determine which annotations to show a new student

Which annotations are shown to a student is decided in our model by a process incorporating trust modeling, inspired by the model of Zhang [5] which determines trustworthiness based on a combination of private and public knowledge (with the latter determined on the basis of peers). Our process integrates i) a restriction on the maximum number of annotations shown per learning object ii) modeling the reputation of each annotation iii) using a threshold to set how valuable any annotation must be before it is shown iv) considering the similarity of the rating behaviour of students and v) showing the annotations with the highest predicted benefit.

Let A represent the unbounded set of all annotations attached to the learning object in focus. Let $r_j^a = [-1, 1]$ represent the *jth* rating that was left on annotation a (1 for thumbs up, -1 for thumbs down and 0 when not yet rated). The matrix R has R^a representing the set of all ratings on a particular annotation, a, which also represents selecting a column from the matrix. To predict the benefit of an annotation for a student s we consider as Local information the set of ratings given by other students to the annotation. Let the similarity[2] between s and $rater$ be $S(s, rater)$. Global information contains all students' opinions about the author of the annotation. Given a set of annotations $A_q = \{a_1, a_2, ..., a_n\}$ left by an annotator (author) q we first calculate the average interest level of an annotation a_i provided by the author, given the set of ratings R^{a_i} to the a_i, as follows:

$$V^{a_i} = \frac{\sum_{j=1}^{|R^{a_i}|} r_j^{a_i}}{|R^{a_i}|} \tag{2}$$

The reputation of the annotator q is then:

$$T_q = \frac{\sum_{i=1}^{|A_q|} V^{a_i}}{|A_q|} \tag{3}$$

which is used as the Global interest level of the annotation.

A combination of Global and Local reputation leads to the predicted benefit of that annotation for the current student. To date, we have used a Cauchy CDF[3] to integrate these two elements into a value from 0 to 1 (where higher values represent higher predicted benefit) as follows:

$$\text{pred-ben}[a, current] = \frac{1}{\pi} \arctan(\frac{(vF^a - vA^a) + T_q}{\gamma}) + \frac{1}{2} \tag{4}$$

where T_q is the initial reputation of the annotation (set to be the current reputation of the annotator q, whose reputation adjusts over time, as his annotations are liked or disliked by students); vF is the number of thumbs up ratings, vA is the number of thumbs down ratings, with each vote scaled according to the similarity of the rater with the current student, according to Eq. 5. γ is a factor which, when set higher, makes the function less responsive to the vF and vA values.

$$v = v + (1 * S(current, rater)) \tag{5}$$

Annotations with the highest predicted benefit (reflecting the annotation's overall reputation) are shown (up to the maximum number of annotations to show, where each must have at least the threshold value of reputation).

---

[2] The function that we used to determine the similarity of two students in their rating behaviour examined annotations that both students had rated and scored the similarity based on how many ratings were the same (both thumbs up or both thumbs down). The overall similarity score ranged from -1 to 1. Other similarity measures that could be explored are raised in the Discussion section.

[3] This distribution has a number of attractive properties: a larger number of votes is given a greater weight than a smaller number (that is, 70 out of 100 votes has more impact than 7 out of 10 votes) and the probability approaches but never reaches 0 and 1 (i.e. there is always a chance an annotation may be shown).

There is real merit in exploring how best to set various parameters in order to enable students to achieve effective learning through exposure to appropriate annotations (and avoidance of annotations which may detract from their learning). In the following section, we present our experimental setting for validating the above framework, focusing on the challenge of "bad" annotations.

3   Experimental Setup

In order to verify the value of our proposed model, we design a simulation of student learning. This is achieved by modeling each student in terms of knowledge levels (their understanding of different concepts in the course of study) where each learning object has a target level of knowledge and an impact [2] that increases when the student's knowledge level is closer to the target. We construct algorithms to deliver learning objects to students in order to maximize the mean average knowledge of the entire group of students (i.e. over all students, the highest average knowledge level of each student, considering the different kinds of knowledge that arise within the domain of application).

As mentioned, one concern is to avoid annotations which may detract from student learning. As will be seen in Figure 2, in environments where many poor quality annotations may be left, if annotations are simply randomly selected, the knowledge levels achieved by students, overall, will decline. This is demonstrated in our experiments by comparing against a Greedy God approach which operates with perfect knowledge of student learning gains after an annotation is shown, to then step back to select appropriate annotations for a student. The y-axis in our graphs shows the mean, over all students, of the average knowledge level attained by a student (so, averaged over the different knowledges being modeled in the domain).

As well as generating a random set of target levels for each learning object, we also generated a random length of completion (ranging from 30 to 480 minutes) so that we are sensitive to the total minutes required for instruction. The x-axis in each graph maps how student learning adjusts, over time. We used 20 students, 100 learning objects and 20 iterations, repeating the trials and averaging the results. For these experiments we ran what is referred to as the raw ecological approach [2] for selecting the appropriate learning object for each new student; this has each student matched with the learning object best predicted to benefit her knowledge, based on the past benefits in learning achieved by students at a similar level of knowledge as in Step 1 of Section 2. Ratings left by students were simulated by having each student exposed to an annotation providing a score of -1 or 1; we simulated this on the basis of "perfect knowledge": when the annotation increased the student learning a rating of 1 was left[4].

---

[4] This perfect knowledge was obtained by running the simulated learning twice, once with the annotation and learning object, and once with just the learning object. A student gave a positive rating if they learned more with the annotation and a negative rating if they learned more without.

The standard set-up for all the experiments described below used a maximum of 3 for the number of annotations attached to a learning object that might be shown to a student; a threshold of 0.4 for the minimum reputability of an annotation before it will be shown; a value of 0.5 as the initial reputation of each student; and a value of 20% for the probability that a student will elect to leave an annotation on a learning object. While learning objects are created by expert educators, annotations created by peers may serve to undermine student learning and thus need to be identified and avoided.

3.1   Quality of Annotations

We performed experiments where the quality of annotations from the group of simulated students varied. For each student we randomly assigned an "authorship" characteristic which provided a probability that they would leave a good annotation (defined as an annotation whose average impact was greater than 0). A student with an authorship of 10% would leave good annotations 10% of the time and bad annotations 90% of the time, while a student with an authorship of 75% would leave good annotations $\frac{3}{4}$ of the time and bad annotations $\frac{1}{4}$ of the time. In each condition, we defined a maximum authorship for the students and authorships were randomly assigned, evenly distributed between 0.0 and the maximum authorship. Maximum authorships of 1.0 (the baseline), 0.75, and 0.25 were used. For these set of experiments, we elected to focus solely on Local information to predict the benefit of annotations, i.e. on the votes for and against the annotations presented by peers (but still adjusted according to rater similarity as in Eq. 5).

The graphs in Figure 2 indicate that our approach for selecting annotations to show to students (referred to as the Cauchy), in general does well to begin to achieve the learning gains (mean average knowledge) attained by the Greedy God algorithm. The random selection of annotations is not as compromised when there is a greater chance for students to leave good annotations (100% authorship) but degrades as a greater proportion of bad annotations are introduced (and does quite poorly when left to operate in the 25% authorship scenario). This reinforces the need for methods such as ours.

Fig. 2. Comparison of Various Distributions of Bad Annotations

3.2   Cutoff Threshold

One approach to removing annotations or annotators from the system is to define a minimum reputation level, below which the annotation is no longer shown to students (or new annotations by an annotator are no longer accepted). A trade-off exists: if the threshold is set too low, bad annotations can be shown to students, if the threshold is set too high, good annotations can be stigmatized.

In order to determine an appropriate level in the context of a simulation, we examined cut-off thresholds for annotations first of 0.2 and then of 0.4. We considered the combination of Local and Global information in the determination of which annotations should be shown (as outlined in Step 3 of Section 2). In conjunction with this, we adjusted the initial reputation of all students to be 0.7. Students were randomly assigned an authorship quality (as described in Section 3.1) evenly distributed between 0.0 and 1.0.

The results in Figure 3 indicate that our algorithm, both in the case of a 0.4 threshold and that of a 0.2 threshold (together with a generous initial reputation rating of 0.7 for annotator reputation), is still able to propose annotations that result in strong learning gains (avoiding the bad annotations that cause the random assignment to operate less favourably).

3.3   Explore vs. Exploit

Even for the worst annotators, there is a chance that they will leave an occasional good comment (which should be promoted), or improve the quality of their commentary (in which case they should have a chance to be redeemed). For this

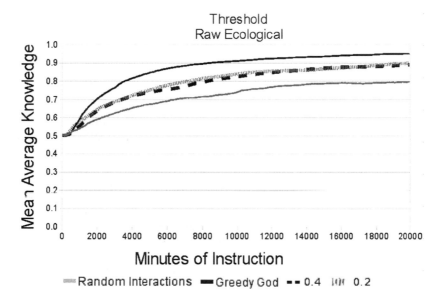

Fig. 3. Comparison of Various Thresholds for Removing Annotations

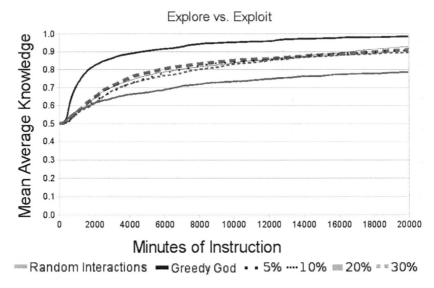

Fig. 4. Explore vs Exploit

experiment, we considered allowing an occasional, random display of annotations to the students in order to give poorly rated annotations and annotators a second chance and to enhance the exploration element of our work. We continued with the experimental setting of Section 3.2, where both Local and Global reputations of annotations were considered. We used two baselines (random and Greedy God again) and considered 4 experimental approaches. The first used our approach as outlined above, the standard authorship of 100%, a cut-off threshold of 0.4 and a 5% chance of randomly assigning annotations. The second used an exploration value of 10%, which meant that we used our approach described above 90% of the time, and 10% of the time we randomly assigned up to 3 annotations from learning objects.We also considered conditions where annotations were randomly assigned 20% and 30% of the time.

Allowing a phase of exploration to accept annotations from students who had previously been considered as poor annotators turns out to still enable effective student learning gains, in all cases. Our algorithms are able to tolerate some random selection of annotations, to allow the case where annotators who would have otherwise been cut off from consideration have their annotations shared and thus their reputation possibly increased beyond the threshold (if they offer an annotation of value), allowing future annotations from these students to also be presented.

4   Discussion

We first note that there is value of being aware of possible bad advice from peers and avoiding it – not just for our context but for peer-based intelligent tutoring in general. In [6] the authors deal with the situation of providing incentives to encourage student participation in learning communities. They use a variable incentive model, based on classroom marks, to encourage behaviours helpful to the community of students. For example, if a student shares a small number of good resources, they will be given a greater incentive to contribute more. In the case of students who contribute a reasonable quantity of low-quality resources, the incentive to contribute is lowered, and the user is prompted with a personalized message to try to have them contribute less and to improve their quality. These incentives do not, however, eliminate scenarios where bad annotations may be left. Our work investigates this consideration. In addition, our approach does not focus on adjusting the contribution frequency of various students, but instead looks to preferentially recommend the more worthwhile contributions.

We contrast with researchers in peer-based intelligent tutoring who are more focused on assembling social networks for ongoing real-time advice [7,6], as we are reasoning about the past experiences of peers. Some suggestions for how to bring similar students together for information sharing from [8] may be valuable to explore as an extension to our current work.

Our research also serves to emphasize the potential value of trust modeling for educational applications (and not just for our particular environment of education based on the selection of learning objects that have brought benefit to similar peers, in the past). As discussed, we are motivated by the trust modeling approach of Zhang [5]. Future work would consider integrating additional variations of Zhang's original model within our overall framework. For example, we could start to flexibly adjust the weight of Local and Global reputation incorporated in the reasoning about which annotation to show to a student, using methods which learn, over time, an appropriate weighting (as in [5]) based on when sufficient Local information is available and can be valued more highly. In addition, while trust modeling would typically have each user reasoning about the reliability of each other user in providing information, we could have each student maintain a local view of each other student's skill in annotation (though this is somewhat more challenging for educational applications where a student might learn and then improve their skill over time and where students may leave good annotations at times, despite occasionally leaving poor ones as well). In general, studying the appropriate role of the Global reputation of annotations, especially in quite heterogeneous environments, presents interesting avenues for future research (since currently this value is not in fact personalized for different users).

Collaborative filtering recommender systems [9,10,11] are also relevant related work. However, intelligent tutoring systems have an additional motivation when selecting appropriate peer advice, namely to enable student learning. Thus, in contrast to positioning a user within a cluster of similar users, we would like to ideally model a continually evolving community of peers where students at a lower level are removed and more advanced students are added as a student works through the curriculum. This is another direction for future research. Some research on collaborative filtering recommender systems that may be of value for us to explore in the future includes that of Herlocker et al. [11] which explores what not to recommend (i.e. removing irrelevant items) and that of Labeke et al. [12] which is directly applied to educational applications and suggests a kind of string-based coding of the learning achieved by students, to pattern match with similar students in order to suggest appropriate avenues for educating these new students.

Several directions for future work with the model and the simulation would also be valuable to explore. As mentioned previously, we simulated students as accurately rating (thumbs up or thumbs down) annotations based on whether the annotation had helped them learn. It would be interesting to provide for a richer student modeling where each student has a certain degree of "insight", leading to a greater or lesser ability to rate annotations. If this were incorporated, each student might then elect to be modeling the rating ability of the other peers and this can then be an influence in deciding whether a particular annotation should be shown. It might also be useful to model additional student characteristics such as learning style, educational background, affect, motivation, language, etc. The similarity calculation would need to be updated for such enhancements; similarity should then ideally be modeled as a multi-dimensional measure where an appropriate weighting of factors would need to be considered. Similarity measures such as Pearson coefficients or cosine similarity may then be appropriate to examine.

Other variations for our simulations are also being explored. Included here is the introduction of a variation of our algorithm for selecting the learning objects for each student based on simulated annealing (with a view to then continue this simulated annealing approach in the selection of annotations as well). This variation is set up so that during the first 1/2 of the trials there is an inverse chance, based on the progress of the trials, that each student would be randomly associated with a lesson; otherwise the raw ecological approach was applied. We expect this to pose greater challenges to student learning in the initial stages but to perhaps result in even greater educational gains at later stages of the simulation.

We note as well that simulations of learning are not a replacement for experiments with human students; however, the techniques explored in this work are useful for early development where trials with human students may not be feasible and future work could look to integrate human subjects as well; we are currently in discussion with possible users in the home healthcare field. While our current use of simulations is to validate our model, we may gain additional insights from the work of researchers such as [13] where simulations help to predict how humans will perform.

In conclusion, we offer an approach for coping with bad advice from peers in the context of peer-based intelligent tutoring, employing a repository of learning objects that have annotations attached by students. Our experimental results confirm that there is value to student learning when poor annotations are detected and avoided and we have demonstrated this value through a series of variations of our experimental conditions. Our general message is that there indeed is value to modeling peer trust in educational settings.

Acknowledgements. Financial support was received from NSERC's Strategic Research Networks project hSITE.

References

1. McCalla, G.: The ecological approach to the design of e-learning environments: Purpose-based capture and use of information about learners. Journal of Interactive Media in Education 7, 1–23 (2004)
2. Champaign, J., Cohen, R.: A model for content sequencing in intelligent tutoring systems based on the ecological approach and its validation through simulated students. In: Proceedings of FLAIRS-23, Daytona Beach, Florida (2010)
3. Briggs, A.L., Cornell, S.: Self-monitoring Blood Glucose (SMBG): Now and the Future. Journal of Pharmacy Practice 17(1), 29–38 (2004)
4. Plant, D.: hSITE: healthcare support through information technology enhancements. NSERC Strategic Research Network Proposal (2008)
5. Zhang, J., Cohen, R.: Evaluating the trustworthiness of advice about seller agents in e-marketplaces: A personalized approach. Electronic Commerce Research and Applications 7(3), 330–340 (2008)
6. Cheng, R., Vassileva, J.: Design and evaluation of an adaptive incentive mechanism for sustained educational online communities. User Model. User-Adapt. Interact. 16(3-4), 321–348 (2006)
7. Read, T., Barros, B., Bárcena, E., Pancorbo, J.: Coalescing individual and collaborative learning to model user linguistic competences. User Modeling and User-Adapted Interaction 16(3-4), 349–376 (2006)
8. Brooks, C.A., Panesar, R., Greer, J.E.: Awareness and collaboration in the ihelp courses content management system. In: EC-TEL, pp. 34–44 (2006)
9. Adomavicius, G., Tuzhilin, A.: Toward the next generation of recommender systems: A survey of the state-of-the-art and possible extensions. IEEE Transactions on Knowledge and Data Engineering 17, 734–749 (2005)
10. Breese, J.S., Heckerman, D., Kadie, C.: Empirical analysis of predictive algorithms for collaborative filtering, pp. 43–52. Morgan Kaufmann, San Francisco (1998)
11. Herlocker, J.L., Konstan, J.A., Terveen, L.G., Riedl, J.T.: Evaluating collaborative filtering recommender systems. ACM Trans. Inf. Syst. 22(1), 5–53 (2004)
12. van Labeke, N., Poulovassilis, A., Magoulas, G.D.: Using similarity metrics for matching lifelong learners. In: Woolf, B.P., Aïmeur, E., Nkambou, R., Lajoie, S. (eds.) ITS 2008. LNCS, vol. 5091, pp. 142–151. Springer, Heidelberg (2008)
13. VanLehn, K., Ohlsson, S., Nason, R.: Applications of simulated students: An exploration. Journal of Artificial Intelligence in Education 5, 135–175 (1996)

Modeling Mental Workload Using EEG Features for Intelligent Systems

Maher Chaouachi, Imène Jraidi, and Claude Frasson

HERON Lab, Computer Science Department
University of Montreal,
2920 chemin de la tour, H3T 1N8, Canada
{chaouacm,jraidiim,frasson}@iro.umontreal.ca

Abstract. Endowing systems with abilities to assess a user's mental state in an operational environment could be useful to improve communication and interaction methods. In this work we seek to model user mental workload using spectral features extracted from electroencephalography (EEG) data. In particular, data were gathered from 17 participants who performed different cognitive tasks. We also explore the application of our model in a non laboratory context by analyzing the behavior of our model in an educational context. Our findings have implications for intelligent tutoring systems seeking to continuously assess and adapt to a learner's state.

Keywords: cognitive workload, EEG, ITS.

1 Introduction

Modeling and developing systems able to assess and monitor users' cognitive states using physiological sensors has been an important research thrust over few past decades [1-5]. These physio-cognitive systems aim to improve technology's adaptability and have shown a significant impact on enhancing users' overall performance, skill acquisition and productivity [6]. Various models tracking shifts in users' alertness, engagement and workload have been successfully used in closed-loop systems or simulation environment [7-9]. By assessing users' internal state, these systems were able to adapt to users' information processing capacity and then to respond accurately to their needs.

Mental workload is of primary interest as it has a direct impact on users' performance in executing tasks [10]. Even though there is no agreement upon its definition, mental workload can be seen in terms of resources or mental energy expended, including memory effort, decision making or alertness. It gives an indication about the amount of effort invested as well as users' involvement level. Hence, endowing systems with workload assessment models can provide intelligent assistance, efficient adaptation and more realistic social communication in the scope of reaching optimal interaction conditions.

Nevertheless, scarce and scattered research has explored these faculties to refine the learning process within educational settings. Intelligent tutoring systems (ITS) are still mainly based on learners' performance in analyzing learners' skill acquisition process

Joseph A. Konstan et al. (Eds.): UMAP 2011, LNCS 6787, pp. 50–61, 2011.

or evaluating their current engagement level and the quality of learning [11-14]. Even though the integration of affective models in ITS added an empathic and social dimension into tutors' behaviors [15-17] there is still a lack of methods helping tutors to drive the learning process and evaluate learners' behavior according to their mental effort. The limited action range offered to learners (menu choice, help, or answers) restricts the ability of forecasting learners' memory capacity and objectively assessing their efforts and implication level [18]. EEG techniques for workload assessment can represent, then, a real opportunity to address these issues. The growing progress in developing non intrusive, convenient and low cost EEG headsets and devices are very promising enabling their use in operational educational environments.

In this paper we model users' workload in a learning environment by developing an EEG workload index and we analyze its behavior in different phases across the learning process. In particular, we performed an experiment with two phases: (1) A cognitive phase, in which users performed different cognitive tasks, was used to derive the workload index. (2) A learning phase during which the developed index was validated and analyzed. We performed data analysis using machine learning techniques and showed that there are identifiable trends in the behavior of the developed index.

The rest of this paper is structured as follows. Section 2 presents previous work on EEG based workload detection approaches. Section 3 presents our experimental methodology. Section 4 discusses our approach and its implications. We conclude in Section 5.

2   Previous Work

Developing EEG indexes for workload assessment is a well developed field especially in laboratory contexts. A variety of linear and non-linear classification and regression methods were used to determine mental workload in different kinds of cognitive tasks such as memorization, language processing, visual, or auditory tasks. These methods use mainly EEG Power Spectral Density (PSD) bands or Event Related Potential (ERP) techniques to extract relevant EEG features [7-9].

Wilson [19] used an Artificial Neural Network (ANN) to classify operators' workload level by taking EEG as well as physiological features as an input. Reported results showed up to 90% of classification accuracy. Gevins and Smith [20] used spectral features to feed neural networks classifying workload of users while performing various memory tasks. In a car driving simulation environment, Kohlmorgen et al. [21] used Linear Discriminant Analysis (LDA) on EEG-features extracted and optimized for each user for workload assessment. Authors showed that decreasing driver workload (induced by a secondary auditory task) improves reaction time. Support Vector Machine (SVM) and ANN were also used to analyze task demand recorded in lecture and meeting scenario as well as in others cognitive tasks (Flanker paradigm and Switching paradigm) using EEG features. Results reached 92% of accuracy in discriminating between high and low workload levels [22, 23].

Berka and colleagues [1, 24] developed a workload index using Discriminant Function Analysis (DFA) for monitoring alertness and cognitive workload in different environments. Several cognitive tasks such as grid location task, arithmetic computing, and image memorization were analyzed to validate the proposed index. The same index was used in an educational context to analyze students' behavior while acquiring skills in a problem solving context [18, 25, 26].

In this paper, we propose to model users' workload from EEG extracted features through a cognitive task activity. The major contribution of this study is to validate the model within a learning activity as opposed to the work of Berka and colleagues [1, 24] where the proposed index was validated only according to purely cognitive tasks. Our study uses Gaussian Process Regression to train workload models in a first phase especially designed to elicit different levels of workload and applied in a second phase, within a learning environment to detect different trends in learners' mental workload behavior. We will now describe our experiment.

3 Methodology

The aim of this study was to model and evaluate mental workload induced during human-computer interaction using features extracted from EEG signals. The experimental process was divided into two phases: a cognitive activity phase including three cognitive tasks designed with incrementally increasing levels of difficulty to elicit increasing levels of required mental workload and a learning activity phase about trigonometry consisting of three main steps. Data gathered from the first phase were used to thoroughly derive a workload index whereas data from the second phase were used to validate the computed index in a "non-laboratory" context. Our experimental setup consists of a 6-channel EEG sensor headset and two video feeds. All recorded sessions were replayed and analyzed to accurately synchronize the data using necessary time markers.

17 participants were recruited for this research. All participants were briefed about the experimental process and objectives and signed a consent form. Participation was compensated with 20 dollars. Upon their arrivals, participants were equipped with the EEG-cap and familiarized with the materials and the environment. All subjects completed a five minutes eyes open baseline followed by another five minutes eyes closed baseline. During this period, participants were instructed neither to be active nor to be relaxed. This widely used technique enabled us to establish a neutral reference for the workload assessment. Then, participants completed the cognitive activity phase. This phase consists of three successive tasks: (1) Forward Digit Span (FDS) (2) Backward Digit Span (BDS) and (3) Logical Tasks (LT). Each task has between three and six difficulty levels. All participants performed these tasks in the same order and were allowed to self-pace with respect to the time required to complete each task.

Forward Digit Span (FDS). This test involves attention and working memory abilities. In this task, a series of single digits were successively presented on the screen. Participants were asked to memorize the whole sequence, then prompted to enter the digits in the presented order. This task included 6 difficulty levels incrementally increasing by increasing the length of the sequence that participants have to retain. Level one consisted of a series of 20 sets of 3 digits, level two: 12 sets of 4 digits, level three: 8 sets of 5 digits, level four: 6 digits and 6 sets, level five: 7 digits and 4 sets and level six: 4 sets of 8 digits.

Backward Digit Span (BDS). The principle of this test is similar to the FDS task. Participants had to memorize a sequence of single digits presented on the screen. The difference was that they were instructed to enter digits in the reverse order from the one presented. Five levels of difficulty were considered by increasing the number of digits in the sequence. The first level consisted of a series of 12 sets of 3 digits; the second level: 12 sets of 4 digits, the third level: 5 digits and 8 series, the fourth level: 6 sets of 6 digits and the fifth level: 4 sets of 8 digits. No time limit was fixed for FDS and BDS tasks.

Logical Tasks (LT). These tasks require inferential skills on information series and are typically used in brain training exercises or in tests of reasoning. In these tasks, participants were instructed to deduce a missing number according to a logical rule that they had to infer from a series of numbers displayed on the screen, within a fixed time limit of 30 seconds. An example of such series is "38 - 2 - 19 - 9 - 3 - 3 - 40 - 4 - ?" and one should deduce that the missing element ("?") would be "10". That is, the logical rule that one should guess is that for each group of three numbers the last number is the result of the division of the first by the second. The logical tasks involved three difficulty levels. Each level consisted of a series of 5 questions and the difficulty level was manipulated by enhancing the difficulty of the logical rule between the data.

After completing the cognitive activity phase, participants took a little break, and then were invited to perform the learning phase during which a trigonometry course was given. This phase consists of three successive steps (1) a pretest session, (2) a learning session and (3) a problem solving session. Before starting these tasks, participants were asked to report their self-estimated skill level in trigonometry (low, moderate or expert).

Pretest. This task involved 10 (yes/no/no-response) questions that covered some basic aspects of trigonometry (for instance: "is the tangent of an angle equal to the ratio of the length of the opposite over the length of the adjacent?"). In this part, participants had to answer to the questions without any interruption, help or time limit.

Learning Session. In this task, participants were instructed to use a learning environment covering the theme of trigonometry and specially designed for the experiment. Two lessons were developed explaining several fundamental trigonometric properties and relationships. The environment provides basic definitions as well as their mathematical demonstrations. Schemas and examples are also given for each presented concept.[1]

Problem Solving. Problems presented during this task are based on participants' ability to apply, generalize and reason about the concepts seen during the learning session. No further perquisites were required to successfully resolve the problem except the lessons' concepts. However a good level of reasoning and concentration is

---

[1] At the end of the experiment, all participants reported that they were satisfied with the quality of the environment as well as the pedagogical strategy used for presenting the materials.

needed to solve the problems. A total of 6 problems with a gradually increasing difficulty level were selected and presented in the same order for all the participants. Each problem is a multiple-choice question illustrated by a geometrical figure. A fixed time limit is imposed for each problem varying according to its difficulty level. Each problem requires some intermediate steps to reach the final solution and the difficulty level was increased by increasing the number of required intermediate steps. For example, to compute the sinus of an angle, learners had first to compute the cosines in the first step. Then, they had to square the result and to subtract it from 1 in the second step. Finally the third step consisted of computing the square root.

The problem solving environment provided a limited number of hints for each problem as well as a calculator to perform the needed computations. All the problems were independent in terms of learned concepts except for problem 4 and 6 that shared the same geometrical rule required to solve the problem (i.e. "the sum of the angles of a triangle is equal to 180 degrees").

3.1 Subjective and Objective Measures of Workload

After completing each task level, participants were asked to evaluate their mental workload both in the cognitive activity phase and the learning activity phase. We used the *NASA-Task Load Index* (NASA-TLX) technique [27]. As for other subjective measures of workload, NASA-TLX relies on subjects' conscious perceived experience with regards to the effort produced and the difficulty of task. NASA_TLX has the advantage of being quick and simple to administer.

In addition to the subjective ratings, other objective factors that may be used for assessing workload were considered in this study, such as performance (i.e. proportion of correct answers in cognitive tasks, pretest and problem solving) and response time.

3.2 EEG Recording

EEG is a measurement of the brain electrical activity produced by synaptic excitations of neurons. In this experiment, EEG was recorded using a stretch electro-cap. EEG signals were received from sites P3, C3, Pz and Fz as defined by the international 10-20 electrode placement system (Jasper 1958). Each site was referenced to Cz and grounded at Fpz. Two more active sites were used namely A1 and A2 typically known respectively as the left and right earlobe. This setup is known as "referential linked ear montage" and is illustrated in figure 1. Roughly speaking, in this montage the EEG signal is equally amplified throughout both hemispheres. Moreover, the "linked ears" setup yields a more precise and cleaner EEG signal by calibrating each scalp signal to the average of the left and right earlobe sites (A1 and A2). For example, the calibrated C3 signal is given by (C3-(A1+A2)/2). Each scalp site was filled with a non-sticky proprietary gel from Electro-Cap and impedance was maintained below 5 Kilo Ohms. Any impedance problems were corrected by rotating a blunted needle gently inside the electrode until an adequate signal was obtained. The recorded sampling rate was at 256 Hz.

Data Preprocessing and Features Extraction. Due to its weakness (on the order of micro volts: 10^{-6} volts), the EEG signal needs to be amplified and filtered. The brain electrical activity signal is usually contaminated by external noise such as environmental interference caused by surrounding devices. Such artifacts alter clearly the quality of the signal. Thus a 60-Hz notch filter was applied during the data acquisition to remove these artifacts. In addition, the acquired EEG signal easily suffers from noise caused by user body movements or frequent eye blinks or movement. Therefore, an artifact rejection heuristic was applied to the recorded data using a threshold on the signal power with regards to the eyes open and eyes closed baseline. If the amplitude of any epoch in any channel exceeded the threshold by more than 25%, the epoch was considered as contaminated and was excluded from subsequent analysis.

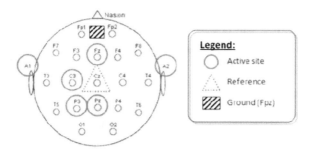

Fig. 1. EEG channel electrode placement

For each participant, EEG data recorded from each channel were transformed into a power spectral density using a Fast-Fourier Transform (FFT) applied to each 1-second epoch with a 50 % overlapping window multiplied by the Hamming function to reduce spectral leakage. Bin powers (the estimated power over 1 Hz) of each channel ranging from 4 Hz to 48 Hz were concatenated to constitute the feature vector.

To sum up, 176 features (4 channels x 48 bins) were extracted from the signal each second. To reduce the data input dimensionality and improve the workload model, a Principal Component Analysis (PCA) was applied on the EEG data of each participant. The number of features was reduced to 25 (78.63% reduction rate) explaining 85.98% to 94.71% of the variability ($M = 90.42\%$, $SD = 3.30\%$). PCA scores were then z-normalized and the resulting vector used as an input for the model.

4 Results and Discussions

The experimental results are presented in the following subsections. The first part is concerned with the cognitive phase data analysis. The second part describes mental workload modeling from the EEG. The third part deals with the validation and evaluation of the model within the learning activity.

4.1 Cognitive Activity Results

In order to evaluate NASA_TLX subjective estimates of mental workload, correlational analysis was performed with regards to the task design and performance and response time objective variables.

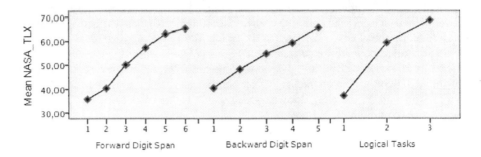

Fig. 2. Mean NASA_TLX workload estimate for each difficulty level for the forward digit span, backward digit span and logical tasks

Repeated measures one-way ANOVA (N =17) was performed in the FDS, LT, and BDS cognitive activities across their associated difficulty levels. Degrees of freedom were corrected using Greenhouse-Geisser estimates of sphericity for FDS and BDS (epsilon = 0.35 and 0.54 respectively) as the assumption of sphericity had been violated (chi-square = 60.11 and 54.40 respectively, p <.05) while Mauchly's test was non significant for the LT. Results revealed significant changes between NASA_TLX scores with regards to the task demand of each level in the three tasks (F(1.73, 27.65) = 25.65, p < 0.001 for FDS, F(2.18, 34.89) = 18.25, p < 0.001 for BDS and F(2, 32) = 43.51, p < 0.01 for LT), showing a significant linear increase of subjective workload estimates as the level of difficulty increased (figure 2).

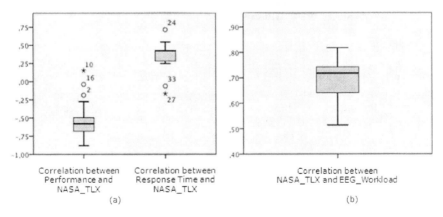

Fig. 3. Bivariate correlations between: (a) NASA_TLX and objective measures (b) NASA_TLX and EEG_Workload

Bi-variate correlations between NASA_TLX and objective measures of task performance and response time are illustrated in figure 3 (a). Correlations were calculated for each individual across the 14 levels (FDS, BDS and LT). The median correlation between NASA_TLX and task performance was -0.58 with a range of -0.89 to 0.15 and the median correlation between NASA_TLX and response time was

0.42 with a range of -0.16 to 0.72. Correlations were also computed for each of the 3 activities across the 17 participants. Performance decreased linearly as the workload increased in FDS ($r = -0.59$, $p < 0.001$) and LT ($r = -0.50$, $p < 0.001$) while the relationship was not linearly significant in the BDS ($r = -0.19$, $p = $ n.s.). Response time increased linearly as a function of workload in FDS ($r = 0.30$ $p < 0.05$) and LT ($r = 0.35$, $p < 0.05$) and did not linearly correlate in BDS ($r = 0.014$, $p = $ n.s.)

To summarize, NASA_TLX workload ratings showed linear relationship with the objective measures except for the BDS tasks. Besides, NASA_TLX accurately tracked the intended pattern of the task design that used incrementally increasing levels of difficulty to elicit increasing levels of mental workload required for the task. This manifest trend suggests that NASA_TLX subjective ratings can be a reliable indicator of mental workload for training the predictive models.

4.2 EEG Mental Workload Index

Our aim was to quantitatively predict the mental workload using EEG extracted features. Specially, we were interested in using workload patterns detected in the cognitive activity phase to analyze the learning activity. An individual model was developed for each participant by training a Gaussian Process Regression (GPR) function [28] with a squared exponential kernel and noise parameter $\sigma^2 = 0.1$. NASA_TLX subjective ratings were introduced as a target variable of the training data in all models.

NASA_TLX workload values were classified into three classes namely low, medium and high (low < 30, 30 <= medium < 70 and high >=70). The same classification was done for the predicted GPR values. A mean accuracy rate of 91% across all the participants was reached with models trained on a split of 90% of the cognitive task data and tested on the other 10%. The mean EEG_Workload indices derived by the model were computed across each task of the learning activity phase.

4.3 Learning Activity Results

Our next objective was to validate the computed EEG_Workload model within the learning context. The box plot in figure 3 (b) illustrates the results of the bi-variate correlations between EEG_Workload and NASA_TLX subjective metrics. Correlations were computed across participants in the pretest, the learning session and each of the six problems revealing significant relationships in the eight activities. The median correlation was 0.72 with a range of 0.52 ($p < 0.001$) for problem 2 to 0.82, ($p < 0.05$) for problem 1. These results provide confirmation of the validity of the computed EEG model of mental workload.

Our next investigation was to evaluate the progression of the workload level across the learning tasks. A repeated measures ANOVA revealed that there were significant changes in the EEG_Workload between the learning activities $F(3.23, 51.61 = 2.76$, $p < 0.05$). Degrees of freedom were corrected using the Greenhouse-Geisser estimates of sphericity (epsilon = 0.46). Post hoc results showed that the EEG_Workload measures significantly increased during the learning session when compared with the pretest ($p < 0.05$). This increase can be explained by the effort produced by learners in understanding concepts and acquiring skills in the learning phase compared to the pretest session where learners responded to questions that did not require particular engagement and concentration levels. In fact, during the pretest no pressure was put on learners who had simply to situate their knowledge in trigonometry.

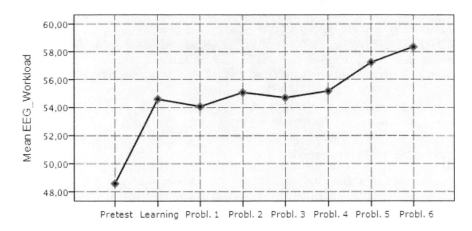

Fig. 4. Mean EEG_Workload for each activity in the learning environment

Significant increases were also registered between the pretest and problems 4, 5 and 6 with the highest workload level (see figure 4) revealing that mental workload significantly increases from the beginning to the end of the learning interaction. A significant increase was also found during problem 5 when compared with problems 1, 3 and 4 suggesting that learning tasks varied in terms of the cognitive workload demand required from the participants.

To summarize, EEG_Workload was validated according to the learners' subjective ratings. The index value increased clearly as learners acquired skills in trigonometry. This trend was significant when we compared the pretest with the learning session and the problem solving tasks.

Our next concern was to evaluate the EEG_Workload model with regards to the objective metrics in the learning environment. A bi-variate correlation was computed between EEG_Workload and response time across participants in the six problems (N = 17 x 6) showing a rather small but significant relationship ($r = 0.21$, $p < 0.05$). Besides, correlational analysis of each problem apart revealed a significant correlation only in problem 5 ($r = 0.56$, $p < 0.05$). Indeed, unlike pure cognitive tasks with strict laboratory conditions and imposed time limits, in a more complex learning environment, learners are less restricted and a longer response time does not necessarily imply higher mental workload which can also be distilled into other mental processes.

Bi-variate correlations were computed between EEG_Workload and performance in the pretest and each problem. Results showed a significant linear relationship between EEG_Workload and performance in the pretest ($r = -1.88$, $p < 0.05$) while no significant correlation was found between EEG_workload and performance in any of the problems. Again, these data suggest that changes in workload are not related to performance in complex learning tasks and that a more complex relationship may exist between mental workload and performance.

Looking at participants' self reported skill levels in trigonometry, ANOVA tests revealed a reliable effect of the skill level on the mean EEG_Workload in the problems ($F(2, 14) = 11.93$, $p < 0.05$). We found that participants with a moderate skill level have had the highest workload values ($M = 68.97$; $SD = 14.16$) as compared to participants with low skill level ($M = 57.25$; $SD = 4.06$) and to expert participants who showed the lowest workload values ($M = 41.35$, $SD = 7.52$). One can explain this result by the fact that learners with moderate skills tend to produce more effort than experts who might be more at ease with trigonometry and do not produce a lot of effort. On the other side, learners with the lowest skill level tend to be rather disengaged in the task compared to learners with moderate to high skills.

Our last investigation dealt with the overall impact of learners' workload, response time and skill level on their performance in the problems. A multiple regression analysis was conducted to measure the influence of each of these parameters. The overall model was significant ($F(3, 98) = 8.48$, $p < 0.01$, $R = 0.41$). Conditional main effect analyzes revealed a positive effect of workload ($\beta = 0.24$, $p < .05$) and skill level ($\beta = .42$, $p < .001$) and a negative effect of response time ($\beta = -0.27$, $p < .05$) suggesting that a combination of these variables can be used to predict learning performance. This result suggests that a combination of several variables can improve the accuracy of systems in assessing learners' skill acquisition process.

5 Conclusion

In this paper we have presented a workload index based on features extracted from EEG signals. 17 participants were recruited for this experiment and were equipped with a 6-channel EEG headset. The developed workload index uses a Gaussian Process Regression model trained on data gathered from purely cognitive tasks with incrementally increasing levels of difficulty to elicit increasing levels of required mental workload. Our model was validated in a learning activity during which learners interacted with an educational environment about trigonometry including a pretest, a learning session and six problem solving tasks and self-reported their workload level. Results showed that our index was significantly correlated to learners' subjective ratings and gradually increased from the pretest to the end of the session. Correlational analysis showed that mental workload was not necessarily, linearly associated to performance and response time objective variables in the learning context, as opposed to the strict laboratory conditions of the cognitive task activity.

Future work involves developing a generalized model and incorporating it within a real time interaction based tutoring system. Further variables from the learners' profile will be considered in the development of the system that will be centered in optimally adapting content, problem level and interactions to learners' mental states.

Acknowledgments. We acknowledge the CRSNG (Conseil de Recherches en Sciences Naturelles et en Génie du Canada) for funding this research.

References

1. Berka, C., Levendowski, D.J., Cvetinovic, M.M., et al.: Real-Time Analysis of EEG Indexes of Alertness, Cognition, and Memory Acquired With a Wireless EEG Headset. International Journal of Human-Computer Interaction 17, 151–170 (2004)
2. Gevins, A., Smith, M.E.: Assessing fitness-for-duty and predicting performance with cognitive neurophysiologic measures. In: Caldwell, J.A., Wesensten, N.J. (eds.) Biomonitoring for Physiological and Cognitive Performance during Military Operations. Proceedings of SPIE, vol. 5797, 18, pp. 127–138 (2005)
3. Murata, A.: An Attempt to Evaluate Mental Workload Using Wavelet Transform of EEG. Human Factors: The Journal of the Human Factors and Ergonomics Society 47, 498–508 (2005)
4. Smith, M.E., Gevins, A.: Neurophysiologic monitoring of mental workload and fatigue during operation of a flight simulator. In: Caldwell, J.A., Wesensten, N.J. (eds.) Proceedings of SPIE Defense and Security Symposium, Biomonitoring for Physiological and Cognitive Performance during Military Operations, pp. 116–126. SPIE, Orlando (2005)
5. Wilson, G.: Operator functional state assessment for adaptive automation implementation. In: Caldwell, J.A., Wesensten, N.J. (eds.) Proceedings of SPIE Defense and Security Symposium, Biomonitoring for Physiological and Cognitive Performance during Military Operations, pp. 100–104. SPIE, Orlando (2005)
6. Parasuraman, R.: Neuroergonomics: the brain at work. Oxford University Press, New York (2005)
7. Pope, A.T., Bogart, E.H., Bartolome, D.S.: Biocybernetic system evaluates indices of operator engagement in automated task. Biological Psychology 40, 187–195 (1995)
8. Prinzel, L.J., Freeman, F.G., Scerbo, M.W.: A Closed-Loop System for Examining Psychophysiological Measures for Adaptive Task Allocation. International Journal of Aviation Psychology 10, 393–410 (2000)
9. Sterman, M.B., Kaiser, D.A., Mann, C.A., et al.: Application of Quantitative EEG Analysis to Workload Assessment in an Advanced Aircraft Simulator. In: Human Factors and Ergonomics, Seattle, Washington, USA, pp. 118–121 (1993)
10. Hancock, P.A., Warm, J.S.: A Dynamic Model of Stress and Sustained Attention. Human Factors and Ergonomics Society 31, 519–537 (1989)
11. Arroyo, I., Woolf, B.: Inferring learning and attitudes from a Bayesian Network of log file data. In: Proceeding of the 2005 Conference on Artificial Intelligence in Education: Supporting Learning through Intelligent and Socially Informed Technology, pp. 33–40. IOS Press, Amsterdam (2005)
12. Baker, R.S., Corbett, A.T., Koedinger, K.R.: Detecting Student Misuse of Intelligent Tutoring Systems. In: Lester, J.C., Vicari, R.M., Paraguaçu, F. (eds.) ITS 2004. LNCS, vol. 3220, pp. 531–540. Springer, Heidelberg (2004)
13. Beck, J.E.: Engagement tracing: using response times to model student disengagement. In: Proceeding of the 2005 Conference on Artificial Intelligence in Education: Supporting Learning through Intelligent and Socially Informed Technology, pp. 88–95. IOS Press, Amsterdam (2005)
14. Johns, J., Woolf, B.: A dynamic mixture model to detect student motivation and proficiency. In: Proceedings of the 21st National Conference on Artificial Intelligence, vol. 1, pp. 163–168. AAAI Press, Boston (2006)

15. Arroyo, I., Cooper, D.G., Burleson, W., et al.: Emotion Sensors Go To School. In: Proceeding of the 2009 Conference on Artificial Intelligence in Education: Building Learning Systems that Care: From Knowledge Representation to Affective Modelling, pp. 17–24. IOS Press, Amsterdam (2009)
16. D'Mello, S., Craig, S., Witherspoon, A., et al.: Automatic detection of learner's affect from conversational cues. User Modeling and User-Adapted Interaction 18, 45–80 (2008)
17. Forbes-Riley, K., Rotaru, M., Litman, D.J.: The relative impact of student affect on performance models in a spoken dialogue tutoring system. User Modeling and User-Adapted Interaction 18, 11–43 (2008)
18. Stevens, R., Galloway, T., Berka, C.: Integrating EEG Models of Cognitive Load with Machine Learning Models of Scientific Problem Solving. In: Schmorrow, D., Stanney, K., Reeves, L. (eds.) Augmented Cognition: Past, Present and Future, pp. 55–65. Strategic Analysis, Inc., Arlington (2006)
19. Wilson, G.F.: An analysis of mental workload in pilots during flight using multiple sychophysiological measures. Int. J. Aviat. Psychol. 12, 3–18 (2004)
20. Gevins, A., Smith, M.E.: Neurophysiological measures of cognitive workload during human-computer interaction. Theoretical Issues in Ergonomics Science 4, 113–131 (2003)
21. Kohlmorgen, J., Dornhege, G., Braun, M., et al.: Improving human performance in a real operating environment through real-time mental workload detection. In: Toward Brain-Computer Interfacing, pp. 409–422. MIT Press, Cambridge (2007)
22. Heger, D., Putze, F., Schultz, T.: Online Workload Recognition from EEG Data during Cognitive Tests and Human-Machine Interaction. In: Dillmann, R., Beyerer, J., Hanebeck, U.D., Schultz, T. (eds.) KI 2010. LNCS, vol. 6359, pp. 410–417. Springer, Heidelberg (2010)
23. Honal, M., Schultz., T.: Determine task demand from brain activity. In: 3rd International Conference on Bio-inspired Systems and Signal Processing (2008)
24. Berka, C., Levendowski, D.J., Lumicao, M.N., et al.: EEG Correlates of Task Engagement and Mental Workload in Vigilance, Learning, and Memory Tasks. Aviation, Space, and Environmental Medicine 78, B231–B244 (2007)
25. Stevens, R., Galloway, T., Berka, C.: EEG-Related Changes in Cognitive Workload, Engagement and Distraction as Students Acquire Problem Solving Skills. In: Conati, C., McCoy, K., Paliouras, G. (eds.) UM 2007. LNCS (LNAI), vol. 4511, pp. 187–196. Springer, Heidelberg (2007)
26. Stevens, R.H., Galloway, T., Berka, C.: Integrating innovative neuro-educational technologies (I-Net) into K-12 science classrooms. In: Proceedings of the 3rd International Conference on Foundations of Augmented Cognition, Beijing, China, pp. 47–56 (2007)
27. Hart, S.G., Staveland, L.E.: Development of NASA-TLX (Task Load Index): Results of Empirical and Theoretical Research. In: Hancock, P.A., Meshkati, N. (eds.) Human Mental Workload, pp. 139–183. North-Holland, Amsterdam (1988)
28. Rasmussen, C.E., Williams, C.K.I.: Gaussian Processes for Machine Learning. MIT Press, Cambridge (2006)

Context-Dependent Feedback Prioritisation in Exploratory Learning Revisited

Mihaela Cocea[1,2] and George D. Magoulas[2]

[1] School of Computing, University of Portsmouth,
Buckingham Building, Lion Terrace, Portsmouth, Hampshire, PO1 3HE, UK
mihaela.cocea@port.ac.uk
[2] London Knowledge Lab, Birkbeck College, University of London,
23-29 Emerald Street, London, WC1N 3QS, UK
gmagoulas@dcs.bbk.ac.uk

Abstract. The open nature of exploratory learning leads to situations when feedback is needed to address several conceptual difficulties. Not all, however, can be addressed at the same time, as this would lead to cognitive overload and confuse the learner rather than help him/her. To this end, we propose a personalised context-dependent feedback prioritisation mechanism based on Analytic Hierarchy Process (AHP) and Neural Networks (NN). AHP is used to define feedback prioritisation as a multi-criteria decision-making problem, while NN is used to model the relation between the criteria and the order in which the conceptual difficulties should be addressed. When used alone, AHP needs a large amount of data from experts to cover all possible combinations of the criteria, while the AHP-NN synergy leads to a general model that outputs results for any such combination. This work was developed and tested in an exploratory learning environment for mathematical generalisation called *eXpresser*.

Keywords: context-dependent personalised feedback, feedback prioritisation, exploratory learning, analytic hierarchy process, neural networks.

1 Introduction

Exploratory learning is characterised by complex tasks such as constructing models and varying their parameters, that can be approached in different ways, leading to equally valid solutions. Although these solutions are varied, they are all characterised by some key points the learners need to address or be aware of. The actions of a learner when solving a task can indicate the points the learner may need help with, however, to be effective, the help that is given should take into consideration the personal characteristics of the learner. Moreover, relevant information could be extracted from the context which can lead to more appropriate feedback. There are many works in the literature that investigate the role of context in a diversity of fields such as recommender systems [2], artificial intelligence [1], educational psychology [40] and ubiquitous computing [27].

Joseph A. Konstan et al. (Eds.): UMAP 2011, LNCS 6787, pp. 62–74, 2011.
© Springer-Verlag Berlin Heidelberg 2011

The definition of context is also diverse, varying from the wide social context to the specificity of network characteristics. In our approach context refers to the stages within a task, with each stage providing essential information about what is currently relevant for the learner.

Exploratory Learning Environments (ELEs) (e.g. SimQuest [22], Adaptive Coach for Exploration (ACE) [7], Vectors in Physics and Mathematics [18]) are characterised by freedom, allowing learners to explore the domain rather than guide their learning in a structured manner. On the other hand, complete lack of guidance in ELEs is not useful for learning [23]. Consequently, the challenge is to provide feedback in such a way that the learner does not feel restrained and at the same time perceives the feedback as relevant with respect to the current activity. This problem is not unique to exploratory learning environments, but also applies to educational simulated environments (e.g. [42]) and games (e.g. [38]) where the challenge is to provide feedback without breaking the flow [13].

This paper addresses the problem of *personalised feedback prioritisation* in ELEs which allow learners a high degree of freedom as opposed to the guided learning offered by more structured learning environments such as intelligent tutoring systems. The approach was developed using an ELE for mathematical generalisation and the prioritisations used to train the neural network are validated by experts in the field of mathematical education.

In previous work [11] [12], we have proposed an approach for feedback prioritisation based on the Analytic Hierarchy Process [35], a popular method in Multicriteria Decision-Making [43]. Due to the large amount of data needed from experts, the AHP approach was developed only for the most frequent combinations of criteria, where criteria refer to task difficulty, experience and arithmetic ability. This meant that when a combination of criteria was not available, the closest match to the available combinations of criteria was found and the prioritisation of the best match was used instead.

To address this issue, in this paper we present a context-dependent personalised feedback prioritisation mechanism using the Analytic Hierarchy Process and Neural Networks [3]. AHP is used to define feedback prioritisation as a multi-criteria decision-making problem, while NN is used to model the relation between the criteria and the order in which the conceptual difficulties should be addressed, i.e. the prioritisation. When used alone, AHP needs a large amount of data from experts to cover all possible combinations of the criteria, while the AHP-NN synergy leads to a general model that outputs results for any such combination. The experimental study aims to establish the feasibility of the AHP-NN approach for the personalised feedback prioritisation problem.

The next section briefly introduces adaptive feedback, mathematical generalisation and the system employed. Section 3 presents the AHP-NN approach, while Section 4 presents the experimental results obtained using the proposed approach. Section 5 discusses the results and concludes the paper.

2   Adaptive Feedback in Our Exploratory Learning Environment

Feedback is usually a response to the actions of a learner aiming to correct future iterations of the actions [30]. It includes information about what happened or did not happen as a consequence of the user's actions in relations to the goal [41]; this information is given to the users to compare their performance with the expected one [21] and to make use of it in the following attempt [41].

In exploratory learning, the freedom given to learners leads to situations when feedback is required on several aspects. This is also the case of *eXpresser*[1] [31] [33], which is an ELE for mathematical generalisation that aims to link the visual with the algebraic-like representation of rules. It enables constructions of patterns, creating dependences between them, naming properties of patterns and creating algebraic-like rules with either names or numbers. Some screenshots are displayed in Figure 1, illustrating the system, two constructions, the *properties list* of a pattern that is dependent on another one, the *properties list* of an independent pattern and two examples of *rules*.

The main area of the screen in Figure 1 displays two constructions. These are solutions of two learners working independently on a task called "footpath", which is typical in the UK curriculum. The task requires to find out the number of green tiles needed to surround *any* pattern of red tiles (representing the footpath). The components of *Construction 1* are displayed separately for ease of understanding; this construction has four patterns: (a) two compact rows of green (lighter colour) tiles and (b) two rows with gaps in between tiles: one green and one red (darker colour). The first two mentioned are the same, and consequently, have the same properties displayed in the *property list* of the highlighted row in *Construction 1*. The first property, i.e. number of iterations, shows that the pattern depends on the red one because the number of iterations of the green tiles is set to 'the number of red tiles multiplied by 2 plus 1'; the *T box* with the name *red* and the corresponding value of 3 is called an *icon variable* and is used to make a pattern dependent on another; the use of *icon variables* leads to general constructions, i.e. they work for any number of red tiles. The second property, *moving left*, is set to 1 and the third property, *moving down*, is set to 0, which makes the pattern a row; for the red pattern *moving left* is set to 2 and *moving down* is set to 0, which makes a row with gaps between the tiles. The last property establishes the number needed to colour all the tiles in the pattern; in the current case it is the same as the number of iterations in the pattern. However, if a pattern is a group of several tiles, this would not be the case anymore; for example, if a pattern is a group of three tiles and is iterated five times, the number required to colour it would be three times five.

Construction 2 is built in a similar fashion, but the compact rows of green tiles do not depend on the red pattern: the first property (number of iterations)

---

[1] Developed in the context of MiGen Project, funded by the ESRC/EPSRC Teaching and Learning Research Programme (RES-139-25-0381); http://www.migen.org.

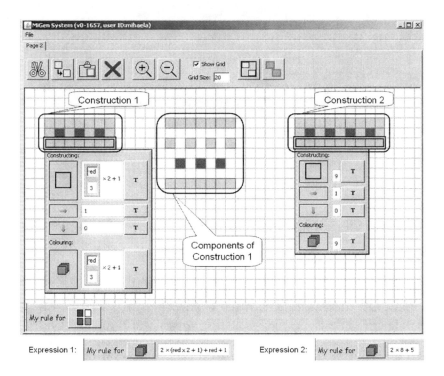

Fig. 1. eXpresser screenshots. The main screenshot includes a toolbar, an area for pattern construction and an area for defining rules/algebraic-like expressions; the toolbar (at the top) allows the following actions: cut, copy, paste, delete, zoom in, zoom out, show grid, grid size (changeable from here or using the zoom tools), group and ungroup; the main area has two constructions for the "footpath" task and two *property lists*; the components of *Construction 1* are also presented separately. The two screenshots at the bottom illustrate the rules defined by the learners who built the two constructions.

from the *property list* is set to 9. At the bottom of Figure 1, two expressions corresponding to the two constructions are displayed. *Expression 1* uses the name *red* for the number of red tiles, while *Expression 2* is numeric.

In the constructions of Figure 1, both learners follow the same strategy in surrounding the footpath: two rows of tiles at top and bottom, and one row of tiles in the gaps of the red pattern; also, for both constructions, the row of green tiles with gaps in between (the middle one) does not depend on the red pattern and the expressions do not correspond to their corresponding constructions. However, there are a few differences: (a) they work with a different number of red tiles, i.e. 3 and 4, respectively; (b) the first learner is very close to a general solution, while the second is still working with the particular case of 4 red tiles; (c) the expression of the first learner (*Expression 1* in Figure 1) is already general, while the expression of the second learner (*Expression 2* in Figure 1) is numeric.

Construction 2 could be used at this point to illustrate how the need for feedback prioritisation emerges during exploration. In this instance, from pedagogical point of view, several issues need to be addressed: (a) the construction is correct only when the red pattern consists of four tiles, i.e. it is specific, whilst the aim of the activity is to create a general construction that would work for any number of tiles; (b) the learner may need to be reminded how to make a pattern dependent on another (i.e. the use of icon variables); (c) the expression does not correspond to the construction and contains a mistake; (d) the expression is specific. To this end, different types of feedback are needed depending on learner's characteristics and contextual information. In the next section, we describe an approach that leads to prioritising feedback on these issues based on a multi-criteria decision making method called the *Analytic Hierarchy Process.*

3   The AHP&NN Feedback Prioritisation Approach

Multicriteria Decision Making (MDM) defines a class of problems where a decision from a predefined set of alternatives needs to be reached by taking into account two or more criteria. Each alternative is evaluated on the set of criteria; the outcomes provide a means of comparison between the alternatives that will facilitate a selection of one or more alternatives, or a ranking between them. Other purposes are classification of alternatives into groups (clustering) and group ranking [43]. Among the possible approaches of decision problems that correspond to this description are: statistical techniques, multi-attribute utility analysis, analytic hierarchy process, knowledge bases, mathematical models, etc.

MDM has many applications in fields where decisions need to be taken. The Analytic Hierarchy Process (AHP) is one of the most popular methods in MDM and is widely applied in a diversity of areas like logistics, military, manufacturing and health-care [20]. Frequently AHP is used in combination with other methods - a recent literature review [20] reports five main categories of tools integrated with AHP: (a) mathematical programming, (b) quality function development, (c) meta-heuristics, (d) SWOT analysis, and (e) data envelopment analysis. Four works related to higher education are reported in areas of IT-based project selection [26], teaching method selection [28], education requirement selection [24] and faculty course assignment [32].

In the area of learner/user modelling, AHP has been used in combination with fuzzy logic [17] for student diagnosis in an adaptive hypermedia educational system and in combination with Multi-Attribute Utility Theory (MAUT), another method from MDM, in recommender systems [37], where the evaluation function from MAUT is used to rate how well each alternative fulfills the decision criteria.

The AHP uses a hierarchy to represent a decision problem and to establish priorities between alternatives depending on a set of criteria involved in the decision process. It includes three main steps: (a) construction of the hierarchy; (b) analysis of priorities and (c) verification of consistency.

The *hierarchy* has the general structure presented in Figure 2. The highest level represents the *goal*, which, in our context, is personalised feedback. The second level includes the *criteria* based on which the decision should be taken; in our case, the criteria refer to the stage in the exploratory task. The third level includes the *alternatives* to be prioritised with respect to the criteria; the alternatives correspond to pedagogical aspects of mathematical generalisation. The first step includes a decomposition of the decision problem into parts defined by all relevant attributes; these attributes are arranged into hierarchical levels so as to reach the hierarchical structure presented in Figure 2.

To obtain a prioritisation of the alternatives, pairwise comparisons are needed between each pair of criteria and between each pair of alternatives. The later requires comparisons with respect to each criteria, i.e. if there are n criteria and m alternatives, $_nC^2$ pairwise comparisons are needed for the criteria and $n *_m C^2$ pairwise comparisons are needed for the alternatives ($_mC^2$ comparisons per criterion). In previous work [12] we have used AHP alone to produce the prioritisation feedback. Due to the amount of pairwise comparisons, however, we have considered as criteria only the stage within the task and produce a pairwise comparisons for different combinations of learner characteristics. This approach was taken because if the learner characteristics would have been introduced in the AHP hierarchy as criteria, it would have led to a vast amount of pairwise comparisons.

The next step in AHP is the verification of consistency, calculated by a set formula based on the pairwise comparisons. If there is a lack of consistency, the pairwise comparisons need to be reviewed and the consistency is checked again. This process is repeated until the consistency criteria is satisfied. Consequently, there could be even more effort needed from the experts at this stage.

To address this limitation, we propose to use the AHP hierarchy with the context, task difficulty and learner characteristics as criteria, and use neural networks to model the relation between the criteria and the prioritisation of alternatives. More specifically, we use a back-propagation network which is a multi-layered feed-forward neural network which is fully connected [15]. Each layer can have several units, with each unit connected to all the units in the next layer. By training the network, the optimal weights between units are learned and therefore, one could say that the knowledge about the aspect being modelled is encoded in these weights. For our purpose, by training a network on instances representing combinations of criteria with their corresponding order of alternatives, the network will learn the association between the two and will be able to output prioritisations for any combination of criteria.

Neural networks have the ability to derive meaning from complex or imprecise data and are used to extract patterns and to detect trends that cannot be noticed by humans due to their complexity [3]. Neural networks have been used in a variety of fields such as medicine [5], biology and chemistry [9], engineering [36], finance [29] and management science [25]. In the area of elearning, neural networks were used for personalised recommendations of learning objects [4].

For our purpose, the neural network will have as input the criteria and as output the prioritisation of alternatives. The criteria are the stages within a task: (1) specific construction; (2) variation of parameters; (3) general construction and (4) expression. To identify the stage a learner is at, a set of rules are used. Basically, for each stage, the presence or absence of certain actions or properties of the construction/expression are used. A learner is considered to be in the *specific construction* stage if he has not used T-boxes yet and the construction is not complete (i.e. it does not fit the mask of the task construction). The *variation of parameters* is indicated by the change in the values of the properties of patterns. The *general construction* stage is identified by the presence of T-boxes, while the *expression* stage is identified by modifications made to the expression. The other criteria are task difficulty and learners' characteristics, i.e. their experience with tasks of various degrees of difficulty and their arithmetic ability.

The alternatives are feedback on the following aspects: (a) correctness of construction (CC); (b) correctness of expression (CE); (c) construction-expression correspondence (C-E); (d) symmetry of construction (Sym); (e) generality of construction (CGen); (f) generality of expression (EGen); (g)linking patterns (LP).

4   Experimental Results

The network has four input nodes and seven output nodes. The inputs are the AHP criteria and the outputs are the AHP alternatives that were introduced in the previous section. The data used for our experiments consists of 108 instances of criteria combinations and their corresponding prioritisations of the alternatives. The criteria and their coding is presented in Table 1. The 108 instances were obtained by combining the number of values for all the criteria: $4 \times 3 \times 3 \times 3$.

The alternatives are the ones mentioned in the previous section and they are coded as 1 to 7 in the order they were introduces, i.e. CC is coded as 1 and LP is coded as 7. Both inputs and outputs are normalised by mapping minimum and maximum values to [-1 1].

One expert produced the prioritisations (i.e. the ranking of the alternatives from 1 to 7) for all instances and two other experts were asked to validate

Table 1. Criteria and their coding

Criteria	Possible values	Coding
Context, i.e. stage	specific construction	1
in the task	variation of parameters	2
	general construction	3
	expression	4
Task difficulty	low	1
	medium	2
	high	3
Experience	low	1
	medium	2
	high	3
Arithmetic ability	low	1
	medium	2
	high	3

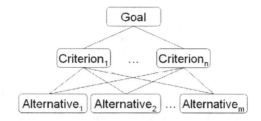

Fig. 2. Hierarchy in the Analytic Hierarchy Process

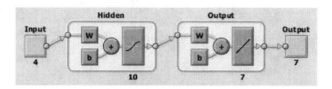

Fig. 3. Network architecture

these prioritisations for 48 instances (approximately 45% of all instances). One expert agreed with 97% of the prioritisations, while the other agreed only with 91%. On the intsances on which there was disagrement, the prioritisations were modified to reflect the agregated opinion of all experts. One could argue that the two experts that validated the prioritisations could have been asked to validate separate sets of prioritisations, thus covering 90% of all instances. This approach, however, could have led to inconsistencies between the prioritisations of the two experts which could affect the performance of the neural network. Therefore, we gave the same set of instances to the two experts to avoid this problem.

The data was randomly partitioned into three sets used for training (55%, i.e. 60 instances), validation (15%, i.e. 16 instances) and testing (32%, i.e. 30 instances). We have tested several networks architectures and found that the best performance is obtained when the number of hidden nodes is 10. The sigmoid function was used as activation function in hidden layer and the linear activation function was used in the output layer - this can be seen in Figure 3. The Levenberg-Marquart [19] algorithm was used for training. Early stopping technique was applied to check the validation error rate periodically during training [34]. The stopping conditions were the gradient magnitude (with a value of 1e-5) and the number of validation error checks (set to 6).

Using the set-up presented above, the network was used in 500 independent trials and the results are given in Table 2. The average number of iterations was 15.81 with a standard deviation of 1.96; the maximum and minimum number of iterations were, respectively, 53 and 5.

Performance refers to correct ranking of the alternatives, while error refers to the means squared error (mse), i.e. the average squared error between the network outputs and the target outputs. For our particular purpose, it is important that the neural network returns a prioritisation according to the context

Table 2. The results of the 500 independent runs

	Training	Validation	Testing
Average performance	0.899	0.902	0.906
Standard deviation	0.101	0.168	0.129
Average error(mse)	0.002	0.002	0.002
Standard deviation	0.033	0.055	0.042
Best performance	0.936	0.982	0.964
Worst performance	0.864	0.795	0.871

and the learning characteristics. Consequently, to judge the performance of the network, we need to measure if the network outputs match the target outputs not in terms of the values returned, but of the order between those values. Therefore, to calculate the network performance, we compared the ranking produced at output with the target ranking.

On the other hand, we are interested in learning the mapping between the inputs and the outputs regardless of the exact ranking because the neural network will be used to rank alternatives on the basis of imprecise information about the criteria, i.e. real values not just integers could be used for task difficulty, experience and arithmetic ability. For example, a learner's experience with tasks of medium difficulty, does not suddenly go from low (coded as 1) to medium (coded as 2), but could have intermediate values such as 1.2 or 1.8. The network should be able to return prioritisations when these intermediate values are used, and therefore, we are interested in the network's performance in terms of the mean squared error.

Looking at the results for the average error and its standard deviation, we can see that the network fits the data well. In terms of performance from ranking point of view, the results show that the network's output is the same as the targets in 91% of the cases.

5   Discussion and Conclusions

In this paper we proposed an AHP-NN approach to address the problem of feedback prioritisation in an exploratory learning environment for mathematical generalisation. In our previous work we used a sole AHP approach and run into difficulties due to the number of pairwise comparisons needed and the amount of time experts would need to spend on providing the pairwise comparisons and validating the outputs of the AHP mechanism.

In this paper we addressed this issue by proposing the use of neural networks that are capable of generalising complex relationships by mapping one data space to another one using a number of examples. Moreover, the AHP-NN approach offers the advantage of returning prioritisations when real values rather than integers are used for criteria. In AHP, the knowledge of the mapping is in the pairwise comparisons and it is only possible to take into account the exact value of a criterion, e.g. a value of 1.2 and a value of 1.8 may be considered the same.

In other works, in AHP an integer actually covers a range of values; for example 2 could be used for any value between 1.51 and 2.49, or between 2.00 and 2.99 (different experts have different views on this). The AHP-NN approach has the advantage of producing more refined prioritisations, i.e. a value of 1.2 for one criterion may lead to a different prioritisation compared with a value of 1.8 of the same criterion.

Due to the nature of our problem, the neural network needed to be tested in terms of how well it generalises, i.e. how well the networks performs with unknown data at the input, with respect to the following two aspects: the mean squared error and the correspondence between the ranking produced at output and the target ranking. The first aspect is the typical way to judge a neural network and the results show that, from this point of view, the performance is very good. The other aspect, however, is equally important and the findings are promising with an overall success of 91%.

The second aspects on which we tested out network is in fact a label ranking problem, i.e. a complex prediction task with the goal to map instances to a total order over a finite set of predefined labels [39]. Several approaches have been used to address this problem such as kernel methods [16], instance-based learning [10], case-based reasoning [6] and log-linear models [14]. We found only one previous work on label ranking using neural networks [8] developed specifically for ranking results returned by internet search engines.

Looking at the worst performing cases for the training, validation and testing sets, we have identified 10 instances that led to high errors. When looking at these instances we found they reflect infeasible combinations of criteria that fall in three categories: combining low experience and low arithmetic ability with the last two stages of the tasks; combining low experience and low arithmetic ability with high task difficulty, and combining low arithmetic ability with the last stage of the task (which requires the development of an arithmetic expression). In reality, in a classroom situation teachers would not expect learners with low arithmetic ability (with or without experience) to solve difficult tasks or finalise the last two stages of the tasks. The last two stages require the use of arithmetic expressions; in the penultimate phase, expressions need to be defined in order to make the construction general, while the last stage requires the learner to define an algebraic expression that corresponds the the construction that s/he built. Therefore, these situations could be compared to learners attempting to solve problems for which they do not have the necessary prerequisites.

To address the issue outlined above, in future work we will work on two possible solutions. One is to filter the input data to detect infeasible situations that could then be dealt with appropriate feedback or by informing the teacher. For example, if low experience and low arithmetic ability is detected the student could be given feedback to redo some stages of the task before going into the the highly difficult part. The other solution that we will investigate is to add an extra output for the neural network that could help the network learn infeasible situations and provide special type of feedback with the highest priority.

In conclusion, the research presented in this paper proposed an AHP-NN approach to address the problem of feedback prioritisation in ELEs. Although tailored for *eXpresser* the approach could be used in other ELEs provided that information is available about the aspects to give feedback on, and experts can provide some representative cases to train the neural network.

References

1. Akman, V., Bouquet, P., Thomason, R.H., Young, R.A. (eds.): CONTEXT 2001. LNCS (LNAI), vol. 2116. Springer, Heidelberg (2001)
2. Anand, S., Mobasher, B.: Contextual recommendation. In: Proceedings of Web-Mine 2006, pp. 142–160 (2007)
3. Anderson, J.A.: An Introduction to Neural Networks. MIT Press, Cambridge (1995)
4. Baylari, A., Montazer, G.: Design a personalized e-learning system based on item response theory and artificial neural network approach. Expert Systems with Applications 36(4), 8013–8021 (2009)
5. Behrman, M., Linder, R., Assadi, A.H., Stacey, B.R., Backonja, M.M.: Classification of patients with pain based on neuropathic pain symptoms: Comparison of an artificial neural network against an established scoring system. European Journal of Pain 11(4), 370–376 (2007)
6. Brinker, K., Hüllermeier, E.: Label ranking in case-based reasoning. In: Weber, R.O., Richter, M.M. (eds.) ICCBR 2007. LNCS (LNAI), vol. 4626, pp. 77–91. Springer, Heidelberg (2007)
7. Bunt, A., Conati, C.: Probabilistic student modelling to improve exploratory behaviour. User Modelling and User-Adaptive Interaction 13(3), 269–309 (2003)
8. Burges, C., Shaked, T., Renshaw, E., Lazier, A., Deeds, M., Hamilton, N., Hullender, G.: Learning to rank using gradient descent. In: Proceedings of the 22nd International Conference on Machine Learning, ICML 2005, pp. 89–96. ACM, New York (2005)
9. Cartwright, H.M.: Artificial neural networks in biology and chemistry the evolution of a new analytical tool. In: Walker, J.M., Lvingstone, D.J. (eds.) Artificial Neural Networks, Methods in Molecular Biology, vol. 458, pp. 1–13. Humana Press, Totowa (2009)
10. Cheng, W., Hühn, J., Hüllermeier, E.: Decision tree and instance-based learning for label ranking. In: Proceedings of the 26th International Conference on Machine Learning, ICML 2009, pp. 161–168. ACM, New York (2009)
11. Cocea, M., Magoulas, G.: Context-dependent personalised feedback prioritisation in exploratory learning for mathematical generalisation. In: Houben, G.-J., McCalla, G., Pianesi, F., Zancanaro, M. (eds.) UMAP 2009. LNCS, vol. 5535, pp. 271–282. Springer, Heidelberg (2009)
12. Cocea, M., Magoulas, G.D.: Hybrid model for learner modelling and feedback prioritisation in exploratory learning. International Journal of Hybrid Intelligent Systems 6(4), 211–230 (2009)
13. Csikszentmihalyi, M.: Finding Flow: The Psychology of Engagement With Everyday Life. BasicBooks, New York (1997)
14. Dekel, O., Manning, C.D., Singer, Y.: Log-linear models for label ranking. Advances in Neural Information Processing Systems 16, 497–504 (2003)

15. Dreyfus, G.: Neural networks: methodology and applications. Springer, Heidelberg (2005)
16. Elisseeff, A., Weston, J.: A kernel method for multi-labelled classification. Advances in Neural Information Processing Systems 14, 681–687 (2001)
17. Grigoriadou, M., Kornilakis, H., Papanikolaou, K.A., Magoulas, G.D.: Fuzzy inference for student diagnosis in adaptive educational hypermedia. In: Vlahavas, I.P., Spyropoulos, C.D. (eds.) SETN 2002. LNCS (LNAI), vol. 2308, pp. 191–202. Springer, Heidelberg (2002)
18. Grigoriadou, M., Samarakou, M., Mitropoulos, D., Rigoutsos, A., Stavridou, E., Solomonidou, C.: Vectors in physics and mathematics. In: Proceedings of the International Conference on Technology and Education, pp. 71–73 (1999)
19. Hagan, M., Menhaj, M.: Training feedforward networks with the marquardt algorithm. IEEE Transactions on Neural Networks 5, 989–993 (1994)
20. Ho, W.: Integrated analytic hierarchy process and its applications – A literature review. European Journal of Operational Research 186(1), 211–228 (2008)
21. Johnson, D., Johnson, R.: Cooperative learning and feedback in technology-based instruction. In: Dempsey, J.V., Sales, G.C. (eds.) Interactive Instruction and Feedback, Englewood Cliffs, NJ, pp. 133–157 (1993)
22. van Joolingen, W.R., King, S., de Jong, T.: The simquest authoring system for simulation-based discovery environments. In: de Boulay, B., Mizoguchi, R. (eds.) Knowledge and Media in Learning Systems, pp. 79–87. IOS, Amsterdam (1997)
23. Kirschner, P., Sweller, J., Clark, R.E.: Why minimal guidance during instruction does not work: An analysis of the failure of constructivist, discovery, problem-based, experiential and inquiry-based teaching. Educational Psychologist 41(2), 75–86 (2006)
24. Koksal, G., Egitman, A.: Planning and design of industrial engineering education quality. Computers & Industrial Engineering 35(3-4), 639–642 (1998)
25. Krycha, K.A., Wagner, U.: Applications of artificial neural networks in management science: a survey. Journal of Retailing and Consumer Services 6(4), 185–203 (1999)
26. Kwak, N.K., Lee, C.W.: A multicriteria decision-making approach to university resource allocation and information infrastructure planning. European Journal of Operational Research 110(2), 234–242 (1998)
27. Kwon, O.: The potential roles of context-aware computing technology in optimization-based intelligent decision-making. Expert Systems with Applications 31(3), 629–642 (2006)
28. Lam, K., Zhao, X.: An application of quality function deployment to improve the quality of teaching. International Journal of Quality and Reliability Management 15(4), 389–413 (1998)
29. Landajo, M., de Andrés, J., Lorca, P.: Robust neural modeling for the cross-sectional analysis of accounting information. European Journal of Operational Research 177(2), 1232–1252 (2007)
30. Mason, B., Bruning, R.: Providing feedback in computer-based instruction: What the research tells us (2001), http://dwb.unl.edu/Edit/MB/MasonBruning.html
31. Noss, R., Hoyles, C., Mavrikis, M., Geraniou, E., Gutierrez-Santos, S., Pearce, D.: Broadening the sense of 'dynamic': a microworld to support students' mathematical generalisation. The International Journal on Mathematics Education 41(4), 493–503 (2009)
32. Ozdemir, M.S., Gasimov, R.N.: The analytic hierarchy process and multiobjective 0–1 faculty course assignment. European Journal of Operational Research 157(2), 398–408 (2004)

33. Pearce, D., Mavrikis, M., Geraniou, E., Gutiérrez, S.: Issues in the design of an environment to support the learning of mathematical generalisation. In: Dillenbourg, P., Specht, M. (eds.) EC-TEL 2008. LNCS, vol. 5192, pp. 326–337. Springer, Heidelberg (2008)
34. Prechelt, L.: Automatic early stopping using cross validation: quantifying the criteria. Neural Networks 11, 761–767 (1998)
35. Saaty, T.: The Analytic Hierarchy Process. McGraw-Hill, New York (1980)
36. Schlechtingen, M., Santos, I.F.: Comparative analysis of neural network and regression based condition monitoring approaches for wind turbine fault detection. Mechanical Systems and Signal Processing (2010) (in Press)
37. Schmitt, C., Dengler, D., Bauer, M.: Multivariate preference models and decision making with the MAUT machine. In: Brusilovsky, P., Corbett, A.T., de Rosis, F. (eds.) UM 2003. LNCS (LNAI), vol. 2702, pp. 297–302. Springer, Heidelberg (2003)
38. Vasilyeva, E.: Towards personalized feedback in educational computer games for children. In: Proceedings of the Sixth Conference on IASTED International Conference Web-Based Education, vol. 2, pp. 597–602. ACTA Press (2007)
39. Vembu, S., Gärtner, T.: Label ranking algorithms: A survey. In: Johannes Fürnkranz, E.H. (ed.) Preference Learning. Springer, Heidelberg (2010)
40. Wang, S., Treat, T., Brownell, K.: Cognitive processing about classroom-relevant contexts: Teachers' attention to and utilization of girls' body size, ethnicity, attractiveness, and facial affect. Journal of Educational Psychology 100(2), 473–489 (2008)
41. Wiggins, G.: Feedback: how learning occurs (2008), http://www.authenticeducation.org/bigideas/article.lasso?artId=61
42. Zigmont, J.J., Kappus, L.J., Sudikoff, S.N.: Theoretical foundations of learning through simulation. Seminars in Perinatology 35(2), 47–51 (2011)
43. Zopounidis, C., Doumpos, M.: Multicriteria classification and sorting methods: A literature review. European Journal of Operational Research 138(2), 229–246 (2002)

Performance Comparison of Item-to-Item Skills Models with the IRT Single Latent Trait Model

Michel C. Desmarais

Polytechnique Montréal
2500, chemin de Polytechnique
Montréal (Québec), Canada
michel.desmarais@polymtl.ca
http://www.professeurs.polymtl.ca/michel.desmarais/

Abstract. Assessing a learner's mastery of a set of skills is a fundamental issue in intelligent learning environments. We compare the predictive performance of two approaches for training a learner model with domain data. One is based on the principle of building the model solely from observable data items, such as exercises or test items. Skills modelling is not part of the training phase, but instead dealt with at later stage. The other approach incorporates a single latent skill in the model. We compare the capacity of both approaches to accurately predict item outcome (binary success or failure) from a subset of item outcomes. Three types of item-to-item models based on standard Bayesian modeling algorithms are tested: (1) Naive Bayes, (2) Tree-Augmented Naive Bayes (TAN), and (3) a K2 Bayesian Classifier. Their performance is compared to the widely used IRT-2PL approach which incorporates a single latent skill. The results show that the item-to-item approaches perform as well, or better than the IRT-2PL approach over 4 widely different data sets, but the differences vary considerably among the data sets. We discuss the implications of these results and the issues relating to the practical use of item-to-item models.

Keywords: IRT, Bayesian Models, TAN, Learner models.

1 Introduction

A number of adaptive applications need a learner model to assess the student skills. They will query this model to find out if a given concept is known, or if a skill is mastered, to perform some adaptation of the learning environment to the user's profile. The skill modelled is an abstraction that cannot be measured directly. A skill is often referred to as a learner's *latent trait* that will determine the successes or failures to some test items or exercises. It is often represented as a probabilistic abstraction, to reflect the fact that stochastic factors like slips and guesses influence the success or failure outcome to item trials.

We explore two means to create such abstractions. One is to integrate skills directly along observable items in a domain model. Hierarchies of skills, where observable items are situated at the bottom of this hierarchy, is a typical example

Joseph A. Konstan et al. (Eds.): UMAP 2011, LNCS 6787, pp. 75–86, 2011.

of a domain model that is commonly found in the literature of intelligent tutoring systems and most often modeled as a Bayesian Network or some hybrid derivative (for eg. [22,5,4]). Standard algorithms for probabilistic inference can then be used to infer the probability of mastery of skills given observed items.

Another approach relies on a Q-matrix [20], which defines which skills are linked to each test items. A familiar example that can be considered as a *summative* assessment with a Q-matrix is a standard questionnaire scoring scheme, where each question is given a weight and the weighted sum of successes to each question yields the assessment of the skill that is intended to be measured by the questionnaire. The skills are the columns of the Q-matrix and the items are the row, and the contribution of each item to a set of skills is given by the weights in the matrix. Assuming a matrix of n rows representing items, and m columns representing skills, and assuming that if a value greater than 0 in cell (i,j) represents the weight of item i to skill j, then we can compute the skill profile of a student through the dot product of the student's item response outcomes vector and the Q-matrix. This product is a skills mastery vector which readily can be normalized to obtain the percent mastery of each skill, for example.

The summative assessment approach to skill assessment with a Q-matrix is not probabilistic in itself, but if the student item outcome matrix contains probabilities of mastery, then the resulting skills assessment is probabilistic.

The choice between the item-to-item approach or the latent traits approach (eg. Bayesian Network) is a compromise between a number of factors to consider, such as knowledge engineering efforts, computational complexity, and most importantly reliability and accuracy of predictions. A number of researchers in the learner modeling field have investigated this issue over the last decade or so [22,5,4,6,1,15].

This paper revisits the issue of assessing item-to-item model performance by comparing the predictive accuracy of standard Bayesian classifier algorithms [10] to create item-to-item learner models with that of the IRT approach (see [21]), which contains a single latent skills. These approaches readily lend themselves to a fair comparison to the extent that each of them are solely data driven and require no knowledge engineering effort for the purpose of predicting item outcome. This would not the case if we wanted to predict the mastery of a set of (unobservable) skills, in which case both approaches would require some knowledge engineering effort, such as defining a Q-matrix or defining the topology of a Bayesian Network, as well as independent means to assess the skills for validation purpose.

Similar studies were conducted by Desmarais et al., [6,7]. These studies respectively compared the performance of a Bayesian Network developed by Vomlel [23] and of the IRT approach with a derivative of a Naive Bayes item-to-item model (POKS). The results showed that for predicting item outcome, POKS performed slightly better than the two other approaches. The current study extends this work by comparing IRT with three standard probabilistic inference techniques: (1) the Tree Augmented Naive Bayes (TAN), (2) a variant of TAN that relies on the K2 search algorithm, and (3) the simple Naive Bayes model. Because the

POKS technique used in the work of Desmarais et al. (2005, 2006) integrates a feature selection algorithm in addition to the probabilistic inference techniques listed, it cannot be directly compared here. However, given that POKS uses a Naive Bayes inference rule, the performance would be expected to be the same as the Naive Bayes technique of this study.

The next two sections describe the IRT model and the item-to-item models. They are followed by the description of the experiments methodology and results.

2   Model with a Single Latent Trait: Item Response Theory

The Item Response Theory (IRT) model [21] is the most widely studied model in psychometrics and routinely used for Computer Adaptive Testing applications. It also gained some adoptions by the intelligent learning community in the last decade or so. This model assumes that the success to all items in a test is determined by a single skill, θ. This skill is referred to as the latent trait. The model can be graphically represented by the network in figure 1.

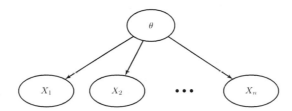

Fig. 1. Generic graphical representation of an IRT model

In the two parameter version of IRT, the probability of success to a single item, X_i, is determined by the logistic function:

$$P(X_i|\theta) = \frac{1}{1 + e^{-a_i(\theta - b_i)}} \tag{1}$$

where parameter a_i is the *discrimination* and b_i is the *difficulty* of item i. A multiplicative factor of 1.7 is often added to a to fit the curve closer to the integration of the normal curve and align it with the so called normal ogive model of the original IRT theory. These parameters are estimated from a training sample and they are specific to each item i (see [3]). This model has a single latent trait (skill) corresponding to θ, which is estimated by maximizing its value according to the observed outcomes to a vector of item nodes **X** and under the assumption of independence of the conditional probabilities $P(X_i|\theta)$:

$$\arg\max_\theta P(\theta|\mathbf{X}) = P(\theta|X_1, X_2, ..., X_n) = \prod^{n} P(X_i|\theta) \tag{2}$$

3   Bayesian Models without Latent Skills

To compare the predictive performance of latent models vs. non latent models, we now consider three types of Bayesian classifier models which do not integrate any latent traits (such as θ in IRT):

Naive Bayes (NB) The Naive Bayes model can be represented as figure 1's network, but the (latent) class node θ is replaced by some node X_k for which we aim to predict the most likely binary value, $\{0, 1\}$ (or predict the probability of each value). Computation follows the structure of equation 2, except that instead of maximizing the conditional probability $P(\theta|\mathbf{X})$, we maximize for X_k:

$$\arg \max_{X_k=\{0,1\}} P(X_k|\mathbf{X}) = \prod_{X_i \in \mathbf{X}} P(X_i|X_k) \qquad (3)$$

where $\mathbf{X}$ can be any subset of test items excluding X_k.

A distinct equation of the form above is constructed for each of the item in the set. Given that there are no latent trait, the link function of equation (1) is replaced by the conditional probability estimate $P(X_i|X_k)$, which is estimated from the observed frequencies. Akin to the IRT model, independence of the conditional probabilities $P(X_i|X_k)$ is assumed.

Tree Augmented Bayesian Network (TAN) To address the issue that some items may be highly correlated, and therefore that the independence assumption between conditional probabilities does not hold, an alternative class of network topologies was proposed by Friedman et al. [10]: the Tree Augmented Bayesian network (TAN). This topology retains the Naive Bayes topology but it adds a tree structure of links among the leaf nodes. Except for the class root node, each node can have two parents, the class and another node among $\mathbf{X}$. The resulting network creates a tree among the children of the class node X_k (see figure 2). As with the Naive Bayes approach, a different model is created for each item. This structures retains much of the simplicity of Naive Bayes while allowing for efficient network topology induction and inference.

Bayesian Network Classifier (BNC) BNC is a variant of the TAN model that uses the K2 algorithm (see [24]) to search for the tree structure among children nodes. We will name this model a Bayesian Network Classifier in accordance with [24], but the reader should keep in mind that it follows the same topological constraints as the TAN.

4   Experiments

The respective performances of the IRT latent trait model and of the non latent Bayesian models are compared by assessing their predictive power in a simulation study. A fixed number of observed item outcomes (success or failure) from a test

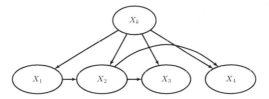

Fig. 2. TAN network example with four predictor items for X_k. In addition to the usual Naive Bayes structure, a tree structure is defined among the leaf nodes, X_1 to X_4.

is fed to the model and we measure the model's ability to correctly classify the outcome of all other observable items from the same individual. These remaining observable items are kept unobserved from the model's perspective, but the real outcome has in fact been recorded, which allows a comparison of the prediction to the reality.

Our choice is to compare predictions over observed data only. Even for the latent model IRT, we do not attempt to derive an independent measure of the skill θ to assess how accurately its estimate/prediction matches. Such procedure was used by Vomlel in an experiment where he asked experts to independently assess concept mastery from test data and compared the assessment of a Bayesian Network over this independent data [23]. Instead, we presume that if θ is correctly estimated, then it will show in the model's ability to predict the observed outcome to items. This approach allows for better experimental replication quality as it is less prone to biases and errors introduced by a few number of experts in assessing skill mastery.

4.1 Data Sets

The experiments are conducted over four sets of real data:

College mathematics: Data from a mathematics test administered in 2005 to freshman engineering students that covers their general knowledge of college mathematics. It spans many topics from algebra to analytical geometry, calculus, trigonometry, and exponentials.

Fraction algebra: This data set is from Vomlel's Bayesian Network study [23]. It was administered to 10-12 year old and covers the basics of fraction algebra. Only the data from the 20 question items tests was used and the concept expert assessment was ignored.

LSAT: This data set is available from the `ltm` package written R [17] which can be obtained through the usual CRAN repository[1]. It corresponds to data from the Law School Admission Test.

UNIX: A questionnaire developed by the author to assess knowledge of the Unix shell commands. It contains question items that cover basic knowledge

---

[1] `http://cran.r-project.org/`

to advanced topics and was administered to respondents having a very large array of expertise. This distribution of item difficulty and respondent expertise allows for strong classification performance.

All these sets are composed of binary success/failure data with few missing values, from 0% to 5%, which were recoded as failure answers.

Table 1 reports a number of statistics and informations about the four data sets:

Nb. items: Size of the questionnaire.

Nb. respondents: Number of questionnaires answered by respondents.

Training size: Number of respondents used in a cross validation (the remaining being used for testing).

Avg. respondent score: Average of respondent success rates.

Stdev. score: Standard deviation of success rates.

Nb. folds: Number of folds in the cross-validation experiments for the results reported in the next section.

Nb. features: Number of items fed to the models as observations. These items are selected based on a simple feature selection, namely the degree of correlation with the class variable. Each item has a different set of "feature" items selected for its prediction by the models. The training of the models is done only on the features selected.

Avg. cor. among features: As a measure of the degree to which the independence assumption of the BN and IRT models is violated, we report the average correlation among the features selected.

We can judge from table 1 that the data sets differ widely among them. LSAT is only a 5 items set but, it contains a large number of respondents, whereas UNIX has larger number of items. With only 48 respondents, the UNIX training is limited to 38 cases and the testing to 10, such that the number of folds was increased to obtain more reliable results from the simulations. The correlation among features is also widespread, ranging from 0.08 for LSAT to 0.62 for UNIX. These differences may explain to some extent the large differences in performance reported in the next section.

4.2   Simulation Methodology

Model performance assessment is done through cross-validations. Each model is trained on a portion of the data and tested on the other. For a single fold, the same training and testing sets are used across models to reduce variance. The IRT 2PL model is based on the `ltm` package implemented in R [17]. All three other models are taken from the Weka data mining package [24] and used within R through `RWeka`[2] [14].

---

[2] RWeka version 0.4-3 and RWeka.jar dated 27 Sept 2010. These packages are available under the CRAN repository. The scripts for the simulations and the data sets are available from this url:
http://www.professeurs.polymtl.ca/michel.desmarais/Papers/UMAP2011/

Table 1. Data sets

	Coll. math	Frac. algebra	LSAT	UNIX
Nb. of items	60	20	5	34
Nb. of respondents	246	149	1000	48
Training size	171	100	900	38
Testing size	75	49	100	10
Avg. respondent score	0.60	0.61	0.76	0.53
Stdev. score	0.15	0.25	0.21	0.29
Nb. of folds	10	10	10	20
Nb. of features	5	5	4	5
Avg. cor. among features	0.17	0.47	0.08	0.62

In accordance with the approach described in section 3, a different model is trained for each item. Although this is not required for the IRT model, for which a single model could be derived for the prediction of all item outcomes, we chose to apply the same methodology throughout all models[3].

Following the usual terminology for classification tasks, we also refer to the predicted item as the target class and to the observed items as features. For each model, 5 features are selected, except for the LSAT data which has only 5 items in total and therefore only 4 other features can be defined. The respective item models are trained only over the selected feature subset. The selection of features for each item is based on the correlation with the target. For a subset of size 5, the top 5 features most correlated with the target nodes are selected. Note that a more sophisticated feature selection algorithm which would take into account intra-features dependencies would likely yield slightly better results from the current experiment for the item-to-item models. However, it remains unclear whether it would favor one item-to-item model over another.

Once a model is trained, the simulation procedure consists in feeding the model with observed items (features). All four models output a probability that the target item will be 0 or 1 and this prediction is compared with the actual respondent's score. Using this probability allows us to derive a ROC curve (Receiver Operating Characteristic), from which the AUC (The Area Under the ROC Curve) score is computed and which serves as one of the performance measure[4]. The other measure reported is the accuracy: if a target node has a probability above 0.5, it is considered true, or false otherwise. Accuracy is reported as percent correct of predictions matched with reality.

5   Results

The simulation methodology described above is run over the 4 data sets and the average AUC and accuracy scores are computed. Table 2 reports the different

---

[3] IRT can predict all items from the same model because θ is the single predictor to all item nodes, whereas for the item-to-item models, a different network is derived for each node.

[4] ROC and AUC analysis are computed with the ROCR package (Sing et al., 2005; available at http://cran.r-project.org/)

Table 2. mean (AUC) results of Models for the four data sets

	TAN	BNC	NB	IRT	AoV significance level		
					All	TAN-IRT	w/o IRT
Coll. math	0.77(.012)	0.76(.012)	0.75(.014)	0.74(.013)	***	***	**
Frac. algebra	0.90(.018)	0.90(.018)	0.88(.018)	0.85(.015)	***	***	**
LSAT	0.59(.038)	0.59(.038)	0.58(.039)	0.57(.041)	-	-	-
UNIX	0.96(.021)	0.96(.023)	0.95(.023)	0.91(.036)	***	***	-[a]

*** $p<0.001$, ** $p<0.01$, * $p<0.05$ - $p>0.05$
[a] Close to significant: $p=0.052$

results of the AUC scores for each model and each data set. Each number represents the mean across AUC values of each run, where each AUC value is the average AUC of all question items for a given data set. The number in parenthesis is the standard error across simulation runs.

Table 2 also reports significance levels for three hypothesis tests based on an analysis of variance (AoV)[5]:

All: all 4 conditions (models)
TAN-IRT: TAN and IRT conditions alone
w/o IRT: without IRT (i.e. TAN+BNC+NB)

The AoV test is performed on the AUC score averaged over students and over items.

The results show that, for AUC scores, apart from the LSAT data set, almost all the hypothesis tests are positive at the level of $p<0.01$ or $p<0.001$. The TAN-IRT condition indicates that TAN performs significantly better than IRT, with differences in AUC ranging from 3% to 5% for Coll. math, Frac. algebra and UNIX data sets, and 1% for LSAT. TAN and BNC have almost exactly the same performance up to the second decimal, so all conclusions regarding TAN applies to BNC.

Note that even if these differences are small, they must be taken into the context that a random prediction would perform at 0.5 for AUC, and that the relative error reduction from 95% to 97.5% is equivalent to the reduction from 80% to 90% (reducing the remaining error rate by half). Considering this, the 3% AUC error reduction for the UNIX data set is in fact more substantial in relative terms than the 5% fraction algebra. This would be reflected when computing confidence intervals in the prediction of test scores, for example, which entails important implications when a tutoring system needs to gauge the certainty of its assessment. In other words, even if the differences are small in absolute terms, they can have a substantial impact in practice.

The "w/o IRT" condition shows that the thee different latent free Bayesian methods do perform at significantly different levels. The NB condition is

---

[5] An analysis of variance is preferred over a Student-t test here to avoid conducting multiple t-tests. Furthermore, the choice of reporting only the TAN-IRT condition over all 6 possible pairs is because TAN seems to yield the best results.

Table 3. Accuracy results of Models for the four data sets

	TAN	BNC	NB	IRT	AoV significance level		
					All	TAN-IRT	w/o IRT
Coll. math	0.64(.044)	0.64(.043)	0.63(.044)	0.65(.036)	-	-	-
Frac. algebra	0.70(.069)	0.70(.068)	0.68(.064)	0.71(.047)	-	-	-
LSAT	0.83(.009)	0.83(.010)	0.83(.012)	0.83(.010)	-	-	-
UNIX	0.93(.016)	0.94(.013)	0.91(.021)	0.86(.029)	***	***	***

*** $p<0.001$, ** $p<0.01$, * $p<0.05$ - $p>0.05$

systematically lower than the other, suggesting that the added value of the more complex topology of TAN and BNC does yield improvement by accounting for internal correlation among predictor items.

Large differences in the AUC scores are found across data sets. Even if large training samples are available for the Coll. math and LSAT experiments, performance over these tests is the lowest. However, the LSAT relative performance differences is by far the lowest. A possible explanation is that large data sets reduces the predictive advantage of the three other techniques.

Table 3 reports the accuracy scores with a cutoff of 0.5 (an item is considered succeeded if the estimated probability is above 0.5). The scores are obtained according to the procedure described in section 5, and the significance levels reported are for the same conditions as the AUC score.

Accuracy scores show no significant differences among models, except for the UNIX data set, and indicate that accuracy is a much less sensitive measure than the AUC results reported in table 2. However, the results concur with the explanation that the size of the data sets has an effect on model performance, since the only significant diffference between the models is for the smallest data set, UNIX, which is composed of only 38 respondants.

6   Discussion

The results of the experiments clearly suggest that the predictive performance of item-to-item models is generally as good, or superior to the well known IRT model that contains a single latent skill to predict performance. Even the simplest of the item-to-item model (NB) performs as well or better than IRT on the AUC scores. However, the accuracy scores show smaller differences than the AUC scores across models.

The improvement over IRT varies considerably between data sets and appear sensitive to sample size, with small samples favoring the Bayesian approaches over IRT. The gain over IRT also coincides with the strength of inter-item correlations reported in table 1, which is to be expected since the item-to-item approach exploits these very correlations in the estimates.

The item-to-item approaches outlined in this paper can therefore offer a valid alternative to an IRT approach, especially for small samples where the item-to-item models appear to outperform IRT. Under this approach, estimating the chances of success to a single item requires building a classifier from a chosen subset of a few observed items. Assessing overall mastery involves estimating the chances of success to each item that is yet to be administred in the test. This overall assessment process can take close to one second, according to the setup we used for this experiment (a combination of non optimized code written over R and Weka and running on an single threaded process on an AMD Phenom II 2.6 GHz processor). On a multicore machine, and granted that the processing time of the simulation code can be improved, we can expect that a signle server can support testing of an averaged size class of around 50 students and more from a single server.

6.1   From Item-to-Item Models to Skills Assessment

The assessment outcome of the item-to-item approach is a set of probabilities, the probabilities that a given student will succeed each test item. Now, item outcome estimates do not constitute, in themselves, a skills assessment. Recall from the introduction that the student's assessment of skills is based on the weighted sum of all item responses, one weighted sum for each skill. This can be conceived as the dot product of the response matrix by the Q-matrix. Implicit to this approach is that the skill domain is covered by the set of items, of which only a subset is actually administered as part of the actual student assessment, and the mastery of the rest of the items is estimated based on the item-to-item model. The assumption is that the estimated probabilities of success to untested items allow for a more accurate assessment of skills. Such framework has been extensively studied by Falmagne, Doignon, and a number of colleagues [8] under the theory of Knowledge Spaces and it has given rise to a widely used commercial intelligent learning environment named ALEKS[6] and to a few academic systems [11,13]. Moreover, Heller and his colleagues [12] have devised a formal framework to define prerequisite relations between items and skills that allows a more sophisticated means of assessing skills with item mastery estimates.

6.2   Q-Matrix vs. Skills as Latent Traits

A Q-matrix is an intuitive concept that is readily understood as a weighted sum of items. Therefore we can assume any teacher or domain expert would be able to construct one without exceptional effort. However, the single latent concept IRT approach is even more simple to the extent that no other artifact like a Q-matrix is necessary to assess the single concept. The discrimination and difficulty parameters of an item indirectly determines its weight to the assessment of this concept, and yet no expert intervention is required given sufficient data. Of course, it is limited to a single concept, but multidimensional IRT models allow for a few skills to be assessed simultaneously, albeit with the aid of an expert that does an item classification that approaches the task of building a Q-matrix. So, in the end, the two approaches must involve a minimum knowledge engineering

---

[6] www.aleks.com. See also [9].

effort to handle multiple skills. Recent work by Pavlik et al. [16], by Stamper et al. [19], and by Liu [15], among others, offer some avenues to automatize the induction of Q-matrices from data, but this work is still in early stage.

However, a difference arises in the fact that the item-to-item approach offers no means to validate the Q-matrix, since item mastery prediction is entirely detached from the skills assessment. With IRT, the item fit method and the procedures used in our experiment allows some assessment of the validity of the skill assessment to predict item outcome, even if we had used a multidimensional (multi-skill) model. This is not possible with the item-to-item approach, as defined here, and it leaves open the question of how to validate the Q-matrix. However, research on automating the construction of a Q-matrix may offer interesting solutions in the future (see for eg. [2]).

References

1. Amershi, S., Conati, C.: Unsupervised and supervised machine learning in user modeling for intelligent learning environments. In: IUI 2007: Proceedings of the 12th International Conference on Intelligent User Interfaces, pp. 72–81. ACM, New York (2007)
2. Ayers, E., Nugent, R., Dean, N.: A comparison of student skill knowledge estimates. In: 2nd International Conference on Educational Data mining, Cordoba, Spain, pp. 1–10 (2009)
3. Baker, F.B.: Item Response Theory Parameter Estimation Techniques. Marcel Dekker Inc., New York (1992)
4. Carmona, C., Millán, E., Pérez-de-la-Cruz, J.-L., Trella, M., Conejo, R.: Introducing Prerequisite Relations in a Multi-layered Bayesian Student Model. In: Ardissono, L., Brna, P., Mitrović, A. (eds.) UM 2005. LNCS (LNAI), vol. 3538, pp. 347–356. Springer, Heidelberg (2005)
5. Conati, C., Gertner, A., VanLehn, K.: Using Bayesian networks to manage uncertainty in student modeling. User Modeling and User-Adapted Interaction 12(4), 371–417 (2002)
6. Desmarais, M.C., Meshkinfam, P., Gagnon, M.: Learned student models with item to item knowledge structures. User Modeling and User-Adapted Interaction 16(5), 403–434 (2006)
7. Desmarais, M.C., Pu, X.: A bayesian inference adaptive testing framework and its comparison with Item Response Theory. International Journal of Artificial Intelligence in Education 15, 291–323 (2005)
8. Doignon, J.P., Falmagne, J.C.: Knowledge Spaces. Springer, Berlin (1999)
9. Falmagne, J.C., Cosyn, E., Doignon, J.P., Thiéry, N.: The assessment of knowledge, in theory and in practice. In: Missaoui, R., Schmidt, J. (eds.) Formal Concept Analysis. LNCS (LNAI), vol. 3874, pp. 61–79. Springer, Heidelberg (2006)
10. Friedman, N., Geiger, D., Goldszmidt, M.: Bayesian network classifiers. Machine Learning 29(2-3), 131–163 (1997)
11. Heller, J., Hockemeyer, C., Albert, D.: Applying competence structures for peer tutor recommendations in CSCL environments. In: Kinshuk, L.C., Sutinen, E., Sampson, D., Aedo, I., Uden, L., Kähkönen, E. (eds.) The 4th IEEE International Conference on Advanced Learning Technologies, pp. 1050–1051. IEEE Computer Society, Los Alamitos (2004)

12. Heller, J., Steiner, C., Hockemeyer, C., Albert, D.: Competence–based knowledge structures for personalised learning. International Journal on E–Learning 5(1), 75–88 (2006)
13. Hockemeyer, C., Held, T., Albert, D.: Rath - a relational adaptive tutoring hypertext www-environment based on knowledge space theory (1997)
14. Hornik, K., Buchta, C., Hothorn, T., Meyer, D., Zeileis, A.: The RWeka package (2006)
15. Liu, C.L.: A simulation-based experience in learning structures of bayesian networks to represent how students learn composite concepts. I. J. Artificial Intelligence in Education 18(3), 237–285 (2008)
16. Pavlik, P.I., Cen, H., Koedinger, K.R.: Learning factors transfer analysis: Using learning curve analysis to automatically generate domain models. In: Barnes, T., Desmarais, M.C., Romero, C., Ventura, S. (eds.) Proceedings of the 2nd International Conference on Educational Data Mining, EDM 2009, Cordoba, Spain, July 1-3, pp. 121–130 (2009), www.educationaldatamining.org
17. Rizopoulos, D.: ltm: An r package for latent variable modelling and item response theory analyses. Journal of Statistical Software 17(5), 1–25 (2006)
18. Sing, T., Sander, O., Beerenwinkel, N., Lengauer, T.: Rocr: visualizing classifier performance in r. Bioinformatics 21(20), 3940–3941 (2005), http://bioinformatics.oxfordjournals.org/content/21/20/3940.abstract
19. Stamper, J.C., Barnes, T., Croy, M.J.: Extracting student models for intelligent tutoring systems. In: AAAI 2007, pp. 1900–1901. AAAI Press, Menlo Park (2007)
20. Tatsuoka, K.K.: Rule space: An approach for dealing with misconceptions based on item response theory. Journal of Educational Measurement 20, 345–354 (1983)
21. van der Linden, W.J., Hambleton, R.K. (eds.): Handbook of Modern Item Response Theory. Springer, Heidelberg (1997)
22. VanLehn, K., Niu, Z., Siler, S., Gertner, A.S.: Student modeling from conventional test data: A bayesian approach without priors. In: Goettl, B.P., Halff, H.M., Redfield, C.L., Shute, V.J. (eds.) ITS 1998. LNCS, vol. 1452, pp. 434–443. Springer, Heidelberg (1998)
23. Vomlel, J.: Bayesian networks in educational testing. International Journal of Uncertainty, Fuzziness and Knowledge Based Systems 12, 83–100 (2004)
24. Witten, I.H., Frank, E.: Data mining. Morgan Kaufmann, Los Altos (2000)

Hybrid User Preference Models for Second Life and OpenSimulator Virtual Worlds

Joshua Eno, Gregory Stafford, Susan Gauch, and Craig W. Thompson

Computer Science and Computer Engineering Department
University of Arkansas
504 J. B. Hunt Building
Fayetteville, AR 72701
{jeno,gstaffor,sgauch,cwt}@uark.edu

Abstract. Virtual world user models have similarities with hypertext system user models. User knowledge and preferences may be derived from the locations users visit or recommend. The models can represent topics of interest for the user based on the subject or content of visited locations, and corresponding location models can enable matching between users and locations. However, virtual worlds also present challenges and opportunities that differ from hypertext worlds. Content collection for a cross-world search and recommendation service may be more difficult in virtual worlds, and there is less text available for analysis. In some cases, though, extra information is available to add to user and content profiles enhance the matching ability of the system. In this paper, we present a content collection system for Second Life and OpenSimulator virtual worlds, as well as user and location models derived from the collected content. The models incorporate text, social proximity, and metadata attributes to create hybrid user models for representing user interests and preferences. The models are evaluated based on their ability to match content popularity and observed user behavior.

Keywords: Content Models, Social Models, Virtual Worlds, Personalization, Recommendations.

1 Introduction

Virtual world environments provide a platform for a wide range of applications, from virtual classrooms to games to mirror versions of the real world. However, many users find their first experiences in virtual worlds to be frustrating. Areas of interest for the user are often difficult to find, and the relatively slow load times for content mean that it may take significant time after moving to a new location to determine whether it will be worth staying. In such an environment, personalization through user models has the potential to improve user experiences by allowing them to find more useful content reliably after identifying a few locations of interest.

Virtual worlds provide a wealth of information for constructing user models to enable a high degree of personalization. In general, users have one or more

Joseph A. Konstan et al. (Eds.): UMAP 2011, LNCS 6787, pp. 87–98, 2011.

persistent identities as avatars, allowing profiles to be built and maintained over time. Movement in public areas is observable by other avatars and scripted objects, providing a means to unobtrusively create user traces. Social networking through group affiliations, friend lists, instant messaging, and both voice and text chat is often a native service and in some cases affiliations are publicly available. In some worlds, even user's personal recommendations to other users are available in avatar profiles.

However, despite the amount of information available, relatively little work has been done to develop user models in virtual worlds. Some researchers have studied avatar movement [1] or social networks[2], but extending user models to incorporate content preferences is still an unexplored area. Even the companies that run virtual worlds and thus have unlimited access to user data have been slow to incorporate this information into user models to improve user experiences. In Second Life, search results and showcased locations are ranked globally based on either popularity or a list created by a group of curators. OpenSimulator lacks even the global popularity ranking. This is unfortunate, because virtual world grids have the easiest access to the information and in the case of Second Life already provide search and topic-based recommendations. The profiles presented here could easily be incorporated into existing search and recommendation systems within closed worlds, though an approach such as ours that gathers externally from several grids would provide the additional utility of being usable across multiple grids.

In this paper, we apply a common approach in hypertext environments of creating content models based on the *tf-idf* values of terms found in the location. We combine these content models with a social feature model to create hybrid profiles for locations. Then, using profiles from previous locations of interest and social affiliations for a user, we create a user preference model. Without access to the back end user databases, we rely on only publicly available location and user information combined with limited user tracking based on seeing other avatars during the content collection process.

The accuracy and coverage would be improved by a server-side implementation with full knowledge of user histories. However, just as we use web crawlers to gather information from across the web and rely on independent ranking functions like PageRank even though each individual web site has full logs and content knowledge, there is some utility in developing a system that does not rely on complete access to internal databases and complete trust of self-reported popularity. Such a system can span multiple worlds, and does not require trusting individual worlds, which have an incentive to inflate popularity metrics. Additionally, some of the challenges in virtual worlds exist regardless of how the data is gathered. Text content in virtual worlds is quite limited. Locations have name and description attributes with maximum lengths of 63 characters and 255 characters, respectively. While other sources of content information are available, each has its own limitations, and the total amount of content from aggregating all available information is still relatively small.

Despite these difficulties, if a successful method for developing virtual world user models can be developed, it has the potential to improve search results and recommendations, making virtual worlds more attractive for a broader audience. Additionally, virtual worlds have similarities to the real world, such as spatial proximity, movement costs, similar activities, and metadata-tagged objects that may allow virtual world models to be applied to the real world. The amount of tagged objects and locations combined with persistent identities and social networks that are easily trackable make virtual worlds a possible test-bed for more advanced virtual and real-world user models, as well.

2 Background

The data for this research was obtained from Second Life, the largest virtual world currently available with dynamic, user-generated content. This section provides some background on several virtual world concepts and their real-world or hypertext analogues. We also discuss prior work on both document-based and location-based user models developed for recommendations or search ranking that are similar to our approach.

2.1 Virtual World Content and Users

The profiles for this research were created using data from Second Life. However, the collection system has also been used in OpenSimulator worlds, and many of the concepts are similar in other virtual worlds where users create their own content, such as Open Wonderland and Open Cobalt. Our OpenSimulator data was too sparse to perform similar analysis. Most virtual worlds, including Second Life and OpenSimulator, are divided into distinct regions that are hosted on different servers. Some regions may be adjacent, and movement between them is often transparent to the user. Others are separated from other regions by un-navigable space and must be teleported to directly. In Second Life and OpenSimulator Users can discover these disconnected spaces either through a world map displaying all available regions, or through searches, landmarks (a kind of shareable bookmark), or directory services. Each region contains one or more parcels, which are locations in the world with their own ownership, access permissions, and metadata. Each parcel is owned by either an avatar or a group. Other metadata for a parcel includes a name, description, category (e.g. shopping, residential, hangout), and several other attributes. In some sense, regions are like blocks in a city, which may be divided among several individuals or may be owned by a single individual or group and may be zoned for different uses.

Avatars represent individual users within the virtual world. They may be controlled by a human using a graphical client, or by a computer program running a client library. The data for this research was collected by a crawler program using the OpenMetaverse[3] client library. Avatars have profiles in the world where they can describe themselves, list group affiliations, and list up to ten picks, which are favorite places they have found in the world. About 38% of the

1.15 million avatars we discovered had picks. Of those with picks, the average number of picks per avatar was 3, but it was a somewhat bi-modal distribution, with most having very just a few and another group using nearly all of their allotted 10.

Researchers have developed models of user mobility and social connections in virtual worlds, though little has been done to develop content preference models or other recommendation systems. La and Michiardi studied user movement traces in Second Life and found that that they closely matched real-world behavior[1]. Varvello and Voelker have developed social models of avatars in Second Life that may differentiate between human users and bots[2].

2.2 Document-Based User Models

Traditional modeling of user behavior in the two-dimensional web space is accomplished by collecting information by tracking user document views, often through browser plug-ins or search engine clicks. Many users take advantage of the ability to set bookmarks of their favorite websites to visit. Although bookmarks can be used to extract a user profile, they may become stale over time if users do not update them frequently. Combining bookmarks with the most visited pages, the PROS personalized ranking system showed significant improvements in profiling accuracy by using user profiles[4]. Second Life avatars may have a list of 'picks' that define their favorite location to visit and may be used in place of bookmarks in the virtual world.

In addition to explicitly user defined information, passive tracking of user browsing or searching can be used to define a user model. Click-through data taken from search engine log files has been shown to provide useful training data by exhibiting relative user preferences[5]. Over time, utilization of web server logs and page hit or view counts can be assessed to modify the rankings of pages in a manner reflecting the user's browsing past. Using this information gained without requiring explicit input from users has been shown to increase the accuracy of a user model[6].

2.3 Location-Based User Models

Because the location models described here rely on proximity, location descriptions and text descriptions of the objects found at the location and users visit locations to shop, hang out, and create virtual homes, the location models are have similarities with geospatial location models for the real world. Ashbrook and Starner[7] used GPS tracks to model spatio-temporal behavior profiles of user movement in order to learn significant locations and predict movement. CitySense[8] identifies high-activity clusters in real-time, allowing users to discover where other users are gathering. Another location activity project, TTI Model[9], attempts to infer user interests from tracking walking speed in urban environments. They found that users often slow down when they see something of interest, and the model attempts to build a user interest model based on walking speed and location histories. In combining multiple models, our system is similar to the Magitti system[10], which uses multiple indicators to create recommendations based on proximity, text associated with locations, and user activity predictions based on context such as weather, time of day, calendar entries.

The Magitti system uses location text from user reviews, store descriptions, web pages, and other sources along with semantic information such as hours of operations and ratings to match users with locations. Other projects have taken a similar approach of using structured information to help users plan activities or find new places of interest. The Mobile Commodities system[11] uses data from Microsoft's MapPoint database to help users plan efficient routes to accomplish plan goals. The PERSONAF system [12] uses multi-level ontologies to provide users with personalized information about people and locations.

3   Collection and Profile Systems

The data for this research was collected over the course of eight days by twenty crawler agents on the main Second Life grid. Section 3.1 provides an overview of the collection system and the data collected. A more complete description of the collection system and data is available in[13]. Once the data was collected, it was used to generate location models for each parcel visited during the crawl. Section 3.2 describes the content and group feature vectors and the methods used to generate user models from locations of interest for the user.

3.1   Collection System

The collection system relies on one or more avatar bots emulating the client/server protocol to connect to the virtual world and explore it just as a normal user would. In this respect it is similar to web crawlers which issue standard HTTP requests to collect web content, rather than relying on direct access to file systems or content databases. During the collection process, the crawlers request information about locations, avatars, objects, and groups. An average of 27 objects with meaningful names or descriptions was used for each parcel. Another source of parcel text content was the text description in avatar picks.

Because the world contains 24,000 regions, and the crawl only involved 20 crawlers, only 31,754 distinct avatars were directly observed, though some were seen more than once, so a total of 49,328 avatar location instances were collected. Most of the avatars were discovered instead through land ownership or group affiliations.

3.2   Profile System

Once the raw data was collected, we created a location model for each of the 310,606 parcels discovered. Location models included general popularity, content, and group components. The content model consisted of a feature vector containing numerical, categorical, and text features. Numerical features included the size, traffic, object utilization, and similar attributes. Categorical features includes some flags, such as whether the parcel was owned by a group, or was for sale, as well as the self-identified category for the parcel, which could be one of 13 categories defined by Second Life (e.g. shopping, residential, hangout). Numerical features were normalized to a 0,1 range, while categorical values and owner IDs were assigned a value of 1 if they were true and 0 otherwise. Text features were assigned a value based on the common *tf-idf* metric, with the inverse document frequency based on the document frequency for the type of field. So a term that occurs frequently in object names but infrequently in location descriptions will have a higher idf value in location descriptions.

Group models for a location were created by starting with a set of groups associated with a location, either because of group ownership or based on the owner's groups. This set was expanded by doing a breadth-first search and adding groups which were closely related (based on shared avatar members) to the initial group or set. The value for a group is given by:

$$\sum \frac{norm(s)}{\alpha * d} \tag{1}$$

Where:

- s is the number of avatars shared between the child and parent group.
- *norm(s)* is normalized between 0 and 1.
- $\alpha * d$ is the distance from the seed set, multiplied by a penalty factor α.

Scores are summed when a group is found through multiple children, but total scores are capped at 1. The BFS for additional groups continues until no more are found or the total number of found groups is ≥ 100 in order to limit the time required to traverse the group graph, and because experiments with larger numbers of groups did not improve scoring accuracy.

The user models were created by combining the content models from a set of locations of interest for the avatar and the groups related to the avatar based on public group affiliations and the same weighting system as locations. If a user had no public group affiliations, the group vectors from the user's associated parcels were summed to create a group vector. Both content and group vectors were normalized, so the maximum cosine similarity score in the hybrid model was 2. In an application, personalized content and group match scores might be combined with both general popularity scores and other factors such as query match scores or proximity scores to rank results overall, but for this work we have focused only on the personalization and general popularity scores.

4   Analysis

The goal of the personalization is to use picks and/or observed locations to infer user interests and identify locations a user might be likely to visit. The data allows us to measure the ability of the created profiles to accomplish those goals in several ways. First, we can measure the ability of a content and metadata-based model to predict popularity in the absence of reliable traffic measurements. We do this by comparing our SVM general popularity model result rankings with known traffic rankings. We also measure how well the model based on a set of picks matches the rest of a user's picks. A failure to match could indicate either inconsistency between picks, or a failure of the model to adequately infer interests.

One concern with pick-base profiles is the inability to know when the picks were created. As a result, even internally consistent pick-based models may not be useful for predicting current user behavior. We explore this question by comparing pick-based profiles to observed user locations. Finally, if pick-based profiles are unreliable because of stale results or picks that do not reflect where users visit, we may find that profiles created based on recent activity are more useful. We use data on avatars who were seen in multiple locations during the 2-week crawl to build observed location profiles to determine if recent activity is more accurate than picks in matching observed behavior.

4.1   General Popularity Scores

Avatar traffic logs provide an accurate measure of location popularity in a closed virtual world, much like web logs do for a single web site. However, self-reported popularity information may not be available or reliable in a cross-world system. PageRank and similar models link-graph models that provide a similar metric in hyperlinked environments are less useful in sparsely linked virtual worlds, so some other general popularity or quality metric must be used to provide a generally available overall location score. In order to determine whether metadata and content data for a location might be useful for generating such a metric, we trained an SVM regression model using the known popularity scores.

The rankings we generated were computed using the regression option of the SVMLight software[14] with a linear kernel. Each location feature vector included metadata features (e.g. category, size, sale price) as well as *tf-idf* text features. Using five-fold validation, four groups were used to train a model that was then used to predict the popularity ranking of the remaining group. The results from all five sets were averaged to determine the overall ranking accuracy of the SVM rankings.

The overall ranking accuracy is measured using the Kendall τ rank correlation coefficient. The results are similar in accuracy to PageRank results found in[15], with the accuracy diminishing as the ranked parcels are restricted to the most popular subsets.

4.2   Pick-Based Personalized Scores

After several preliminary tests of the personalized feature vectors, it was found that including only the term, avatar, and category features produced the most accurate predictions.

We performed several tests to determine which individual fields provided the best accuracy, and to determine how accurate the full model was when constructed from different sources or compared to different parcels of interest to the user.

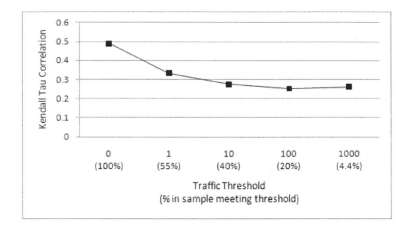

Fig. 1. Rank Correlations for Parcels with Traffic Above Threshold

Table 1. Average Scores for Picks vs. Random Parcels

Attribute	Pick Mean	Random Mean	Mean Difference
Category	0.762	0.326	0.436
Parcel Name	0.107	0.006	0.101
Parcel Description	0.135	0.016	0.119
Note Cards	0.085	0.052	0.033
Object Name	0.122	0.039	0.083
Object Description	0.140	0.041	0.990
Pick Text	0.115	0.012	0.103
Landmark Text	0.071	0.042	0.029
Owner	0.095	0.001	0.094
Groups	0.161	0.068	0.093

Profiles were generated based on a user's picked parcels and group affiliations. While a user may list as many as 10 picks, we also tested to see how the performance degraded as profiles with fewer picks were included.

Individual Component Analysis. In order to determine which field provided the most information individually, we generated feature vectors that included information from a single source, such as parcel names, or object names. In general, we attempted to test against a sample of 5,000 avatars, though in some cases information was available for less than 5,000 profiles. For groups, we used 500 avatars because of the time required to compute the group features from the group graph.

The absolute match scores are generally small, primarily because the feature vectors are quite sparse. With dictionary sizes of several hundred thousand words, but only a few words per attribute, the cosine similarity tends to be

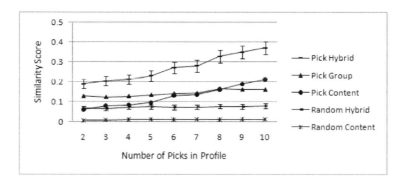

Fig. 2. Profile match scores with increasing picks per profile

quite small. Some attributes, such as users, landmarks, and note cards, are so sparse that the scores are particularly small and variable. The most promising individual fields in terms of difference between the pick and random parcels are categories, groups, and the names and descriptions of both parcels and objects. These are also the most frequently available features. Category matches skew higher because most parcels are either shopping or residential.

Hybrid Profile Analysis. The next analysis is to determine the effectiveness of a hybrid profile, which combines text, category, owner, and group data. The same leave-one-out analysis was done, except the term features were combined into a single set of features with the term value set to the sum of the *tf-idf* values across all fields to form the content feature vector. Because few users have the maximum 10 picks, profiles using as few as one pick were used.

Increasing the number of pick parcels improves both the overall match score and the difference between the picks and the random comparison set. Error bars were added to the hybrid profile scores to indicate the 95% confidence interval for the mean. The match scores for random parcel groups were omitted to reduce clutter, but can be inferred from the difference between the hybrid and content scores. Group scores were largely flat regardless of the number of picks used, while content matches improved as more information from picks was added. We also tested a set with no pick text to see if the model was relying heavily on the avatar's own description of the picked parcels, but he results were not significantly different, particularly when close to ten picks were used.

Results for Non-pick Parcels. The results for the hybrid profile show that the user model is capable of discriminating between random parcels and parcels which the user is likely to select as a pick. The next question is whether the pick-based profile matches with observed user behavior. In order to test this question, we computed the similarity between the user profile and the parcels we observed the avatars visiting. The analysis includes three data series. In the

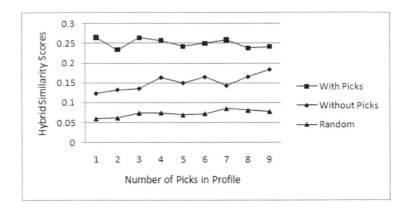

Fig. 3. Profile match scores for observed avatar locations

first, we compared the scores across all avatar locations, but this included some parcels which were actually listed in the avatar's picks. The second data series shows the results with the pick parcels removed, resulting in a lower average score. The final data set is against a random set of locations.

The match scores that included some parcels that were also avatar picks used in the profile were consistent regardless how many were used in the profile. In the series with no picks included, we again see an improvement as more picks are used to build the profile, though the improvement is not so pronounced as in the leave-one-out analysis. The mismatch between pick profiles and observed behavior may indicate that picks become obsolete and no longer reflect user interests.

4.3   Observed Location Personalized Scores

Although picks are a natural source for building a profile, many users never add them, and they may become obsolete over time. Another option is to use observed avatar locations to build a profile. We performed the same leave-one-out analysis as with the pick-based profile, but because relatively few avatars were observed on more than one parcel, the number available to perform the analysis decreases as more locations are required. 4 includes 95% confidence interval error bars for both the random and observed location hybrid profiles.

Avatar's observed locations show a greater degree of similarity than was observed in the picks. For more than 7 locations, the sample sizes were too small to draw firm conclusions, though the trend continued. We also cannot rule out some selection bias, where the actively mobile avatars we observed more times were more closely tied to parcel groups than is typical. However, the data is suggestive of some differences between pick-based and observed-location profiles. In contrast to the pick-based profiles, content matches were relatively flat, while

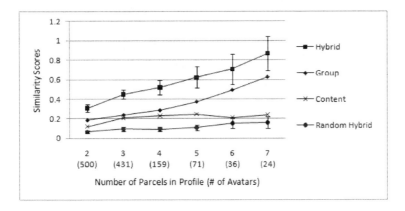

Fig. 4. Observed Location Profile Scores

group matches improved as more locations were used. One possible explanation is that content is more important for determining what an user adds as a profile pick, while social factors are a greater factor in where they visit regularly.

5   Conclusion

The results show that the SVM popularity model is able to provide location popularity rankings with similar accuracy to the popular PageRank algorithm for the Web, without requiring an extensive link graph. However, the traffic information needed to train the model will still be difficult to collect in a distributed environment without global knowledge. In cases where sufficient samples of user activity are not available to train a global ranking model, personalized models such as those presented here appear to provide good performance with a smaller and less universal training set. Even in environments where completely accurate global popularity is available, a combination of global popularity and personalized relevance scores might significantly increase the quality of search results and recommendations. Further research and user studies with users actively ranking newly recommended locations are needed to provide more validation of the model and to gain insights into how it could be improved.

While further refinements to feature weights, input sources, and additional data will continue to improve the results of the proposed user model, it has already demonstrated the ability to differentiate between the majority of uninteresting locations for each user and the few highly relevant locations. Both the pick-based and location-based approaches achieved viable results with limited training examples. The next step will be creating an interactive system that users can access within the world to get either general recommendations or personalized search results.

Acknowledgments. This research is partially supported by the NSF grant EAGER-1050801: Mapping Three-Dimensional Virtual Worlds.

References

1. La, C.-A., Michiardi, P.: User Mobility in Second Life. In: 2008 ACM Workshop on Online Social Networks. ACM, Seattle (2008)
2. Varvello, M., Voelker, G.M.: Second Life: A Social Network of Humans and Bots. In: 20th International Workship on Network and Operating Systems Support for Digital Audio and Video. ACM, Amsterdam (2010)
3. OpenMetaverse Foundation, http://openmetaverse.org
4. Chirita, P.-A., Olmedilla, D., Nejdl, W.: PROS: A Personalized Ranking Platform for Web Search. In: De Bra, P.M.E., Nejdl, W. (eds.) AH 2004. LNCS, vol. 3137, pp. 34–43. Springer, Heidelberg (2004)
5. Joachims, T.: Optimizing Search Engines using Clickthrough Data. In: 8th ACM SIGKDD International Conference on Knowledge Discovery and Data Mining. ACM, New York (2002)
6. Sugiyama, K., Hatano, K., Yoshikawa, M.: Adaptive Web Search Based on User Profile Constructed without any Effort from Users. In: 13th International Conference on World Wide Web (WWW 2004). ACM, New York (2004)
7. Ashbrook, D., Starner, T.: Using GPS to LEarn Significant Locations and Predict Movement Across Multiple Users. J. Personal and Ubiquitous Computing 7(5), 275–286 (2003)
8. Loecher, M., Jebara, T.: CitySense:Multiscale Space Time Clustering of GPS Points and Trajectories. In: 2009 Joint Statistical Meeting (2009)
9. Sato, C., Takeuchi, S., Imbe, T., Ishibashi, S., Inami, M., Inakage, M., Okude, N.: TTI Model: Model Extracting Individual's Curiosity Level in Urban Spaces. In: 8th ACM Conference on Designing Interactive Systems. ACM, New York (2010)
10. Bellotti, V., Begole, B., Chi, E.H., Ducheneaut, N., Fang, J., Isaacs, E., King, T., Newman, M., Partridge, K., Price, B., Rasmussen, P., Roberts, M., Schiano, D., Walendowski, A.: Activity-Based Serendipitous Recommnendations with the Magitti Mobile Leisure Guide. In: 26th SIGCHI Conference on Human Factors in Computing Systems. ACM, New York (2008)
11. Horvitz, E., Koch, P., Subramani, M.: Mobile Opportunistic Planning: Methods and Models. In: Conati, C., McCoy, K., Paliouras, G. (eds.) UM 2007. LNCS (LNAI), vol. 4511, pp. 228–237. Springer, Heidelberg (2007)
12. Niu, W.T., Kay, J.: PERSONAF: Framework for Personalized Ontological Reasoning in Pervasive Computing. J. User Modeling and User-Adapted Interaction 20(1), 1–40 (2010)
13. Eno, J., Gauch, S., Thompson, C.: Agent-Based Search and Retrieval in Virtual World Environments. In: Soro, A., Vargiu, E., Armano, G., Paddeu, G. (eds.) Information Retrieval and Mining in Distributed Environments. SCI, vol. 324, pp. 125–143. Springer, Berlin (2011)
14. Joachims, T.: Making Large-Scale SVM Learning Practical. In: Schölkopf, B., Burges, C., Smola, A. (eds.) Advances in Kernel Methods - Support Vector Learning. MIT-Press, Cambridge (1999)
15. Meiss, M., Menczer, F., Fortunato, S., Flammini, A., Vespignani, A.: Ranking Web Sites with Real User Traffic. In: International Conferend on Web Search and Web Data Mining, pp. 65–76. ACM, Palo Alto (2008)

Recipe Recommendation: Accuracy and Reasoning*

Jill Freyne, Shlomo Berkovsky, and Gregory Smith

Tasmanian ICT Center, CSIRO
GPO Box 1538, Hobart, 7001, Australia
firstname.lastname@csiro.au

Abstract. Food and diet are complex domains for recommender technology, but the need for systems that assist users in embarking on and
engaging with healthy living programs has never been more real. One key
to sustaining long term engagement with eHealth services is the provision
of tools, which assist and train users in planning correctly around the
areas of diet and exercise. These tools require an understanding of user
reasoning as well as user needs and are ideal application areas for recommender and personalization technologies. Here, we report on a large
scale analysis of real user ratings on a set of recipes in order to judge the
applicability and practicality of a number of personalization algorithms.
Further to this, we report on apparent user reasoning patterns uncovered in rating data supplied for recipes and suggest ways to exploit this
reasoning understanding in the recommendation process.

Keywords: Collaborative filtering, content-based, machine learning,
recipes, personalization.

1   Introduction

The World Health Organisation is predicting that the number of obese adults
worldwide will reach 2.3 billion by 2015, a statistic which is attracting increased
attention [1]. Much of this attention is being paid to online diet monitoring systems, which have been replacing traditional pen-and-paper programs in recent
years. These systems, which often include informative content and services to
persuade users to alter their behaviour, gather a vast amount of user preference
information that could be harnessed to personalize interactive features in order to
increase engagement with the online system, and in turn with the diet program.
Dieters use these systems to acquire knowledge, to plan and to record dietary
intake. A personalized service ideally suited to informing diet and lifestyle is a
personalized recipe recommender. This recommender could exploit explicit food

* This research is jointly funded by the Australian Government through the Intelligent Island Program and CSIRO Food and Nutritional Sciences. The Intelligent
Island Program is administered by the Tasmanian Department of Economic Development, Tourism, and the Arts. The authors acknowledge Mealopedia.com and
Penguin Group (Australia) for permission to use their data.

Joseph A. Konstan et al. (Eds.): UMAP 2011, LNCS 6787, pp. 99–110, 2011.
© Springer-Verlag Berlin Heidelberg 2011

ratings, food diary entries, and browsing behaviour to inform its recommendations and assist dieters with one of the biggest challenges of successful lifestyle change.

The domain of food is varied and complex and presents many challenges to the recommender systems community. There are many factors that will impact on a user's opinion on foods, some of which will be more important to some individuals than others. The obvious contributory factors are *cooking methods, ingredients, costs* and *availability, cooking complexity, preparation time, nutritional breakdown, ingredient combination effects*, as well as *user goals, cultural* and *social factors*. Add to these factors the sheer number of available ingredients, the fact that eating often occurs in groups, that the sequencing is crucial, and the complexity of challenge becomes clear.

In this work, we follow on from earlier preliminary analysis on the suitability of traditional personalization algorithms for recommendations in the food domain. We explore the possibilities of using machine learning and analyse trends in users' reasoning, which uncover user traits that could have significant impact in many dimensions of recommender techniques. Thus, the contributions of this work are (1) an analysis reporting on the applicability of various personalized techniques for rating prediction, and (2) a report on the observed trends of reasoning uncovered by machine learning feature selection algorithm.

The paper is structured as follows; Section 2 positions this work in relation to other work in the field, Section 3 provides details of the recommendation algorithms implemented. In Section 4 we discuss algorithm accuracy and performance and the trends uncovered in the ratings sets of users. We conclude with a discussion of our findings and present an outline of future plans.

2   Related Work

Initial efforts to address the challenge of intelligent support in meal planning resulted in systems, such as Chef [6] and Julia [9], which rely heavily on domain knowledge for recommendations. More recently, works concentrating on social navigation, ingredient representation and recipe modeling have come to the fore. A recipe recommender system based on user browsing patterns is presented by Svensson et al. [14]. They use social navigation techniques and apply collaborative filtering to predict ratings. While users reported liking the system, formal analysis of its predictive power is not reported.

Freyne et al. investigated the performance of collaborative, content-based, and hybrid recommender strategies, which break down recipes into ingredients in order to generate recommendations [2,3]. Their results showed that solicitation of recipe ratings, which are transferred to ingredient ratings, is an accurate and effective method of capturing ingredient preferences, and that the introduction of simple intelligence can improve the accuracy of recommendations.

Zhang et al. also make use of an ingredient representation but, in contrast, distinguish three levels of importance, which are manually assigned [17]. Using this mechanism, ingredients that are considered to be more important have the largest contribution to the similarity score. Once again, a level of domain expertise is required for this process. We would argue that the importance of an ingredient in a recipe is likely to be user dependent rather than a generic rule. Pixteren et al. do take a user-centered approach to recipe modeling rather than making a priori assumptions about the characteristics that determine the perceived similarity, such as ingredients or directions [15]. They derive a measure, which models the perceived similarity between recipes by identifying and extracting important features from the recipe text. Based on these features, a weighted similarity measure between recipes is determined.

3   Recommender Strategies

This work aims to investigate how individuals reason in relation to food and in particular recipes. We examine real user rating data to see if patterns of reasoning exist for individuals. This analysis presented here aims to understand reasoning on recipes only, as a first step, and disregards the context of meal planning and scheduling. We acknowledge that other factors are at play when planning meals but it is crucial to get the foundations right before embarking on a total solution to this complex problem.

Each recipe in our corpus has a basic structure including a *Title*, *Ingredient List* and *Instructions*. From this basic information we automatically extract additional information. We decipher two indicators of recipe complexity: the *number of ingredients* and the *number of steps* required to complete the recipe. In addition, we manually annotate each recipe with simple domain knowledge in the form of a *general cuisine type*, a *specific cuisine type*, and a *broad category*, containing options traditionally used to classify a dish. The options for cuisine types and categories are in Table 1.

We implemented three personalized recommender algorithms: two standard recommender strategies and one machine learning strategy suitable for rating prediction. A standard *collaborative filtering* algorithm [10] assigns predictions, $pred(u_a, r_T)$, for user u_a for a target recipe, r_T, based on the weighted ratings of a set of N neighbours. Briefly, each user's similarity to u_a is determined as shown in Equation 1 and the users with the top N similarity scores make up the neighbours. Predictions for r_T are generated using Equation 2.

Table 1. Metadata features and values

General Cuisine	Specific Cuisine	Category
African, American, Asian, European, International, Oceania	African, Australian, Chinese, Eastern European, French, German, Greek, Indian, International, Italian, Japanese, Mexican, Middle Eastern, South East Asian, Southern, Spanish, UK&Ireland	beef, pork, lamb, chicken, veal, fish, vegetables, fruit

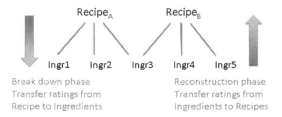

Fig. 1. Recipe - ingredient breakdown and reconstruction

$$sim(u_a, u_b) = \frac{\sum_{i=1}^{k}(u_{a_i} - \overline{u_a})(u_{b_i} - \overline{u_b})}{\sqrt{\sum_{i=1}^{k}(u_{a_i} - \overline{u_a})^2}\sqrt{\sum_{i=1}^{k}(u_{b_i} - \overline{u_b})^2}} \tag{1}$$

$$pred(u_a, r_T) = \frac{\sum_{n \epsilon N} sim(u_a, u_n)rat(u_n, r_T)}{\sum_{n \epsilon N} sim(u_a, u_n)} \tag{2}$$

The second algorithm is a *content-based* algorithm [3], which breaks down each rated recipe into ingredients $ingr_1, ..., ingr_x$ (see Figure 1) and assigns the provided rating to each ingredient according to Equation 3. We transfer the ratings gathered for each recipe to each ingredient listed in the recipe equally. The strategy then applies a content-based algorithm shown in Equation 4 to predict a score for the target recipe based on the average of all the scores provided by the user on ingredients $ingr_1, ..., ingr_j$ making up the target recipe.

$$score(u_a, ingr_i) = \frac{\sum_{r \epsilon recipes(ingr_i)} rat(u_a, r)}{\#recipes(ingr_i)} \tag{3}$$

$$pred(u_a, r_t) = \frac{\sum_{i \epsilon ingredients(r_t)} score(u_a, i)}{\#ingredients(r_t)} \tag{4}$$

Our third algorithm is a sophisticated prediction algorithm using the open source data mining tool Weka [5]. We used the logistical decision tree algorithm M5P [16,13] to predict scores based on the recipe content and metadata. The M5P algorithm can be applied to all or a subset of the recipe features, including the presence and absence of ingredients and the associated metadata.

M5P is a binary tree classifier, where each leaf predicts a numeric quantity using linear regression [13]. Each data instance is a set of features $\{a_1, ..., a_{N+1}\}$, where each feature may be numeric or nominal, but a_{N+1} is the class label and must be numeric. Predictions are made based on the smoothed tree by tracing the path to a leaf and using a linear interpolation of predictions made by the nodes on the path. Each non-leaf node performs a binary test of a single feature from $\{a_1, ..., a_N\}$, partitioning instances into those to be classified by the right and left sub-tree. Each leaf node is a most specific generalisation that contains a linear regression model, predicting the class label for those instances that are classified by this leaf, such the set of leaves of the tree collectively predicts the class label over the whole space.

Model tree induction by M5P occurs in three stages. In the first stage, nodes are recursively split using a criterion that minimizes the intra-subset variation in the class values down each branch. For each candidate feature to test at that node, the expected reduction in error resulting from testing that feature is computed. A node is split on the best feature if the highest expected reduction in error is large enough. In the second stage, the tree is simplified by pruning. Linear models are computed for non-leaf nodes, starting at the bottom, and error estimates are compared to the corresponding leaf nodes. If the non-leaf is chosen, that sub-tree is pruned and replaces with a new leaf node.

4 Evaluation

We gathered a dataset of recipe ratings through Mechanical Turk, Amazon's online task facilitator (www.mturk.com). A corpus of 343 recipes was obtained from the CSIRO Total Wellbeing Diet books [11,12] and from the meal planning website Mealopedia.com (www.mealopedia.com).

Online surveys, each containing 35 randomly selected recipes, were posted to the system. Responses for each of the 35 recipes displayed were required and users could answer as many of the published surveys as they wished. Each question asked users to report on how much a recipe appealed to them on a 5-Likert scale, spanning from "not at all" to "a lot". Overall, we gathered 101,557 ratings of 917 users, such that the density of the obtained ratings matrix was 33%. 15% (15191) of recipes were rated *not at all*, 14% (14425) – *not really*, 20%(19840) – *neutral*, 25% (25593) – *a little*, and 26% (26508) – *a lot*.

On average, each recipe was made up of 9.52 ingredients (stdev 2.63) and the average number of recipes that each ingredient was found in was 8.03 (stdev 19.8). On average, each user rated 109 recipes (stdev 81.9), with the minimum number of ratings per person being 35 and the maximum being 336.

4.1   Set-up

We conducted a number of experiments on the dataset collected using traditional recommender and machine learning approaches, to determine algorithm accuracy for recipe rating predictions. For the collaborative filtering (CF) and content based (CB) algorithms, we employed a traditional leave-one-out analysis, which removed each tuple $\{u_i, r_t, rat(u_i, r_t)\}$ from the user's profile and used the algorithms to predict the rating $rat(u_i, r_t)$. A set of 20 neighbours were selected only once for each user, based on the entire set of ratings provided. The M5P algorithm was run separately on the ratings of each user. Each user profile was split into 90% training and 10% test set and the ratings $rat(u_i, r_t)$ in the test set were predicted. 10 iterations were carried out for different selections of the test set. We present the average MAE [8] score obtained by each algorithm.

4.2   Algorithm Accuracy

Table 2 shows the average MAE of the prediction scores for each algorithm presented in section 3. The results of the CF and CB algorithms match earlier

Table 2. MAE of personalized algorithms

Content Based Filtering	Collaborative Filtering	Machine Learning (M5P)
1.2083	1.2614	0.9774

results from a similar analysis on an smaller dataset presented in previous works [3,2]. The accuracy of CF and CB recommenders is similar, with an increase in accuracy of only 0.05 over CF obtained by CB. A comparison between the CF algorithm, which treats each recipe as one entity and ignores its ingredients, and the CB algorithm, which considers the ingredients, shows that even the uniformly weighted break down and reconstruction offer increases in accuracy.

The best performing algorithm is the M5P algorithm, which in this case takes only the recipe metadata into consideration to determine recipe ratings. The M5P algorithm is the most accurate, with an MAE of 0.98. It is worth noting that we also ran this analysis using a linear regression algorithm, but the results were very similar to those of the M5P algorithm and the results provided by the M5P algorithm facilitated a more in-depth analysis of user behaviour, thus we omitted the results and discussion due to space limitations.

In terms of the coverage of each algorithm [8], the *M5P* strategy achieved a 100% coverage for each user, whereas the CB strategy obtained 92% coverage and the CF strategy only 83.8%. Thus, the machine learning approach appears to be the best performer overall.

4.3   Reasoning on User Input

While knowing which algorithm performs best is valuable, we embarked on further investigation into the reasons behind the improved performance of the M5P algorithm. By understanding the differences in performance we can affect other dimensions of recommender systems such as information gathering for user profiling, hybridization of recommendation algorithms, and persuasive explanation of recommendations.

As mentioned, we use three classes of metadata: *complexity data* that details the number of steps and ingredients in a recipe, *cuisine* data that categorises recipes according to their cuisine type, and the *broad category* which categorises recipes according to the main food type included in the recipe.

We employed a Corrleation-based Feature Selection algorithm (CFS) to compute a heuristic measure of the "merit" of feature subsets from pair-wise feature correlations. Merit is quantified by

$$M_S = \frac{k\overline{r_{cS}}}{\sqrt{k + k(k-1)\overline{r_S}}} \tag{5}$$

where k is the number of features in the selected set S, $\overline{r_{cS}}$ is the mean feature-class correlation over class c and set of features S, and $\overline{r_S}$ is the average feature-feature intercorrelation over S. The correlation is calculated using symmetrical uncertainty:

Table 3. Distribution of Predictors

	1 predictor	2 predictors	3 predictors	4 predictors
profiles	172	327	187	147
% of total	20.6%	39.2%	22.4%	17.7%

$$u(X, Y) = 2\left[\frac{g(X, Y)}{h(Y) + h(X)}\right] \tag{6}$$

where h is entropy of a feature and g is information gain of a class given a feature [4]. Thus, selection of a feature as a predictor depends on the extent to which it predicts classes in areas of the instance space not yet predicted by other features.

We analyzed the set of predictive features selected for each user in our dataset. 20.6% of users have one predictive feature, 39.2% have two, 22.4% have three and 17.7% have four predictive features, as seen in Table 3. We hypothesize that the different number of predictors reflects different levels of reasoning employed by users when providing ratings. To ascertain whether the number of predictive features is related to the number of user's ratings, we calculated the correlation between the density of a user's rating vector and the number of features selected. The correlation coefficient was -0.031, showing no patterns between the number of ratings provided by a user and the number of predictive features.

20.6% of users have one predictive feature selected. For 93% of this group, the feature identified was the *broad category* feature, i.e. the presence of a certain key ingredient. We assume that users in this group assign ratings to recipes based primarily on the main ingredient of the recipe. Simple rational following this reasoning is: *"I like chicken recipes, I dislike fish recipes, I love beef recipes, etc"*.

39.2% of users have two predictive features selected and we assume are reasoning on two levels. In 96% of these profiles, the *broad category* feature was selected, this time in conjunction with an additional feature. The additional feature selected was the *general cuisine* feature in 48.6% of cases, the *specific cuisine* in 37.3% of cases, or *number of ingredients* in 10.4% of cases. Table 4 shows how this breaks down for the various combinations of features. The dominance of the *broad category* feature changes depending on its coupling with other features. For example, when coupled with *general cuisine*, the *broad category* feature is the most predictive feature in 57.2% of cases. So, with respect to the *broad category* and *general cuisine* features, 57.2% of users are rationalizing according to the statements *"I like beef and I love it when its included in a Chinese style dish"* and 42.8% of according to *"I love Chinese dishes, especially ones which contain beef"*. When the *specific cuisine* feature is a predictor in conjunction with the *broad category*, in 81.9% of cases the *broad category* is the most predictive feature and only in 18.1% of cases the *specific cuisine* feature is most predictive. The opposite is the case when the *number of ingredients* feature is present. It is the dominating predictive feature in 74.6% of cases, while the *broad category* is the most predictive feature in 26.4% of cases.

Table 4. Combinations and dominance of features when two predictive features exist

Predictive features (feat1,feat2)	% of profiles applicable	most predictive feat1	most predictive feat2
(broad category, general cuisine)	48.62%	57.2%	42.8%
(broad category, specific cuisine)	37.31%	81.9%	18.1%
(broad category, number of ingredients)	10.40%	26.4%	74.6%
other	5.37%		

Table 5. Combinations and dominance of features when three predictive features exist

Predictive features (feat1, feat2, feat3)	% of profiles applicable
(number of ingredients, general cuisine, specific cuisine)	43.28%
(number of ingredients, specific cuisine, broad category)	20.90%
(number of ingredients, general cuisine, broad category)	18.51%
(general cuisine, specific cuisine, broad category)	11.94%
other	5.37%

20% of users have three predictive features selected. When users are reasoning on three features, the *broad category* is *not* a predictive feature in 43.3% of cases. This suggests that when users are applying complex reasoning processes to provide well thought ratings, their focus is on the fine grained details of cuisine type and cooking complexity, rather than simply on the main ingredient of the recipe itself. These users are likely to reason along the lines of *"I like Asian dishes, in particular Thai dishes, but only ones with a small number of ingredients"*. Table 5 shows the break down of the three predictive features.

4.4   Applications of reasoning knowledge

One of the challenges of recommender systems is that of the cold start problem, where insufficient user information has been attained to generate accurate recommendations. One way of combatting this is to gather ratings for items that are seen to attract varied ratings from users (i.e items that some love and others hate, rather than items that most tend to like or dislike). Gathering ratings on these items maximises the information gained from each individual rating [7]. To achieve similar goals, we consider using the feature selection process as an indicator for the number and type of reasoners that a user is using when providing rating recipes. This information would allows us to (1) obtain ratings that provide maximal differentiation across the desired features, and (2) determine how many of these ratings are required for accurate user profiling as well as influencing other areas of the recommendation process.

In the following analysis we concentrate on users with more than 100 ratings in their profiles. For each user, the number of features on which they reason is determined by examining the first 100 ratings provided. In this experiment, we

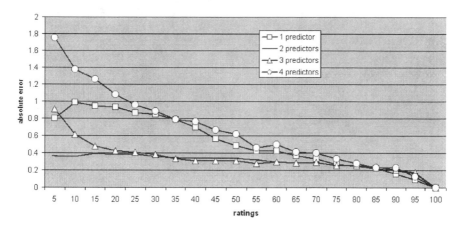

Fig. 2. Predictor stability over time

grow the number of ratings in the profile, k, from 5 to 100 in randomly selected increments of 5 ratings. For each k we carry out the feature selection process and compare the number of selected features to the number of features selected when all 100 ratings in the profile are considered. We repeat this process 10 times and report on the average error between the two. We compute the error separately for groups of users reasoning on 1, 2, 3, and 4 features. Figure 2 shows the average error for various values of k.

The highest error is obtained for users reasoning on 4 features. We observe an error rate of 1.75 for $k = 5$, an initial steep drop off followed by a steady decline. The same trend is seen for users reasoning on 3 features, although the error at $k = 5$ is half that of the previous group. This curve levels off at 0.4 when $k = 25$. A very consistent error line is observed for users reasoning on 2 features, showing that the feature selection is accurate even when a small number of ratings is available. In contrast to the emerging trend, the error rates are high for users reasoning on only 1 feature. The error hovers around the 0.8, ..., 1 mark until 35 ratings are received and then steadily decreases. Note that when a user is reasoning on 1 feature, the error can only be positive (i.e., the algorithm selected multiple features), whereas in other cases it could over or under predict. Thus, the feature selection is mostly predicting that the users are reasoning on two features rather than one for $k < 35$. We believe that this is caused by the lack of dominance of the main feature, when insufficient ratings are available for the feature's merit score to be sufficient independent.

Figure 3 shows the MAE of predictions made using the selected features for user profiles of different sizes of 5, .., 100. For each value of k, feature selection was completed on 90% of the user profile and the selected features used to predict the remaining 10%. 10 runs of each were carried out and the average MAE across users in each group are reported. Note that a similar accuracy is obtained for users reasoning on two and three features when $k > 5$. However, there is a distinct difference in the accuracy of predictions for users reasoning

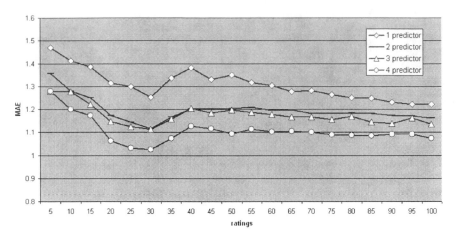

Fig. 3. MAE of predictions made using feature selection at various k

on one feature and four features. These groups had very similar absolute errors in Figure 2, but the error has affected the prediction accuracy in different ways. The average error observed for the number of selected features (Figure 2) across users reasoning on one feature at $k = 10$ was 1.0. This error however, was always a positive error and the number of selected features was being over predicted, resulting in an additional layer being added to the decision tree. Similarly, at $k = 10$ the average error for users reasoning on four features was 1.4, and this was always a negative error. Hence, the number of selected features was under predicted and a shallower tree, of on average 2.6 levels, was generated. So, in the overestimated cases, noise was added to the tree, and in the underestimated cases the tree was incomplete.

We examined the changes of merit scores when additional noisy data is added to a tree and when information is missing from a tree. The analysis shows a 10% reduction in merit score when an additional feature was selected. Thus, the correlation between the features in the tree and the ratings is 10% lower. However, missing information from the tree has a weaker effect. In this case, the information loss associated with one missing feature is 2% and with two missing features is 4%. Thus, it appears better to underestimate the number of predictors rather than overestimate them. Hence, the MAE scores obtained for users with four predictive features are lower than those obtained for users with one predictive feature.

4.5   Summary

The results of this exploratory work have uncovered several useful and informative trends in how users approach a recipe rating task and on which domain features they are reasoning. We uncovered four groups of users, each reasoning on recipes on different levels. The first group, which consisted of 20.6% of users, reasoned on the most general metadata – the *broad category* of the recipes. The largest group of users (39.2%) reasoned on two features, and in most cases the features in question related to the *broad category* and *cuisine type* metadata, showing a deeper reasoning process. When users reasoned on three features (22.4%), they often did not reason on the *broad category* but preferred other more detailed features such as recipe complexity measures as well as cuisine types. Finally, 17.4% of users reasoned on four features.

Further analysis showed that it is easy to select the features, on which users reasoning on two features actually reason, even with few ratings. On the contrary, selecting features that users reasoning on one feature and on four features requires more ratings. Finally, we noted that the accuracy of the feature selection technique has different effects depending on whether too many or two few features are selected. This is explained by the decision tree based prediction mechanism employed by M5P.

5   Conclusions and Future Work

In this work we have investigated the applicability of recommender techniques to generate recipe recommendations and identified the performance enhancements achieved by using machine learning techniques. Analyses of the results have shown that users reason on various levels when rating recipes and that various combinations of metadata are seen to have different predictive qualities for different users. This information assists us in understanding how users provide recipe ratings and suggests ways in which this knowledge could be used to benefit recommender algorithms.

As mentioned, implications of knowing how users reason are obvious in the recommender domain. Informative rating acquisition is a logical next step for evaluation. We will develop an active learning model, which will determine a user's reasoning level and adapt the ratings requested accordingly, in order to obtain the most high value user information. Item diversity is another example of where knowing the reasoning process is important, particularly when sequencing recommendations as in the food domain. Recipe diversity could depend on the user, rather than just on the recipe similarity. In a similar way, persuasive techniques aiming to increase the uptake of recommendations could be made more effective, if the user's reasoning process is known.

References

1. Chronic disease information sheet, http://www.who.int/mediacentre/factsheets/fs311/en/index.html (accessed June 2010)
2. Freyne, J., Berkovsky, S.: Intelligent Food Planning: Personalized Recipe Recommendation. In: Proceedings of the 2010 International Conference on Intelligent User Interfaces (IUI 2010), pp. 321–324 (2010)
3. Freyne, J., Berkovsky, S.: Recommending Food: Reasoning on Recipes and Ingredients. In: De Bra, P., Kobsa, A., Chin, D. (eds.) UMAP 2010. LNCS, vol. 6075, pp. 381–386. Springer, Heidelberg (2010)

 4. Hall, M.: Correlation-based feature selection for machine learning. PhD thesis, Citeseer (1999)
 5. Hall, M., Frank, E., Holmes, G., Pfahringer, B., Reutemann, P., Witten, I.H.: The Weka Data Mining Software: An Update. ACM SIGKDD Explorations Newsletter 11(1), 10–18 (2009)
 6. Hammond, K.: CHEF: A Model of Case-Based Planning. In: Proceedings of the Fifth National Conference on Artificial Intelligence, vol. 1 (1986)
 7. Herlocker, J.L., Konstan, J.A., Borchers, A., Riedl, J.: An algorithmic framework for performing collaborative filtering. In: SIGIR, pp. 230–237 (1999)
 8. Herlocker, J.L., Konstan, J.A., Terveen, L.G., Riedl, J.T.: Evaluating collaborative filtering recommender systems. ACM Trans. Inf. Syst. 22(1), 5–53 (2004)
 9. Hinrichs, T.R.: Strategies for adaptation and recovery in a design problem solver. In: Proceedings of the Workshop on Case-Based Reasoning (1989)
10. Konstan, J.A., Miller, B.N., Maltz, D., Herlocker, J.L., Gordon, L.R., Riedl, J.: GroupLens: applying collaborative filtering to Usenet news. Communications of the ACM 40(3), 87 (1997)
11. Noakes, M., Clifton, P.: The CSIRO Total Wellbeing Diet Book. Penguin Group, Australia (2005)
12. Noakes, M., Clifton, P.: The CSIRO Total Wellbeing Diet Book 2. Penguin Group, Australia (2006)
13. Quinlan, J.: Learning with continuous classes. In: Proceedings of the 5th Australian Joint Conference on Artificial Intelligence, pp. 343–348. Citeseer (1992)
14. Svensson, M., Höök, K., Laaksolahti, J., Waern, A.: Social navigation of food recipes. In: CHI 2001: Proceedings of the SIGCHI Conference on Human Factors in Computing Systems, pp. 341–348. ACM, New York (2001)
15. van Pinxteren, Y., Geleijnse, G., Kamsteeg, P.: Deriving a recipe similarity measure for recommending healthful meals. In: Proceedings of the 2011 International Conference on Intelligent User Interfaces, IUI 2011, pp. 105–114 (2011)
16. Wang, Y., Witten, I.: Induction of model trees for predicting continuous classes (1996)
17. Zhang, Q., Hu, R., Namee, B., Delany, S.: Back to the future: Knowledge light case base cookery. Technical report, Dublin Institute of Technology (2008)

Tag-Based Resource Recommendation in Social Annotation Applications

Jonathan Gemmell, Thomas Schimoler, Bamshad Mobasher, and Robin Burke

Center for Web Intelligence, School of Computing, DePaul University
243 South Wabash Ave, Chicago, Illinois 60604
{jgemmell,tschimoler,mobasher,rburke}@cdm.depaul.edu

Abstract. Social annotation systems enable the organization of online resources with user-defined keywords. The size and complexity of these systems make them excellent platforms for the application of recommender systems, which can provide personalized views of complex information spaces. Many researchers have concentrated on the important problem of tag recommendation. Less attention has been paid to the recommendation of resources in the context of social annotation systems. In this paper, we examine the specific case of tag-based resource recommendation and propose a linear-weighted hybrid for the task. Using six real world datasets, we show that our algorithm is more effective than other more mathematically complex techniques.

1 Introduction

The surge in popularity of social media systems shows no sign of abating. These systems leverage vast amounts of user-generated content, enhancing the user's ability to organize information, explore resources and build communities. One class of these applications is the social annotation system in which user-generated content takes the form of tags, arbitrary labels applied by users to online resources. Social annotation systems are popular in part because they allow users to tag resources with any tag they wish, free from any preconceived conceptual hierarchy.

The freedom and richness of social annotation systems does not come without a cost. Because the number of users, resources and tags in these systems is often measured in the millions, the sheer volume of data can quickly burden the user with information overload. The unrestricted nature of the tagging function is liberating, but also means that the resulting tag data will be noisy. Ambiguous tags abound: one user may apply "jaguar" only to cars, another only to large felines [17]. Redundant tags including synonyms and mis-spellings cannot be prevented and make it more difficult for a user to choose tags on which to search.

For these reasons, recommender systems, which can take into account the user's interests and context, have much to offer social annotation systems. However, the recommendation function in social annotation systems is considerably more complex than in the e-commerce applications to which it has typically been applied. Tags represent user interest and preference in a detailed, multi-dimensional way, as compared to scalar ratings, but they also make comparisons between users and between items more difficult.

Joseph A. Konstan et al. (Eds.): UMAP 2011, LNCS 6787, pp. 111–122, 2011.
© Springer-Verlag Berlin Heidelberg 2011

We address the problem of tag-based resource recommendation. This task looks a lot like a standard information retrieval problem, in which the user supplies a tag, like a query, and the task of the system is to find matching items. However, because of the challenges of ambiguity and redundancy in tagging systems, it is recognized that a personalized approach is needed: our car-lover's "jaguar" should not match the pages on the feline predator, but might instead match pages tagged "XJ12". Thus, the task of retrieving pages becomes a recommendation problem requiring a personalized interpretation of tags in both queries and annotations. Unlike previous work in tag-based recommendation, our general approach does not assume access to external information, is amenable to a variety of query types, and is easily adaptable to other related tasks, such as recommendation of tags or recommendation by example.

This paper describes our formulation of the resource recommendation task. We outline our linear weighted algorithm, which is a variant of that previously proven successful for tag recommendation [8] and the more general case of basic resource recommendation problem without any requirements such as a tag [9,10]. We also introduce a competing algorithm based on tensor factorization. We then show the performance of the algorithms on six real-world datasets.

2   Background and Definitions

A social annotation system is essentially a collection of labeled bookmarks that users share with one another. Each annotation records the application by a user u of one or more tags $t_1,...,t_n$ to a resource r. The set of all bookmarks A – together with the sets U, R and T of users, resources and tags – forms a complete representation of the system. It is sometimes useful to view a social annotation system as a tensor URT in which an entry $URT(u, r, t)$ is 1 if u has tagged r with t.

We define resource recommendation as the production of an ordered list of resources likely to be of interest to a particular user. Such a list might be requested in a variety of ways through a system's interface and may need to incorporate constraints that the user imposes. For example, if the user clicks on the tag "jaguar", the recommender system should take that tag (and its user-specific meaning) as a requirement that the resource being retrieved should meet.

For maximum generality, therefore, we view any resource recommendation algorithm as a function $\phi : U \times Q \times R \rightarrow \mathbb{R}$ which operates on a user $u \in U$, a set of requirements $q \in Q = \mathcal{P}(U \cup T \cup R)$, and a resource $r \in R$, and produces a real-valued result p, which is the predicted value of r for u: $\phi(u, q, r) = p$. A system capable of computing such a function can use it to rank items and return the top-ranked ones as recommendations.

As noted in previous efforts [4], user requirements in recommendation can take a variety of forms. In our definition, we assume that the set of requirements q can be any set made up of the basic annotation elements: tags, resources or even users. The simplest case of resource recommendation is the one where no requirements are imposed and the recommender must find resources based only on the identity of the user: $\phi(u, \emptyset, r)$. We will refer to this task as *basic resource recommendation*.

An important special case of resource recommendation is one in which the user supplies a requirement in the form of a single tag. This special case we call *tag-based resource recommendation*, defined as the function $\phi(u, \{T\}, r)$, where $q = \{T\}$, a set of tags. In our evaluation we examine the case where the set of tags contains a single tag, $q = \{t\}$, simulating the commonly occurring scenario in which a user selects a tag to see what resources are related to it.

3   Related Work

Resource recommendation in social annotation systems has yet to be studied in a systematic manner. Some authors assume the basic form of resource recommendation. Others assume the tag-based variant or perhaps other forms. Often algorithms designed for one kind of requirement are not compatible with others. Adding to this confusion is the fact that algorithms which perform well for other tasks such as tag recommendation perform poorly when applied to resource recommendation.

Starting from the well-known PageRank algorithm [20], researchers have derived Adapted PageRank and FolkRank [15, 14] for tag recommendation. These algorithms demonstrated the importance of an integrative framework in social annotation systems: users, resources and tags were treated as nodes and were connected based on their occurrence in annotations. For tag recommendation the approach works particularly well. However for resource recommendation the algorithm suffers from the fact that potential recommendations are several steps away from the activated nodes (those resources immediate the activated nodes are known to the user and cannot be recommended). The computational requirements of this approach is also daunting, requiring the calculating of the PageRank vector for each query.

Instance-based collaborative filtering has been modified to resource recommendation in social annotation systems by extending the ratings matrix to include tag information [27], although most efforts do not assume access to ratings data. User-based collaborative filtering [16, 24] has been adapted for recommending tags. Users can be modeled as a vector of resources, a vector of tags, a combinations of the two, or feature vectors such as those calculated through singular value decomposition [11]. Item-based collaborative filtering [3, 22] has also been adapted for tag-recommendation [7, 8]. In this work we extend these instance-based methods to tag-based resource recommendation in social annotation systems.

Matrix factorization approaches that have been found successful in e-commerce recommendation depend on the two-dimensional structure of the *ratings matrix*, in which users and resources form the axes and the values of the matrix are known ratings. Researchers have begun exploring tensor factorization to reduce the dimensionality of the social data. Tucker decomposition is one approach, factoring the three-dimensional tagging data into three feature spaces and a core residual tensor [26]. However the model-building phase is highly computationally-intensive.

A pair-wise interaction tensor factorization model has also been proposed. It offers far more reasonable run times in both the construction of the model and the generation of recommendations [21]. Given its effectiveness, this technique is considered one the state-of-the-art approaches for tag recommendation. In this work, we adapt this method to construct an ordered list of resources for a given user-tag pair and use it for comparative purposes.

Clusters of tags can represent topic areas [1]. These clusters have been used as inter-mediaries between users and resources allowing the recommendation of resources [12, 19,25]. Such recommenders can accommodate both the basic and tag-based constraints of resource recommendation. Clustering tags is also useful for overcoming the problem of redundancy [6] as well as ambiguity found in user-centric tag models [28].

Hybrid models [2] have been used to generate integrative models by combining sev-eral component recommenders like those above into a larger framework. One approach demonstrated that a graph-based model may be improved by incorporating item-based collaborative filtering [7]. A similar effort designed a hybrid for the PKDD-ECML 2009 Challenge [5]. Hybrid models composed of both user-based and item-based collabora-tive filtering algorithms were shown to match or outperform the state-of-the-art pair-wise interaction tensor factorization model in tag recommendation [8]. Another effort incorporating hybrids predicts user ratings in MovieLens, one of the few systems that contains both ratings and tags [23]. We build on these efforts proposing a flexible and easily extensible hybrid model for tag-based resource recommendation.

4   Tag-Based Resource Recommendation Algorithms

Our definition of resource recommendation centers on the function ϕ, which assigns a real-valued score to each resource describing the relevance of the resource to the user (and, if supplied, the requirements.) In this work we focus on tag-based resource recommendation in which the requirement is a single tag. In this section, we describe the linear-weighted hybrid algorithm that we propose for this task, the components from which the hybrid is constructed, and we will also describe the implementation of our comparative benchmark, an integrative approach based on tensor factorization.

4.1   Linear-Weighted Hybrid

A linear-weighted hybrid is composed of recommendation components κ_1 through κ_k, whose output is combined by computing a weighted sum [2]. We assume that each component κ_i has its own computation of the function $\phi_i(u, q, r)$, producing output in the range $[0..1]$, and a weight α_i in the same range. We further require that the α-values sum to 1. The hybrid is therefore defined as: $\phi(u, q, r) = \sum_{i=1}^{k} \alpha_i \phi_i(u, q, r)$.

To obtain the correct α_i for each component, we use a simple and efficient random-restart hill climbing technique. A subset of the data is selected as a holdout set for learning the algorithm parameters, including the α values. (See Methodology descrip-tion in Section 5.2 below.) The α vector is initialized with random positive numbers constrained such that the sum of the vector equals 1. The recommender then operates over the holdout set, and uses hill-climbing based on the calculated precision over the holdout set to modify the α vector until a stable point is reached. The algorithm is then restarted to avoid local minima.

The components within the hybrid are created by reducing the dimensionality of the URT matrix into two dimensional projections. A more detailed account of these projections can be found in our previous work [8, 9, 10] as well as other efforts [15, 18] in social annotation systems.

$PopTag$: This algorithm reduces the recommendation problem to a non-personalized production of the most popular items for the given tag. Although this is a simple, non-personalized, algorithm, the hybrid algorithm performed better across all datasets with it included.

KNN_{ur} , KNN_{ut} : These algorithms operate like the well-known user-based collaborative filtering algorithm [16,24]. We obtain a matrix of user profiles by making a two-dimensional projection of the URT matrix. The UR projection defines a user profile as the binary vector with a 1 for each resource the user has tagged and a 0 for those untagged. The UT projection is a weighted vector with the count of times that a user has applied a given tag. Depending on which projection is used, we refer to either the KNN_{ur} or KNN_{ut} component. To make recommendations, we filter the users to only those who have used the selected tag. We perform cosine similarity to find peer users, and use these peers to recommend resources with the restriction that the resources were annotated with the selected tag.

KNN_{ru} , KNN_{rt} : These algorithms are analogous to item-based collaborative filtering [3,22], which relies on discovering similarities among resources rather than among users. We make projections similar to the user-based ones described above – this time to create RU (resources as vectors of users) and RT (resources as vectors of tags) matrices. We filter resources that have been tagged with the query tag and use cosine similarity to score the resemblance of resources to those found in the user profile..

TS_{tt} : Because users apply tags and resources have tags applied to them, we can represent users and resources in a shared tag space. In the case of tag-based resource recommendation, the question is whether the query tag is represented similarly in the resource's profile as in the user's profile. We measure this with a degenerate form of cosine similarity using only the values associated with the query tag in the numerator.

4.2   Pair-Wise Interaction Tensor Factorization

Another approach to incorporate several dimensions of the data is to perform dimensionality reduction on the three-dimensional matrix as a whole. As a basis for comparison with our algorithm, we chose the pair-wise interaction tensor factorization [21] algorithm, which was developed for the task of tag recommendation and is considered among the start-of-the-art tag recommenders. Our adaptation of the model to resource recommendation simply exchanges the roles of resources and tags with respect to each other. This model-based approach generates a set of factor matrices which resembles a special case of the Tucker decomposition of a tensor. The tensor itself is not directly induced by the data, but rather reflects a ranking over the resources for each user-tag pair. Thus, it is important to note that this model is applicable only to the special case of tag-based resource recommendation, and not for resource recommendation tasks with other requirements.

The model is built by considering observations in the data of the form (u, r_+, r_-, t), where (u, r_+, t) is a triple which is found in the data (a positive example of resource selection) and (u, r_-, t) is a triple *not* found in the data (a negative example of resource selection). An iterative gradient-descent algorithm is employed to optimize a ranking function that prefers positive examples in the data over negative ones. Each of four related matrices is updated until convergence is found. The matrices represent the factor-reduced components of the specialized tensor factorization $M = U_k R_k^U + T_k R_k^T$, where U_k is the user factor matrix, T_k is the tag factor matrix, R_k^U is the resource factor matrix with respect to users and R_k^T is the resource factor matrix with respect to tags, k is the selected number of factors, and M is the personalized resource-ranking tensor.

Generating a resource recommendation for a given user u and tag t is simply a matter of referring to the appropriate user-tag column of the ranking tensor M. The relevance score of a resource given a user-tag pair is calculated as: $\phi(u, \{t\}, r) = \sum_{i=1}^{k} U_k[u][i] R_k^U[r][i] + T_k[t][i] R_k^T[r][i]$.

5   Experimental Evaluation

In this section we describe the methods used to gather and pre-process our datasets and our evaluation metrics and methodology. Then we examine the results for each dataset, and finally draw some general conclusions.

5.1   Datasets

We have collected six real-world tagging datasets on which to perform our testing. Each dataset has been post-processed to retain a p-core [15] in order to eliminate noise and create a denser dataset. Making recommendations in the long tail of the data is a worthwhile endeavor but lies outside the scope of this paper. In all cases we ensured that the p-core contained enough data on each user to create five partitions. We chose $p = 20$ to generate the core, when possible; some datasets did not contain a 20-core, so instead we constructed a 5-core.

Bibsonomy enables its users to annotate both URL bookmarks and journal articles. This data set has been made available online by the system administrators [13], who have pre-processed the data to remove anomalies. A 5-core was taken. It contains 13,909 annotations with 357 users, 1,738 resources and 1,573 tags.

Citeulike is a popular online tool used by researchers to manage and catalog journal articles. The site owners make their dataset freely available to download. Once a 5-core was computed, the remaining dataset contains 2,051 users, 5,376 resources, 3,343 tags and 105,873 annotations.

MovieLens is a data set gathered from the corresponding MovieLens Web site and is administered by the GroupLens research lab at the University of Minnesota. It contains users, rating of movies, and tags. A 5-core was generated from the data resulting in 35,366 annotations with 819 users, 2,445 resources and 2,309 tags.

Delicious is a popular Web site in which users annotate URLs. Profiles from 524,790 users were collected in late 2008. Due to memory and time constraints, 10% of the user profiles was randomly selected, and a 20-core taken for experiments. The dataset is our largest, containing 7,665 users, 15,612 resource and 5,746 tags. It contains 720,788 annotations.

Amazon is America's largest online retailer. The site includes a myriad of ways for users to express opinions of the products. Recently Amazon has added social annotations to this list. After taking a 20-core of the data, it contained 498,217 annotations with 8,802 users, 10,679 resource and 5,559 tags.

LastFM users upload their music profiles, create playlists and share their musical tastes online. Users have the option to tag songs, artists or albums. The tagging data here is limited to album annotations. A p-core of 20 was drawn from the data. It contains 2,368 users, 2,350 resources, 1,141 tags and 172,177 annotations.

5.2 Methodology

For each data set, we started with a complete collection of annotations A. Two phases are required for the evaluation. First, the parameters must be learned including the number of neighbors for the collaborative filtering approach, the number of features for $PITF$ and the α values for the linear-weighted hybrid. The annotations are divided into five equal partitions P_1 though P_5. The partitions were generated randomly, but the process ensured that each user is represented in each partition. One partition was used for the learning of the parameters. That partition was then discarded and four-fold cross-validation was performed using these remaining partitions. One partition P_h was selected as a holdout set of annotations and the remaining partitions served as training data for the recommenders.

To evaluate the tag-based resource recommendation algorithms, we need to provide both a user and a tag and evaluate the system's ability to find a resource to which the user has applied that tag. We started with the holdout partition P_h and operated on one annotation at a time. Each annotation contains a user u, a resource r and a collection of tags t_1 through t_k. We select one tag at random, and generate a recommendation set using this tag and the user. This is the set R.

For this approach, we measure recall in the top 10 items: $recall = |R_h \cap R|/|R_h|$. For any given annotation, the measure will be either 1 (if the resource appears in the recommendation list) or 0 (if not.) We average over all annotations in the test set and over all folds. Since there is only one resource in the holdout set, R_h, this measure is also know as *hit ratio*.

The values chosen for k in the instance-based collaborative algorithms was selected after experimenting with values in the range 1 through 100. They are shown in the legend of Figure 1. $PITF$, the pair-wise interaction tensor factorization model, was built with 64 features and a learning rate of 0.03. Improvement could not be achieved by increasing the number of features or tuning the learning rate. It was trained until convergence.

5.3 Experimental Results

The tag-based resource recommenders accept as input a user and a single tag (representing the additional requirements). The output is a set of resources aligned with the user's interests and relevant given the required tag and the user profile. Figure 1 presents the results for eight algorithms across our six datasets.

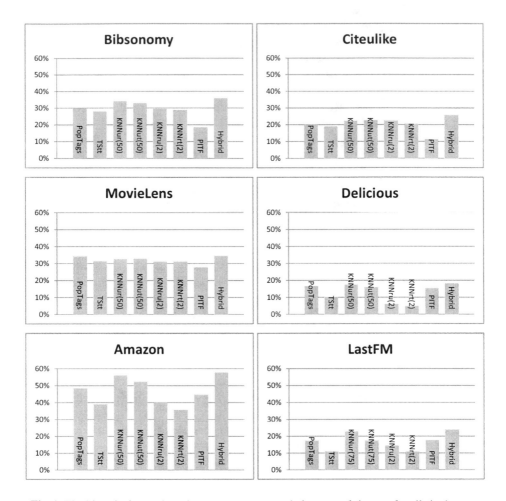

Fig. 1. The hit ratio for tag-based resource recommendation sets of size ten for all six datasets

The requirements of the selected tag can narrow the potential resource pool considerably. $PopTags$ which ignores the user model and simply recommends the resources most often annotated with the selected tag performs relatively well. Similarly TS_{tt} which considers only the query tag's relative occurrence in the user profile does well in many cases. Due to the usage of cosine similarity TS_{tt} may recommend infrequently annotated resources.

KNN_{ur} is consistently a top performer. It does well in part because it captures several dimensions of the data. It models users as resource and uses the selected tag to filter both neighbors and resources. It consequently includes information from the user-resource, user-tag and resource-tag dimensions.

In nearly all cases KNN_{ut} is either equivalent or second to KNN_{ur}. This algorithm estimates the similarity between users by modeling them over the tag space instead of the resource space. It too filters the potential resources by the selected tag, and then relies on neighbors for recommendations.

The item-based collaborative filtering techniques, KNN_{ru} and KNN_{rt}, model resources as either users or tags. In both cases, the neighborhood of resources is restricted to those that have been annotated by the user with the selected tag. Item-based collaborative filtering performs well when compared to the user-based techniques in MovieLens but fairs much worse in Delicious.

These experimental results reveal several key findings. First, not all social annotation systems are equivalent. In Amazon the hit ratio is nearly 60% while in Delicious and LastFM the results are much poorer. The performance of the individual algorithms varies as well. These differences may be explained by considering the dynamics of user interaction with the system.

Bibsonomy originally allowed its users to annotate journal articles. Later it was expanded to include Web sites, but the focus of the system largely remains on scientific research topics. In this system the users are motivated to organize their resources for later retrieval. They often focus on their area of expertise and use tags reflecting concepts from their discipline. The result is a social annotation system with several strong dimensions of the data. The experimental results bear this out; algorithms relying on different dimensions of the data all perform relatively well.

Citeulike offers a more specific example of a focused resource-centric annotation system. Its users annotate only journal articles. In this dataset we again see several strong recommenders each relying on different aspects of the data. This likely occurs because users most often annotate articles from their area of research and agree with their fellow users on how to annotate those resources. The tight-knit communities make users a good model for resources just as the agreement on tags make them a good model for resource description.

MovieLens provides a platform for users to annotate movies. Similar to Citeulike its users often agree on tags often drawn directly from the genre or actor's name. Moreover users often focus on particular types of movies; some may prefer sci-fi while others prefer romantic-comedies. This type of behavior strengthens the user-resource dimension of the data. Consequently several of the recommenders perform well each exploiting different dimensions of the data.

Delicious users are able to annotate any Web page on the Internet. In terms of variance across topics, this system provides the broadest focus. User are often motivated to organize resources for later retrieval rather than share resources among friends. Their interests are varied and the tags they use are often idiosyncratic or ambiguous. As a result this dataset presents a difficult target for resource recommendation. The noise in the tag space is so great that KNN_{ru} and TS_{rt} perform much worse than the nonpersonalized recommender based on popularity.

In contrast, Amazon allows almost 60% recall for a recommendation set of size 10. The average user focuses on a narrow selection of categories making the recommendation task easier. Furthermore tags, often manufacturer names or product categories, dramatically reduce the search space and provide a clear picture of the user's intention. These observations suggest that it is easier to model users whether by resources or tags. We see in the performance of KNN_{ur} and KNN_{ut} the value of incorporating the neighbors.

The results for LastFM reveal yet another example of how the manner in which users interact with the system effects the characteristics of the data. KNN_{ur} performs the best. Both this recommender concentrates on the user-resource relation. There is a wide gulf between this approaches and the remaining constituents to the hybrid. KNN_{ut}, KNN_{rt} and TS_{rt} all perform nearly as bad or as worse as the recommender based on popularity. This may be due to the fact that its users do not store or organize their music within the LastFM application. Rather than using the application for organizing and exploring music through the tag space, users often employ the system to find new music and friends through the resource and user space. Visual examination of the tag space reveals that when users do annotate albums, the tags are often overly generic, such as "rock," or not descriptive of the resource, such as "album i own." In terms of tag-based resource recommendation, this analysis explains why tags would offer little utility.

In all cases the linear-weighted hybrid outperforms its constituent parts as well as the comparative recommender based on pair-wise interaction tensor factorization. The largest relative improvement is seen in Bibsonomy and Citeulike where all of the components do well. In datasets where some of the components do not perform well, such as Delicious and LastFM, the hybrid does not provide the same benefit. These results point to the conclusion the hybrid is most effective when it can exploit component recommenders that draw on complimentary dimensions of the data.

The $PITF$ approach provides a relevant point of comparison to our hybrid algorithm. In many cases, it is competitive to the hybrid model, although in Bibsonomy and Citeulike, it performs poorly. In tag recommendation, where $PITF$ has been shown to perform quite well, the algorithm can combine tags from the user profile as well as the selected resource profile. In tag-based resource recommendation, on the other hand, the algorithm can promote resources from the selected tag profile but not from the user profile since these resources are treated as positive examples and all other resources (including the ones that might be recommended) are treated as negative examples. $PITF$ is consequently ill suited for the tag-based resource recommendation task. This finding coupled with the drawback that it is not universally applicable to all resource recommendation tasks underscore the need for a more flexible recommendation algorithms in social annotation systems, such as the hybrid approach proposed here.

6 Conclusions

This paper has formalized the notion of resource recommendation in social annotation systems. The notion of requirements for the recommendation tasks is a flexible construct which covers many cases common in these systems. We provided experimental results in the special case of tag-based resource recommendation, and we analyzed the results across six real-world datasets with different characteristics. A linear-weighted hybrid framework for making recommendations was also proposed and shown to be effective.

These results motivate several conclusions. First, the way users interact with a system can dramatically affect the underlying characteristics of the data, and as a result the performance of recommendation algorithms. Secondly, a linear-weighted hybrid recommender provides a flexible, general, and effective approach to capitalize on strong relationships across different dimensions of a dataset. When constructed from simple yet fast components, the hybrid itself maintains these properties, offering a highly scalable and easily updatable solution for many recommendation tasks. Thirdly, the hybrid also offers extensibility. This work focused on recommenders which rely on the URT data model, but other recommenders could be incorporate recency, context or content. Other integrative techniques proposed to date do not provide this level of simplicity, flexibility and extensibility while achieving the presented accuracy.

References

1. Begelman, G., Keller, P., Smadja, F.: Automated tag clustering: Improving search and exploration in the tag space. In: Collaborative Web Tagging Workshop at WWW 2006, Edinburgh, Scotland (2006)
2. Burke, R.: Hybrid recommender systems: Survey and experiments. User Modeling and User-Adapted Interaction 12(4), 331–370 (2002)
3. Deshpande, M., Karypis, G.: Item-Based Top-N Recommendation Algorithms. ACM Transactions on Information Systems 22(1), 143–177 (2004)
4. Felfernig, A., Burke, R.: Constraint-based recommender systems: technologies and research issues. In: International Conference on Electronic Commerce, Innsbruck, Austria (2008)
5. Gemmell, J., Ramezani, M., Schimoler, T., Christiansen, L., Mobasher, B.: A fast effective multi-channeled tag recommender. In: European Conference on Machine Learning and Principles and Practice of Knowledge Discovery in Databases Discovery Challenge, Bled, Slovenia (2009)
6. Gemmell, J., Ramezani, M., Schimoler, T., Christiansen, L., Mobasher, B.: The impact of ambiguity and redundancy on tag recommendation in folksonomies. In: RecSys 2009: Proceedings of the Third ACM Conference on Recommender Systems, New York (2009)
7. Gemmell, J., Schimoler, T., Mobasher, B., Burke, R.: Improving folkrank with item-based collaborative filtering. In: Recommender Systems & the Social Web, New York (2009)
8. Gemmell, J., Schimoler, T., Mobasher, B., Burke, R.: Hybrid tag recommendation for social annotation systems. In: 19th ACM International Conference on Information and Knowledge Management, Toronto, Canada (2010)
9. Gemmell, J., Schimoler, T., Mobasher, B., Burke, R.: Resource Recommendation in Collaborative Tagging Applications. In: E-Commerce and Web Technologies, Bilbao, Spain (2010)
10. Gemmell, J., Schimoler, T., Ramezani, M., Christiansen, L., Mobasher, B.: Resource Recommendation for Social Tagging: A Multi-Channel Hybrid Approach. In: Recommender Systems & the Social Web, Barcelona, Spain (2010)
11. Gemmell, J., Schimoler, T., Ramezani, M., Mobasher, B.: Adapting K-Nearest Neighbor for Tag Recommendation in Folksonomies. In: 7th Workshop on Intelligent Techniques for Web Personalization and Recommender Systems, Chicago, Illinois (2009)
12. Gemmell, J., Shepitsen, A., Mobasher, B., Burke, R.: Personalizing Navigation in Folksonomies Using Hierarchical Tag Clustering. In: 10th International Conference on Data Warehousing and Knowledge Discovery, Turin, Italy (2008)
13. Hotho, A., Jaschke, R., Schmitz, C., Stumme, G.: BibSonomy: A social bookmark and publication sharing system. In: Proceedings of the Conceptual Structures Tool Interoperability Workshop at the 14th International Conference on Conceptual Structures, Aalborg, Denmark (2006)
14. Hotho, A., Jäschke, R., Schmitz, C., Stumme, G.: Information Retrieval in Folksonomies: Search and Ranking. In: Sure, Y., Domingue, J. (eds.) ESWC 2006. LNCS, vol. 4011, pp. 411–426. Springer, Heidelberg (2006)

15. Jäschke, R., Marinho, L., Hotho, A., Schmidt-Thieme, L., Stumme, G.: Tag Recommendations in Folksonomies. In: Kok, J.N., Koronacki, J., Lopez de Mantaras, R., Matwin, S., Mladenič, D., Skowron, A. (eds.) PKDD 2007. LNCS (LNAI), vol. 4702, pp. 506–514. Springer, Heidelberg (2007)
16. Konstan, J.A., Miller, B.N., Maltz, D., Herlocker, J.L., Gordon, L.R., Riedl, J.: GroupLens: Applying Collaborative Filtering to Usenet News. Communications of the ACM 40(3), 87 (1997)
17. Mathes, A.: Folksonomies-Cooperative Classification and Communication Through Shared Metadata. Computer Mediated Communication (Doctoral Seminar), Graduate School of Library and Information Science, University of Illinois Urbana-Champaign (December 2004)
18. Mika, P.: Ontologies are us: A unified model of social networks and semantics. Web Semantics: Science, Services and Agents on the World Wide Web 5(1), 5–15 (2007)
19. Niwa, S., Doi, T., Honiden, S.: Web page recommender system based on folksonomy mining for itng'06 submissions. In: Third International Conference on Information Technology: New Generations, ITNG 2006, Las Vegas, Nevada (2006)
20. Page, L., Brin, S., Motwani, R., Winograd, T.: The pagerank citation ranking: Bringing order to the web (1998)
21. Rendle, S., Schmidt-Thieme, L.: Pairwise Interaction Tensor Factorization for Personalized Tag Recommendation. In: Proceedings of the Third ACM International Conference on Web Search and Data Mining, New York (2010)
22. Sarwar, B., Karypis, G., Konstan, J., Reidl, J.: Item-Based Collaborative Filtering Recommendation Algorithms. In: 10th International Conference on World Wide Web, Hong Kong, China (2001)
23. Sen, S., Vig, J., Riedl, J.: Tagommenders: connecting users to items through tags. In: Proceedings of the 18th International Conference on World Wide Web, Madrid, Spain (2009)
24. Shardanand, U., Maes, P.: Social Information Filtering: Algorithms for Automating "Word of Mouth". In: SIGCHI Conference on Human Factors in Computing Systems, Denver, Colorado (1995)
25. Shepitsen, A., Gemmell, J., Mobasher, B., Burke, R.: Personalized Recommendation in Social Tagging Systems using Hierarchical Clustering. In: ACM Conference on Recommender Systems, Lausanne, Switzerland (2008)
26. Symeonidis, P., Nanopoulos, A., Manolopoulos, Y.: Tag recommendations based on tensor dimensionality reduction. In: Proceedings of the 2008 ACM Conference on Recommender Systems, Lausanne, Switzerland (2008)
27. Tso-Sutter, K., Marinho, L., Schmidt-Thieme, L.: Tag-aware recommender systems by fusion of collaborative filtering algorithms. In: Proceedings of the 2008 ACM Symposium on Applied Computing, Ceara, Brazil (2008)
28. Wetzker, R., Zimmermann, C., Bauckhage, C., Albayrak, S.: I tag, you tag: translating tags for advanced user models. In: WSDM 2010: Proceedings of the Third ACM International Conference on Web Search and Data Mining, New York (2010)

The Impact of Rating Scales on User's Rating Behavior

Cristina Gena, Roberto Brogi, Federica Cena, and Fabiana Vernero

Dipartimento di Informatica, Università di Torino
Corso Svizzera 185; 10149 Torino, Italy
{gena,cena,vernerof}@di.unito.it

Abstract. As showed in a previous work, different users show different preferences with respect to the rating scales to use for evaluating items in recommender
systems. Thus in order to promote users' participation and satisfaction with recommender systems, we propose to allow users to choose the rating scales to use.
Thus, recommender systems should be able to deal with ratings coming from heterogeneous scales in order to produce correct recommendations. In this paper we
present two user studies that investigate the role of rating scales on user's rating
behavior, showing that the rating scales have their own "personality" and mathematical normalization is not enough to cope with mapping among different rating
scales.

1 Introduction

Recommender systems help users overcome the information overload by automatically
selecting potentially relevant items, based either on their similarity with items users
liked in the past (content-based approach) or on the preferences of people with similar tastes (collaborative filtering approach). Recommender systems usually collect user
preferences by means of "rating scales", i.e. graphical widgets that allow a user to express her preferences by means of a numerical score. According to [5], rating scales
should ideally be devised so that users can express their preferences in an easy and
meaningful way, and a smooth translation should be possible from the granularity of
true user preferences, i.e., the number of levels among which users wish to distinguish,
to the range and granularity provided by rating scales themselves [9].

Recommender systems usually provide the same rating scale to all their users. However, in a user experiment we carried out [3], we found that users have different preferences with respect to the rating scales to use for the topic they are evaluating, and
that they prefer different rating scales for evaluating different topics. Thus, in order to
improve users' satisfaction and promote their participation, we proposed to allow users
to choose the rating scales to use in recommender systems.

This opportunity presents some challenges. In fact, recommender systems must be
able to deal with ratings expressed by means of heterogeneous scales, mapping them
to an internal representation, in order to generate correct recommendations. [5] found
a high correlation among ratings for the same items given by means of rating scales
which differ for their granularity, numbering, and visual metaphor. Consequently, they
concluded that designers can safely allow users to choose any scale they prefer, since
they only need to compute the ratings to use in the recommendation process by means

Joseph A. Konstan et al. (Eds.): UMAP 2011, LNCS 6787, pp. 123–134, 2011.

of a normalisation based on mathematical proportion. This is in contradiction with our findings in a similar experiment [3], where we observed that ratings expressed on different rating scales may depart considerably from mathematical proportion, motivating the idea that rating scales actually have an influence on user ratings. This insight is also confirmed by related work in the field of survey design, which reports the effect of scales on user ratings [7,6,2].

Given the importance of rating scales for recommender systems, and considering the controversial results reported in the state of the art and previous work by the authors, in this paper we decided to further investigate the issue of normalizing ratings given on heterogeneous rating scales.

As a first step, we aimed at experimentally confirming our past observation that rating scales actually have an influence on user ratings, and pure mathematical normalisation is not enough. To this purpose, we chose the gastronomy domain as a use case and carried out an experiment where users were asked to repeatedly assess a set of N recipes, using N different rating scales. We then confronted average user ratings on each rating scale, and we correlated all the ratings. We actually found that some rating scales are characterized by ratings that are higher or lower than average ratings. This allowed to calculate a coefficient for each scale, that filters out the effects due to the use of a specific rating scale. This can be used to capture the actual meaning of user ratings, and to accurately represent user preferences.

As a second step, we aimed at confirming the results of the first experiment in a more realistic setting, i.e. in the context of use of a real recommender system. Thus, we wanted to validate i) that mathematical normalization is not sufficient, and ii) the rating scale coefficients we calculated. Therefore we carried out a controlled experiment wherein users were asked to rate a number of recipes they liked with different rating scales. We have contextualized this experiment using I-Cook, a recommender system in the gastronomy domain which builds user models based on user ratings of system-provided recipes and which offers customizable rating scales. We should notice that I-Cook currently manages ratings coming from different rating scales using mathematical proportion.

The paper is organized as follows. We start by presenting the state of the art of rating scales studies in Section 2. Then, in Section 3 we present our definition of the main concepts we refer to in the paper. We present our experiments in Section 4: the first one is presented in Section 4.1, while the second one in Section 4.2. Finally, section 5 concludes the paper.

2   State of the Art

The role of rating scales is crucial in recommender systems where suggestions are generated by predicting ratings for items users are unaware of, based on ratings users explicitly provided for other items. It is commonly accepted that different users may use rating scales differently, and some sort of average adjusting is usually adopted in order to compensate for such an idiosyncratic behaviour (see for example [9,1,8,11]). On the other hand, relevant work in the area of recommender systems also focused on the choice of appropriate scales for collecting user ratings ([12,9,13])

Referring to the design of the rating process as a whole, in [12] the authors suggested to adopt a mix of different types of questions (e.g., expressing binary liking versus rating items on a Liker-like scale) and provide constant feedback on user contributions in order to keep users from getting bored or frustrated.

Distinguishing between domain features (which refer to the content being recommended) and inherent features of recommender systems, [9] points out that the granularity of true user preferences with respect to recommended contents may be different from the range and granularity of user ratings which are managed by a specific recommender system. An appropriate rating scale for a certain domain should allow users to distinguish among exactly as many levels of liking as it makes sense to them.

In [13], the authors defined the main elements that determine the design of interface aspects (corresponding to rating scales, according to our framework) aimed at presenting system predictions and at collecting explicit user feedback in the context of a TV recommender system: 1) presentation form (which quite closely corresponds to what we will call the "visual metaphor" in the rest of the paper); 2) scale of the prediction or rating (including range, precision, symmetric versus asymmetric and continuous versus discrete); 3) visual symmetry or asymmetry; and 4) use of colour. They also found that most users prefer to have predictions presented by means of five-star interfaces, while they are less in agreement as far as interfaces to provide feedback are concerned, consistently with our findings [3].

Differently from our approach, however, these works do not focus on the possible effect of different rating scales on user ratings and on ways to deal with it. Instead, starting from the consideration that a good rating scale should support users in expressing their preferences in a meaningful way and without much effort, in [5] the authors explicitly investigated the effect of rating scales on user ratings. More specifically, they asked their experimental subjects to re-rate each of three sets of movies they had already evaluated by means of the original MovieLens five-position rating scale on one of the following rating scales: a binary scale providing only thumbs up or down, a no-zero scale ranging from -3 to +3, and a half-star scale ranging from 0.5 to 5. Notice that, the authors did not explicitly focus on the possible effects of numbering and visual metaphors (unlike our case, as it will be seen later on in the paper), although they did use rating scales which differ with respect to these aspects. The authors found that ratings on all three scales correlated well with original user ratings, with no need for specific countermeasures, and suggested that designers might allow users to choose their favourite rating scale and compute recommendations by means of mathematically normalized scores. However, they also observed that users tended to give higher mean ratings on the binary and on the no-zero scales, and that new ratings on the binary scale correlated less strongly with original ratings (r = 0,706) than new ratings on the no-zero and half-star scales (r = 0,827 and r = 0,829, respectively).

The effect of rating scales on user ratings, on the contrary, is often reported in work in the domain of survey design.

In [7], the author produces some evidence that the presence or absence of a neutral point on a scale produces some distortion in the results. In particular, they found that some respondents may choose the mid-point in order to provide a less negative answer, because of a social desirability bias. On the other hand, rating scales with no mid-point force the real indifferent to make a choice, causing a distortion the polarity of which is content-specific.

Various factors which can cause a rating scale to be biased are examined in [6], including: 1) category labels (either words or numbers); 2) effects of response alternatives on question interpretation; 3) forced choices (e.g., no neutral point is available); 4) imbalance in the number of positive and negative responses; 5) order of responses (there is evidence of a bias towards the left side of a scale) and 6) granularity.

The possible effects of numeric category labels are also investigated in [2]. In particular, the authors show that the negative-evaluation side of a scale is perceived as more negative when it is labeled with negative rather than positive numbers (e.g., -4 rather than 1), and this causes more positive evaluations and higher average ratings when scales with negative numerical labels are used.

3   A General Approach for Defining Rating Scales

In this Section, we first define the three grounding concepts for our approach: rating scales, rating scale personality and user rating. Then, we describe how we deal with rating scale personality.

We define **rating scales** as complex widgets which are characterized by the following features: i) granularity, ii) numbering, iii) visual metaphor, iv) presence of a neutral position. For "granularity", we mean the number of positions of the scale: this can be coarse (e.g., a 3-point scale where only negative, neutral/intermediate and positive ratings are possible) or fine (e.g., a 10-points scale). For "numbering", we mean the numbers, if any, which can be associated to each position in a rating scale (e.g., three different 3-point rating scales might be numbered 0,1,2; 1,2,3; or -1,0,+1). For "visual metaphor", we mean the visualization form which is used to suggest the behaviour of rating, and which influences the emotional connotation of each scale: for example, a thumb rating scale shows a metaphor related to human behaviour; a star rating scale conveys a metaphor which relies heavily on cultural conventions (as with hotel ratings), while a slider rating scale is based on a technological metaphor which reminds, for example, of volume tuners. For "neutral position", we mean that an intermediate, neutral point, indicating that users have no definite opinion, is provided.

All these features contribute to define what we call the **personality** of rating scales, i.e., the way rating scales are perceived by users and affect their behaviour. In fact, we claim that rating scales are not neutral tools, but they exert an influence on people who are using them to express their preferences. Rating scales personality causes a certain rating scale to have a specific influence on user ratings, e.g., it stimulates users to express tendentially higher/lower ratings than other scales. Therefore, mappings based on mathematical proportion alone do not allow to capture the actual meaning of user ratings. We assume that rating scale personality may be defined at two levels. First, at an **aggregate** level, it is determined according to the behaviour of all users of a recommender system, and it reflects general tendencies in the use and perception of rating scales (e.g., according to [2], scales with negative numerical labels cause users to give higher ratings on average). Second, at an **individual** level, it is determined according to the behaviour of each specific user, and it reflects personal idiosyncrasies in the use and perception of rating scales (e.g., a certain user might consistently give higher ratings when using a specific rating scale, but this behaviour might not be generalize to the whole user community). In this paper, we focused on the aggregate level.

According to our approach, **user ratings** are therefore determined by at least three elements:

- the item which is being rated;
- the personality of the user who is rating;
- the personality of the rating scale in use.

The first point is straightforward: the influence of the items being rated on user ratings is meant to represent real user preferences for such items.

By user personality we mean the fact that users may tend to use rating scales differently, for example, optimistic users may tend to assign very positive ratings for the most part. User personality has been dealt with extensively in literature (see Section 2 for references on classical approaches which adopt *average adjusted* ratings for use in collaborative filtering systems) and we do not treat it further in this paper. On the contrary, the novel aspect we focus on here is rating scale personality.

Rating scale personality should be taken into account in various scenarios. For example, in content-based and collaborative filtering recommender systems, if users are expected to change the rating scales they use over time, or to assign specific ratings, given with different rating scales, to different aspects of items (e.g., quality of food and atmosphere for a restaurant), and such specific ratings are to be somehow aggregated in a general item rating. In content-based recommender systems, considering scale personality is useful when users are expected to use different rating scales for different types of items which map to common domain categories. For example, restaurants and recipes might be mapped to a common taxonomy based on their cuisine, as for restaurants, and on their nationality or primary ingredient, as for recipes. Thus a recommender system might be able to infer the level of user interest on French (or vegetarian) restaurants based on user ratings of French (or vegetarian) recipes. Finally, in collaborative filtering systems, rating scale personality should be taken into account if different users are expected to use different rating scales from one another (even if they may not change the scale they use over time, their ratings have to be compared in order to generate recommendations).

In this paper, we investigate the impact of *aggregate* rating scale personality in two users studies, which will be presented in the following section.

4   The Experiments

In this section, we present two user studies we performed:

1. A first preliminary experiment was carried out in order to: a) validate our assumption that rating scales have different personalities, i.e., they exert an influence on user ratings, and b) define numeric coefficients which formally describe rating scale personality at an aggregate level (aggregate personality coefficients) .

2. A second controlled experiment was carried out in order to further assess our approach, focusing on the scenario of a content-based recommender system where users are expected to change the rating scales they use over time.

4.1 The First Experiment

The goal of our experiment was to investigate the issue of normalizing ratings given on heterogeneous rating scales. Our starting idea is that mathematical normalization is not enough for mapping user ratings expressed with different rating scales. In a previous experiment [3] we observed that ratings expressed on different rating scales depart considerably from mathematical proportion, and so that rating scales actually have an influence on user ratings. It is worth noting that in that experiment 40% of ratings departed considerably from mathematical proportion, showing that mathematical proportion is not enough to make a mapping which is able to capture the actual meaning of user ratings. We believe that each rating scale has a specific personality that may influence the rating (even if this is in contrast with other works which found different results, as described in Section 2).

In order to confirm our past results, we have designed an experiment where users have been asked to repeatedly assess a set of N recipes presented in a cuisine web site, using N different rating scales. We then confronted user ratings on each rating scale. We chose the gastronomy domain presenting common recipes as a use case since is quite likely that user has already had experience with the recipe (because she has already eaten or cooked it) and if she does not she may obtain a good idea of the recipe just reading its description (ingredients, preparation, etc.).

For this experiment, we have considered seven rating scales (see Figure 1): thumb-up/thumb-down, thumb-up/thumb-down/thumb-medium, 3-points stars, 5-points stars, 10-points stars, 3-points slider, and 10-points slider. These rating scales are different for i) the granularity they provide in selecting values: they range from a minimum of two position to a maximum of 10 position; ii) the numbering; iii) the visual

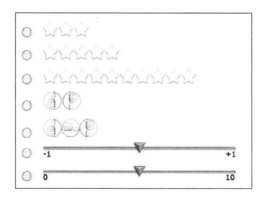

Fig. 1. The rating scales used in the two experiments

metaphor (thumb, star, slider); iv) the presence of a neutral position (thumb-up/thumb-down/thumb-medium, 3-points slider). Notice that the experiment was counterbalanced in order to avoid order effects. See later for details.

Hypothesis. We have hypothesized that user ratings may vary depending on the rating scale in use and thus ratings may depart from mathematical proportion. We have also hypothesized that this deviation could be ascribed to what we defined as the "personality" of each rating scale.

Experimental Design. Single factor within subjects design. The independent variable was the rating scale manipulated according to four levels: visual metaphor, granularity, numbering, and presence of neutral position. In the first treatment condition we manipulated both visual metaphor and granularity of the rating scale asking users to perform a rating task using three rating scales differing for visual metaphor and for granularity: thumb-up/thumb-down, 10-points slider, and 5-points stars. In the second treatment condition we only manipulated the granularity using the same visual metaphor (stars). In this second condition we presented to the users the following three rating scale: 3-points stars, 5-points stars, 10-points stars. In the third treatment condition we manipulated the visual metaphor (thumb, stars, slider) leaving the same granularity (3-point scale), and adding the presence of a neutral position (in thumbs and slider). One rating scale (the slider) has a negative value. In this last condition we proposed to the users the following rating scales: thumb-up/thumb-down/thumb-medium, 3-points stars, 3-points slider. Subjects were randomly assigned to all the three treatment conditions.

Subjects. 21 subjects, 22-26 years old, 11 male and 10 female, students at the School of Multimedia, Arts, and Humanities, University of Turin, recruited according to an availability sampling strategy.

Measures and Material. A series of nine web pages was prepared, grouped according to the three different treatment conditions. Each page presented a set of eight recipes to be rated with a single rating scale per page, and randomly presented to each subject. We randomly varied the order of the pages in each condition, and the order of the condition served from each user. We recorded users' performance with a screen capture video, and we registered user's ratings. Users received the instruction for experimental tasks directly on the web page presenting the experiment.

Experimental task. Users were asked to read the recipes (belonging to a imaginary friend's blog) and then rate them taking into account the description, and if they would cook/eat or not the recipe. Since their friend would like to know which rating scale to use in her blog, they were asked to rate the same recipe several times with different rating scales. At the end of the test every recipe had been rated with all the eight rating scales (3-point stars were used twice).

Results. We have collected in total 1512 ratings. All scales were normalized to a zero-to-one range. We computed mean ratings (see Figure 2, first row), and we correlated original values by means of Pearson correlation in order to compare the rating behavior of the users on different scales. We found the following significant correlations (all significant at the 0.01 level). The reader should notice that we only consider correlations equal or beyond a given threshold (0.5):

- in the 3rd treatment, **thumb-up/thumb-down/thumb-medium** and **3-points slider**: $r=0.861$. Single values showed that users gave often the same values when using these scales. When values do not co-vary, we observed the medium value of the thumb frequently corresponds to the maximum value in 3-points slider. Even if the granularity is the same, the negative numbering influences the rating, pushing slider values up, as sustained in [2];
- **thumb-up/thumb-down/thumb-medium** (3rd treatment) and **thumb-up/thumb-down** (1st treatment): $r=0.666$. Confirming general expectations, these two rating scales tend to vary together. When values do not co-vary the, 3-points scale shows mean values lower than the 2-points scale due to the presence of neutral position;
- **thumb-up/thumb-down** (1st treatment) and **3-points slider** (3rd treatment): $r= 0.658$. More than the previous correlations, these two scales co-vary also for higher values. The maximum value of the slider frequently corresponds to maximum value of the thumb;
- in the first treatment, **5-points stars** and **10-points slider**: $r= 0.631$. This correlation is lower than one could expect, and looking at single values we have noticed that, when not correlated, stars promote higher values than sliders;
- **5-points stars** (1st treatment) and **5-points stars** (2nd treatment): $r= 0.616$. This correlation is lower than expected: users rated the same items with the same scale but gave different ratings depending on the treatment condition. In the second treatment 5-point stars showed values slightly higher, and this trend is also confirmed by the next correlation;
- in the second treatment, **5-points stars** and **10-points stars**: $r= 0.575$. As in the case of stars/sliders, the correlation is lower than one could expected. Looking at single values we notice that, when not correlated, 5-points stars promote higher values.

In order to have a measure of the impact of the rating scale on the way the user rates, we have calculated a *coefficient* for each rating scales. This numeric coefficient is calculated as a ratio between the average ratings of each scale and the average ratings of 10-points stars rating scale. This scale was chosen for the recognized acceptance of the star metaphor and because scales with a fine granularity are considered more reliable [4], provided that users can handle such granularity (which certainly holds true for 10-points rating scales, see for example [5]). The coefficients we found are summarized in Table 4.1. We believe that these rating scales coefficients could represent the role of rating scales in the users ratings.

However, most of users ratings do not correlate, and when they do they do not correlate very well. Thus, we can affirm that these correlations do not reflect a mathematical proportion. Visual metaphor, granularity, numbering, and presence of neutral position seem to have an influence on the way the users rate. However, i) rating the same item

Table 1. Coefficients for rating scales in the two experiments

	2-p. thumb	10-p. slider	5-p. stars	3-p. stars	10-p. stars	3-p. thumb	3-p. slider
1st *experiment*	1.12	0.99	1.02	1.04	1	0.84	1.17
2nd *experiment*	1.05	0.92	0,98	1.08	1	1.08	0.77

would bias the way the user mapped her ratings on each scale, and ii) as shown in previous experiments (see [5] and [10]), the correlation between re-ratings ranges between 0.8 and 0.7. These reasons could have affected final results. Thus we have designed a second experiment wherein user can perform less constrained tasks in a more realistic setting.

4.2   The Second Experiment

Hypothesis. We have hypothesized that mathematical normalization would have failed also in a experimental setting less artificial than the one of the previous experiment, and we wanted to validate the rating scales coefficients we calculated in the previous experiment.

Experimental Design. Single factor within subjects design. The independent variable was the rating scale manipulated according to 4 levels: visual metaphor, granularity, numbering, and presence of a neutral position. The rating scales presented to the subjects were the seven scales of the previous experiment (see Figure 1). Users were asked to choose a rating scale, then to rate five courses (appetizer, first dish, second dish, side dish, desserts) they like using that scale. After that, they had to choose another scale, and do the same tasks. Scales were presented to the user in a random order, as well as courses.

Subjects. 32 subjects, 20-69 years old, 15 male and 17 female, skilled Internet users, recruited according to an availability sampling strategy.

Measures and Material. Users were given written instructions, then they were asked to connect to I-Cook recommender system[1] and perform the experimental tasks. Users' performance was recorded with a screen capture video, they were observed in real time by the experimenter, and their ratings were registered on a database.

Experimental task. Users were asked to connect to I-Cook, then to register on the web site. After that they were asked to choose a rating scale, and to rate an appetizer, a first dish, a second dish, a side dish, a dessert they like using that scale. After that, users were asked to select another rating scale and perform the same task. User were asked to use 7 rating scales (see Figure: thumb-up/thumb-down, thumb-up/thumb-down/thumb-medium, 3-points stars, 5-points stars, 10-points stars, 03-points slider, 10-points slider) presented in a random order. At the end they had to fill in a questionnaire, and to answer a set of questions asked by the experimenter.

Results. We have collected in total 1120 ratings. We calculated mean values for every user/rating scale, then we correlated values using Pearson correlation (See Figure 2, second row). The reader should notice that in the previous experiment all values were

---

[1] I-Cook is a recommender system which suggests recipes according to user preferences inferred by the user's rating behavior. Recipes are described by several features, relating to their course (appetizer, first dish, second dish, side dish, desserts), nationality (Italian, French, Chinese, Japanese, Spanish), main ingredient (meat, fish, etc), difficulty (easy, medium, hard) and preparation time (short, medium, long). Moreover, recipes can be characterized as vegetarian and gluten free. Differently from existing systems, I-Cook allows users to use the rating scale they prefer (http://brogiroberto.altervista.org/)

	2p.thumb	10-p.slider	5-p.stars	3-p. stars	10-p stars	3-p.thumb	3-p.slider
Mean 1st exp.	0.67	0.59	0.60	0.63	0.60	0.50	0.70
Mean 2nd exp.	0.68	0.60	0.64	0.70	0.65	0.70	0.50

Fig. 2. Mean ratings in the two experiments

comparable, since all the users rated the same item with the same rating scale. In this experiment mean values refer to the average values obtained from all the recipes rated by users with the same rating scales. So mean values represent the general trend of ratings obtained by using the same rating scale. The effect of the item to be rated on the total number of ratings has been neutralized by the high number of well-known recipes to be rated. We found the following significant correlations, all significant at the 0.01 level:

- **10-points slider** and **5-points stars**: $r=0.579$. This correlation was already present in the previous experiment, but with an higher value. The values expressed with these two rating scales correlate quite strongly. However, when not correlated, slider values are lower then star values, as in shown the previous experiment;
- **10-points stars** and **5-points stars**: $r=0.486$. This correlation was already present in the previous experiment, but with an higher value. 10-points stars slightly promote higher values;
- **10-points stars** and **3-points stars**: $r=0.472$. This correlation was not present in the previous experiment. 3-points stars mean values tend do be higher than 10-points ones;
- **thumb-up/thumb-down/thumb-medium** and **3-points stars**: $r=0.458$. This correlation was not present in the previous experiment. Thumbs mean values tend do be close to the ones in 3-point stars especially when users rate medium/higher values;
- **5-points stars** and **3-points stars**: $r=0.472$. This correlation was not present in the previous experiment. However, when not correlated, 3-points stars values tend to be higher than 5-points stars;

   More than in the previous experiment we can affirm that these correlations do not reflect mathematical proportion. To investigate the impact of single scales on ratings, we have calculated coefficient also for these rating scales. The coefficients we found are summarized in Table 4.1 (2nd experiemnt row). Comparing these new values with the older ones we can make the following considerations. Some trend in the coefficients is confirmed, but with some are slight different: i) thumb-up/thumb-down promote high ratings, and the new coefficient is lower than the old one; ii) 10-points slider promotes low ratings, and the new value is lower than the old one; iii) 3-points star promotes higher ratings, and the new value is higher than the old one; iv) 5-points star values are quite close to the ones expressed with 10-points star values, but in this experiments they tend to be lower. Some other value shows an opposite trend: i) thumb-up/thumb-down/thumb-medium new values seem to promote higher ratings, while in the old experiment they promoted low ratings. As noticed above, in this experiment users exploit this scale as the 3-stars one, considering its medium value close to the one expressed by the one of 2-points star; ii) 3-points slider promotes low ratings, while in the previous experiment promoted higher ones, as also sustained in [2]. This different trend could partly be explained by experiment design. We have noticed that users, knowing that they could change the rating scale, prefer giving negative values using the 3-points slider. Some user thinking-aloud said "I do not like this recipes, I will rate it after with the slider".

Regarding the preferences for the rating scales, the most favourite is the 5-point stars (with 16 preferences), followed by 10-points stars (with 9 preferences). All the other scales had few preferences (all 2). The worst is thumb-up/thumb-down with only one preference. This confirms the results of [13]. Most of the users (25) claimed that they appreciate the possibility to choose the rating scale. Two users did not have an opinion about this, and 5 did not like this opportunity.

We can conclude this analysis with some general insight. In general, we believe that the coefficients for capturing the actual personality of rating scales should be learnt by users' behaviour with a specific system, and cannot be calculated at priori. However, concerning the design of recommender interfaces, we notice that, in general, stars promote high ratings, especially 3-points stars, wherein 2-stars scores are largely used for items the user likes. Sliders promote low ratings - we can hypothesize that its design constraints encourage the criticism - and with negative labels are preferred for expressing negative ratings. Thumbs promotes high ratings, especially when used in thumb-up/thumb-down version.

5 Conclusions

In this paper we investigated the problem of how a recommender system can properly deal with values coming from heterogeneous rating scales. We presented two experiments that confirm the idea that a normalization process for mapping preferences expressed with different rating scales onto a unique system representation should consider the personality of the rating scale. The main contributions of the paper are the following: i) we experimentally confirmed the idea that scales have their own "personality" and mathematical normalization is not enough, ii) we discovered that the coefficients for capturing the actual personality of rating scales should be learnt by users' behavior with a the specific system, and cannot be calculated at priori.

The benefit is that designers of recommender systems now can be aware of these issues, and should take them into account in the creation of novel enhanced recommenders.

We presented our results in a context of content-based recommender systems. However, our solution could be applied as well to collaborative filtering systems in order to compare the rating on an item given by two users using different rating scales. This could be useful to compute similarity among users, which takes into account the ratings given by the users on the same items. The coefficients we have proposed could be used to compensate the variations caused by the use of different rating scales by adjusting users' ratings.

Another aspect we should take into account in our future work is the fact that individual ratings in some case can simply depend on the evaluated item (i.e., the rating on an item is low not for the ratings scale personality or for the user personality, but because the user does not really like the item itself). Thus, it becomes necessary to consider this aspect, in order not to confuse the effect of the rating scale with the effect of the evaluated item. For example, if the user uses an optimist scale for voting items she does not like, her ratings will be higher than using other more pessimistic scales, but the average could be low, as if the scale were pessimistic. To avoid this, some kind of semantic description of item is useful, in order to be able to compare the items and see if the users rate similar objects in a similar way.

Finally, we are planning to experiment the case of rating scale personality at the *individual* level, i.e. consider the specific rating behaviour of the individual user. Thus we will investigate to use machine learning techniques.

References

1. Adomavicius, G., Tuzhilin, A.: Toward the next generation of recommender systems: A survey of the state-of-the-art and possible extensions. IEEE Trans. on Knowl. and Data Eng. 17, 734–749 (2005)
2. Amoo, T., Friedman, H.H.: Do Numeric Values Influence Subjects Responses to Rating Scales? Journal of International Marketing and Marketing Research 26, 41–46 (2001)
3. Cena, F., Vernero, F., Gena, C.: Towards a customization of rating scales in adaptive systems. In: De Bra, P., Kobsa, A., Chin, D. (eds.) UMAP 2010. LNCS, vol. 6075, pp. 369–374. Springer, Heidelberg (2010)
4. Churchill, J., Gilbert, A., Peter, J.P.: Research design effects on the reliability of rating scales: A meta-analysis. Journal of Marketing Research 21(4), 360–375 (1984)
5. Cosley, D., Lam, S.K., Albert, I., Konstan, J.A., Riedl, J.: Is seeing believing?: how recommender system interfaces affect users' opinions. In: Proceedings of the SIGCHI Conference on Human Factors in Computing Systems, CHI 2003, pp. 585–592. ACM, New York (2003)
6. Friedman, H.H., Amoo, T.: Rating the rating scales. Journal of Marketing Management 9(3), 114–123 (1999)
7. Garland, R.: The Mid-Point on a Rating Scale: Is it Desirable. Marketing Bulletin 2, 66–70 (1991)
8. Goldberg, K.Y., Roeder, T., Gupta, D., Perkins, C.: Eigentaste: A constant time collaborative filtering algorithm. Inf. Retr. 4(2), 133–151 (2001)
9. Herlocker, J.L., Konstan, J.A., Terveen, L.G., Riedl, J.: Evaluating collaborative filtering recommender systems. ACM Trans. Inf. Syst. 22(1), 5–53 (2004)
10. Hill, W., Stead, L., Rosenstein, M., Furnas, G.: Recommending and evaluating choices in a virtual community of use. In: Proceedings of the SIGCHI Conference on Human Factors in Computing Systems, CHI 1995, pp. 194–201. ACM Press/Addison-Wesley Publishing Co., New York, NY, USA (1995)
11. Schafer, J.B., Frankowski, D., Herlocker, J., Sen, S.: Collaborative filtering recommender systems. In: Brusilovsky, P., Kobsa, A., Nejdl, W. (eds.) Adaptive Web 2007. LNCS, vol. 4321, pp. 291–324. Springer, Heidelberg (2007)
12. Swearingen, K., Sinha, R.: Interaction design for recommender systems. In: Proceedings of Designing Interactive Systems 2002. ACM Press, New York (2002)
13. van Barneveld, J., van Setten, M.: Designing Usable Interfaces for TV Recommender Systems. In: Ardissono, L., Kobsa, A., Maybury, M. (eds.) Personalized Digital Television. Targeting Programs to Individual Users, pp. 259–285. Kluwer Academic Publishers, Dordrecht (2004)

Looking Beyond Transfer Models: Finding Other Sources of Power for Student Models

Yue Gong and Joseph E. Beck

Computer Science Department, Wrcester Polytechnic Institute,
100 Institute Road, Worcester, MA, 01609, USA
{ygong,josephbeck}@wpi.edu

Abstract. Student modeling plays an important role in educational research. Many techniques have been developed focusing on accurately estimating student performances. In this paper, using Performance Factors Analysis as our framework, we examine what components of the model enable us to better predict, and consequently better understand, student performance. Using transfer models to predict is very common across different student modeling techniques, as student proficiencies on those required skills are believed, to a large degree, to determine student performance. However, we found that problem difficulty is an even more important predictor than student knowledge of the required skills. In addition, we found that using student proficiencies across all skills works better than just using those skills thought relevant by the transfer model. We tested our proposed models with two transfer models of fine- and coarse-grain sizes; the results suggest that the improvement is not simply an illusion due to possible mistakes in associating skills with problems.

Keywords: performance factors analysis, question difficulty, student overall proficiencies, predicting student performance.

1 Introduction

Many computer-based tutoring systems use student modeling techniques to track student knowledge and predict student performance or behaviors in order to individualize instruction, such as supporting mastery learning [1]. A study shows that, from a 'most-wanted' list of specific features, students primarily require an ITS to provide individualized teaching and learning [2]. In order to promote student feelings of being tutored in an individualized manner, high predictive accuracy of the applied student model is important. There have been many efforts focusing on developing student modeling techniques. The knowledge tracing model (KT) [3] is a generative model and can be implemented by a Hidden Markov Model [4], which uses student performance to estimate student knowledge. In addition, there is another group of models, which are discriminative models, such as Learning Factors Analysis (LFA, [5]). The LFA model uses three predictors, taking the form of a logistic regression to predict student performance. A new model, which is a variant of LFA, and is competitive with knowledge tracing, is the Performance Factors Analysis model (PFA) [6]. It modifies LFA model to incorporate item difficulty and the effects of student prior performance.

Joseph A. Konstan et al. (Eds.): UMAP 2011, LNCS 6787, pp. 135–146, 2011.
© Springer-Verlag Berlin Heidelberg 2011

Although LFA/PFA and KT differ markedly in their functional forms (HMM vs. logistic regression), one constant between them is only paying attention to the skills required to answer the question. That is, they consider only those skills noted in the transfer model and ignore all other skills (also called knowledge components in this paper). Specifically, LFA estimates a single parameter capturing the learning rate for each skill and a parameter representing skill difficulty, while PFA estimates two parameters to represent the effects of prior successes and prior failures on each skill.

To determine which skills are required in a question, a transfer model maintains the associations between skills and questions. It is usually created by domain experts, yet can also be learnt automatically by algorithms [7, 9]. Given that almost all student modeling techniques use transfer models, it is reasonable to infer that transfer models are fundamental to student modeling. In this paper, rather than taking the importance of transfer models for granted, we try to answer a basic question: what components are important to a student model for better predicting student performance. Specifically, our goal is to determine whether there are other factors that are equally as (or even more) important than transfer models.

2   Predictive Factors for Student Modeling

Although the skills required to answer a question are presumably important, two questions can use the same skills but vary in difficulty; which leads to a natural question: compared to the predictive power from a transfer model, does *question* difficulty deserve equal, or even more attention? This research question motivates us for the following two reasons. First, to our knowledge, the PFA model using question difficulty [6] has never been evaluated in terms of the model's predictive accuracy [Pavlik, personal communication]. The second reason is originated from our prior work [8], where we compared the PFA model against KT and found that PFA is considerably superior to KT with respect to making more accurate predictions on unseen student's performances: 0.16 vs. 0.06 in R^2 and 0.75 vs. 0.66 in AUC (Area Under the Curve) of the ROC (Receiver Operating Characteristic) curves. In this study, we are interested in digging deeper to explore the reason for PFA's superior performance. We hypothesize that the difference may come from question difficulty, as although the two models take different modeling forms, from a more general view, what is the same between PFA and KT is the utilization of the transfer model, while the major difference is that PFA alone takes question difficulty into account. In this study, we want to test the hypothesis of whether PFA capturing question difficulty is responsible for the large gain in accuracy.

In addition to focusing on examining the predictive powers of question difficulty and transfer models we, from a scientific standpoint, also question the assumption of using transfer models to predict. The common use of transfer models assumes that student proficiencies on, and only on, the required skills, as specified by a transfer model, have impact on solving the question. Note that the assumption only holds when the following corollary is also true: student performance on the problem is independent of student proficiencies on non-required skills. However, the corollary could fail to be true, perhaps due to the possibility that there are relationships between required skills and non-required skills that are not well captured by the transfer model, or perhaps problems involve a broader range of skills than the subject matter expert believed and encoded in the transfer model. Therefore, it is reasonable for us to relax the assumption and design a model acknowledging that the probability a student successfully solves a problem might also depend on his proficiencies on "non-required" skills. Therefore, we propose a model where student proficiencies on *all* skills are considered as possibly relevant for making predictions.

There is another reason for us to incorporate student proficiencies on all skills: in some student modeling techniques, student ability is viewed as a factor helpful for producing higher model accuracy. Some models, such as LFA, have incorporated student ability by estimating a parameter for each individual student based on examining the student's overall proficiencies. Recently, [10] proposed an individualized knowledge tracing model, which enhances the traditional knowledge tracing model by considering student's individual difference and leads to higher predictive accuracy than the classic KT model.

Thus, it appears that considering the student's individual ability is reasonable to other researchers. Since student proficiencies across all skills is a reasonable proxy for student ability, we suspect it will likewise be a useful predictor. In a sense, it is reasonable to assume that an overall stronger student is more likely to produce a correct response than a weaker student, even if neither has practiced the skills required for the problem. Therefore, considering student overall proficiencies as an indicator of student ability forms the second reason for us to design a model incorporating student overall proficiencies.

Moreover, it is worth pointing out that there is a thorny problem with the approaches that utilize an explicit parameter to represent student ability (such as LFA): in those approaches, a student's ability is represented as a specific value based on examining all of the student's performances, so the value cannot be applied to a new student. This leads to the model's lack of ability to adapt to new incoming students. The model presented by Pardos, et al.[10] solves the problem by using the new student's first performance as a piece of evidence to initialize the model.

The requirement of handling new students is not negligible in applications of intelligent tutoring systems, as findings should generalize to new students. Our model can accommodate new students as, rather than trying to estimate student ability, it instead estimates the *effects* of student proficiencies on all skills. Therefore, it is able to reuse those estimated effects when making predictions for new students. In this way, since the student parameter is no longer necessary, the model doesn't require peeking into the future at all of the student's performances.

3   The Models

We used the performance factors analysis as our framework, for the reason that it has been shown to work well on our data [8], as well as it takes the form of logistic regression, so it is straightforward to incorporate more (or different) variables.

3.1   Performance Factors Analysis

Performance Factors Analysis (PFA), a new student modeling approach, was developed by Pavlik et al. [6]. Briefly speaking, PFA takes the form of a logistic regression model for making predictions with student performance as the dependent variable. PFA reconfigures LFA on its independent variables, by dropping the student variable and replacing the knowledge component difficulty with the question difficulty (i.e. one parameter per question). The PFA model can also be viewed as a learning decomposition [11] model in that it estimates the different effects on performance of getting a practice opportunity correct or incorrect.

$$m(i,\ j,\ q \in questions,\ s,\ f) = \beta_q + \sum_{j \in required\_KCs} (\gamma_j s_{i,j} + \rho_j f_{i,j}) \tag{1}$$

As shown in Equation 1, m is the logit representing the accumulated strength of student i practicing on a series of problems. The model estimates a parameter (β), representing the difficulty of question q, and two parameters (γ and ρ) for each skill j reflecting the effects of the prior successes and prior failures achieved for that skill. The terms $s_{i,j}$ and $f_{i,j}$ represent the counts of the prior successful and failed attempts by student i on skill j. Unlike LFA, the PFA model doesn't capture student ability. However, by dropping the student ability term it gains the ability to make predictions about new students.

The following example illustrates the factors used in the PFA model and how they are organized. Suppose there are two skills in the data set. Table 1 shows a sequence of performances, extracted from the middle of the input file. These questions are answered by a single student and organized in chronological order. In each row, the counts of prior successes and prior failures, achieved by the student in the past for the corresponding skills, are shown in the last four columns. Note that in the PFA model, the counts for a skill are only non-zero when that skill is required in the question. Consequently, as a correct data format for the PFA model, all the cells with two numbers separated by a slash should be set to 0s (the number preceding the slash), as the transfer model does not believe performance on that skill impacts performance on the question. For example, in the second row, even though the student has generated 5 correct and 3 incorrect responses for skill 1 in the past, when the model deals with the question with ID = 53, since this question requires no ability about skill 1, the student proficiency on skill 1 is ignored, thus two zeros should be assigned for the number of prior success and failures (columns 4 and 5). In this way, the model follows the assumption of using transfer models to predict: student proficiencies on non-required skills are irrelevant.

3.2   The Overall Proficiencies Model

As we argued in Section 1.2, student proficiencies on all skills, not just on required skills, could be important in terms of providing more predictive power. Our model is built based on the assumption that student proficiencies on certain specific skills are less important than his overall proficiencies. Therefore, we reconfigured the PFA model's predictors, keeping question difficulty, yet replacing the student proficiencies on required skills to those on all skills. We call this new model the overall proficiencies model. Its formula is shown as follows.

$$m(i,\ j,\ q \in questions,\ s,\ f) = \beta_q + \sum_{j \in ALL\_KCs} (\gamma_j s_{i,j} + \rho_j f_{i,j}) \tag{2}$$

Table 1. Input data formats of the PFA model and the <u>overall proficiencies model</u>

Question ID	skills	correct	prior successes skill 1	prior failures skill 1	prior successes skill 2	prior failures skill 2
1004	1	Yes	4	3	0 / <u>10</u>	0 / <u>4</u>
53	2	No	0 / <u>5</u>	0 / <u>3</u>	10	4
5	1,2	Yes	5	3	10	5
214	2	No	0 / <u>6</u>	0 / <u>3</u>	11	5

The skills taken into account by the model differentiate our proposed model from the original PFA model (note: the set which skill j is drawn from—all KCs vs. required KCs). In this new model, student proficiencies on all skills are believed to have effects on student performance. This modification enables the model to break the limitations due to the potential failure of the assumption underlying transfer models, namely that student performance is independent of non-required skills. Furthermore, it also incorporates student overall ability as a predictor of student performance. In the example of Table 1, the data format of this model is different from that of the PFA model in using the underlined values to the right of the "/" in those cells with two numbers—it considers performance data for all skills.

3.3   A Hybrid Model – The Overall Student Proficiencies Model Emphasizing the Transfer Model

The original PFA model solely pays attention to the skills in the transfer model, as it follows the assumption that student proficiencies on non-required skills are not helpful. The overall proficiencies model takes the opposite approach and makes no assumption about which skills are more important for a particular problem. Compared to the well-established models, this model acknowledges the effects of student overall proficiencies, yet overlooks the importance of transfer models in prediction. Ignoring the transfer model could be an issue, as empirically almost all existing student modeling techniques make use of it, suggesting its effectiveness in prediction. Furthermore, it is reasonable to believe that student proficiencies on those required (at least according to the transfer model) skills would be more important predictors than an average skill. Towards this issue, we designed a hybrid model which considers both student overall proficiencies and his proficiencies on the required skills. The model is built based on the overall proficiencies model, meanwhile combining the idea of emphasizing the skills noted in the transfer model.

$$m(i, j, k, q, s, f) = \beta_q + \sum_{j \in ALL\_KCs} (\gamma_j s_{i,j} + \rho_j f_{i,j}) + \sum_{k \in required\_KCs} (\gamma'_k s_{i,k} + \rho'_k f_{i,k}) \qquad (3)$$

As shown in Equation 3, the first part remains the same as the overall proficiencies model, while the effects of student's proficiencies on skills in the transfer model are included in the second part of the equation. The problem with this model is that when there are a large number of skills, the number of estimated parameters is also very large. There are two parameters for each skill in the original PFA model (γ and ρ), while in this hybrid model the number increases to 4 for each skill (γ, ρ, γ' and ρ'). The first two parameters, γ and ρ captures the effects of practices on a skill, when those practices are treated as evidence of student overall proficiencies, while the other two, γ' and ρ', are corresponding to the effects of student proficiency on the required skill. Considering that if we add additional $2*n$ (n=# of skills) columns in the input data, most cells in a single row would be 0s, as among n skills, only a small number of skills are required in a question, to reduce the sparseness we compressed the $2*n$ columns to $2*x$ columns, where x is the maximum number of required skills of a question across all questions in our data set. For the second part of the model, for each row, the spaces for non-required skills are removed and all the followings are moved forward, until the preceding cell has been filled in and corresponding to another required skill, so that all effective counts are maintained in those $2*x$ columns.

Table 2 shows the data format under the scenario where there are n skills and at most a question requires x skills. Due space limitations, we use abbreviations for the titles: s-s$_1$ is short for the number of prior successes of skill 1; the counterpart is f-s$_1$. Req-s-s$_1$ is short for the number of prior successes of the first required skill; while for failures, the abbreviation is req-f-s1.

Table 2. Input data format of the hybrid model

Question ID	skills	correct	s-s$_1$	f-s$_1$	...	s-s$_n$	f-s$_n$	req-s-s$_1$	req-f-s$_1$	...	req-s-s$_x$	req-f-s$_x$
1004	1	Yes	4	3	...	0	0	8	7	...	0	0
53	2	No	0	0	...	10	4	15	24	...	10	4
5	1,2	Yes	5	3	...	10	5	15	8	...	10	5
214	2	No	0	0	...	11	5	17	8	...	11	5

Note that for those x columns, the counts in a single column could correspond to different skills in different rows. For example, suppose in the first row, the values of 8 and 7 in the cells of req-s-s$_1$ and req-f-s$_1$ are of the skill of Addition; in the second row, the values in the corresponding cells, 15 and 24 could be the counts of the same, or any other skill, such as Subtraction, Multiplication, etc. Thus, this model has an issue where the model parameters of γ' and ρ' lose the meanings of the effects of practices on a specific, named skill, but acquires the interpretation of the effects of practices on a skill with a specific position (first, second, third, ...).

In order to preserve semantic meaning for a particular position in the table, and thus have interpretable model parameters, we need some way to order the required skills. There are several reasonable approaches we can take. If we assume that in a multiple skill question, all the required skills are equally important in terms of contributing an accurate prediction of student performance, then we could use a random ordering. However, in the case where even if multiple skills are required, if the proficiency on one skill is more important than the others, we could put the more important skill earlier. In such a model, the first skill is the most important, and presumably the most difficult, skill required in the question. To determine difficulty, we could use student initial knowledge of skills, or the grade when the skill is taught, based on the assumption that an easier skill is taught earlier. We used the latter in this study; specifically the highest grade-level skill is req-s1, the second highest level skill is req-s2, etc. Our subject matter expert provided, as part of the domain model, the grade level where different skills are typically introduced. Thus, the coefficient for req-s1 is not interpretable in terms of a particular skill, but instead refers to the impact of the most advanced skill related to the problem.

4   Experiments and Results

We used data from ASSISTments [12], a web-based math tutoring system. The data are from 445 twelve- through fourteen- year old 8th grade students in urban school districts of the Northeast United States. They were from four classes. These data consisted of 113,979 problems completed in ASSISTments during Nov. 2008 to Feb. 2009. Performance records of each student were logged.

It is worth pointing out that the results of this study might be sensitive to the transfer model we used. Imagine that if the transfer model has many mistakes in associating skills to questions, it could lead to opportunities for the all skills or hybrid models being a better classifier than the original PFA model built with student proficiencies on the skills in the transfer model. Therefore, in order to reduce the possibility of using a poor transfer model, we used two transfer models with different grain sizes. The fine-grained transfer model has 104 math skills, including area of polygons, Venn diagram, division, etc. The other has 31 coarser math skill categories, such as Data-Analysis-Statistics-Probability: understanding-data-generation-techniques, Data-Analysis-Statistics-Probability: understanding-data-presentation-techniques, Geometry: understanding-polygon-geometry, etc. It is much less likely for a problem to be mistagged in the coarse- than in the fine-grained model since there are fewer possible skills with which to tag it.

A source of bias could be how affected our data are by the transfer model itself. For example, if ASSISTments is making pedagogical decisions based on the transfer model, it could impact how students perform. For this dataset, ASSISTments did not make use of the transfer model for any adaptation techniques (e.g., no mastery learning, although this feature has been since added to ASSISTments). For this study, the only way the transfer model was used was to group questions into problems sets that contained related questions. The impact of such problem grouping is probably minimal, as it is also the most common method of assigning math problems to students both in computer tutors and for school work.

We did a 4-fold cross validation at the level of students, and tested our models on unseen students. We hold out data at the student level since that results in a more independent test set. In the next section, we report the comparative results by providing mean test-set performance across all four folds (all reported results are for unseen students in the test set). To evaluate the models, we perform paired two-tailed t-tests using the results from the cross validation with degrees of freedom of N-1, where N is the number of folds (i.e. df=3, except where noted).

In this study, we focus on the student model's accuracy in predicting student performance. Predictive accuracy is the measure of how well the instantiated model predicts the test data. We used two metrics to examine the model's predictive performance on the unseen test data: R^2 and AUC. R^2 is a measure of how well a model performs in terms of accurately predicting values for each test data point, where the baseline it compares to is a model using the test data mean to predict; 0

indicates that the model has no predictive power once knowing the mean value of the target to be predicted, and 1 indicates prefect prediction. AUC of ROC curve evaluates the model's performance at differentiating students' positive and negative responses. An AUC of 0.5 is the baseline, which suggests random prediction: there is no relationship between the predicted value and the true value.

4.1   Question Difficulty vs. Transfer Model

We examine the predictive power provided by the property of questions: question difficulty, and the traditionally-believed important factor: student proficiencies on the skills identified by the transfer model as being necessary to answer the question. We compare predictive accuracy between the two variants of PFA, one of which is fitted by only using question identity to capture question difficulty (i.e. it ignores student performance). The other is fitted by just using the observation counts of prior successes and prior failures on each skill and ignores all information about question difficulty. The first model reflects the effect of question difficulty on predicting student performance, while the second examines the model's predictive performance in the case of solely relying on transfer models. The latter is trained and tested using both the fine-grained and coarse-grained transfer models (the first model makes use of neither transfer model).

Table 3 shows that, as indicated by the mean values of both metrics, the model using question difficulty is able to achieve higher predictive accuracy than the models just using the transfer models with different granularities. Based on the statistical tests using the results from the cross validation, for the comparison of the model with question difficulty vs. the one with the fine-grained transfer model, the difference in R^2 is statistically reliable with $p<0.05$, while $p=0.06$ for AUC. In the other comparison concerning the coarse-grained transfer model, the superiority of the model with question difficulty is reliable, supported by the t-tests of both metrics with $p<0.01$. The results suggest that divergent from the traditional belief that transfer models deliver a large amount of predictive ability to prediction of student performance, at least on our data sets, question difficulty is a more powerful source.

Table 3. Comparisons between the models with question difficutly and with transfer models

	R^2	AUC
Question_Difficulty	0.101	0.689
Transfer_Model-Fine	0.076	0.668
Transfer_Model-Coarse	0.061	0.650

4.2   Student Proficiencies on Required Skills vs. Student Overall Proficiencies

We proposed that estimating the effects of student overall proficiencies might contribute to more accurate predictions. To test that, we compared the proposed student overall proficiencies model against the original PFA model, which, in order to predict student performance on a question, only uses the skills in the transfer model.

Table 4 shows the comparative results with the models sorted by predictive accuracy. For the models using the coarse-grained transfer model, the results in the first and the fifth rows, the mean values of the two metrics suggest that the overall proficiencies model is superior to the PFA model. The t-tests yielded p values for R^2 and AUC less than 0.005, indicating that the differences are reliable.

For the models using the fine-grained transfer model, the second and third rows, the overall proficiencies model seems to outperform the PFA model in both metrics, but we failed to find any reliable differences between these two models, even though there is a suggestive trend in the mean values that the proposed model is probably better than PFA. We have encountered this problem previously [8], as the issue is one of relatively low statistical power of the t-tests, as we only have four independent observations (one for each fold of the cross validation).

Table 4. Comparisons between the original and our proposed PFA models

	Transfer model	Overall proficiencies	Grain Size	R^2	AUC
PFA-Coarse	Yes	No	Coarse	0.162	0.740
PFA-Fine	Yes	No	Fine	0.167	0.745
Overall proficiencies-Fine	No	Yes	Fine	0.181	0.756
Hybrid-Fine	Yes	Yes	Fine	0.189	0.760
Overall proficiencies -Coarse	No	Yes	Coarse	0.191	0.762
Hybrid-coarse	Yes	Yes	Coarse	0.194	0.763

Given that the statistical tests might not be sensitive to detect differences due to small number of observations, increasing the sample size is a cure. We grouped the measurement values from the models with fine and coarse grain size together. For instance, for the R^2 values, the number of observations increased to 8 (4 from each model). Taking the 8 observations, we were able to conduct paired two-tailed t-tests (df=7) with a larger sample size. The p values of 0.005 in R^2 and 0.001 in AUC suggest that the overall proficiencies model is reliably better.

One interesting pattern in the data is summing the R^2 values of the Question Difficulty and Transfer Models in Table 3 is approximately equal to the R^2 of a model that uses both components (as seen in the second row of Table 4 for the fine-grained PFA model and the first row for the one using coarse granularity). With the fine-grained model, 0.101+0.075=0.176 is fairly close to 0.167, while for the coarse-grained model, 0.101+0.061=0.162 equals to that of the PFA model. This fact suggests that the variance covered by question difficulty and the variance covered by the transfer model contain little overlap. In other words, estimating question difficulty can provide unique coverage of variance in student problem-solving performance.

4.3   A Hybrid Model: Combining Overall Proficiencies and Transfer Models

Our results showed that the overall proficiencies model is reliably more accurate than the original PFA model. However, the overall proficiencies model treats skills that are peripherally related to solving the problem as having equal importance as those most likely to be helpful in solving the problem. Since focusing on relevant skills might be able to improve model accuracy, we combined the transfer and all proficiencies into a hybrid model (see Section 3.3).

We compared the overall proficiencies and the hybrid models, showing the results in the last four rows of Table 4. For both model granularities and for both performance metrics, the hybrid model is more accurate on unseen test data. P-values from paired two-tailed ttests confirmed that the differences are reliable: p=0.043 in R^2 for the fine-grained transfer model, while the value of the coarse-grained model is 0.01. P values in AUC for both comparisons are both less than 0.005.

It is worth noticing that the improvement from incorporating transfer models into the overall proficiencies model is fairly small, less than 1%. Thus, once the model knows question difficulty and student overall proficiencies, student proficiencies on required skills contain little predictive power in terms of modeling student performance. Therefore, we question whether student proficiencies on required skills in the transfer models are overrated in the traditional student modeling approaches, especially considering evidence in Section 3.1, where we showed that using transfer models alone produced less accuracy than question difficulty alone.

5   Contributions

This paper made several contributions to student modeling.

First, this work determined what knowledge is fundamental to student modeling by examining the impacts of different sources of power on student model accuracy. Many components have been believed helpful for more accurately predicting student performance, and have consequently been incorporated by various student modeling techniques, such as question difficulty in LFA[5], PFA[6], as well as student overall proficiency (individual difference) in LFA and an augmented KT model, the prior per student model[10]. Nevertheless, few studies (e.g. [10]) have explored impacts of those components, i.e. model accuracy contributed by those factors, even though it is an important guideline for designing student models. Our study found that question difficulty is capable of accounting for more variance in our data than the skills labeled as necessary by the transfer model. More important is that question difficulty's predictive power is orthogonal to the variance accounted for by transfer model; thus they provide unique sources of information. Therefore, we recommend including question difficulty in student models for higher predictive accuracy. In addition, there are several existing techniques that have already incorporated notions of student overall proficiencies, usually also referred as student ability or student individual difference. This study, by conducting the comparisons between models with and without a means of considering student overall proficiencies, showed that the predictive power of student overall proficiencies is better than using the required skills for the problem.

Second, we proposed a new model on the basis of the PFA model, enabling it to incorporate student overall proficiencies on skills beyond those in the transfer model and showed that it reliably raised the student model accuracy. The model's advantage is its ability to capture the relationships, if there are any, between the problem and skills that are not specified by the transfer model as being relevant. Also the model works under the assumption that student overall proficiency impacts student performance. Unlike most existing models of student overall proficiency, our model is able to rapidly use partial data as it becomes available: rather than estimating a parameter summarizing the student, instead it estimates the effects of student prior performances on each skill. Since the model just needs to apply the effects so as to make the prediction, it is able to work immediately for new students.

Finally, we found that using the transfer model to predict is one of the least useful sources of predictive accuracy. While transfer models are often treated as a key component of student models, its importance is not supported by our results. We showed that both question difficulty and student overall proficiencies are able to capture more variance of student performance than transfer models. More than that, using transfer models to predict provides little additional power over using question difficulty and student overall proficiencies.

6   Future Work and Conclusions

Our study leaves several interesting questions deserving more effort. The overall proficiencies model works well, but it is uncertain regarding the source of its power. As we pointed out, there are at least two possible mechanisms explaining why the all proficiencies model works well. First, the all proficiencies model might be capturing the underlying structure of skills, where relationships between skills exist, yet are not captured by the transfer model. Second, the overall proficiency model could be capturing the overall competence of the student rather than properties of the domain. It is an important step to determine which, or the relative combination of each, is the key to the improvement.

It is also interesting to understand what other sources of predictive power are. The R^2 values of all of the models are relatively low, but that is where the field is at the moment; KT and PFA are the established baseline techniques, and although we certainly wish we had more accurate models, that is an open challenge for the user modeling community. Finding other factors that are able to account for student performance variability is a key challenge. One possibility is recent student performance, based on the assumption that recent performances are more predictive of the next performance than those that occurred further back in time. Student seriousness could also be key, as a student performance is not entirely determined by the student's ability, or the question's difficulty, but could be affected by his attitude.

To sum up, this work, based on the Performance Factors Analysis model, examines the components of student modeling in terms of their abilities to produce higher model accuracy. Although we need transfer models to build student models, using transfer models to predict appears to not be very helpful. We showed that question difficulty is a more important factor. Incorporating student performances on all skills, rather than those in the transfer model, also substantially benefits the predictions. Therefore, our results suggested that the effect of student proficiencies on the skills in the transfer model is overrated, and other factors that influence student performance should be considered.

Acknowledgments. For the full list of over a dozen funders please see http://www.webcitation.org/5xp605MwY.

References

1. Koedinger, K.R., Anderson, J.R., Hadley, W.H., Mark, M.A.: Intelligent Tutoring Goes to School in the Big City. Int. J. Artificial Intelligence in Education (1997)
2. Harrigan, M., Kravčík, M., Steiner, C., Wade, V.: What Do Academic Users Really Want from an Adaptive Learning System? In: Houben, G.-J., McCalla, G., Pianesi, F., Zancanaro, M. (eds.) UMAP 2009. LNCS, vol. 5535, pp. 454–460. Springer, Heidelberg (2009)
3. Corbett, A.T., Anderson, J.R.: Knowledge Tracing: Modeling the Acquisition of Procedural Knowledge. User Modeling and User-Adapted Interaction 4, 253–278 (1995)
4. Reye, J.: Student Modelling Based on Belief Networks. International Journal of Artificial Intelligence in Education 14, 63–96 (2004)
5. Cen, H., Koedinger, K.R., Junker, B.: Learning Factors Analysis – A General Method for Cognitive Model Evaluation and Improvement. In: Ikeda, M., Ashley, K.D., Chan, T.-W. (eds.) ITS 2006. LNCS, vol. 4053, pp. 164–175. Springer, Heidelberg (2006)
6. Pavlik, P.I., Cen, H., Koedinger, K.: Learning Factors Transfer Analysis: Using Learning Curve Analysis to Automatically Generate Domain Models. In: Proceedings of the 2rd International Conference on Educational Data Mining, pp. 121–130 (2009)
7. Barnes, T.: The q-matrix method: Mining student response data for knowledge. In: Proceedings of the AAAI 2005 Workshop on Educational Data Mining (2005)
8. Gong, Y., Beck, J.E., Heffernan, N.T.: How to Construct More Accurate student models: Comparing and Optimizing Knowledge Tracing and Performance Factor Analysis. International Journal of Artificial Intelligence in Education (to appear)
9. Winters, T.: Topic Extraction from Item-Level Grades. In: AAAI 2005 Workshop on Educational Data Mining (2005)
10. Pardos, Z.A., Heffernan, N.T.: Modeling individualization in a bayesian networks implementation of knowledge tracing. In: De Bra, P., Kobsa, A., Chin, D. (eds.) UMAP 2010. LNCS, vol. 6075, pp. 255–266. Springer, Heidelberg (2010)
11. Beck, J.E., Mostow, J.: How who should practice: Using learning decomposition to evaluate the efficacy of different types of practice for different types of students. In: Woolf, B.P., Aïmeur, E., Nkambou, R., Lajoie, S. (eds.) ITS 2008. LNCS, vol. 5091, pp. 353–362. Springer, Heidelberg (2008)
12. Razzaq, L., Feng, M., Nuzzo-Jones, G., Heffernan, N.T., Koedinger, K.R., Junker, B., Ritter, S., Knight, A., Aniszczyk, C., Choksey, S., Livak, T., Mercado, E., Turner, T.E., Upalekar, R., Walonoski, J.A., Macasek, M.A., Rasmussen, K.P.: The Assistment project: Blending assessment and assisting. In: Proceedings of the 12th Artificial Intelligence in Education, pp. 555–562 (2005)

Using Browser Interaction Data to Determine Page Reading Behavior

David Hauger[1], Alexandros Paramythis[1], and Stephan Weibelzahl[2]

[1] Institute for Information Processing and Microprocessor Technology
Johannes Kepler University, Altenbergerstrasse 69, A-4040, Linz, Austria
{hauger,alpar}@fim.uni-linz.ac.at
[2] School of Computing, National College of Ireland,
Mayor Street, IFSC, Dublin 1, Ireland
sweibelzahl@ncirl.ie

Abstract. The main source of information in most adaptive hypermedia systems are server monitored events such as page visits and link
selections. One drawback of this approach is that pages are treated as
"monolithic" entities, since the system cannot determine what portions
may have drawn the user's attention. Departing from this model, the
work described here demonstrates that client-side monitoring and interpretation of users' interactive behavior (such as mouse moves, clicks and
scrolling) allows for detailed and significantly accurate predictions on
what sections of a page have been looked at. More specifically, this paper provides a detailed description of an algorithm developed to predict
which paragraphs of text in a hypertext document have been read, and
to which extent. It also describes the user study, involving eye-tracking
for baseline comparison, that served as the basis for the algorithm.

Keywords: interaction monitoring, modeling algorithm, eye-tracking,
empirical study.

1 Introduction

Server-side data collection is the most common source of information in adaptive
hypermedia systems (AHS). The main drawback of relying solely on request-
based information is that requesting a page is not necessarily equivalent to reading everything that is presented on this page. Therefore, more recent systems
also utilize time between requests [1] and / or semantic information embedded
in the requests to improve on derived assumptions.

Client-side user behavior has long been identified as a potential additional
source of information, but due to technical limitations it was difficult to access.
Early attempts used custom browsers [2] or browser plugins [3] to enable client-
side monitoring. With JavaScript now established as a commonly supported
in-browser technology, more recent systems used this to reliably capture mouse
and keyboard events on the client side. For instance, mouse movements have
been used to identify learning types [4] [5] or as input for a neural network to

Joseph A. Konstan et al. (Eds.): UMAP 2011, LNCS 6787, pp. 147–158, 2011.

calculate a "level of activity" for a page [3]. Within "The Curious Browser" [6], Claypool et al. found that the amount of scrolling and the time spent on a page may be used to identify interests, and that the absence of individual scrolling actions or mouse clicks helped to identify the least interesting pages.

More recent work by the authors has examined the premise that increased granularity of information on a user's client-side activities might help not only in making inferences on a page as a whole, but also in splitting pages and treating the resulting fragments separately [7]. A first user study conducted to this end [8] addressed the question of whether browser events (resulting from user interaction) are generally suited for differentiating the user's reading behavior in distinct parts of a page. In this study, users were asked to read a single news page including several short articles. Their behavior was recorded with a purposely developed JavaScript monitoring library. Results showed that some events (especially clicks and text selections) are well suited to identifying whether the related text fragment has been read, although the lack of explicit interactions reduces the accuracy of assumptions. For instance, a selection in a paragraph is a strong indicator that the paragraph has been read; however, the more common case of "no selections" provides hardly any information at all. On the other hand, in some cases it is trivial to determine that something has not been read (e.g., the user never scrolled to a part of the page), but increasing times of visibility of text fragments –above the estimated time required for reading– by themselves, only slightly change the probabilities that something has been read. Using the amount of time the mouse pointer has hovered over articles was found to give some additional information on whether some paragraph might have been read.

Following these first encouraging results, we went on to examine whether it is possible to increase the accuracy of predicting what a user has read while at a page, by identifying and interpreting specific patterns in the user's interactive behavior. A primary objective in this second study has been to perform the monitoring unobtrusively, allowing the user to behave naturally (in contrast to approaches that enforce specific user behavior, such as blurring the screen and highlighting only the area around the mouse pointer, to force the user to "read with the mouse" [9]). Our overall goal was to find out how the observation of users' normal and unencumbered mouse and keyboard behavior could be related to what users are currently reading. Correlations of mouse and eye positions in situations with many "required" mouse interactions like web browsing [10] and within search interfaces [11] [12] have already been measured. The same is true for repeated visitation patterns [13] [14]. Our own results [15] showed a potential for learning environments as well, and we have been able to prove a number of hypotheses based on interaction patterns that were then used as a basis for an algorithm that associates such patterns with the users' reading behavior.

This paper reports on the aforementioned second study, along with the hypotheses tested and the results obtained; the prediction algorithm developed on the basis of these results; and the performance of the algorithm. The paper is concluded with a discussion of the algorithm's strengths and limitations, and an outlook of our ongoing and forthcoming work in this area.

2   Method and Experimental Setup

2.1   Hypotheses

As a first step in developing an algorithm for predicting what users read on a page, we examined a number of hypotheses that attempted to relate specific interaction patterns with reading behavior. These included (imprecise terms used are defined in section 2.3, after discussing the experimental setup):

H1: For pages where users moved their mouse frequently: (a) there is strong correlation between the positions of the mouse pointer and the users' gaze; (b) there is strong correlation between the positions of the mouse pointer and the users' gaze, while the users are moving the mouse; (c) the paragraph under the mouse pointer tends to be the same as the one being read; (d) the paragraph under the mouse pointer tends to be the same as the one being read, while the users are moving the mouse; and, (e) if the frequent movement is vertical, the mouse pointer's position is strongly correlated with the position of the users' gaze.

H2: An indicator for the user's current reading position is: (a) moving the mouse; (b) clicking on text; and, (c) selecting text.

H3: For users using their mouse frequently, the mouse position may be used to identify the relative position within the screen (e.g., top, middle, bottom) they most likely pay attention to (using the mouse position as indicator)

H4: After scrolling up, users are more likely to focus their attention on the items that became visible and were not visible before.

H5: Users scrolling down at small increments, tend to read mostly within a relative area of the screen (top / center / bottom).

2.2   Experiment Setup

To test these hypotheses, we designed a study that allowed us to compare users' reading behavior when encountering different types of text, to their interactive behavior while reading these texts in a browser. Reading behavior was determined through eye-tracking (described in more detail later), whereas interactive behavior was recorded through the purposely developed JavaScript library. The study involved a total of 13 participants (6 male, 7 female) in Ireland. Participants were given five tasks to perform, each based on a different type of text typically encountered online (one main task with seven pages of instructions and information for a board game, and four additional single-page tasks: a multiple choice questionnaire on the board game, a set of search results, a health-related article, and a set of news items). User interaction with the texts, as well as with all other study-related materials and instructions, was through a browser.

The main task involved the users learning about, and answering questions regarding, the game of "Go". The seven different pages comprised text (ca. 7010 words), graphics (11) and pictures (5). A typical page is shown in Fig. 1. Participants were free to navigate between pages, using the navigation bar or hyperlinks

Fig. 1. Excerpt of page on basic game rules for the game of "Go"

in the text. In order to motivate participants to read this text carefully, they were told in advance that they would have to sit a quiz on the content afterwards. Web pages were presented through the Internet Explorer browser (in "kiosk" mode with only a minimal set of browser controls visible in a toolbar at the top of the page). Descriptions of tasks and instructions were also included in web pages. All material was presented through a TFT screen, running at a resolution of 1280x1024 (1280x996 effective, excluding browser navigation bar). Gaze position was determined with an SMI RED4 remote eye-tracker. Gaze data, as well as data about web pages presented, was collected through the so called Experiment Center Suite software.

2.3   Evaluation of the Hypotheses

In the briefly described first step of our analysis [15], we tested the hypotheses to identify interaction patterns suitable for developing an algorithm. In total 112 page requests were recorded, with a page being visited for 2 to 1096 seconds with a mean of 122 ($\sigma = 116s$). On average, each user spent 17.54 minutes on the information on the game of Go. Before proceeding to discuss the results obtained, we need to more precisely define some of the terms used in the hypotheses.

To start with, several of the hypotheses refer to "mouse moves". For this study we defined a "mouse move" to be any set of changes in the mouse pointer's position, preceded and followed by at least one second of idle time. This definition was derived empirically and subsequently verified on the basis of the collected data, coupled with direct observation of recorded video of the users' sessions. Moves outside the viewing area (e.g., users dragging the scrollbar) were filtered out. "Frequency" of mouse moves on a per page basis was defined to be the ratio of time during which the mouse pointer moved, vs. the total time spent on the page (including idle time); e.g., a frequency of 25% indicates that the pointer moved for a quarter of the time a page was viewed. With these definitions at hand, we can now proceed to discuss the findings.

Table 1. Correlations of pixel positions of mouse cursor and eye gaze, depending on the frequency of mouse usage

	Frequency of mouse moves	Correlation $r_{eye_{vs}mouse}$	N	Regression model constant	weight	sig.
vertical	baseline	.250	89739	345.133	.228	.000*
	all; weighted by frequency	.528	89739	233.106	.494	.000*
	$frequency > 25\%$	.608	39134	211.082	.567	.000*
	$frequency > 50\%$	.658	21906	173.328	.613	.000*
	$frequency > 75\%$	.746	16360	165.461	.666	.000*
horizontal	baseline	.101	89739	577.499	.75	.000*
	all; weighted by frequency	.284	89739	461.427	.248	.000*
	$frequency > 25\%$	.393	39134	385.193	.386	.000*
	$frequency > 50\%$	.493	21906	241.912	.604	.000*
	$frequency > 75\%$	.560	16360	188.254	.727	.000*

H1: *Are mouse pointer position and gaze position correlated?* Analyzing across all users and including idle times, we found weak correlations both horizontally and vertically (see baseline in Table 1). However, these correlations are too weak to make reliable predictions on what has been read. We thus explored how predictions may be improved based on the frequency of movements.

H1.a: *Is it possible to improve prediction of gaze by considering the frequency of mouse usage on a page?* We found that, the higher the percentage of mouse movements, the lower the distance between mouse and gaze positions – see Table 1. Including mouse frequency as a weight (see rows "all" in Table 1 in comparison to baseline) raises the correlation significantly. When events are filtered by the level of frequency of mouse movements (e.g., greater than 25%), the correlation increases even further. As one might expect, the more restrictive the filter, the higher the correlation. In accordance with the baseline, the correlations in the vertical direction are higher than in the horizontal. In summary, predictions of the gaze position will be more accurate for users who use their mouse frequently on a page, than for those using the mouse less often.

H1.b: *Are H1.a predictions better while the mouse is in motion?* To analyze this hypothesis, we identified those events where the mouse was actually in motion. In comparison to the previous model, correlations increase yet again – see Table 2. In line with the results above, correlations also increase with more restrictive frequency filters. This suggests that prediction of the gaze position will be more accurate while the mouse is in motion.

Table 2. Correlations of pixel positions of mouse cursor and eye gaze while the mouse is being moved, depending on the frequency of mouse usage

	Frequency of mouse moves	Correlation $r_{eye_{vs}mouse}$	N	Regression model constant	weight	sig.
vertical	baseline	.250	89739	345.133	.228	.000*
	all; weighted by frequency	.752	59857	137.826	.723	.000*
	$frequency > 25\%$	.746	36202	142.850	.725	.000*
	$frequency > 50\%$	.751	21401	139.159	.701	.000*
	$frequency > 75\%$	.777	21270	153.598	.696	.000*
horizontal	baseline	.101	89739	577.499	.75	.000*
	all; weighted by frequency	.521	59857	252.650	.596	.000*
	$frequency > 25\%$	.513	36202	265.610	.579	.000*
	$frequency > 50\%$	.551	21401	202.246	.682	.000*
	$frequency > 75\%$	.580	21270	170.052	.764	.000*

Table 3. Frequency of element hovered by mouse matches element currently being looked at based on frequency of mouse moves – overall and while mouse being moved

Frequency level of mouse moves	overall			filter: while mouse moved		
	Frequency: match	Standard Deviation	N	Frequency: match	Standard Deviation	N
0%-25%	21,00%	.404	24331	59,00%	.493	12555
25%-50%	51,00%	.500	9461	60,00%	.490	8512
50%-75%	70,00%	.458	3478	82,00%	.387	3314
75%-100%	72,00%	.451	13921	72,00%	.449	13844
Total	26,00%	.441	51191	65,00%	.477	38225

H1.c: *Do gaze and mouse point at the same paragraph on the screen?* In general, the element pointed at with the mouse coincides with the paragraph looked at in 26% of the cases. When limiting the analysis to cases where people use the mouse a lot, this rises up to 72% (see Table 3). Again, more restrictive frequency filters increase the likelihood that the paragraphs are the same.

H1.d: *Are H1.c predictions better while the mouse is in motion?* In line with H1.b results, predicting which paragraph has been looked at is easier when the mouse is in motion. In particular, for users that do not use the mouse a lot (frequency level 0% − 25%), prediction increases strongly (compare columns "overall" and "filter: while mouse moved" in Table 3).

H1.e: *If vertical predictions are better, should we select vertical moves rather than just frequent moves in any direction?* While in all cases the predictions were better than the baseline and followed the same trends as the previous results (e.g., in motion better than not in motion), frequency of vertical movements did not improve prediction over the levels observed for general frequency of mouse movements (e.g., $r = .397$ for vertical moves vs. $r = .528$ for general moves).

H2.a-c: *When the mouse is actively used, users are likely to look at the region the mouse is positioned.* The mean distance of mouse and eye position reduces to less than 50% when users are clicking, selecting text, or when the mouse is moving (see Tables 4 and 5). Again, the horizontal correlation is lower than the vertical. This is in particular true for text selection activities, where users seem to read left to right, but keep the mouse at one end of the selected text. However, this improvement of prediction comes at the expense of very limited coverage. In short, when mouse actions occur, predictions will be good, but clicks, selections and movements occur only for a fraction of the total observation time.

H3, H4, H5: While we could not establish statistically significant support for these hypotheses, this may partly be due to the type of task we set. For

Table 4. Mean distances in pixels between mouse cursor and eye gaze for selected types of interactions

		N	mean distance	Std. Error	F	Sig
click	no	86838	383.9	.746	796.5	.000*
	yes	2901	163.4	7.77		
select	no	89706	382.0	.746	26.31	.000*
	yes	33	136.3	47.8		
in move	no	29882	404.7	.768	7063.5	.000*
	yes	59857	222.1	2.033		

Table 5. Regression models for user interactions

	event filter	Correlation $r_{eye_{vs}mouse}$	N	Regression model constant	weight	sig.
vertical	baseline	.250	89739	345.133	.228	.000*
	click	.873	2901	83.245	.820	.000*
	select	.986	33	64.388	.826	.000*
	in move	.672	59857	161.966	.659	.000*
horizontal	baseline	.101	89739	577.499	.075	.000*
	click	.808	2901	98.057	.774	.000*
	select	.494	33	334.191	.579	.004*
	in move	.436	59857	330.684	.435	.000*

instance, we observed only a limited number of scrolling-up events (H4) and very few instances of small increment scrolling (H5). The analysis for relative areas on the screen (e.g., top, middle, bottom) seems to be invalidated by the fact that almost everybody gazed at the middle part of the screen for the majority of time (H3) (see Fig. 2); this finding (i.e. users tend to scroll down just for a few lines while they are reading to keep the currently read item at the center of the screen), however, is in itself also quite useful in establishing a prediction algorithm as we see later.

3   From Hypotheses to Algorithm

3.1   General Structure of the Algorithm

Based on the findings outlined in the previous section, an algorithm was developed to calculate the extent to which paragraphs (or more generally: text fragments) of a page have been read. The main premise of the algorithm is the "splitting" of the time spent reading between the items visible at that time. Therefore each page view is split into "scroll windows", i.e. the time window where the visible items and their relative position on the screen remain constant (identified as the time spans between load, scroll or resize events).

For each such scroll window, the algorithm first calculates the "estimated time spent reading" (T_E). This is based on the measured "available" duration of the

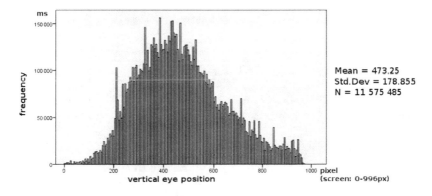

Fig. 2. Histogram of vertical eye position within the screen

scroll window (T_A), but also takes into consideration interaction data that may provide additional information. For instance, if users usually exhibit considerable mouse activity, and then suddenly stop interacting, it is possible that they have not been continuously reading. The motivation behind the introduction of T_E is the derivation of a time measure that potentially more accurately represents the *real* time that users spent reading during a scroll window.

To get the time spent reading for each visible fragment ($\overrightarrow{TSR}$), T_E is split among the visible page fragments by multiplying it with a vector defining the percentage of time that should be assigned to each fragment. This vector is a weighted average of a number of normalized distributions of time ($\overrightarrow{TD_N}$) created by different modifier functions (hereforth referred to as "modifiers"), each focusing on a different aspect, for instance, the number of words in the different paragraphs, the number of interactions, the relative position of the paragraph within the screen, etc (see section 3.2). Each modifier receives as input the interaction data of the scroll window, and provides the following output values:

- w_{INT}: The internal weight of the modifier, which provides an indication of the modifier's relative significance for a given scroll window. For instance, a modifier based on text selections would return a w_{INT} of zero if no selections were made during a scroll window, as it can not provide any predictions.
- $\overrightarrow{TD_N}$: The modifier's normalized distribution of time over the text fragments (partially or entirely) visible during the scroll window. The result is a vector of weights for each such fragment.
- $T_\%$: The modifier's estimated percentage of the total available time (T_A) the user spent reading in a scroll window.
- w_{TIME}: A weight to be used in association with $T_\%$. Similar to the internal weight for the time distribution this value is the internal weight for the estimation on the percentage of time a user spent reading.

Further to the above, each modifier has an "external weight" (w_{EXT}), which denotes the relative significance of a modifier over others. A modifier based on text selections for instance provides stronger indicators of reading behavior than one based on fragment visibility.

Based on the above, T_E is defined as follows:

$$T_E = T_A \cdot \frac{\sum_{i=1}^{N_M} w_{EXT_i} \cdot T_{\%_i} \cdot w_{TIME_i}}{\sum_{i=1}^{N_M} w_{EXT_i} \cdot w_{TIME_i}}$$

where N_M is the total number of modifiers applied. The final algorithm can then be described as follows:

$$\overrightarrow{TSR} = T_E \cdot \frac{\sum_{i=1}^{N_M} w_{EXT_i} \cdot w_{INT_i} \cdot \overrightarrow{TD_{N_i}}}{\sum_{i=1}^{N_M} w_{EXT_i} \cdot w_{INT_i}}$$

where $\overrightarrow{TSR}$ is the column vector containing the calculated time spent reading for each visible text fragment.

The external weight of the modifiers is the only part of the algorithm that is not directly derived from user interaction. Our first experiments had already shown which interactions should get stronger weights (e.g., text selections). Combining these results with the more recent findings (specifically with the identified strength of the correlation for confirmed hypotheses), allowed us to arrive at a set of weights that were used to derive the results described in section 4. Note that we do not consider these weights to be final or absolute. We expect that adjustments may be needed to cater for specific characteristics of the reading context. Nevertheless, there are two points that merit attention: (a) the derived weights appear to have only little sensitivity over the type of text being read; and, (b) even in a "worst case" scenario with all weights set to 1 (equivalent to no knowledge of the expressiveness of different interaction patterns) the algorithm still classified 73.3% of the paragraphs correctly (92.9% with a maximum error of 1 level); please refer to Section 4 for a discussion of these percentages.

3.2   The Weight Modifiers

Currently there are six implemented modifiers focusing on different aspects of the interaction data. Due to lack of space we provide here only a brief outline of each modifier, along with its base hypotheses and external weight:

M_{Select}: This modifier is based on text tracing, i.e., selecting portions of text while reading [16], which is a strong indicator of current reading. In all our experiments it was both the strongest indicator, but also the least frequent type of interaction. (H2.c, $w_{EXT} = 150$)

M_{Click}: Based on mouse clicks, which, like text selections, are a strong indicator of current reading. If users click on fragments / paragraphs, this modifier splits the available time among them. (H2.b, $w_{EXT} = 70$)

M_{Move}: Based on the users' tendency to move their mouse while reading. This modifier sets weights according to the time the mouse cursor has been moved above a fragment. The more users tend to move their mouse, the stronger the weight of this modifier. (H1.a-d and particular H1.c-d, $w_{EXT} = 45$)

$M_{MousePositions}$: Even if the mouse is not moved the position of the cursor may be used to identify the area of interest. This modifier considers the placement of the mouse over a fragment, as well as its placement in at a position that falls within the vertical constraints of the fragment (e.g., in the white-space area next to the text). (H1.e, $w_{EXT} = 45$)

$M_{ScreenAreas}$: Even if there are only few interactions we may make further assumptions on what has been read. Most people prefer to read in the center of the screen, so if the page is long enough that a user could scroll up or down (the first and last paragraphs of a page definitely have to be read while on top/bottom of the screen), this modifier puts its weight on the centered 80% of the page. A more fine-grained distribution over different parts of the screen or additional knowledge on the user's preferred reading area might improve a future version of this modifier. (adjusted H3 as per Fig. 2, $w_{EXT} = 5$)

$M_{Visibility}$: The simplest modifier, this one just splits the time among all visible paragraphs based on the number of words they contain. ($w_{EXT} = 1$)

Table 6. Classification distance of para- graphs in the Go course

Dist.	# Par.	%	Cumulative %
0	746	78.7%	78.7%
1	143	15.1%	93.8%
2	47	5.0%	98.7%
3	12	1.3%	100.0%
Total	948	100.0%	

Table 7. Classification distance of para- graphs in Questions page

Dist.	# Par.	%	Cumulative %
0	41	85.4%	85.4%
1	3	6.3%	91.7%
2	2	4.2%	95.8%
3	2	4.2%	100.0%
Total	48	100.0%	

Table 8. Classification of paragraphs split by the actual reading level (L0-3) – context: Go course

L0	# Par.	%	L1	# Par.	%	L2	# Par.	%	L3	# Par.	%
L0	596	89.1%	L0	23	26.7%	L0	7	8.0%	L0	0	.0%
L1	46	6.9%	**L1**	34	39.5%	L1	15	17.2%	L1	14	13.2%
L2	15	2.2%	L2	18	20.9%	**L2**	43	49.4%	L2	19	17.9%
L3	12	1.8%	L3	11	12.8%	L3	22	25.3%	**L3**	73	68.9%
Total	669	100.0%	Total	86	100.0%	Total	87	100.0%	Total	106	100.0%

4   Results

In order to evaluate our algorithm we measured the reading speed of each user (rate of words per minute). We used that rate, along with the number of words in each paragraph, to estimate the time the user would require for reading it ($T_{p_{req}}$). We then used that in conjunction with the time the user spent on the paragraph, as per the algorithm's predictions ($T_{p_{pred}}$), to define four "levels" of reading for paragraphs:

- level 0 (paragraph skipped): $T_{p_{pred}} < 0.3 \cdot T_{p_{req}}$
- level 1 (paragraph glanced at): $0.3 \cdot T_{p_{req}} \leq T_{p_{pred}} < 0.7 \cdot T_{p_{req}}$
- level 2 (paragraph read): $0.7 \cdot T_{p_{req}} \leq T_{p_{pred}} < 1.3 \cdot T_{p_{req}}$
- level 3 (paragraph read thoroughly): $1.3 \cdot T_{p_{req}} \leq T_{p_{pred}}$

The user's fixations have been used to calculate the baseline reading level our algorithm should be compared against. Table 6 shows the absolute distances between the calculated reading level and the baseline from the eye tracking data. In 78.7% of all cases the algorithm was able to classify the paragraph correctly. However, not only the exact matches, but also the difference between the baseline category and the level selected is important. In 93.8% of all cases this distance is only 0 or 1.

Table 8 shows in more detail how paragraphs of each level have been categorized by the algorithm. The highest precision was reached for paragraphs that have been skipped or read thoroughly. However, even for the intermediate levels the algorithm classified most paragraphs correctly.

The focus of our experiment was to test the algorithm in the context of reading learning materials. Nevertheless, it is worth noting that the algorithm performs comparably well in the other contexts tested. For example, on pages where users answered questions (a task that inherently requires more interaction), the algorithm performed even better than in the case of the Go course (see Table 7). However, we concentrate on the learning scenario where it is more difficult to get valid information due to reduced requirements for interaction.

5   Conclusions and Ongoing Work

This paper has demonstrated that it is possible to predict, with satisfactory precision, the users' reading behavior on the basis of client-side interaction. In our experiments, users visited all pages of provided hypertext material. A traditional AHS might, thus, assume everything has been read. In contrast, using the proposed approach, we were able to determine that 70% of the paragraphs were not read, and users focused on certain paragraphs instead of reading entire pages. Our experiment has shown that the algorithm, using mouse and keyboard events, can correctly identify a paragraph's "reading level" in 78.7% of all cases (and in 93.8% of the cases calculate the correct level ± 1).

The algorithm, in its current form, has weaknesses that need to be addressed. To start with, it is geared towards pages that contain one main column of text. While this may be typical for learning content, enhancements are required before the algorithm can satisfactorily handle multi-column page content. A related question is how well the algorithm might perform in mobile settings, with different screen factors (and, therefore, different amounts of text visible at a time) and potentially different interaction patterns (brought forth by the screen factor, or by alternative input techniques available). Another area that requires further work is the establishment of the effects of external modifier weights in different reading contexts (e.g., with less text visible at a time, the visible part of a page may be a stronger indicator on what is currently being read).

Among the strengths of this algorithm is its extensibility. For example, additional input devices may be easily integrated through client-side "drivers" and the introduction of corresponding modifiers (e.g. a webcam, eye tracking, etc.). The same is true for interaction patterns that may be established as evidence for reading behavior in the future.

Further to the above, and specifically in the domain of learning, we intend to test the effects of having access to predictions of reading behavior on learner models and their use in adaptive educational hypermedia systems. Our next experiment will use the presented algorithm to make predictions on which questions relating to course content a learner is likely to be able to answer, based on what that learner has (been predicted to have) read from that content.

Finally, as soon as the algorithm has matured and been shown to be of general applicability, we intend to make the implementation (along with the accompanying JavaScript library for monitoring) publicly available.

Acknowledgments. The work reported in this paper is partially funded by the "Adaptive Support for Collaborative E-Learning" (ASCOLLA) project, supported by the Austrian Science Fund (FWF; project number P20260-N15).

References

1. Hofmann, K., Reed, C., Holz, H.: Unobtrusive Data Collection for Web-Based Social Navigation. In: Workshop on the Social Navigation and Community based Adaptation Technologies (2006)
2. Stephanidis, C., Paramythis, A., Karagiannidis, C., Savidis, A.: Supporting Interface Adaptation: The AVANTI Web-Browser. In: Stephanidis, C., Carbonell, N. (eds.) Proc. of the 3rd ERCIM Workshop "User Interfaces for All" (1997)
3. Goecks, J., Shavlik, J.W.: Learning Users' Interests by Unobtrusively Observing Their Normal Behavior. In: Int. Conference on Intelligent User Interfaces - Proc. of the 5th Int. Conference on Intelligent User Interfaces, pp. 129–132 (2000)
4. Spada, D., Sánchez-Montañés, M.A., Paredes, P., Carro, R.M.: Towards Inferring Sequential-Global Dimension of Learning Styles from Mouse Movement Patterns. In: Nejdl, W., Kay, J., Pu, P., Herder, E. (eds.) AH 2008. LNCS, vol. 5149, pp. 337–340. Springer, Heidelberg (2008)
5. Cha, H.J., Kim, Y.S., Park, S.-H., Yoon, T.-b., Jung, Y.M., Lee, J.-H.: Learning Styles Diagnosis Based on User Interface Behaviors for the Customization of Learning Interfaces in an Intelligent Tutoring System. In: Ikeda, M., Ashley, K.D., Chan, T.-W. (eds.) ITS 2006. LNCS, vol. 4053, pp. 513–524. Springer, Heidelberg (2006)
6. Claypool, M., Le, P., Wased, M., Brown, D.: Implicit interest indicators. In: Intelligent User Interfaces, pp. 33–40 (2001)
7. Hauger, D.: Using Asynchronous Client-Side User Monitoring to Enhance User Modeling in Adaptive E-Learning Systems. In: Houben, G.-J., McCalla, G., Pianesi, F., Zancanaro, M. (eds.) UMAP 2009. LNCS, vol. 5535. Springer, Heidelberg (2009)
8. Hauger, L.D., Van Velsen, L.: Analyzing Client-Side Interactions to Determine Reading Behavior. In: Adaptivity and User Modeling in Interactive Systems, ABIS 2009, Darmstadt, Germany, pp. 11–16 (2009)
9. Ullrich, C., Melis, E.: The Poor Man's Eyetracker Tool of ActiveMath. In: Proceedings of the World Conference on E-Learning in Corporate, Government, Healthcare, and Higher Education (eLearn 2002), Canada, vol. 4, pp. 2313–2316 (2002)
10. Chen, M.C., Anderson, J.R., Sohn, M.H.: What can a mouse cursor tell us more?: correlation of eye/mouse movements on web browsing. In: CHI 2001: CHI 2001 Ext. Abstracts on Human Factors in Computing Systems, pp. 281–282. ACM, New York (2001)
11. Chee, D.S.L., Khoo, C.S.: Users' Mouse/Cursor Movements in Two Web-Based Library Catalog Interfaces. In: Khalid, H., Helander, M., Yeo, A. (eds.) Work with Computing Systems, pp. 640–645. Damai Sciences, Kuala Lumpur (2004)
12. Rodden, K., Fu, X., Aula, A., Spiro, I.: Eye-mouse coordination patterns on web search results pages. In: CHI 2008: CHI 2008 Extended Abstracts on Human Factors in Computing Systems, pp. 2997–3002. ACM, New York (2008)
13. Mueller, F., Lockerd, A.: Cheese: tracking mouse movement activity on websites, a tool for user modeling. In: CHI 2001: CHI 2001 Extended Abstracts on Human Factors in Computing Systems, pp. 279–280. ACM, New York (2001)
14. Liu, C.C., Chung, C.W.: Detecting Mouse Movement with Repeated Visit Patterns for Retrieving Noticed Knowledge Components on Web Pages. IEICE - Transactions on Information and Systems E90-D, 1687–1696 (2007)
15. Hauger, D., Paramythis, A., Weibelzahl, S.: Your Browser is Watching You: Dynamically Deducing User Gaze from Interaction Data. In: De Bra, P., Kobsa, A., Chin, D. (eds.) UMAP 2010. LNCS, vol. 6075, pp. 10–12. Springer, Heidelberg (2010)
16. Hijikata, Y.: Implicit user profiling for on demand relevance feedback. In: IUI 2004: Proceedings of the 9th International Conference on Intelligent User Interfaces, pp. 198–205. ACM, New York (2004)

A User Interface
for Semantic Competence Profiles

Martin Hochmeister and Johannes Daxböck

Electronic Commerce Group, Vienna University of Technology
Favoritenstraße 9-11/188-4, 1040 Vienna, Austria
martin.hochmeister@ec.tuwien.ac.at,
johannes.daxboeck@student.tuwien.ac.at

Abstract. Competence management systems are increasingly based on ontologies representing competences within a certain domain. Most of these systems represent a user's competence profile by means of an ontological structure. Such semantic competence profiles, often structured as a hierarchy of competences, are difficult to navigate for self-assessment purposes. The more competences a user profile holds, the more challenging the comprehensive presentation of profile data is. In this paper, we present an integrated user interface that supports users during competence self-assessment and facilitates a clear presentation of their semantic competence profiles. For evaluation, we conducted a usability study with 19 students at university. The results show that users were mostly satisfied with the usability of the interface that also represents a promising approach for efficient competence self-assessment.

Keywords: User Interface, User Profile, Semantic Competence Profile, Profile Editing, Ontology.

1 Introduction

Today, competence management systems (CMSs) play an important role in corporate efforts to ensure the achievement of strategic goals and thus gain sustainable competitive advantage. The major task of a CMS is the provision of information describing an individual's competences. This information is used to support tasks like expert finding or workforce planning [8]. A user's competence information is also used for personalization. For instance, in learning management, recommendations for future learning activities are personalized based on a user's competences.

In recent years, CMSs adopted competence ontologies for the representation of competences [4] [18]. Such an ontology consists of competence concepts and the relations between them. Liao et al. [12] use competence ontologies to empower a knowledge-based system to effectively find individuals to accomplish a certain business task. Individuals are represented with competence profiles that contain sets of instances from the underlying competence ontology. Since competences are hierarchically structured, the representation with ontologies seems

Joseph A. Konstan et al. (Eds.): UMAP 2011, LNCS 6787, pp. 159–170, 2011.

very suitable. Due to the relations between competences, it is possible to infer additional knowledge about competences. For instance, Sieg et al. [16] use additional knowledge gained from ontological reasoning to improve web search personalization. In the following, we address a competence profile based on a competence ontology as a semantic competence profile.

To gain user acceptance for a CMS, it is necessary to leave the ultimate control of profiles to the users [13]. Even though competences may be derived implicitly, the users should be able to maintain them. A review of CMSs [8] reports that employees are increasingly supplied with self-service portals to self-assess competences.

Besides competence management, Bull and Kay [3] describe a similar trend in opening profiles to users in the field of intelligent tutoring systems. Giving learners greater control over their learner models may aid learning by supporting the reflection of competences and the planning of future educational activities. There is a need for tools allowing individuals to maintain their competence profiles.

Competence ontologies are mostly very large in both breath and depth. The navigation through such ontologies as well as the presentation of semantic competence profiles are major challenges in the design of user interfaces [5] [1]. As for navigation, a conventional tree view of concepts is very cumbersome to handle. A user starts at the top of the tree and navigates to the bottom of it. If this navigation leads to a path the user is not interested in, the user must go back all the way to the starting point. Regarding the presentation of a competence profile, users may quickly lose their sense of the big picture as more concepts are available in their profile. In this paper, we address the following two questions in order to make competence self-assessment easier:

1. How can we support a user in navigating a competence ontology, selecting concepts and assigning values to these concepts?
2. How can we achieve a useful competence profile presentation for the users?

In answering these questions, we propose a novel user interface that consists of (1) a navigation and (2) a presentation component. The navigation component helps users to easily select concepts from a competence ontology, to assign them a competence score and finally to store the competence profile to the database. The presentation component aims to provide a comprehensive view of competences as well as several options to adapt this view to personal preferences.

Regarding the research method, we adhere to the constructive approach and started out with developing a prototype by means of an iterative design process. We compiled various user interface elements from literature and reviewed their usability. For evaluation, we set up a usability study with 19 master students enrolled in a computer science program at university. Within a tutorial on knowledge management, students were asked to assess their competences in the field of internet technologies by using the proposed interface. We focused mainly on the level of user satisfaction by means of a quantitative feedback. However, there was room for qualitative feedback as well. We logged all user interactions in order to interpret user behavior and analyze problems that might occur during user testing.

This research is part of a larger project that visions a system which recommends courses to students based on their competence profile. Students may also benefit from finding other students with the same interests for building learner groups. The integration of this system with the university's career platform may bring further value for both students and potential employers.

The remainder of this paper is organized as follows. The next section discusses related work concerning ontology navigation and approaches how to present profile data. Section 3 describes the components that build up the prototype system and introduce the structure of the competence ontology. In Section 4 and 5 we propose the integrated user interface for competence self-assessment. The setup of the usability study as well as the results are presented in Section 6. We conclude in Section 7 and come up with ideas for future work.

2   Related Work

A survey regarding ontology visualization shows that ontologies are predominantly structured as hierarchies [11]. However, in many domains ontologies tend to be quite large and complex, which makes them difficult to explore and present [17].

The *Visual Information Seeking Mantra* tackles the problem of representing large data in three steps including overview first, then zoom and filter and show details-on-demand [15]. When dealing with large unknown data, the concept of *Information Scents* [14] and its application in the form of scented widgets [19] improves traditional user interface elements. Information scents provide users with more context and help them to accomplish tasks more efficent. Crowder et al. [5] make use of content dependent filtering, an autocompletion text box and partial segments using drop-down lists for ontology navigation.

With regards to the cognitive support for ontology navigation, d'Entremont and Storey [6] suggest principles to provide overview and context, reduce the complexity, indicate points of interest and support incremental exploration. They further introduce a plugin for the ontology editor Protégé using these principles in providing *Visual Orientation Cues* for user relevant content. The user interface Jambalaya [17], also based on Protégé, employs the concept of nested interchangeable views to allow a user to explore multiple perspectives of information at different levels of abstraction.

Based on the reviewed principles, Bakalov et al. [1] present a rich-interaction interface enabling users to inspect and alter their user profiles. The interface provides an overview of terms representing user interests, allows for zooming/filtering and displays additional term information like a term's relationship with other terms.

To the best of our knowledge, none of the reviewed approaches support an ontology navigation that allows users to reflect and compare values between

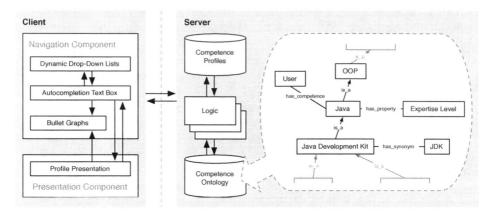

Fig. 1. System architecture and competence ontology

several ontology concepts. They also do not facilitate a clear procedure to assign values to ontology concepts.

3   System Architecture

Figure 1 shows the architecture of our prototypical implementation that is based on a three-tier model commonly used for web applications. We iteratively developed the user interface elements into more advanced ones for ontology navigation, competence self-assessment and competence profile presentation. For navigation, competence concepts are retrieved from the ontology on demand. The competence ontology may grow without affecting the interface's performance. For this retrieval task, AJAX-methods effectively decrease user waiting time and thus increase efficiency. Once users assign competences to their profiles, the whole profile is transferred to the server for data storage. Dorn and Hochmeister [7] introduce a competence ontology as the foundation for their competence mining approach. We use this ontology as a starting point for the ontology design. The ontology represents competence concepts within the domain of internet technologies structured in a hierarchical order. The more general/specific a competence concept is, the higher/lower its place in the hierarchy is. In order to support the assessment of competences, ontology concepts are enhances with a property that holds a value reflecting the expertise level of a competence.

The right side of Figure 1 depicts a snippet of the final competence ontology. An ontology instance describes a user who is competent in one or more topics, each with a certain level of expertise. Our ontology design adheres to the overlay model presented by Brusilovsky and Millan [2], where a user's knowledge is represented as a subset of a domain model. After modification, the competence ontology holds 422 competences and 224 synonyms. The synonyms are used for the autocompletion feature that supports ontology navigation as described in the next section.

4   Navigation Component

In this section, we assemble the elements that allow users (1) to navigate through the competence ontology in order to find a desired competence concept and (2) to assign a value to a selected competence representing the user's expertise level.

4.1   Versatile Ontology Navigation

Crowder et al. [5] present autocompletion text boxes and interconnected drop-down lists as means for ontology navigation. We take these user interface elements as a starting point for our work.

Once a user enters a word in the autocompletion text box, the underlying ontology is queried for concepts that match the user's input at best. The query string will be enhanced with wildcards and the returned result set is further expanded with its concepts children [5]. The resulting list is directly displayed below the text box. We extended the result list with competence values assigned by the user. The left side of Figure 2 shows an example of the autocompletion text box. Eventually, the user selects the desired competence from the list and is able to modify its value. Conventional drop-down lists show all concepts available. This is cumbersome for navigation purpose since they do not maintain the overview of hierarchy. To solve this, interconnected drop-down lists limit the

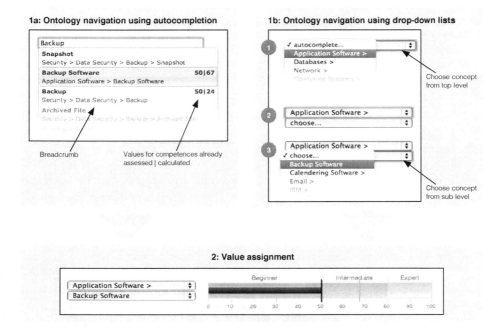

Fig. 2. Two ways of competence selection leading to value assignment

number of elements to the number of hierarchy levels. When a user selects a competence from the list, another drop-down list will pop up including all concepts from the selected competence above as illustrated on the right side of Figure 2. Selecting the option *choose...* causes the lower drop-down lists to disappear.

In order to offer the user a versatile ontology navigation, we combine the autocompletion text box with interconnected drop-down lists. According to Ernst et al. [9], a top-down approach especially helps users unfamiliar with the ontology. On the other hand, advanced users might directly dig into the ontology by selecting a particular concept they assume or even know to exist. Using the combined approach, users can choose their preferred way to explore the ontology. The system starts with a drop-down list of top level ontology concepts shown in Figure 2. The autocompletion text box may be activated by choosing the item *autocomplete...* in the drop-down list, which is then replaced by an autocompletion text box. The drop-down list can be restored by double-clicking on the autocompletion text box. After selecting a competence in the autocompletion text box, the navigation component switches back to the interconnected drop-down lists providing a competence's full path to the root of the hierarchy. The user interface presents the current value of the selected competence as shown in the bottom part of Figure 2. For the presentation and modification of competence values, we utilize a graphical element called bullet graph introduced in the next section.

4.2   Assigning Values to Competences

During self-assessment, users assign numeric values between 0 and 100 points to selected competences. To illustrate this task, we introduce an interface element that is based on bullet graphs [10]. Originally, a bullet graph consists of a content box, which represents a qualitative scale, a quantitative scale and a bar illustrating a value. Additionally, a cross bar may indicate a comparative value to qualify the value shown by the bar element.

A bullet graph is usually not intended to be interactive. Thus, we build up an interactive bullet graph using widget elements that allows users to drag the value bar to a desired level of expertise. Furthermore, we add labels to describe the fields of the qualitative scale. The comparative value can be used for different purposes, for instance, to represent supervisors' opinions about the expertise level of their employees. Figure 3 shows the bullet graph including our modifications.

5   Presentation Component

To display a user's competence profile, we introduce a table including competences, their values and the relation amongst them. Since our ontology represents only hierarchical relations, we make use of an hierarchical approach for profile presentation using a HTML table element as a base. Figure 4 illustrates the presentation of a user's competence profile. We proceed by incorporating the ideas

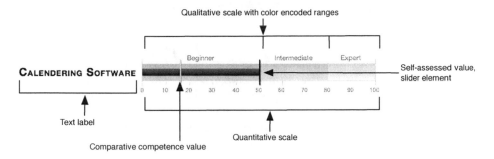

Fig. 3. Adapted bullet graph for competence self-assessment

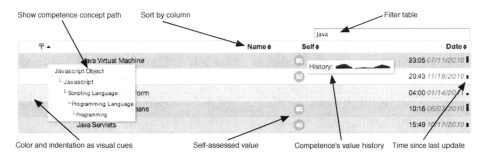

Fig. 4. A user's competence profile table

of the visual information seeking mantra by Shneiderman [15] as well as information scented widgets [19]. We also consider the principles of cognitive support for ontology navigation by means of visual cues [6]. By using hierarchical visual cues, we adapt the intensity of background color in each table row according to how deep a concept is located in the ontology. A tooltip at the left border of each row shows the path in the ontology leading to the concept in reverse order. For the same purpose, we indent the competence labels. In order to distinguish two succeeding items on the same level but with different top levels, we separate the respective two rows with a thicker grey line. Competence values are represented by circled numbers. When moving the mouse over a competence value, a graphical tooltip visualizes how the value changed over time by means of a filled line chart. The last column of the profile table shows the date of the last modification together with a bar chart representing the time passed since the last update. Users can personalize their competence profile table with filtering and sorting options. A filter text box allows users to filter competences towards a string in a concept's full path represented by this row. The users can also sort each column to their personal preferences.

The components for navigation and presentation are displayed within the same view. This means, the user can search for competences, assign competence values and refer to the competence profile at the same time. The functionalities of both components are linked together as well. A click on the profile table causes the navigation component to refresh and to show the selected competence.

6 Evaluation

In order to evaluate usefulness and usability of the proposed user interface, we conducted a usability study with students at university. When referring to usability, we measure user satisfaction and investigate how efficient users may perform competence self-assessment using the interface. The study had a duration of 22 days and took place in a knowledge management course at university. 19 master students of computer science participated in the study. In order to ensure easy access to the user interface, we published the service on the web. The students were free to access the user interface as often and as long as they wanted.

We asked the students to self-assess their competences by navigating through the competence ontology, selecting desired competences and assign values to these competences. We provided a short user guide describing the main features of the interface, but did not recommend strategies on how to use it.

At the end of the study, the students had to fill out a questionnaire that primarily focused on the measurement of usefulness and user satisfaction. By means of the users' feedbacks we aimed to interpret the following questions.

1. How satisfied are users with navigating the competence ontology and the selection of competences?
2. How useful is the presentation of self-assessments based on bullet graphs that show values on two different scales?
3. How useful is the presentation of a user's profile based on the profile table that displays competence values as well as the relations amongst competences?
4. How useful are the sorting and filter functions to adapt a user's competence profile?

Students were also asked to give their opinion about likes and dislikes of the user interface. The interpretation of these feedbacks may reveal further details on how the navigation and presentation of competences can be improved.

6.1 Results and Findings

During the study, users self-assessed 1267 competences. Figure 5 shows the results regarding the quantitative part of the questionnaire. A significant majority was mostly satisfied with the interface for ontology navigation and perceived the bullet graph as useful to specify a competence's expertise level. As for the competence profile table, the users were predominantly convinced of its usefulness and have used the sorting and filtering functions to adapt the profile table to their preferences. The user opinions mainly confirm the results shown in Figure 5. Some said that the visual navigation cues in the profile table were not clear to them. Others appreciated the extensive use of AJAX for navigation and profile presentation.

Figure 6 illustrates the users' competence self-assessments on a timeline. We aggregated the data in time clusters to better show the total number of assessed

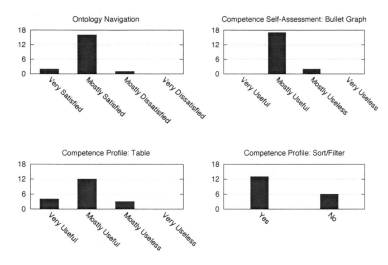

Fig. 5. Results regarding usability and usefulness

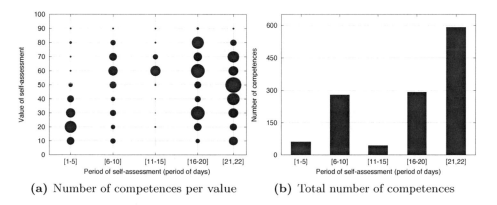

(a) Number of competences per value   (b) Total number of competences

Fig. 6. Analysing log data to measure efficiency

competences. The size of the dots in Figure 6a represents the number of competences related to a certain expertise level. Figure 6a shows that users did not use minimum or maximum values for self-assessment. We expected that users would not assign minimum values since they were not asked to declare competences they do not possess. As for the maximum values, Figure 6a confirms the well-known phenomenon that experts seldom assign maximum expertise scores to themselves. It is assumed, experts know better than less competent people that there might be something they do not know.

Figure 6a as well as Figure 6b show that the number of assessed competences increases over the course of the study. Is this evidence strong enough to prove the interface to be an efficient support for self-assessment?

We could interpret the rise of competence assessments as an indication that the more competences are assessed by users, the faster the self-assessments were performed. This interpretation may be supported by the fact that only one task was given to the users at the beginning of the study. From this point on, the users were free to undertake self-assessment in the given time period and were not asked for further tasks.

We can rule out the possible bias that students assessed more competences in favor of getting better marks since students were not required to finish the task with a profile holding a certain number of competences. There certainly is a shortcoming in our study design. Students might have been curious in the first place about how the interface is built up and just started to try it out. While attending other courses students may stick to a plan on when to accomplish tasks for particular courses. This plan could lead to a larger workload in the end of some courses assuming that all courses started at the same time. This might have biased our results. Another limitation of this study is that its participants are to some extent familiar with the domain and the notion of ontologies. We plan to conduct the next user study with students from different study programs to possibly gain more reliable results.

Assuming that these biases did not remarkably affect the results, we could interpret that the proposed user interface helps to maintain the overview of competences since this would definitely be a challenge the more competences are assessed. However, for the current stage of our research, it is not totally clear if the interface can be proved as efficient support for self-assessment. We have to consider this issue for a future user study.

7 Conclusion and Future Work

Based on the problem that large competence ontologies are difficult to navigate for self-assessment, we propose an integrated user interface that allows users to easily find competences by various navigation options. In order to assign values to competences, we make use of bullet graphs, which offer a quantitative as well as a qualitative scale to qualify competence scores. We further introduce a competence profile table to display assessed competences and their relations to adjacent competences. The proposed components for navigating and presenting competence profiles are functionally linked together, which allows users to approach competence self-assessment in various ways.

We conducted a usability study with 19 master students enrolled in a computer science program. The results show that the users were mostly satisfied with navigating the competence ontology. They perceived the bullet graph for competence assessment as useful and were satisfied with the presentation of competences and its options to adapt it to personal preferences.

We could not fully prove if the proposed user interface provides efficient competence self-assessment. Efficient means that the interface speeds up the process of self-assessment. Probable biases affecting the results may have been too dominant for a solid claim. However, the results are promising under certain assumptions and motivate the further investigation of proper evaluation methods to measure efficiency.

Regarding future work, we will evaluate the use of a score propagation mechanism to recommend values for competences not scored yet based on competences already assessed by the user. This may increase the efficiency of the self-assessment procedure. Introducing tool tips, little information chunks displayed on mouseover, may provide a more detailed competence description on demand. This was an argued desire from some of the participants. Another idea considers the use of a query language applied in the autocompletion text box. For instance, a user could query *::recommended* competences gained from score propagation mentioned before.

Acknowledgments. This research is part of the project SeCoMine, which calculates users' competence scores based on their contributions and social interactions in online communities. SeCoMine is fully funded by the Österreichische Forschungsförderungsgesellschaft mbH (FFG) under the grant number 826459.

References

1. Bakalov, F., König-Ries, B., Nauerz, A., Welsch, M.: Introspectiveviews: An interface for scrutinizing semantic user models. User Modeling, Adaptation, and Personalization, 219–230 (2010)
2. Brusilovsky, P., Millán, E.: User models for adaptive hypermedia and adaptive educational systems. The Adaptive Web, 3–53 (2007)
3. Bull, S., Kay, J.: Open learner models. Advances in Intelligent Tutoring Systems, 301–322 (2010)
4. Colucci, S., Di Noia, T., Di Sciascio, E., Donini, F., Ragone, A.: Measuring core competencies in a clustered network of knowledge. In: Knowledge Management: Innovation, Technology and Cultures: Proceedings of the 2007 International Conference on Knowledge Management, Vienna, Austria, August 27-28, p. 279. World Scientific Pub. Co. Inc., Singapore (2007)
5. Crowder, R., Wilson, M.L., Fowler, D., Shadbolt, N., Wills, G., Wong, S.: Navigation over a large ontology for industrial web applications. In: International Design Engineering Technical Conferences and Computers and Information in Engineering Conference. DETC2009-86544 (2009), http://eprints.ecs.soton.ac.uk/17918/
6. d'Entremont, T., Storey, M.A.: Using a degree of interest model to facilitate ontology navigation. In: IEEE Symposium on Visual Languages and Human-Centric Computing, VL/HCC 2009, pp. 127–131 (2009)
7. Dorn, J., Hochmeister, M.: Techscreen: Mining competencies in social software. In: The 3rd International Conference on Knowledge Generation, Communication and Management, Orlando, FLA, pp. 115–126 (2009)
8. Draganidis, F., Mentzas, G.: Competency based management: a review of systems and approaches. Information Management & Computer Security 14(1), 51–64 (2006)
9. Ernst, N., Storey, M., Allen, P.: Cognitive support for ontology modeling. International Journal of Human-Computer Studies 62(5), 553–577 (2005)

10. Few, S.: Information dashboard design: the effective visual communication of data. O'Reilly Media, Inc., Sebastopol (2006)
11. Katifori, A., Halatsis, C., Lepouras, G., Vassilakis, C., Giannopoulou, E.: Ontology visualization methods—a survey. ACM Computing Surveys 39(4), 10 (2007)
12. Liao, M., Hinkelmann, K., Abecker, A., Sintek, M.: A competence knowledge base system as part of the organizational memory. In: Puppe, F. (ed.) XPS 1999. LNCS (LNAI), vol. 1570, pp. 125–137. Springer, Heidelberg (1999)
13. Lindgren, R., Henfridsson, O., Schultze, U.: Design principles for competence management systems: a synthesis of an action research study. MIS Quarterly 28(3), 435–472 (2004)
14. Pirolli, P.: Information foraging theory: Adaptive interaction with information. Oxford University Press, USA (2007)
15. Shneiderman, B.: The eyes have it: A task by data type taxonomy for information visualizations. In: Proceedings of the IEEE Symposium on Visual Languages, 1996, pp. 336–343. IEEE, Los Alamitos (2002)
16. Sieg, A., Mobasher, B., Burke, R.: Web search personalization with ontological user profiles. In: Proceedings of the Sixteenth ACM Conference on Conference on Information and Knowledge Management, pp. 525–534. ACM, New York (2007)
17. Storey, M., Musen, M., Silva, J., Best, C., Ernst, N., Fergerson, R., Noy, N.: Jambalaya: Interactive visualization to enhance ontology authoring and knowledge acquisition in protégé. In: Workshop on Interactive Tools for Knowledge Capture (K-CAP 2001), Citeseer (2001)
18. Tarasov, V., Sandkuhl, K., Henoch, B.: Using ontologies for representation of individual and enterprise competence models. In: 2006 International Conference on Research, Innovation and Vision for the Future, Ho Chi Minh City, Vietnam, February 12-16. IEEE Operations Center, Piscataway (2006)
19. Willett, W., Heer, J., Agrawala, M.: Scented widgets: Improving navigation cues with embedded visualizations. IEEE Transactions on Visualization and Computer Graphics, 1129–1136 (2007)

Open Social Student Modeling: Visualizing Student Models with Parallel IntrospectiveViews

I-Han Hsiao[1], Fedor Bakalov[2], Peter Brusilovsky[1], and Birgitta König-Ries[2]

[1] School of Information Sciences, University of Pittsburgh. 135 N. Bellefield Ave.,
Pittsburgh, PA 15260, USA
[2] Institute for Computer Science, University of Jena,
Ernst-Abbe-Platz 2, 07743 Jena, Germany
{ihh4,peterb}@pitt.edu;
{fedor.bakalov,birgitta.koenig-ries}@uni-jena.de

Abstract. This paper explores a social extension of open student modeling that we call open social student modeling. We present a specific implementation of this approach that uses parallel IntrospectiveViews to visualize models representing student progress with QuizJET parameterized self-assessment questions for Java programming. The interface allows visualizing not only the student's own model, but also displaying parallel views on the models of their peers and the cumulative model of the entire class or group. The system was evaluated in a semester-long classroom study. While the use of the system was non-mandatory, the parallel IntrospectiveViews interface caused an increase in all of the usage parameters in comparison to a regular portal-based access, which allowed the student to achieve a higher success rate in answering the questions. The collected data offer some evidence that a combination of traditional personalized guidance with social guidance was more effective than personalized guidance alone.

Keywords: Open User Model, Visualization, Parameterized Self-Assessment, Open Student Model.

1 Introduction

Engaging students with social learning technologies has become an important trend in modern e-learning. One of the biggest challenges is to provide support in the context of social learning, while at the same time allowing students to feel in control. One popular solution to address the issue of control is the so-called open student modeling, an approach that permits the students to observe and reflect on their progress. In particular, visual approaches for open student modeling were explored to provide students with an easy-to-grasp and holistic view of their progress [1-3]. However, most of the open student modeling research focuses on the representation of an individual student -- ignoring the social aspect of learning. In contrast, several social visualization approaches which were explored in an e-learning context [4] focus mainly on student communication and collaboration rather than on the student's progress. Our work attempts to explore the potential of open student modeling and

Joseph A. Konstan et al. (Eds.): UMAP 2011, LNCS 6787, pp. 171–182, 2011.

student progress visualization in the context of modern social e-learning. The goal is to extend the benefits of visualizing the student models from the cognitive aspects to the social aspects of students. We investigate using an *open social student modeling* approach (which offers parallel views of multiple student models) to guide students to the most appropriate learning content. In this paper, we explore a specific implementation of the open social student modeling approach based on IntrospectiveViews [12] visualization. We do so in the context of a semester-long classroom study. In the next section, we provide a short review of the related work on open user modeling and social learning. The system and study design are presented in Section 3. Then we report the evaluation results. Finally, we summarize this work and discuss the future research plan.

2 Related Work

There are two main streams of work on open student models. One stream focuses on visualizing the model to support students' self-reflection and planning; the other one encourages students to participate in the modeling process, such as engaging students through negotiation or collaboration on the construction of the model [2]. Representations of the student model vary from displaying high-level summaries (such as skill meters) to complex concept maps or Bayesian networks. A range of benefits of opening the student models to the learners have been reported, such as increasing the learner's awareness of the developing knowledge, difficulties and the learning process, and students' engagement, motivation, and knowledge reflection [1-3]. Dimitrova et al. [5] explore interactive open learner modeling by engaging learners in negotiating with the system during the modeling process. Chen et al. [6] investigated active open learner models in order to motivate learners to improve their academic performance. Both individual and group open learner models were studied; they both demonstrated an increase in reflection and helpful interactions among teammates. Bull & Kay [7] described a framework to apply open user models in adaptive learning environments and provided many in-depth examples. In our own work on the QuizGuide system [11] we embedded open learning models into the adaptive link annotation and demonstrated that this arrangement can remarkably increase student motivation to work with non-mandatory educational content.

To support social learning, it is common to see the use of the average values of a group to represent a particular aspect in the model. Open group modeling enables students to compare and understand their own states of learning. Such group models have been used to support the collaboration between learners among the same group, and to foster competition in a group of learners [8]. Vassileva and Sun [8] investigated the community visualization in online communities. They summarized that social visualization allows peer-recognition and provides students with the opportunity to build trust in others and in the group. Bull & Britland [9] used OLMlets to research the problem of facilitating group collaboration and competition. The results revealed that optionally releasing the models to their peers increased the discussion among students and encourages them to start working sooner. CourseVis [10] is one of the few systems providing graphical visualization for multiple groups of users to teachers and learners. It helps instructors to identify problems early on, and to prevent some of the common problems in distance learning. Therefore, it motivates us to further investigate the effectiveness of social visualization techniques in the open student model systems.

3   QuizJET Meets IntrospectiveViews

To explore the value of open social student modeling, we extended the educational system *QuizJET* with an open social student modeling interface based on a modified version of the *IntrospectiveViews* visualization tools. QuizJET is a system for authoring and delivery of parameterized questions on Java programming language. It generates parameterized questions for assessment and self-assessment of students' knowledge on a broad range of Java topics. The implementation and functionalities of QuizJET were described in detail in [11]. The IntrospectiveViews visualization approach was first proposed for scrutinizing semantically-enriched user interest models in [12]. The interface visualizes user interests as a set of keywords displayed on a circular surface gradually painted in shades between red and blue, where the gradient colors denote different degrees of interest. It also allows grouping the items into circular sectors by type, i.e., the semantic class they belong to (e.g. person, company, country, etc.).

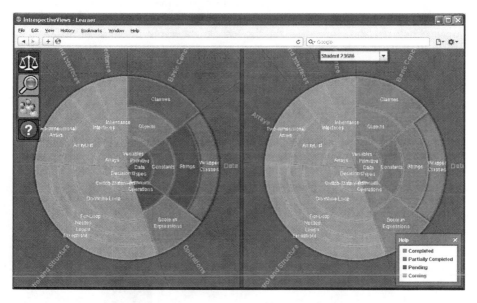

Fig. 1. Parallel IntrospectiveViews. Left pane – visualization of the student's own progress; right pane – visualization of a peer's progress. The circular sectors represent the lectures and the annular sectors represent the topics of individual lectures. The shades of the sectors indicate whether the topic has been covered and for the covered subjects, they denote the progress the student has made. Color screenshots available at: http://www.minerva-portals.de/research/introspective-views/.

In [14] we presented an adapted version of IntrospectiveViews, which was modified to fit the context of social learning. This version visualizes learner progress rather than user interests and offers parallel views of two student models so that the user can see not only her own model, but also the models of her peers and the class on average. Below, we briefly describe the application of parallel IntrospectiveViews for visualizing student progress on QuizJET questions. For a more detailed description refer to [14].

Figure 1 shows parallel IntrospectiveViews for a student in a class on Object-Oriented Programming (OOP). The visualization consists of two panes: the left pane displays the student's own progress and the right one displays the progress of someone else. Each pane visualizes the respective student's progress as a pie chart. The pie chart representation was chosen because of its capability to visually convey the chronological order of items and their size. The pie chart consists of several circular sectors each representing a class lecture. The lectures are displayed in a clockwise order denoting their pre-requisite sequence, i.e., the order they are taught in class. Lectures may consist of one or several topics, which are represented as annular sectors placed within the circular sector of the corresponding lecture. The radius (width) of annular sectors denotes the amount of readings, quizzes, and exercises assigned to the topic. In a similar way, the span of circular sectors indicates the amount of learning content assigned to the corresponding lecture. Such representation allows the student to easily estimate the amount of work she has to spend on each individual topic or lecture. The shade of each annular sector denotes whether the topic has been covered and, for the covered ones, indicates the progress the student has made with respect to the topic. The sectors painted grey represent the topics that have not been covered yet, whereas the sectors painted a shade from the color range red to green represent the sectors that have been already covered. For the covered topics, the interface displays the student progress. The progress, in the current implementation, is a ratio of successfully completed quizzes to the total quiz count in the topic. If the ratio equals 0, i.e., no quiz has been successfully completed, the sector is painted red. If it equals 1, i.e., all quizzes have been completed, the sector appears green. The shades in the range between red and green denote partial completion of the quizzes.

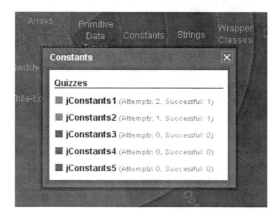

Fig. 2. Quizzes of the selected topic

The interface allow the user to see the contents of the corresponding topic by clicking on a particular sector. In the current implementation, the list of questions on the topic is presented when selected (Figure 2). For each question, the interface provides a visual cue indicating the student's progress and displays the total number of attempts the student has made on the quiz and the number of successful attempts. By clicking on a quiz label, the interface will display the quiz in a new window.

Our hypothesis is that such visualization can help the student to plan her class work by providing an overview of her progress in the class and showing the topics that she has already completed as well as those yet to be worked on. In addition to that, we believe that the ability to view someone else's progress can help the student to quickly find the peers that can help with a difficult topic or quiz. The class study described in the next section reveals whether or not this hypothesis is true.

4   The Classroom Study and the Results

To assess the impact of our technology, we have conducted a thorough evaluation in a semester-long classroom study. The study was performed in an undergraduate Object-Oriented Programming course offered by the School of Information Sciences, University of Pittsburgh in the Fall semester of 2010. All students received access to self-assessment quizzes through the IntrospectiveViews (IV) interface. The system was introduced to the class at the beginning of the course and served as a non-mandatory course tool over the entire semester. Of the 32 students enrolled in the course, 18 actively used the system. All student activity with the system was recorded. For every student attempt to answer a question, the system stored a timestamp, the user's name, the question, quiz, and session ids, and the results (right or wrong). We also recorded the frequency and timing of student model access and comparisons. Pre- and post- tests were administered at the beginning and the end of the semester in order to measure the gain in students' learning. At the end of the semester, the students were asked to provide their subjective feedback about the system and its features by completing the evaluation questionnaire.

4.1   Effects on System Usage

On average, each student attempted 113 different questions and achieved a success rate of 71.35% on answering the questions. On average, students tried 9 out of 17 distinct topics and 36.5 out of 103 distinct question. The data is summarized in Table 1. Following our prior experience with open student modeling in JavaGuide [11], we expected that the ability to view student knowledge progress would encourage the students to work more with the system. To assess it, we compared the student usage of self-assessment quizzes through IV (Column 1 in Table 1) with the data from a comparable class that accessed quizzes using a traditional course portal with no progress visualization (Column 2 in Table 1) and another class accessing quizzes through an adaptive hypermedia system JavaGuide (Column 3 in Table 1). We found that the social visualization of student models with IntrospectiveViews resulted in a 39% increase in the average attempts compared to the traditional course portal. The students also explored more topics, tried more distinct questions, and accessed the system more frequently. In brief, we observed an increase in all usage parameters similar to that it was observed in a very different JavaGuide interface. At the same time, the increase in usage was not as high as in the case of JavaGuide. As a result, no significant difference on the usage level was found between IV and the portal as well as between IV and JavaGuide.

Table 1. Summary of Basic Statistics of System Usage

		1	2	3
		QuizJET w/ IV	QuizJET w/ Portal	JavGuide
	Parameters	n=18	n=16	n=22
Average User Statistics	Attempts	113.05 ± 15.17	80.81 ± 22.06	125.50 ± 20.04
	Success Rate	71.35% ± 3.39%	42.63% ± 1.99%	58.31% ± 7.92%
	Distinct Topics	9.06 ± 1.39	7.81 ± 1.64	11.77 ± 1.19
	Distinct Questions	36.5 ± 5.69	33.37 ± 6.50	46.18 ± 5.15
Average User Session Statistics	Attempts	27.51	21.55	30.34
	Distinct Topics	2.20	2.31	2.85
	Distinct Questions	8.88	8.9	11.16
Average Sessions		4.11 ± 0.70	3.75 ± 0.53	4.14 ± 0.75
Pre-test score (M ±SE)		6.38 ± 1.12	9.56 ± 1.29	4.97 ± 0.85
Post-test score (M ±SE)		13.71 ± 1.00	17.12 ± 0.86	
Normalized Knowledge Gain		0.43 ± 0.07	0.36 ± 0.05	
IntrospectiveViews				
Average Comparison mode	Class on Average	3.33 ± 0.71		
	Peers	6.83 ± 2.25		
	Topics	4.00 ± 0.79		
	Questions	4.67 ± 1.36		

Since the student own knowledge visualization was relatively similar in IV and JavaGuide, a slighter increase in student activity in IV could be attributed to the social side of open social student modeling. While the access to social data could encourage less active users to do more work, it can also discourage very active users from jumping too much ahead of the class. As a result, the difference between the most active and least active users is getting smaller. Evidence that this is really happening is the observed 25% decrease in standard deviations for the number of attempts. In turn, the class as a whole became a bit less adventurous than in non-social JavaGuide, exploring fewer questions and topics (this is because the variety of topics come to some extent from more active users who run ahead of the class). This effect can be also observed in IV, especially the session level. While the amount of work per session increases for IV, question and topic coverage stays the same.

In sum, as a whole, social guidance provided by the access to class progress mediates the motivating effect of progress visualization by making the whole class a bit less adventurous and more conservative than without social guidance tools. An interesting question is whether a more conservative increase in the amount of work and variety of explored context is a good or a bad thing. Our evidence shows that it might actually be a good thing. As Table 1 shows, students using social visualization in IV achieved the highest success rate (a ratio of correct solutions to total attempts) among all conditions. This is significantly higher than for the portal case, $F(1,32)=$ 11.303, $p<.01$. The growth of the success rate demonstrates that knowledge-based and social guidance combined are more effective in guiding the students to appropriate questions that they are ready to handle than knowledge-based guidance alone. The community wisdom does matter.

4.2 The Use of Peer Guidance

The assumptions about the impact of social features of IV can be validated only if we can show some evidence that these features were really used by students. To collect this evidence, we looked at how students use the provided ability to compare their models with those of their peers' models. We found that students compared their own models to the models of their peers on the average of 6.83 times on average. This is strong evidence that the social features were used and that they had a chance to provide social guidance by affecting student question selection. But can we really argue that peer progress data could guide the student to appropriate topics and questions? Could it be just curiosity? To answer this question, we checked how many times a topic and a question were accessed from the peer model chart rather than from the students' own model of knowledge. We found that on average, students compared to their peers on 4 topics and made 4.67 attempts on the questions initiating from the peers' chart. The final question is whether the guidance obtained by visiting progress data of their peers benefited student learning. We found a correlation between the frequency of peer model comparisons and the learning gain. The more the students compared to their peers, the higher post-quiz scores they received ($r= 0.34$ $p=0.004$).

4.3 Effects on Student Learning

A study of educational innovation is not complete without the analysis of its impact on student learning. To ensure that the student cohorts were comparable, we first examined the students' pre-test scores. We found no significant differences between groups before using the systems, $F(2, 53)=1.644$, $p= .203$, $\eta^2= .057$. The assumption of homogeneity of variance was met, Brown-Forsythe $F(2, 53)= 1.644$, $p= .207$. We found that in both conditions (IV and portal), the students achieved a significant knowledge growth as measured by pre- and post- test scores, $t_1(17)= 7.203$, $p< .01$; $t_2(15)= 6.108$, $p<.01$. To compare learning gains under these two conditions, we calculated the Normalized Knowledge Gain (NKG) based on formula (1). While the average NKG was slightly higher in the IV group, we did not find significant differences between these two conditions. It should be noted, however, that our experiment was performed in a non-controlled classroom context where the systems were used as just supplementary course tools. The students were able to learn the subject by many ways with the QuizJET/Portal system being just one of many factors which may have contributed to the learning.

$$NKG = \frac{posttest - pretest}{\max score - pretest} \qquad (1)$$

Table 2. Questionnaire

Usefulness	
A.1.	The interface helps me to understand how the class content is organized.
A.2.	The interface helps me to identify my weak points.
A.3.	The interface helps me to plan my class work.
A.4.	The interface helps me to access quizzes.
A.5.	The comparison mode of the interface motivates me to progress on the quizzes.
A.6.	The comparison mode of the interface helps me to find the classmates who can help on difficult topics.
Ease of Use	
B.1.	The interface is easy to use.
B.2.	The interface is user friendly.
B.3.	The interface requires the fewest steps possible to accomplish what I want to do with it.
Ease of Learning	
C.1.	I learned how to use the interface quickly.
C.2.	I easily remember how to use the interface.
C.3.	It is easy to learn how to use the interface.
Satisfaction	
D.1.	I am satisfied with the interface.
D.2.	The interface is fun to use.
D.3.	The interface is pleasant to use.
D.4.	I would recommend the interface to my classmates.
Privacy and Data Sharing	
E.1.	I like the idea of comparing my progress with other students.
E.2.	I feel comfortable sharing my progress with others.
E.3.	I do not mind that my progress is displayed anonymously in the average progress of the entire class.
E.4.	I would like to view progress of other students because: 1. S/He and I are friends 2. I know s/he is a good student 3. I know s/he is good at specific topic 4. I am just curious 5. Other_____
E.5.	I am willing to share: 1. My overall progress with: no one / selected classmates / everyone 2. My good progress topics with: no one / selected classmates / everyone 3. My overall success rate with: no one / selected classmates / everyone 4. My good success rate topics with: no one / selected classmates / everyone. 5. Selected topics with: no one / selected classmates / everyone. 6. Other_____

4.4 Subjective Evaluation Results

Out of the 18 IV users, 13 completed the questionnaire. For the purpose of analysis, we classified 17 questions into 5 categories (Table 2). From the *usefulness* perspective, 84.5% of the students strongly agreed or agreed that the clockwise pie-chart design helped them to understand how the class content is organized. 76.9% of the students agreed or strongly agreed that the interface helped them to identify their weak points. 84.6% of the students agreed that the interface helped them to access the quizzes. 61.5% of the students agreed that the comparison mode motivated them to progress on the quizzes. However, there were 76.9% of students who did not think the comparison mode allowed them to identify a classmate to help them on difficult topic regardless of the positive effects of using the comparison mode (proven in the previous section). The results suggested that the students generally had a high opinion of agreement on the usefulness of the system and indentified the system's inability to find a comparable peer from the current design. Considering the *Ease of Use & Ease of Learning* in the system, students found it easy to learn how to use the system (92.3%), easy to remember how to use it (92.3%) and learned how to use it quickly (84.6%). They considered that the interface was easy to use (76.9%), it was user friendly (69.2%) and required fewest steps to accomplish the task[1] (66.7%). There was not a single strong disagreement with the questions of this category. In the category of *Satisfaction*, students liked the system. 76.9% were strongly satisfied with the system. They determined that the interface was fun (69.2%) and pleasant (76.9%) to use. 91.3% of the students would recommend it to their classmates. In terms of *Privacy and Data Sharing*, 84.6% of the students appreciated the feature of comparing their progress with others. 69.2% of them felt comfortable in sharing their progress with others. However, some of them had concerns on sharing the data with others. 15.4% of them do not want to share any data with others at all. 30.8% of them would like to selectively share data with others, for example, display the model anonymously or selectively share the data (either their progress or success). We also investigated the reasons of why students view the progress of other students. We found that 46.2% of the students viewed others progress out of curiosity. 46.2% of them knew the ones they viewed are good students or are good at specific topic. To extend the current model on aspects other than progress, we also collected students' opinions on such attributes as success rate, selected topics, good progress and good success rate. 46.2% of the students are willing to share everything to everyone. 23.1% arc willing to share their overall progress to selected people. 23.1% of them would only share the good progress or success rate to everyone. Only 1 student (7.6%) was extremely private and was not willing to share anything to anyone. The results indicated that students were generally positive toward the data sharing idea provided the privacy management to make them feel in charge. Figure 3 shows the detail percentages for each question.

---

[1] One of the survey participants did not answer this question (B.3). The percentile was calculated based on the responses from the remainder of the participants.

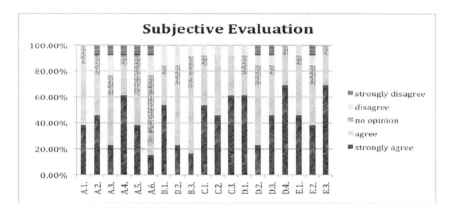

Fig. 3. Subjective evaluation results

5 Summary and Future Work

In this paper, we presented a specific implementation of the open social student modeling approach based on the parallel IntrospectiveViews interface. This interface was used to provide access to QuizJET parameterized self-assessment questions in an introductory programming class. The parallel IntrospectiveViews interface allowed the students to visualize not only the student's own model, but also to display parallel views of the models of their peers and the cumulative model of the entire class. The system was evaluated in a semester-log classroom study. While the use of the system was non-mandatory, it has been used very actively. Moreover, the social features provided by the interface were used for both progress comparison and navigation. We observed that the parallel IntrospectiveViews interface caused an increase in all the usage parameters in comparison to a regular portal-based access system. While the increase was slightly smaller and conservative in comparison to the similar increase caused by our earlier system (JavaGuide) non-social open student modeling interface of our earlier system JavaGuide, the IntrospectiveViews interface allowed the student to achieve a higher success rate in answering the questions. In addition, the system and most of its features were highly praised by the students.

Our current results are encouraging and suggest new challenges for the future work. Based on our experience, we identified five areas for improvement in the future.

(1) *Adaptive navigation support:* based on our previous experiences [11] adaptive navigation support can dramatically increase the likelihood of answering the questions correctly. Therefore, the current design can be further improved with the additions of adaptive navigation support feature such as providing icon abstractions etc.

(2) *Personalized guidance:* the positive correlation between comparison with peers and learning gain encourages us to further look at the effects of comparison between students with different levels of knowledge; for example, a recommendation about whose models to explore.

(3) *Privacy management:* students have different levels of concerns about the privacy side for data sharing. Therefore, in the future, we have to enable the privacy setting in a sensitive manner to accommodate assorted scenarios.

(4) *Visualizing models of multiple peers:* to help users to navigate through the peers' models, the interface should be able to display multiple models at a time. The next version will contain a pane listing miniature copies of progress pie charts of all classmates. The user will be able to sort peers by overall progress, progress in a given topic, name, and other attributes.

(5) *Collaboration features*: in order to facilitate collaboration among students, we plan to add a feature for sending messages from the interface and a feature allowing students to set the status indicating their willingness to help.

Acknowledgment. This research was supported in part by the National Science Foundation under Grant No. 0447083.

The development of IntrospectiveViews was carried out in the Minerva Context-Adaptive Portals project funded by the IBM Deutschland Research & Development GmbH.

References

1. Bull, S.: Supporting learning with open learner models. In: Proceedings of 4th Hellenic Conference on Information and Communication Technologies in Education, Athens, Greece, September 29-October 3, pp. 47–61 (2004)
2. Mitrovic, A., Martin, B.: Evaluating the Effect of Open Student Models on Self-Assessment. Int. J. of Artificial Intelligence in Education 17(2), 121–144 (2007)
3. Zapata-Rivera, J.D., Greer, J.E.: Visualizing and inspecting Bayesian belief models. International Journal of Artificial Intelligence in Education IJCAI 14, 1–37 (2004)
4. Vassileva, J.: Toward Social Learning Environments. IEEE Transactions on Learning Technologies 1(4), 199–214 (2008)
5. Dimitrova, V., Self, J., Brna, P.: Applying Interactive Open Learner Models to Learning Technical Terminology. In: Bauer, M., Gmytrasiewicz, P.J., Vassileva, J. (eds.) UM 2001. LNCS (LNAI), vol. 2109, pp. 148–157. Springer, Heidelberg (2001)
6. Chen, Z.H., Chou, C.Y., Deng, Y.C., Chan, T.W.: Active Open Learner Models as Animal Companions: Motivating Children to Learn through Interaction with My-Pet and Our-Pet. International Journal of Artificial Intelligence in Education 17(3), 217–226 (2007)
7. Bull, S., Kay, J.: Student Models that Invite the Learner In: The SMILI Open Learner Modelling Framework. International Journal of Artificial Intelligence in Education 17(2), 89–120 (2007)
8. Vassileva, J., Sun, L.: Using Community Visualization to Stimulate Participation in Online Communities. e-Service Journal 6(1), 3–40 (2007)
9. Bull, S., Britland, M.: Group Interaction Prompted by a Simple Assessed Open Learner Model that can be Optionally Released to Peers. In: Brusilovsky, P., Grigoriadou, M., Papanikolaou, K. (eds.) Proceedings of Workshop on Personalisation in E-Learning Environments at Individual and Group Level, User Modeling 2007 (2007)
10. Mazza, R., Dimitrova, V.: CourseVis: a graphical student monitoring tool for supporting instructors in web-based distance courses. International Journal of Human-Computer Studies 65(2), 125–139 (2007)

11. Hsiao, I., Sosnovsky, S., Brusilovsky, P.: Guiding Students to the Right Questions: Adaptive Navigation Support in an E-learning System for Java Programming. Journal of Computer Assisted Learning 26(4), 270–283 (2010)
12. Bakalov, F., König-Ries, B., Nauerz, A., Welsch, M.: IntrospectiveViews: An interface for scrutinizing semantic user models. In: De Bra, P., Kobsa, A., Chin, D. (eds.) UMAP 2010. LNCS, vol. 6075, pp. 219–230. Springer, Heidelberg (2010)
13. Bakalov, F., König-Ries, B., Nauerz, A., Welsch, M.: Scrutinizing User Interest Models with Introspective Views. In: Adjunct Proc. of the 18th Intl. Conf on User Modeling, Adaptation and Personalization (2010)
14. Bakalov, F., Hsiao, I., Brusilovsky, P., König-Ries, B.: Visualizing Student Models for Social Learning with Parallel IntrospectiveViews. In: Proc. of the Workshop on Visual Interfaces to the Social and Semantic Web at the International Conference on Intelligent User Interfaces (2011)
15. Vassileva, J.: Open Group Learner Modeling, Interaction Analysis and Social Visualization. In: Dimitrova, V., Tzagarakis, M., Vassileva, J. (eds.) Proceedings of Workshop on Adaptation and Personalisation in Social Systems: Groups, Teams, Communities. Held in Conjunction with UM 2007 (2007)

Location-Adapted Music Recommendation Using Tags

Marius Kaminskas and Francesco Ricci

Free University of Bolzano,
Piazza Domenicani 3, 39100 Bolzano, Italy
{mkaminskas,fricci}@unibz.it

Abstract. Context-aware music recommender systems are capable to suggest music items taking into consideration contextual conditions, such as the user mood or location, that may influence the user preferences at a particular moment. In this paper we consider a particular kind of context aware recommendation task — selecting music content that fits a place of interest (POI). To address this problem we have used emotional tags attached by a users' population to both music and POIs. Moreover, we have considered a set of similarity metrics for tagged resources to establish a match between music tracks and POIs. In order to test our hypothesis, i.e., that the users will reckon that a music track suits a POI when this track is selected by our approach, we have designed a live user experiment where subjects are repeatedly presented with POIs and a selection of music tracks, some of them matching the presented POI and some not. The results of the experiment show that there is a strong overlap between the users' selections and the best matching music that is recommended by the system for a POI.

Keywords: recommender systems, location-aware, context, music, social tagging, emotions.

1   Introduction

Music recommender systems are decision support tools that reduce the information overload by retrieving relevant music items based on a user's profile. The recommendation process can be content-based, i.e., using features of the music liked by the user to predict what the target user may like [4], or collaborative-based, which finds users with similar music preferences and recommend to the target user items liked by these users [7]. However, most of the available music recommender systems suggest music regardless of the contextual conditions which can be important to predict the user's preferences at a particular moment. In fact, a study on users' musical information needs [6] has shown that people often seek music for a contextual situation like an occasion, an event or an emotional state rather than by artist or song information. To cope with these needs, recently there has been an emerging interest in contextual, or situational music selection [8,2]. The idea of such music selection is to recommend music

Joseph A. Konstan et al. (Eds.): UMAP 2011, LNCS 6787, pp. 183–194, 2011.

depending on the user's actual situation, emotional state, or any other contextual condition that might be relevant to increase the user's satisfaction for the selected music.

In this line of research, we are considering the problem of retrieving music that fits the surroundings of the user, and more specifically, we are looking for effective ways to match musical content with places of interest (POIs). For instance, a Vivaldi's concerto seems a better choice for a "calle" (a narrow street) in Venice than a Schubert's lied, that may better suit an old street in Vienna. Being able to select music for a place can be used for creating new engaging location-aware music delivery services. In particular, we are considering a scenario where a tourist is sightseeing a city using a mobile city guide (Android). It recommends a walking itinerary and, while the user is visiting the suggested POIs, it plays music that, according to the technique described in this paper, matches the visited POIs. The goal is to enhance the user's experience and create a more engaging travel guide tool. This application will be described in a forthcoming paper; here we want to focus on the enabling music to POI adaptation technologies.

It is clearly challenging to match music to a place so that the user can recognize this adaptation or, even without explicitly recognizing it, the user can appreciate such a selection and prefer it to other music not explicitly matching the place. The core technical issue to be solved is related to the fact that music and POIs are different objects and there is no obvious way to match one with the other. In recommender systems literature, it is normal to establish the similarity of two items, either using their feature based descriptions [11], or using their ratings given by a set of users [14]. The first approach requires that the two items, whose similarity is sought, share a common set of features, while the second one requires that a large number of users co-rated the two items. The first approach is therefore difficult to apply when the two items are not of the same type, while the second would only predict that a user that likes (dislikes) the first item will also like (dislike) the second. But this is not really a sign that the two items match together and they can, for instance, be recommended together. The problem of matching POI with a music track is more closely related to that found in cross-selling, e.g., recommending a type of boots that suit a kind of ski. This is a rather unpopular recommendation problem, that have only be considered by applications that recommend a good bundling of items, e.g., a travel planning [13] or music compilation [1].

In the research described here we decided to use the first approach mentioned above, and we looked for a common set of tags as shared representation for music and POIs. With such a representation the matching can then be performed by comparing the tag profiles of the two items. Since emotionally related tags can be used both for POIs and music we decided to explore this path. Music and places can both raise emotions and we conjectured that the commonality of the raised emotions could provide the base for establishing a degree of match between a place and a music track. Moreover, using tags to describe both music and POIs is a promising and viable approach since there is a rapid growth of the amount of user-generated tagging data (a phenomena also known as social, or collaborative tagging) [3,15].

In a previous work [5] we conducted a preliminary user study aiming at verifying that matching music to places can enhance the user satisfaction for recommended itineraries. In that study the tags used for describing music and POIs were not only describing emotions and included a standard set of English descriptive adjectives. Furthermore, we used a rather simple similarity metric without comparing it to other competing metrics. This paper extends substantially that early work in three directions:

- A well founded set of emotional tags, suggested by recent studies on music cognition [16] is used for representing music and POIs.
- A set of similarity metrics, which were previously tested in a different setting [10], is evaluated first offline, comparing them in term of the generated ranked music recommendations for a POI, and then with a live user study where users expressed their subjective evaluations for the proposed match between music and POI.
- The matching of music to POIs is carefully evaluated for each considered POI as opposed to the previous study where the user feedback was collected for itineraries, i.e., a collection of three POIs.

In conclusion, in this paper we show that matching POIs with music is feasible. We have found that the proposed approach can recommend music tracks that users consider more suitable for a POI, compared to other apparently similar tracks but not matching the POI. This is an interesting result as it makes it possible to develop context-aware music retrieval systems that can enhance the user experience in many practical applications, such as travel guides, music recommender systems, automatic soundtrack generation systems.

The rest of this paper is structured as follows. We first describe the process of collecting the tagging data for music and POIs as well as present the statistics of collected data. Then we describe the used similarity metrics and the process of evaluating our matching strategies with real users. We then review some of the related work, and finally we draw conclusions and discuss some future work.

2   Tagging Music and POIs

As we mentioned above, in this research we have investigated if emotional tags attached to music and POIs can be used as a common set of descriptive features for establishing a match between these two types of items. Since emotionally tagged music tracks or POIs are not directly available, we have designed a web interface to collect this type of tagging data (Figure 1). We have considered 75 classical music tracks and movie soundtracks, and 50 POIs in the city of Bolzano and surrounding areas. The tagging was performed by volunteer users; mostly students and researchers at the Free University of Bolzano. The users were asked to tag the items using a restricted tag vocabulary consisting of adjectives from

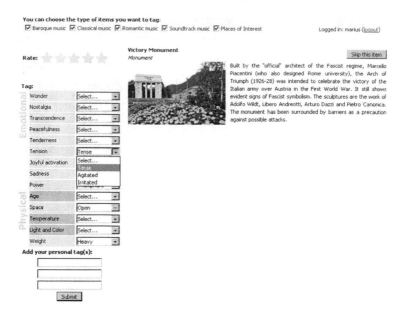

Fig. 1. Tagging interface

Table 1. Emotional tags from the GEMS model

Category	Tags
Wonder	Allured, Amazed, Moved, Admiring
Transcendence	Fascinated, Overwhelmed, Thrills, Transcendence
Tenderness	Mellowed, Tender, Affectionate, In love
Nostalgia	Sentimental, Dreamy, Melancholic, Nostalgic
Peacefulness	Calm, Serene, Soothed, Meditative
Power	Triumphant, Energetic, Strong, Fiery
Joyful Activation	Joyful, Animated, Bouncy, Amused
Tension	Tense, Agitated, Irritated
Sadness	Sad, Tearful

the Geneva Emotional Music Scale (GEMS) model described in [16]. The GEMS model consists of nine groups of emotions, each group having 2-4 emotional tags (Table 1). In addition to the emotional tags from GEMS model, we used tags describing physical characteristics of items that proved to be useful in a previous user study [5]. These are: Ancient, Modern — Colorful, Bright, Dark, Dull — Open, Closed — Light, Heavy — Cold, Mild, Warm.

The tagging was performed by 32 volunteer users. In total, 817 tags were collected for the POIs (16.34 tags per POI on average) and 1025 tags for the music tracks (13.67 tags per track on average). We call the tag-based description of an item its tag-profile. Figure 2 shows tag usage statistics grouped by tag categories. These results show that certain types of emotional tags have been applied to both music tracks and POIs with similar probabilities. This particularly applies to the categories "Peacefulness" and "Power". Whereas some

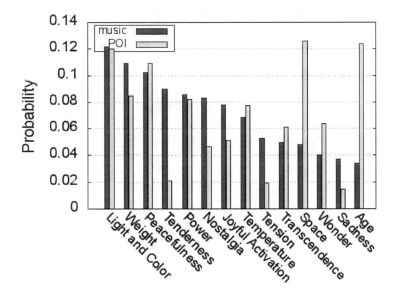

Fig. 2. Tag usage probability across tag categories

other categories were clearly used more often for music than POIs. These include "Tenderness", "Nostalgia", "Tension", and "Sadness". Tags in these categories are not likely to be useful for direct matching of music and POI, at least for our selection of POIs. From the physical tag categories, "Light and Color", "Weight" and "Temperature" are the most likely to be useful due to the similar usage of such tags in both music and POI profiles. Contrastingly, tags describing age and space of items were applied mostly to POIs. These findings are interesting per se, but also indicate that an effective similarity metric for this task should be robust against the differences in the overall tags distributions observed for the two types of items. We observe that in previous research works that used tag-based similarity metrics this was not an issue as the items to be matched were confined to be in a single domain. Observing that the tags in the same emotion category are synonyms, we have also considered a simpler model where the original tags are replaced with their emotion category. For instance, the tags *allured*, *amazed*, *moved* and *admiring* appearing in any item tag-profile were substituted with *wonder*. Such merging of tags improved the tag coverage and reduced the dimensionality of item profiles from 46 (the initial number of individual tags) to 22 (9 emotion categories + 13 physical tags). In the next section we will present some similarity metrics that are either using the original tag-profile or this more compact tag-profile based on the adjectives' categories.

3   Similarity Metrics

In order to match POIs with music, we decided to consider a well established set of similarity metrics that are applicable to tagged resources. Markines et al. [10]

evaluated the performance of some similarity metrics using classical IR evaluation measures, when computing the similarity between tagged resources. However, this study was conducted on a single folksonomy data set (BibSonomy.org — a social bookmarking system), with the task being to predict URL-to-URL similarity. The ground truth for resources' similarity was the graph-based similarity of URLs. Since our task was to match tagged objects from different domains (music and POIs) where the ground-truth similarity could only be assessed by subjective users' evaluations, we could not directly rely on the outcome of that study; we had to evaluate these metrics for our specific task.

In the following definitions, u and v represent items (either a music track or a POI), y represents a tag, X_u — the set of tags with not null frequency in the tag-profile of the item u, w_{uy} — the frequency of tag y in the item's u tag-profile and $p(y)$ — the fraction of items (both music tracks and POIs) annotated with y.

- The Matching similarity between two items is defined as:

$$MatchingSim(u,v) = \frac{\sum_{y \in X_u \cap X_v} log\ p(y)}{\sum_{y \in T} log\ p(y)}$$

  where T is the set of all tags in the database.
- The Overlap similarity:

$$OverlapSim(u,v) = \frac{\sum_{y \in X_u \cap X_v} log\ p(y)}{max(\sum_{y \in X_u} log\ p(y), \sum_{y \in X_v} log\ p(y))}$$

- The Jaccard similarity:

$$JaccardSim(u,v) = \frac{\sum_{y \in X_u \cap X_v} log\ p(y)}{\sum_{y \in X_u \cup X_v} log\ p(y)}$$

- The Dice similarity:

$$DiceSim(u,v) = \frac{2\sum_{y \in X_u \cap X_v} log\ p(y)}{\sum_{y \in X_u} log\ p(y) + \sum_{y \in X_v} log\ p(y)}$$

- The Cosine similarity:

$$CosineSim(u,v) = \frac{\sum_y w_{uy} w_{vy}}{\sqrt{\sum_y w_{uy}^2} \sqrt{\sum_y w_{vy}^2}}$$

- The TF-IDF similarity: in addition to the above metrics, we have introduced a variation of Cosine similarity metric, where the tag frequencies w_{uy} in an item profile X_u are replaced with the TF-IDF weight of tag y. In order to compute the TF-IDF weights, for each item u all the tags assigned to the item (with repetitions) are considered as a document representing the item.

The usage of logarithms in the first four metrics is related to Shannon information theory. Intuitively, a very common tag will have a high probability and therefore a very small log probability. Thus, it will bring a small contribution to the similarity score. We observe that all six metrics range in $[0,1]$, making their comparison easier. Moreover, we note that they can be applied both to the original tag-profiles and to the merged tag-profiles mentioned previously. As a result, we have 12 different ways to compute the similarity between a music track and a POI.

4   System Evaluation

Since there is no accessible ground-truth telling if a music track suits a POI, we designed a live user study were the user is requested to assess that relationship. However, since a user cannot express many of these subjective judgments in a single session we had to narrow down the number of similarity metrics compared in the live user study. For that reason, the full evaluation of the effectiveness of the matching computed by the considered similarity metrics was carried out in two steps. First, we computed the correlation of the ranked lists produced by the considered similarity metrics when matching (scoring) the available music tracks to a given POI. The more correlated two rankings are the more similar will be the recommended music tracks for a given POI. This initial analysis allowed us to study the general properties of the metrics, and to discard some redundant metrics. Second, the selected metrics were used in the live user experiment to collect the users' subjective evaluations, i.e., if a music track suits a POI.

4.1   Offline Similarity Metrics Comparison

In order to compare the considered similarity metrics, without relying on sub-jective user-based evaluations, we sorted the music tracks recommended for a given POI using the different similarity metrics and we computed, pairwise, the Spearman's correlation of these ranked lists produced by the different metrics. Averaging, for each pair of metrics, the correlation of the ranked lists of music tracks generated by two metrics for all the POIs in our database we produced an average correlation score between every pair of metrics.

When comparing the similarity metrics, using the original tag-profiles, i.e., without merging the count for the tags in the same emotional category, we observed two clusters of metrics: [Matching, Overlap, Jaccard, Dice] all have an average correlation higher than 0.8 between each other. Likewise, Cosine and TF-IDF similarities have a correlation higher than 0.7, but were less correlated with the metrics in the first cluster (e.g., correlation of TF-IDF with Overlap was 0.64, Cosine with Jaccard — 0.68). The same clusters of metrics were observed when we compared the similarity metrics computed on the merged tag-profiles. Hence, relying on these results we have selected one representative metric for each cluster; i.e., Jaccard for the first and Cosine for the second. We observe that there is a major difference between these two metrics: cosine considers tag frequency in items' profiles while Jaccard only considers each co-occurring tag once. In the online evaluation study with real users, which is described later, we used these two metrics.

Table 2. Average Spearman's correlation of different similarity metrics. The asterisk marks similarity computed when merging the emotional tags. Grey cells indicate an average correlation lower than 0.7.

	Matching	Overlap	Jaccard	Dice	Cosine	TF-IDF	Matching*	Overlap*	Jaccard*	Dice*	Cosine*	TF-IDF*
Jaccard	0.94	0.92	1.00	1.00	0.82	0.70	0.70	0.60	0.72	0.72	0.64	0.70
Cosine	0.78	0.78	0.82	0.82	1.00	0.73	0.64	0.58	0.67	0.67	0.76	0.73
Jaccard*	0.75	0.65	0.72	0.72	0.67	0.88	0.93	0.83	1.00	1.00	0.68	0.85
Cosine*	0.63	0.60	0.64	0.64	0.76	0.83	0.62	0.63	0.68	0.68	1.00	0.83

The effect of merging the tag profiles is evident by looking at Table 2, where the average correlation of the four selected metrics with all the initially considered similarity metrics is shown. The average correlation of the ranking produced by using the merged tag-profiles and the original tag-profiles is much lower; this can be seen by comparing the figures shown in the first (second) and third (fourth) rows of this table (e.g., Jaccard-Matching is 0.94, vs. Jaccard*-Matching is 0.75). Whereas the differences in the correlation between the same pair of metrics, when applied to a merged or not merged pair of tag-profiles, is not large. This can be seen comparing the first six entries of the first (second) row with the corresponding last six entries of the third (fourth) row. In other words, if two metrics are correlated when using the not merged tag-profiles they are still correlated when using the merged profiles.

4.2   Online User Study

In the final and more important evaluation experiment we measured whether the users consider the music tracks with largest similarity to a POI as those really better suited for that POI. In order to perform this evaluation we have designed a second web interface (Figure 3). Here, the users were repeatedly asked to consider a POI (taken from a POI collection), and while looking at this POI, to listen to some selected music tracks. The user was asked to check all the tracks that in her opinion suit that POI.

During each evaluation step the music recommendations for a POI were selected using two out of the four considered similarity metrics. The selected tracks included the two best matching tracks for each metric (highest similarity). In addition, we introduced in the recommendation lists two tracks that were mostly different from the matching tracks, i.e., having low similarity to the given POI. Introducing the low similarity tracks allowed us to directly compare tracks that were supposed to fit the POI with those not. In total a maximum of six tracks were suggested for each POI, but usually less tracks were shown as the tracks selected by the similarity metrics often overlap.

The goal of this analysis was to see whether the users actually agree with the music-to-POI matching computed using our approach. We note that the outcome

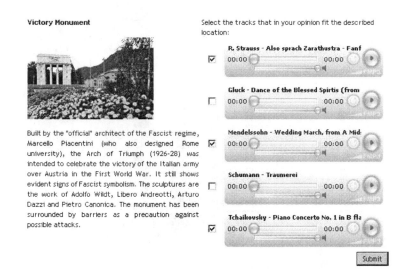

Fig. 3. The interface for evaluating music matching to POI

of this evaluation was not evident at all, since with a superficial evaluation, even the less similar tracks could be considered as suited and there are not large differences among the considered tracks (all of them are popular classical music tracks).

For example, consider the evaluation step shown in Figure 3. The POI Victory Monument was tagged as *bright, heavy, open, strong, triumphant, tense,* etc. In this case, the two metrics used to select the tracks are: Jaccard (suggesting tracks 1 and 5), and Jaccard with merged tag profiles (suggesting tracks 3 and 5). The low similarity tracks are tracks 2 and 4. Track 1 has been tagged as *open, heavy, triumphant, amazed* etc.; track 3 — *open, bright, agitated, bouncy, in love, triumphant,* etc.; track 5 — *open, heavy, triumphant, strong, cold,* etc. Contrastingly, tracks 2 and 4 have been tagged as *serene, light, colorful* etc. Looking at the tag profiles, it is easy to understand why the similarity metrics suggest tracks 1,3 and 5. However, the user is neither aware of the items' tag profiles, nor of the different ways the tracks were selected. It was therefore crucial to see if a person, just by listening to the selected music tracks, would agree with the match produced by our approach.

The online evaluation was carried out by 10 users in total performing 154 evaluation steps, that is, each user considered on average 15.6 POIs and the music suggested for these POIs. In order to compare the effectiveness of different metrics in selecting the best tracks, we have computed the probability that a metric produces a music track that is considered suited for a POI by the users. The probability was computed as the ratio of the number of times any track produced by a metric was selected over the total number of evaluation steps where this metric was used, i.e., tracks produced by this metric were presented.

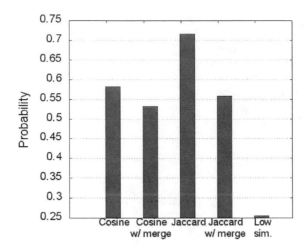

Fig. 4. The selection probability for the five evaluated matching approaches

Note that each time a music track, which was suggested by multiple metrics, was selected as appropriate for a POI, the probabilities for all these metrics were increased.

Looking at the results of this experiment (see Figure 4) it is clear that all the four tested similarity metrics performed significantly better than the low similarity matching (99% confidence level of the two-proportion z-test). Among the 4 metrics, Jaccard performs significantly better than the others (95% confidence level of the two-proportion z-test). A possible reason for the better performance of Jaccard compared to Cosine is that Jaccard metric in contrast to Cosine uses the probability that a tag can be found in a corpus; thus a frequent tag contributes to the similarity score less than a rare tag. In conclusion, we can affirm that the users consider the music tracks suggested by our approach as more suited for POIs than other not matching tracks. Furthermore, Jaccard selects the tracks that the users most frequently choose as suited for the illustrated POIs.

5   Related Work

Matching music with the user's location has not been investigated so far. The most closely related works are in the area of context-aware music recommendation. For instance, in [12,8] music is adapted to environment parameters, such as the location of the user, the time or the weather conditions. In other research works emotions have been used as a link between music and other types of content, e.g., websites [2] and images [9]. [2] mined emotions directly from textual representation of websites and music tracks, while [9] used a machine learning approach trained on hand labeled training data. We note that these works used emotion models that are different from the one used in our work.

Other research activities have been conducted on tagging behavior and tag distribution in social tagging systems [3,15]. However, to the best of our knowledge the usage of social tags for matching heterogeneous objects has not been investigated so far. We have used the similarity measures presented in [10] as a reference point, but we could not rely on their evaluation results since our study deals with different types of resources and a different ground truth. However, in [10], Matching, Overlap, Dice and Jaccard metrics performed slightly better than Cosine metric — a result that was also observed in our experiment.

6 Conclusions and Future Work

In this paper we have analyzed a new problem in music recommendation, i.e., recommending music tracks that suit a place of interest (POI). We have developed an approach that exploits user assigned emotional tags to both music tracks and POIs. We have collected and analyzed the tagging data obtained from real users through a custom developed interface that enables users to uniformly tag both music tracks and POIs. Then, we have performed an online experiment where the users were required to evaluate the appropriateness of the music selected by the system for POIs. The results show that users tend to agree with the matching produced using our proposed approach. Moreover, Jaccard similarity measure was shown to produce the matching preferred by most of the users.

We are currently testing the music-to-POI matching approach on a mobile device. We have developed a mobile tourist guide for the city of Bolzano. The guide offers an itinerary and plays matching music tracks as the user approaches a POI. We intend to collect the user feedback and further explore the effects of such matching on users' experience. An important next step is understanding if certain tags (emotions) contribute more to the perceived match between a POI and a music track (currently all tags have equal importance). Another important future step is to move from manually labeled data towards automatic tag acquisition for both music and POIs. We intent to investigate public folksonomies (e.g., Flickr, Last.fm) and blogs as possible data sources. Additionally, we want to study if personal preferences should be taken into account in this task as currently the same match is provided for all the users. Furthermore, we intend to use ontologies as an additional way to match music with POIs.

References

1. Baccigalupo, C., Plaza, E.: Case-based sequential ordering of songs for playlist recommendation. In: Roth-Berghofer, T.R., Göker, M.H., Güvenir, H.A. (eds.) ECCBR 2006. LNCS (LNAI), vol. 4106, pp. 286–300. Springer, Heidelberg (2006)
2. Cai, R., Zhang, C., Wang, C., Zhang, L., Ma, W.-Y.: Musicsense: contextual music recommendation using emotional allocation modeling. In: Proceedings of the 15th International Conference on Multimedia, pp. 553–556. ACM, New York (2007)
3. Golder, S.A., Huberman, B.A.: Usage patterns of collaborative tagging systems. Journal of Information Science 32(2), 198 (2006)

4. Hoashi, K., Matsumoto, K., Inoue, N.: Personalization of user profiles for content-based music retrieval based on relevance feedback. In: Proceedings of the Eleventh ACM International Conference on Multimedia, pp. 110–119. ACM, New York (2003)

5. Kaminskas, M., Ricci, F.: Matching places of interest with music. In: Workshop on Exploring Musical Information Spaces, WEMIS 2009, pp. 68–73. University of Alicante (2009)

6. Kim, J.Y., Belkin, N.J.: Categories of music description and search terms and phrases used by non-music experts. In: Proceedings of the 3rd International Conference on Music Information Retrieval, Paris, France (2002)

7. Konstas, I., Stathopoulos, V., Jose, J.M.: On social networks and collaborative recommendation. In: Proceedings of the 32nd International ACM SIGIR Conference on Research and Development in Information Retrieval, pp. 195–202. ACM, New York (2009)

8. Lee, J.S., Lee, J.C.: Context awareness by case-based reasoning in a music recommendation system. In: Ichikawa, H., Cho, W.-D., Chen, Y., Youn, H.Y. (eds.) UCS 2007. LNCS, vol. 4836, pp. 45–58. Springer, Heidelberg (2007), http://dx.doi.org/10.1007/978-3-540-76772-5_4

9. Li, C.-T., Shan, M.-K.: Emotion-based impressionism slideshow with automatic music accompaniment. In: Proceedings of the 15th International Conference on Multimedia, pp. 839–842. ACM, New York (2007)

10. Markines, B., Cattuto, C., Menczer, F., Benz, D., Hotho, A., Stumme, G.: Evaluating similarity measures for emergent semantics of social tagging. In: Proceedings of the 18th International Conference on World Wide Web, pp. 641–650. ACM, New York (2009)

11. Pazzani, M.J., Billsus, D.: Content-based recommendation systems. The Adaptive Web, 325–341 (2007)

12. Reddy, S., Mascia, J.: Lifetrak: music in tune with your life. In: HCM 2006: Proceedings of the 1st ACM International Workshop on Human-centered Multimedia, pp. 25–34. ACM, New York (2006)

13. Ricci, F., Cavada, D., Mirzadeh, N., Venturini, A.: Case-based travel recommendations. In: Fesenmaier, D.R., Woeber, K.W., Werthner, H. (eds.) Destination Recommendation Systems: Behavioural Foundations and Applications, pp. 67–93. CABI (2006)

14. Schafer, J.B., Frankowski, D., Herlocker, J.L., Sen, S.: Collaborative filtering recommender systems. The Adaptive Web, 291–324 (2007)

15. Sen, S., Lam, S., Rashid, A., Cosley, D., Frankowski, D., Osterhouse, J., Harper, F., Riedl, J.: Tagging, communities, vocabulary, evolution. In: Proceedings of the 20th Anniversary Conference on Computer Supported Cooperative Work, pp. 181–190. ACM, New York (2006)

16. Zentner, M., Grandjean, D., Scherer, K.R.: Emotions evoked by the sound of music: Characterization, classification, and measurement. Emotion 8(4), 494–521 (2008)

Leveraging Collaborative Filtering to Tag-Based Personalized Search

Heung-Nam Kim, Majdi Rawashdeh, and Abdulmotaleb El Saddik

School of Information Technology and Engineering, University of Ottawa,
800 King Edward, Ottawa, Ontario, K1N 6N5, Canada
{hnkim,majdi,abed}@mcrlab.uottawa.ca

Abstract. In recent years, social media services with social tagging have become tremendously popular. Because users are no longer mere consumers of content, social Web users have been overwhelmed by the huge numbers of social content available. For tailoring search results, in this paper, we look into the potential of social tagging in social media services. By leveraging collaborative filtering, we propose a new search model to enhance not only retrieval accuracy but also retrieval coverage. Our approach first computes latent preferences of users on tags from other similar users, as well as latent annotations of tags for items from other similar items. We then apply the latency of tags to a tag-based personalized ranking depending on individual users. Experimental results demonstrate the feasibility of our method for personalized searches in social media services.

Keywords: Personalized Search, Social Tagging, Collaborative Filtering.

1   Introduction

The prevalence of social media services has brought voluminous, previously-unavailable content through daily additions. Accordingly, users on the social Web are still overwhelmed by the content and have trouble finding the most desirable content suited to their needs. Personalized searches, which have emerged in response to this problem, generates users' search results based partially on their personal interests and/or past search histories; thus it can display different search results to different users to make the search more relevant to users' needs [14, 15]. With the current popularity of social tagging (also known as *folksonomy*), a number of researchers have recently concentrated on personalized searches with social tagging [2, 9, 19, 20, 22, 23]. Because modern social media services allow users to freely annotate their resources (e.g., images in Flickr[1], music in Last.fm[2], videos in YouTube[3], and bookmarks in Delicious[4]) with descriptive tags, the users tend to use the tags to annotate resources that they are interested in [7]. Consequently, social tagging has

---

[1] http://www.flickr.com/
[2] http://www.last.fm/
[3] http://www.youtube.com/
[4] http://www.delicious.com/

Joseph A. Konstan et al. (Eds.): UMAP 2011, LNCS 6787, pp. 195–206, 2011.
© Springer-Verlag Berlin Heidelberg 2011

become a popular way to share and organize social resources, in turn leading to a sizeable amount of user-generated metadata [3].

Recent studies, such as [3, 12, 20], observed that a set of aggregated user-generated tags on resources is rich and compact enough to characterize and describe the main concepts of content in the resource. Additionally, popular query terms and tags tend to overlap significantly [8]. These observations indicate that social tagging aggregated by community users contains important and useful information that can make search results more relevant. Ideally, personalized search algorithms should discover not only accurate resources suited to users' needs, but also a wide range of desirable resources for users' queries. However, because users employ a small portion of the total number of tags and often use personal and self-reference tags, mostly helpful for themselves, it is not enough to model an individual user via tags only used by him/her. Similarly, since resources are usually annotated with a small portion of the total number of tags, users may fail to find valuable resources if they retrieve solely those resources that already have tags contained in the query (e.g., query matching).

To deal with these limitations, in this paper, we introduce a new method of personalized searches that incorporates collaborative filtering techniques into social tagging. Collaborative filtering, which is one of the most successful technologies in recommender systems, utilizes community collaboration for resource recommendations, rather than analysis of the actual content itself [1]. Our method explores not only individual interests but also social wisdom that profited by collaborative filtering for ranking social resources in tag-based searches. After determining the similarities between users and between items, we build two latent models: i) a latent preference of a user for a certain tag and ii) a latent annotation of a tag for a certain item. Finally, for a given query (i.e., a set of tags) issued by a user, we apply the models to a personalized item ranking for the user. The remainder sections are organized as follows: Section 2 briefly review previous studies related to social search using social tagging. In Section 3, we provide a detailed description of building models and exploiting the models for tailoring search results. In Section 4, we present experiment evaluations comparing our approach with state-of-the art methods. Finally, we conclude our study with future work in Section 5.

2   Related Work

In this section, we mainly review literatures closely relevant to personalized searches that make use of social tagging to enhance search results. Some early work in using social tagging for information retrieval is presented by Hotho et al. [9]. The authors presented a formal model and a new graph-based search algorithm for folksonomies, called *FolkRank*. The *FolkRank* explored folksonomy structure for ranking search requests within tagging systems. Wu et al. [21] took emergent semantics of social tags into consideration to apply the semantics to search Web bookmarks. They proposed a global semantic model that could help disambiguate tags and group synonymous tags together in concepts. Two algorithms are proposed in [2], *SocialSimRank* and *SocialPageRank*. The former exploited the similarity between user queries and tags whereas the latter captured page popularity based on its annotations. Levy and

Sandler [12] investigated several latent semantic models, such as Latent Semantic Analysis (LSA) and Probabilistic LSA, for uncovering emergent semantics from tags labeled to music.

There are some recent studies that have inspired us to design our algorithm. Xu et al. [22] studied a personalized search framework incorporated with social tagging. The authors took into consideration two aspects, a query term matching and a topic matching, for the rank of an item by regarding social tags as topics. Differing from our approach, Xu et al.'s approach adopted two different ranking methods that operate separately; thus both of them for a query of a user have to be aggregated to obtain a final ranked list. Similar to our work, Zanardi and Capra [23] proposed a social ranking mechanism incorporated with collaborative filtering techniques, namely *Social Ranking*, to find content relevant to a user's query. It exploited users' similarity by tag overlap to improve accuracy, as well as tags' similarity based on their association to the content to increase coverage. The main difference between this study and our study is that our study does not expand a user's query explicitly. Instead, our model itself implicitly contains the effect of the query expansion. More importantly, their work did not consider a user's preference for tags when the tags were expanded for a given query. More recently, Wetzker et al. [20] proposed a user-centric tag model (*UCTM*) that maps personal tag vocabularies on the corresponding tag vocabularies used by all users using resources as intermediates. The main difference between this model and our model is our approach makes the best use of collaborative filtering technologies that identify not only similar users but also similar items. We will further discuss the differences in more detail through comparison experiments.

3   Tag-Based Personalized Search

To support an accurate tag-based search depending on individual users, we build two latent tag models by leveraging two well-known collaborative filtering techniques: a user-based approach [4] and an item-based approach [6]. Before going into further detail, some definitions of matrices are introduced. In this paper, matrices are denoted using boldface upper-case letters, such as $\mathbf{R}$, whereas the corresponding italic letters with two subscript indices, such as $R_{u,i}$, represent the entries of the matrices. We henceforth use the term *items* to refer to resources. In general, for a list of l users $U = \{u_1, u_2, ..., u_l\}$, a list of m tags $T = \{t_1, t_2, ..., t_m\}$, and a list of n items $I = \{i_1, i_2, ..., i_n\}$, a folksonomy can be represented as three projected matrices: an $l \times n$ user-item matrix $\mathbf{R}$, an $l \times m$ user-tag matrix $\mathbf{A}$, and an $m \times n$ tag-item matrix $\mathbf{G}$ [20]. Each entries of the matrices are denoted by $R_{u,i}$, $A_{u,t}$, and $G_{t,i}$, respectively, where $R_{u,i}$ is an indicator variable which is equal to 1 if user u tagged item i and 0 otherwise, $A_{u,t}$ represents the number of items that user u has tagged with tag t, and $G_{t,i}$ represents the number of users who have tagged item i with tag t.

3.1   Building a Model for Latent Tag Preference

The basic idea of computing latent tag preferences starts from assuming that a certain user is likely to prefer tags that have been used by him/her or other similar users. To determine similar users, vector cosine similarity, which quantifies the similarity of two vectors according to their angle, is employed to measure the similarity values between a certain user and every other user. The vectors used in our study are row vectors from the user-tag matrix $\mathbf{A}$. Finally, for l users, the similarity of users can be represented as an $l \times l$ user-user similarity matrix $\mathbf{S}$. Analogous to a user-based collaborative filtering, we also take k *nearest neighbors* of each user into consideration. To this end, in the similarity matrix $\mathbf{S}$, the entry $S_{u,v}$, which represents the u-th user for the v-th user, is set to the cosine similarity value between a pair of users u and v if the corresponding similarity value is greater than the k highest similarity value in the v-th column of $\mathbf{S}$, and 0 otherwise. In other words, each column in the matrix $\mathbf{S}$ contains at most k non-zero values indicating the similarity values between the corresponding column user and k nearest neighbors. Note that all entries on the main diagonal in the matrix are equal to 1, i.e., for any two users, a and b, where $a \in U$ and $b \in U$, if a is equal to b, then $S_{a,b} = 1$. This matrix is denoted by $\mathbf{S}^k$ where k is the number of similar users.

First model, namely a latent tag preference model, reflects the tendency of how a particular tag has been tagged by users similar to a certain user. For that, we build a new user-tag matrix derived by the product of two matrices, $\mathbf{A}$ and $\mathbf{S}$. Before building the model, each row vector of users in the user-tag matrix $\mathbf{A}$ is normalized as $\| \mathbf{u}_v \|_2 = 1$, for $v = 1, 2, \ldots, l$. Formally, for a given entry $A_{u,t}$, a normalized value of $A_{u,t}$ is computed by:

$$\tilde{A}_{u,t} = A_{u,t} \Big/ \sqrt{\sum\nolimits_{j=1}^{m} (A_{u,j})^2} \tag{1}$$

Let $\tilde{\mathbf{A}}$ denote a normalized matrix of $\mathbf{A}$. Then, a model of latent tag preferences $\mathbf{M}$ can be built by:

$$\mathbf{M} = \tilde{\mathbf{A}}^\mathrm{T} \mathbf{S}^k \tag{2}$$

where $\tilde{\mathbf{A}}^\mathrm{T}$ is a transpose matrix of the normalized matrix $\tilde{\mathbf{A}}$ of $\mathbf{A}$. More precisely, let $\tilde{\mathbf{a}}_t$ denote the t-th column vector of $\tilde{\mathbf{A}}$ and $\mathbf{s}_u$ the u-th column vector of $\mathbf{S}^k$. Then, an entry of the u-th column of the t-th row in $\mathbf{M}$ can be filled by the dot product of the two column vectors:

$$M_{t,u} = \tilde{\mathbf{a}}_t \cdot \mathbf{s}_u = \sum\nolimits_{v=1}^{l} \tilde{A}_{v,t} \times S_{v,u} \tag{3}$$

where $M_{t,u}$ implies a latent preference value of user u on tag t with respect to k nearest neighbors of him/her. The more a neighbor v is similar to user u, the more influence the neighbor has for computing the preference value. In addition, by normalizing each row in $\mathbf{A}$, users who have used numerous tags present less contribution than users who have used a small number of tags.

3.2   Building a Model for Latent Tag Annotation

For the second model, called a latent tag annotation model, we capture the tendency of how a certain tag has been labeled to items similar to a particular item. Analogous to the concept of an item-based collaborative filtering, we first identify groups of items that are similar to each item using the tag-item matrix $\mathbf{G}$. With respect to an item-item similarity between two items, two column vectors in the matrix $\mathbf{G}$ are used for vector cosine similarity. Let $\mathbf{H}$ denote an $n \times n$ item-item similarity matrix.

Analogous to k nearest neighbors, we take account of k' *most similar items*; the resulting matrix is denoted by $\mathbf{H}^{k'}$ in which each column stores at most k' non-zero similarity values. Note that all entries on the main diagonal in the similarity matrix are equal to 1.

Finally, a model of latent tag annotations $\mathbf{W}$ can be constructed by the product of two matrices:

$$\mathbf{W} = \hat{\mathbf{G}}\,\mathbf{H}^{k'} \tag{4}$$

where $\hat{\mathbf{G}}$ refers to a normalized matrix of $\mathbf{G}$. For a given element of i-th column of t-th row, $G_{t,i}$, a normalized value is calculated by:

$$\hat{G}_{t,i} = G_{t,i} \bigg/ \sqrt{\sum_{j=1}^{m}(G_{j,i})^2} \tag{5}$$

More precisely, let $\hat{\mathbf{g}}_t^T$ denote the t-th row vector of $\hat{\mathbf{G}}$ and $\mathbf{h}_i$ the i-th column vector of $\mathbf{H}^{k'}$. Then, an entry of the i-th column of the t-th row in $\mathbf{W}$ can be filled by the dot product of the two vectors:

$$W_{t,i} = \hat{\mathbf{g}}_t^T \cdot \mathbf{h}_i = \sum_{j=1}^{n} \hat{G}_{t,j} \times H_{j,i} \tag{6}$$

where $W_{t,i}$ implies a latent annotation value of tag t on item i with respect to k' most similar items of item i. Items that are more similar to item i contribute more to estimating the latent annotation value of the item. In addition, through the normalization of each column in $\mathbf{G}$, items annotated with lots of tags can present less contribution in Equation 6 than items annotated with a small number of tags.

3.3   Personalized Searching and Ranking

In our study, we assume that a query submitted by users consists of a set of tags. Because every user has different tastes on items, different items in search results may be considered to be relevant to the user despite the same query.

For tailoring search results, we propose a new ranking method depending on a user and his/her query. Formally, a given query q submitted by user u, a ranking score of item i is computed by:

$$Rank_{u,q}(i) = \sum_{t \in q} M_{t,u} \times W_{t,i} \tag{7}$$

where $M_{t,u}$ is the value of u-th column (user) of t-th row (tag) in the matrix $\mathbf{M}$ and $W_{t,i}$ is the value of i-th column (item) of t-th row (tag) in the matrix $\mathbf{W}$. In Equation 7, the value $M_{t,u}$ provides latent preference of user u on tag t contained in the query; thus it separates the ranking result for user u from ranking results for different users who submit the same tags as a query. Moreover, the value $W_{t,i}$ is the result that reflects tag t's usages of all users on items similar to item i. The more tag t is labeled to items similar to a certain item, the higher ranking score the item obtains. By incorporating the two models, $\mathbf{M}$ and $\mathbf{W}$, into personalized searches, items that a user would like the most can be discovered regardless of whether query tags are explicitly annotated in the items. For a given query of user u, once our strategy computes a ranking score of items which have not previously been tagged by him/her, the items are ranked in descending order of the score. Figure 1 shows the overall process of computing a ranking score of an item for given query tags of a search user.

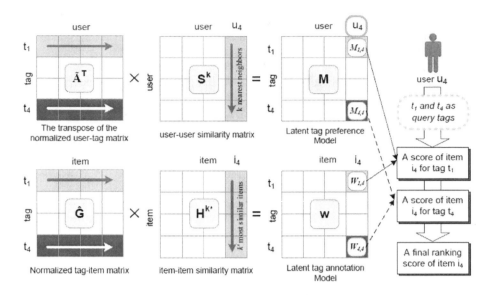

Fig. 1. Computing an item ranking score for given query tags of a user

3.4   Computational Complexity

We analyze the computational complexity of our retrieval method according to the number of users l, the number of items n, the number of tags m, the number of similar users k, and the number of similar items k'.

Prior to building the models, the user-user similarity matrix $\mathbf{S}$ and the item-item similarity matrix $\mathbf{H}$ have to be computed. The complexities of these steps are, in the worst case, $O(l^2 m)$ and $O(mn^2)$, respectively. For computing $\mathbf{M}$ and $\mathbf{W}$, we additionally require approximately $O(klm)$ and $O(k'mn)$, respectively; therefore, the total complexity of building the model $\mathbf{M}$ becomes $O(l^2 m + klm)$ whereas that of building the model $\mathbf{W}$ becomes $O(mn^2 + k'mn)$. However, as pointed out in several studies [22, 23], because the user-tag matrix $\mathbf{A}$ and the tag-item matrix $\mathbf{G}$ are extremely sparse in practice, the actual computational complexity tends to be significantly reduced. The complexities of the matrix $\mathbf{S}$ is closer to $O(lm)$, since almost user vectors contain a relatively small number of tags. Analogously, The complexities of the matrix $\mathbf{H}$ is reduced to $O(mn)$, as most items have been labeled with a very small number of tags. Therefore, the complexities of $\mathbf{M}$ and $\mathbf{W}$ are approximately reduced to $O(lm + klm) \cong O(lm)$ and $O(mn + k'mn) \cong O(mn)$, respectively; consequently the total computational complexity becomes $O(lm + mn)$ during the model building phase. Note that the building the models, which are most time-consuming tasks, can be accomplished offline.

With respect to personalized searches, for w tags contained in a user's query, the computational complexity required to compute a *ranking score* of a particular item is given as $O(w)$; accordingly the total complexity of computing n items becomes $O(wn) \cong O(n)$.

4   Experiment Results

The experimental data comes from BibSonomy[5], which is a social tagging application allowing users to organize, annotate, and share scholarly references. The dataset used in this study is the p-core at level 5 [10, 11]. After we removed 63 duplicate data, the dataset contains 10,085 tag assignments on 412 items from 116 users with 361 tags. We projected the tag assignments onto three two-dimensional matrices: 2406 non-zero entries of the user-item matrix $\mathbf{R}$, 3696 non-zero entries of the user-tag matrix $\mathbf{A}$, and 5347 non-zero entries of the tag-item matrix $\mathbf{G}$.

4.1   Experiment Design and Metrics

To evaluate the performance of our search model, we followed the evaluation procedure described in [23]. For each user, we randomly withheld one of his/her posted items and his/her tags annotated in that item, and subsequently used those tags as a test query for the user. And the remaining tag assignments were used as a training set for building the models and finding the hidden item for each user. To ensure that our results are not sensitive to a particular test query for each user, we conducted five different runs in which each run with a different test query; thus the values reported in the experimental results are the averages of five runs with a 95% confidence interval.

Evaluation Metrics. To measure the retrieval accuracy with the ability of ranking relevant items, we employed Mean Reciprocal Rank at top-N [19], *MRR@N*, which is obtained by:

$$MRR @ N = \frac{1}{|U|} \sum_{u=1}^{|U|} \left(\sum_{i \in (T_u \cap R_u^N)} \frac{1}{r(i)} \right) \tag{8}$$

where T_u is a set of items tagged by user u in the test data whereas R_u^N is a set of top-N returned items for a query of user u. In addition, $r(i)$, $1 \leq r(i) \leq N$, refers to the rank of item i within a top-N list of user u. The higher the *MRR@N* value, the more accurately an algorithm ranks relevant items to users. Note that the value of MRR@1 is exactly same as that of *precision* at top-1.

In addition to the *MRR@N*, we also reported *coverage*, a measure of the ratio of relevant items an algorithm can discover for given queries [23]. That is, for computing coverage, we returned all items for a given query if an algorithm was able to compute a ranking score of the items.

Baseline Methods. For comparison purposes, we also conducted experiments with three state-of-the art methods: i) *Social Ranking* without query expansion (denoted as *SRk0*) and with query expansion using k most similar tags (denoted as *SRk5*), described in [23], ii) A User-Centric Tag Model (denoted as *UCTM*) presented in [20], and iii) BM25-based personalization model (denoted as *CosBM25*) described in [19] and [22]. Because these algorithms are mostly tailored to our personalized search scenario with social tagging, we implemented them to the best of our knowledge based on the published papers.

---

[5] http://bibsonomy.org

As for the Social Ranking, it exploited users' similarities for improving accuracy and tags' similarities for improving search coverage by expanding users' queries. When the query expansion was performed, the accuracy of a resulted set tended to decrease but it increased coverage. For fair comparisons, we tested two versions of Social Ranking when $k=0$ (i.e., no query expansion) and $k=5$ (query expansion using 5 most similar tags). With respect to the UCTM, Wetzker et al. [20] demonstrated that the UCTM outperformed *Adapted PageRank* [10] and *FolkRank* [9]. However, it originally took a single-tag query into account whereas our study considered a set of tags as a query. Accordingly, we extended the UCTM that could be possible to work a multi-tag query according to the suggestion in [20]. In the case of CosBM25, the final ranked list was provided by combining query matching based on the cosine similarity and topic matching based on BM25 weighting scheme using CombSUM as a ranking aggregation method [18].

4.2   Sensitivity to Parameters

Prior to running comparison experiments, we first investigated how our accuracy was sensitive to the number of similar users k and similar items k' used in building the latent models, $\mathbf{M}$ and $\mathbf{W}$, respectively. As described in Section 3, we expected that the number of similar users and the number of similar items could be significant factors affecting the accuracy of personalized searches because the models $\mathbf{M}$ and $\mathbf{W}$ are built depending on the values k and k', respectively.

Table 1 shows the MRR values at top-10 as the parameter values increase. The first row represents the value of k and k'. For example, the second column labeled "10" means we used 10 nearest neighbors (i.e., $\mathbf{S}^{10}$) and 10 most similar items (i.e., $\mathbf{H}^{10}$) when building the models $\mathbf{M}$ and $\mathbf{W}$, respectively. We also ran the experiment with all users (i.e., $\mathbf{S}^{116}$) and all items (i.e., $\mathbf{H}^{412}$).

Table 1. MRR according to variation of k and k' values (95% Confidence Intervals)

k, k'	10	20	30	40	50	60	70	all
MRR@10	0.250	0.259	0.253	0.245	0.242	0.230	0.229	0.212
95% C.I.	±0.010	±0.013	±0.025	±0.029	±0.025	±0.028	±0.027	±0.023
Coverage (%)	94.8	99	99.7	99.8	99.8	99.8	99.8	100
95% C.I.	±1.2	±0.3	±0.4	±0.3	±0.3	±0.3	±0.3	-

The experiment result shows that small values of k and k' yielded good performance enough. MRR tended to improve slightly as k and k' value increased from 10 to 20; beyond this point, the MRR values decreased. Importantly, when compared to the MRR value applied all users and all items (k=all and k'=all), the MRR values applied the small values (e.g., $k=10$ and $k'=10$) was significantly better. This result indicates that a relatively small values of similar users and items lead to good search accuracy while decreasing the computation cost. With respect to coverage, it tended to increase as the values of k and k' increased; however, similar to the MRR result, small values also provided reasonably good coverage. To avoid not only increasing unnecessary computation cost but also including superfluous information, $k=20$ and $k'=20$ were selected in our comparison experiment.

4.3   The Impact of Normalizations

In this experiment, we examined the impact of the matrix normalization on retrieval accuracy. To this end, we carried out experiments with a non-normalized approach that employs the matrix $\mathbf{A}^T$ in Equation 2 and the matrix $\mathbf{G}$ in Equation 4 instead of $\tilde{\mathbf{A}}^T$ and $\hat{\mathbf{G}}$, respectively. Subsequently, the MRR results of this approach were compared with the results obtained by the normalized approach in Section 4.2.

Table 2. MRR improvements over a non-normalized method (MRR@10)

k, k'	10	20	30	40	50	60	70	all
Improvement	0.029*	0.027**	0.024*	0.019*	0.021**	0.019*	0.019**	0.015**

(* Significant at $p < 0.5$, ** Significant at $p < 0.01$)

Table 2 summarizes MRR improvements of the normalized approach over the non-normalized one. Similar to the results of the normalized approach, small values of k and k' provided reasonably good MRR values. Comparing the MRR values obtained by the normalized case and the non-normalized one, the former was found to be superior to the latter at all variations of k and k' values. To analyze statistical significance, we also conducted two-tailed paired t-tests on the MRR results. As a result, we observed that there are statistically significant differences between the two approaches.

4.4   Comparisons with Baseline Methods

To compare our ranking method to the baseline methods described in Section 4.1, we investigated how well each algorithm makes a relevant item to be positioned at a higher rank for a given user's query. For this, we selectively examined MRR results at top-1, top-5, and top-10 positions (i.e., N=1, 5, and 10).

Figure 2 depicts the comparison results, showing how our method outperformed the baseline methods at the selected top-N positions. We also plotted confidence intervals on each bar chart. Comparing results of MRR@1, it was apparent that our method and the other methods had significant MRR disparity. This result implied that the proposed model could indeed put items relevant to user interests on a top rank in a searched list. Similar to the situation in the top-1 position, improvements over *SRs* and *UCTM* at the top-5 and top-10 results were quite considerable. Two-tailed paired t-tests were also performed to determine whether there were significant differences. As a result, the differences between our method and *SRk0* (or *SRk5*) were statistically significant ($p < 0.001$). Comparing the t-tests on our method and *UCTM*, the differences also appeared to be statistically significant at a level of 5% ($p < 0.05$). The same significant levels were obeserved by performing the t-tests on our method and *CosBM25*.

We continued to examine coverage of each algorithm. Table 3 summarizes the result shown with a 95% confidence interval. As a result, our method obtained approximately 7.9%, 4.5%, 13.8%, and 1.6% improvement on coverage, compared to *SRk0*, *SRk5*, *UCTM*, and *CosBM25*, respectively.

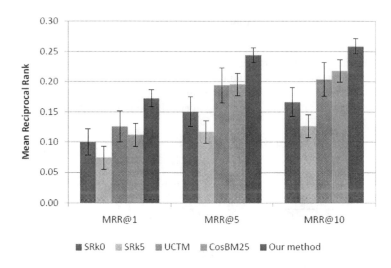

Fig. 2. Comparisons of Mean Reciprocal Rank at different top-N results

Table 3. A comparison ofcoverage of the five methods (95% Confidence Intervals)

	SRk0	SRk5	UCTM	CosBM25	Our method
Coverage (%)	91	94.5	85.2	97.4	99
95% C.I.	±1.4	±0.4	±1.2	±0.9	±0.3

Basically, *SRk0* can only find items that have been labeled with at least one of tags contained in a query. On the other hand, it is theoretically possible that the other methods, including our approach, can retrieve some items not previously tagged with query tags. *SRk5* expands a query by utilizing five most similar tags to each tag contained in the query; thus it could find items that have annotated with tags contained in the extended query. As can be seen from the result, such query expansion indeed helped improve coverage, compared to *SRk0*. In the case of *CosBM25*, it performs the two ranking processes, a query term matching process and a topic matching process, to generate a final ranked list. The topic matching process determines how a search user is interested in items in terms of tags labeled to the items; accordingly, items annotated with tags used by a search user could be searched even though those ranks within searched results might be low. As for *UCTM*, it first translates a query tag used by a search user to other co-occurrence tags which can be represented by a vector. Thus, items labeled with the translated vector could be retrieved. Nevertheless, in our experiment we failed to translate personal test tags for some of test users to global tags; consequently coverage of *UCTM* was rather worse than the other methods. In the case of our method, although a query tag has not been annotated in a particular item, we could search that item if the query tag once was labeled to items similar to the item. Analogously, personal preference of a search user for a query tag could be inferred from the tag's usage of users similar to the searcher; Contrary to *UCTM*, accordingly, our approach could easily represent query tags as a vector regardless of whether the searcher had used them.

These comparison experiments clearly showed that our method could offer considerable performance in terms of both ranking accuracy and coverage, compared to the state-of-the art baseline methods.

5   Conclusions and Future Work

In this paper, we propose a new tag-based method for personalized searches incorporated with a user-based and an item-based collaborative filtering. By exploiting similar users and similar items, we build the latent model for tags with respect to both individual users and individual items, facilitating more accurate search results. The major advantage of the proposed method is that it can search and rank items regardless of whether query tags are annotated in the items. The experimental results demonstrate that the proposed algorithm indeed offers significant advantages in improving retrieval accuracy and coverage. In addition, our method can provide more suitable items with a higher rank in searched results.

In future work, we plan to carry out further experiments using large-scale different datasets because tag usage of users might be different according to a type of items (e.g., Web pages, music, videos, and photos). In addition, we intend to compare our approach to other state-of-art methods that use tensor factorization [5, 17] or dimensionality reduction techniques [12]. It would also be interesting to apply our method to different scenarios such as tag or item recommendations. For example, when assuming that a particular user submits all tags as his/her query, we could compute a preference score of the user on an item using the dot product of the column vector of the corresponding user in the latent tag preference model and the column vector of the corresponding item in the latent tag annotation model. We plan to apply the proposed models to the item recommendation scenario in the future.

References

1. Adomavicius, G., Tuzhilin, A.: Toward the Next Generation of Recommender systems: A Survey of the State-of-the-art and Possible Extensions. IEEE Transactions on Knowledge and Data Engineering 17(6), 734–749 (2005)
2. Bao, S., Wu, X., Fei, B., Xue, G., Su, Z., Yu, Y.: Optimizing Web Search Using Social Annotations. In: 16th International Conference on World Wide Web, pp. 501–510 (2007)
3. Bischoff, K., Firan, C.S., Nejdl, W., Paiu, R.: Can All Tags be Used for Search? In: 17th ACM Conference on Information and Knowledge Management, pp. 203–212 (2008)
4. Breese, J.S., Heckerman, D., Kadie, C.: Empirical Analysis of Predictive Algorithms for Collaborative Filtering. In: 14th Annual Conference on Uncertainty in Artificial Intelligence, pp. 43–52 (1998)
5. Cai, Y., Zhang, M., Luo, D., Ding, C., Chakravarthy, S.: Low-order Tensor Decompositions for Social Tagging Recommendation. In: 4th ACM International Conference on Web Search and Data Mining, pp. 695–704 (2011)
6. Deshpande, M., Karypis, G.: Item-based Top-N Recommendation Algorithms. ACM Transactions on Information Systems 22(1), 143–177 (2004)
7. Golder, S.A., Huberman, B.A.: Usage Patterns of Collaborative Tagging Systems. Journal of Information Science 32(2), 198–208 (2006)

8. Heymann, P., Koutrika, G., Garcia-Molina, H.: Can Social Bookmarking Improve Web Search? In: 1st International Conference on Web Search and Web Data Mining, pp. 195–206 (2008)
9. Hotho, A., Jäschke, R., Schmitz, C., Stumme, G.: Information Retrieval in Folksonomies: Search and Ranking. In: 3rd European Semantic Web Conference, pp. 411–426 (2006)
10. Jäschke, R., Marinho, L., Hotho, A., Schmidt-Thieme, L., Stumme, G.: Tag Recommendations in Social Bookmarking Systems. AI Communications 21(4), 231–247 (2008)
11. Knowledge and Data Engineering Group, University of Kassel: Benchmark Folksonomy Data from BibSonomy, version of April 30th, http://www.kde.cs.uni-kassel.de/bibsonomy/dumps/
12. Levy, M., Sandler, M.: Learning Latent Semantic Models for Music from Social Tags. Journal of New Music Research 37(2), 137–150 (2008)
13. Li, X., Guo, L., Zhao, Y.E.: Tag-based Social Interest Discovery. In: 17th International Conference on World Wide Web, pp. 675–684 (2008)
14. Liu, F., Yu, C.T., Meng, W.: Personalized Web Search for Improving Retrieval Effectiveness. IEEE Transactions on Knowledge and Data Engineering 16(1), 28–40 (2004)
15. Ma, Z., Pant, G., Sheng, O.R.L.: Interest-based Personalized Search. ACM Transactions on Information Systems 25(1), Article 5 (2007)
16. Markines, B., Cattuto, C., Menczer, F., Benz, D., Hotho, A., Stumme, G.: Evaluating Similarity Measures for Emergent Semantics of Social Tagging. In: 18th International Conference on World Wide Web, pp. 641–650 (2009)
17. Rendle, S., Schmidt-Thieme, L.: Pairwise Interaction Tensor Factorization for Personalized Tag Recommendation. In: 3rd ACM International Conference on Web Search and Data Mining, pp. 81–90 (2010)
18. Shaw, J.A., Fox, E.A.: Combination of Multiple Searches. In: Text REtrieval Conference, pp. 243–252 (1993)
19. Vallet, D., Cantador, I., Jose, J.M.: Personalizing Web Search with Folksonomy-based User and Document Profiles. In: 32nd European Conference on Information Retrieval, pp. 420–431 (2010)
20. Wetzker, R., Zimmermann, C., Bauckhage, C., Albayrak, S.: I Tag, You Tag: Translating Tags for Advanced User Models. In: 3rd ACM International Conference on Web Search and Data Mining, pp. 71–80 (2010)
21. Wu, X., Zhang, L., Yu, Y.: Exploring Social Annotations for the Semantic Web. In: 15th International Conference on World Wide Web, pp. 417–426 (2006)
22. Xu, S., Bao, S., Fei, B., Su, Z., Yu, Y.: Exploring Folksonomy for Personalized Search. In: 31st Annual International ACM SIGIR Conference on Research and Development in Information Retrieval, pp. 155–162 (2008)
23. Zanardi, V., Capra, L.: Social Ranking: Uncovering Relevant Content Using Tag-based Recommender Systems. In: 2008 ACM Conference on Recommender Systems, pp. 51–58 (2008)

Modelling Symmetry of Activity as an Indicator of Collocated Group Collaboration

Roberto Martinez[1], Judy Kay[1], James R. Wallace[2], and Kalina Yacef[1]

[1] School of Information Technologies, J12, University of Sydney,
1 Cleveland St. NSW 2006, Australia
{roberto,judy,kalina}@it.usyd.edu.au
[2] Department of Systems Design Engineering, University Waterloo,
200 University Ave. West, Waterloo, Ontario, Canada N2L 3G1
jrwallac@uwaterloo.ca

Abstract. There are many contexts where it would be helpful to model the collaboration of a group. In learning settings, this is important for classroom teachers and for students learning collaboration skills. Our approach exploits the digital and audio footprints of the users' actions at collocated settings to automatically build a model of symmetry of activity. This paper describes our theoretical model of collaborative learning and how we implemented it. We use the Gini coefficient as a statistical indicator of symmetry of activity, which is itself an important indicator of collaboration. We built this model from a small-scale qualitative study based on concept mapping at an interactive tabletop. We then evaluated the model using a larger scale study based on a corpus of coded data from a multi-display groupware collocated setting. Our key contributions are the model of symmetry of activity as a foundation for modelling collaboration within groups that should have egalitarian participation, the operationalisation of the model and validation of the approach on both a small-scale qualitative study and a larger scale quantitative corpus of data.

Keywords: tabletop, group modelling, groupware, collaborative learning, collocated collaboration, clustering.

1   Introduction

There are important reasons for building effective models of the collaborative process of small teams of people who are using electronic tools as part of collocated activities. This is particularly important in those educational contexts where the goal of the learning activity is to develop learners' collaboration skills. If we can build accurate models which reflect the levels of key aspects of collaboration, this can be valuable for teachers, learners or learning management systems to improve the learning process. There are many situations where people need to work collaboratively in small groups, both at the workplace and informal settings. In many cases, all members of the group should be active in the collaboration: for example, to draw upon the different expertise and background of each member or to find solutions to problems by negotiation and discussion of competing possibilities.

Joseph A. Konstan et al. (Eds.): UMAP 2011, LNCS 6787, pp. 207–218, 2011.

This makes it important to be able to build models that indicate whether a group is collaborating effectively. Emerging technologies that can support small groups have the potential to provide the data that could be used to create such group models of collaboration. Previous work in user modelling research has articulated the importance of capturing a user model according to the users' interactions around the tabletop in order to adapt and improve the support to the group activities [1].

Drawing on the considerable work on collaborative learning theories [2] and collaborative learning supported by desktop computers [3], an objective and useful indicator of collaboration is the notion of *symmetry*. We build upon that work, and constructivist theories of *group cognition* [4] to create a theoretical model of *symmetry of activity* of the group in small collocated settings, such as at interactive tabletops. We argue that the measure of the symmetry of participation of collocated group members can provide insights into the extent of collaboration of the group, and that this measure can be extracted automatically from log and audio traces. This paper describes our exploration of ways to create helpful models of collaboration based upon indicators of symmetry.

We begin by describing some theoretical foundations and outlining important elements of the collaboration model. We then describe our model in terms of our exploratory study based on concept mapping at the tabletop and show how we have implemented it by defining measures of symmetry of activity. We then evaluate the model using a larger scale trial drawing on a corpus of coded data from a multi-display groupware collocated setting based on a problem-solving activity.

The remainder of the paper is organised as follows. The next section presents a short overview of related work. Next, we describe our exploratory study in terms of the collaborative learning theory Afterwards, the extraction of the model is presented, with Section 4 describing the creation of our model of symmetry, and Section 5 presenting the clustering work to validate such a model. Then, we discuss the results of the analysis with reflections on how the indicators of symmetry ought to be included in the learner model of the group to improve teaching and learning. Finally, we conclude with the discussion and future work.

2 Related Work

There has been relatively limited research exploring how to make use of the digital footprints of the learners' activity to infer indicators that could help build models of collocated collaboration; these could be used in many ways to help groups to learn work more collaboratively and effectively. Previous work in this area has focused mostly on supporting group collaborative tasks within e-learning systems.

The Narcissus system [5] gives support to groups working collaboratively through the Trac[1] web-based collaborative system. It allows teams to interact with their group model of activity, helping learners and their tutors gain insights on how the group has operated. Anaya and Boticario [6] described a domain-independent collaborative learning modelling method based on statistical quantitative data. This was evaluated using two data mining techniques, clustering and decision trees. This approach aims to classify and group individuals according to their collaboration level. Perera et.al.

---

[1] Trac Open Source Project: http://trac.edgewall.org/

[7] also modelled key aspects of teamwork and collaboration, using machine learning techniques but focusing on clustering groups according to various indicators of collaboration and exploring the sequential patterns of interaction. Soller and Lesgold [8] modelled the *process* of collaborative learning supported by an online shared workspace. They presented a modelling approach based on Hidden Markov Models to recognise the communication networks within groups classifying the sequences of interaction that distinguish the effective sharing knowledge episodes. Casillas and Daradomius [9] described another approach for extracting and modelling behavioural patterns in collaborative settings building on Social Network Analysis.

3 Theoretical Foundations: Group Cognition and Symmetry of Action

Group cognition theory builds upon many other theories based on the concept of constructing meaning through language and social interactions [10]. According to these theories, a group of people working collaboratively externalise and negotiate their different viewpoints. Sometimes the flux of interactions results in the creation of external artefacts such as texts, conceptual maps, diagrams, sculptures and other objects. These social artefacts embody the group's understanding. Figure 1 depicts the elements in the process of group cognition starting with the personal understanding cycle (1), which occurs inside individuals' minds, and the social knowledge building cycle (2), which includes all the sub-processes that may be present when building shared understanding. In face to face interactions, these sub-processes can generate a huge quantity of cognitive artefacts in short periods of time. Group members have to articulate their thoughts to convince others or to explain their point of view. They negotiate, share, revise and externalise their standpoints to other participants, leaving more digital evidence of the collaboration process than in individual learning settings. These are the digital tracks of the process of the interaction that we aim to exploit.

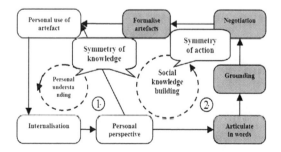

Fig. 1. Simplified model of collaborative knowledge building adapted from [10]

Dillenbourg [2] points to the importance of high levels symmetry of action, knowledge and status for successful collaboration in learning contexts.. Symmetry of action is the degree to which users perform the same level of activity; we can capture this aspect from actions at a tabletop or at a multi-display setting. Symmetry of knowledge refers to the extent to which users have the same level of skills and knowledge. In Figure 1 we depict these two dimensions of symmetry as related directly to the collaborative process. Finally, the symmetry of status is associated with the relative position that each user has in their community.

We investigate whether assessing key aspects of the *symmetry of action* in group's logs and audio traces can determine important aspects of collaboration in the group. Key features of this symmetry can easily be captured, whereas the symmetry of knowledge is highly domain dependent and therefore difficult to assess in a generic way. Similarly, the symmetry of status is a complex social phenomenon that cannot be entirely tackled from a quantitative perspective.

We collected data from two sources: the logs of interactions (touches on the tabletop or clicks in a multi-display setting), obtained directly from the application, and the audio traces, obtained using microphones [11]. From these two sources of data, we identified four measures of action that we aim to use to model the degree of symmetry of action: the number and total duration of verbal interventions, and the number and total duration of physical interaction with the system.

In addition to these measures, we used the *Gini Coefficient* [12], a measurement of statistical dispersion which has been successfully used to estimate equity of participation of students in learning environments [13] and also for measuring levels of participation at multi-touch devices [14]. The Gini Coefficient (G) is an indicator of dispersion that ranges between 0 and 1. A coefficient value of 1 indicates total asymmetry or dispersion and 0 indicates total symmetry or perfect equality.

This indicator can be defined as the mean of the difference between every pair of participants (n= 3 or 4 in this study), divided by the mean size μ (1). In essence, our approach requires a way to translate the logs of interactions into Gini coefficients for representing symmetry of activity.

$$G = \frac{\sum_{i=1}^{n} \sum_{j=1}^{n} |x_i - x_j|}{2\,n^2 \mu} \tag{1}$$

Our methodology consists of, first, conducting a qualitative and statistical exploration in a small study to refine a model of group collaboration based on these measures (in the form of rules), and then, evaluating this model through a large-scale study.

4   Model of Symmetry

4.1   Context of the Study

We designed a case study on a multi-touch tabletop interface. Multi-touch tabletops offer the promise of supporting rich face to face collaboration. Importantly, they can capture digital footprints of the users' activity.

Groups were recruited for the first part of the analysis to build an artefact collaboratively at the tabletop using Cmate, as shown in Figure 2. Cmate is a tabletop application designed for collaborative *concept mapping* [15]. One of the advantages of the concept maps is that through these tools learners can construct understanding in their own terms, discuss relationships between concepts and reflect on alternative perspectives. The implementation of the Cmate interface is described in detail in [16].

Task. In the first part of the experiment, participants were asked to create an individual concept map, capturing their own understanding of a topic using their own concept set. After studying the same text titled: *Recycling, cost-benefit analysis,* participants were requested to draw maps answering the focus question: *does recycling help the environment?* These initial individual artefacts were built on desktop computers, using CmapTools[2], and preloaded into the tabletop. In the second (and collaborative) part of the experiment, each group was asked to build a common group concept map at the tabletop. After the group had discussed their individual maps, participants could use Cmate to perform basic actions such as adding concepts, creating directed links between two concepts, moving and deleting concepts/links, and editing node words by double tapping a node and modifying the word using a virtual keyboard, all these with the purpose of creating a combined group map.

Fig. 2. Our tabletop application being used to build group concept maps

Population and data collection. Every touch on the tabletop was logged, along with the user who made it, and all sessions were video recorded. Sound was recorded with individual microphones worn by each participant. The study involved five groups, each of 3 or 4 participants, for a total of 18 participants. They were students predominantly enrolled in engineering courses and were aged between 20 and 27. Group members were familiar with one another. Each group had thirty minutes to build the concept map and five additional minutes to discuss the ideas and formalise which propositions should remain in the final map. Groups performed between 1450 and 2360 actions per session, for 8500 recorded touches. We also obtained a total of 6296 seconds of active verbal participation.

In Table 1 we present two example excerpts from group session logs. The fragment at the left corresponds to a collaborative group. In this case students combined talking with actions at the tabletop, dedicating some time to discussion before making changes. A different group, non collaborative this time, is shown in the excerpt at the right; this group dedicated most of the time to perform physical actions rather than discussing their ideas. Both fragments where extracted from the starting part of their respective sessions to illustrate the nature of the available data.

---

[2] Institute for Humans and Machine Cognition. CmapTools: http://cmap.ihmc.us/

Table 1. Simplified fragments of the combined log (application log + audio log). Left: collaborative group. Right: Non-collaborative group.

	Collaborative group			Non-collaborative group	
Author	Time	Log	Author	Time	Log
2	5:59:13	audio participation 4 sec	4	2:49:06	app "add concept" 32 "production"
1	5:59:15	audio participation 4 sec	4	2:49:07	app "move concept" 32 " production "
4	5:59:16	audio participation 1 sec	2	2:49:06	app "scroll menu m44
1	5:59:18	app "scroll menu" m9	3	2:49:10	app "move concept" 32 "production"
3	5:59:18	app "move menu" m10	3	2:49:15	app "add concept" 33 "consumption"
4	5:59:19	app "add link " 1 "waste"	4	2:49:16	app "delete concept" 32 "production "
1	5:59:20	app "scroll menu" m10	3	2:49:16	app "move concept"33 "consumption "
3	5:59:24	app "scroll menu" m11	2	2:49:17	app "scroll menu m44
4	5:59:29	audio participation 2 sec	2	2:49:18	app "add link" 35 "is"
3	5:59:31	app "move menu" m11	3	2:49:20	audio participation 1 sec
4	5:59:35	audio participation 2 sec	4	2:49:21	audio participation 2 sec
3	5:59:36	app "add concept gesture" m12	3	2:49:26	app "edit concept" 33 "consumption "

4.2 Model of Symmetry as an Indicator of Collaboration

In this section, we describe the statistical and qualitative approach to obtain the measurements of symmetry. Before any quantitative technique was performed, the data and video recordings were examined to see whether any simple statistics could discriminate symmetric groups in terms of their collaborative behaviour. We could observe that a couple of groups were highly collaborative. They were distinguished from others in terms of their consistent verbal communication and awareness of others' physical actions, discussing most of the actions each group member intended to perform. The other three groups displayed behaviour that ranged from moments of collaboration to periods of partial or non-existent communication. Most of the time, these participants worked individually, either not communicating with others or involving just a couple of participants in the discussion, leaving others working independently with the tabletop interface in a small region.

During the non-collaborative moments, participants split the work and worked in their personal space without awareness of others actions. These moments were characterised by high amounts of physical activity with each participant performing similar amount of actions, but low levels of verbal communication in very irregular amounts. This means that we expect the Gini coefficient in the physical dimension to be quite low (reflecting symmetry) whereas in the audio dimension it should be high (reflecting asymmetry). By contrast, the collaborative periods, especially for the groups that were generally collaborative, were characterised by high levels of verbal communication with a somewhat egalitarian distribution of participation in this dimension (hence a low Gini coefficient). However, as they were focused on the discussion and observing others' actions, the level of physical actions was lower compared with the non-collaborative groups. We could additionally observe that in some groups participants were keen to partially collaborate, leaving one or two members as spectators, or, at the extreme, one participant tended to do all the work by himself (hence a high Gini coefficient).

Another way to explore the symmetry of activity was to examine the *radars of activity* [17], giving a more summarised view of the activity. We generated a pair of radars, one for the physical events on the tabletop, measured in terms of the quantity of touches; and time of verbal participation, measured in seconds. For this study the time window for each visualisation was 90 seconds. Figure 3 shows three pairs of radars of a collaborative group (left) and a non collaborative group (right). Each coloured circular marker corresponds to one learner at their circular personal space: orange, yellow, green and purple for participants 1, 2, 3 and 4 respectively. The position of these markers indicates the level of participation: the closer the marker is to the centre, the less active they were in that period of time. The shape of the radars gives an indication of the symmetry of activity. Through these visual aids, we confirmed what we had observed from the videos. The collaborative group had more verbal participation but a low level of physical actions at the tabletop (see pairs of radars 1, 2 and 3 at the left of the figure). By contrast, the members of the non collaborative group performed high amounts of physical actions without externalizing their thoughts too much.

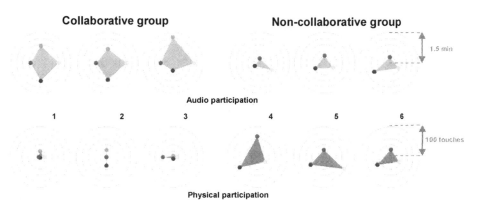

Fig. 3. Radars of activity for three different episodes, for both a collaborative and a non very collaborative group. They illustrate the symmetry and amount of audio (radars at the top of the figure) and touch participation (radars at the bottom).

These visualisations helped to assess whether groups were collaborating or not relying not just on the symmetry of groups but also in the extent of their participation (verbal and physical). In fact, our approach aims to quantify this information so that it can be incorporated and exploited in a group model. The quantitative information needed to draw these radars corresponds to the metrics we are evaluating as indicators of symmetry. Table 2 shows these measures for the episodes shown in Figure 3. They are: talking time, Gini coefficient of verbal participation, number of touches and the Gini coefficient of the quantity of touches.

Our initial analysis indicated that our metrics of symmetry can model facets of group collaboration. Based on the observations offered by this dataset, we hypothesise a set of rules, in terms of numeric metrics, as follows:

$$(low)P_{talk} + (high)G_{talk} + (high)P_{physical} + (low)G_{physical} \rightarrow Non\ Collaborative\ situations \qquad (2)$$

$$(high, medium)P_{talk} + (high)G_{talk} + (high)P_{physical} \rightarrow Partial\ collaboration \qquad (3)$$

$$(high)P_{talk} + (low)G_{talk} + (low)P_{physical} + (high, med)G_{physical} \rightarrow Collaborative\ situations \qquad (4)$$

Table 2. Tabletop data log grouped in pieces of 90 seconds. These values correspond to the visualisations showed in Figure 2.

Attribute	Collaborative group			Non-collaborative group		
Radar #	1	2	3	4	5	6
P_{talk} (seconds)	53	51	56	21	23	28
G_{talk} (Gini coeff.)	0.131	.132	0.315	0.400	0.129	0.347
$P_{physical}$ (touches)	17	24	25	72	69	47
$G_{physical}$ (Gini coeff.)	0.488	0.678	0.587	0.214	0.357	0.242

where P_{talk} corresponds to verbal participation, $P_{physical}$ to physical participation (touches, clicks), G_{talk} to the Gini coefficient as indicator of symmetry of talk and $G_{physical}$ as an indicator of symmetry of physical actions.

Indeed, after inspecting the correlation between these metrics of symmetry we found interesting relationships. There was a negative correlation between physical and verbal participation – corr. -0.441, (see chart at the left of Figure 4) and a stronger negative correlation between physical participation and the Gini coefficient of physical action - corr, -0.611 (Figure 4, right). In other words, when groups talk they do not perform many actions and, additionally, when they perform many actions, this physical activity is more egalitarian. However, in order to confirm that these observations are valid across collocated domains, and that the metrics are correlated with the extent of collaboration of the group, we used a second large-scale dataset based on a corpus of coded data.

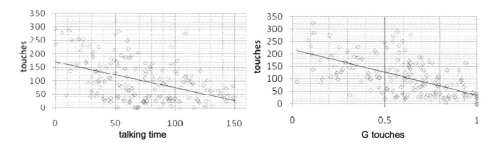

Fig. 4. Left: Scatter plot of physical and verbal participation. Right: Scatter plot of number and the Gini coefficient of physical participation.

5   Evaluation

5.1   Experiment and Data Collection

We evaluated the rules described in the subsection 4.2 using a dataset from groups performing a Job Shop Scheduling (JSS) task, an optimisation problem previously used for evaluating group interactions [18]. In this case, participants have to optimise the scheduling of six jobs, each one composed of six operations. These operations require the use of six resources that cannot be used by two or more operations at the same time. Participants modify the schedule by arranging the position of the resource pieces with the purpose of setting up the completion of all six jobs in the minimum time. A detailed description of the implementation of the interface can be found in [19]. The physical setting for these trials included a large shared display projected on a nearby wall and personal laptops with external mice for each participant, through which they could perform individual actions. Data from 19 trials were considered. The participants were students aged between 18 and 27 years. Groups of three were formed for each trial. Each group performed between 100 and 600 actions per solution, for a total of 9800 recorded interactions with the JSS software. The actions corresponded mostly to dragging resource pieces into position. In addition to the application data, we also transcribed verbal communication for each trial from video recordings. These transcripts included a total of 4836 utterances.

The video recordings of each trial were observed and coded manually. A coding label was assigned to each 90 seconds block of activity for each group. These time frame size was chosen based on the observations of the videos of the sessions in a parallel study [20]. Each block of activity was coded as corresponding to one of three possible values, according to the following guidelines. A block was labelled *collaborative* (C) if all participants participated to some extent and were aware of their peers' actions during that period of time. *Medium collaboration* (M) was used if one or two members of the group were unaware of their peer's actions and the group communication was partial. Finally, a block was labelled *non-collaborative* (NC) if the group split the task, working separately without awareness of each other. Three raters, including a domain expert, coded the blocks according to the descriptions detailed above. Inter reliability was tested on 15% of the sample (Cohen's, k = 0.69). This dataset is very similar, in terms of definition of data, to our tabletop dataset (see Table 2). Therefore, we grouped the log lines and calculated the same attributes we used for the first dataset. In this case, the difference is that we have an additional label for each 90 seconds of activity block. This additional information and the larger size of the dataset served to apply our unsupervised machine learning techniques and supervise the results to validate the hypotheses posed in the previous section.

5.2 Clustering Group Interactions According to Their Collaboration and Symmetry

We used a clustering machine learning technique to reveal the relationship between the rules of our model described in the previous section and the extent of collaboration of the groups. The features used were verbal participation (P_{talk}), physical participation ($P_{physical}$, number of clicks) and Gini coefficients as indicators of symmetry of talk (G_{talk}) and symmetry of physical actions ($G_{physical}$). Clustering has been used in a collaborative learning setting such as in [21], where authors aimed at grouping students according to their individual collaboration within their groups. In contrast, we use clustering to assess whether our rules can be applied to other domains with the aim of obtaining meaningful information about the symmetry and collaboration of collocated groups. It is important to highlight that in our approach we cluster segments of activity rather than the entire groups.

We used the clustering algorithm k-means with Euclidean distance measure. This algorithm is simple and effective if the number of clusters is previously known. However, k-means is sensitive to the initial seed. To mitigate this limitation we ran k-means 10 times using the 4 attributes specified in the rules of our model. Additionally, we also ran a secondary algorithm, the Expectation Maximisation (EM), using the same settings (k=3 clusters), obtaining similar results as with k-means (see Table 3). After the clusters from both algorithms were obtained, we compared the presence of collaborative, non- collaborative or moderately collaborative blocks in each cluster. The results of this comparison defined cluster 0 as the group with more collaborative blocks, cluster 1 as medium collaboration blocks and cluster 2 with the non collaborative blocks. The percentage of correct grouping was around 60% for both algorithms. This indicates that our clusters are not excellent classifiers but classification is not the purpose of our approach this time.

Table 3. Clustering results. Cluster-0 (C), Cluster-1 (M), Cluster-2 (NC).

Attribute	Clusters running 10 times k means				Clusters running EM			
	Full data	Cluster-0	Cluster-1	Cluster-2	Full data	Cluster-0	Cluster-1	Cluster-2
P_{talk}	28.668	**32.524 (h)**	34.999 (h)	**17.231 (l)**	28.668	**29.719 (h)**	37.099 (h)	**11.233 (l)**
G_{talk}	0.5304	**0.359 (l)**	0.610 (h)	**0.694 (h)**	0.5304	**0.444 (l)**	0.592 (m)	**0.753 (h)**
$P_{phvsical}$	36.714	**33.787(l)**	30.680 (l)	**46.25 (h)**	36.714	**37.691 (l)**	27.741 (l)	**47.463 (h)**
$G_{physical}$	0.3502	**0.305(m)**	0.528 (h)	**0.246 (l)**	0.3502	**0.267 (l)**	0.586 (h)	**0.284 (l)**

6 Discussion

The comparison of Table 3 with the rules posed in section 4 revealed that every cluster formed by the second dataset followed similar numerical behaviour than the tabletop dataset. The rules (2), (3) and (4) presented in the previous section are defined in non numerical terms (high, low, medium levels of participation and Gini coefficients). For the Gini coefficient attributes (G_{talk} and $G_{physical}$) the quantitative equivalent to *low* and *high* can be translated into the quantitative equivalences *below 0.5* (more symmetric) and *above 0.5* (less symmetric). But for the numerical attributes (P_{talk} and $P_{physical}$) the parameter to define the terms *low* and *high* are the correspondent average of the attributes across the complete dataset (P_{talk} =28.668, and $P_{physical}$ = 36.714, see columns *Full data* in Table 3).

$(low)P_{talk} + (high)G_{talk} + (high)P_{physical} + (low)G_{physical} \rightarrow$ ***Non Collaborative situations.*** We found that all parts of the rule are confirmed by the clustering information obtained from the two algorithms (see columns *Cluster-2*, Table 3). The non collaborative situations are characterised by low level of talk, asymmetry in the conversation and high levels of physical action compared with the average across groups. Therefore, we can accept the rule hypothesised in (2).

$(high, medium)P_{talk} + (high)G_{talk} + (high)P_{physical} \rightarrow$ ***Partial collaboration .***

In educational terms is not easy to define when a group is collaborating, even if experts observe directly the activity of groups. Even though, we observed that when a partial collaboration within the group exists it is because one or two members "leaded" the activity in both physical and verbal participation. However, even when the clustering results for partial collaboration (see columns *Cluster-1*, Table 3) shows high levels of asymmetric verbal participation, it is hard to define what happened with the physical dimension, obtaining low level of physical actions and undefined symmetry ($G_{physical}$ around exactly 0.5). Therefore, we cannot accept the rule hypothesised in (3) as is.

$$(high)P_{talk} + (low)G_{talk} + (low)P_{physical} + (high)G_{physical} \rightarrow Collaborative\ situations.$$

In this case the major part of the rule is confirmed by the clustering information obtained from the two algorithms (see columns *Cluster-0*, Table 3). Collaborative situations are characterised by high levels of symmetric conversation and less physical actions compared with the average across groups. We were expecting more asymmetry in the physical actions caused by the variable flux of the conversation. We learnt from this rule that collaborative moments tend to be symmetrical in both the physical and verbal layers. Thus, even when the hypothesised rule was not perfectly matched, most of its factors were present. Then, we can accept the rule hypothesised in (4).

7 Conclusions and Future Work

We have presented our research to validate the significance of the notion of symmetry of activity for modelling the presence of collaboration within small groups of people. We illustrated how the theoretical model we built upon and our methodological basis can give insight on the groups' collaborative process, first, with a small-scale qualitative study at the tabletop, and then, evaluating in a larger dataset of collocated interactions. Our approach applies qualitative assessment, statistical analysis for the formulation of the model and machine learning techniques for the evaluation.

Our evaluation demonstrates that both amount and symmetry of verbal and physical participation are good indicators of collaborative and non-collaborative moments. The symmetry of participation is just one dimension of the complex collaborative process; however, it provides useful information that would be an essential part of the group model. In order to asses collaboration in a more effective way, the future research agenda of this project includes evaluating the indicators of symmetry of knowledge and enriching the group model by including the different facets of the collaborative process besides the levels of interactions.

References

1. Martín, E., Haya, P.A.: Towards Adapting Group Activities in Multitouch Tabletops, in adj. In: De Bra, P., Kobsa, A., Chin, D. (eds.) UMAP 2010. LNCS, vol. 6075, pp. 28–30. Springer, Heidelberg (2010)
2. Dillenbourg, P.: What do you mean by 'collaborative learning'? In: Collaborative Learning: Cognitive and Computational Approaches, pp. 1–19. Elsevier Science, Amsterdam (1998)
3. Jeong, H., Hmelo-Silver, C.E.: An Overview of CSCL Methodologies. In: Proc. ICLS 2010, Chicago, USA, pp. 920–921 (2010)
4. Stahl, G.: Collaborative learning through practices of group cognition. In: Proc. CSCL 2009, pp. 33–42 (2009)
5. Upton, K., Kay, J.: Narcissus: Group and individual models to support small group work. In: Houben, G.-J., McCalla, G., Pianesi, F., Zancanaro, M. (eds.) UMAP 2009. LNCS, vol. 5535, pp. 54–65. Springer, Heidelberg (2009)

6. Anaya, A., Boticario, J.: Content-free collaborative learning modeling using data mining. User Modeling and User-Adapted Interaction 1(20), 1–36 (2010)
7. Perera, D., Kay, J., Koprinsca, I., Yacef, K., Zaiane, O.: Clustering and Sequential Pattern Mining of Online Collaborative Learning Data. IEEE TKDE 21, 759–772 (2009)
8. Soller, A., Lesgold, A.: Modeling the process of collaborative learning. The Role of Technology in Proc. CSCL 2007, 63–86 (2007)
9. Casillas, L., Daradoumis, T.: Knowledge extraction and representation of collaborative activity through ontology based and Social Network Analysis technologies. J. Business Intelligence and Data Minining 4(2), 141–158 (2009)
10. Stahl, G.: Group Cognition: Computer Support for Building Collaborative Knowledge. MIT Press, Cambridge (2006)
11. Bachour, K., Kaplan, F., Dillenbourg, P.: An Interactive Table for Supporting Participation Balance in Face-to-Face Collaborative Learning. IEEE Transactions on Learning Technologies 3(3), 203–213 (2010)
12. Thomas, V., Wang, Y., Fan, X.: Measuring Education Inequality: Gini Coefficients of Education (2000)
13. Belgiorno, F., Ilaria, M., Giuseppina, P., Vittorio, S.: Free-Riding in Collaborative Diagrams Drawing. In: Sustaining TEL: From Innovation to Learning and Practice, pp. 457–463 (2010)
14. Harris, A., Rick, J., Bonnett, V., Yuill, N., Fleck, R., Marshall, P., Rogers, Y.: Around the table: are multiple-touch surfaces better than single-touch for children's collaborative interactions? In: Proc. CSCL 2009, pp. 335–344 (2009)
15. Novak, J.: Concept maps and Vee diagrams: two metacognitive tools to facilitate meaningful learning. Instructional Science 19(1), 29–52 (1990)
16. Martinez, R., Kay, J., Yacef, K.: Collaborative concept mapping at the tabletop. In: Proc. ACM ITS, p. 207 (2010)
17. Martinez, R., Kay, J., Yacef, K.: Visualisations for longitudinal participation, contribution and progress of a collaborative task at the tabletop, pp. 2–11 (2011)
18. Tan, D., et al.: Using job-shop scheduling tasks for evaluating collocated collaboration. Personal and Ubiquitous Computing 12(3), 255–267 (2008)
19. Wallace, J., Scott, S., Stutz, T., Enns, T., Inkpen, K.: Investigating teamwork and taskwork in single-and multi-display groupware systems. Personal and Ubiquitous Computing 13(8), 569–581 (2009)
20. Martinez, R., Wallace, J., Kay, J., Yacef, K.: Modelling and identifying collaborative situations in a collocated multi-display groupware setting. In: Proc. AIED 2011 (2011)
21. Anaya, A., Boticario, J.: Clustering learners according to their collaboration. In: Proc. CSCWD 2009, pp. 540–545 (2009)

A Dynamic Sliding Window Approach for Activity Recognition

Javier Ortiz Laguna, Angel García Olaya, and Daniel Borrajo

Departamento de Informática, Universidad Carlos III de Madrid,
Avda. de la Universidad. 30, 28911 Leganés, Madrid, Spain
{jortiz,agolaya}@inf.uc3m.es, dborrajo@ia.uc3m.es
http://www.uc3m.es

Abstract. Human activity recognition aims to infer the actions of one or
more persons from a set of observations captured by sensors. Usually, this
is performed by following a fixed length sliding window approach for the
features extraction where two parameters have to be fixed: the size of the
window and the shift. In this paper we propose a different approach using
dynamic windows based on events. Our approach adjusts dynamically
the window size and the shift at every step. Using our approach we
have generated a model to compare both approaches. Experiments with
public datasets show that our method, employing simpler models, is able
to accurately recognize the activities, using fewer instances, and obtains
better results than the approaches used by the datasets authors.

Keywords: Human Activity Recognition, Sliding Window, Sensor Networks, Wearable Systems, Ubiquitous Computing.

1 Introduction

Generally speaking, human activity recognition (AR) can be defined as the automatic recognition of an activity or a state of one or more persons based on
observations coming from sensor readings. Usually, AR problems are tackled as a
machine learning problem where the observations collected by the sensors are the
inputs, the performed activities are the classes, and the learning techniques generate classifiers. Sensors produce data streams that can be seen as a simple time
series, a collection of observations made sequentially in time. So, the recognition
system must process the inputs to extract the learning instances, their feature
values and the classes. The features depend on the available sensors. Thus, in [12]
RFID sensors are used and the features extracted are the RFID tags detected
by the RFID reader. In [8], two-state sensors are used and the features are the
states of all sensors. Other types of sensors like accelerometers produce continuous data streams and the features must be extracted from those. For instance,
the features extracted in [1] are the mean, energy, frequency-domain entropy,
and correlations of the other features. In [6], they use similar features as well as
the magnitude of the mean, variance, energy, spectral entropy, and the discrete
Fast Fourier Transform (FFT) coefficients.

Joseph A. Konstan et al. (Eds.): UMAP 2011, LNCS 6787, pp. 219–230, 2011.
© Springer-Verlag Berlin Heidelberg 2011

Independently of the sensors used, in the feature extraction step most AR systems use a sensory sequence segmentation based on a fixed-size sliding window [1,15,14]. In those cases, many of the classification errors come from the selection of the sliding window length [4]. For instance, an incorrect length may truncate an activity instance. In many cases, errors appear at the beginning or at the end of the activities, when the window overlaps the end of one activity and the beginning of the next one. In other cases, the window length may be too short to provide the best information for the recognition process. In [6], the authors studied different features and window lengths. They showed that the best performance is achieved when different window lengths and features are chosen separately for each activity.

Besides, the static sliding window approach generates many identical consecutive temporal windows with exactly the same features and the same activity performed when the user executes the same activity during a long period of time. Those repetitive instances do not contribute to solve the problem better. Instead, they produce higher scores of the activities during which those instances are generated. But they do not help to recognize other activities, and the systems have to classify the identical instances over and over again.

For those reasons, we hypothesize that a different segmentation approach based in non-fixed length windows may achieve better results. Thus, we propose an approach based in events to generate dynamic sliding windows to infer the activities. So, instead of defining a static fixed-length window, we define the events that will be used to define the boundaries of the dynamic windows employed to extract the features. Hence, when a specific event in the sensors readings is detected, we extract the features to classify what the user did between that event and the previous one. Those features are always the same, but the size of the windows changes based on when the events happen. So, the size of the window is dynamically established by the events. Thus, the windows are dynamic in time although the number of events in a window is always the same. In addition, our method does not create any temporal window if no events are detected.

The events we use are domain dependent and rely on the sensors the system uses. In the case of Radio Frequency Identification (RFID) or reed switch sensors, an event could be any sensor state change. That is the case of the datasets used in this paper. Using sensors producing continuous data like accelerometers, magnetometers, gyroscopes or GPS's, one or several thresholds could be set in order to detect the events. Since there is no evidence that this method would work using this kind of sensors, in the near future, we plan to test the method using data from this type of sensors.

The goal of this paper is to learn the actions that users perform, using the dynamic window method based on state changes on public datasets, and to compare the results with other approaches. For our experiments, we used data from two different sources. The first dataset used was presented in [8]. It uses a set of two state sensors deployed in a house. The second dataset is the one used in [12]. In this dataset, RFID readers and a set of RFID tags installed in the environment are used to detect the activities. We built models using some state-of-the-art algorithms for classifying the activities and models used by the authors of the datasets in order to compare their models and ours.

The rest of the paper is organized as follows. In Section 2 we describe models generated for testing. In Section 3 we report on the results of the approaches used. Section 4 discusses related work. Finally, in Section 5 we summarize our findings.

2   Dynamic Windows Based on State Changes

Given a network of N sensors, N sequences will be generated by the AR system where each sequence can be represented as a vector $X^s =< .., x_i^s, .. >$ of readings of sensor s. x_i^s is the sensor reading at time i of sensor s. So, the first task consists of defining a function f_1 that takes the N sequences and produces Z vectors of features $\boldsymbol{F_i}$. Each vector is labeled with the activity a that the user performed during the period of time from i to $i+l$ in which the features in $\boldsymbol{F_i}$ were extracted. The second task is to learn a function f_2 that takes as inputs those vectors $\boldsymbol{F_i}$ produced by f_1 and builds a classifier to infer the activities performed.

The static sliding window approach uses fixed-length temporal windows that shift to create instances. Each window position produces a segment that is used to isolate data for later processing. It uses two parameters: the windows length l and the shift r. Figure 1 shows an example of sliding windows where $l = r$, i is the timestamp at which the first window starts and $i + l$ is the timestamp at which it finishes and the next temporal window starts.

So, using this method, the function f_1 may be defined as follows. Given a network of N sensors, N sequences of data are generated. Each sequence is segmented in Z temporal windows or time slices of l seconds in length defined as $W_i^s =< x_i^s, ..., x_{i+l-1}^s >$ of contiguous readings from the sensor s starting at time i. The window shift, r, defines the next temporal window as $W_{i+r}^s =< x_{i+r}^s, ..., x_{i+r+l-1}^s >$. The segments that start at time i are grouped in the matrix $W_i =< W_i^1, .., W_i^N >$. These temporal windows are represented as squares in the

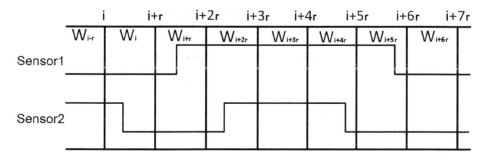

Fig. 1. Temporal segmentation on time series of two sensors by the sliding window method

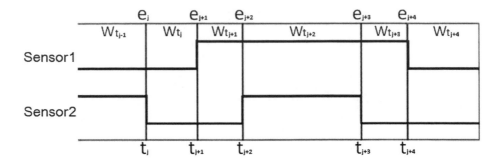

Fig. 2. Temporal segmentation on a time series of two sensors by the dynamic window method

figure 1. Then, the features are extracted from W_i to build the vector F_i which is labeled with the activity $a \in A = \{a_1, a_2, ..., a_n\}$ that the user performed during W_i. Thus, given a set of n activities $A = \{a_1, a_2, ..., a_n\}$ (classes), every temporal window W_i produces a vector F_i that is labeled with an activity $a \in A$. Then, the function f_2 builds a classifier to find the mapping between F_i and the activity in A that was performed by the user.

In contrast, our approach generates the learning instances, given by f_1, from a temporal window created by using as boundaries what we call *significant* events. So, it uses the last m *significant* events to generate the learning instances. Also, instead of sliding, it uses the next events to fix the boundaries of the next instance. Hence, the approach relies on the events detected by the sensors that the system uses instead of the window length. Figure 2 shows an example of our method using as significant events all the changes in the values of the sensors.

Thus, our method does not set values for l, the size of the window, and r, the shift. These values change over time. The function f_1 can be formulated as follows. Given N sequences of sensors readings as above, X^s, we generate one sequence of significant events $E = < e_0, e_1, .., e_j, .. >$ that are detected at time steps $T = < t_0, t_1, .., t_j, .. >$ where t_j is the timestamp of event e_j. The events are detected from all sensors readings, but they are merged in E. Then, the sequences of all sensors are segmented by the events $e_x \in E$, from all sensors. Those events will divide the sequences in Z temporal windows $W_{t_j}^s = < x_{t_j}^s, .., x_{t_{j+m-1}}^s >$ where $W_{t_j}^s$ will contain all the readings of sensor s from t_j to t_{j+m-1}, being m the number of significant events used to build the windows. The next window will be defined as $W_{t_{j+1}}^s = < x_{t_{j+1}}^s, .., x_{t_{j+1+m-1}}^s >$ so the shift at every step will be set dynamically as $r_{j+1} = t_{j+1} - t_j$. Then, $W_{t_j} = < W_{t_j}^1, .., W_{t_j}^N >$ will be the segments of the N sensors in the time t_j. The figure 2 show this segments W_{t_j} as squares where $m = 2$. Events will divide the sequences of all sensors, even the sequences of the sensors that did not detect such event.

Once the temporal windows are delimited, the features F_{t_j} are extracted and they are labeled with an activity $a_j \in A$. The activity that will label the window W_{t_j} will be the activity that the user performed between the last two events t_{j+m-2} and t_{j+m-1}. Finally, the function f_2 is performed.

One of the main differences between both methods is that our approach generates a new window just when a new event is detected, whereas the other approach continues creating new windows even when the sensor readings do not change; temporal windows created with no changes in the sensors are identical. It can be seen in the figure 1 where the window W_{i+3r} does not contain any event, so the vector F_{i+3r} will be identical to the vector F_{i+2r} generated by the previous window W_{i+2r}.

In order to test our approach, we generated models based on the sensors used to record the datasets. Hence, for each dataset we chose different *significant* events to generate the classification instances. In the first dataset we generated models following the dynamic window approach. We compared our models with the fixed-length sliding-window approach employed by the authors. We used the second dataset in a similar way. We generated models using our approach and we compared our models with the model that got better results from the ones generated by the authors of the dataset. Next, we describe the models generated for our experiments in detail.

2.1 Kasteren Dataset

The first dataset was recorded and used by Kasteren and colleagues in [8]. The sensor network consists of wireless network nodes to which simple off-the-shelf sensors can be attached. Each sensor sends an event when the state of the digital input changes or when some threshold of the analog input is reached. The dataset was recorded in the house of a 26-year-old man living alone in a three-room apartment where 14 state-change sensors were installed. Locations of sensors included doors, cupboards, refrigerator and a toilet flush sensor. Sensors were left unattended, collecting data for 28 days in the apartment. The dataset contains 2638 sensor events and 245 activity instances. Activities were annotated by the subject himself using a bluetooth headset as described in [8]. Seven different activities were annotated, namely: *Leave house, Toileting, Showering, Sleeping, Preparing breakfast, Preparing dinner* and *Preparing a beverage*. Times where no activity is annotated are referred to as *Idle*. The dataset is public and can be downloaded with its annotations.

2.2 Kasteren Models

We executed three experiments with this dataset. In the first one, we reproduced the model that achieved the best results in [8]. They employed temporal probabilistic models and divided the data in slices of constant length, 60 seconds, without overlapping. So, the parameters used were $l = 60$ seconds and $r = 60$ seconds. A vector of features was generated for each slice. The vector contained one entry for each sensor, where the values of the sensors could be 0 or 1. They performed four experiments. We will focus in the one that got better results. In that experiment they used two representations in parallel that they called *change point* and *last*. In the *change point* representation the sensor gives a 1 to time slices where the sensor reading changed. In the *last* representation the last sensor that changed its state continues to give 1 and changes to 0 when a different sensor changes state. In our experiments we recreated this in the first experiment but we used a Dynamic Bayesian network (DBN) equivalent to the Hidden Markov Model (HMM) used by them since an HMM is a simple DBN. To do so, we added the id of the last activity performed to the vector of features.

In order to test our approach, we built some models using the same representation over the same dataset, but generating the instances using the dynamic window approach and using a different representation. To use this approach, we considered as a significant event any change in the sensor readings. That is, when a sensor changes its state from *1* to *0* or vice versa. Since we used changes in the sensors readings instead of slices of constant length, we generated our instances from the last *10* changes. A way to select the length of the temporal window is using the average time spent performing an activity in the data, as in [12]. Instead of using the time, we used the events. So, we divided the state changes of the dataset, 2638, by the number of activities 245 and we obtain $m = 10$. There were 14 sensors, so the features were a vector $\boldsymbol{F_{t_j}} = < F_j^1, ..., F_j^{14} >$ for the event e_j where $F_j^n \in \{0, 1\}$. The F_j^n was set to 1 if the sensor n changed its state at least once between t_j and t_{j+9} since m is set to 10. Also, we kept to 1 the last sensor that changed its state. This way we reproduced the representations *change point* and *last* used by the author. Additionally, we added the id of the last activity performed to the vector of features to learn activity transitions like the HMM does. This experiment was called *DSW-1-K* for Dynamic Sliding Window using Kasterens dataset. For the third experiment, *DSW-2-K*, we created a new model using a different representation and features. Instead of using the state of all sensors during the temporal window, whether the sensor changes its state or not, in this model we construct the vector using the identifier of the sensors that produced the last 10 events. So, the features of the segment that starts in e_i were $\boldsymbol{F_{t_j}} = < s_{t_j}, ..., s_{t_{j+9}} >$ where $s_{t_n} \in \{1, ..., 14\}$ since there were 14 different sensors. The s_{t+9} is set to the identifier of the sensor that produced the event e_{j+9} and s_{t_j} is the identifier of the sensor that produced the event e_j. If a sensor is not responsible for any event in the last 10 ones it is not included. Also, if a sensor produced k events, the identifier of that sensor is included k times. So, for example, if in the current temporal window W_{t_j} the sensors that changed its state were $1, 2, 3, 4, 1, 2, 3, 4, 5, 6$ then the features used would be $\boldsymbol{F_{t_j}} = < 1, 2, 3, 4, 1, 2, 3, 4, 5, 6 >$.

Then, we tried to reduce the number of features extracted from the sensors performing a feature selection method by computing the Information Gain Ratio [5] for each of the features and then ranking them from highest to lowest. Afterwards, we created and tested a model using all the features. The worst feature according to the ranking was eliminated and a new model was generated and tested with the remaining features. All the features were progressively eliminated until none is left. All generated models are compared and the features employed in the best model were kept. Using this feature selection method, we reduced the size of the vector from 10 to the last two sensor state changes $\boldsymbol{F_{t_j}} = < s_{t_{j+8}}, s_{t_{j+9}} >$ being $s_{t_{j+8}}$ and $s_{t_{j+9}}$ the id of the sensors that detected the last 2 events. Later, we added the id of the last activity performed like in the other models. Since we are interested in comparing probabilistic models with others models more easily readable by humans, *DSW-1-K* and *DSW-2-K* were generated using *PART* [3], an algorithm that generates rule sets, and *C4.5* [13], a decision-trees learning algorithm, instead of a DBN. We use these two algorithms because the model they generate can be transformed into a simple computer program that may be used to decide the activity performed by the user.

2.3   Patterson Dataset

The second dataset used is the one in [12]. The experiments performed with this dataset focused on routine morning activities which used common objects and are normally interleaved. The 11 activities which were observed are: *Using the bathroom, Making oatmeal, Making soft-boiled eggs, Preparing orange juice, Making coffee, Making tea, Making or answering a phone call, Taking out the trash, Setting the table, Eating breakfast* and *Clearing the table*. To create the dataset, one of the authors performed each activity 12 times in two contexts: twice in isolation, and then on 10 mornings all of the activities were performed together in a variety of patterns.

In order to capture the identity of the objects being manipulated, the kitchen was outfitted with 60 RFID tags placed on every object touched by the user during a practice trial. Data are in the form: <objectID> <activityID>. This dataset is more challenging than the previous one; most tasks were interleaved with or interrupted by others during the 10 full data collection sessions. In addition, the activities performed shared objects in common. This made interleaved AR much more difficult than associating a characteristic object with an activity. The dataset is public and can be downloaded.

2.4   Patterson Models

We also executed three experiments using this dataset. In the first experiment we used the fixed-length sliding-window approach used by the authors of this dataset. We also used their features and representation. They divided the data in slices of constant length, where the mean length of each uninterrupted portion of the interleaved tasks was 74 seconds. At each second they generated a vector of features with the data of the last 74 seconds. So, the parameters used were $l = 74$ seconds and $r = 1$ seconds. The vector contained 74 entries, one for each second, where the values of each entry could be *object-X-touched* when an object was detected or *no-object-touched* when no objects were detected. They used temporal probabilistic models too. They tested four different models. We have reproduced one of the most accurate models they generated; an HMM equivalent to the one used by Kasteren in the previous dataset. So, in order to replicate the results we created a DBN equivalent to the HMM used by the authors as with the Kasteren dataset.

In *DSW-1-P*, we used our approach with the same representation. We used a vector with the last 74 significant events to recognize the activity that was performed between the last two events. In this case, we considered as significant event when the RFIDs change the object detected or no objects are detected. So, the features used were the id of the new object detected or *no-object*. The dataset just provides information about the objects detected and the timestamps. Therefore, to detect the *no-object* state we assumed that when two readings are found in the dataset and the time interval between them is one second or more there is at least a state with no objects detected.

We also generated a new model using a simpler representation in *DSW-2-P*. We used a vector of features composed of the last 74 events like in the previous setup. Then, we applied the same feature selection method that we used in the previous dataset to find the optimal combination of features. That way we obtained a very accurate model using just the last two events instead of 74.

Like in the other dataset, we generated the models that use our approach, *DSW-1-P* and *DSW-2-P*, employing the *C4.5* and *PART* algorithms. We added the activity performed previously to the vector of features used in these experiments to learn activity transitions like we did in the previous dataset.

3   Experimental Results

In summary, we have performed six experiments, using the models described in the previous section. We used two metrics to evaluate the models using 10-fold cross-validation for estimating the error: precision and recall averaged over all activities. We have used these two metrics instead of accuracy, used by the authors of the datasets, because the datasets are unbalanced. So, accuracy is not a good metric as described in [2]. Hence, we have used precision and recall as recommended by Kasteren in [16,2]. The measures are calculated as follows:

$$\text{Precision} = \frac{1}{C} \sum_{c=1}^{C} \left\{ \frac{tp_c}{tp_c + fp_c} \right\} \qquad \text{Recall} = \frac{1}{C} \sum_{c=1}^{C} \left\{ \frac{tp_c}{tp_c + fn_c} \right\}$$

in which tp_c are the true positives of the class c, fp_c are the false positives of the class c, fn_c are the false negatives of the class c and C is the number of classes. So, what we call precision was used as a metric by Kasteren but he called it *ClassAccuracy*.

The learning algorithms we used were *DBN* to learn the models that replicate the models used by the authors of both datasets and *C4.5* and *PART* to learn our models.

Table 1 shows the average precision and recall obtained by each setup, and the number of instances generated by each model. In addition, we have included a column with the percentage of times that the temporal window generated by the segmentation method contains at least one event able to change the state of the sensors and produce an instance different from the one produced in the previous window. That is, any change in the sensors readings that generates one instance different from the previous one. This counter measures the diversity of the temporal windows from which the instances are created since the values of the sensors in the temporal windows without state changes will be the same as in the previous window.

Table 1. Precision, recall, number of instances and diversity for all Setups

	Precision	Recall	N. Instances	Diversity
Kasteren DBN	80.55	80.08	40003	3.16%
DSW-1-K C4.5	92.16	91.15	2638	68.35%
DSW-1-K PART	92.28	90.85	2638	68.35%
DSW-2-K C4.5	93.05	91.34	2638	68.35%
DSW-2-K PART	92.61	91.38	2638	68.35%
Patterson DBN	78.90	86.57	16280	27.16%
DSW-1-P C4.5	94.80	94.48	5408	100%
DSW-1-P PART	97.72	96.76	5408	100%
DSW-2-P C4.5	94.80	94.49	5408	100%
DSW-2-P PART	97.69	95.32	5408	100%

As we can see from the results of both datasets, the precision and recall of the static sliding-window approach, *Kasteren DBN* and *Patterson DBN*, are much lower than the dynamic window, *DSW-1-K*, *DSW-2-K*, *DSW-1-P* and *DSW-2-P*. The table shows that the different models generated using the dynamic window approach obtain similar results. The feature selection improved slightly the results in the first dataset, though not in the second dataset. The precision of *Kasteren DBN* is 80.55%, quite similar to the result reported by Kasteren in [8] which is 79.4%. The DBN we used needs some parameters to be defined, so the difference probably is due to dissimilarities in those parameters. We can not compare our results with those reported by Patterson in [12] since they do not report on precision and recall.

The table shows as well that the number of instances created by each method is very different. The static sliding-window approach creates many more instances than our approach in both datasets. Our method creates an instance just when an specific event is detected, while the static sliding-window approach creates instances for every time slide even when the user is not at home, or is sleeping and no events are detected. That is the case of the first dataset. The behavior in the second dataset is similar; many instances are created when the system does not detect any event, since one instance is created every second. So, most of the instances are generated without changes in the sensor readings. This fact is shown in the last column of the table where our models generated higher percentages of different temporal windows. Notice that the diversity of the dynamic window in the first dataset is not 100% like in the second dataset because some of the significant events produced the same feature. When a sensor changed its state from 1 to 0 or vice versa the value of the feature extracted was 1 in both cases because of the *change point* representation. Thus, some consecutive instances generated were identical. In any case, using near 5% of the instances generated by the sliding window approach, we obtain better precision and recall.

A deeper analysis of the models shows that the sliding window fails more often when the activity changes. Comparing the *Kasteren DBN* and *DSW-2-K PART* we see that the first one fails in the 96.37% of the instances when the activity changes, whereas the second one fails in 48.12%. The results are similar in the second dataset, so *Patterson DBN* fails in 86.58% whereas the *DSW-2-P PART* fails in 42.13%. Thus, the activities with fewer instances reach a lower precision and recall, whereas the activities with many instances like *leave house* and *sleep* in the first dataset and *Making soft-boiled eggs* in the second get better results.

The experiments show that the different classification algorithms obtained similar results. Although experiments with Pattersons dataset show that PART obtained better results than C4.5, the differences are small in both datasets.

4   Related Work

In relation to sensor data segmentation approaches, most AR systems use a sensory sequence segmentation based on a static sliding window for extracting the relevant features. In [1] the feature vectors were computed on 512 sample windows of acceleration data with 256 samples overlapping between consecutive windows. In others [15], the duration for each feature vector was the average duration for each activity computed from all the activities and the shift in the feature window was half of the duration of the quickest activity. In [14], the sensors used in [1,15] are combined. Each feature is computed over a sliding window shifted in increments of 0.5 seconds. They evaluated the performance of the features both individually and in combination, and over different window lengths (0.5sec-128sec). In [6], different features and window lengths are studied to recognize some activities. They show that the best performance is achieved when different window lengths and features are chosen separately for each activity.

So, using different deployments or different types of sensors, the common approach is to extract the features over a fixed length sliding window. Since a fixed length temporal feature slice is not the optimal solution [6], in our system we do not use them to compute the features. Instead, we compute the features every time a *significant* event is detected in the system. In that way we avoid the limitations of the static sliding windows approach.

Although the static sliding window is the most commonly used method, it is not the only one. For example, an approach that does not use sliding windows and instead employs events can be found in [7]. They use a two-stage method which consists of a preselection stage that aims to localize and preselect sections in the continuous signal and a second stage that classifies the candidate sections selected in the previous stage. The preselection stage looks for relevant motion events, which is very similar to what we do with our *significant* events approach. Ours is different because we try to find the events that mark the beginning and the end of one activity and they try to find one event that marks the whole activity, since it tries to recognize very short actions. Other different approaches that are not based on sliding windows may be found in [10,11].

5   Conclusions

In this paper we have presented a different approach to create the learning instances for AR. The novelty of this approach relies on the fact that our system uses the changes in the information captured by the sensors to create the instances for classification instead of the temporal sliding-window approach. We have compared our approach in public datasets used in the past by other researchers and we have shown a good performance. The results show that our approach obtains higher scores in precision and recall in the datasets used to test the approach.

The main advantage of the dynamic window approach is that it provides accurate models using much fewer number of learning instances and features. This makes this approach suitable to be used online and in situations where computation times are important, since fewer instances would be evaluated and the instances will be processed faster. Also, it is independent of the time granularity.

One limitation is that instances depend on the sensors accuracy. So, whenever the sensors do not capture a significant change in the environment, the system does not detect the state change and it does not create the corresponding instance. Anyway, this case is equivalent to the case when the temporal window is too long and contains two activities instead of just one. In [9] the author has shown some of the limitations of RFID in extensive use. However, other sensor modalities like accelerometers or magnetometers can be used to recognize the activities.

We have described how models can be used for AR employing this method to extract the information from the sensor readings. The generated models are able to predict transition probabilities better by recording the last objects observed in each activity. So, good results can be obtained by using just the last two objects detected by the RFID or the last two reed switch sensor that changed the value. While there are still technical challenges to overcome, this work shows that AR using the significant events approach to generate the instances and just some of the changes in the states of the sensors as features can be a good choice.

For our future work, we will try our approach with sensors that produce continuous signals, like accelerometers, in order to test the method with other type of sensor and features. Also, we will test the method to recognize short length activities like gestures. This is called activity spotting by some researchers [7]. We believe our approach may obtain good results in such task too.

References

1. Bao, L., Intille, S.: Activity recognition from user-annotated acceleration data. In: Ferscha, A., Mattern, F. (eds.) PERVASIVE 2004. LNCS, vol. 3001, pp. 1–17. Springer, Heidelberg (2004)
2. Chawla, N.: Data mining for imbalanced datasets: An overview. In: Data Mining and Knowledge Discovery Handbook, pp. 875–886 (2010)
3. Frank, E., Witten, I.: Generating accurate rule sets without global optimization. In: Proceedings of the Fifteenth International Conference on Machine Learning, pp. 144–151. Citeseer (1998)

4. Gu, T., Wu, Z., Tao, X., Pung, H., Lu, J.: epSICAR: An Emerging Patterns based approach to sequential, interleaved and Concurrent Activity Recognition. In: Proceedings of the 2009 IEEE International Conference on Pervasive Computing and Communications, pp. 1–9. IEEE Computer Society, Los Alamitos (2009)
5. Hall, M., Smith, L.: Practical feature subset selection for machine learning. Computer Science 98, 4–6 (1998)
6. Huynh, T., Schiele, B.: Analyzing features for activity recognition. In: Proceedings of the 2005 Joint Conference on Smart Objects and Ambient Intelligence: Innovative Context-Aware Services: Usages and Technologies, p. 163. ACM, New York (2005)
7. Junker, H., Amft, O., Lukowicz, P., Tröster, G.: Gesture spotting with body-worn inertial sensors to detect user activities. Pattern Recognition 41(6), 2010–2024 (2008)
8. Kasteren, T., Athanasios, N., Englebienne, G., Kröse, B.: Accurate activity recognition in a home setting. In: UbiComp 2008: Proceedings of the 10th International Conference on Ubiquitous Computing, pp. 1–9. ACM, New York (2008)
9. Logan, B., Healey, J., Philipose, M., Tapia, E., Intille, S.: A long-term evaluation of sensing modalities for activity recognition. In: Krumm, J., Abowd, G.D., Seneviratne, A., Strang, T. (eds.) UbiComp 2007. LNCS, vol. 4717, pp. 483–500. Springer, Heidelberg (2007)
10. Modayil, J., Bai, T., Kautz, H.: Improving the recognition of interleaved activities. In: Proceedings of the 10th International Conference on Ubiquitous Computing, pp. 40–43. ACM, New York (2008)
11. Ortiz, J., García, A., Borrajo, D.: A Relational Learning Approach to Activity Recognition from Sensor Readings. In: 4th International IEEE Conference Intelligent Systems, IS 2008, vol. 3 (2008)
12. Patterson, D., Fox, D., Kautz, H., Philipose, M.: Fine-grained activity recognition by aggregating abstract object usage. In: Ninth IEEE International Symposium on Wearable Computers, pp. 44–51 (2005)
13. Quinlan, J.: C4.5: programs for machine learning. Morgan Kaufmann, San Francisco (2003)
14. Stikic, M., Huynh, T., Van Laerhoven, K., Schiele, B.: ADL recognition based on the combination of RFID and accelerometer sensing. In: 2nd International Conference on Pervasive Computing Technologies for Healthcare (2008)
15. Tapia, E., Intille, S., Larson, K.: Activity Recognition in the Home Setting Using Simple and Ubiquitous Sensors. LNCS, pp. 158–175 (2004)
16. Van Kasteren, T., Englebienne, G., Kröse, B.: Towards a Consistent Methodology for Evaluating Activity Recognition Model Performance

Early Detection of Potential Experts in Question Answering Communities

Aditya Pal[1], Rosta Farzan[2], Joseph A. Konstan[1], and Robert E. Kraut[2]

[1] Department of Computer Science & Engineering
University of Minnesota, Minneapolis, MN 55455, USA
{apal,konstan}@cs.umn.edu
[2] Human-Computer Interaction Institute
Carnegie Mellon University, Pittsburgh, PA 15213, USA
{rfarzan,robert.kraut}@cs.cmu.edu

Abstract. Question answering communities (QA) are sustained by a handful of experts who provide a large number of high quality answers. Identifying these experts during the first few weeks of their joining the community can be beneficial as it would allow community managers to take steps to develop and retain these potential experts. In this paper, we explore approaches to identify potential experts as early as within the first two weeks of their association with the QA. We look at users' behavior and estimate their *motivation* and *ability* to help others. These qualities enable us to build classification and ranking models to identify users who are likely to become experts in the future. Our results indicate that the current experts can be effectively identified from their early behavior. We asked community managers to evaluate the potential experts identified by our algorithm and their analysis revealed that quite a few of these users were already experts or on the path of becoming experts. Our retrospective analysis shows that some of these potential experts had already left the community, highlighting the value of early identification and engagement.

Keywords: Question Answering, Potential Experts, Expert Identification.

1 Introduction

Question answering communities (QA) are excellent knowledge sources which enable their users to create value while participating in social interactions with one another. There is a core group of users also referred to as experts in these communities who are the key contributors of knowledge. The experts constitute a small percentage of the community members and are responsible for a large percentage of the answers [9]. We also see the evidence of this in TurboTax Live Community (TTLC)[1]. TTLC allows users to ask and answer tax-related and TurboTax product related questions. The TTLC dataset is a complete dump of

---

[1] http://ttlc.intuit.com

Joseph A. Konstan et al. (Eds.): UMAP 2011, LNCS 6787, pp. 231–242, 2011.

Table 1. Participation characteristics of the two types of users in TTLC

	no. users	no. questions	no. answers	no. best answers
superuser	83 (0.01%)	1,963 (0.31%)	177,427 (45%)	43,059 (78%)
user	604,900 (99.99%)	630,522 (99.69%)	218,366 (55%)	12,385 (22%)

questions and answers from the time period July 2006-April 2009. It contains 83 superusers (or experts), 604,900 ordinary users, 633,112 questions, and 688,390 answers. Superusers constitute 0.01% of the population yet they have provided 78% of the best answers and close to 45% of all answers. They differ drastically from the ordinary users in terms of how they participate, as depicted in table 1. Needless to say, the superusers are the drivers of community answer-production and are extremely important for this community to function.

Intuit[2] recognizes these superusers, making their status visible to other community members. This recognition adds a stamp of trust to their answers and keeps them motivated to carry on the good work. It is important to note that these users are not paid for their answers and do not have any association with Intuit. Intuit takes special care in identifying the superusers. They have employees that manually evaluate top answerers for qualities such as tax knowledge, quality of their answers, politeness and clarity of responses and writing ability. If a user has some professional experience in the tax domain, that is also a plus. Based on these assessments, a user can get promoted to superuser. Through April, 2009 Intuit has recognized 83 superusers; they acknowledge that there are likely many more qualified users, but due to the manual evaluation process, they have not yet identified them. The human evaluation process highlights two important limitations:

- Humans usually evaluate long-time contributors; as a result recently joined users with high potential are not considered.
- The evaluation process is slow, which leads to the risk of high-potential users leaving the community due to the lack of recognition of their efforts.

These limitations highlight the need for a screening tool to filter through tens of thousands of users to recommend potential superusers to human evaluators. Specifically, we use machine learning to identify high-potential users in the first few weeks of their participation. Early identification of potential experts can benefit the community in several ways. It enables measures to nurture experts and retain them. The proper training of potential experts could also improve their skills and improve the overall quality of the participation in the community.

The primary difficulty in finding potential experts early on is that the markers that reflect expertise of a person, e.g., number of answers, number of best answers, etc., are not that strong for a newly joined user. As a result not much prior work has been done in finding potential experts in early-stage in QA. Panciera et al. [6] show that initial contributions of experts are measurably different from contributions of ordinary users in communities like Wikipedia. The question

---

[2] Intuit is the company that launched TurboTax live community (TTLC).

arises whether early experts behavior is different in QA communities? Is there an untapped set of potential experts that we could develop - users who might otherwise leave the community due to lack of recognition? Our research seeks to address this challenge.

In this paper, we propose several different measures that could be used for identifying potential experts based on their early participation. We look at the behavioral characteristics of current experts when they joined the community and use predictive and ranking algorithms to estimate their potential. This helps answer several questions. Do the experts differ from ordinary users since the day they joined the community or did they improve over a period of time? What abstract qualities are required for users to become experts in general? What qualities are important to become an expert in a domain specific QA like TTLC? How effective can algorithms be in identifying potential experts early on?

2   Related Work

Several other researchers have addressed the question of expert identification in QA communities. Zhang et al. [9] modified PageRank [4] to propose an algorithm, ExpertiseRank. Their algorithm considers whom a person answered in addition to how many people a person answered. They combined the number of answers (a) and number of questions (q) of a user in one score, Z-score ($z = \frac{a-q}{\sqrt{a+q}}$). A person with high Z-score is considered to have higher expertise than a person with low Z-score value. They used a dataset from the Java developer forum to validate several ranking algorithms against a ground truth of human evaluation. Their analysis indicated that a simple measure such as Z-score outperforms complex graph based algorithms such as ExpertiseRank, PageRank, and HITS in the assessment of the expertise of the users.

Expertise measures such as Z-score and ExpertiseRank typically provide a ranking of users in terms of decreasing expertise levels. They do not instruct how many users should be selected as experts from the ranked list. Bouguessa et al. [1] addressed this issue. The authors considered number of best answers as an indicator of user expertise. Based on this indicator they modeled authority scores as a mixture of gamma distributions and used Bayesian Information Criteria (BIC) to estimate the appropriate number of mixture components and the parameters using the Expectation Maximization algorithm. Their results on Yahoo Answers dataset resulted in two mixtures of users, suggesting that the Yahoo Answers community contains two types of users: {experts, non-experts}.

Jurczky et al. [3] performed link analysis over the question-answer interconnections among users of Yahoo Answers. Their analysis showed that the HITS algorithm outperforms classical graph measures such as in-degree, out-degree, and centrality for the identification of expertise. More recently, Pal et al. [5], proposed a model to estimate the question selection bias of the answerers. They showed that the experts differ from the normal users in their selection biases; this bias was used to identify experts.

Our work differs from prior research as we focus on early identification of potential experts. As a result, we use users' activity during the first few weeks

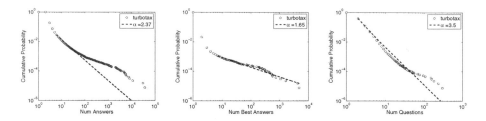

Fig. 1. Log-Log distribution of participation characteristics of users

of their participation. We propose that motivation and ability to help others should be ideally present among potential experts, and model them using several abstract measures. As per our literature survey, we are the first to show that classification and ranking models can be built successfully to detect potential experts early on and provide a useful baseline for further work in this direction.

3   Dataset Description

TurboTax Live Community (TTLC) is a question and answering online service that allows users to ask and answer tax-related and TurboTax's product related questions. It has the same basic structure as popular Q&A websites like Yahoo Answers and Stackoverflow.com. We have TTLC question and answer data from July 2006 - April 2009. The dataset contains 633,112 questions asked by 525,143 users and 688,390 answers provided by 130,770 users. The dataset has 83 users explicitly marked as superusers by Intuit employees.

Superusers play a vital role by answering tax questions of thousands of users (43,059 best answers - Table 1). Fig. 1 shows the distribution of participation characteristics of users in TTLC. These plots follow power-law distribution as is the case with most online Q&A systems [9]. The power-law distribution is an indicator of an uneven participation where a large section of users contribute in a small proportion and a small section contributes in large proportion.

We selected users who gave 10 or more answers and discarded the remaining, to ensure that we have sizable data to evaluate each user. This led to a selection of 1,367 users out of which 83 were superusers and other 1,284 ordinary users. These 1,367 users represented less than 1% of all the community members yet they have provided 76% of all the answers.

4   Qualities of Potential Experts

Taking a cue from the participation characteristics of experts, a potential expert should be highly motivated to help others (*motivation*) and she should have the required capability to answer questions correctly (*ability*). Motivation in this context means the willingness of the person to help others. Ability aims to assess

Table 2. Indicators of user qualities

Quality	Indicators
Motivation	M1: *Quantity of contributions.* M2: *Frequency of contributions.* M3: *Commitment towards the community.*
Ability	A1: *Domain knowledge of the user.* A2: *Trustworthiness of user's answers.* A3: *Politeness and clarity in response.*

the quality of the help a person can provides. Table 2 mentions several indicators of these qualities in the context of a QA. Based on our domain knowledge and interaction with the domain experts, we selected the following features to estimate these indicators of quality.

- **M1**: Quantity of the contributions made by the user is reflected from the *number of answers, number of questions.*
- **M2**: Frequency of the contributions is reflected from the *average time elapsed between two answers.* This parameter is estimated by taking the ratio of total number of answers given in a session by session time averaged for the sessions.
- **M3**: Commitment towards the community is indicated from *how many times a user logs into the system* (#login) and *how much time she spends in the community* (login span).
- **A1**: Domain knowledge of the user is hard to estimate as there are no direct measures to tell how much a user knows in the given domain. We use an indirect measure: *number of best answers* to approximate it.
- **A2**: Trustworthiness of user's answers can be determined from the *number of votes on answers, number of positively voted answers, ratio of answers with negative votes to positively voted answers.* Votes are the ratings provided by the community members in QA and they can be positive as well as negative.
- **A3**: In order to estimate the politeness and clarity in response we perform a language analysis of the answers provided by the user and choose 56 language dimensions. The most prominent of those are 1) presence of typos, spelling mistakes, bad words, sms language, 2) usage of singular pronouns (I,You,They), 3) usage of negative terms like not, discard, reject, hate, etc, 4) usage of greetings like hi, hello, proper-noun (usernames). 5) usage of special characters (?,!,#,etc).

We used all the features described above to represent the six abstract qualities. Next, we present our models for identifying potential experts based on the selected features.

5   Early Identification of Potential Experts

To perform an early identification of potential experts, we select the first n weeks of data per user. For a given user, the start of her association is measured from the timestamp of her first answer. We use all the features defined previously and user labels {superuser, ordinary user} to build predictive models to identify potential experts. The models are described below, followed by their performance.

5.1 Learning Model

We use Support Vector Machines (SVM) [2] and C4.5 Decision Tree (DTree) [8] over the features mentioned in the previous section to find potential experts. Both the algorithms are generally known to perform well for supervised learning. SVM is a maximum margin classifier that maximizes the decision boundary margins; leading to better generalization performance. We use the sequential mining optimization approach to train SVM [7]. DTree splits the training set into subsets based on a feature using some splitting criteria. This process is repeated to create further subsets until all the subsets at a given level have the same class or fall below a certain threshold. Then pruning is applied to the tree so that it doesn't overfit the training data. In order to construct the training data, we use 10-fold cross-validation. Cross-validation ensures that the models do not overfit the data and they report the true generalization accuracy.

5.2 Model Performance

Fig. 2 shows the performances of the two models in predicting potential experts. We measure the performance of the models using three standard measures: Precision (p), Recall (r) and F-Measure ($\frac{2*p*r}{p+r}$). The precision of SVM is consistently better than of DTree but it has a lower recall and the F-measure of DTree is marginally better than SVM.

The user labeling can be considered to be noisy as several of the worthy superusers are not yet labeled due to the manual process. The limitation of the SVM model in this case is that it considers the labeling as ground truth and optimizes the decision boundary accordingly. As a result it misses out a lot of experts (leading to low recall) as well as a lot of potential experts. On the other hand DTree based model prunes a lot of branches and avoids overfitting, hence it is able to recall a lot of experts. The lower precision on DTree indicates that it identifies a lot more potential experts (otherwise labeled ordinary users). This makes the predictions of DTree as an attractive choice for further analysis.

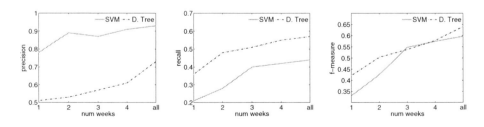

Fig. 2. Model performance over first N weeks of dataset

Consider the DTree model over 2 weeks of data. It predicts 75 users as potential experts out of which 40 are actually labeled as superusers ($p = 40/75$, $r = 40/83$). Based on this, we make these two key observations:

- There are 35 ordinary users who showed the potential to be an expert but were not labeled as experts. They are either false positives or missed by the manual evaluators at Intuit. We asked Intuit to evaluate these users manually (described in next section), and found that 27 of these 35 ordinary users were almost ready to be a superuser. The lack of due recognition runs the risk of their disassociation from the community and indeed several of them had already either left or reduced their activity.
- There are 43 out of 83 (52%) superusers who did not show potential early on. Further, the recall performance over time suggests that even by considering activity over a time period as large as 1 or 2 years, we can successfully recall only 60% of the experts. This result suggests that our model only captures part of the behavior recognized in superuser status, but promisingly shows that this behavior often manifests early in a user's life-cycle.

The experiment described here shows promise that user modeling and machine learning can be useful in finding high potential users as early as within 2 weeks of their joining.

Furthermore, if we consider the entire time period for which the data is available to compute the features, the model performance expectedly improves significantly. However the performance still does not reach 100%. This suggests two possibilities: a) Our models do not precisely capture the human evaluation process to identify experts, and b) There are many more users worthy of superuser status than currently awarded that status. We believe both of these reasons to be true. The models only approximated the key indicators such as domain knowledge based on the participation characteristics without looking at the context of the question and other answers provided on it. Moreover the model does not take the user's background and professional experience into account (not part of the dataset).

5.3   Balance Between Quality Measures

In the previous subsection, we saw that the two qualities *motivation* and *ability* are important in identifying potential experts. In this subsection, we assess how these qualities perform individually. Table 3 shows the performance of the models

Table 3. Model performance over 2 week data over different user qualities

	Motivation		Ability		Motivation + Ability	
	SVM	DTree	SVM	DTree	SVM	DTree
precision	0.70	0.56	0.70	0.50	0.89	0.53
recall	0.10	0.42	0.10	0.44	0.23	0.48
f-measure	0.18	0.48	0.18	0.47	0.37	0.50

over 2 week data. The two quality measures performed comparably when used individually - nearly identical for SVM. The combination of the two, however resulted in marginally better performance for DTree and substantially better for SVM. Since DTree is used with pruning it could not utilize the additional features as effectively as SVM. This can be good as it avoids over fitting of the model in higher dimensional space and issues of sparsity.

Overall this result indicates that the two qualities represent two different aspect of user's potential and they are roughly equally important in early identification of potential experts.

5.4   Ranking Users on Quality Measures

The purpose of early identification of potential experts is to provide mentoring opportunities and encouragement to the users. However this cannot be provided to all the users due to cost and time constraints. Hence it could be desirable to rank the users on their potential and provide these opportunities to the top ranked users only. Another reason to choose the ranking method is that the underlying user labeling is noisy and hence the results of the classification models cannot be highly reliable. We propose a ranking mechanism based on the observations drawn from the previous results.

As we saw earlier the two qualities are equally weighted by the classification algorithms, so it makes sense to have an un-weighted ranking between them. We first pick 6 best features (using Information Gain) that represent each abstract quality (see Table 4). One feature per quality ensures that we do not overweight a quality by selecting multiple features representing it. For all the features a higher score is preferred except however for the A3 feature. To handle this we multiply the value of the A3 feature by -1. A Gaussian Cumulative Distribution Function based ranking is used which measures how high a user scores on a given feature in comparison to the overall population over that feature. The following formula shows how the scores for all the features are combined:

$$R_G(x_i) = \prod_{f=1}^{d} \int_{-\infty}^{x_i^f} N(x; \mu_f, \sigma_f) \tag{1}$$

where $N(x; \mu_f, \sigma_f)$ is the Gaussian distribution with parameters μ_f indicating mean value of all users for feature f and σ_f represents the corresponding standard deviation. The integral is performed to compute the Gaussian CDF value for a given user feature. All the CDF values are then multiplied to get a one-dimensional score for each user. In order to contrast with the DTree model, we select the top 75 ranked users as potential experts, then 33 of them turn out be superusers ($p = 33/75$, $r = 33/83$) leading to slightly lower performance than DTree but still significant. Table 5 shows the expertise score of different types of users over the 2 week dataset. The average score indicates that potential experts have scores similar to experts and some of them are even better than the current experts in their expertise score. We see that ranking can also be used in conjunction with classification models to surface potential experts. This ranking further helps us in selecting users for human evaluation.

Table 4. Information gain of the top most feature per user quality

Abstract Quality	Feature	Info. Gain
M1	Number of answers	0.084
A2	Number of votes	0.081
A1	Number of best answers	0.076
M3	Frequency of login	0.074
M2	Avg. time elapsed between answers	0.024
A3	Usage of pronoun - I	0.017

Table 5. Average expertise scores of different types of users using 2 week data

	mean	std	min	max
experts	0.28	0.12	0.14	0.44
35 potential experts (D. Tree)	0.22	0.12	0.1	0.41
35 top users (excluding potential experts)	0.09	0.10	0.01	0.34

6   Human Evaluation

In order to estimate the effectiveness of the proposed prediction and the ranking models, we consider human evaluation of the identified potential experts. We created a stimuli sample by selecting the 35 potential users (DT) identified by DTree, top 35 ranked users (CDF) (excluding DT users) by the ranking algorithm, and 35 randomly selected users (RND) (excluding DT and CDF users) to create a stimuli sample for human evaluation.

Survey Users. We asked those Intuit employees who actually evaluate users for promotion to superusers to take the survey. These evaluators exactly know what skills are required in a TTLC superuser. Each evaluator was presented with a list of 12-15 users selected equally from DT, CDF, and RND and were ordered randomly. The evaluators were not aware of the algorithms' predictions. The evaluators looked at all the answers (and not just first two weeks) provided by these users including the complete question thread (answers of other users provided on those threads) to estimate users' expertise. On an average they took 15 minutes per user and each evaluator took 3-4 hours to complete the survey. Every user was evaluated by 2 judges. The inter-rater reliability measured by Cronbach α was 0.86 which presents a high reliability on evaluator ratings.

Survey Design. The evaluators rated users on the two main criteria:

- **Q1**: "This user has the potential to become a successful superuser" - The evaluators marked their responses on a 5-point Likert scale where 1 indicates strong disagreement, 3 indicates that they neither agree or disagree (neutral), and 5 indicates strong agreement.
- **Q2**: "What is your assessment of this user's potential to become a TTLC SuperUser?" - The evaluators responded on a 5-point Likert scale where 1

Table 6. Evaluators' rating of users over the questions: Q1 and Q2. We picked the maximum rating that a user received.

Q1: This user has the potential to become a successful superuser					
	strongly disagree	disagree	neither agree or disagree	agree	strongly agree
DT	3	3	11	10	8
CDF	8	8	10	7	2
RND	11	9	10	3	2
Q2: What is your assessment of this user's potential to become a TTLC SuperUser?					
	no potential	some potential	shows potential - not ready	almost ready	ready to be superuser
DT	1	2	5	18	9
CDF	2	7	8	14	4
RND	5	10	11	7	2

indicates no potential demonstrated, 3 indicates user shows potential but is not ready yet and 5 indicates that the user is ready to be a superuser.

The questions Q1 and Q2 are similar in nature but are added for the robustness of the responses. Pearson correlation of evaluator ratings on Q1-Q2 is 0.867 which is significant at $p < 0.01$ (2-tailed). We also asked participants to rate a user on a 5-point Likert scale, where 5 being the highest, for the following 6 criteria: 1) Tax knowledge, 2) Product knowledge, 3) Solving problems, 4) Writing, 5) Social skill, 6) Quality of responses.

6.1   User Ratings

Table 6 presents the evaluation details of users over Q1 and Q2. 18 (51%) DT users have demonstrated potential to become a superuser (Q1) and 27 (77%) of them are almost ready to be superuser (Q2). Evaluators suggested that they would like to wait a little and analyze a few more answers of the users coded as "almost ready" (4 on Q2). The result of the human evaluation strengthens our confidence in the classification models and indeed shows their effectiveness in identifying potential experts early on.

The ranking algorithm also found several worthy users which were missed by the DTree algorithm. Put together they discovered 45 out of 54 potential experts who were almost ready to be superusers (Q2) and 27 out of 32 users who showed potential to become successful superusers (Q1). Thus a conjunction of the two algorithms is an effective way to find potential experts.

The 32 users (30% of 105) were rated 4 or more on Q1 and 54 (51% of 105) were rated 4 or more on Q2. Our retrospective analysis shows that some of these potential experts had already left the community. The evaluators suggested that these users could be nurtured and retained by providing them some feedback and encouragement - highlighting the need of automated tools to find the potential experts early on.

Table 7. Wald Chi Square assessment of the likelihood of a user's potential over different rating aspects

Rating Aspects	Sig.	Wald Chi-Square
Tax knowledge	.000	**26.11**
Product knowledge	.035	**4.43**
Solving problems	.012	**6.37**
Writing	.307	1.04
Social	.512	0.425
Quality of responses	.001	**10.50**

6.2   Assessment of Rating Aspects

Survey takers evaluated users on 6 core aspects they consider necessary to become a TTLC superuser. We use them and the rating of users on Q2 to run a Wald Chi-Square test. The test assesses the likelihood of a user's potential to become a superuser with the user's assessment on the given rating aspect. Table 7 shows significant effect of tax knowledge, product knowledge, quality of responses, and solving problems on the judgment of the evaluators. The features proposed by us (see Table 4) also assess these qualities and indeed the high agreement between the human evaluators and our algorithms over the identified potential experts indicate that automated filters can be built to align as per the expectations of the humans.

7   Conclusion and Future Work

In this paper, we model users' behavior based on their early participation in the community and show that we could use classification as well as ranking algorithms to identify potential experts. The evaluation by community managers revealed that quite a few of the identified potential experts were already experts or on the path of becoming experts. A word of encouragement could put them to speed to reach the desired goal and stop them from leaving the community.

We showed that a person with potential should demonstrate *motivation* and *ability* to help others. These qualities are equally important and help us devise a ranking algorithm to measure the expertise of the users. We advocate using a mix of classification and ranking algorithms to find potential experts. We propose using Decision Tree based model over SVM conditioned on the fact that the labeling is noisy. Our approach to select the predicted potential experts by the classification model and then using the ranking algorithm to sweep the top ranked from the remaining, would identify a majority of the potential experts if not all. The benefit of the early identification of experts could be long lasting. The identified users could be elevated to intermediate user status to keep them motivated in the community. For a community like TTLC which has only 83 superusers, an addition of 32 worthy superusers is a significant addition. Even for communities with larger number of experts, it would only improve the quantity and the quality of the interactions.

Though our results are encouraging the study has certain limitations. We only consider TTLC - a single Q&A sites with a narrow purpose and an active team of professional behind the scene. TTLC has a small number of hand labeled experts - it is a future task to see how to generalize our findings to communities with large number of experts. Our work depends on the human labeling and evaluation of user contributions, which used only two coders per user. Finally we do not attempt to exhaustively evaluate different models and machine learning strategies. This work focuses on demonstrating the potential for early detection of experts, and we leave optimization as future work.

Our results suggested that early identification of experts in QA communities is possible. We would like to see the application of this in different types of QA. We are conducting a second round of studies on TTLC, testing alternate volunteer-development strategies on users, such as, promotion to intermediate user status; providing training materials; providing mentoring; developing feedback and task driven mechanism.

Acknowledgments. We would like to thank Intuit and their employees for providing the dataset and putting their time for useful discussions. We would also like to thank the anonymous reviewers for providing their valuable feedback on the paper. This work was supported by the National Science Foundation, under grants IIS 08-08692 and IIS 08-08711.

References

1. Bouguessa, M., Dumoulin, B., Wang, S.: Identifying authoritative actors in question-answering forums: the case of Yahoo! answers. In: ACM International Conference on Knowledge Discovery and Data Mining, KDD, pp. 866–874 (2008)
2. Cortes, C., Vapnik, V.: Support-Vector Networks. Journal of Machine Learning, 273–297 (1995)
3. Jurczyk, P., Agichtein, E.: Discovering authorities in question answer communities by using link analysis. In: ACM International Conference on Information and Knowledge Management, CIKM, pp. 919–922 (2007)
4. Lawrence, P., Brin, S., Motwani, R., Winograd, T.: The PageRank Citation Ranking: Bringing Order to the Web. Technical Report, Stanford InfoLab (1999)
5. Pal, A., Konstan, J.A.: Expert identification in community question answering: exploring question selection bias. In: ACM International Conference on Information and Knowledge Management, CIKM, pp. 1505–1508 (2010)
6. Panciera, K., Halfaker, A., Terveen, L.: Wikipedians are born, not made: a study of power editors on Wikipedia. In: ACM International Conference on Supporting Group Work, GROUP, pp. 51–60 (2009)
7. Platt, J.C.: Fast training of support vector machines using sequential minimal optimization. In: Advances in Kernel Methods, pp. 185–208. MIT Press, Cambridge (1999)
8. Quinlan, J.R.: C4.5: programs for machine learning. Morgan Kaufmann Publishers Inc., San Francisco (1993)
9. Zhang, J., Ackerman, M.S., Adamic, L.: Expertise networks in online communities: structure and algorithms. In: ACM International Conference on World Wide Web, WWW, pp. 221–230 (2007)

KT-IDEM: Introducing Item Difficulty to the Knowledge Tracing Model

Zachary A. Pardos and Neil T. Heffernan

Department of Computer Science, Worcester Polytechnic Institute,
100 Institute Road, Worcester, MA 01609 USA
{Zpardos,nth}@wpi.edu

Abstract. Many models in computer education and assessment take into account difficulty. However, despite the positive results of models that take difficulty in to account, knowledge tracing is still used in its basic form due to its skill level diagnostic abilities that are very useful to teachers. This leads to the research question we address in this work: Can KT be effectively extended to capture item difficulty and improve prediction accuracy? There have been a variety of extensions to KT in recent years. One such extension was Baker's contextual guess and slip model. While this model has shown positive gains over KT in internal validation testing, it has not performed well relative to KT on unseen in-tutor data or post-test data, however, it has proven a valuable model to use alongside other models. The contextual guess and slip model increases the complexity of KT by adding regression steps and feature generation. The added complexity of feature generation across datasets may have hindered the performance of this model. Therefore, one of the aims of our work here is to make the most minimal of modifications to the KT model in order to add item difficulty and keep the modification limited to changing the topology of the model. We analyze datasets from two intelligent tutoring systems with KT and a model we have called KT-IDEM (Item Difficulty Effect Model) and show that substantial performance gains can be achieved with this minor modification that incorporates item difficulty.

Keywords: Knowledge Tracing, Bayesian Networks, Item Difficulty, User Modeling, Data Mining.

1 Introduction

Many models in computer education and assessment take into account difficulty. Item Response Theory (IRT) [1] is one such popular model. IRT is used in Computer Adaptive Testing (CAT) and learns a difficulty parameter per item. This makes IRT models very powerful for predicting student performance; however the model learning processes is expensive and is not a practical way of determining when a student has learned a particular skill because it does not model learning. Despite the predictive power of IRT, the Cognitive Tutors [2] employ standard Knowledge Tracing (KT) [3] to model students' knowledge and determine when a skill has been learned. Knowledge Tracing is used because it is a cognitively diagnostic form of

Joseph A. Konstan et al. (Eds.): UMAP 2011, LNCS 6787, pp. 243–254, 2011.
© Springer-Verlag Berlin Heidelberg 2011

assessment which is beneficial to both student and teacher. The parameters for a KT model need only be learned once, typically at the beginning of the school year (based on the past year's data) and the inference of individual student' knowledge of a skill can be executed with very little computation. Models like IRT that take into account item difficulty are strong at prediction, and model such as KT that infer skills are useful for their cognitively diagnostic results. This leads us to our research question: Can KT be effectively extended to capture item difficulty and improve predictive?

There have been a variety of extensions to KT in recent years. One such extension was Baker's contextual guess and slip model [4]. While this model has shown positive gains over KT in internal validation testing, it has not performed well relative to KT on unseen in-tutor data or post-test data; however, it has proven a valuable model to use alongside other models. Likewise, the contextual slip model [5] also suffered the same inadequacies on in-tutor data prediction. The contextual guess and slip model increased the complexity of KT by adding regression steps and feature generation. The added complexity of feature generation across datasets may have hindered the performance of this model. Therefore, one of the aims of our work in this paper was to make the most minimal of modifications to the KT model in order to add item difficulty and keep the modification limited to slight changes to the topology of the model.

1.1 Knowledge Tracing

The standard Bayesian Knowledge Tracing (KT) model has a set of four parameters which are typically learned from data for each skill in the tutor. These parameters dictate the model's inferred probability that a student knows a skill given that student's chronological sequence of incorrect and correct responses to questions of that skill thus far. The two parameters that determine a student's performance on a question given their current inferred knowledge are the guess and slip parameters and these parameters are where we will explore adding question level difficulty. The guess parameter is the probability that a student will answer correctly even if she does not know the skill while the slip parameter is the probability that the student will answer incorrectly when she knows the skill. Skills that have a high guess rate can be thought of, intuitively, as easy (a multiple choice question for example). Likewise, skills that have a low guess and/or a higher rate of mistakes (high slip) can be thought of as hard. Based on this intuition we believe a questions' difficulty can be captured by the guess and slip parameter. Therefore, we aim to give each question its own guess and slip thereby modeling a difficulty per item.

Figure 1 depicts the standard KT model. The three latent nodes representing knowledge are above the three observable nodes representing questions in the tutor. The depiction is showing an unrolled dynamic Bayesian topology for modeling a sequence of three questions but this chain can continue for an arbitrary number of questions a student answers. The guess and slip parameters are represented by $P(G)$ and $P(S)$ respectively. The two knowledge parameters, which dictate the state of the knowledge node, are the probability of learning, $P(T)$, and probability of initial knowledge, $P(L_o)$, also referred to as prior probability of knowledge or just *prior*. $P(L_o)$ is the probability that a student knows the skill before answering the first question and $P(T)$ is the probability that a student will transition from not knowing the skill to knowing it.

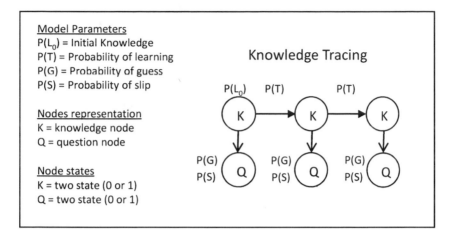

Fig. 1. The standard Knowledge Tracing model

While knowledge is modeled as a binary variable (a student is either in the learned or unlearned state), the inferred probability of knowledge is a continuous value. Once that probability reaches 0.95, the student can be assumed to have learned the skill. The Cognitive Tutors use this threshold to determine when a student should no longer be asked to answer questions of a particular skill.

2   Knowledge Tracing: Item Difficulty Effect Model (KT-IDEM)

One of our stated goals was to add difficulty to the classical KT model without going outside of the Bayesian topology. To do this we used a similar topology design to that which was demonstrated in Pardos & Heffernan's student individualization paper [6]. In that work a multinomial node was added to the Bayesian model that represented the student. The node(s) containing the parameters which the authors wished to individualize were then conditioned based on the student node, thus creating a parameter per student. For example, if one wished to individualize the prior parameter, the student node would be connected to the first knowledge node since this is where the prior parameter's CPT is held. A separate prior could then be set and learned for each student. Practically, without the aid of a pre-test, learning a prior for every student is a very difficult fitting problem, however, simplifying the model to represent only two priors and assigning students to one of those priors based on their first response has proven an effective heuristic for improving prediction by individualizing the prior.

In a similar way that Pardos & Heffernan showed how parameters could be individualized by student, we individualized the guess and slip parameter by item. This involved creating a multinomial item node, instead of a student node, that represents all the items of the particular skill being fit. This means that if there were 10 distinct items in the skill data, the item node would have values ranging from 1 to 10. These values are simply identifiers for the items which can arbitrarily be assigned. The item node is then connected to the question node (Fig 2) in the topology, thus conditioning the question's guess/slip upon the value of the item node. In the example of the 10 item dataset, the model would have 10 guess parameters, 10 slip parameters, a learn rate and a prior, totaling 22 parameters versus standard KT's 4 parameters. It is possible that this model will be over parameterized if a sufficient amount of data points per item is not met; however, there has been a trend of evidence that suggests models that have equal or even more parameters than data points can still be effective such as was shown in the Netflix challenge [11] and 2010 KDD Cup on Educational Data Mining [12].

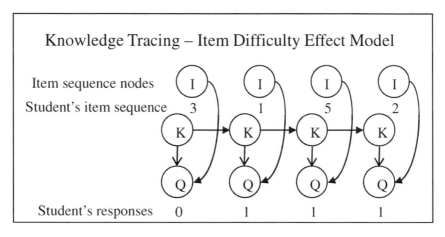

Fig. 2. The KT-IDEM topology depicting how the question node (and thus the guess/slip) is conditioned on the item node to add item difficulty to the KT model

Figure 2 illustrates how the KT model has been altered to introduce item difficulty by adding an extra node and an arc for each question. While the standard KT model has a single $P(G)$ and $P(S)$, KT-ITEM has a $P(G)$ and $P(S)$ for each item, for example $P(G/I=1)$, $P(G/I=2)$... $P(G/I=10)$, stating that there is a different guess parameter value given the value of the item node. In the example in Figure 2, the student sees items with IDs 3, 1, 5 and then 2. This information is fully observable and is used in model training, to fit appropriate parameters to the item $P(G/I)$ and $P(S/I)$, and in model tracing (prediction), to inform which items a particular student has encountered and make the appropriate inference of knowledge based on the answer to the item. By setting a student's item sequence to all 1s during training and tracing, the KT-IDEM model represents the standard KT model, therefore the KT-IDEM model, which we have introduce in this paper, can be thought of as a more general KT model. This model can also be derived by modifying models created by the authors for detecting the learning value of individual items [7].

3   Datasets

We evaluate the KT and KT-IDEM models with two datasets from two separate real world tutors. The datasets will show how the models perform across a diverse set of different tutoring scenarios. The key factor of KT-IDEM is modeling a separate guess and slip parameter for every item in the problem set. In these two datasets, the representation of an item differs. In the ASSISTments dataset, a problem template is treated as an item. In the Cognitive Tutor dataset, a problem, which is a collection of steps, is treated as an item. The sections bellow provide further descriptions of these systems and the data that were used.

3.1 The ASSISTments Platform

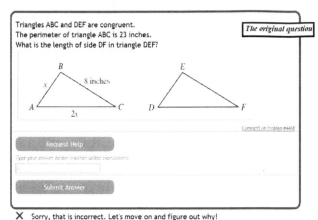

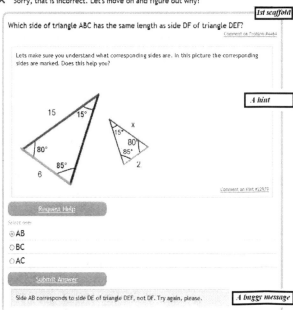

Our first dataset consisted of student responses from ASSISTments [8], a web based math tutoring platform which is best known for its 4th-12th grade math content. Figure 3 shows an example of a math item on the system and tutorial help that is given if the student answers the question wrong or asks for help. The tutorial help assists the student in learning the required knowledge by breaking each problem into sub questions called scaffolding or giving the student hints on how to solve the question. A question is only marked as correct if the student answers it correctly on the first attempt without requesting help.

Item templates in ASSISTments
Our skill building dataset consists of responses to multiple questions generated from an item template. A template is a skeleton of a problem created by a content developer in the web based builder application. For example, a template could

Fig. 3. An example of an ASSISTments item where the student answers incorrectly and is given tutorial help

specify a Pythagorean Theorem problem, but without the numbers for the problem filled in. In this example the problem template could be: "What is the hypotenuse of a right triangle with sides of length X and Y?" where X and Y are variables that will be filled in with values when questions are generated from the template. The solution is also dynamically determined from a solution template specified by the content developer. In this example the solution template would be, "Solution = sqrt(X^2+Y^2)". Ranges of values for the variables can be specified and more advance template features are available to the developer such as dynamic graphs, tables and even randomly selected cover stories for word problems. Templates are also used to construct the tutorial help of the template items. Items generated from these templates are used extensively in the skill building problem sets as a pragmatic way to provide a high volume of items for students to practice particular skills on.

Skill Building Datasets

Skill building is a type of problem set in ASSISTments that consists of hundreds of items generated from a number of different templates, all pertaining to the same skill or skill grouping. Students are marked as having completed the problem set when they answer three items correctly in a row without asking for help. In these problem sets items are selected in a random order. When a student has answered 10 items in a skill building problem set without getting three correct in a row, the system forces the student to wait until the next calendar day to continue with the problem set. The skill building problem sets are similar in nature to mastery learning [9] in the Cognitive Tutors; however, in the Cognitive Tutors, mastery is achieved when a knowledge-tracing model believes that the student knows the skill with 0.95 or better probability. Much like the other problem sets in ASSISTments, skill builder problem sets are assigned by the teacher at his or her discretion and the problem sets they assign often conform to the particular math curriculum their district is following.

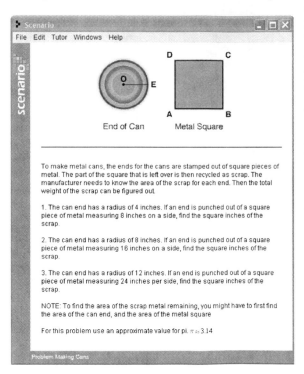

Fig. 4. A Geometry problem within the Cognitive Tutor

We selected the 10 skill builder datasets with the most data from school year 2009-2010, for this paper. The number of students for each problem set ranged from

637 to 1285. The number of templates ranged from 2-6. This meant that there would be at max 6 distinct sets of guess/slips associated with items in a problem set. Because of the 10 item/day question limit, we only considered a student's first 10 responses per problem set and discarded the remaining responses. Only responses to original questions were considered. No scaffold responses were used.

3.2 The Cognitive Tutor: Mastery Learning Datasets

Our Cognitive Tutor dataset comes from the 2006-2007 "Bridge to Algebra" system. This data was provided as a development dataset in the 2010 KDD Cup competition [10]. The Cognitive Tutor is designed differently than ASSISTments. One very relevant difference to this work is that the Cognitive Tutor presents a problem to a student (Fig 4) that can consist of questions (also called steps) of many skills. Students may enter their answers to the various questions pertaining to the problem in an answer grid (Fig 5). The Cognitive Tutor uses Knowledge Tracing to determine when a student has mastered a skill. A problem in the tutor can also consist of questions of differing skill. However, once a student has mastered a skill, as determined by KT, the student no longer needs to answer questions of that skill within a problem but must answer the other questions which are associated with the unmastered skill(s).

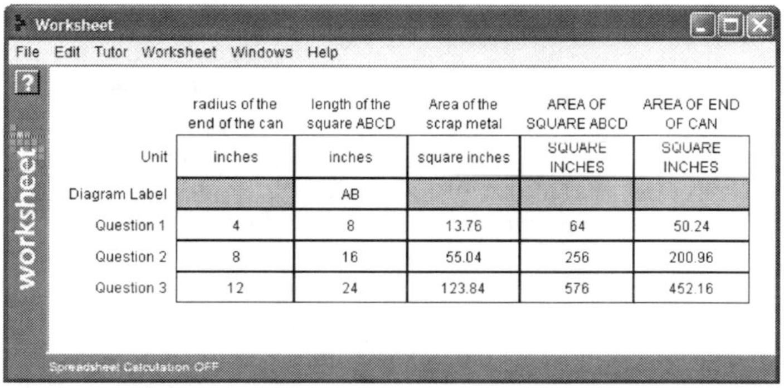
Worksheet
File Edit Tutor Worksheet Windows Help
worksheet
radius of the end of the can
length of the square ABCD
Area of the scrap metal
AREA OF SQUARE ABCD
AREA OF END OF CAN
Unit
inches
inches
square inches
SQUARE INCHES
SQUARE INCHES
Diagram Label
AB
Question 1
4
8
13.76
64
50.24
Question 2
8
16
55.04
256
200.96
Question 3
12
24
123.84
576
452.16
Spreadsheet Calculation OFF

Fig. 5. Answer entry box for the Geometry problem in Fig 4

The number of skills in this dataset was substantially larger than the ASSISTments dataset. Instead of processing all skills, a random sample of 12 skills were selected. Some questions consisted of multiple skills. Instead of separating out each skill, a set of skills associated with a question was treated as a separate skill. The Cognitive Tutor separates lessons into pieces called Units. A skill name that appears in one Unit was treated as a separate skill when appearing in a different Unit. Some skills in the Cognitive Tutor consist of trivial tasks such as "close-window" or "press-enter". These types of non-math related skill were ignored. To maintain consistency with the per student data amount used in the ASSISTments dataset, the max number of responses per student per skill was also limited to the first 10.

4 Methodology

A five-fold cross-validation was used to make predictions on the datasets. This involved randomly splitting each dataset into five bins at the student level. There were five rounds of training and testing where at each round a different bin served as the test set, and the data from the remaining four bins served as the training set. The cross-validation approach has more reliable statistical properties than simply separating the data in to a single training and testing set and should provide added confidence in the results since it is unlikely that the findings are a result of a "lucky" testing and training split.

4.1 Training the Models

Both KT and KT-IDEM were trained and tested on the same cross-validation data. The training phase involved learning the parameters of each model from the training set data. The parameter learning was accomplished using the Expectation Maximization (EM) algorithm. EM attempts to find the maximum log likelihood fit to the data and stops its search when either the max number of iterations specified has been reached or the log likelihood improvement is smaller than a specified threshold. The max iteration count was set to 200 and threshold was set to the BNT default of 0.001. Initial values for the parameters of the model were set to the following, for both models: $P(G)$ of 0.14, $P(S)$ of 0.09, $P(L_0)$ of 0.50, and $P(T)$ of 0.14. This set of values were found to be the average parameter values across skills in a previous analysis of ASSISTments data using students from

4.2 Performing Predictions

Each run of the cross-validation provided a separate test set. This test set consisted of students that were not in the training set. Each response of each student was predicted one at a time by both models. Knowledge tracing makes predictions of performance based on the parameters of the model and the response sequence of a given student. When making a prediction on a student's first response, no evidence was presented to the network except for the item identifier associated with the question. Since no individual student response evidence is presented on the first response, predictions of the first response are based on the models' *prior* and *guess/slip* parameters alone. This meant that, within a fold, KT will make the same prediction for all students' first response. KT-IDEM's first response may differ since not all students' first question is the same and the *guess/slip* differs based on the question. When predicting the student's second response, the student's first response was presented as evidence to the network, and so on, for all of the student's responses 1 to N.

5 Results

Predictions made by each model were tabulated and the accuracy was evaluated in terms of Area Under the Curve (AUC). AUC provides a robust metric for evaluating predictions where the value being predicted is either a 0 or a 1 (incorrect or correct), as is the case in our datasets. An AUC of 0.50 always represents the scored achievable by random chance. A higher AUC score represents higher accuracy.

5.1 ASSISTments Platform

The cross-validated model prediction results for ASSISTments are shown in Table 1. The number of students as well as the number of unique templates in each dataset is included in addition to the AUC score for each model. A Delta column is also included which shows the KT-IDEM AUC subtracted by the KT AUC score. A positive Delta indicates that there was an improvement in accuracy by using KT-IDEM instead of standard KT. A negative indicates that accuracy declined when compared to KT.

Table 1. AUC results of KT vs KT-IDEM on the ASSISTments datasets. The Delta column reports the increase (+) or decrease (–) in accuracy by using KT-ITEM.

Skill	#students	#templates	AUC		
			KT	KT-IDEM	Delta
1	756	3	0.616	0.619	+0.003
2	879	2	0.652	0.671	+0.019
3	1019	6	0.652	0.743	+0.091
4	877	4	0.616	0.719	+0.103
5	920	2	0.696	0.697	+0.001
6	826	2	0.750	0.750	- - - - -
7	637	2	0.683	0.689	+0.006
8	1285	3	0.718	0.721	+0.003
9	1024	4	0.679	0.701	+0.022
10	724	4	0.628	0.684	+0.056

The results from evaluating the models with the ASSISTments datasets are strongly in favor of KT-IDEM (Table 1) with KT-IDEM beating KT in AUC in 9 of the 10 datasets and tying KT on the remaining dataset. The average AUC for KT was 0.669 while the average AUC for KT-IDEM was 0.69. This difference was statistically significantly reliable (p = 0.035) using a two tailed paired t-test.

5.2 Cognitive Tutor

The cross-validated model prediction results for the Cognitive Tutor are shown in Table 2. The number of students, unique problems and data points in each skill dataset are included in addition to the AUC score for each model. The ratio of data points per problem (the number of data points divided by the number of unique problems) is also provided to show the average amount of data there was per problem.

The overall performance of KT vs. KT-IDEM is mixed in this Cognitive Tutor dataset. The average AUC of KT was 0.6457 while the average AUC for KT-IDEM was 0.6441; however, this difference is not statistically reliably difference (p = 0.96). As alluded to earlier in the paper, over parameterization is a potential issue when creating a guess/slip per item. In this dataset this issue becomes apparent due to the considerably high number of problems (avg. 311) compared to the number of templates in ASSISTments (avg. 3). Because of the high number of problems, and thus high number of parameters, the data points per problem ratio (dpr) becomes highly important. The five of the twelve datasets with a dpr > 6 were all predicted more accurately by KT-IDEM, with most showing a substantially higher accuracy over KT (+ 0.10 avg. AUC improvement). Among these five datasets, the average AUC of KT was 0.6124 and the average AUC of KT-IDEM was 0.7108. This difference was statistically reliably (p = 0.02). For the skill datasets with dpr < 6, the loss in accuracy was relatively low (~0.04) with the exception of skill 6 that produced a KT-IDEM AUC of 0.497 a score which was 2 standard deviations lower than the mean KT-IDEM score for Cognitive Tutor. This skill dataset had 396 problems with the most frequent problem accounting for 25% of the data points and the 2nd most frequent problem accounting for only 0.3%. This was exceptionally unbalanced relative to the other skill sets and served as an example of the type of dataset that the KT-IDEM model does not perform well on.

Table 2. AUC results of KT vs KT-IDEM on the Cognitive Tutor datasets. The AUC of the winning model is marked in bold.

Skill	#students	#prob	#data	#data/#prob	AUC		
					KT	KT-IDEM	Delta
1	133	320	1274	3.98	0.722	0.687	- 0.035
2	149	102	1307	12.81	0.688	0.803	+0.115
3	116	345	1090	3.16	0.612	0.605	- 0.007
4	116	684	1062	1.55	0.694	0.653	- 0.041
5	159	177	1475	8.33	0.677	0.718	+0.041
6	116	396	1160	2.93	0.794	0.497	- 0.297
7	133	320	1267	3.96	0.612	0.574	- 0.038
8	116	743	968	1.30	0.679	0.597	- 0.082
9	149	172	1431	8.32	0.585	0.720	+0.135
10	148	177	1476	8.34	0.593	0.626	+0.033
11	149	172	1431	8.32	0.519	0.687	+0.168
12	123	128	708	5.53	0.574	0.562	- 0.012

6   Discussion and Future Work

The training of the models in this paper was accomplished by splitting up a cohort of students into a test and training set through cross-validation. If a previous year's cohort of students were used instead, this may increase the number of training samples due to not requiring a portion of the data to be held out. This will also raise the issue of which guess and slip values to use for an item that has been added after the previous year's data was collected and thus was not in the training set. One approach is to use the average of all the learned guess/slip values or use the standard KT model guess/slip values for that question.

The results for the Cognitive Tutor showed that the average number of data points per problem largely determined if the accuracy of KT-IDEM would be greater than KT. It could be that some problems within a skill dataset have high amounts of data while some problems have low amounts. To improve the accuracy of KT-IDEM, the guess/slip values for the low data problems in the model could be replaced with KT's guess/slip values. This would ensure that when predicting performance on high data items, KT-IDEM parameters would be used and KT parameters would be used on low data items. The model parameter fitting could potentially be improved by using information such as average percent correct and number of hints requested to set the initial guess/slip values for each item instead of using default guess/slip values.

An open area for future work would be to improve assessment speed by choosing items based on their guess/slip values learned with KT-IDEM. The standard computer adaptive testing paradigm is focused on assessment, not learning. To accomplish quick assessment, these tests select the questions that give the optimal amount of information about a student's ability based on their response. In an IRT model, this criterion is called item discrimination. A response to an item with high discrimination results in a larger change in the student's assessed ability level than a response to a lower discrimination item. Likewise, in KT-IDEM, guess and slip can also capture discrimination. When an item has a zero guess and zero slip, the student's response is completely representative of their knowledge; however, when the guess and slip are closer to 0.50, the response has less of an impact on the updated probability of knowledge. In order to optimize the selection of questions for assessment, questions can be selected that maximize the change in probability of knowledge given an incorrect response and the change in probability of knowledge given a correct response to the selected question. Questions eligible for selection should have had sufficient data used to train their guess/slip values, otherwise erroneously high or low guess/slip values are likely to be learned and would not represent the true discrimination of the item. While this method could minimize the number of questions needed to assess a student, the questions which lead to the most learning do not necessarily correspond to the questions which are best for assessment. The Item Effect Model [7] has been used to determine item learning value with a Knowledge Tracing approach and could compliment KT-IDEM for choosing the appropriate questions which blend assistance and assessment.

7 Contribution

With the ASSISTments Platform dataset, KT-IDEM was more accurate than KT in 9 out of the 10 datasets. KT scored an AUC of 0.669 on average while KT-IDEM scored an AUC of 0.699 on average. This difference was statistically significant at the $p < 0.05$ level. With the Cognitive Tutor dataset, overall, KT-IDEM is not statistically reliably different from KT in performance prediction. When dpr is taken into account, KT-IDEM is substantially more accurate (0.10 average gain in AUC over KT). This improvement when taking into account dpr is also statistically reliable at the $p < 0.05$ level.

We have introduced a novel model for introducing item difficulty to the Knowledge Tracing model that makes very minimal changes to the native topology of the original mode. This new model, called the KT Item Difficult Effect Model (IDEM) provided reliably better in-tutor performance prediction on the ASSISTments Skill Builder dataset. While overall, the new model was not significantly different from KT in the Cognitive Tutor, it was significantly better than KT on datasets that provided enough data points per problem.

We believe these results demonstrate the importance of modeling item difficulty in Knowledge Tracing when sufficient data is available to train the model. The real world implication of improved accuracy in assessment is less student time spent over practicing and improved accuracy of skill reports given to teachers. Accurate guess and slip parameters per item with KT-IDEM also opens up the capability for a tutoring system to select questions with low guess and slip and thus optimizing the number of questions needed for assessment while remaining inside the model tracing paradigm.

Acknowledgements. This research was supported by the National Science foundation via grant "Graduates in K-12 Education" (GK-12) Fellowship, award number DGE0742503 and CAREER award. Funding was also provided by the Department of Education IES Center for Mathematics and Cognition grant. We would like to thank Hanyuan Lu, Matt Dailey and the Pittsburg Science of Learning Center for the datasets and dataset preparation.

References

1. Johns, J., Mahadevan, S., Park Woolf, B.: Estimating Student Proficiency Using an Item Response Theory Model. In: Ikeda, M., Ashley, K.D., Chan, T.-W. (eds.) ITS 2006. LNCS, vol. 4053, pp. 473–480. Springer, Heidelberg (2006)
2. Koedinger, K.R., Corbett, A.T.: Cognitive tutors: Technology bringing learning science to the classroom. In: Sawyer, K. (ed.) The Cambridge Handbook of the Learning Sciences, pp. 61–78. Cambridge University Press, New York (2006)
3. Corbett, A.T., Anderson, J.R.: Knowledge Tracing: Modeling the Acquisition of Procedural Knowledge. User Modeling and User-Adapted Interaction 4, 253–278 (1995)
4. Baker, R.S.J.d., Corbett, A.T., Aleven, V.: More accurate student modeling through contextual estimation of slip and guess probabilities in bayesian knowledge tracing. In: Woolf, B.P., Aïmeur, E., Nkambou, R., Lajoie, S. (eds.) ITS 2008. LNCS, vol. 5091, pp. 406–415. Springer, Heidelberg (2008)
5. Baker, R.S.J.d., Corbett, A.T., Gowda, S.M., Wagner, A.Z., MacLaren, B.A., Kauffman, L.R., Mitchell, A.P., Giguere, S.: Contextual Slip and Prediction of Student Performance after Use of an Intelligent Tutor. In: De Bra, P., Kobsa, A., Chin, D. (eds.) UMAP 2010. LNCS, vol. 6075, pp. 52–63. Springer, Heidelberg (2010)
6. Pardos, Z.A., Heffernan, N.T.: Modeling Individualization in a Bayesian Networks Implementation of Knowledge Tracing. In: De Bra, P., Kobsa, A., Chin, D. (eds.) UMAP 2010. LNCS, vol. 6075, pp. 255–266. Springer, Heidelberg (2010)
7. Pardos, Z., Dailey, M., Heffernan, N.: Learning what works in ITS from non-traditional randomized controlled trial data. The International Journal of Artificial Intelligence in Education (in Press, 2011)
8. Razzaq, L., Feng, M., Nuzzo-Jones, G., Heffernan, N.T., Koedinger, K.R., Junker, B., et al.: The Assistment project: Blending assessment and assisting. In: Looi, C.K., McCalla, G., Bredeweg, B., Breuker, J. (eds.) Proceedings of the 12th Artificial Intelligence in Education, pp. 555–562. ISO Press, Amsterdam (2005)
9. Corbett, A.T.: Cognitive computer tutors: Solving the two- sigma problem. In: Bauer, M., Gmytrasiewicz, P.J., Vassileva, J. (eds.) UM 2001. LNCS (LNAI), vol. 2109, pp. 137–147. Springer, Heidelberg (2001)
10. Pardos, Z.A., Heffernan, N.T.: Using HMMs and bagged decision trees to leverage rich features of user and skill from an intelligent tutoring system dataset. To appear in Journal of Machine Learning Research W & CP (in Press)
11. Bell, R., Koren, Y.: Lessons from the Netflix Prize Challenge. SIGKDD Explorations 9, 75–79 (2007)
12. Yu, H.-F., Lo, H.-Y., Hsieh, H.-P., Lou, J.-K., McKenzie, T.G., Chou, J.-W., et al.: Feature Engineering and Classifier Ensemble for KDD Cup 2010. In: Proceedings of the KDD Cup 2010 Workshop, pp. 1–16 (2010)

Walk the Talk

Analyzing the Relation between Implicit and Explicit Feedback for Preference Elicitation

Denis Parra[1] and Xavier Amatriain[2]

[1] School of Information Sciences, University of Pittsburgh
Pittsburgh PA 15260, USA
dap89@pitt.edu
[2] Telefonica Research, Diagonal 00, Barcelona 08019, Spain
xar@tid.es

Abstract. Most of the approaches for understanding user preferences or taste are based on having explicit feedback from users. However, in many real-life situations we need to rely on implicit feedback. To analyze the relation between implicit and explicit feedback, we conduct a user experiment in the music domain. We find that there is a strong relation between implicit feedback and ratings. We analyze the effect of context variables on the ratings and find that *recentness* of interaction has a significant effect. We also analyze several user variables. Finally, we propose a simple linear model that relates these variables to the rating we can expect to an item. Such mapping would allow to easily adapt any existing approach that uses explicit feedback to the implicit case and combine both kinds of feedback.

1 Introduction

The rise of recent web applications such as online social networks and e-commerce has uncovered the unforeseen potential of user mining and modeling. Applications such as Recommender Systems [1] rely on understanding user preferences in order to tailor the response and produce a personalized output. User preferences are modeled by taking into account either *explicit* or *implicit* user feedback.

Implicit feedback [2] is obtained by measuring the interaction of the user with the different items. Implicit feedback is obtained without incurring into any overhead on the user, since it is obtained from direct usage [3]. However, it is not clear that we can trust a simple one-to-one mapping between usage and preference [4]. On the other hand, explicit feedback is obtained by directly querying the user, who is usually presented with an integer scale where to quantify how much she likes the items. In principle, explicit feedback is a more robust way to extract preference, since the user is reporting directly on this variable, removing the need of an indirect inference. However, it is also known that this kind of feedback is affected by user inconsistencies known as *natural noise* [5]. Besides, the fact that we are introducing a user overhead, makes it difficult to have a complete view on the user preferences [6].

Joseph A. Konstan et al. (Eds.): UMAP 2011, LNCS 6787, pp. 255–268, 2011.

Therefore, none of the two existing strategies clearly outperforms the other. Ideally, we would like to use implicit feedback, minimizing the impact on the user, but having a robust and proven way to map this data to the actual user preference. Our target scenario is one in which by sampling a few ratings given by some of the users we can design an appropriate mapping. This would allows us to then use implicit feedback with any method proved valid for explicit ratings.

2   Preliminaries and Related Work

Although implicit feedback is much more readily available in practical applications, most of the research literature focuses on the use of explicit feedback input. The main reason is that this explicit feedback is considered the ground truth on the user preferences and the recommender problem is then assimilated into a predictive model. The current work is motivated by some of our previous work in doing contextual recommendations based on implicit feedback [7]. In that case, we modeled implicit data following the approach by Celma [8] in which playcounts are directly binned into ratings. However, we found results to be unsatisfactory and uncovered the need for more work in this area.

In one of the few papers addressing the implicit feedback recommendation problem [9], Hu *et al.* list their observations regarding implicit feedback: (1) **There is no negative feedback**. In explicit feedback, users may rate items they like or they don't. In implicit feedback, we cannot assume zero feedback means the user did not like the item. (2) **Implicit feedback is noisy**. We would like to directly relate amount of implicit feedback to level of preference. But this might not always true. (3) **Preference vs. Confidence**. The numerical value of explicit feedback indicates preference while the numerical value of implicit feedback indicates confidence on whether the user likes the item. (4) **Evaluation of implicit feedback**. There is a lack of clear metrics for evaluating a recommender system using implicit feedback.

Our approach starts off from different hypothesis, some of which in fact contradict the previous. In particular: (1) While it is true that you cannot interpret no implicit feedback as negative feedback – and this is true also for explicit feedback–, implicit data can include negative feedback. As long as the granularity of the items is comparable, and there is enough variability, you should be able to assume that *low* feedback is negative feedback. For example, if you are comparing TV series, you can assume that the user did not like a series she watched only once. You could not assume this with cinema movies, since most users will only watch movies once and therefore there is not enough variability. However, you could group them into, for instance, genres, and again assume that the user does not like least watched genres. (2) Implicit feedback is noisy but, as we showed in previous work [5], so is explicit feedback. (3) The numerical value of implicit feedback can be directly mapped to preference given the appropriate mapping and this is the main goal of our work. On the other hand, we do agree that there is no appropriate evaluation approaches for implicit feedback and this is in fact one of the motivations of our work: if we find an appropriate way to map implicit to explicit feedback we can ensure an evaluation that is as good as the one we have in the explicit case.

Our hypothesis that there is some observable correlation between implicit and explicit feedback can be tracked in the literature. Already in 1994, Morita and Shinoda [10] proved that there was a correlation between reading time on online news and self-reported preference. Konstan *et al.* [11] did a similar experiment with the larger user base of the Grouplens project and again found this to be true. Oard and Kim [12] performed experiments using not only reading time but also other actions like printing an article to find a positive correlation between implicit feedback and ratings. Koh *et al.* did a thorough study of rating behavior in two popular websites [13]. They hypothesize that the overall popularity or average rating of an item will influence raters. The conclusion on this issue is that, while there is an effect, this depends on the cultural background of the raters.

There are two recent works that are worth mentioning since they approach the issue of implicit feedback in the music domain. Jawasher *et. al* analyze the characteristics of user implicit and explicit feedback in the context of last.fm music service [14]. The authors also report on some experiments using standard Collaborative Filtering techniques on both implicit and explicit data. However, their results are not conclusive due to limitations in the dataset. In particular, it should be noted that they only used explicit feedback available in the last.fm profiles, which is limitted to the *love/ban* binary categories. This data is very sparse and, as the authors report, almost non-existant for some users or artists. On the other hand, Kurdomova *et. al* use a Bayesian approach to learn a classifier on multiple implicit feedback variables [15]. Using these features, the authors are able to classify liked and disliked items with an accuracy of 0.75, uncovering the potential of mapping implicit feedback directly to preferences.

All these previous works, provide a qualitative intuition of the potential of implicit feedback and its relation to explicit ratings. However, they do not measure the significance of the effect of the variables, nor propose a predictive model for ratings. In this context, the main contributions of our work are: (1) A study of the relation between implicit and explicit feedback in the music domain; (2) An analysis of the effect of other context and user variables; (3) A predictive linear model that can be used to infer unknown user ratings given their implicit feedback; (4) A general approach to building such a linear mapping in other domains.

3 Experimental Setup

We conducted an online user study among users of the last.fm music service. The goal of the study was to gather explicit feedback on music albums to compare to the user implicit feedback we obtained by directly crawling the last.fm page related to the user taking the survey. Explicit feedback was obtained by asking users to rate albums on a 1 to 5 star scale – see Figure 1. The items to rate were obtained from the list of albums in the user's playlist so that users responded to a personalized survey.

Fig. 1. Rating interface screenshot

User Demographics. To be accepted to the study, users had to (a) be 18 years old, and (b) have 5000 songs in their lastfm listening history. The reason for this latter requirement is that we wanted to ensure a meaningful sampling of the listening habits for the users selected in the study. This is not a limitation of the approach, but rather a way to ensure the model is derived from meaningful data. 151 users started the user experiment, and 127 completed the process. We filtered out outliers which did not present a meaningful variance in their ratings so our final study is based on 114 users.

Before starting the rating exercise, we queried users about a number of demographic variables. Out of the final users, 82% were male and 18% were female. Although we had representatives from 23 different countries, the sample was biased towards three countries: Spain (25 users), U.S. (15 users), and UK (16 users).

When asked about their internet use, more than 80% admitted to be heavy users with 20 or more hours per week. The percentage of heavy music listeners was lower, but still noticeable, with more than 50% of our users listening to music for over 20 hours per week. Almost 9% responded that they did not attend music concerts while, on the opposite end, 30% went to 11 or more concerts a year. 35% of our subjects said that they only read music magazines or blogs *sometimes*. However, the most involved music enthusiasts who read them at least every week accounted for over 20%. Over 50% of our subjects admitted rating music online never or seldom. And only 9% reported doing so consistently (often or every week). 45% of our subjects said they bought 1 to 10 physical records a year, and a non-negligible 18% said they did not buy any. On the other extreme, only 5% reported buying more than 21 records a year. Looking at online music shopping, more than 35% report never doing so, but 8% say they do it once a month or more. Finally, since we are asking users to report on their preferences on "albums", we wanted to verify whether they usually listened to albums as a whole or to single songs. Only 14% of our subjects preferred to listen to single tracks while over 45% preferred listening to full albums. The other 40% reported listening to music either way.

Item Sampling. We were interested in analyzing how a number of variables influence the relation between implicit and explicit feedback. On the other hand, we want our users to face a reasonable number of items to rate.

We decided to control the following variables: user popularity, general popularity, and recentness. Our initial hypothesis is that implicit feedback is directly correlated with user explicit feedback. However, global popularity might also affect since users might feel the *social pressure* to rate higher, items with more popular acceptance. In a similar way, we hypothesize that users might rate higher those items that have been listened to recently. Our main variables are therefore: (1) *Implicit Feedback (IF)*: playcount for a user on a given item; (2) *Global Popularity (GP)*: global playcount for all users on a given item; (3) *Recentness (R)* : time elapsed since user played a given item.

Depending on the user's listening habits, a naive, random sampling strategy might yield only very popular items. Therefore, both the number of control variables and the sampling strategy that we adopt is critical. For each of the three control variables we define three bins – *low*, *medium*, and *high*. This effectively defines 27 buckets, where we place all items for a given user. Bins are not defined by simply dividing the scale for each variable in three. All these variables follow a powerlaw-like distribution. Therefore, our bins are defined logarithmically in order to guarantee that the number of items in a bucket remains reasonably homogeneous. We then follow a random sampling strategy for each bucket. Some particular combinations of variables are more unlikely than others. Therefore, and despite of our goal of having a homogeneous distribution, we obtain buckets that include anywhere from 1 to 8% of the total number of items.

4   General Analysis

Are User Ratings Related to Implicit Feedback? Our initial assumption is that we have a dependent variable – the explicit rating given by the user – that depends on the user implicit feedback but also on the two other in dependent variables – overall popularity and recentness. In this initial qualitative analysis we shall first look at how these three variables affect the user ratings. We leave quantitative and significance analysis to the next section where we shall make use of multiple regression.

Figure 2 illustrates the relation between implicit feedback and ratings. Note how there is a clear correlation between the distribution of ratings and the implicit feedback. As we can see, the more implicit feedback, the higher the rating value where the distribution of ratings is centered. Note that ratings are quantized to the closest integer and this forces the median for implicit feedback of 2 and 3 to be located at 4. However, the mean, also depicted as an asterisk, clearly shows an ascending trend.

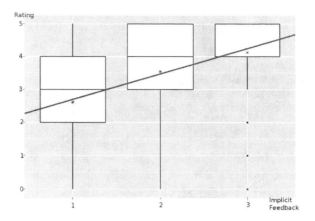

Fig. 2. Relation between implicit feedback and explicit ratings

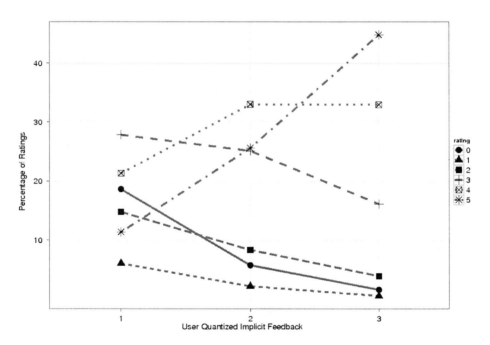

Fig. 3. Distribution of ratings given different values of implicit feedback

Figure 3 depicts the distribution of user ratings given different values for implicit feedback. Implicit feedback – *i.e.* how much they have listened to the album – is quantized as explained in the previous section and increases from 1 to 3 in the horizontal axis. We see that positive ratings that users give to the albums – ratings 4 and 5 – increase proportionally to the implicit feedback

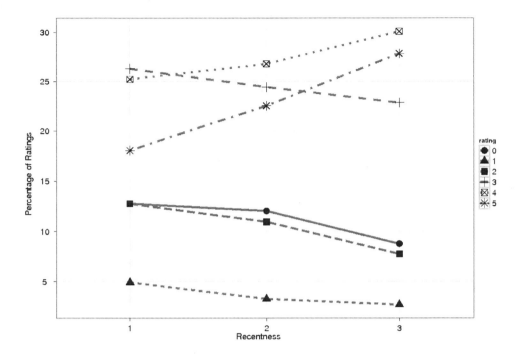

Fig. 4. Distribution of ratings given different values of recentness

while negative ratings – ratings 1 and 2 – decrease. Rating 0 – the especial case where the user decided not to rate an item – also decreases with user feedback. Interestingly, the middle rating – *i.e.* 3 – also decreases with implicit feedback.

If we look into more details, we see that the descending slope for negative ratings 1 and 2 is constant and approximately the same. On the other hand, rating 3 is more or less stable from user feedback 1 to 2 and rapidly decreases for 3. In other words, the probability a user rates an album that she has listened to *a lot* with a 3 is significantly lower than one with an average number of listens. However, there is little difference between albums with medium and low implicit feedback.

For positive ratings we see a clear and almost constant ascending slope for the 5. However, the 4 has a different behavior that is somewhat complementary to the 3. There is a significant difference between the proportions of 4 given to low and medium feedback, but this proportion remains constant between medium and high feedback.

4.1   Effect of Other Independent Variables on Ratings

Recentness. We look at the effect of the recentness factor in Figure 4. We see that this factor has a noticeable effect on all ratings. For positive ratings 4 and 5, the percentage increases almost linearly with the quantized recentness.

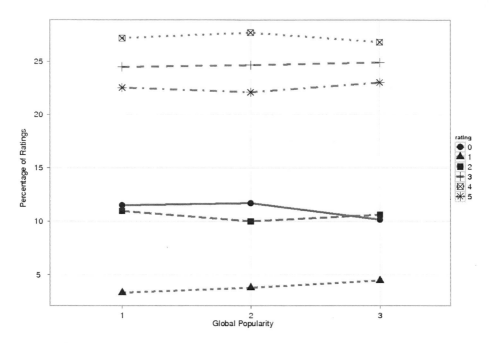

Fig. 5. Distribution of ratings given different values of overall popularity

All negative ratings and 3 decrease their percentage for more recent ratings. In other words, albums that were listened to more recently tend to receive more positive ratings and less negative ones. And, differently to what we saw with the implicit feedback variable, descending and ascending lines seem to have a similar and approximately constant slope.

Overall Popularity. We also analyze the effect of overall popularity in Figure 5. We don't see a significant effect of the independent variable for any of the ratings. Therefore, this first rough analysis seems to discard the effect of overall popularity in the user explicit rating.

Interaction Analysis. Next, we analyze the possible interaction between different pairs of variables by analyzing the corresponding interaction plots – we cannot include these figures due to space constraints. The only two variables that showed some coupling were recentness and implicit feedback. In particular, we found that for albums listened to more recently, the user needs a higher number of listens to give them a high rating. When we analyze the detailed effects of this coupling, however, we see that its effect on the average rating are not very significant.

Effect of User Variables. In the previous analysis, we are assuming that users rate items in a similar way, regardless of their demographic or musical background. However, it may well be that these variables influence and are somehow

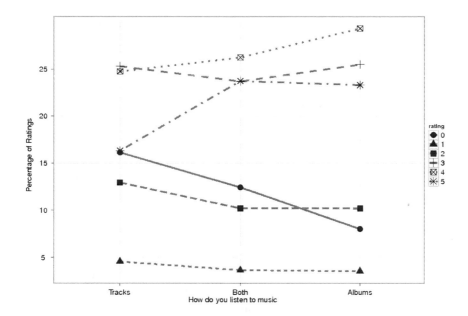

Fig. 6. Effect of listening style on percentage of ratings.

correlated with the user response to some items. In order to analyze these possible effects, we perform a multi-way ANOVA analysis on the different user variables we gathered from our initial survey.

By analyzing these results, we realize that there is only one variable with a significant contribution to explain the variance of our data – *p-value* below 0.05. The variable, *listen to tracks or albums*, encodes the way in which users listen to music. In particular, we were asking users whether they tend to listen to full albums, single tracks – e.g. through a radio stream –, or both. There was a significant difference on the average rating among the levels of *listen to tracks or albums*, $F(2, 62) = 3.949$, p $= 0.024$[1]. In order to further inspect this possible effect, we look at the relation between this variable and the different ratings in figure 6.

We see a number of clear trends. First, the percentage of zeros – *i.e.* not rated – is much higher for users that listen to tracks. In fact, the percentage of unrated items for users who listen to tracks 16% doubles the percentage in users who listen preferably to albums. This might be an expected effect since these users might not have a well-formed opinion on the quality of the album or even of its content. However, we also see significant differences in other ratings. In particular, users who tend to listen to tracks seem to have a much more critical opinion of albums since we observe a clear decrease in the percentage of positive ratings. The highest rating – 5 – captures around 23% of the ratings

---

[1] In our survey, in order to obtain an appropriate level of granularity, we only asked users to rate albums, not tracks.

for the users who listen to albums and even a bit more for those who listen to albums and independent tracks. But it only corresponds to 16% of the ratings for users who listen preferably to tracks.

We conclude that, except for the user listening style, all demographic and usage variables seem to have little or no effect on the rating of items. But the kind and granularity of the interaction of the user with content should be taken into account when interpreting implicit feedback.

5   Predicting ratings

Our ultimate goal is to come up with a general model that can directly map implicit data to explicit ratings. We aim at having some kind of parametric model that given input data on implicit user feedback is able to predict the rating that the user would give.

We approach our goal by performing a regression analysis in order to capture which independent variable (IV) or combination of IVs better accounts for the variations in the rating, the dependent variable (DV). In order to obtain fully meaningful results from a regression analysis, the model needs to observe some assumptions [16]. Given the way that our model is constructed, we cannot guarantee that it observes all the conditions. However, we conduct the regression analysis with the goal of having a preliminary idea. We shall then evaluate the models directly and verify our preliminary findings using a hold-out method to measure prediction error.

Types of variables. In this analysis, the IVs – implicit feedback, global popularity, and recentness –, which take values either 1, 2, or 3, are considered continuous. The DV, rating, although it is rigorously an ordinal variable, is also considered continuous in order to assess the model using a common measure such as RMSE, which will make results comparable with previous research. Note that, initially, we do not consider the special case of the 0 value – *i.e.* unrated – as part of this ordinal scale. However, we will analyze the effect of including or excluding this variable in the predictive power of the derived model at the end of this Section.

Model Comparison and Selection. After removing observations where the albums were unrated, we performed a regression analysis comparing 4 models using the remaining 10122 ratings. In all of the models, the DV is rating, but the IVs are respectively for models 1 through 3: i) implicit feedback (IF), ii) implicit feedback and recentness (RE) iii) implicit feedback, recentness and global popularity (GP). In the last model we check for possible interactions between implicit feedback with recentness. The exact formulation of each model is as follows:

- Model 1: $r_{iu} = \beta_0 + \beta_1 \cdot if_{iu}$
- Model 2: $r_{iu} = \beta_0 + \beta_1 \cdot if_{iu} + \beta_2 \cdot re_{iu}$
- Model 3: $r_{iu} = \beta_0 + \beta_1 \cdot if_{iu} + \beta_2 \cdot re_{iu} + \beta_3 \cdot gp_i$
- Model 4: $r_{iu} = \beta_0 + \beta_1 \cdot if_{iu} + \beta_2 \cdot re_{iu} + \beta_3 \cdot if_{iu} \cdot re_{iu}$

Table 1. Regression Results. R^2, F-value, and p-value for the 5 models.

Model	R^2	F-value	p-value	β_0	β_1	β_2	β_3
1	0.125	$F(1, 10120) = 1146$	< 0.001	2.726	0.499	-	-
2	0.1358	$F(2, 10019) = 794.8$	< 0.001	2.491	0.484	0.133	-
3	0.1362	$F(3, 10018) = 531.8$	< 0.001	2.435	0.486	0.134	0.0285
4	0.1368	$F(3, 10018) = 534.7$	< 0.001	2.677	0.379	0.038	0.053

Table 2. Predictive power including (RMSE1) and excluding (RMSE2) unrated items

Model	RMSE1	RMSE2
User average	1.5308	1.1051
1	1.4206	1.0402
2	1.4136	1.034
3	1.4130	1.0338
4	1.4127	1.0332

Table 1 presents the results of each model. The results show that all models significantly explain the variance in the data. Besides, there are clear trends in the results. By including the variable **recentness** as a predictor, model 2 increases the amount of variability of the DV explained by the model in 10% with respect to model 1, which is reflected in the R^2 value. Although including the variable **global popularity** as a predictor increases the value of R^2, this increment is very small. This result, in addition to the fact that global popularity is not correlated to the other two IVs, supports our assumptions that the variables implicit feedback and recentness are more strongly related to rating, and subsequently, would be more useful to predict it. We see that model 4, which considers the interactions between implicit feedback and recentness, shows an important improvement over model 2. This supports our initial finding of such an interaction reported in Section 4.1. Note also that the β coefficients remain fairly constant throughout the models giving always much more importance to implicit feedback.

Predictive Power of the Models. Finally, to test our findings in the regression analysis, we fit the 4 linear models described in the previous section using 80% of the observations, and then by doing 10-fold cross validation, we compare the predictive power of our models. We do so by measuring the root-mean squared error (RMSE) between our predictions and the actual ratings. The results in Table 2 show that all of our models improve the user average baseline significantly – 7% in the worst case. The improvement in performance when introducing other variables, is less clear. In the best case, introducing recentness, improves our accuracy in 0.5%. And, as we would expect, introducing global popularity does not improve the results significantly.

Predicting known ratings. The above results refer to a model that predicts both ratings and non-ratings. The zero value in our ratings refers to the user not

Table 3. Predictive power of the regression models depending on the user interaction style. Values represent RMSE of 10-fold cross validation

Model	Tracks	Tracks/Albums	Albums
User average	1.1501	1.1833	1.1306
1	1.0579	1.0417	1.0257
2	1.0512	1.0383	1.0169
3	1.0507	1.0386	1.0159
4	1.049	1.0384	1.0159

giving any feedback. Therefore, we are deriving models in which we can not only predict what the rating will be but also if the user decided to rate or not. However, we are also interested in evaluating the predictive capabilities of the models on known ratings. That is, given a pair of user and item for which we know there is the rating, how well can we predict its rating?

By comparing the results in columns 2 and 3 in Table 2, we can see that by excluding non-rated items our models have a significant gain in predictive power (RMSE decreases in more than 25%). However, relative performance of each model remains approximately the same. The improvement over the baseline predictor of user average is 6.5%.

Adding effect of user interaction style. In Section 4.1, we found that the average user rating showed a significant difference only among the levels of the listening/interaction style variable (*i.e.* listen to tracks or albums). We also identified a difference in the distribution (percentage) of ratings among the three levels of this variable. Our hypothesis is that our models should be able to predict better ratings for users who interact with music at the album level. In order to check this, we split our data into three different sets: (a) those who interact at the track level; (b) those who interact at the album level; and (c) those who interact either way.

In Table 3 we see that all of our models perform better when predicting users that listen preferably to albums. The decrease in RMSE is around 10%. This finding is supported when comparing the results to those obtained for the whole dataset and reported in Table 2 and finding a general improvement for users who listen to albums despite the fact that the user average baseline decreases its performance for this population. In fact, the average improvement of our predictive models over the baseline user average predictor is over 10% when segmenting the population into these three groups.

6   Conclusions and Future Work

Our analysis shows a clear relation between the amount of times users listen to an album, and the rating they report. We also find that the time elapsed since the user interacted with the album, have a significant effect but others, but the global item popularity does not influence the rating. We analyze the effect of several demographic and usage variables and find that only the granularity of the interaction style has a significant effect: .

Using the results of our analysis, we create a predictive model in which we can predict a user rating, given information of how the user interacted with an item. We perform a regression analysis to come up with several linear models and evaluate their fit to this purpose. We conclude that we can predict user ratings with an acceptable level of accuracy using a simple model that takes into account implicit feedback and recentness. In the best case, we measure an improvement over the baseline user average predictor of more than 10%.

The same approach to create a linear mapping could be applied to any domain for which we have a sample of ratings, and information about relevant context and user variables. Our results open up many possibilities for using implicit feedback in predictive tasks, especially in the context of recommender systems. Since we have a model that relates this implicit feedback to ratings, we can think of applying any of the methods used for explicit feedback on implicit data. Nevertheless, the particular model should be validated on other domains and datasets. In future work, we also plan on exploring other possible parametric approaches such as hierarchical or Bayesian models.

References

1. Ricci, F., Rokach, L., Shapira, B., Kantor, P.B.: Recommender Systems Handbook. Springer, Heidelberg (2011)
2. Oard, D.W., Kim, J.: Implicit feedback for recommender systems. In: AAAI Workshop on Recommender Systems (1998)
3. Potter, G.: Putting the collaborator back into collaborative filtering. In: 2nd KDD Workshop on Large-Scale Recommender Systems and the Netflix Prize Competition (2008)
4. Nichols, D.M.: Implicit rating and filtering. In: Proceedings of the Fifth DELOS Workshop on Filtering and Collaborative Filtering, pp. 31–36 (1997)
5. Amatriain, X., Pujol, J.M., Oliver, N.: I like it... I like it not: Evaluating user ratings noise in recommender systems. In: Houben, G.-J., McCalla, G., Pianesi, F., Zancanaro, M. (eds.) UMAP 2009. LNCS, vol. 5535, pp. 247–258. Springer, Heidelberg (2009)
6. Jawaheer, G., Szomszor, M., Kostkova, P.: Characterisation of explicit feedback in an online music recommendation service. In: Proceedings of the Fourth ACM Conference on Recommender Systems, RecSys 2010, pp. 317–320 (2010)
7. L., Baltrunas, X.A.: Towards time-dependant recommendation based on implicit feedback. In: Workshop on Context-Aware Recommender Systems (CARS 2009) in ACM Recsys 2009 (2009)
8. Celma, O.: Music recommendation and discovery in the long tail (2008)
9. Hu, Y., Koren, Y., Volinsky, C.: Collaborative filtering for implicit feedback datasets. In: Proceedings of ICDM 2008 (2008)
10. Morita, M., Shinoda, Y.: Information filtering based on user behavior analysis and best match text retrieval. In: SIGIR 1994: Proceedings of the 17th Annual International ACM SIGIR Conference, pp. 272–281. Springer-Verlag New York, Inc., Heidelberg (1994)

11. Konstan, J.A., Miller, B.N., Maltz, D., Herlocker, J.L., Gordon, L.R., Riedl, J.: Grouplens: applying collaborative filtering to usenet news. Commun. ACM 40(3), 77–87 (1997)
12. Oard, D., Kim, J.: Modeling information content using observable behavior. In: Proc. of the ASIST Annual Meeting, pp. 481–488 (2001)
13. Koh, N.S., Hu, N., Clemons, E.K.: Do online reviews reflect a product's true perceived quality? - an investigation of online movie reviews across cultures. Electronic Commerce Research and Applications (2010)
14. Jawaheer, G., Szomszor, M., Kostkova, P.: Comparison of implicit and explicit feedback from an online music recommendation service. In: Proceedings of the 1st International Workshop on Information Heterogeneity and Fusion in Recommender Systems (2010)
15. Kordumova, S., Kostadinovska, I., Barbieri, M., Pronk, V., Korst, J.: Personalized implicit learning in a music recommender system. In: De Bra, P., Kobsa, A., Chin, D. (eds.) UMAP 2010. LNCS, vol. 6075, pp. 351–362. Springer, Heidelberg (2010)
16. Kutner, M., Nachtschiem, C., Wasserman, W., Neter, J.: Applied Linear Statistical Models, 4th edn. McGraw-Hill, New York (1996)

Finding Someone You Will Like and Who Won't Reject You

Luiz Augusto Pizzato, Tomek Rej, Kalina Yacef,
Irena Koprinska, and Judy Kay

School of Information Technologies
University of Sydney, NSW 2006, Australia
luiz.pizzato@sydney.edu.au

Abstract. This paper explores ways to address the problem of the high cost problem of poor recommendations in reciprocal recommender systems. These systems recommend one person to another and require that both people like each other for the recommendation to be successful. A notable example, and the focus of our experiments is online dating. In such domains, poor recommendations should be avoided as they cause users to suffer repeated rejection and abandon the site. This paper describes our experiments to create a recommender based on two classes of models: one to predict who each user will like; the other to predict who each user will dislike. We then combine these models to generate recommendations for the user. This work is novel in exploring modelling both people's likes and dislikes and how to combine these to support a reciprocal recommendation, which is important for many domains, including online dating, employment, mentor-mentee matching and help-helper matching. Using a negative and a positive preference model in a combined manner, we improved the success rate of reciprocal recommendations by 18% while, at the same time, reducing the failure rate by 36% for the top-1 recommendations in comparison to using the positive model of preference alone.

1 Introduction

Modelling what users *like* has allowed recommender websites to provide personalised recommendations of products they might want to purchase. There has been relatively little work that explicitly modelled negative preferences, independently of the positive model. This issue is somewhat subtle, because recommenders make use of both positive and negative ratings to build their preference models. These models are successful if they are effective in providing recommendations that have a high proportion of good recommendations. It may not matter if there is a small proportion of poor recommendations within this set.

However, for recommenders that focus on matching people to people, the cost of a poor recommendation can be quite high. This type of recommender is called *reciprocal recommender* [9] because it involves establishing reciprocal relationships between people in domains such as in online dating sites, employment

Joseph A. Konstan et al. (Eds.): UMAP 2011, LNCS 6787, pp. 269–280, 2011.

websites (which aim to match employees and employers), mentor-mentee matching and matching helper and helpees. So, for example, consider a scenario where a user, *Bob*, is recommended to another user, *Alice*; this recommendation is only successful if both *Alice and Bob* reciprocally agree that the recommendation is good. Importantly, the interaction is staged. At the first stage, it is like other recommenders in the fact that *Alice* is presented with a set of recommendations and she can simply ignore the one for *Bob* if she does not like that recommendation (*Bob* may never know that he was recommended). However, it can be highly costly to the system if *Alice* initiates a contact with *Bob* and he then rejects her. If the same situation happens repeatedly, it may cause *Alice* to feel the anguish of repeated rejection.

Because the cost of poor reciprocal recommendations can be high, it seems likely that it will be valuable to build a model of negative preferences for such domains. Some key attributes of reciprocal recommenders make this seem rather important, compared to conventional recommenders. Notably, it is important to avoid overloading any individual. This is partly because each person only needs a small number of recommendations of people they should consider more seriously, for example, moving to establishing contact. It is also important from the recommendee perspective as it increases the risk of them being ignored or rejected by a popular person. Another key property of reciprocal recommenders is that they must involve every user in recommendations: every user must be given recommendations, and the system should recommend every user to others, no matter how unpopular they might be. This might mean that, compared with conventional recommenders, the reciprocal recommender may need to find recommendations that may not be a particularly good match to the user's preference model; in this case, the explicit modelling of negative preferences, may help avoid making recommendations that are more likely to incur the risk of rejection.

In this paper, we explore the impact of building and combining positive and negative preference models for online dating. We need to introduce some terminology for this context. The first stage of the recommendation process involves presenting a user (such as *Alice* in our scenario) with a set of recommendations. If this is successful, and the user likes one or more of the recommendations, the user can send an expression of interest (EOI) to the people they like. The EOI for our system is one of a set of short, pre-defined messages. The second stage involves the person who receives an EOI (*Bob* in our scenario), who can respond to an EOI with one of a small set of pre-defined messages. The response of an EOI can be either *positive* or *negative* indicating whether the recipient *likes* or *dislikes* the person who sent the EOI. At this second stage, a positive response indicates the recommendation process is proceeding successfully. The third key step is that one of the users can purchase a token allowing both users to exchange unconstrained messages that might contain contact details. After this stage users can meet face to face, or simply communicate outside the online dating website using standard electronic means.

The remainder of this paper is structured as follows. Section 2 reviews the literature in reciprocal recommenders for online dating and the use of negative indications of preference. Section 3 describes the main characteristics of the content-based reciprocal recommender used in this study, including the way we have incorporated negative indications of preferences. Section 4 presents the evaluation setup and the evaluation results, including how much negative preferences influenced the results, and especially its effect on preventing rejection. Finally, Section 5 discusses the results and their implications for other reciprocal recommenders.

2   Literature Review

Although online dating had not received much attention in recommender systems research in the past, the last year has seen several papers on the subject. These include our work [9] which introduced the notion or reciprocal recommenders, identified their distinctive characteristics and created RECON, a recommender we used to explore the effect of taking reciprocity into account. There was also the quite independent work of Diaz et al. [5] as well as McFee and Lanckriet [8], which focussed on finding a list of users whose chance of a positive interaction with another user is higher for those users near the top of the list than for those users near the bottom (i.e. a ranking problem). We will return to these in more detail after reviewing key work in modelling negative preferences.

There has been a range of research into use of negative preferences. For instance, the Adaptive Radio [4] is one example of work that explored the value of explicitly modelling negative preferences for group recommendation. The work of Kim et al. [7] creates a people recommendation system for a social network website where users can reply positively or negatively to other users. Kim et al. create groups of users based on common attributes and by comparing the communication between these groups, they find rules that can be applied to generate recommendations. They highlight that it is important to consider both sides of the recommendation process. They have shown that for the reciprocal domain of social networks, recommendation can improve by considering the preferences of the object of the recommendation. However, they did not report any particular use of the negative interactions, nor did they attempt to minimise negative responses.

Similarly, the collaborative filtering technique named SocialCollab [3] was also in the context of a social network. But they make no mention of negative interactions. Their algorithm combines two network of users: (1) users with similar "taste", and (2) users with similar "attractiveness". Similar taste is defined in terms of the users who send messages to the same group of users, while similar attractiveness relates to those users who receive messages from the same group of users. By combining these two strategies, they report improved performance, indicating the importance of reciprocity in a people to people recommender.

The work of Akehurst et al. [1] makes use of positive and negative responses to an EOI. Akehurst found that similar users, in terms of the attributes of the users, like and dislike similar groups of users. Using this information, Akehurst deals with the cold start problem by finding a set of users who were liked by a group of similar users, and used a ranking strategy that accounts for the number of positive and negative responses given by these users. This strategy means that the system aims to recommend people who send more positive replies and few negative replies to the set of similar users. This work used a hybrid approach, that combined collaborative filtering to generate recommendations, and content-based recommender algorithms to compute the list of similar users.

Brozovsky and Petricek [2] applied collaborative filtering in an online dating system. They used variations of user-user and item-item collaborative filtering algorithms and several different benchmarks using a dataset to predict the ratings that users would give for each other's appearance in an online dating service. The use of positive and negative indications are implicit in the ratings given by the user.

Taking an information retrieval and machine learning approach to finding good matches in an online dating scenario, McFee and Lanckriet [8] used structural support vector machine (SVM) to learn distance metrics optimised for different ranking measures. Because structural SVMs require positive and negative examples, McFee and Lanckriet used positive interactions as positive indications and then treated all other interactions (not necessarily known to be negative) as negative examples. Although McFee and Lanckriet reported better results than the baseline, the difference in the results is small.

Diaz et al. [5] focus on learning a reciprocal ranking function that maximises the chance of a positive interaction between online dating users. They describe the reciprocal aspects in the research as two-sided relevance. They used structured and unstructured profile features, including the information about the user's explicit preferences (the user "query") and the positive and negative interactions between users.

In this paper, we go beyond the class of the work discussed above by exploring the modelling of negative preferences, as well as positive preferences. We use these models to generate recommendations that we are most confident the user *likes* balanced by the need to present recommendations for people who are least likely to *dislike* the user.

3   RECON

As this work builds from the earlier RECON [9], we now describe it. RECON is a content-based reciprocal recommender system for online dating. It uses positive user interactions to build the model used to generate recommendations. RECON is a reciprocal recommender, meaning that it considers the preference models of both sides before a match is suggested to the user.

Consider the set of users with whom a user A has positively interacted. This is any user to whom A has sent an EOI or, the user has sent an EOI to A, who then replied positively. We extract the values of all profile features of these users. We store these values as a collection of counts and build a model of positive preferences M_A^+, which is then used to calculate the positive compatibility

$C^+(A, B)$ of a user A with any user B. This positive compatibility is calculated by checking how many times each attribute value of B's profile occurred in M_A^+. These values are normalised by the number of users used to build the preference model and by the number of attributes in the user profile.

For instance, Alice has sent EOIs to 10 men with the following characteristics: 7 singles, 2 divorced, 1 separated; 5 smokers, 5 non smokers. The positive compatibility between Alice and a user Bob who is single and a non smoker is:

$$C^+(Alice, Bob) = \frac{7 + 5}{10 \times 2} = 0.6$$

The reciprocal part of the recommendation is created by finding the top-N highest reciprocal compatibility scores between all A, B pairs of users. The reciprocal positive compatibility scores is the harmonic mean between $C^+(A, B)$ and $C^+(B, A)$. Essentially, RECON learns who to recommend to a user Alice, by learning the people whom Alice is likely to like and, of these people, selecting those most likely to like her. It does this by making use only of the positive actions of Alice (people she has sent an EOI or replied positively to) and the positive actions of other users.

3.1   RECON Using Negative Preferences

The same approach can be used create a model based on the negative interactions between the users (i.e. indications that someone does not like someone else). These negative models can be used to generate recommendations that are less likely to be disliked by the users.

Similarly to the positive preference model, given the set of negative user interactions of a user A, we define a negative preference model M_A^-. This negative preference model is used to calculate the negative compatibility $C^-(A, B)$ of a user A with any user B. This is essentially a model that measures the similarity between a user and the people whom Alice has negatively replied to their EOI.

Given a positive and negative compatibility, we can calculate the combined compatibility of a user A with a user B using A's positive and negative models of preference by subtracting the negative compatibility score from the positive compatibility score, with a normalisation step to obtain a compatibility score between 0 and 1. The formula is as follows:

$$C^\pm(A, B) = \frac{1 + C^+(A, B) - C^-(A, B)}{2} \tag{1}$$

In this way, it is possible to measure how much a user Bob matches the positive compatibility of a user Alice (i.e. how strongly the model predicts that Alice will like Bob) and how much Bob matches the negative compatibility of Alice (i.e. how strongly the model predicts that Alice will dislike Bob).

By combining both scores, we define a combined compatibility score that will give high scores for matches that are similar to the positive preference model and different from the negative preference model. Combined compatibility scores close to 0.5 are likely to be users who match the positive and the negative

Table 1. Example of recommendations and compatibility scores for a user x (ranking of recommendations for user x according to each compatibility score is shown in brackets)

$y =$	$C^+(x,y)$	$C^-(x,y)$	$C^\pm(x,y)$	$C^+(y,x)$	$C^-(y,x)$	$C^\pm(y,x)$	$C^+_{rec}(x,y)$	$C^\pm_{rec}(x,y)$
j	0.80 (1)	0.30 (2)	0.75 (1)	0.40	0.80	0.30	0.53 (2)	0.43 (4)
p	0.75 (2)	0.75 (5)	0.50 (3)	0.80	0.30	0.75	0.77 (1)	0.60 (1)
z	0.55 (3)	0.50 (3)	0.53 (2)	0.30	0.70	0.30	0.39 (4)	0.38 (5)
w	0.30 (4)	0.70 (4)	0.30 (5)	0.90	0.30	0.80	0.45 (3)	0.44 (3)
k	0.20 (5)	0.20 (1)	0.50 (3)	0.20	0.30	0.45	0.20 (5)	0.47 (2)

preference model equally. By contrast, combined scores close to zero indicate users who highly match someone's negative model and are a poor match to that person's positive model. Table 1 shows examples of these scores.

Similar to RECON, reciprocal recommendation can be created as the harmonic mean of the combined compatibility scores such that:

$$C^\pm_{rec}(A, B) = \frac{2}{\frac{1}{C^\pm(A,B)} + \frac{1}{C^\pm(B,A)}} \tag{2}$$

between all pairs of users A and B. We use harmonic mean because it is desirable to favour low compatibility scores over high scores when two users have distinctly different levels of compatibility. For instance, if *Bob* likes *Alice* a lot, and *Alice* does not like *Bob* at all, there is a very little chance that this reciprocal relationship will be successful; therefore, we want to have a reciprocal compatibility score more similar to *Alice*'s score than to *Bob*'s score.

In Table 1, we demonstrate how the values of the different compatibility scores relate to each other. For example, user p, who has a high positive compatibility score with user x (ranked second using $C^+(x,y)$) and a high negative score (ranked last[1] using $C^-(x,y)$), only ranks third in a combined score using $C^\pm(x,y)$. The same third position is occupied by k with a low $C^+(x,y)$ and a low $C^-(x,y)$. Also in the example of Table 1, we can observe that user j has the highest combined compatibility score with user x (highest $C^\pm(x,y)$); however because x's combined compatibility score with j (i.e. $C^\pm(j,x)$) is low, j has a low reciprocal compatibility score ($C^\pm_{rec}(x,y)$) in comparison to the other users in this example.

4   Evaluation

We have conducted our research in the context of one of the largest online dating websites in Australia. For the experiments described in this paper, we used one month of interactions (EOIs sent and their replies) between users to train our models, and the subsequent month to evaluate them. All experiments were clearly divided into training and testing data. For the purpose of evaluating

---

[1] Notice that the negative ranking is from the lowest value to the highest value.

Table 2. Data set used in these experiments

	Training	Testing
Users	11,921	11,495
EOIs	360,498	560,595
Positive Replies	56,080	93,810
Baseline Success Rate	(15.56%)	(16.73%)
Negative Replies	164,880	309,211
Baseline Failure Rate	(45.74%)	(55.16%)

the impact of negative preference model, we selected users who had both positive and negative preference models; that is, users who have sent at least one EOI or replied positively to one EOI (a positive indication of preference), *and* who have replied negatively to at least one other user. In order to run different types of experiments in a timely manner and because location is one of most important factors in online dating, we only selected users who lived in the Sydney area. The size of the data set is shown in Table 2. The training and test sets are similar in size. The baseline success rate of is calculated by dividing the positive replies by the total number of EOIs. Similarly, the baseline failure rate is the number of negative replies as a percentage of all EOIs.

4.1   Evaluation Metrics

We evaluated our systems using EOI precision at N ($P@N$), success rate at N ($S@N$), and failure rate at N ($F@N$). EOI precision at N (Equation 3), measures the proportion of the top-N recommendations to whom the user sent an EOI in the test data. EOI precision at N can tell us how well the ranking works in terms of the rate of acceptance of the recommendations by the user receiving the recommendation.

$$P@N = \frac{|EOIs \cap Recommended|}{|Recommended|} \tag{3}$$

Success rate at N ($S@N$) measures the rate of success (EOI with positive replies) among all EOIs in the top-N recommendations (Equation 4). Success rate at N can tell us whether the first N recommendations, if accepted by the users receiving them, are likely to have positive responses.

$$S@N = \frac{|EOIs \cap Recommended \cap PositiveResponse|}{|EOIs \cap Recommended|} \tag{4}$$

Failure rate at N is a similar measure to $S@N$, and is calculated using all EOIs that had negative responses against all EOIs in the top-N recommendations (Equation 5). Failure rate can tell us whether a ranking strategy can help minimise negative responses if the first N recommendation were accepted by the users. Therefore, $F@N$ is particularly important for evaluating a strategy which aims to minimise user dissatisfaction. Note that an EOIs can have a positive response, a negative response or they may have no response at all; so $F@N$ is not the complement of $S@N$.

$$F@N = \frac{|EOIs \cap Recommended \cap NegativeResponse|}{|EOIs \cap Recommended|} \qquad (5)$$

4.2   Results

We analyse how well the compatibility scores correlate with the users actual responses to each other by observing if higher positive compatibility $C^+(A, B)$ between all users A and B translate into more EOIs sent between users A and B.

We observed that all compatibility scores are normally distributed across the number of EOIs sent. We also noticed a higher average positive compatibility score (average: 0.45, standard deviation: 0.07) than the average negative compatibility score (average: 0.40, standard deviation: 0.09). Most EOIs are sent between users with combined compatibility higher than 0.5, meaning that their positive scores are higher than their negative scores. The average combined score is 0.51 with a standard deviation of 0.07, meaning that the positive compatibility scores between the sender and receiver of EOIs is mostly higher than their negative compatibility score. The higher standard deviation for the negative compatibility scores is likely due to the user's lack of control over who sends them an EOI. This means that people receive messages from users with a wider ranger of attributes, compared to the range of attributes found in the positive preference models.

In order to understand how negative models of preference can help avoiding undesired recommendations, we used a set of users who have both a positive preference model (have sent at least one EOI) and a negative preference model (have sent at least one negative reply). For these users, we observed no significant difference in $P@N$ when including the combining positive and negative preferences in comparison to positive preferences only as shown in Figure 1. The few EOI-precision points that we are losing are recommendations with high positive compatibility scores and with similarly high negative compatibility scores. As shown in example of Table 1 with recommendations p, a highly positive recommendation based on $C^+(x, p)$ are pushed down the ranking on $C^\pm(x, p)$, because the negative compatibility score $C^-(x, p)$ is equally high.

It is important to highlight that because we are evaluating over historical data, the values of $P@N$ are lowerbound values. For instance, from all recommendations that we generate, we are only certain of those that are present in the historical data, most recommendations were not seen by the user and therefore nothing can be inferred for those. Therefore, if we generate 100 recommendations and only 5 appear in the historical data, we can say for certain that we have a 5% lowerbound precision, but we cannot say anything regarding the remaining 95 recommendations.

Because the negative preference model of a user *Alice* is based on the few users who sent EOIs to her and to whom she sent negative responses, the majority of the online users will not match *Alice*'s negative preference model. For

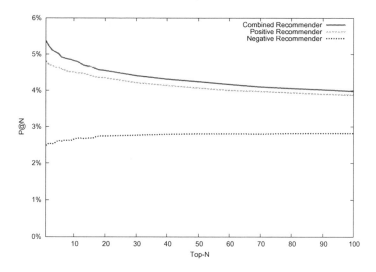

Fig. 1. EOI precision for different number of recommendations given

instance, *Alice* may not want to date users over 50 years of age, but because she has not receive any EOI from users of this age group (and as a consequence, she has not rejected them), we cannot infer a negative compatibility score for them. Therefore, most random pairs of online dating users will have unknown negative compatibility scores. In our strategy unknown scores are given the value of zero (meaning *not disliked*). Because of this, we evaluated the negative preference model scores using all recommendations B where the positive compatibility $C^+(A, B)$ is greater than zero (i.e. users we predict A likes to at least some degree). For this recommender – referred to as 'Negative Recommender' – we ranked all recommendations such that the recommendation B with the lowest negative compatibility score $C^-(A, B)$ (least disliked) appears first and the B with highest negative compatibility score appears last.

We observed in Figure 1 that the 'Negative recommender' seems to have constant EOI precision, which indicates that the negative compatibility scores by itself does not provide a good ranking for a recommender. Also, we observed that many users have low negative compatibility scores, which indicate that this model contains many ties, which will harm the precision of such a recommender. Another reason why negative compatibility scores cannot predict EOIs is that the negative compatibility model is trained over responses of EOIs and not EOIs that were not sent (information that we do not possess). For the same reason, the combined recommender has similar EOI precision to the positive recommender.

Unlike other recommendations, reciprocal recommendations benefit from negative preferences as can be seen in Figure 2. This occurs because negative preferences are modelled using negative *responses*, therefore improving measures that account for the response of the users. We can observe that the use of negative preferences in the reciprocal recommender gives a better success rate for

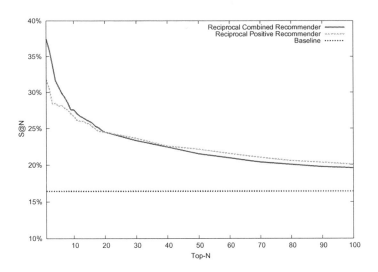

Fig. 2. Success rate for different number of recommendations given

top-1 and for top-5, while for top-10 and for top-100 they are virtually the same. The results for the reciprocal combined recommender for top-1 and for top-5 are 37.46% and 30.77% respectively, while the corresponding results for the reciprocal positive-only recommender are 31.78% and 28.09%. We ran the Mann-Whitney-Wilcoxon test on both data sets, for different values of N, to see whether the success rate improvement of the negative preference reciprocal recommender was statistically significant. We found that the difference is significant to a 95% confidence interval from top-1 to top-5 but is not significant at higher N. Importantly, the success rates of both recommenders are higher than the baseline success rate, which is the ratio between the number of positively replied EOIs and the number of EOIs in the test set. These results are important for our domain, particularly for the case of unpopular users, for whom we may have small numbers of good recommendations. These results are also important as the very top recommendations are critical because people are most likely to focus time and attention on the first set of items presented to them [6].

Matching these results for success rate, there is a lower failure rate for reciprocal preferences when negative preferences are used, compared to the case when only positive preferences are used (Figure 3). We can observe that for all values of N the combined positive and negative recommender consistently outperforms the positive only recommender. But at top-100, the failure rate increases above the baseline level of 54.19%, which indicates that the reciprocal recommender provides recommendations with lower chance of rejection only for lower numbers of N.

Overall these results show that exploiting negative preferences is a promising approach for fine tuning reciprocal recommendations. As the negative preference compatibility score is subtracted from the positive one, the effect is in fact only

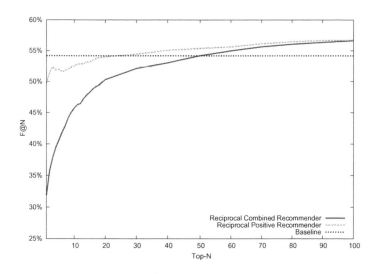

Fig. 3. Failure rate for different number of recommendations given

pushing recommended users down the list, not promoting users to be recommended who did not already have a very high positive score. This is why the EOI precision is not statistically different. However for top-1 to top-5, the success rate is higher and the failure rate considerably lower than using the positive preferences only. This means that our combined recommender does indeed help with our goals of reducing the chance of rejection.

5   Concluding Remarks

The driver for this exploration of modelling both negative and positive preferences was to reduce the risk of people being rejected in a reciprocal recommender system. Our broader goal was to gain greater understanding of how the negative preference model affects the performance of a reciprocal recommender. Accordingly, we defined models for both positive and negative preferences and explored ways to combine these to select recommendations and then for ranking them.

We have conducted our research in the context of a large online dating site. In our study, we created a model of negative user preferences and evaluated the use of this model in conjunction with the use of a positive model of user preferences in order to generate and to rank recommendations for an online dating recommender. We observed that, despite the fact that negative preferences do not help to increase the number of EOI sent (observed using $P@N$), they do help to make recommendations with a higher chance of success and lower chance of failure. Therefore, by accounting for *dislikes* as well as *likes*, the addition of negative preferences in a reciprocal recommender can reduce the risk of repeated rejection that some users experience in online dating. Since other reciprocal recommender domains also involve a risk of rejection, these results are a contribution to improving understanding of how to create better reciprocal recommenders.

Acknowledgments. This research was funded by the Smart Services Co-operative Research Centre.

References

1. Akehurst, J., Koprinska, I., Yacef, K., Pizzato, L., Kay, J., Rej, T.: CCR - A Content-Collaborative Reciprocal Recommender for Online Dating. In: Proc. of the 22nd International Joint Conference on Artificial Intelligence (IJCAI), Barcelona (2011)
2. Broovsk, L., Petek, V.: Recommender system for online dating service. CoRR abs/cs/0703042 (2007)
3. Cai, X., Bain, M., Krzywicki, A., Wobcke, W., Kim, Y., Compton, P., Mahidadia, A.: Collaborative filtering for people to people recommendation in social networks. In: Li, J. (ed.) AI 2010. LNCS, vol. 6464, pp. 476–485. Springer, Heidelberg (2010)
4. Chao, D.L., Balthrop, J., Forrest, S.: Adaptive radio: achieving consensus using negative preferences. In: Proc. of the 2005 International ACM SIGGROUP Conference on Supporting Group Work, GROUP 2005, pp. 120–123. ACM, New York (2005)
5. Diaz, F., Metzler, D., Amer-Yahia, S.: Relevance and ranking in online dating systems. In: SIGIR 2010: Proc. of the 33rd International ACM SIGIR Conference on Research and Development in Information Retrieval, pp. 66–73. ACM, New York (2010)
6. Joachims, T., Granka, L., Pan, B., Hembrooke, H., Gay, G.: Accurately interpreting clickthrough data as implicit feedback. In: Proc. of the 28th Annual International ACM SIGIR Conference on Research and Development in Information Retrieval, SIGIR 2005, pp. 154–161. ACM, New York (2005)
7. Kim, Y., Mahidadia, A., Compton, P., Cai, X., Bain, M., Krzywicki, A., Wobcke, W.: People recommendation based on aggregated bidirectional intentions in social network site. In: Kang, B.-H., Richards, D. (eds.) PKAW 2010. LNCS, vol. 6232, pp. 247–260. Springer, Heidelberg (2010)
8. McFee, B., Lanckriet, G.: Metric learning to rank. In: Proc. of the 27th International Conference on Machine Learning (ICML 2010) (June 2010)
9. Pizzato, L., Rej, T., Chung, T., Koprinska, I., Kay, J.: Recon: a reciprocal recommender for online dating. In: RecSys 2010: Proc. of the Fourth ACM Conference on Recommender Systems, pp. 207–214. ACM, New York (2010)

Personalizing the Theme Park:
Psychometric Profiling and Physiological Monitoring

Stefan Rennick-Egglestone[1], Amanda Whitbrook[2], Caroline Leygue[3],
Julie Greensmith[1], Brendan Walker[4], Steve Benford[1], Holger Schnädelbach[1],
Stuart Reeves[3], Joe Marshall[1], David Kirk[1], Paul Tennent[1],
Ainoje Irune[1], and Duncan Rowland[5]

[1] School of Computer Science, University of Nottingham, Jubilee Campus,
Wollaton Road, Nottingham, NG8 1BB
{sre,jqg,sdb,hms,jqm,dsk,pxt,aai}@cs.nott.ac.uk
[2] BAE Systems, Systems Engineering Innovation Centre, University of Loughborough,
Holywell Park, Loughborough, LE11 3TU
a.m.whitbrook@lboro.ac.uk
[3] Horizon Digital Economy Research, Sir Colin Campbell Building,
University of Nottingham Innovation Park, Triumph Road, Nottingham, NG7 2TU
Aerial, 258 Globe Road, London, E2 0JD
info@aerial.fm
[4] School of Computer Science, University of Lincoln, Brayford Pool, Lincoln, LN6 7TS
drowland@lincoln.ac.uk

Abstract. Theme parks are important and complex forms of entertainment, with
a broad user-base, and with a substantial economic impact. In this paper, we
present a case study of an existing theme park, and use this to motivate two
research challenges in relation to user-modeling and personalization in this
environment: developing recommender systems to support theme park visits,
and developing rides that are personalized to the users who take part in them.
We then provide an analysis, drawn from a real-world study on an existing ride,
which illustrates the efficacy of psychometric profiling and physiological
monitoring in relation to these challenges. We conclude by discussing further
research work that could be carried out within the theme park, but motivate this
research by considering the broader contribution to user-modeling issues that it
could make. As such, we present the theme park as a microcosm which is
amenable to research, but which is relevant in a much broader setting.

Keywords: Psychometrics, physiological monitoring, theme park.

1 Introduction

Leisure and entertainment is a topic of interest for researchers involved in user-
modeling and personalization. One application is e-commerce systems such as
Amazon or eBay. These provide personalized, collaborative recommendations for
leisure items such as books, DVDs and computer games, generated through an analysis
of on-line activities [1]. Other applications include the personalized recommendation

Joseph A. Konstan et al. (Eds.): UMAP 2011, LNCS 6787, pp. 281–292, 2011.
© Springer-Verlag Berlin Heidelberg 2011

of leisure activities to partake in whilst on holiday [2], or the recommendations of playlists of music [3]. Working within a framework of affective computing [4], there have been attempts to model human emotions such as frustration [5], based on data collected from sensors. Prototypes of games that detect and respond to these emotions have then been built, using a variety of sensing devices and prosthetics to gather data (for example, [6]).

Approaching the theme of leisure and entertainment from a novel direction, this paper motivates the application of personalization technologies to *theme parks*, which are highly complex entertainment spaces that contain a wide variety of different forms of attraction. As a whole, the theme park industry caters for hundreds of millions of visitors every year [7], and theme park operators have significant budgets to spend on novel forms of entertainment. Although the theme park provides enormous scope for computational interventions, there are few examples of published research in the theme park. An exception is [8], and the authors have also developed a number of publications around the theme park. So far, these have focused on issues such as building novel interfaces for spectators [9], and the prototyping of new forms of ride [10,11]. An initial investigation into the use of user-profiling technologies in the theme park has also been published [12].

Building on this research program, this paper makes a contribution to research through a detailed exploration of the personalization of theme park experiences for visitors. It begins by providing a case-study of a typical theme park environment, which is used to highlight the potential benefits to visitors and to park operators that can be provided user-modeling and personalization technologies. This section is used to introduce two themes of research which the authors are interested in – namely the development of recommender systems for the theme park environment, and the development of novel forms of ride that are capable of responding to those that ride them. The section outlines a set of research challenges related to the themes of user-modeling and personalization. It then provides an overview of research which the authors have conducted in this space.

Following on from this section, this paper presents two analyses of a novel corpus of data which was collected in the theme park, through a study involving 56 participants who took part in a single ride. This data contains a detailed profile of these participants, which include assessments against two standard psychometric personality tests – the Big Five and the Sensation Seeking Scale, which are introduced later in this paper. It also includes a series of physiological measurements which were captured through wearable computing technologies. Analysis presented in this paper is then used to highlight the predictive power of psychometric profiles for experience on the ride, suggesting the inclusion of psychometric measures in a profile of theme park visitors which could be used by a recommender system. It is also used to demonstrate the efficacy of using physiological data to measure experience on a ride, suggesting the use of physiological measurements to personalize ride experiences.

Finally, after having presented these analyses, the paper concludes by discussing further work required to make the personalization of theme park experiences a reality. It also considers the broader contributions to knowledge that can be made through research in the theme park, therefore emphasizing its wider applicability.

2 The Theme Park Environment

Theme parks are a popular form of entertainment around the world, and their design differs substantially. To provide a solid grounding for the remainder of this paper, this section now provides a case-study of a particular theme park with which the authors have interacted. Details presented in this case-study have been drawn from interviews with park management and other staff. Having presented this case-study, we then highlight the potential interest of the theme park environment to researchers interested in user-modeling and personalization, by setting two research challenges. The remainder of this paper is then structured around these research challenges.

2.1 An Overview of Alton Towers

Alton Towers [13] is a theme park in the UK. It attracts more than 2 million visitors every year, with a daily capacity of 30,000 visitors. Figure 1 shows the stylized map that is provided to visitors on arrival. This highlights the various attractions at the park. These include a large number of thrilling and family-orientated rides, restaurants, shops, a formal garden (which existed before the theme park) and a hotel complex. Cameras have been installed onto many rides, and shops already provide souvenirs that have been personalized with photographs or video of riders. Alton Towers has a consistent theming, which is known internally as "Fantastical Escapism". This theming begins with "Towers Street", the single entry point to the park, and continues throughout.

Fig. 1. Alton Towers map

The rides at Alton Towers are the big draw for most visitors, and because of their limited capacity, queues can be large (sometimes longer than an hour for new rides). To reduce queuing, the most popular rides are distributed around the furthest edge of the park, so that crowds have spread out by the time they get there. There are also boards illustrating queuing times for these rides, which are updated manually once an hour. Staff at the park believe that many visitors walk move in an anti-clockwise direction around the park, causing queuing problems at particular locations. Queuing is also worse at peak times, or at particularly new rides.

Additionally, for many visitors, their interaction with a particular park visit begins on-line – through a ticket purchasing system that offers discounts in comparison to the gate price. Visitors can also purchase extra tickets that allow them to jump to the front of queues all day (most expensive option) or on individual rides (cheapest option). On-line information provided by Alton Towers allows visitors to plan their day, and additional information can be found on a variety of fan-sites (for example, [14]). Alton Towers also maintains a presence on Facebook and Twitter.

2.2   Challenges for User-Modeling and Personalization in the Theme Park

Having provided a short case-study of a particular theme-park, we now outline two research challenges which involve user-modeling and personalization. Section 3 of this paper then presents initial studies that provide knowledge in relation to these.

Challenge one: The theme park recommendation system
A day at a theme-park can be an expensive investment for a family, potentially involving travel costs, park entry fees, food and accommodation. Once at the park, there is an enormous selection of entertainment on offer. However, given the time taken to traverse the park, and given the possibility of large queues that has been outlined above, there is a significant potential for a frustrating experience. This suggests the challenge of creating an information system that assists visitors, and which recommends a personalized experience. Such a system might embed aspects of collaborative recommendation [15]. It might also interface with future park systems that monitored visitor movements, with on-line systems for booking tickets, or with information collected during previous visits.

Challenge 2: Personalized experiences on rides
Many of the rides at Alton Towers are thrilling, but each provides essentially the same experience to all visitors. However, developments in ride technology provide the potential for personalized ride experiences - for example, some rides now embed CAVE-like motion-platform and projection technologies [16], whilst others provide for individual actuation of seat movements [17]. In addition, technologies such as RFID that allow for the identification of visitors are already in operation at Alton Towers, for the purposes of identifying video sequences that feature particular riders, which are then used to produce souvenirs. This suggests the challenge of developing rides that can be personalized to individual riders, or to groups of riders. Such rides may draw on information collected by on-line systems, or during previous visits.

3   Results of Studies Constructed around These Challenges

Having motivated two research challenges relating to the theme park, we now present two analyses which contribute knowledge in relation to these. Both draw on data collected during a single study by the authors in the theme park, which involved 56 participants. During this study, each had one ride on Oblivion, a major attraction at Alton Towers. Before this ride, a personal profile was collected for each rider, and during the ride, wearable equipment was used to record aspects of their physiological response. Oblivion is constructed around a vertical drop into a tunnel, and a photograph of this drop is shown in figure 2. This figure also shows an abstract map of the ride, which has been labeled with 10 key points. Immediately after the ride, participants used paper forms to provide a numerical assessment of their emotional state at each of these points against the circumplex model [18], which is defined by two dimensions, *arousal* and *valence*. This model is commonly used in research requiring the quantification of emotion, and seems particularly relevant to intense experiences such as theme park rides. In the context of this study, arousal was defined on a scale of 0 to 10 as being how much the rider felt "alert, with your body pumped up and buzzing, ready for action", whilst valence was defined on a scale of -5 to +5 as being how much the rider felt "positive or good" or "negative or bad". Data collected against this model has been used in both analyses presented below.

Fig. 2. Beginning of vertical drop (left) and map of ride (right): *1*: Loading bay *2-3*: Lift hill *4-5*: Drop *6-7*: Tunnel *8*: Curves *9-10*: End of ride

3.1   Analysis One: Relationships between Personal Profiles and Ride Experience

A key component of a system constructed in response to challenge one (the theme park recommendation system) could be a module that uses a profile of a user to recommend a series of rides that they will enjoy, and which assimilates geographic information about the layout of rides and the size of queues. For users who have visited parks before, such a profile may draw on records of previous visits. However, an alternative approach is required for first-time visitors. For this group, we have been investigating the efficacy of including demographic and psychometric personality data in a visitor profile. Whilst the use of demographics in profiling is well-accepted, the use of personality data in personal profiles for recommender systems is a current topic of user-modeling research [19], where it is appropriate for the recommendation of experiences that are mediated by personality. In this section, we provide proof-of-concept evidence that this is the case in the theme park.

Our approach in gathering this evidence has been to use data collected during the Oblivion study, allowing us to investigate relationships between demographic and psychometric dimensions and self-reported experience on a single ride. Psychometric personality profiling requires users to fill out a questionnaire, from which numeric scores on a set of pre-determined personality dimensions are produced. Informed by discussions with psychology colleagues, we chose two commonly-used psychometric personality profiling tools for this study: the Big Five [20], a general-purpose test, and the Sensation Seeking Scale [21], a test designed for investigations into thrilling experiences. Table 1 below summarizes dimensions in our profile. When working with this data, we have used correlation analysis to identify a candidate set of dimensions with significant relationships to self-reported experience. We have then used this candidate set to cluster participants into groups, and tested for significant differences in self-reported experience between groups.

Table 1. Profile (ride count = number of previous rides on Oblivion)

Demographics	Psychometrics – Big 5	Psychometrics – SSS
Age	Openness	Thrill seeking
Gender	Conscientiousness	Experience seeking
ride count	Extraversion	Disinhibition
	Agreeableness	Boredom susceptibility
	Neuroticism	

To implement the method described above, we first tested for normality (using Shapiro-Wilks). This failed to provide evidence for normality for almost all profiling dimensions in table 1, so we chose to use the Spearman rank correlation, a non-parametric correlation co-efficient, to search for relationships between dimensions shown in table 1 and self-reports of emotion. To add depth to our analysis, we grouped some points in the map shown in figure 1, to generate a set of categories shown in table 2. Only those correlations between personality dimensions and these categories that are significant at a confidence level of $p=0.001$ are then shown in table 3. The choice of this more stringent confidence level (than the more commonly-used level of $p=0.05$) reduces the possibility of seemingly significant correlations occurring by chance when calculating such a large number of correlations.

Based on these correlations, *ride count, thrill seeking, extraversion* and *openness* were chosen as candidate dimensions for a future profile. A further investigation was then carried out using the k-means clustering algorithm as implemented by SPSS. After an exploratory analysis, three useful methods of clustering participants were identified (clustering on *ride count* alone, clustering on *thrill seeking* alone, and clustering on *extraversion* and *openness* together). An analysis of the self-reports of experience provided by members of these groups has demonstrated that there is a significant difference between these self-reports (table 4 - Kruskall-Wallis test, $p=0.05$). Collectively, these statistics provide further evidence for the use of these dimensions in a future personal profile for a theme park recommender system.

Table 2. Category definitions

Whole ride	Pre-drop	Hanging	Drop	Post-drop
1-10	1-3	4	5-7	8-10

Table 3. Significant correlations between categories and profiling dimensions

	Extraversion	Openness	Thrill seeking	Gender	Ride count
whole_ride_arousal	-	0.12	-0.14	-	-0.19
pre_drop_arousal	-	-	-0.24	-	-
hanging_arousal	-	-	-	-	-
drop_arousal	-	0.21	-	-	-0.31
post_drop_arousal	-	-	-	-	-0.29
whole_ride_valence	0.24	0.11	-	-0.15	-
pre_drop_valence	0.30	-	0.24	-	-
hanging_valence	-	-	-	-	0.36
drop_valence	0.23	-	-	-0.30	-
post_drop_valence	-	0.23	-	-	-0.28

Table 4. p-values showing significant differences in experience between clusters, generated by three different methods. cs1=clustering by *ride count*, cs2=clustering by *thrill seeking*, cs3=clustering by *extraversion* and *openness*.

	cs1	cs2	cs3
whole_ride_arousal	0.000	0.003	0.007
pre_drop_arousal	0.040	0.001	-
hanging_arousal	-	0.005	-
drop_arousal	0.003	0.017	0.003
post_drop_arousal	0.003	-	0.004
whole_ride_valence	0.000	0.005	0.000
pre_drop_valence	-	0.000	0.000
hanging_valence	-	0.025	0.029
drop_valence	0.001	-	0.001
post_drop_valence	0.009	-	0.006

3.2   Analysis Two: Proof-of-Concept Evidence for Heart-Rate Monitoring

Challenge 2 involves the design of rides that are personalized to participants. This could simply make use of a profile, gathered in advance, to select from a number of pre-defined ride programs. However, we have been investigating a more challenging form of personalization which involves the ride adapting dynamically to the responses of its participants. This raises the question of what responses to monitor, how to model these responses, and how to use these models in personalization algorithms. Informed by the field of affective computing [4], we have chosen to investigate the potential of using wearable computing equipment to measure heart-rate response on the ride described above. Heart-rate relates directly to physiological arousal, a measure of body's level of preparation for exciting or fearful situations. Building a ride that responds to individual levels of this arousal is a promising approach, and this section provides proof-of-concept evidence for measuring heart-rate on a ride.

Given our choice of heart-rate, the collection of proof-of-concept evidence for its use in a dynamically-adaptive ride involves a number of questions. Question 1: does the ride actually affect heart-rate sufficiently for it to be a usable measure in this context? Question 2: is there sufficient variability between riders for this measure to be useful in personalization of experience? Question 3: are there any relationships between heart-rate and emotional experience? In the remainder of this section, we present evidence in relation to all three of these questions.

Figure 3 begins to address the first two, through a plot that shows the distribution of all the individual heart-rates values that were recorded from participants, during six phases of the experience of taking part in the ride. This plot shows an ascending pattern for the sample median throughout most of this experience, with a local maximum whilst waiting to board the ride. The Wilcoxan Rank Sum test was used (at p=0.05) to compare the distribution of heart-rate between these boxes, and shows a significant difference between all. In addition, the plot suggests a significant amount of variation in heart-rate across the sample. Box 2, for example, contains some outliers with heart-rates around 60 beats per minute (BPM), and some outliers with heart-rates around 160 BPM, and also has a large inter-quartile range. A careful analysis of heart-rate data traces has convinced us that these outliers represent true heart-rates, rather than the results of equipment failures such as drop-outs.

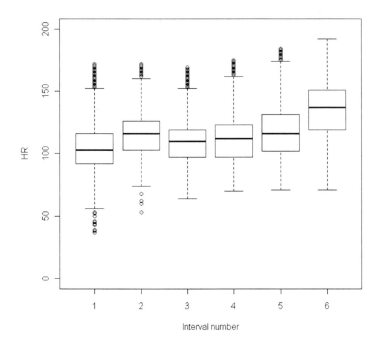

Fig. 3. Distribution of individual heart-rate values (BPM) 1: arrival at loading bay 2: waiting to board ride 3: waiting for ride to move 4: ascent of lift hill 5: progress around top 6: drop and remainder of ride

Further evidence for variation across the sample is provided in the scatter plots shown in figure 4, which compare median heart-rate for participants in different phases of the ride. These show an extreme variation in levels of physiological arousal, far higher than what would be expected in normal life (for which a heart-rate between 60 and 100 BPM is more usual). In addition, they suggest a linear relationship between median heart-rate early in the experience and median heart-rate later in the experience. A regression analysis, at a confidence level of p=0.05, confirms the predictive nature of heart-rate both on arrival and during the lift-hill for heart-rate during the drop and the remainder of the ride. Therefore, although the ride clearly affects heart-rate, and although there is sufficient variation in the sample to suggest the value of measuring it, there is more evidence for the measurement of heart-rate before the ride begins, as an indicator of physiological arousal, rather than measuring it whilst the ride is moving. This may reflect the fact that many riders are already fearful or excited before the ride begins, and who are therefore more likely to be fearful or excited throughout the remainder of their experience.

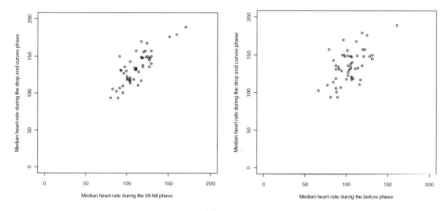

Fig. 4. Scatter plots showing distribution of median heart-rates. Left: ascent of lift-hill (x-axis) against drop and remainder of ride (y-axis) Right: arrival at loading bay (x-axis) against drop and remainder (y-axis).

Finally, in relation to question 3, an analysis which involves the use of correlation to search for linear relationships between median heart-rate in the different phases and self-reports of emotional experience has produced mixed results. No significant correlations were found for the first five phases defined in figure 3 above. However, for the final phase, a significant positive correlation was found between self-reported arousal and heart-rate, and a significant negative correlation was found between valence and heart-rate. This phase was then split into four intervals, each of five seconds in duration. The following significant correlations were obtained:

Table 5. Significant correlations during the final phase of the ride

Time in final phase	Correlation with arousal	Correlation with valence
0-5 seconds	-	0.30
5-10 seconds	0.29	0.34
10-15 seconds	0.39	0.31
15-20 seconds	0.36	-

4   Discussion

In this paper, we have presented analyses of data collected during a single study, and related them to research challenges in the theme park environment. The first analysis provides proof-of-concept evidence for the use of psychometric personality testing in profiles designed for a theme park recommender system, based on its ability to predict experience on a single ride. The second provides evidence for the use of heart-rate as a profiling tool in the queue of a ride, with the potential to identify participants who are relaxed or highly aroused. As an initial piece of research in this novel application domain, these analyses have raised a significant number of research questions, whose investigation could provide knowledge to support the implementation of real theme-park systems in the future. In this final section, we present a selection of these questions, and then conclude by discussing their relevance to user modeling research.

4.1   Extending the Analysis to Multiple Rides

A limitation of the initial studies presented in this paper is that they only consider data in relation to a single ride, and interesting research questions might be constructed around their extension to multiple rides. For example, it would be interesting to know whether particular dimensions in our chosen personality tests had particularly strong relationships with experience on different rides, and whether there are other personality tests that are useful in this context. Equally, it would be interesting to know whether heart-rate in the queue is always a predictor for heart-rate later in other rides, or whether variables such as fatigue are more important in some situations.

4.2   Considering Groups in the Design of Future Systems

Analyses presented in this paper have focused on treating participants individually. However, it is clear from our interviews and observations that many people experience theme park rides in groups (e.g. of family or friends). A recommender system for a day at the park would need to consider the needs of a group rather than just the needs of individuals that compose it; the design and evaluation of such a system might contribute more generally to group-orientated recommender systems research. Similarly, a system that personalizes a ride to its participants might need to consider all the individuals in a particular carriage, rather than just being able to consider participants on an individual basis. Future research might consider different tactics for modeling groups, and selecting programs of operation for them.

4.3   Repeat Visits

Analyses presented in this paper have considered a single ride on Oblivion. However, interviews with park management suggest a high number of repeat visits, raising the question of how to construct profiles that build over time, and which therefore provide a stronger basis for recommendation or adaption. For example, a user-profile might combine psychometric and demographic profiling with records of physiological monitoring or self-report. Such a profile could use identification mechanisms such as RFID, or even be integrated with on-line systems relating to ticket sales. These kinds of profile are a current topic of research, especially given the ever-expanding digital footprint that many people are generating. As such, research work in the theme park might contribute more generally to research in this field, especially given the significant number of visits to theme parks that are made by individuals.

4.4 Optimization of the Use of Psychometric Personality Profiling

Data in this paper relates to two specific personality tests: the Big Five and the Sensation Seeking Scale. There are a number of interesting issues around the use of these kinds of test that might be considered in future research. In particular, in common with other personality tests, there are a number of different versions of the Sensation Seeking Scale, each of which utilizes a different length questionnaire, and each of which provides a different level of modeling of respondents' personality. There is clearly a trade-off here between the length of time taken to fill out a test and the information that it provides, and such trade-offs may be interesting to investigate in future research. An example of these trade-offs outside of the theme park is present in a number of on-line dating services, such as Match Affinity [23]. Such sites often use quite complex personality tests, and may therefore provide interesting research data for the user-modeling community in relation to their success.

5 Conclusions

Most of this paper has focused on the theme park. Two research challenges have been established, and a set of analyses, drawn from a single study, have presented initial knowledge in relation to these. However, the theme park can be seen as a microcosm in which research that is relevant to the wider world can be conducted, potentially aided by theme park infrastructures that support visiting by guests, but which can also provide data for research. Therefore, although research in the theme park is clearly specialized, it has implications that can make a broader contribution, and it is therefore a setting which should be of interest to other researchers.

Acknowledgments. This work was supported by the Horizon Digital Economy Hub (EP/G065802/1) and by an EPSRC platform award to the Mixed Reality Laboratory (EP/F03038X/1).

Reference

1. Schafer, J.B., Konstan, J., Riedi, J.: Recommender systems in e-commerce. In: 1st ACM Conference on Electronic Commerce. ACM, New York (1999)
2. Duchenaut, N., Partridge, K., Huang, Q., Price, B., Roberts, M., Chi, E.H., Bellotti, V., Begole, B.: Collaborative filtering is not enough? Experiments with a mixed-model recommender for leisure activities. In: Houben, G.-J., McCalla, G., Pianesi, F., Zancanaro, M. (eds.) UMAP 2009. LNCS, vol. 5535, pp. 295–306. Springer, Heidelberg (2009)
3. Hansen, D., Golbeck, J.: Mixing it up: recommending collections of items. In: 27th Annual SIGCHI Conference on Human Factors in Computer Systems (2009)
4. Picard, R.: Affective Computing. MIT Press, Cambridge (1997)

5. Klein, J., Moon, Y., Picard, R.W.: This computer responds to user frustration: Theory, design, and results. Interacting with Computers 14(2) (2002)
6. Emotiv Epoch interface device, http://www.emotiv.com/
7. Attraction attendance report published by the Theme Entertainment Association, http://www.connectingindustry.com/downloads/pwteaerasupp.pdf
8. Pausch, R., Snoddy, J., Taylor, R., Watson, S., Haseltine, E.: Disney's Aladdin: first steps towards storytelling virtual reality. In: 23rd International Conference on Computer Graphics and Interaction Techniques (1996)
9. Schnädelbach, H., Rennick Egglestone, S., Reeves, S., Benford, S., Walker, B.: Performing Thrill: Designing telemetry systems and spectator interfaces for amusement rides. In: 26th Annual SIGCHI Conference on Human Factors in Computer Systems (2008)
10. Rennick Egglestone, S., Marshall, J., Walker, B., Rowland, D., Benford, S., Rodden, T.: The Bronco: A proof-of-concept adaptive fairground ride. In: Annual Conference on Advances in Computer Entertainment Technology (2009)
11. Marshall, J., Rowland, D., Rennick Egglestone, S., Benford, S., Walker, B., McAuley, D.: Breath control of amusement rides. In: 29th Annual SIGCHI Conference on Human Factors in Computer Systems (2011)
12. Rennick Egglestone, S., Whitbrook, A., Greensmith, J., Walker, B., Benford, S., Marshall, J., Kirk, D., Schnadelbach, H., Irune, A., Rowland, D.: Psychometric profiling in the theme park. In: Annual Conference on Advances in Computer Entertainment Technology (2010)
13. AltonTowers corporate website, http://www.altontowers.com/
14. Towers Almanac fan-site, http://www.towersalmanac.com/
15. Adomavicius, G., Tuzhilin, A.: Towards the next generation of recommender systems: a survey of the state-of-the-art and possible extensions. IEEE Transactions on Knowledge and Data Engineering 17(6) (2005)
16. Charlie and the Chocolate ride at Alton Towers contains a motion platform with projectors, http://www.towersalmanac.com/areas/rides.php?id=85
17. RoboCoaster ride systems, http://www.robocoaster.com
18. Larsen, R.J., Diener, E.: Promises and Problems with the Circumplex Model of Emotion. Review of Personality and Social Psychology (13) (1992)
19. Hu, R., Pu, P.: A study on user perception of personality-based recommender systems. In: De Bra, P., Kobsa, A., Chin, D. (eds.) UMAP 2010. LNCS, vol. 6075, pp. 291–302. Springer, Heidelberg (2010)
20. John, O.P., Donahue, E.M., Kentle, R.L.: The Big Five Inventory—Versions 4a and 54. Institute of Personality and Social Research, University of California, Berkeley (1991)
21. Zuckerman, M.: Behavioural Expressions and Biosocial Bases of Sensation Seeking. Cambridge University Press, Cambridge (1994)
22. Carlson, N.R.: Physiology of behavior, 8th edn. Pearson, London
23. Match Affinity dating website, http://www.matchaffinity.com/

Recognising and Recommending Context in Social Web Search

Zurina Saaya, Barry Smyth, Maurice Coyle, and Peter Briggs

CLARITY: Centre for Sensor Web Technologies
School of Computer Science and Informatics
University College Dublin, Ireland
firstname.lastname@ucd.ie
http://www.clarity-centre.org

Abstract. In this paper we focus on an approach to social search, HeyStaks that is designed to integrate with mainstream search engines such as Google, Yahoo and Bing. HeyStaks is motivated by the idea that Web search is an inherently social or collaborative activity. Heystaks users search as normal but benefit from collaboration features, allowing searchers to better organise and share their search experiences. Users can create and share repositories of search knowledge (so-called search staks) in order to benefit from the searches of friends and colleagues. As such search staks are community-based information resources. A key challenge for HeyStaks is predicting which search stak is most relevant to the users current search context and in this paper we focus on this so-called stak recommendation issue by looking at a number of different approaches to profiling and recommending community-search knowledge.

Keywords: social search, context recommendation.

1 Introduction

The *social web* is represented by a class of web sites and applications in which user participation is the primary driver of value. Discussions of the social web often use the phrase *collective intelligence* or *wisdom of crowds* to refer to the value created by the collective contributions of all these people writing articles for Wikipedia[1], sharing tagged photos on Flickr[2], sharing bookmarks on Delicious[3], streaming their personal blogs into the open seas of the blogosphere and using and sharing the search knowledge in collaborative environment[3].

Recently ideas from the social web has begun to exert their influence beyond content creation and on to content curation and information discovery. In short, many researchers have begun to consider the role of collaboration during information search and content discovery; see for example the work of Ariadne [10], SearchTogether[6] and CoSearch[1]. Golovchinsky et al. [2] proposes a taxonomy

---

[1] http://www.wikipedia.org
[2] http://www.flickr.com
[3] http://www.delicious.com

Joseph A. Konstan et al. (Eds.): UMAP 2011, LNCS 6787, pp. 293–304, 2011.

of collaborative information sharing highlight key dimensions such as the *intent, depth, concurrency,* and *location* for a variety of collaborative information services. Very briefly, for example, Golovchinsky et al. distinguish between services that support *implicit* versus *explicit* collaboration, services that over shallow UI-based collaboration versus deeper algorithmic support for collaboration, services that support *synchronous* versus *asynchronous* collaboration , and finally those services that assume information seekers are *co-located* versus those that assume *remote* collaboration.

In this paper we will focus on HeyStaks, the details of which have been previously published in [8]. In short, HeyStaks brings a layer of collaboration to mainstream search engines, via a browser plugin which allows searchers to organise and share their search experiences and to collaborate with others as they search. HeyStaks is a collaborative web search service that offers elements of implicit and explicit intent among searchers. It provides for a range of UI enhancements to support collaborating searchers as well as deeper algorithmic components in order to identify relevant results from a community of collaborators. Finally, it assumes asynchronous, remote collaboration: searchers do not need to be co-located and collaboration can occur overtime as recent searchers benefit from recommendations that originate from earlier search sessions.

Here we are emphasised on a key challenge for HeyStaks and its users. Specifically, the central concept in HeyStaks is the notion of a *search stak*, which acts like a folder for our search experiences. Briefly, a user can create a search stak on a topic of their choosing and they can opt to share this stak with other users. Now, as they search (using HeyStaks and their favourite mainstream search engine) the results that they select (or tag or share) will be associated with their active stak so that these results can be subsequently recommended to other stak members in the future when appropriate. In this way, stak members can benefit from the past searches of friends or colleagues who share their staks. A key problem here for HeyStaks to ensure that the right stak is chosen for a given search session. One way to solve this is to ask the user to pick their stak at the start of their search session, but since many users forget to do this, this is not a practical solution in reality. The alternative is to use information about the user's current search session as the basis for automatically selecting and recommending an appropriate stak at search time. In this paper then we focus on this stak selection problem and in what follows we describe and evaluate a recommendation-based strategy that works well enough in practice to automatically suggest relevant staks to the user at search time, or even automatically switch users into a likely stak without their intervention.

2   A Review of HeyStaks

In designing HeyStaks our primary goal is to provide social Web search enhancements, while at the same time allowing searchers to continue to use their favourite search engine. HeyStaks adds two basic features to any mainstream search engine. First, it allows users to create *search staks*, as a type of folder

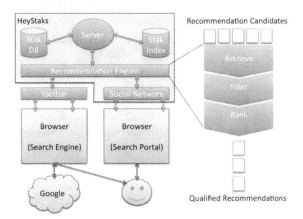

Fig. 1. The HeyStaks system architecture and outline recommendation model

for their search experiences at search time, and the creator can invite initial members by providing their email addresses. Staks can be configured to be *public* (anyone can join) or *private* (invitation only). Second, HeyStaks uses staks to generate recommendations that are added to the underlying search results that come from the mainstream search engine. These recommendations are results that stak members have previously found to be relevant for similar queries and help the searcher to discover results that friends or colleagues have found interesting, results that may otherwise be buried deep within Google's default result-list.

As shown in Figure 1, HeyStaks takes the form of two basic components: a client-side *browser toolbar* and a back-end *server*. The toolbar (see Figure 2) allows users to create and share staks and provides a range of ancillary services, such as the ability to tag or vote for pages. The toolbar also captures search result click-thrus and manages the integration of HeyStaks recommendations with the default result-list. The back-end server manages the individual stak indexes (indexing individual pages against query/tag terms and positive/negative votes), the stak database (stak titles, members, descriptions, status, etc.), the HeyStaks social networking service and, of course, the recommendation engine.

In the following sections we review how HeyStaks captures search activities within search staks and how this search knowledge is used to generate and filter result recommendations at search time; more detailed technical details can be found in [9,8].

2.1   Profiling Stak Pages

Each stak in HeyStaks captures the search activities of its stak members within the stak's context. The basic unit of stak information is a result (URL) and each stak (S) is associated with a set of results, $S = \{r_1, ..., r_k\}$. Each result is also anonymously associated with a number of implicit and explicit interest

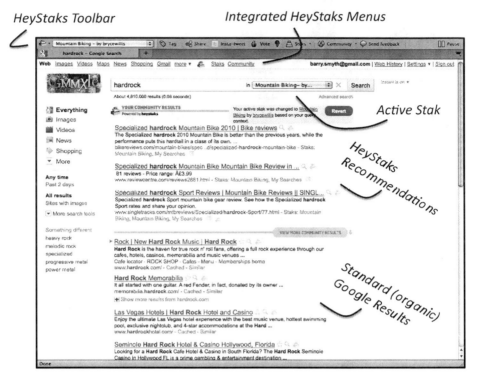

Fig. 2. The searcher is looking for information from a specialist mountain biking brand, Hard Rock, but Google responds with results related to the restaurant/hotel chain. HeyStaks recognises the query as relevant to the the searcher's *Mountain Biking* stak and presents a set of more relevant results drawn from this stak

indicators, based on the type of actions that users can perform on these pages, which include:

– *Selections (or Click-thrus)* – that is, a user selects a search result (whether *organic* or *recommended*). Similarly,
HeyStaks allows a user to *preview* a page by opening it in a frame (rather than a window), and to *popout* a page from a preview frame into a browser window;
– *Voting* – that is, a user positively votes on a given search result or the current web page;
– *Sharing* – that is, a user chooses to share a specific search result or web page with another user (via email or by posting to their Facebook wall etc.);
– *Tagging/Commenting* – that is, the user chooses to tag and/or comment on a particular result or web page.

Each of these actions can be associated with a degree of confidence that the user finds the page to be relevant for example, *implicit* actions such as result selections are weaker than *explicit* actions, such as tagging or sharing a page. Each result page r_i^S from stak S, is associated with these indicators of relevance, including the total number of times a result has been selected (Sl), the query terms ($q_1, ..., q_n$) that led to its selection, the terms contained in the snippet of the selected result ($s_1, ..., s_j$), the number of times a result has been tagged (Tg), the terms used to tag it ($t_1, ..., t_m$), the votes it has received (v^+, v^-), and the number of people it has been shared with (Sh) as indicated by Equation 1.

$$r_i^S = \{q_1...q_n, s_1...s_j, t_1...t_m, v^+, v^-, Sl, Tg, Sh\} . \tag{1}$$

Importantly, this means each result page is associated with a set of *term data* (query terms and/or tag terms) and a set of *usage data* (the selection, tag, share, and voting count). The term data is represented as a Lucene (*lucene.apache.org*) index, with each result indexed under its associated query and tag terms, and this provides the basis for retrieving and ranking *recommendation candidates*. The usage data provides an additional source of evidence that can be used to filter results and to generate a final set of recommendations.

2.2 Recommending Results: Relevance and Reputation

At search time, the searcher's query q_T and current stak S_T are used to generate a list of recommendations to be returned to the searcher. There are two key steps when it comes to generating recommendations. First, a set of *recommendation candidates* are retrieved from S_T by querying the corresponding Lucene index with q_T. This effectively produces a list of recommendations based on the overlap between the query terms and the terms used to index each recommendation (query, snippet, and tag terms). Second, these recommendations are filtered and ranked. Results that do not exceed certain activity thresholds are eliminated as candidates; e.g., results with only a single selection or results with more negative votes than positive votes (see [8]). The remaining recommendation candidates are then ranked according to two key factors: *relevance* and *reputation*. Essentially each result is evaluated using a weighted score of its relevance and reputation score as per Equation 2; where w is used to adjust the relative influence of relevance and reputation and is usually set to 0.5.

$$score(r, q_T) = w \times rep(r) + (1 - w) \times rel(q_T, r) . \tag{2}$$

The relevance of a result r with respect to a query q_T is computed based on Lucene's standard *TF*IDF* metric [4] as per Equation 2. The reputation of a result is a function of the reputation of the stak members who have added the result to the stak. And their reputation in turn is based on the degree to which results that they have added to staks have been subsequently recommended to, and selected, by other users; see [5] for additional information.

3   Recognising Context and Recommending Staks

In this paper we are not concerned with recommending individual result pages to HeyStaks users. Rather, our focus is on the so-called *stak selection* task.

Briefly, the success of HeyStaks depends critically on users correctly identifying an appropriate stak for their searches at search time. As in the example in Fig. 2, as the user search for mountain bike related information they need to choose *Mountain Biking* as their current stak. If they do this consistently then HeyStaks will learn to associate the right pages with the right staks, and be in a position to make high quality recommendations for stak members. However, the need to manually select a stak at the start of a new search session is an extra burden on the searcher. To make this as easy as possible, HeyStaks integrates its stak-lists as part of the mainstream search engine interface (see Fig. 2) but still many users, especially during the early stages forget to do this, and this means that a majority of search sessions are associated with the searcher's default stak (*My Searches*) rather than a more specific and appropriate stak of which they are a member.

The solution to this problem, which is the main contribution of this paper, is to proactively predict and recommend a suitable stak to the user at search time. To do this we draw on ideas from recommender systems and traditional information retrieval. As described above, each stak is a separate search index that is made up of documents that have been selected, tagged, and/or shared by stak members. For our stak recommendation solution we treat each stak index itself as a type of *summary* document; effectively the terms and URLs contained in the stak index become the terms of the summary document and in this way a collection of staks can be represented as a collection of documents. Using Lucene, these documents can then be transformed into a *stak summary index* (or *SSI*); see Fig. 3. Then, at search time, we can use the searcher's query as a probe into this stak summary index to identify a set of staks that most relevant to the query; in this work we focus only on staks that the user is currently a member of but a similar technique could be used to recommend other third-party staks in certain circumstances. These recommended staks can then be suggested directly to the user as a reminder to set their appropriate stak context; or, alternatively, we can configure HeyStaks to automatically pre-select the top ranking recommendation as the current stak context, while providing the searcher with an option to undo this if they deem the stak to be incorrect.

In the above we assume that the user's own search query (q_T) is used as the SSI query (or *stak query*), but in fact there are a number of additional sources of information that can be usefully harnessed for this. For example, at search time, the initial set of search engine results represents a valuable source of additional context information. This approach also has been used in [7] to classify the queries with text classification algorithm.

For instance, the terms in the title and snippets (R_{S+T}), and URLs (R_{URL}) of the result-list can also be used in addition to the user's short search query, during stak recommendation. For this reason we refer to three basic *types* of stak recommendation strategy – *query, snippet, URL* – depending on which sources of information form the user's stak query (S_Q).

At stak recommendation time we use Lucene's standard TF*IDF weighting model as the basis for scoring recommended staks as shown in Equations 3 and

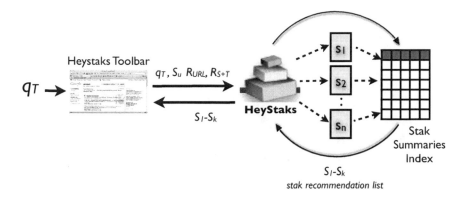

Fig. 3. Stak Recommendation

4. Effectively, terms in the stak summary index (SSI) are scored based on the TF*IDF model, which prefers terms that are frequent within a given stak but infrequent across the user's staks (S_U) as a whole.

$$RecList(S_Q, S_U, SSI) = \frac{SortDesc(Score(S_Q, S, SSI))}{\forall S \epsilon S_U} \qquad (3)$$

$$Score(S_U, S, SSI) = \sum_{t \epsilon S_U} tf(t, S) \times idf(t, SSI) \qquad (4)$$

In this way we can generate different recommendation lists $(RL_{URL}, RL_{query}, RL_{S+T},)$ by using different sources of data as the stak query (S_Q); for example, we can use the terms in result titles and snippets as the stak query, which will lead to staks being recommended because they contain lots of distinctive title and snippet terms. Of course we can also look to combine these different sources of query terms, for example, by ranking recommended staks according to their position across the recommendation lists produced by different sources of query terms. For instance, we can define the *rank score* of a given stak, across a set of recommendation lists, to be the sum of the positions of the stak in the different recommendation lists with a simple penalty assigned for lists that do not contain the stak as per Equations 5 and 6. The final recommendation list is then sorted in ascending order of the rank scores of recommended staks.

$$RankScore(s, RL_1 - RL_n) = \sum_{RL_i \epsilon RL_1 - RL_n} PositionScore(s, RL_i) \qquad (5)$$

$$PositionScore(s, RL) = \begin{cases} Position(s, RL) \text{ if } s \epsilon RL; \\ Length(RL) + 1 \text{ otherwise.} \end{cases} \qquad (6)$$

We have described a general purpose approach to stak recommendation, which accommodates different sources of query data, and provides for a flexible way to combine multiple recommendation lists to generate an ensemble recommendation

Table 1. Staks Categories

# URLs	Size	# Staks	% of Staks
1 - 10	Small	378	63%
11 - 100	Medium	178	30%
101 - 500	Large	31	5%
500+	X-Large	11	2%

list. The intuition of course is that by combining different sources of query data we will generate better recommendations, which we shall look at in the following evaluation.

4 Evaluation

In this section we evaluate the different forms of our stak recommendation approach, based on live-user search data, and focusing in particular on the overall recommendation accuracy of the different techniques, and combinations of techniques, across different stak types.

4.1 Setup

The data for this evaluation stems from HeyStaks usage logs generated during the period October 2008 - October 2009. The sample data used contains 114,109 individual, timestamped search activities. Each refers to a specific search query submitted by a particular user in a given stak context. For the purpose of this evaluation we limit our interest to only those activities that are associated with non-default search staks; this means that we focused on search sessions where the user did select a specific stak for their search. There are 8,100 of these activities across 158 unique users and, on average, users were members of 6.94 staks each. We also collect data on the size of each of these staks, based on the number of URLs they contain to categorise staks as either *small, medium, large* or *extra-large* as per Table 1.

For the purpose of this study we evaluate a range of different recommendation strategies based on our three basic techniques, namely, *query, snippet, URL* and including all combinations of these techniques. In addition we also evaluate a baseline *random* recommendation strategy, which suggests staks at random from the user's stak-list. This leads to a total of eight different recommendation alternatives. To evaluate these alternatives, we generate a recommendation list for each of the 8,100 search instances and compute the percentage of times that the known active stak is recommended among the top k recommendations ($k = 1 - 5$).

4.2 Overall Recommendation Precision

To begin with we will look at the overall success rate across the different recommendation alternatives. This data is presented in Fig. 4 as a graph of success

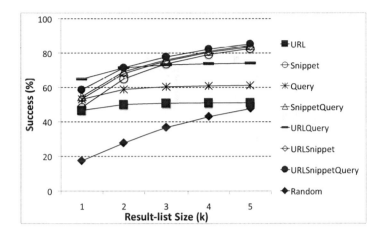

Fig. 4. Recommendation success rate

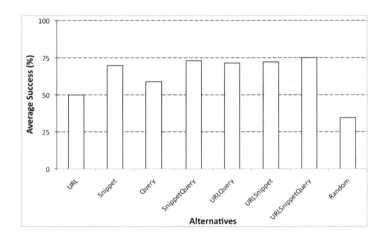

Fig. 5. Mean average success rate

rate against recommendation-list size (k). Each recommendation technique is represented as an individual line-graph based on its success rate for the different values of k. For clarity we also present the mean average success rate across the different values of k in Fig. 5.

The results highlight a considerable variation in performance across the different recommendation strategies. As expected *random* performs poorly as the baseline, with a success rate of between 17 and 48% depending on k; as expected, success rates grow with increasing k since there are more opportunities to recommend the correct active stak. Generally speaking the ensemble approaches, which combine multiple basic techniques, tend to outperform individual techniques on their own. For example, one of the best performing strategies is the combination of *URL*, *snippet*, and *query* with success score ranging from 60%

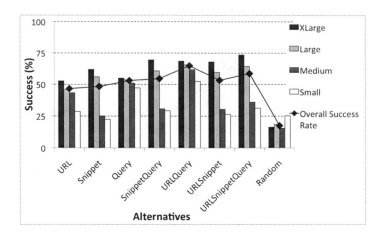

Fig. 6. Success rate by stak size where $k = 1$

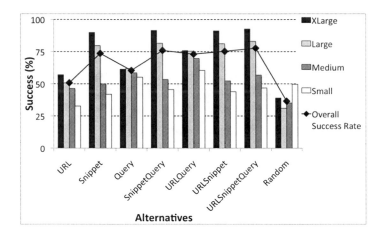

Fig. 7. Success rate by stak size where $k = 3$

$(k = 1)$ to 85% $(k = 5)$, compared to the less impressive performance of say the URL technique on its own, which varies from about 47% $(k = 1)$ to just 51% $(k = 5)$.

It is interesting to pay special attention to the $k = 1$ results because the ideal strategy for HeyStaks would be to automatically switch the user into a correct stak, rather than present a set of stak options. This would require a reasonably high success rate at $k = 1$ to avoid user frustration in the case of incorrect stak switches. Unfortunately, it appears from the results in Fig. 4 that the success rates at $k = 1$ do not support such an automatic switching approach. For example, the best performing strategy at $k = 1$, which combines URL and $query$ techniques, achieves a success rate of 65%, which does not seem high enough to support an automatic stak switching.

4.3   Precision vs. Stak Size

Of course the above results refer to recommendation success across all staks. But not all staks are created equally. For example, as per Table 1, the majority of staks (63%) contain relatively few URLs (1-10 URLs) which provides a much weaker basis for indexing. It seems likely that this will have a great impact on stak recommendation effectiveness compared to larger staks. To test this, in Fig. 6 and Fig. 7 we present the recommendation success rate for each of the recommendation alternatives, by stak size (comparing *small, medium, large* and *extra-large* staks) for recommendation lists of size 1 (Fig. 6) and 3 (Fig. 7). It is clear that there are significant differences in recommendation accuracy across the various stak sizes. For example, looking at the combination of *URL, snippet, query* we see a success rate of about 75% at $k = 1$ for the extra-large staks and 70% for the large staks, compared to only 36% and 31% for the medium and small staks respectively. This is encouraging because, from a engineering standpoint, it suggests that it may be practical to implement a reliable automatic stak switching policy, at least for large staks which contain more than 100 URLs. When we look at the results for $k = 3$ (see Fig. 7) we see similar effects, only this time many ensemble techniques are achieving success rates in excess of 90%, for a number of recommendation combinations across the extra-large staks.

4.4   Conclusions

HeyStaks facilitates partitioned collaboration between searchers, by allowing users to create and share their own search staks, and it does this by integrating with mainstream search engines rather than expecting the user to change to a new search engine. The main contribution of this work has been to highlight a practical problem facing HeyStaks — the need to automatically predict the right stak for users at search time — and to propose and evaluate a feasible solution in the form of a stak recommendation strategy. To this end we have described a general framework for stak recommendation. It is based on the indexing of user staks, which accommodates a variety of different recommendation alternatives using different types of query data at search time, such as search query terms, title and snippet terms of search results, the URLs of search results, and usage data from staks. We have described the results of a comprehensive evaluation of a wide variety of recommendation strategies, based on live user search data, and the results speak to the practical effectiveness of this overall approach to stak recommendation. In particular, the success scores achieved across the larger staks speak to the potential for a reliable automatic stak switching mechanism, and at the very least it is possible to generate a short-list of stak recommendations that are accurate up to nearly 90% of the time.

Acknowledgments. This work is supported by Science Foundation Ireland under grant 07/CE/I1147, HeyStaks Technologies Ltd, Ministry of Higher Education Malaysia and Universiti Teknikal Malaysia Melaka.

References

1. Amershi, S., Morris, M.R.: Cosearch: a system for co-located collaborative web search. In: Proceeding of the Twenty-sixth Annual SIGCHI Conference on Human Factors in Computing Systems, CHI 2008, pp. 1647–1656. ACM, New York (2008)
2. Golovchinsky, G., Pickens, J., Back, M.: A taxonomy of collaboration in online information seeking. In: JCDL Workshop on Collaborative Information Retrieval, pp. 1–3 (2008)
3. Gruber, T.: Collective knowledge systems: Where the social web meets the semantic web. Web Semantics: Science, Services and Agents on the World Wide Web 6(1), 4–13 (2008); Semantic Web and Web 2.0
4. Hatcher, E., Gospodnetic, O.: Lucene in action. Manning Publications (2004)
5. McNally, K., O'Mahony, M.P., Smyth, B., Coyle, M., Briggs, P.: Towards a reputation-based model of social web search. In: IUI 2010: Proceeding of the 14th International Conference on Intelligent User Interfaces, pp. 179–188. ACM, New York (2010)
6. Morris, M.R., Horvitz, E.: Searchtogether: an interface for collaborative web search. In: Proceedings of the 20th Annual ACM Symposium on User Interface Software and Technology, UIST 2007, pp. 3–12. ACM, New York (2007)
7. Shen, D., Pan, R., Sun, J.-T., Pan, J.J., Wu, K., Yin, J., Yang, Q.: Query enrichment for web-query classification. ACM Trans. Inf. Syst. 24, 320–352 (2006)
8. Smyth, B., Briggs, P., Coyle, M., O'Mahony, M.: Google shared. a case-study in social search. In: Houben, G.-J., McCalla, G., Pianesi, F., Zancanaro, M. (eds.) UMAP 2009. LNCS, vol. 5535, pp. 283–294. Springer, Heidelberg (2009)
9. Smyth, B., Briggs, P., Coyle, M., O'Mahony, M.P.: A case-based perspective on social web search. In: McGinty, L., Wilson, D.C. (eds.) ICCBR 2009. LNCS, vol. 5650, pp. 494–508. Springer, Heidelberg (2009)
10. Twidale, M.B., Nichols, D.M., Paice, C.D.: Browsing is a collaborative process. Information Processing & Management 33(6), 761–783 (1997)

Tags as Bridges between Domains: Improving Recommendation with Tag-Induced Cross-Domain Collaborative Filtering

Yue Shi, Martha Larson, and Alan Hanjalic

Multimedia Information Retrieval Lab, Delft University of Technology,
Mekelweg 4, 2628CD Delft, Netherlands
{y.shi,m.a.larson,a.hanjalic}@tudelft.nl

Abstract. Recommender systems generally face the challenge of making predictions using only the relatively few user ratings available for a given domain. Cross-domain collaborative filtering (CF) aims to alleviate the effects of this data sparseness by transferring knowledge from other domains. We propose a novel algorithm, Tag-induced Cross-Domain Collaborative Filtering (TagCDCF), which exploits user-contributed tags that are common to multiple domains in order to establish the cross-domain links necessary for successful cross-domain CF. TagCDCF extends the state-of-the-art matrix factorization by introducing a constraint involving tag-based similarities between pairs of users and pairs of items across domains. The method requires no common users or items across domains. Using two publicly available CF data sets as different domains, we experimentally demonstrate that TagCDCF substantially outperforms other state-of-the-art single domain CF and cross-domain CF approaches. Additional experiments show that TagCDCF addresses data sparseness and illustrate the influence of the number of tags used by users in both domains.

Keywords: Collaborative filtering, cross domain collaborative filtering, matrix factorization, tag, recommender systems.

1   Introduction

Collaborative filtering (CF) is one of the most successful techniques in recommender systems [1]. The idea of CF is to make use of the user-item rating matrix to predict items that individual users may like in future [4]. However, users usually rate a very limited number of items, giving rise to the widely-known data sparseness problem, which characterizes most recommender system tasks. Specifically to address the data sparseness problem, recent research has started to investigate cross-domain CF [6][7][9][16], which makes use of rating data from other domains to benefit a target domain. The key challenge in cross-domain CF is to discover linkage among domains (e.g., shared knowledge or common characteristics) that allows different domains to benefit each other effectively. Typically, domains are mutually exclusive, each involving a certain type of product (e.g., movies, music or books) and a set of users whose identities or identifiers are largely unique to the domain. As a result, it is difficult to directly extract common characteristics among users and items from different

Joseph A. Konstan et al. (Eds.): UMAP 2011, LNCS 6787, pp. 305–316, 2011.
© Springer-Verlag Berlin Heidelberg 2011

domains. Here, we turn to a novel source of information to link domains: user-generated tags. Many of today's recommender systems address tasks involving users who not only rate items, but also annotate items with tags denoting characteristics of items or their own personal preferences. Our approach is based on the insight that different users in different domains may use the same tags to describe items or express their opinions about items. We expect domains that share high-level characteristics, such as notions of plot and genre, to exhibit particularly useful overlap with respect to user-deployed tags. For example, tags such as "sci-fi", "fast-paced" and "romance" can be used by users to annotate items in both a movie domain and a book domain. Users with similar patterns of usage and preference can be assumed to have similar tagging patterns, which we anticipate to hold across domains. In sum, it is potentially beneficial to exploit tags shared between domains in order to transfer knowledge between those domains for the purpose of recommendation.

In this paper, we propose a novel tag-induced cross-domain collaborative filtering (TagCDCF) algorithm that exploits shared tags to link different domains, alleviating data sparseness in each individual domain and improving recommendation performance. TagCDCF uses an explicit encoding of the relationships between domains in the form of user-to-user and item-to-item similarity matrices based on tags shared between the domains to be linked. We formulate the TagCDCF from a probabilistic point of view, leading to an extended matrix factorization framework. The user-item matrices of different domains are factorized into domain-specific latent user features and latent item features. The latent features are linked across domains using the explicit tag-induced cross-domain similarities.

The contribution of this work is twofold: First, we present a novel cross-domain CF algorithm that is able to exploit explicit user-to-user and item-to-item similarities. Second, we show that using tags to bridge domains is able to address data sparseness and outperform state-of-the-art CF and cross-domain CF approaches.

The remainder of the paper is structured as follows. In the next section, we summarize related work and position our work in its context. We present the proposed TagCDCF algorithm in detail in Section 3, after which we evaluate its performance through a series of experiments. The last section sums up the key aspects of the proposed algorithm and briefly discusses directions for future work.

2   Related Work

Collaborative filtering. Collaborative filtering approaches can generally be categorized as memory-based or model-based. Memory-based approaches first compute similarities among users or among items based on a given user-item rating matrix, and then use these similarities to recommend items to a given user, either in terms of preferences of like-minded users (i.e., user-based CF (UBCF) [4]) or in terms of similarity to already rated items (i.e., item-based CF [11]). Model-based approaches first learn a prediction model based on a training set from the user-item rating matrix, and then apply this model to predict unknown preferences for users on items. Matrix factorization (MF) techniques [5] have become one of the most popular model-based CF approaches, due to the advantages of accuracy and scalability. Generally, MF techniques learn latent features of users and items from the observed ratings in a user-item matrix. The learned features are then further used to predict unobserved ratings.

Collective matrix factorization [13] is proposed to factorize multiple matrices representing the same domain that share common latent user or item features. Probabilistic matrix factorization (PMF) [10] approaches factorization in a single domain from a probabilistic point of view. TagCDCF builds on the PMF concept, but goes beyond existing CF approaches by tackling the cross-domain CF problem rather than using only a single domain.

Exploiting Tags for CF. Recently, researchers in recommender systems community have started investigating the usefulness of user-generated tags in improving recommendation quality. Tags have been exploited to enhance item recommendations by several means, e.g., via tensor factorization for user-tag-item triplet data [14], via similarities between users or items in terms of associated tags [12][17], and via representing users and items with weighted tags that have been de-noised [8]. However, our work goes beyond the scope of the aforementioned works, since we make use of tags to bridge different domains in order to enable knowledge transfer from one domain to another.

Cross-Domain CF. Finally, we note that several cross-domain CF approaches have been proposed recently. Coordinate system transfer [9] is proposed to adapt learned latent features of users and items from auxiliary domains and use them to regularize the learning of latent features of users and items in the target domain. However, it requires that either users or items are shared between the domains, which is, as already mentioned above, a condition not commonly encountered in practical applications. Codebook transfer (CBT) [6] and the rating-matrix generative model [7] both learn an implicit cluster-level rating pattern that could be shared between different domains. The learned implicit rating pattern is then used to transfer knowledge between domains to alleviate data sparseness. Similarly, multi-domain CF is proposed to extend probabilistic matrix factorization in multiple domains together with learning an implicit correlation matrix [16], which is assumed to link different domains for knowledge transfer. Compared to all the aforementioned cross-domain CF approaches, the proposed TagCDCF is substantially different in that we exploit explicit common characteristics, i.e., common tags, between different domains for knowledge transfer, rather than learning implicit cross-domain relationships. It is expected that the explicit common characteristics could lead to a more reliable and effective cross-domain CF than the implicit ones.

3   Tag-Induced Cross-Domain Collaborative Filtering

We present Tag-induced cross-domain collaborative filtering (TagCDCF), first introducing cross-domain user-to-user similarity and item-to-item similarity and then presenting the central mechanism of TagCDCF, a matrix factorization approach that incorporates explicit cross-domain similarities to bridge different domains. Matrix factorization uses known data to estimate latent features representing users and items and is the key objective that determines the recommendation accuracy. The integration of tag-induced cross-domain similarities guides the factorization process and leads to improved recommendation performance. Although TagCDCF could be used to incorporate multiple domains, we concentrate in this paper on combining two domains.

3.1   Definition of Tag-Induced Cross-Domain Similarity

TagCDCF makes use of two types of tag-induced cross-domain similarities, item-to-item similarity and user-to-user similarity, which are defined over the tags that are shared between the domains to be combined. As mentioned before, different domains, e.g., a movie recommender system and a book recommender system may have completely different users and items. However, it is still possible that some users in different domains use the same tags to annotate items of interest, and that some items in different domains are tagged by same tags that encode their similar properties. For this reason, we can assume cross-domain user-to-user similarity in terms of common tags the users apply, and cross-domain item-to-item similarity in terms of that items are annotated with.

In the kth domain, we denote the set of users by M_k and the set of items by N_k. The totality of tags used by the users to tag the items is the tag set, $T^{(k)}$, consisting of L_k different tags. The user-tag indicator matrix in the kth domain, $\mathbf{A}^{(k)}$, is an $M_k \times L_k$ matrix, in which $A_{il}^{(k)} = 1$ if user i used tag l, and is otherwise 0. Similarly, the item-tag indicator matrix in the kth domain, $\mathbf{B}^{(k)}$, is a $N_k \times L_k$ matrix, in which $B_{jl}^{(k)} = 1$ if item j is tagged by tag l, an is otherwise 0.

In order to compute the tag-induced cross-domain similarities, we first extract a shared tag set CT that contains all tags in both domains, i.e., $CT=T^{(1)} \cap T^{(2)}$. Then, we define the cross-domain user-to-user similarity $S_{ip}^{(U)}$ (i.e., between user i in the first domain and user p in the second domain) and cross-domain item-to-item similarity $S_{jq}^{(V)}$ (i.e., between item j in the first domain and item q in the second domain) using the cosine similarity measure, as shown below:

$$S_{ip}^{(U)} = \frac{\sum_{t \in CT}\left(A_{ix(t)}^{(1)} A_{py(t)}^{(2)}\right)}{\sqrt{\sum_{t \in CT}\left(A_{ix(t)}^{(1)}\right)^2}\sqrt{\sum_{t \in CT}\left(A_{py(t)}^{(2)}\right)^2}} \quad , \quad S_{jq}^{(V)} = \frac{\sum_{t \in CT}\left(B_{jx(t)}^{(1)} B_{qy(t)}^{(2)}\right)}{\sqrt{\sum_{t \in CT}\left(B_{jx(t)}^{(1)}\right)^2}\sqrt{\sum_{t \in CT}\left(B_{qy(t)}^{(2)}\right)^2}} \tag{1}$$

Note that we use $x(t)$ to denote the index of tag t in the first domain, and $y(t)$ the index of tag t in the second domain.

3.2   Formulation of Tag-Induced Cross-Domain Collaborative Filtering

We denote user-item matrix in kth domain as $\mathbf{R}^{(k)}$, which is an $M_k \times N_k$ matrix containing ratings from M_k users on N_k items. Ratings in each domain are normalized to be within the range from 0 to 1. We adopt the convention of denoting the non-zero entries in a matrix $\mathbf{X}$ as $|\mathbf{X}|$. The latent user features in the kth domain are collected in $\mathbf{U}^{(k)}$, a $d \times M_k$ matrix, whose ith column indicates the d-dimensional latent feature vector for user i. Similarly, the latent item features in the kth domain are represented by $\mathbf{V}^{(k)}$. This is a $d \times N_k$ matrix, whose jth column indicates the d-dimensional latent feature vector for item j.

We first present TagCDCF in a graphical model that illustrates relationships among all variables, as shown in Fig.1. The latent features of users and items, i.e., $\mathbf{U}^{(1)}, \mathbf{V}^{(1)}, \mathbf{U}^{(2)}, \mathbf{V}^{(2)}$, are unknown variables that need to be estimated. As can be seen, the sub-graph that only involves $\mathbf{U}^{(k)}, \mathbf{V}^{(k)}, \mathbf{R}^{(k)}$ ($k =1$ or 2) is equivalent to PMF [10] in a single domain. The tag-induced cross-domain similarities $\mathbf{S}^{(U)}$ and $\mathbf{S}^{(V)}$ actually bring the two domains together, which can be seen as a key innovation in this paper.

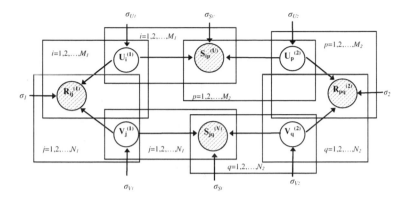

Fig. 1. Graphical model for the proposed TagCDCF

We can further interpret the graphical model from a probabilistic point of view. According to the graphical model theory [2], the joint distribution of all variables in the graph can be expressed as:

$$
\begin{aligned}
&p\left(U^{(1)},V^{(1)},U^{(2)},V^{(2)},R^{(1)},R^{(2)},S^{(U)},S^{(V)},\sigma_1,\sigma_2,\sigma_{U_1},\sigma_{V_1},\sigma_{U_2},\sigma_{V_2},\sigma_{S_U},\sigma_{S_V}\right) \\
&= p\left(R^{(1)}\mid U^{(1)},V^{(1)},\sigma_1\right)p\left(R^{(2)}\mid U^{(2)},V^{(2)},\sigma_2\right)p\left(S^{(U)}\mid U^{(1)},U^{(2)},\sigma_{S_U}\right) \\
&\quad p\left(S^{(V)}\mid V^{(1)},V^{(2)},\sigma_{S_V}\right)p\left(U^{(1)}\mid\sigma_{U_1}\right)p\left(V^{(1)}\mid\sigma_{V_1}\right)p\left(U^{(2)}\mid\sigma_{U_2}\right)p\left(V^{(2)}\mid\sigma_{V_2}\right) \\
&\quad p(\sigma_1)p(\sigma_2)p\left(\sigma_{U_1}\right)p\left(\sigma_{V_1}\right)p\left(\sigma_{U_2}\right)p\left(\sigma_{V_2}\right)p\left(\sigma_{S_U}\right)p\left(\sigma_{S_V}\right)
\end{aligned}
\tag{2}
$$

After applying the product rule to the left side of Eq. (2), and neglecting the influence of constant prior probabilities, we have:

$$
\begin{aligned}
&p\left(U^{(1)},V^{(1)},U^{(2)},V^{(2)}\mid R^{(1)},R^{(2)},S^{(U)},S^{(V)},\sigma_1,\sigma_2,\sigma_{U_1},\sigma_{V_1},\sigma_{U_2},\sigma_{V_2},\sigma_{S_U},\sigma_{S_V}\right) \\
&\propto p\left(S^{(U)}\mid U^{(1)},U^{(2)},\sigma_{S_U}\right)p\left(S^{(V)}\mid V^{(1)},V^{(2)},\sigma_{S_V}\right)\prod_{k=1}^{2}p\left(R^{(k)}\mid U^{(k)},V^{(k)},\sigma_k\right)p\left(U^{(k)}\mid\sigma_{U_k}\right)p\left(V^{(k)}\mid\sigma_{V_k}\right)
\end{aligned}
\tag{3}
$$

The conditional distribution over observed ratings in each domain can be defined as:

$$
p\left(R^{(k)}\mid U^{(k)},V^{(k)},\sigma_k\right)=\prod_{i=1}^{M_k}\prod_{j=1}^{N_k}\left[\mathcal{N}\left(R_{ij}^{(k)}\mid U_i^{(k)T}V_j^{(k)},\sigma_k^2\right)\right]^{I_{ij}^{R^{(k)}}}
\tag{4}
$$

where $\mathcal{N}\left(x\mid\mu,\sigma^2\right)$ denotes the probability density function for a Gaussian distribution with mean μ and variance σ^2. For a matrix $\mathbf{X}$, the indicator function I_{ij}^X is equal to 1 if $X_{ij}>0$, and is otherwise 0.

We also define conditional distributions over observed cross-domain similarities as:

$$
\begin{aligned}
p\left(S^{(U)}\mid U^{(1)},U^{(2)},\sigma_{S_U}\right)&=\prod_{i=1}^{M_1}\prod_{p=1}^{M_2}\left[\mathcal{N}\left(S_{ip}^{(U)}\mid U_i^{(1)T}U_p^{(2)},\sigma_{S_U}^2\right)\right]^{I_{ip}^{S^{(U)}}}, \\
p\left(S^{(V)}\mid V^{(1)},V^{(2)},\sigma_{S_V}\right)&=\prod_{j=1}^{N_1}\prod_{q=1}^{N_2}\left[\mathcal{N}\left(S_{jq}^{(V)}\mid V_j^{(1)T}V_q^{(2)},\sigma_{S_V}^2\right)\right]^{I_{jq}^{S^{(V)}}}
\end{aligned}
\tag{5}
$$

Finally, we use the zero-mean spherical Gaussian priors [15] to represent a latent user and movie features in each domain:

$$p\left(U^{(k)} \mid \sigma_{U_k}\right) = \prod_{i=1}^{M_k} \mathcal{N}\left(U_i^{(k)} \mid 0, \sigma_{U_k}^2 I\right) \quad , \quad p\left(V^{(k)} \mid \sigma_{V_k}\right) = \prod_{j=1}^{N_k} \mathcal{N}\left(V_j^{(k)} \mid 0, \sigma_{V_k}^2 I\right) \tag{6}$$

We substitute Eq. (4-6) into Eq. (3) and estimate latent user and item features in Eq. (3) by maximizing the posterior, which is equivalent to minimizing the negative log-posterior as shown below:

$$-\ln p\left(U^{(1)}, V^{(1)}, U^{(2)}, V^{(2)} \mid R^{(1)}, R^{(2)}, S^{(U)}, S^{(V)}, \sigma_1, \sigma_2, \sigma_{U_1}, \sigma_{V_1}, \sigma_{U_2}, \sigma_{V_2}, \sigma_{S_U}, \sigma_{S_V}\right)$$

$$= \sum_{k=1}^{2} \left(\frac{1}{2\sigma_k^2} \sum_{i=1}^{M_k} \sum_{j=1}^{N_k} I_{ij}^{R^{(k)}} \left(R_{ij}^{(k)} - U_i^{(k)T} V_j^{(k)}\right)^2 \right) + \frac{1}{2\sigma_{S_V}^2} \sum_{j=1}^{N_1} \sum_{q=1}^{N_2} I_{jq}^{S^{(V)}} \left(S_{jq}^{(V)} - V_j^{(1)T} V_q^{(2)}\right)^2$$

$$+ \frac{1}{2\sigma_{S_U}^2} \sum_{i=1}^{M_1} \sum_{p=1}^{M_2} I_{ip}^{S^{(U)}} \left(S_{ip}^{(U)} - U_i^{(1)T} U_p^{(2)}\right)^2 + \sum_{k=1}^{2} \left(\frac{1}{2\sigma_{U_k}^2} \sum_{i=1}^{M_k} U_i^{(k)T} U_i^{(k)} + \frac{1}{2\sigma_{V_k}^2} \sum_{j=1}^{N_k} V_j^{(k)T} V_j^{(k)} \right) + C \tag{7}$$

Note that C is a term containing rating variances, similarity variances and prior variances, which are independent of latent features. In order to simplify the model, we can assume that the variance of the user preferences in the two domains are comparable and that the user ratings (which have been normalized to the same scales in both domains) can be assumed to have equal variance, i.e., $\sigma_1^2 = \sigma_2^2$. We also assume that prior variances are the same across all the latent features, i.e., $\sigma_{U_1}^2 = \sigma_{V_1}^2 = \sigma_{U_2}^2 = \sigma_{V_2}^2$.
Therefore, we can define the objective function $F(\mathbf{U}^{(1)}, \mathbf{V}^{(1)}, \mathbf{U}^{(2)}, \mathbf{V}^{(2)})$ as:

$$F\left(U^{(1)}, V^{(1)}, U^{(2)}, V^{(2)}\right)$$

$$= \frac{1}{2} \sum_{k=1}^{2} \sum_{i=1}^{M_k} \sum_{j=1}^{N_k} I_{ij}^{R^{(k)}} \left(R_{ij}^{(k)} - U_i^{(k)T} V_j^{(k)}\right)^2 + \frac{\alpha}{2} \sum_{j=1}^{N_1} \sum_{q=1}^{N_2} I_{jq}^{S^{(V)}} \left(S_{jq}^{(V)} - V_j^{(1)T} V_q^{(2)}\right)^2$$

$$+ \frac{\beta}{2} \sum_{i=1}^{M_1} \sum_{p=1}^{M_2} I_{ip}^{S^{(U)}} \left(S_{ip}^{(U)} - U_i^{(1)T} U_p^{(2)}\right)^2 + \frac{\lambda}{2} \sum_{k=1}^{2} \left(\left\|U^{(k)}\right\|_{Fro}^2 + \left\|V^{(k)}\right\|_{Fro}^2 \right) \tag{8}$$

in which we have $\alpha = \sigma_1^2 / \sigma_{S_V}^2$, $\beta = \sigma_1^2 / \sigma_{S_U}^2$, and $\lambda = \sigma_1^2 / \sigma_{U_1}^2$. α and β are tradeoff parameters that control the influence of cross-domain item-to-item similarity and user-to-user similarity, respectively. λ is a regularization parameter that is usually used to penalize the complexity of latent feature matrices in order to alleviate over-fitting.

A local minimum solution for minimizing the objective function in Eq. (8) can be achieved by gradient descent with alternatively fixed $\mathbf{U}^{(1)}$, $\mathbf{V}^{(1)}$, $\mathbf{U}^{(2)}$, and $\mathbf{V}^{(2)}$. The gradients can be computed as below:

$$\frac{\partial F}{\partial U_i^{(1)}} = \sum_{j=1}^{N_1} I_{ij}^{R^{(1)}} \left(U_i^{(1)T} V_j^{(1)} - R_{ij}^{(1)}\right) V_j^{(1)} + \beta \sum_{p=1}^{M_2} I_{ip}^{S^{(U)}} \left(U_i^{(1)T} U_p^{(2)} - S_{ip}^{(U)}\right) U_p^{(2)} + \lambda U_i^{(1)},$$

$$\frac{\partial F}{\partial V_j^{(1)}} = \sum_{i=1}^{M_1} I_{ij}^{R^{(1)}} \left(U_i^{(1)T} V_j^{(1)} - R_{ij}^{(1)}\right) U_i^{(1)} + \alpha \sum_{q=1}^{N_2} I_{jq}^{S^{(V)}} \left(V_j^{(1)T} V_q^{(2)} - S_{jq}^{(V)}\right) V_q^{(2)} + \lambda V_j^{(1)},$$

$$\frac{\partial F}{\partial U_i^{(2)}} = \sum_{j=1}^{N_2} I_{ij}^{R^{(2)}} \left(U_i^{(2)T} V_j^{(2)} - R_{ij}^{(2)}\right) V_j^{(2)} + \beta \sum_{p=1}^{M_1} I_{pi}^{S^{(U)}} \left(U_p^{(1)T} U_i^{(2)} - S_{pi}^{(U)}\right) U_p^{(1)} + \lambda U_i^{(2)},$$

$$\frac{\partial F}{\partial V_j^{(2)}} = \sum_{i=1}^{M_2} I_{ij}^{R^{(2)}} \left(U_i^{(2)T} V_j^{(2)} - R_{ij}^{(2)}\right) U_i^{(2)} + \alpha \sum_{q=1}^{N_1} I_{qj}^{S^{(V)}} \left(V_q^{(1)T} V_j^{(2)} - S_{qj}^{(V)}\right) V_q^{(1)} + \lambda V_j^{(2)} \tag{9}$$

The learned latent features of users and items can be multiplied to compute the recommendation, i.e., predict unobserved ratings in each domain. By exploiting data sparseness, the complexity of TagCDCF is $O(d(|\mathbf{R}^{(1)}|+|\mathbf{R}^{(2)}|+|\mathbf{S}^{(U)}|+|\mathbf{S}^{(V)}|))$, which is linear with the total number of non-zeros in the user-item rating matrices and cross-domain similarity matrices. Such reasonable complexity reflects the ability of TagCDCF to scale up to use cases involving large sets of rating data.

4   Experimental Evaluation

We carry out a series of experiments to demonstrate that TagCDCF improves recommendation for both of the combined domains over state-of-the-art single domain CF and cross-domain CF approaches. Further experiments examine the ability of TagCDCF to address the data sparseness problem as faced in the case of users who have rated relatively few items. A final set of experiments, explores the dependence of TagCDCF performance on the number of tags shared between domains.

4.1   Experimental Framework

Data sets. We evaluate the proposed TagCDCF algorithm on two different domains represented by two publicly available data sets: the MovieLens data set (http://www.grouplens.org/node/73) [4], with ca. 10 million ratings, and the LibraryThing data set (http://homepage.tudelft.nl/5q88p/LT) [3], with ca. 750 thousand ratings. Both of the data sets have 5-star rating scale, with half star increments. In addition, the MovieLens data set contains 16529 unique tags with 95580 tag assignments from users to movies, and the LibraryThing data set contains 10559 unique tags with ca. 2 million tag assignments from users to books. There are in total 2277 tags common to the two domains.

Our experiments are conducted on the first 5000 users chosen according to the identifiers in the original data sets from the 71567 MovieLens users and the 7279 LibraryThing users and on the first 5000 items from the 10681 MovieLens movies and the 37232 LibraryThing books. This selection of subsets was necessary in order to implement a full-range of baselines for comparison, including the computationally expensive UBCF and CBT. We avoided random selection to facilitate future reproducibility. The experimental subsets are denoted here as ML (from MovieLens) and LT (from LibraryThing). We note that their size is comparable to that of the largest data set used to date for cross-domain CF [9]. The rating data sparseness is 97.7% in ML, and 99.3% in LT.

Experimental Protocol. For each data set, we generate a data partition by randomly selecting 80% ratings as training set, and using the remaining 20% ratings as the test set. In this way, for each data set we generated six data partitions, one of which is randomly selected for validation, i.e., for tuning the parameters, and the other five for testing, i.e., for reporting the performance of the proposed algorithm and comparing it with other approaches. We set the dimensionality d of latent features to 10 for the TagCDCF. Experimental investigation revealed that the performance did not substantially change when further increasing d, due to which 10 is a good choice in terms of model complexity. The regularization parameter is tuned to 0.01, which is the same value as used for the baseline approach PMF.

Evaluation Metric. To be consistent with recent studies [6][7][9][16] on this topic, we also use mean absolute error (MAE) as the evaluation metric, defined as:

$$MAE = \sum_{(i,j)\in Ts} \left| \hat{R}_{ij} - R_{ij} \right| / |Ts| \tag{10}$$

where Ts denotes the set of user-item pairs whose ratings need to be predicted in the test set. We denote by $|Ts|$ the size of the set Ts. $\hat{R}_{ij}$ denotes the predicted rating for user i on item j. Note that the lower MAE means better recommendation performance.

4.2   Experimental Results

Impact of Tradeoff Parameters. Our first experiment investigates the impact of tradeoff parameters in the proposed TagCDCF. This experiment is conducted on the validation partition in each domain. We first set the tradeoff parameter $\beta=0$ and investigate the impact of the tradeoff parameter α. The change in MAE caused by varying the value of α in each data set is shown in Fig.2(a) and (b). The influence of α on MAE confirms that exploiting the cross-domain item-to-item similarity could introduce performance gain in both domains. Then, we fix the tradeoff parameter α with the optimal value as 0.001, and investigate the impact of β, shown in Fig.2(c) and (d). The influence of β (with the optimal value as 0.001) confirms that additional improvement can be achieved in both domains by introducing the cross-domain user-to-user similarity. Summarizing, we find both domains stand to benefit by exploitation of tag-induced cross-domain similarities via TagCDCF.

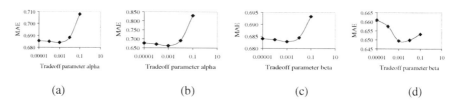

(a)   (b)   (c)   (d)

Fig. 2. Impact of tradeoff parameters on TagCDCF: (a) α on ML, (b) α on LT, (c) β on ML, and (d) β on LT

Performance Comparison. Next, we compare the performance of the TagCDCF with other baseline approaches, using the five test partitions in each data set. Note that the tradeoff parameters used are the optimal ones, as tuned using the validation partition. The baseline approaches are listed below:

UBCF: User-based collaborative filtering [4] is used as a representative of a conventional memory-based CF approach. The neighborhood size is set to 50, determined to be the best-performing neighborhood size using the validation partition.

PMF: Probabilistic matrix factorization [10] is used as a representative of a state-of-the art model-based CF approach. In a single domain, PMF is equivalent to the TagCDCF when both tradeoff parameters are set to 0. The regularization parameter is tuned to 0.01, which achieved optimal performance on the validation partition. Note that both UBCF and PMF are CF approaches that use only a single domain.

CBT: Codebook transfer [6] is used to represent a state-of-the-art cross-domain CF approach. Here, one domain is the auxiliary domain, which is used to construct the codebook, and the other is the target domain in which the predictions are carried out. We use ML as the source of the auxiliary domain for LT predictions and LT as the source of the auxiliary domain for ML predictions. In each case, we follow the protocol used in [6] and select the 500 users and the 500 items with most ratings to constitute the auxiliary domain, while setting the number of user and item clusters to 50.

The performance of the TagCDCF and the baseline approaches are shown in Table 1. Note that the MAE is averaged across all the five test partitions.

Table 1. Performance comparison between TagCDCF and baseline approaches (MAE ± std.)

Data set	UBCF	PMF	CBT	TagCDCF
ML	0.691 ±0.002	0.686 ±0.001	0.688 ±0.002	**0.684 ±0.001**
LT	0.682 ±0.002	0.677 ±0.004	0.671 ±0.003	**0.653 ±0.004**

The results demonstrate that TagCDCF significantly outperforms other approaches in both data sets—improvements in Table 1 are statistically significant according to the Wilcoxon signed rank significance test with p<0.01. TagCDCF achieved an improvement over CBT on both data sets, indicating that the explicit tag-induced relationships between two domains could be more effective than the hypothesized implicit relationships solely learned from rating data. We notice that the improvement achieved by TagCDCF on the LT data set is substantial, i.e., up to 4.4%, and is larger than the improvement on the ML data set, i.e., up to 1% improvement. The difference reflects the smaller number of ratings (i.e., the higher sparseness) mentioned in Section 4.1 in the LT data set, meaning that there is a greater potential for TagCDCF to introduce improvement. Note that the performance of CBT is even worse than PMF on the ML data set, meaning that solely relying on rating data for linking domains is not effective in the case that the auxiliary domain (i.e., LT in this case) is sparser in rating data than the target domain (i.e., ML).

Performance for Different Users. We further investigate the performance of TagCDCF for users with different characteristics. Our investigation is focused on the LT data set, which we take to be representative of a case that derives particular benefits from TagCDCF, as suggested by the results above. Although we report the results obtained on one randomly selected partition, the same trend can be observed on the other partitions. Our first goal is to understand the ability of TagCDCF in alleviating data sparseness. For this reason, we analyze the performance of the TagCDCF and other baseline approaches for users with different number of rated items (cf. Fig. 3).

As can be seen from Fig. 3(a), most users rated limited number of items, i.e., <20 items, while much fewer users rated a lot of items, e.g., >100 items, a common situation in recommender systems. The "<20" group of users usually contains those who are most likely to suffer from the data sparseness problem. For this group of users, the TagCDCF achieves over 8% improvement, compared to the single domain CF approaches, i.e., UBCF and PMF, as shown in Fig. 3(b). These results indicate that TagCDCF could be particularly helpful for users with sparse rating profiles. The other cross-domain CF approach, CBT, also shows a more modest benefit than TagCDCF, but still can be seen to perform particularly well for users with sparse rating profiles. This similarity confirms that TagCDCF shares the same advantage as other cross-domain CF approaches in specifically addressing the data-sparseness problem. In addition, we can see that for users with relatively more rated items, CBT fails to outperform single domain CF approaches. In contrast, the improvement introduced by TagCDCF consistently outperforms single domain CF approaches across the board, indicating that the improvement introduced when tag-induced cross-domain similarities are exploited as a source of information to link domains could be robust for users with different rating profiles.

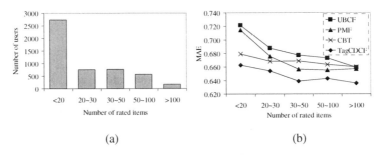

(a)   (b)

Fig. 3. (a) User distribution of the number of rated items. (b) Performance for users with different number of rated items.

Impact of number of tags shared between domains. Our final goal is to investigate the impact of the number of tags shared between domains on the performance of TagCDCF. Here, we again report experimental results on a randomly selected partition from the LT data set. We analyze the performance of TagCDCF for users who use a different number of tags from the set of tags shared between domains (cf. Fig.4).

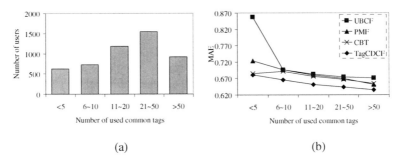

(a)   (b)

Fig. 4. (a) User distribution of the number of used common tags. (b) Performance for users with different number of used common tags.

We notice that the MAE decreases when users use more tags that are shared between domains. This result indicates that the greater the number of tags used by the user that are common across the domains, the more benefits could be introduced by exploiting tag-induced cross-domain similarities. UBCF demonstrates a marked performance deterioration on users using very limited number of shared tags, i.e., <5. This spike suggests that users using fewer shared tags use less tags in general, and are perhaps also not very active with respect to assigning ratings. Lack of adequate numbers of assigned ratings would make these users challenging to the UBCF approach, which depends on ratings to reliably calculate user neighborhoods. We also observe that when the user only used very limited number of common tags, i.e., <5 common tags on the LT data set, the performance of TagCDCF is close to the CBT, indicating that the benefits introduced by tags are limited. However, as can be seen in Fig. 4(a), the number of users making use of a limited number of shared tags is not the majority. Most users use more than 5 common tags and are able, as shown in Fig. 4(b), to benefit more from TagCDCF than from competing approaches.

5   Conclusions and Future Work

We have presented TagCDCF, a novel algorithm that is able to improve recommendation performance in multiple domains by linking them via user-assigned tags. TagCDCF extends a matrix factorization approach to collaborative filtering by making use of tags as a source of explicit information that connects users and items across domains. Cross-domain similarities calculated on the basis of user-assigned tags are used to constrain matrix factorization, resulting in improved recommendation performance. Experimental investigation demonstrated that TagCDCF improved the performance in both domains being linked, with more dramatic performance improvements observed in the domain with greater data sparseness. TagCDCF was shown to outperform baselines representative of conventional single-domain CF approaches as well as a state-of-the-art cross-domain CF approach. The relative size of improvement achieved for users with few rated items demonstrates the ability of TagCDCF to address the sparse-data problem. A final set of experiments showed that the improvement offered by TagCDCF is related to the number of tags used by a user that are common to the domains being linked. TagCDCF was observed to outperform other approaches once a user made use of a relatively small number of shared tags.

Our future work will involve further investigation of specific characteristics of recommendation domains. Here, we have seen that the number of tags shared between domains makes an important contribution to TagCDCF performance. We are also interested in discovering additional properties that make two domains particularly suited to benefit each other via TagCDCF. As formulated here, TagCDCF exploits tags to calculate independent item-to-item and user-to-user similarities. We intend to explore whether integrating information on user-tag co-occurrences can be used to refine these similarities. Finally, although TagCDCF was designed and developed to exploit user-contributed tags in the recommender systems domain, the framework is also potentially applicable to cases in which other explicit comparisons can be made between users and between items. We will investigate the effectiveness of alternate information sources, e.g., information derived from content analysis, as the basis for cross-domain linkage within the TagCDCF framework.

Acknowledgements. The research leading to these results was carried out within the PetaMedia Network of Excellence and has received funding from the European Commission's 7th Framework Program under grant agreement n° 216444.

References

1. Adomavicius, G., Tuzhilin, A.: Toward the next generation of recommender systems: A survey of the state-of-the-art and possible extensions. IEEE TKDE 17(6), 734–749 (2005)
2. Bishop, C.M.: Pattern Recognition and Machine Learning. Springer, Heidelberg (2006)
3. Clements, M., de Vries, A.P., Reinders, M.J.T.: The influence of personalization on tag query length in social media search. Inf. Process. Manage. 46(4), 403–412 (2010)
4. Herlocker, J., Konstan, J., Borchers, A., Riedl, J.: An algorithmic framework for performing collaborative filtering. In: SIGIR 1999, pp. 230–237 (1999)
5. Koren, Y., Bell, R., Volinsky, C.: Matrix factorization techniques for recommender systems. IEEE Computer 42(8), 30–37 (2009)
6. Li, B., Yang, Q., Xue, X.: Can movies and books collaborate?: cross-domain collaborative filtering for sparsity reduction. In: IJCAI 2009, pp. 2052–2057 (2009)
7. Li, B., Yang, Q., Xue, X.: Transfer learning for collaborative filtering via a rating-matrix generative model. In: ICML 2009, pp. 617–624 (2009)
8. Liang, H., Xu, Y., Li, Y., Nayak, R., Tao, X.: Connecting users and items with weighted tags for personalized item recommendations. In: HT 2010, pp. 51–60 (2010)
9. Pan, W., Xiang, E., Liu, N., Yang, Q.: Transfer learning in collaborative filtering for sparsity reduction. In: AAAI 2010, pp. 230–235 (2010)
10. Salakhutdinov, R., Mnih, A.: Probabilistic matrix factorization. In: NIPS 2008, p. 20 (2008)
11. Sarwar, B., Karypis, G., Konstan, J., Reidl, J.: Item-based collaborative filtering recommendation algorithms. In: WWW 2001, pp. 285–295 (2001)
12. Sen, S., Vig, J., Riedl, J.: Tagommenders: connecting users to items through tags. In: WWW 2009, pp. 671–680 (2009)
13. Singh, A.P., Gordon, G.J.: Relational learning via collective matrix factorization. In: KDD 2008, pp. 650–658 (2008)
14. Symeonidis, P., Nanopoulos, A., Manolopoulos, Y.: A Unified Framework for Providing Recommendations in Social Tagging Systems Based on Ternary Semantic Analysis. IEEE TKDE 22(2), 179–192 (2009)
15. Tipping, M.E., Bishop, C.M.: Probabilistic principal component analysis. Technical Report NCRG/97/010, Neural Computing Research Group, Aston University (1997)
16. Zhang, Y., Cao, B., Yeung, D.-Y.: Multi-domain collaborative filtering. In: UAI 2010 (2010)
17. Zhen, Y., Li, W.-J., Yeung, D.-Y.: TagiCoFi: tag informed collaborative filtering. In: RecSys 2009, pp. 69–76 (2009)

User Modeling – A Notoriously Black Art

Michael Yudelson, Philip I. Pavlik Jr., and Kenneth R. Koedinger

Human Computer Interaction Institute, Carnegie Mellon University,
5000 Forbes Avenue, Pittsburgh PA 15213, USA
ppavlik@andrew.cmu.edu, {yudelson,koedinger}@cmu.edu

Abstract. This paper is intended as guidance for those who are familiar with user modeling field but are less fluent in statistical methods. It addresses potential problems with user model selection and evaluation, that are often clear to expert modelers, but are not obvious for others. These problems are frequently a result of a falsely straightforward application of statistics to user modeling (e.g. over-reliance on model fit metrics). In such cases, absolute trust in arguably shallow model accuracy measures could lead to selecting models that are hard-to-interpret, less meaningful, over-fit, and less generalizable. We offer a list of questions to consider in order to avoid these modeling pitfalls. Each of the listed questions is backed by an illustrative example based on the user modeling approach called Performance Factors Analysis (PFA) [9].

Keywords: User modeling, educational data mining, model selection, model complexity, model parsimony.

1   Introduction

Fitting a mathematical model of user's behavior to the data is a notoriously black art. While this statement typically is agreed to by expert modelers, it is very difficult to convey exactly what it means to modelers who, while having a fair knowledge of the domain being modeled, do not possess a solid knowledge of statistics. Inexperienced modelers often transfer classroom knowledge of statistics directly into the cognitive domain, which typically results in multiple confusions. Consider, for example, the Akaike information criterion (AIC) or Bayesian information criterion (BIC). These statistics are routinely output by many statistical packages, but over-reliance on these criteria could lead a modeler to making inappropriate inferences, since user modeling data is very infrequently independent, as required by the definitions of AIC and BIC.

In reality, observations are often dependent and are nested by user, by location, or by content items users interact with. Thus, AIC (which gives preference to models with fewer parameters) and BIC (which, in addition, ranks models build using a smaller sample) cannot always account for these nested dependencies. Other frequently used statistics, such as log-likelihood, mean absolute error, r^2, precision, recall, F-measure, or A' (area under the ROC curve), provide empirical assessments of model's fit, that, although useful for determining whether

Joseph A. Konstan et al. (Eds.): UMAP 2011, LNCS 6787, pp. 317–328, 2011.
© Springer-Verlag Berlin Heidelberg 2011

each new parameter provides additional explanatory power, offer little support in deciding whether the model makes sense and/or supports a prior theory.

In order to make a better decision on model usefulness, the modeler needs to use other criterions for practical model selection and is faced with a series of questions that need to be posed throughout the modeling process. These questions must be kept foremost in the modeler's mind otherwise the risk exists that the implications of the model will be misinterpreted. These questions are.

1. What factors of the data are used to estimate predictive parameters, and which are used to estimate descriptive parameters?
2. What components of the model are fixed effects of the design, and which are random effects due to the selection from the environment?
3. Is the model complex enough in its identification of parameters with user constructs and user experience?
4. Is the model parsimonious in its identification? Namely, is there little or no polysemy among the parameters?

Attention to the questions in the list above is as important as seeing the effect of changes in the model on the model fit. As we will see in the following user modeling report, it is relatively easy to produce models with better fit (as per, for example, AIC, BIC, r^2, or A' metrics) if these issues are ignored, but these models will be less useful to the modeler and the user modeling community alike. Our goals are similar with those of the authors of [10], for we are arguing against making a compromise when utilizing mentioned metrics, but rather highlighting the cases when their brute-force use truly leads to conflicting conclusions.

The rest of the paper is organized around the items in our checklist in the order their appearance. First, predictive vs. descriptive modeling is addressed. A brief description of our modeling dataset follows. Then, fixed vs. random effects modeling of user-specific parameters is discussed. Finally we talk about model complexity and parsimony.

2   Predictive vs. Descriptive Modeling

Whether the model parameters are estimated in a predictive or descriptive manner is an important aspect of model building, but is often overlooked or ignored. The choice of the way the data is organized and parameters are constructed could have a tangible effect on properties of the model being built. An example of what we mean by predictive and descriptive parameters is given in Table 1 It is a rigged-up snippet of the user data where *PercCorr1* is the mean success rate - mean of *Correct* - over prior user trials including the current one. *PercCorr2* is the mean success rate over trials strictly prior to the current one. *PercCorr3* is the percent correct over all user trials.

PercCorr2 is an example of strictly predictive coding of the data, since at user trial t no information about performance of trial t is directly or indirectly incorporated into it. A model that would estimate a parameter for *PercCorr2* would capture the predictive nature of this value. *PercCorr1* and *PercCorr3* are

Table 1. Predictive vs. descriptive parameters (rigged up example)

User ID	Trial No.	Correct	PercCorr1	PercCorr2	PercCorr3
u11	1	1	1.00	null	0.60
u11	2	0	0.50	1.00	0.60
u11	3	0	0.33	0.50	0.60
u11	4	1	0.50	0.33	0.60
u11	5	1	0.60	0.50	0.60

the examples of descriptive coding of the data. *PercCorr1* incorporates the user performance and the current trial t and *PercCorr3* aggregates user performance over all trials: past, current, and future. Although *PercCorr1* and *PercCorr2* look much the same, models built using one or the other can differ greatly.

Clearly, predictive coding of the data is only possible when repeated measures are made. If each user contributes just one data point, only descriptive parameters can be constructed. There is no universal recipe for deciding when to include predictive or descriptive parameters into the model. From our experience, models that are built from repeated measures data (arguably, most of the user models are) and include both predictive and descriptive parameters are more stable and less prone to over-fitting than those that only include descriptive parameters.

3   Data

The dataset that we will use in this paper contains student activity recorded by a modified Bridge to Algebra (BTA) tutor by Carnegie Learning[1]. It was collected in several sixth and seventh grade classes at Pinecrest Academy Charter Middle School and covers 10 warmup sessions added to the main BTA curriculum of 61 existing BTA sections. Warmup sessions addressed the same topic as the forthcoming BTA tutor section. In each of the warmups, users (11-13 year old kids) were presented with 16 simple unscaffolded math problems randomly drawn from a pool of 24. Subjects were distributed across several experimental conditions differing in what accompanied problems 5 through 12 (worked problem, hint, or nothing at all). Subjects in a special *inference* condition were only given 8 problems.

For our modeling we used a subset of the data: the first warmup session addressing least common multiples. This data is comprised of 3616 problem trials (fill-in-the-blank exercises, worked problems, and hints were excluded) belonging to 255 students that completed all 16 assigned problems (8 in case of *inference* condition). Texts of two of the problems are given below as examples.

> *Problem example 1. Sally visits her grandfather every 4 days and Molly visits him every 6 days. If they are visiting him together today, in how many days will they visit together again?*

> *Problem example 2. What is the least common multiple 4 and 9?*

---

[1] http://www.carnegielearning.com/secondary-curricula/bta/

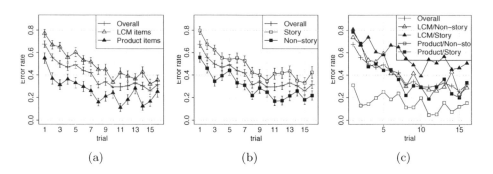

Fig. 1. Error rates comparisons. Serifs in (a) and (b) depict 95% confidence intervals.

The problem examples above have two important properties. First, problem 1 is a so-called *story* problem and problem 2 is a *non-story* problem. Story problems require additional abstraction or a use of a concrete strategy. In the literature, there could be found conflicting evidence on whether *story* problems were more difficult or not (see, for example [6,5]). In our case, story problems are generally harder: overall mean success rate for *story* problems is 0.50 which is lower than the overall mean success rate for *non-story* problems that is 0.69. Out of 24 problems in the first warmup pool, 12 were *story* problems and 12 were *non-story* problems.

A second and, arguably, more important property of the problems is that in some cases the least common multiple (LCM) could be correctly obtained by multiplying the two inputs. In this case, the problem can be solved by applying *partial* problem-solving strategy. However, not all LCM's are equal to the product of the inputs. Problem example 2 is such problem, where LCM of 4 and 9 is $36 = 4 \times 9$. Problem example 1 is a case that requires *full* problem-solving strategy and a product of the inputs would give an erroneous result. Here, LCM of 4 and 6 is $12 \neq 4 \times 6$. In the problem pool, 10 were the problems that could be solve by multiplying the inputs. We will be calling them *Product* problems. In our data set, 14 problems were the ones, for which product of the inputs would yield and incorrect result. We will be referring to them as *LCM* problems. Naturally, *LCM* problems were harder and had 0.50 mean overall success rate, as compared to *Product* problems with 0.73 mean overall success rate.

Fig. 1 shows comparisons of error rate curves (compliment of the learning curve). As we can see in Fig. 1(a) and Fig. 1(b), *LCM* problems' and *story* problems' error rate curves respectively are reliably higher. When these two properties are crossed and four error rate curves are produced (Fig. 1(c)), *LCM/story* problems represent the most hard combination of the properties and *Product/non-story* - the least hard. Respective error rate curves are the highest and the lowest on the graph. The other two – *LCM/non-story* and *Product/story* – are close to the overall curve.

4 Subject Parameters as Fixed vs. Random Effects

Mixed effects modeling approaches are now commonly used in many areas of science. Among other things, these approaches prescribe treating participant-specific model parameters as random effects [1]. A random effect is an effect that is sampled from a population to which statistical inferences are to generalize. Subjects are treated as random factors, because the goal of modeling is to capture effects pertaining not only to the individuals participating in a particular experiment, but to the subject population in general. Entering users as fixed factors (referred to as *fixed fallacy* in [3]), due to sampling variability, could make the model less generalizable and results would not transfer to similar datasets.

This argument may also apply to problem items as well that are often prescribed to be entered as random effects crossed with users (see, for example, [1]). In our dataset, however, problem items were not randomly drawn from a larger problem pool. Problem set was fixed by experimenters. Using random effects for problem items may refine the model further, based on the same principals that led us to use random effects for users. However, we leave determining a possible benefit of it for the further work.

In this section we are going to demonstrate the value of entering user proficiency parameters as random factors. We will do that on the basis of the Performance Factors Analysis (PFA) [9]. PFA is an educational data mining model. It was developed as an elaboration of the Additive Factors Model (AFM) [2] that in its turn is an extension of the Rasch item response model [7].

4.1 PFA Models

The PFA model uses the numbers of prior correct and incorrect responses as indicators of the strength of the student's mastery of a knowledge component (KC). Inclusion of the number of correct responses, in addition to capturing learning, allows PFA to track strength of students knowledge: the more correct responses are produced, the more it is likely that student's knowledge is already high. The number of incorrect plays the role of reflecting learning from errors and also acts as counter-balance, since errors are indicative of the relative weakness of the student's knowledge. Together, both corrects and incorrects not only make model sensitive to the quantity of each, but also the ratio of one to the other.

PFA's standard multiple logistic regression form is shown in Equation (1). Here, Pr denotes probability, *inv.logit* is an inverse logistic function: $inv.logit(x) = 1/(1 + e^{-x})$, Y_{ij} denotes the response of student $i \in [1, U]$ on $KC_j \in [1, K]$, θ_i - coefficient of proficiency of user i, β_j - coefficient of difficulty of KC_j, γ_j - coefficient for the number of correct responses of the KC_j (success rate parameter), ρ_j - coefficient for the number of incorrect responses of the KC_j (failure rate parameter), s_{ij} - user i success rate with KC_j, f_{ij} - user i failure rate with KC_j.

$$p_{ij} = \Pr(Y_{ij} = 1|\theta, \beta, \gamma, \rho) = inv.logit[\ (\theta_i + \sum_j (\beta_j + \gamma_j s_{ij} + \rho_j f_{ij}))\ ] \quad (1)$$

θ and β parameters in PFA are always estimated in a descriptive fashion, since they capture overall KC difficulties and overall user proficiencies. Number of correct (s) and incorrect KC attempts (f) could be computed either descriptively or predictively (thus defining how success (γ) and failure (ρ) rate parameters are estimated). In this paper, we always compute attempt counts and respective success/failure rate parameters as predictive (like PercCorrect2 in Table 1).

Based on the PFA model shown in Equation (1), we build several variants. First one is the PFA without coefficient of user's proficiency (parameter θ_i, present in standard PFA is excluded). We will refer to it as PFA *ns* (no subject). This model is shown in Equation (2). Although this model disregards variability in user proficiency entirely, it is still potentially able to offer useful insights based on KC difficulties and success/failure rate parameters alone. Another variant of PFA, treats user proficiency parameters θ_i as random effects. Instead of estimating user proficiencies directly, it estimates their respective variance. In all other aspects this model is identical to the standard PFA model in Equation (1).

$$p_{ij} = \Pr(Y_{ij} = 1 | \beta, \gamma, \rho) = inv.logit[\ \sum_j (\beta_j + \gamma_j s_{ij} + \rho_j f_{ij})\ ] \qquad (2)$$

In our dataset problems (denoted by j subscript in the PFA model) initially were not indexed with KC's like in the original work on PFA [9]. We are going to use problem-solving strategies instead of KC's and will call them [problem] itemtypes, as was done in a later version of the PFA model [8]. Thus, we have two different itemtypes: *Product* - for the problems, where using a partial strategy is permissible, and *LCM* - where only the use of the full strategy would produce a correct result.

4.2   Model Comparison Results

Table 2 presents a summary of several fit statistics for the three PFA models. Namely, number of parameters (Par.) log-likelihood (LL), Bayesian Information Criterion (BIC), correlation of actual and expected accuracy across students (r_{AE}), area under ROC curve (A$'$) and sum of squared residuals (SSR). Judging just from these values, PFA seems to have an edge: LL and SSR are the lowest, r_{AE} and A$'$ are the highest. BIC, however, is the highest of all three models. PFA *ns* is the least successful and PFA *re* is roughly between the other two models. However, as our main thesis of the paper suggests, the *surface* statistics in Table 2 are not enough.

Table 3 is a summary of actual model parameters. Across all three models, *Product* itemtypes are consistently harder than *LCM* itemtypes: β_P intercepts are higher than β_L intercepts. In PFA *ns* model, success rate parameters γ_P and γ_L are both reliably above zero reflecting that users do learn from correct responses as expected, more from corrects on *LCM* itemtypes. Errors on *Product* itemtypes *hurt* student performance ($\rho_P \leq 0$, p-value=0.000), while errors on *LCM* itemtypes (ρ_L), do not have a significant effect.

Table 2. Fit statistics of PFA models

Model	Par.	LL	BIC	r_{AE}	A′	SSR
PFA ns	6	-2133	4323	0.860	0.739	728.527
PFA	261	-1768	5674	1.000^2	0.836	581.637
PFA re	7	-2123	4296	0.984	0.800	646.908

Table 3. Parameters of PFA models. Subscripts $_P$ and $_L$ refer to *Product* and *LCM* itemtypes respectively.

	PFA ns			PFA			PFA re	
	Par.	Std.Err.	p-value[3]	Par.	Std.Err.	p-value	Par.	Std.Err.	p-value
β_P	0.452	0.077	0.000***	-0.569	0.098	0.010**	0.386	0.082	0.000***
β_L	-0.647	0.073	0.000***	-1.989	0.770	0.000***	-0.800	0.089	0.000***
γ_P	0.118	0.026	0.000***	-0.179	0.046	0.000***	0.046	0.033	0.162
ρ_P	-0.110	0.037	0.003**	0.716	0.082	0.000***	0.075	0.050	0.134
γ_L	0.354	0.026	0.000***	0.018	0.041	0.660	0.274	0.032	0.000***
ρ_L	-0.028	0.021	0.189	0.367	0.043	0.000***	0.081	0.028	0.004**
θ_i	N/A	N/A		-0.003	3.381		-0.008	0.731	
	Mean Std.Dev.			Mean Std.Dev.			Mean Std.Dev.		

While PFA *ns* seems to be generally acceptable, there is one thing that raises caution. Namely, the model fits failure rate parameters to have negative or no effect on students' future performance and, while it seems plausible to expect at least a hint at learning from errors (cf. [4]). Instead, users actually get worse after failing the *Product* problems. Our explanation for it is that ρ_P in PFA *ns* model compensates for the absence of user proficiency parameters. The only way for PFA *ns* to distinguish higher achieving students (with fewer errors) from lower achieving students (with more errors) is to resort to error tracking. As a result, ρ_P is reliably negative. Because of that, PFA *ns* is not complex enough.

The PFA model presents quite a radical picture. Both failure rate parameters (ρ_P and ρ_L) are positive and very high, success rate parameter for *LCM* (γ_L) is indistinguishable from zero, while success rate parameter for *Product* (γ_P) is reliably negative. In addition, standard deviation of the user proficiency coefficient θ_i is dubiously high. Our intuition is that such parameter value *reversal* originates from optimizing the early performance using the fixed subject proficiency factors. A user will tend to perform at this fixed base performance level, which, if already high, will need little change across practice (hence a low γ parameter). In contrast, if the fixed base is low, learning must still occur to capture the general increase in performance in the data. Since correct results are infrequent with low initial strength, the learning is forced to be captured by the ρ parameters.

The PFA *re* model is, arguably, the most accurate of the three and we argue that this is mainly due to the fact that user proficiencies are entered as random

---

[2] The actual value is smaller than 1.000 and is equal to 0.999999999999998668.

[3] Significance codes are: . – p≤0.1, * – p≤0.05, ** – p≤0.01, *** – p≤0.001.

Table 4. Cross-validation of PFA models

Model	Data	mean(LL)	mean(BIC)	r_{AE}	A$'$	MSE
PFA ns	train	-0.590	1.196	0.859	0.739	0.201
	test	-0.594	1.243	0.852	0.735	0.203
PFA	train	-0.489	1.553	1.000	0.836	0.161
	test	-0.518	2.940	-0.723	0.544	0.308
PFA re	train	-0.587	1.193	0.984	0.800	0.179
	test	-0.585	1.234	0.567	0.716	0.209

factors. Success/failure rate parameters for *LCM* itemtype are reliably greater than zero. Failure rate parameter ρ_L is almost four times smaller than success rate parameter γ_L. Nevertheless, the model detects some learning from mistakes as well. Success and failure rate parameters for *Product* itemtype are indistinguishable from zero now. A possible explanation for this could be that the model is not complex enough and results reported in Section 5.2 support this hypothesis. Variability of the user proficiency parameters looks reasonably constrained. At this point there seems to be no indication of problems with parsimony.

To investigate the source of PFA's radical parameter values, we performed a cross-validation of the three PFA models discussed in this section. We performed 20 independent runs during which a 5-fold cross-validation was performed. Folds were stratified by users: 80% of the users were randomly chosen for training, 20% of the users were retained for testing. During each of the 20 runs, only one random split was performed. Model fit statistics reported in Table 4 are averaged across these 20 training and testing runs. When computing statistics for PFA and PFAre models, user proficiencies were set to zero value (mean of user proficiencies in Table 3) for the test dataset, since users in test dataset were not seen by these models before.

As we can see from Table 4, PFA no longer has the edge over PFA ns and PFA re. Despite, mean log-likelihoods having smaller absolute values for PFA model, the rest of the metrics put it at disadvantage. Mean BIC for test dataset as compared to training dataset goes up only slightly for PFA ns and PFA re, while for PFA it almost doubles. r_{AE} of PFA model in train dataset drops radically from 1.000 to -0.723 while remaining hight and positive for PFA ns and PFA re. A$'$ for PFA's test dataset drops almost to the random-guessing baseline level of 0.500, while changes from train to test dataset do not shrink A$'$ for PFA ns and PFA re models considerably. Mean squared error for PFA doubles on the test and only goes up a little for PFA ns and PFA re.

As a result, PFA model with fixed-factor user proficiencies seems to be terribly over-fit. At the same time PFA ns and PFA re hold quite well. A relatively worse behavior of PFA re revealed in steeper drops of A$'$, MSE, and especially r_{AE} between train and test sets, can be attributed to the fact that in training set user proficiencies are effectively removed (set to zero). User proficiency agnostic PFA ns performs on the test set performs slightly better. Despite this, PFA ns is our preferred model, for we think that its abilities to reflect learning from errors and account for variability in user proficiencies are very important.

5   Model Complexity and Parsimony

The results of fitting PFA models from the previous sections show that there is room for improvement, at least in terms of complexity. In this section we are going to suggest two extensions to the PFA re model and discuss resulting changes with respect to complexity and parsimony. Building on the results of the previous section, we will only fit models with user proficiencies entered as random factors.

5.1   Extended PFA Models

Our first extension to the PFA re model addresses the definition of itemtypes. In Section 4.2 above, we specified itemtypes according to problem-solving strategies: *Product* and *LCM*. However, another property of the problems - whether it is a story problem or not - was disregarded. As it is known from literature, students might react to story problems differently (cf. [6,5]). Incorporating information of whether a problem is a story problem into the model could potentially benefit it and help reflect the problem semantics more comprehensively. This extended PFA, that we will refer to as ext PFA1 re is virtually identical to the PFA re. The difference is that the itemtypes are now four: *Product story*, *Product non-story*, *LCM story*, and *LCM non-story*.

In a second extended model we are going to use four problem itemtypes types again. In addition, a new term that captures running percent correct on all prior problem itemtypes will be entered. Current attempt will be excluded and on the first attempt the value of the percent correct would be set to 0.5. This model will be referred to as ext PFA2 re and is shown in Equation (3). There, c_i denotes user's percent correct on prior problem attempts, and δ is the model coefficient for it.

$$p_{ij} = \Pr(Y_{ij} = 1|\theta, \beta, \gamma, \rho, \delta) = inv.logit[\, \theta_i + \delta c_i + \sum_j (\beta_j + \gamma_j s_{ij} + \rho_j f_{ij})\,]\ (3)$$

5.2   Model Comparison Results

As we can see from Table 5, both extended models have an edge over PFA in terms of log-likelihood, BIC, A′, and SSR statistics. When compared to each other, extended models are hardly distinguishable from each other, although, according to χ^2 test, ext PFA2 re has an edge ($\chi^2 - 5.394$, p-value-0.020). Let us, however, turn to Table 6 and compare model parameters.

Table 5. Fit statistics of extended PFA models

Model	Par.	LL	BIC	r_{AE}	A′	SSR
PFA re	7	-2123	4296	0.984	0.800	646.908
ext PFA1 re	13	-2030	4149	0.983	0.826	604.700
ext PFA2 re	14	-2016	4152	0.967	0.812	626.857

Table 6. Parameters of extended PFA models. Subscripts P, L, s, and nS refer to *Product*, *LCM*, *story*, and *non-story* itemtypes and their combinations respectively.

	PFA re				ext PFA1 re				ext PFA2 re		
	Par.	Std.Err.	p-value		Par.	Std.Err.	p-value		Par.	Std.Err.	p-value
β_P	0.386	0.082	0.000***	β_{PnS}	0.945	0.086	0.000***		0.687	0.085	0.000***
				β_{PS}	-0.140	0.085	0.000***		-0.382	0.084	0.000***
β_L	-0.800	0.089	0.000***	β_{LnS}	-0.335	0.099	0.000***		-0.572	0.142	0.000***
				β_{LS}	-1.419	0.084	0.000***		-1.642	0.083	0.000***
γ_P	0.046	0.033	0.162	γ_{PnS}	0.004	0.052	0.943		-0.032	0.054	0.549
				γ_{PS}	0.142	0.060	0.017*		0.125	0.059	0.032*
ρ_P	0.075	0.050	0.134	ρ_{PnS}	0.071	0.105	0.500		0.045	0.100	0.656
				ρ_{PS}	0.086	0.065	0.186		0.085	0.053	0.181
γ_L	0.274	0.032	0.000***	γ_{LnS}	0.347	0.050	0.000***		0.321	0.050	0.000***
				γ_{LS}	0.226	0.061	0.000***		0.226	0.060	0.000***
ρ_L	0.081	0.028	0.004**	ρ_{LnS}	0.251	0.052	0.000***		0.244	0.051	0.000***
				ρ_{LS}	-0.058	0.047	0.220		-0.034	0.047	0.461
				δ_i	N/A	N/A	N/A		0.606	0.240	0.012*
θ_i	-0.008	0.547			-0.008	0.780			-0.006	0.660	
	Mean	Std.Dev.			Mean	Std.Dev.			Mean	Std.Dev.	

In Table 6 we see that β itemtype complexity intercepts in extended models are lower for *LCM* itemtype than for a corresponding *Product* itemtype, just like in PFA models (see Table 3). However, *story* property adds additional differentiation. Within *LCM/Product* levels, *story* intercepts are always lower reflecting the fact that, in our dataset, story problems are harder. This phenomenon can be traced to some other pairs of *story* and *non-story* significant parameters (e.g. $\gamma_{LS} < \gamma_{LnS}$ in *ext* PFA1 *re* model). In addition, in both extended models *LCM/non-story* has lower intercept than *Product/story*.

The first extended PFA model (*ext* PFA1 *re*) provides and interesting specification of the PFA model (PFA *re*). The γ_P – success rate parameter for *Product* itemtypes – had no significant effect in PFA. When split in the first extended model, the *story* part of it (γ_{PS}) is now significant. Namely, successes on *Product/story* problems are indicative of student performance. Failure rate parameters for *Product* remain having no detectable effect.

Success rate parameters for *LCM* itemtypes remain positively predictive of student successes. Success rate parameter for *LCM/story* being smaller than for *LCM/non-story*, suggesting that for the *LCM/story* itemtypes being the hardest complexity inhibits the benefit of correct responses. This phenomenon could also be seen in failure rate parameters. This is too reflected in that errors for *LCM/non-story* itemtypes (ρ_{LnS}) have positive effect on learning, while errors for *LCM/story* itemtypes (ρ_{LS}) have no statistically detectable influence. Overall we can conclude that the complexity that the first extended PFA model adds to the PFA model not only improves the fit, but also facilitates better understanding of student learning and problem domain properties.

The second extended PFA model (*ext* PFA2 *re*) that has one additional parameter – users overall problem percent correct – is in our case an example of lack of parsimony. Although the new parameter is a significant predictor of student performance, it does not bring any additional insights into better understanding of student learning, since it is highly correlated with the individual learning rates that come from the same data. All it does is reduce variance of most of the model parameters from first extended model (including random-effect user proficiencies) while significance levels of the model parameters mostly stay the same. Thus, the value of increased complexity of the model *ext* PFA2 *re* as compared to the model *ext* PFA1 *re* is questionable at best.

6   Conclusions

The motto of the statistical modeling, repeated by scores of instructors, is that every model should be checked against a preconceived theory rather than judged solely by model fit statistics. In this paper we tried to trace that statement to a list of possible pitfalls that user modelers could find themselves in if they do the opposite. The list of potential problems is, likely, incomplete, but the ones we mentioned, if avoided, would arguably make researchers' life a lot easier. Namely, models would be more meaningful and interpretable, would generalize better, and would be less prone to over-fitting.

Throughout the paper, we used a user modeling approach called Performance Factors Analysis (PFA) as an method. The advantages and drawbacks of PFA and its variations that we constructed are most likely specific to PFA only. Should other user modeling methods be used, the magnitude of the effects we discussed or the effects themselves could change. Similarly, the nature of outcomes could change too if a different dataset is used, with richer problem attributes' semantics, for example. However, because of the generality of the issues we addressed, following the advice in this paper is likely benefit most efforts to understand data using mathematical modeling.

Acknowledgments. This research was supported by the U.S. Department of Education (IES-NCSER award #R305B070487) and was also made possible with the assistance and funding of Carnegie Learning Inc., the Pittsburgh Science of Learning Center, DataShop team (NSF-SBE award #0354420) and Ronald Zdrojkowski.

References

1. Baayen, R.H., Davidson, D.J., Bates, D.M.: Mixed-effects modeling with crossed random effects for subjects and items. Journal of Memory and Language 59(4), 390–412 (2008)
2. Cen, H., Koedinger, K.R., Junker, B.: Comparing Two IRT Models for Conjunctive Skills. In: Woolf, B.P., Aïmeur, E., Nkambou, R., Lajoie, S. (eds.) ITS 2008. LNCS, vol. 5091, pp. 796–798. Springer, Heidelberg (2008)

3. Clark, H.H.: The language-as-fixed-effect fallacy: A critique of language statistics in psychological research. Journal of Verbal Learning and Verbal Behavior 12, 335–359 (1973)
4. Corbett, A.T., Anderson, J.R.: Locus of feedback control in computer-based tutoring: impact on learning rate, achievement and attitudes. In: Proceedings of CHI 2002, Human Factors in Computing Systems, Seattle, WA, USA, March 31-April 5, pp. 245–252. ACM, New York (2001)
5. Cummins, D.D., Kintsch, W., Reusser, K., Weimer, R.: The role of understanding in solving algebra word problems. Cognitive Psychology 20, 405–438 (1988)
6. Koedinger, K.R., Nathan, M.J.: The real story behind story problems: Effects of representation on quantitative reasoning. Journal of the Learning Sciences 13, 129–164 (2004)
7. van der Linden, W.J., Hambleton, R.K. (eds.): Handbook of Modern Item Response Theory. Springer, New York (1997)
8. Pavlik, P.I., Cen, H., Koedinger, K.R.: Learning factors transfer analysis: Using learning curve analysis to automatically generate domain models. In: Barnes, T., Desmarais, M., Romero, C., Ventura, S. (eds.) Proceedings of The 2nd International Conference on Educational Data Mining, Cordoba, Spain, pp. 121–130 (2009)
9. Pavlik Jr., P.I., Cen, H., Koedinger, K.R.: Performance factors analysis – A new alternative to knowledge tracing. In: Dimitrova, V., Mizoguchi, R. (eds.) Proceedings of the 14th International Conference on Artificial Intelligence in Education, Brighton, England (2009)
10. Pitt, M.A., Myung, I.J., Zhang, S.: Toward a method of selecting among computational models of cognition. Psychological Review 109(3), 472–491 (2002)

Selecting Items of Relevance in Social Network Feeds[*]

Shlomo Berkovsky, Jill Freyne, Stephen Kimani, and Gregory Smith

Tasmanian ICT Centre, CSIRO,
Hobart, Australia
firstname.lastname@csiro.au

Abstract. The success of online social networking systems has revolutionised online sharing and communication, however it has also contributed significantly to the infamous information overload problem. Social Networking systems aggregate network activities into chronologically ordered lists, Network Feeds, as a way of summarising network activity for its users. Unfortunately, these feeds do not take into account the interests of the user viewing them or the relevance of each feed item to the viewer. Consequently individuals often miss out on important updates. This work aims to reduce the burden on users of identifying relevant feed items by exploiting observed user interactions with content and people on the network and facilitates the personalization of network feeds in a manner which promotes relevant activities. We present the results of a large scale live evaluation which shows that personalized feeds are more successful at attracting user attention than non-personalized feeds.

1 Introduction

The quantity and variety of information available online has far exceeded expectations, and yet there seems to be no end to the growth and diversity of emerging online content. A recent contributor to this relentless growth is the social web which has firmly established itself as *the* platform for sharing and consuming user contributed content. While a key focus of social media is the facilitation of communication between friends, social networking systems such as Facebook and Twitter are fast becoming locations where highly valuable content is found. The volume of content produced is overwhelming and the challenge for users is to keep up with a ferociously fast changing environment and locate items of interest.

Not all relationships on social networks (SN) are equivalent and not all shared content is interesting to all users. Consider the dimensions of online social relationships; some are family based, some involve colleagues or professional connections, some reflect real world friendships and others exist exclusively online. It is natural that the strength and nature of an online relationship will influence the interest that one user has in the activities of another. In a similar vein, some users will have a preference for particular content types over others. Facebook's attempts to keep users informed of the activities of others is to summarise *all* of the performed activities of *all* of an

---

[*] This research is jointly funded by the Australian Government through the Intelligent Island Program and CSIRO. The Intelligent Island Program is administered by the Tasmanian Department of Economic Development, Tourism and the Arts. The authors thank Nilufar Baghaei, Emily Brindal, and Mac Coombe for their contribution to this work.

Joseph A. Konstan et al. (Eds.): UMAP 2011, LNCS 6787, pp. 329–334, 2011.

individuals friends in a chronologically ordered *Network Feed*. This could be an effective tool if it were not for the average users' 130 friends and their 90 pieces of contributed content per month, but in the current circumstances this list is ineffective communication medium.

This work reports on an approach to personalizing the items in a user's Network Feed in order to promote relevant updates. The personalization technique presented exploits learned user-to-user tie strength and user-to-action activity strength indicators in order to judge the relevance of each item in a network feed [2]. We report on an evaluation of our model as part of a large-scale live user study of an experimental eHealth portal. We logged all user interaction with the portal and analysed the uptake of the feeds. Initial results show that the uptake of the personalized feeds is higher than of the non-personalized ones and call for future work on the impact of feed ranking and accuracy of the relevance scoring mechanism.

2   Related Work

The sheer growth of SN contributes highly to the information overload problem, which can be only partially addressed by simple activity feeds. Hence, we have seen a move toward the development of predictive models which examine the relationships between individuals and other users, as well as content types on a social network. For the most part work in this area has concentrated on determining the predictive models rather than exploiting these models to benefit users.

Gilbert and Karaholios developed a *tie strength* model [3], which classified the strength of the relationship between users as weak or strong based on 74 Facebook factors, divided into seven categories: intensity, intimacy, duration, reciprocal services, structure, emotion, and social distance. Paek *et al.* used SVM-based classifiers to elicit a set of most predictive features and then used these features to compute the importance of activities included in Facebook news feeds [5]. The predictive models were accurate in both cases, but the factors included were specific to the type of social networking systems on which they were generated. The evaluations were conducted with small cohorts of users whereas our work reports on a large-scale evaluation.

Wu *et al.* developed a model for computing professional, personal, and overall closeness of users of an enterprise SN [6]. 53 observable SN factors were derived and divided into five categories: user factors, subject user factors, direct interaction factors, mutual connection factors, and enterprise factors. Freyne *et al.* developed a system for recommending SN activities of an interest based on long- and short-term models of content viewed and activities performed by users [2], they simulated feed personalization using offline logs, whereas our work reports on a live user evaluation.

3   Activity Relevance Score Computation

Network activity feeds present a target user T with a list of activities performed by other users of the SN. Each feed item, I, consists of at least two components: the user u_x who performed the activity and the action a_z that was performed. Typically, both the user and action are hyperlinked, facilitating access to the profile of the user who performed the activity and the content viewed/contributed by the activity (see Figure 1). The overall relevance score of the feed activity $S(T,I)$ is computed as a weighted combination of the relevance scores of the two components:

$$S(T,I)=w_1S_U(T,u_x)+w_2S_A(T,a_z)$$

where w_1 and w_2 denote the relative weights of the components. In our case we assign $w_1=0.8$ and $w_2=0.2$, to emphasise activities performed by relevant users. In the rest of this section we elaborate on the computation of user-to-user $S_U(T,u_x)$ and user-to-action $S_A(T,a_z)$ relevance scores.

Fig. 1. Example activity feed

For the computation of the user-to-user friendship score $S_U(T,u_x)$, we adopt the weighting model developed by Wu *et al.* in [6]. The enterprise factors are inapplicable to our eHealth portal and, therefore, we use four categories of factors:

- User factors (UF) – online behaviour and activity of the target user T.
- Subject user factors (SUF) – online behaviour and activity of the subject user u_x.
- Direct interaction factors (DIF) – direct communication between T and u_x.
- Mutual connection factors (MCF) – communication between T and $\{u_y\}$ and between u_x and $\{u_y\}$, where $\{u_y\}$ is the set of common friends of T and u_x.

The user-to-user relevance score $S_U(T,u_x)$ is computed as a weighted combination of the scores of the four categories:

$$S_U(T,u_x)=w_3S_{UF}(T,u_x)+w_4S_{SUF}(T,u_x)+w_5S_{DIF}(T,u_x)+w_6S_{MCF}(T,u_x)$$

Since the features of the system presented in [6] were similar to those provided by our eHealth portal, we assign to the four categories relative weights proportional to the weights derived there: $w_3=0.178$, $w_4=0.079$, $w_5=0.610$, and $w_6=0.133$.

Category scores $S_{UF}(T,u_x)$, $S_{SUF}(T,u_x)$, $S_{DIF}(T,u_x)$, and $S_{MCF}(T,u_x)$ are computed as a weighted combination of the scores of the factors in each category. Overall, we derived 32 factors for the UF and SUF categories and 28 factors for the DIF and MCF categories. The score for each factor is computed based on the observed user interaction with the SN and normalised to the [0,1] range. Table 1 presents the four factors with the highest relative weights within each category. Note that SUF factors are identical to UF, but the score is computed for u_x rather than for T. Similarly, MCF factors are identical to DIF, but the score is averaged across all mutual friends $\{u_y\}$.

The frequency of performing actions is considered the main indicator of user-to-action relevance. We denote by $f(T,a_z)$ the frequency of user T performing action a_z, by $f(T)$ the average frequency of all actions performed by T, by $f(a_z)$ the average frequency of all users performing a_z, and by $f()$ the average frequency of all actions performed by all users. The user-to-action relevance score $S_A(T,a_z)$ is computed by

$$S_A(T,a_z) = \frac{f(T,a_z)}{f(T)} / \frac{f(a_z)}{f()}$$

Hence, we first computed the relative relevance of a_z for T and then normalised it by the relevance of a_z for all users.

Table 1. User-to-user relevance factors and their weights

UF		SUF		DIF		MCF	
factor	weight	factor	weight	factor	weight	factor	weight
# forum posts added by T	0.02031	# forum posts added by u_x	0.00899	Has T friended u_x	0.07627	Has T friended $\{u_y\}$	0.01656
# posts in T's blog	0.02031	# posts in u_x's blog	0.00899	# days T interacted with u_x	0.04576	Average # days T interacted with $\{u_y\}$	0.00994
# T's comments in blogs of others	0.01015	# u_x's comments in blogs of others	0.00449	# T's posts in u_x's blog	0.03814	Average # posts in members of $\{u_y\}$'s blog	0.00828
# images in T's profile	0.01015	# images in u_x's profile	0.00449	# mutual friends of T and u_x	0.02670	Average # mutual friends of T and members of $\{u_y\}$	0.00580

4 Evaluation

We evaluated the feed relevance prediction computation in a live study involving users of an experimental eHealth portal. 2,813 users participated in the study for a period of 12 weeks, from September to November of 2010. The users were randomly divided into several groups, such that about half of them were exposed to personalized and half to non-personalized activity feeds. No personalized feeds were provided during the first week, due to the bootstrapping phase required to determine the relevance scores. From week 2 onwards, users in the personalized groups were exposed to personalized feeds, as presented in Section 3. Users in the non-personalized groups were presented with activities ordered in reverse chronological order. User-to-user and user-to-action scores were calculated offline nightly. Figure 1 depicts the feed interface. By default, the feeds presented 20 activities (with the highest relevance score or most recent timestamp), but users could adjust the number of items.

The results below address our initial findings that focus on the uptake of the feeds, as reflected by the observed click-through rate. Table 2 summarises the number of users, sessions, sessions with feed clicks, feed clicks, and two computed click-through rates (CTR_u – number of clicks per user and CTR_s – number of clicks per session with feed clicks), as observed for both groups from week 2 onwards. As can be seen, the uptake of the personalized feeds was higher than that of the non-personalized feeds.

This is supported by observing the CTR_s score over time. Figure 2 depicts the average CTR_s in both groups for the entire duration of the study. Only days, for which four clicks or more were logged for each group, are included. Due to the variability of the CTR_s values (spikes of activity were originated by email reminders sent to all users and by bursts of SN activity that affected both groups of users similarly), we plotted also the logarithmic regression curves. The uptake curve of the personalized feeds was steadily superior to the curve of the non-personalized feeds. The difference between the groups was statistically significant, $p=0.0195$. This indicates that the activities in the personalized feeds were deemed more relevant than in the non-personalized ones.

Table 2. Overall uptake of the feeds

	users	sessions	sessions$_{cl}$	clicks	CTR$_u$	CTR$_s$
personalized	1,397	12,193	390	901	0.6450	2.3103
non-personalized	1,416	11,386	382	805	0.5685	2.1073

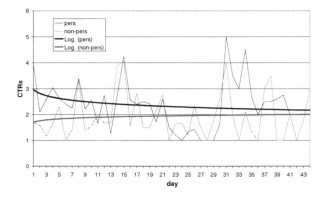

Fig. 2. Feed click-through rates over time

We also computed the number of sessions that included multiple feed clicks. Table 3 summarises the number of feed clicks in a session and the number of sessions that included this (or higher) number of clicks, as was observed for both groups. As can be seen, the number of sessions with multiple clicks in the personalized group was higher than in the non-personalized group. The difference between the groups, however, was not statistically significant. This strengthens our conclusion that the activities in the personalized feeds were deemed more relevant than in the non-personalized feeds.

Table 3. Multiple feed clicks in a session

number of clicks	2	3	4	5	6	7	8	9	10	11	12	13	14	15
personalized	154	87	55	45	33	30	25	20	16	15	9	6	4	4
non-personalized	157	82	53	36	20	14	11	10	7	5	4	2	2	1

Finally, we computed the user-to-user, user-to-action, and overall relevance scores of the clicked activities, as evolved for the entire duration of the study. Figure 3 depicts the average relevance scores of the clicked feeds items, again only for days with four or more clicks. Once again, we plotted the logarithmic regression curves due to the variability of the relevance scores.

The user-to-action relevance scores stabilise rapidly and remain stable for the entire duration of the study. However, the user-to-user relevance scores steadily increase over time and, as a result, overall relevance scores, which are dominated by the user-to-user relevance, also increase over time. This is in line with earlier personalization research findings, which indicate that the accuracy of personalization improves as the amount of information available about the users increases.

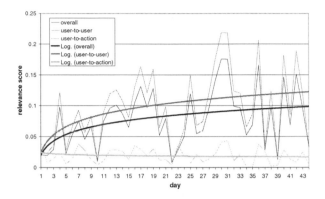

Fig. 3. User-to-user, user-to-action, and overall relevance scores over time

5 Conclusions and Future Work

This work was motivated by the growing volume of information included in SN activity feeds. We developed a personalized model for predicting the relevance score of each activity in the feed and re-ranking the feed accordingly. The model was evaluated with a large set of users for an extensive period of time. Initial analyses of the results showed that the uptake of the personalized feeds is higher than of the nonpersonalized ones and that the relevance of the clicked activities increases over time.

In future analyses, we plan to address the impact of ranking on the uptake of activities. High-ranked activities are normally clicked more frequently than low-ranked ones and we will revise our model to factor out the effect of ranking. Also, we will revisit the weighting model adopted from [6], and will derive a new model appropriate for the eHealth application domain in general and our portal in particular.

References

1. Facebook Statistics,
   http://www.facebook.com/press/info.php?statistics
   (accessed January 2011)
2. Freyne, J., Berkovsky, S., Daly, E.M., Geyer, W.: Social Networking Feeds: Recommending Items of Interest. In: Proceedings of RecSys, Barcelona (2010)
3. Gilbert, E., Karahalios, K.: Predicting Tie Strength with Social Media. In: Proceedings of CHI, Boston (2009)
4. Noakes, M., Clifton, P.: The CSIRO Total Wellbeing Diet. Penguin Publ. (2005)
5. Paek, T., Gamon, M., Counts, S., Chickering, D.M., Dhesi, A.: Predicting the Importance of Newsfeed Posts and Social Network Friends. In: Proceedings of AAAI, Atlanta (2010)
6. Wu, A., DiMicco, J.M., Millen, D.R.: Detecting Professional versus Personal Closeness using an Enterprise Social Network Site. In: Proceedings of CHI, Atlanta (2010)

Enhancing Traditional Local Search Recommendations with Context-Awareness

Claudio Biancalana, Andrea Flamini, Fabio Gasparetti, Alessandro Micarelli,
Samuele Millevolte, and Giuseppe Sansonetti

Artificial Intelligence Laboratory, ROMA TRE University,
Via della Vasca Navale, 79, 00146 Rome, Italy
http://ai-lab-02.dia.uniroma3.it/groups/aigroup

Abstract. Traditional desktop search paradigm often does not fit mobile contexts. Common mobile devices provide impoverished mechanisms for text entry and small screens are able to offer only a limited set of options, therefore the users are not usually able to specify their needs. On a different note, mobile technologies have become part of the everyday life as shown by the estimate of one billion of mobile broadband subscriptions in 2011.

This paper describes an approach to make context-aware mobile interaction available in scenarios where users might be looking for categories of points of interest (POIs), such as cultural events and restaurants, through remote location-based services. Empirical evaluations shows how rich representations of user contexts has the chance to increase the relevance of the retrieved POIs.

Keywords: context-awareness, local search, location-based services, mobile devices.

1 Introduction

Internet location-based services such as Yelp (www.yelp.com), Where.com (where.com), Zagat (www.zagat.com) or Google Maps (maps.google.com) are information services accessible with mobile devices that utilize the ability to make use of the current location, acquired by common embedded GPS units, to answer requests about businesses, general information or objects of interest. With 486 million of estimated location-based services users by 2012[1], context awareness makes LBS applications very interesting compared to other mobile technologies. According to the Kelsey Group[2], local search spending forecasts for 2008-2013 are estimated in 130.5% annual growth rate while incomes from local search will surpass 50% of mobile search revenues.

Context is any information that can be used to characterize the current situation of the user environment (1). The whole user context cannot be easily

---

[1] www.emarketer.com/Report.aspx?code=emarketer_2000510
[2] www.kelseygroup.com/press/pr090224.asp

Joseph A. Konstan et al. (Eds.): UMAP 2011, LNCS 6787, pp. 335–340, 2011.

identified, analyzed and used during human-computer interaction. Current user needs and goals are complex and dynamic factors to represent, therefore the location becomes the only element of the context that can be easily measured more or less accurately depending on the positioning system. Even though there are several additional factors that potentially affect the interaction with the location-based service and the ranking of search results, a few prototypes provide a better representation of the user context and evaluate the potential benefits in real scenarios.

The paper introduces a neural network approach to make context-aware mobile interaction available in LBSs. Users are able to obtain POIs related to the current context in traditional map-based user interfaces. In the following section (Sect. 3) we describe the proposed approach, while results of the experimental evaluation is provided in Section 4.

2   Related Work

To the best of our knowledge, there are very few attempts to investigate the integration of context-awareness technologies in location-based services for mobile environments. SmartCon (2) shares some ideas with the proposed approach, namely, the feature-based representations of POIs and neural networks to match them with the current user context. The authors do not take into consideration a traditional scenario where mobile phones interact with web LBSs but they consider customized mobile services and sensors in health monitoring context. The social pervasive recommender named SPETA (5) uses vector representations to draw distances between POIs and user preferences. It collects features of frequently visited POIs and use them for user profiling. Console *et al.* (4) devise and architecture for providing personalized services on-board vehicles. The recommendation is performed according with stereotypes of users. *CareDB* (8) follows a similar approach, where a so-called query rewriting module translates preferences and context into db query operators. Unfortunately, both of the approaches do not include any evaluation in real mobile scenarios.

3   Context-Aware Recommendation for LBS

The proposed context-aware recommendation engine is based on artificial neural networks. In this case, context-aware recommendation gives high weights to objects which are the most relevant to the given context. The highly ranked results are shown highlighted on the map-based user interface (see for example Fig. 3). The advantage of this approach is to employ machine learning algorithms to automate the process of determining the connections between the contextual factors and features related to the available POIs. Domain experts do not have to write long hand-coded rules or triggers used to specify how context-aware influence the selection criteria of POIs.

Almost any information available at the time of an interaction can be seen as context information. Examples are spatial and temporal information, e.g.,

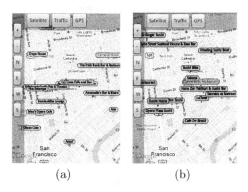

(a)   (b)

Fig. 1. A snapshot of the Google Maps GUI during a search for restaurants (a) and restaurants suggested by our recommender system where darker colors are associated to the most important results (b) (©2011 Google - Map data ©2011 Google)

current location, orientation and current time. Further factors of these kinds can be induced by querying public information services, such as weather, traffic reports and forecast services, or inferred by analyzing the obtained information, e.g., speed and day of the week.

As the user activity is crucial for many applications, context awareness has been lately focused more deeply in the activity recognition field (3). An activity is a sequence of actions conducted by human beings aimed at achieving a certain goal. Along with location and time, the activity is account to be one of the most important contextual factors in understanding mobile user needs (9).

We employ a richer contextual description that besides traditional physical and environmental factors focuses also on the classification of basic human activities or scenarios. In spite of the obvious relevance of this information for providing tailored results, location-based services for mobile devices based on activity recognition approaches have still to be deeply investigated. One of the reasons is undoubtably the complexity of representations and analysis of multiple specific sensor data in the recommendation task.

Even though there are accurate algorithms to estimate the user's physical activity or his social environment (e.g., sitting, standing, walking, in a restaurant or lecture), most of them analyze data collected by wearable sensors such as accelerometers or microphones. One requirement of the system is traditional smart phones as standard devices.

For our purpose, we limited our activity representation to coarse locations and user situations, namely: *1.* working, when the user is engaged in work or he is in the neighborhood of the office; *2.* traveling, when the user is moving between two places; *3.* other, that is, unknown activities or known activities with likelihoods under a given threshold.

The approach proposed by Liao *et al.* (7) is based on Relational Markov Networks (RMN) and raw location data collected by embedded GPS units of mobile devices to build personal maps and associate one of the above-mentioned activities to the current context. The rest of factors included in the context representation correspond to information about the weather and the time of the day. We can summarize them as follow:

- *Current activity*: (working, traveling, other)
- *Time of the day*: (morning, lunch, afternoon, dinner, night)
- *Mode of transportation*: (foot, car)
- *Weather*: (bad, good)

Pre-processing of the raw data having the characteristic of consecutive data, for instance, time and speed, is done in order to abstract them into a set of concepts, for example, *bad weather* or *traveling by car*.

In order to match the current context with the POIs of a LBS, we first use the location as query to retrieve the list of POIs in the user neighbor. The user is able to select one of the available categories, such as restaurant, night club and event. For each category of objects there is a set of features that characterizes some of the relevant information that has the chance to alter the recommendation ranking. For the sake of argument, in the case of restaurant recommendation, we queried Yelp services via its API obtaining 10 features. The available boolean features are: *restaurants with a private parking, fastfood/restaurant, dress code, take-out, waiter service, outdoor sits, take reservation, breakfast, lunch, dinner*. Two more features, namely, the *distance* and *time before closing*, are drawn assessing the two contextual features *user location* and *current time* along with the user location and opening hours of the restaurant.

The contextual features and the above-mentioned features of POIs are given as input to the neural network. The output layer is composed of 5 nodes representing how much close a given restaurant is to the current user context. Basically, the first node is associated to a *not interesting* recommendation and the fifth to *very interesting*. A supervised learning algorithm based on gradient descent and 10-fold cross-validation trains the neural network organized with a feed-forward multi-layer perceptron with one hidden layer.

As for training data used during the unsupervised learning, we collected the user feedback on a set of restaurants from a group of users according with random combinations of contextual factors.

4   Evaluation

We chose restaurants as popular points of interest users usually look for on mobile devices. A group of 15 college students familiar with mobile interfaces were asked to rate three lists of 20 restaurants, each list built querying the Yelp LBS. The three lists are related to restaurants in the neighbor of one specific location (i.e., an intersection road) in three U.S. cities respectively. The same evaluation can be performed with different LBSs so long as they provide a developer interface for obtaining POIs and related features given a location.

Table 1. Comparison of recommendation algorithms in term of NDCG@n

	$NDCG@1$	$NDCG@5$	$NDCG@10$
$Distance$	$0,097$	$0,269$	$0,295$
$YelpLBS$	$0,079$	$0,309$	$0,252$
$Context - Aware$	$0,324$	$0,564$	$0,737$

Each tester were asked to rate the three lists order according with three different contexts: *1.* You are going by car in the evening, you want to have dinner and weather is good, restaurants will be open for at least two hours; *2.* You are going on foot in the evening, you want to have dinner and weather is good, restaurants will be open for at least two hours; *3.* You are going on foot, you want to have lunch, and weather is good, you are just out of your place of work/study or in its surroundings, restaurants will be closed in 30 minutes, one hour. A preliminary analysis of mobile interactions with a popular LBS performed by some testers let us choose these three common contexts that represent quite different situations.

The order of restaurants to rate were previously randomized. The testers were free to browse Internet to acquire additional information useful for the task, e.g., price, photos, reviews. Of course, there is no overlap between contexts used for training and testing.

The rates are in Likert scale: *non-significant, significant, very significant.* The performance is evaluated by means of the Discounted Cumulative Gain NDCG of the top n items NDCG@n (6), a popular measure for search engine algorithms. The limit of the top n is justified since it is unlikely that mobile users will scroll long lists of retrieved items.

A comparison with a location-based ranking (Distance) and with the rank provided by Yelp, which likely balances distance and number positive reviews, shows that the gain for context-aware ranker is the largest. In other words, the recommendations provided by the system get closer to the ideal ranking proposed by users. All results were tested for statistical significance by using a paired 2-tailed t-test with p-value < 0.05.

5   Conclusions

We have presented a recommender system for context-aware mobile services. The system infers contextual data to provide users with personalized recommendations about POIs in the surroundings of the current position. The results of an evaluation performed on users show that the proposed approach provides significant benefits in terms of effectiveness of recommendations in comparison with traditional location-based services. In other words, the highly ranked results are the ones judged more appropriate for the current context. We are currently investigating the utility of information extraction and social network analysis to exploit networks of relationships in the recommendation process.

References

1. Adomavicius, G., Tuzhilin, A.: Context-aware recommender systems. In: Proceedings of the 2008 ACM Conference on Recommender Systems, RecSys 2008, pp. 335–336. ACM, New York (2008), http://doi.acm.org/10.1145/1454008.1454068
2. Al-Masri, E., Mahmoud, Q.H.: Smartcon: a context aware service discovery and selection mechanism using artificial neural networks. Int. J. Intell. Syst. Technol. Appl. 6, 144–156 (2009), http://portal.acm.org/citation.cfm?id=1497600.1497609
3. Bettini, C., Brdiczka, O., Henricksen, K., Indulska, J., Nicklas, D., Ranganathan, A., Riboni, D.: A survey of context modelling and reasoning techniques. Pervasive Mob. Comput. 6(2), 161–180 (2010)
4. Console, L., Torre, I., Lombardi, I., Gioria, S., Surano, V.: Personalized and adaptive services on board a car: An application for tourist information. J. Intell. Inf. Syst. 21, 249–284 (2003), http://portal.acm.org/citation.cfm?id=939823.940055
5. García-Crespo, A., Chamizo, J., Rivera, I., Mencke, M., Colomo-Palacios, R., Gómez-Berbís, J.M.: Speta: Social pervasive e-tourism advisor. Telemat. Inf. 26, 306–315 (2009), http://portal.acm.org/citation.cfm?id=1514442.1514676
6. Järvelin, K., Kekäläinen, J.: Cumulated gain-based evaluation of ir techniques. ACM Trans. Inf. Syst. 20, 422–446 (2002), http://doi.acm.org/10.1145/582415.582418
7. Liao, L., Patterson, D.J., Fox, D., Kautz, H.: Building personal maps from gps data. Annals of the New York Academy of Sciences 1093(1), 249–265 (2005)
8. Mokbel, M.F., Levandoski, J.J.: Toward context and preference-aware location-based services. In: MobiDE 2009: Proceedings of the Eighth ACM International Workshop on Data Engineering for Wireless and Mobile Access, pp. 25–32. ACM, New York (2009)
9. Sohn, T., Li, K.A., Griswold, W.G., Hollan, J.D.: A diary study of mobile information needs. In: CIII 2008: Proceeding of the Twenty-sixth Annual SIGCHI Conference on Human Factors in Computing Systems, pp. 433–442. ACM, New York (2008)

Gender Differences and the Value of Choice in Intelligent Tutoring Systems

Derek T. Green[1], Thomas J. Walsh[1],
Paul R. Cohen[1], Carole R. Beal[1], and Yu-Han Chang[2]

[1] Department of Computer Science, The University of Arizona
P.O. Box 210077, Tucson, AZ 85721-0077
[2] University of Southern California, Information Sciences Institute
4676 Admiralty Way, #909, Marina del Rey, CA 90292
dtgreen@email.arizona.edu

Abstract. Students interacted with an intelligent tutoring system to learn grammatical rules for an artificial language. Six tutoring policies were explored. One, based on a Dynamic Bayes' Network model of skills, was learned from the performance of previous students. Overall, this policy and other intelligent policies outperformed random policies. Some policies allowed students to choose one of three problems to work on, while others presented a single problem at each iteration. The benefit of choice was not apparent in group statistics; however, there was a strong interaction with gender. Overall, women learned less than men, but they learned different amounts in the choice and no choice conditions, whereas men seemed unaffected by choice. We explore reasons for these interactions between gender, choice and learning.

Problem-oriented Intelligent Tutoring Systems (ITS) teach a subject by presenting problems to students to solve (e.g., [10,4]). One form of intelligence in these systems is the *policies* that decide which problem(s) to present. Generally speaking, subjects comprise skills that should be acquired in a strict or partial order, as some skills will depend on others. Good policies will respect these dependencies, and students who work under good policies will learn more than those who don't. This paper discusses two aspects of policies: whether they offer students choices, and whether they are constructed by hand or learned from data. Our research is primarily concerned with learning policies, and our experiments have been designed primarily to test the efficacy of learned strategies. However, the bulk of this paper is devoted to some surprising and consequential empirical results: Giving students choices has an effect mediated by gender, and when our ITS learned a strategy, it helped men more than women.

Section 1 describes the task domain for which the ITS was developed. Section 2 sketches the ITS and summarizes six policies for teaching the domain content, including one learned automatically from observations of students using the ITS. Sections 3 and 4 describe our experiment design and results.

Joseph A. Konstan et al. (Eds.): UMAP 2011, LNCS 6787, pp. 341–346, 2011.

1   The Task Domain

An artificial domain was used to allow us to evaluate tutoring policies without the confounds associated with prior knowledge and expectations of familiar domains. Our interest is skill learning in general and this domain focused on learning the syntax and semantics of an artificial language. We plan to implement this work on a larger scale in real world tutoring domains (not necessarily language related) after verifying that we are able to improve skill learning by planning.

The language used contains few words, but these can be ordered to construct phrases with very different meanings. There are three types of words: nouns, color modifiers, and quantity modifiers. Three nouns (N) refer to shapes: "*bap*" = □, "*muq*" = △, "*fid*" = ○. Three color modifiers (C) refer to colors (e.g. "*duq*" = orange) and are used as postfix operators on nouns (e.g. "*muq duq*" = ▲).

The three quantity modifiers (Q) are polysemous, having the following meanings: "*oy*" = {small, one, light}, "*op*" = {large, many, very}, "*ez*" = {not, none, non}. The specific meaning of a Q-modifier depends on context. As a prefix to an N (i.e. QN) it signifies the size of the noun, (e.g. "*op muq*" = ▲, "a large triangle"). As a suffix to an N (i.e. NQ), it signifies the cardinality of the N, (e.g. "*muq oy*" = ▲, "one triangle"). As a suffix to a C (i.e. CQ), it signifies the intensity or saturation of the C (e.g. "*muq duq op*" = ▲, "a very orange triangle"). Multiple Q-modifiers can be used in a single phrase as in "*op muq op nef oy*" = ▲ ▲ ▲, or "many large light-green triangles".

The skills in the domain are the abilities to construct or understand 14 legal syntactic forms of phrases up to length 5. The skill set is

$$\mathcal{S} = N, C, NC, QN, NQ, CQ, QNQ, QNC, NQC, NCQ,$$
$$QNQC, QNCQ, NQCQ, QNQCQ.$$

The *dependency structure* for this skill set links every skill s of length l to any skill of length $l - 1$ that is a substring of s.

2   The ITS and Its Policies

We built an ITS called BLAST to teach the language described in Sect. 1. BLAST presents students with *training problems* or *hints*. Training problems are multiple-choice items with four choices in which students must either choose the phrase in the language that describes a given scene (e.g. three triangles), or choose the scene that matches a given phrase. Roughly 10% of BLAST's actions are hints.

Since one of our research questions concerns the pedagogical value of choice, every student was either in a *NoChoice* condition in which BLAST presents one problem at a time, or a *Choice* condition where it presents a menu of three problems and allows the student to choose which one to solve. The skill of each problem (or hint) is selected according to a *policy*.

Random and Expert Policies. Two *Random* policies served as control conditions. Each selects a skill from S at random and presents either one (*NoChoice*) or three (*Choice*) problems of that skill to the student.

Three *Expert* policies were constructed. Each relies on the dependencies between skills in S and on the student's estimated *mastery* of the skills. Briefly, the expert policies don't introduce "the next skill" until the student's problem-solving performance suggests that prerequisite skills have been mastered. The *ExpertNoChoice* policy selects a single problem and presents it to the student. The *ExpertChoice* policy selects three problems at the same skill level and lets the student decide which to solve. The *ExpertChoiceZPD* policy selects two problems at the "current" skill level and one at a higher skill level (this is not indicated to the student) and lets the student decide which to solve.

Learned Policy. We trained 75 students using these five policies and applied a machine learning algorithm to learn a new policy. The algorithm is described in detail in [8]. Very briefly, it learns which skill to present next given the student's mastery of other skills. The state of the student is encoded as a Dynamic Bayes' Network [7], so the policy is called the *DBN* policy. Whereas the expert policies hard-code the order in which skills should be presented, the *DBN* policy orders skills to optimize skill mastery. Similar ideas have been proposed in [1,3,5,6].

3 Experiment Protocol

Participants spent roughly one hour working with BLAST. On average, students were able to solve 133 *training problems* during this time. Students were given the correct answer after each training problem. A single test, comprising 20 multiple choice problems that tested most of the skills in S, was administered at four points during the hour, one very close to the beginning of the hour, one at the end, with the others equally spaced between. Students received no feedback on their answers to test questions. We refer to the first and last tests as *pretest* and *posttest*. Each test got a fractional score between 0/20 and 20/20. We define *improvement* to be the difference between the posttest and pretest scores.

As noted, 75 students (50 men and 25 women) participated in five experimental conditions to collect training data for the *DBN* policy. All were recruited from the Psychology pool at the University of Arizona. An additional 35 students were recruited and distributed between the *DBN* and other expert conditions.

4 Results

Overall, students improve between pretest and posttest in *Expert* and *DBN* conditions but not in *Random* conditions. Mean scores on each of the four tests are plotted by condition in Fig. 1 (left). In the *Random* conditions, student performance on the tests hovers around chance (0.25) and does not improve. This establishes that the policy for presenting problems matters: with a random policy, students don't learn; if it is an expert or DBN policy, they do.

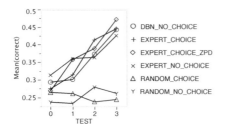

	Female	Male	Mean
DBN	0.046	0.328	0.15
Expert No Choice	0.044	0.19	0.125
Expert Choice	0.145	0.20	0.171
Expert Choice ZPD	0.155	0.25	0.202
Mean	0.099	0.236	

Fig. 1. Mean test scores by condition and Mean improvement by condition and gender

Comparing DBN with Other Expert Policies. The amount and rate at which students learn in the *Expert* and *DBN* conditions do not seem very different. Students in these conditions start at roughly chance performance on the first test and are able to answer roughly 45% of the questions correctly on the final test. A two-way analysis of variance comparing *DBN* with the other *Expert* policies crossed with test number shows a main effect of test number ($p < .0001$) and no main effect of *DBN* or an interaction effect. That is, students improve from one test to the next but whether they work under the *DBN* policy or any other expert policy makes no difference to their improvement.

So is the *DBN* policy as good as the other expert policies? This is not a hypothesis testing question, as hypothesis testing can only show that the policies are unlikely to be equal. It is, however, a confidence interval question: We will show that the confidence interval around the difference between the policies is small and contains zero.

Let $\chi_{s,q,t} = [0, 1]$ represent whether student s answered question q on test t correctly (1) or incorrectly (0). Let $\pi_{\bullet,q,t} = (\Sigma_s \chi_{s,q,t})/N$ be the mean number of correct answers, averaged over N students, for question q on test t, and let $\iota_q = \pi_{\bullet,q,3} - \pi_{\bullet,q,0}$ be the mean *improvement* on question q between the first test (test 0) and the last (test 3). The value of ι_q is quite variable because it is harder to improve on some test questions than on others. The average value of ι_q is 15% for *DBN* students and 16% for the other expert policies. The confidence interval around ι_q is $[-0.06, 0.09]$. This means that, by question, the difference in improvement under the *DBN* and expert policies ranges from -6% to 9% with 95% confidence. In fact, by comparing mean squares in a two-way analysis of variance, we estimate that the test questions themselves have roughly ten times the influence on the width of the confidence interval around ι_q than the policy.

In sum, the *DBN* policy is indistinguishable from the other expert policies, at least with respect to improvement from the pretest to the posttest. This result establishes that a problem-oriented ITS, which repeatedly decides which skill to present to a student, can learn how to teach.

Differences due to Choice and Gender. *Choice* and *gender* interact in unexpected ways to influence how much students learn. Figure 1 (right) shows the mean improvement by condition and gender. Overall, women improve significantly less than men ($p < 0.0045$, two-tailed t test), and women do better in the two *Choice* conditions than in the two *NoChoice* conditions ($p < 0.052$, two-tailed t test). A two-way analysis of variance with *Choice* and *Gender* as factors shows a strong main effect of *Gender* ($p < 0.003$), no effect of *Choice*, and a marginal interaction effect ($p < 0.18$).

These results show that there is no simple answer to how choice affects learning nor to how the DBN strategy performs relative to the other policies. Women are clearly at a disadvantage with the *NoChoice* policies, especially the *DBN* policy. Looking at men only, there is little effect of *Choice*, and the *DBN* policy outperforms the others (though the difference is not statistically significant, due to the small samples). For women, choice matters, though the *DBN* policy is no better or worse than the *ExpertNoChoice* policy.

We can only speculate about the reasons for these gender differences, and our explanations are post-hoc and await prospective experiments to test them. We built regression models to predict improvement and found that factors in these models had different effects depending on gender. The five factors in the models were:

TotalTime   The total number of seconds spent in the experiment
NumProblems The number of training problems done by a student
Test0Score   The score on the first test
Success   The fraction of training problems solved correctly
Test3Time   The number of seconds spent on test 3

We built saturated regression models for men and women, then selectively deleted factors, observing the resulting changes in R^2, the percentage of variance in improvement accounted for by the models. The saturated models had R^2 of 41% and 54% for women and men, respectively. For men, removing *NumProblems* reduced R^2 by one half, to 27.6%, but for women, removing *NumProblems* had a negligible effect ($R^2 = 40\%$). For men, removing *Test0Score* had a small effect ($R^2 = 46\%$), but for women, removing this factor had a large effect ($R^2 = 27\%$). Removing *Success* had a large effect for women and men, and removing *TotalTime* had essentially no effect at all. Apparently, where a woman starts out (*Test0Score*) influences her improvement but the number of problems she solves has little effect, whereas the opposite is true of men.

The story is similar for models that predict *Success* instead of improvement. For women, the most important factor is the *Test0Score* and *NumProblems* has little effect, whereas this pattern is reversed for men. Yet, we are not quite ready to say that our tutoring policies do not work for women. One intriguing result is that the *Choice* policies on which women did the best are also those on which all students, men and women, spent the most time per problem.

Gender differences in performance under ITS tutelage have been previously noted. Differences in responses to different forms of instruction were shown in [2,9]). We note that women and men select problem types in different proportions in our system; however, this difference is not predictive of test performance.

Perhaps women fared poorly in the *NoChoice* conditions because they felt rushed – women and men both did 138 problems in the *NoChoice* conditions compared with 113 and 105 problems, respectively, in the *Choice* conditions. A three-way analysis of variance with factors *Choice*, *Gender*, and whether the student solved more than 110 training problems yields a marginal three-way interaction effect ($p < 0.06$), suggesting that all three factors contribute to the story of how a tutoring system helps students learn.

4.1 Discussion

The promise of ITSs is that they will adapt and modify themselves, learning from data provided by previous students, always improving the quality of individualized instruction they give to each student. This is the first study, that we are aware of, to show that ITSs can learn to do the right thing for some students and the wrong thing for others. Perhaps it is not a coincidence that the *DBN* policy, which was trained with data from 50 men and 25 women, helped men more than women. And while it is true that women improved less under all policies than men, this difference was amplified, not diminished, by the learned policy. Our next experiments will prospectively train separate policies on data for women and men, and test their efficacy in two conditions: "Like" policies, where men and women learn under policies trained on data from their own sex, and "unlike" policies, where women learn on policies trained by men and vice versa. We look forward to a time when ITSs provide high quality, individualized instruction to every student, but now we know that this will not be an inevitable outcome of ITSs learning policies.

Acknowledgements. This work was supported by DARPA HR 0011-09-C-0032 (any opinions expressed in this publication are those of the authors).

References

1. Almond, R.G.: Cognitive modeling to represent growth (learning) using markov decision processes. Technology, Instruction, Cognition and Learning 5, 313–324 (2007)
2. Arroyo, I., Woolf, B., Beal, C.R.: Addressing Cognitive Differences and Gender During Problem Solving. Technology, Instruction, Cognition and Learning 4, 31–63 (2006)
3. Barnes, T., Stamper, J.: Toward automatic hint generation for logic proof tutoring using historical student data. In: Woolf, B.P., Aïmeur, E., Nkambou, R., Lajoie, S. (eds.) ITS 2008. LNCS, vol. 5091, pp. 373–382. Springer, Heidelberg (2008)
4. Beal, C.R., Arroyo, I., Cohen, P.R., Woolf, B.P.: Evaluation of AnimalWatch: An intelligent tutoring system for arithmetic and fractions. Journal of Interactive Online Learning 9, 65–77 (2010)
5. Beal, C.R., Qu, L.: Relating machine estimates of students' learning goals to learning outcomes: A DBN approach. In: AIED (2007)
6. Beck, J.E., Woolf, B.P., Beal, C.R.: Learning to teach: A machine learning architecture for intelligent tutor construction. In: AAAI (2000)
7. Dean, T., Kanazawa, K.: A model for reasoning about persistence and causation. Computational Intelligence 5, 142–150 (1989)
8. Green, D.T., Walsh, T.J., Cohen, P.R., Chang, Y.: Learning a Skill-Teaching Curriculum with Dynamic Bayes Nets. In: IAAI (2011)
9. Woolf, B., Arroyo, I., Beal, C.R., Murray, T.: Gender and Cognitive Differences in Help Effectiveness During Problem Solving. In: Tech., Instr., Cog. and Learning (2006)
10. Woolf, B.P.: Building intelligent interactive tutors. Morgan Kaufmann, San Francisco (2008)

Towards Understanding How Humans Teach Robots

Tasneem Kaochar, Raquel Torres Peralta, Clayton T. Morrison, Ian R. Fasel,
Thomas J. Walsh, and Paul R. Cohen

The University of Arizona, Department of Computer Science,
Gould-Simpson Building, 1040 E. 4th Street, Tucson, AZ 85721-0077
{tkaochar,rtorres,clayton,ianfasel,twalsh,cohen}@cs.arizona.edu

Abstract. Our goal is to develop methods for non-experts to teach complex
behaviors to autonomous agents (such as robots) by accommodating "natural"
forms of human teaching. We built a prototype interface allowing humans to teach
a simulated robot a complex task using several techniques and report the results
of 44 human participants using this interface. We found that teaching styles varied considerably but can be roughly categorized based on the types of interaction,
patterns of testing, and general organization of the lessons given by the teacher.
Our study contributes to a better understanding of human teaching patterns and
makes specific recommendations for future human-robot interaction systems.

1 Introduction

Robots and other intelligent devices capable of carrying out highly complex procedures
are becoming ubiquitous in the home and workplace. However, changing the behavior
and capabilities of these devices typically requires direct programming by specially
trained engineers. While machine learning (ML) algorithms offer the allure of allowing
machines to improve their knowledge and behavior from experience, ML algorithms
still require considerable expertise to use in practice.

To bridge this gap, *human-instructable computing* seeks to develop intelligent devices that can be *taught* by natural human instruction. By "natural," we mean those
patterns of communication that humans use every day while teaching each other. For example, humans provide explicit *definitions* as well as *examples* of concepts, *describe*
and provide *demonstrations* of procedures, give *examples* or *definitions* of rules and
conditions, and provide various kinds of *feedback* based on student behavior. We refer to these patterns of instruction as *natural instruction* methods or *natural modes of
interaction*. The focus of this paper is on understanding what it would take to automatically map natural human instructions to state-of-the-art ML techniques, so that we can
incorporate ML into an end-to-end human-instructable machine.

Prior work in machine learning has studied aspects of human-instructable computing through the lens of single instruction modes such as demonstration [1], teaching
concepts by examples [4,5], and human-provided reinforcement [3,6]. In each of these,
instruction sessions must be carefully set-up by an expert. In this paper we tested a new
interface that allows the user to flexibly switch between all 3 natural instruction modes
as well as an explicit testing phase. This was done with the goal of answering several
questions about how a human *teacher* interacts with an *electronic student*: (1) What

Joseph A. Konstan et al. (Eds.): UMAP 2011, LNCS 6787, pp. 347–352, 2011.
© Springer-Verlag Berlin Heidelberg 2011

natural instruction methods do humans actually use and in what proportion? (2) When and how often do humans switch between instruction modes? (3) How much teaching is implicit rather than explicit? (4) Are there identifiable teaching patterns that we can utilize to better model and design human-robot interaction systems?

Using our new multi-modal instruction interface, we conducted a study of non-expert users and observed how they taught a task in a simulated flight environment to an electronic student they believed was capable of learning. We report on a number of characteristic teaching patterns and styles that were revealed in the teaching sessions.

2   Methodology and Protocol

To answer the above questions, we need to ask novice human participants to teach a series of inter-dependent concepts and tasks to an electronic student. Ideally we would allow humans to use any form of interaction they like while a system learned from their instruction in real-time. However, the current sophistication of natural language processing is insufficient for this task and general ML systems that learn from natural human interaction have not yet been developed.

We therefore designed an interface that enables subjects to flexibly choose among a variety of teaching methods, but using interface elements that can plausibly be interpreted by state-of-the-art machine learning algorithms without requiring natural language understanding. We then asked 44 University of Arizona students to interact and teach an "electronic student" using our interface; to simulate a competent learning agent, the electronic student was actually secretly controlled by a confederate human (the *wizard*), in a so-called "Wizard of OZ" protocol.

Wizard of OZ Experimental Setup: Each teaching session consisted of a participant, who had no prior knowledge of the goals of the project, taking on the role of the *Teacher* while a researcher played the role of the *Student*. The Teacher was led to believe that he/she was interacting with an electronic student. The Teacher was first trained (by a second *Experimenter*) on the use of the interface and then presented with the teaching task outlining the knowledge the Student should attain by the end of the teaching session. The actual teaching sessions lasted from 25 to 35 minutes. The same two researchers took on the role of the Student and the Experimenter, respectively, across all experiments in order to ensure consistent training and Student/Wizard behavior.

The task took place in an Intelligence, Surveillance and Reconnaissance (ISR) domain in which the Student controls a simulated unmanned aerial vehicle (UAV) and is taught to carry out missions. The simulated environment includes a terrain map with objects that can be scanned using two sensors: a *high-resolution camera* (provides detailed object information, such as whether a boat has a cargo hold), and a *radiation sensor* (detects the radiation level of an object in range). The Student can only perceive the world through the sensors and the Teacher must teach the Student how to use the UAV sensors in the appropriate circumstances.

Our interface provides the Teacher three tools to teach the Student: (A) the Instruction Command Interface (ICI), which sends commands to the Student; (B) a Timeline Display that shows a list of all prior Teacher instructions; and (C) a Map Display providing information about world objects, UAV sensor state and range and UAV flight path. Action commands (from the ICI) direct the Student's control of the UAV and examples include *use camera to track object, fly to location*, etc. Four modes of instruction are supported by the ICI: (1) *Teaching by demonstration*: Teacher can label a sequence of actions as an example of a procedure. This can be done either by labeling the beginning and end of the procedure while providing a demonstration, or after the fact by selecting already executed actions from the timeline. Teacher can provide multiple examples of a single procedure and each instance can be labeled as a positive or negative trace of a specific procedure demonstration. (2) *Teaching concepts by examples*: Teacher can define object concepts (such as "cargo boat") by selecting an object on the map interface and giving it a label. Again, positive and negative examples of an object label can be given. (3) *Teaching by reinforcement*: Teacher can give feedback to Student at any time, in the form of 1-3 "happy faces" or 1-3 "frowny faces". Teacher can also label goals and indicate when they have been met. (4) *Testing*: Teacher can test the Student's learning by giving commands that ask the Student to provide a label for an object or execute a previously defined procedure.

Teaching Task: In each of the teaching sessions, there were two kinds of objects, cargo boats and fishing boats; the Teacher was asked to teach the Student how to distinguish them, to use the radiation sensor only on cargo boats, and to generate a report of the readings. Although this task is very simple, it requires teaching multiple object concepts and procedures that depend on one another. Teaching sessions were recorded and a transcript of the Teacher-Student interaction was generated for each teaching session.

3   Results: Analysis of Transcripts

We analyzed the transcripts with the aim of answering the key questions raised in Section 1. We discovered a number of quantifiable patterns, including three major findings:

1. Humans use multiple modes of instruction and these modes are often tightly interleaved. (This observation appears to be independent of the teaching task since it was noted also in our prior pilot studies [2]).
2. We found at least 4 distinct patterns used to switch between teaching and testing of the electronic student.
3. We observed at least 3 categories of human teaching "style" based on the level of organization of the Teacher's instructions.

3.1   Modes of Instruction

In order to answer our first question regarding how often natural instruction methods are used by human teachers, we counted the occurrences of the *label object* (mode: teaching concept by example), *define procedure* (mode: teaching by demonstration) and *give feedback* (mode: teaching by reinforcement) constructs. We found that more than half of our participants (57%) made use of all three modes of teaching while 32% taught using only two modes of instruction (7% demonstration and concepts, 14% demonstration and reinforcement, 11% concepts and reinforcement). 11% taught using only teaching by demonstration (2%) or concepts by examples (9%), the latter of which was insufficient for completing the teaching task. Teaching by reinforcement was never employed by itself and in the 82% of cases where it was used, it followed another teaching type in all but 2 cases. Fifty-eight percent of the teachers who used feedback used it exclusively after testing. This indicates that reinforcement feedback is most useful in this task for fine tuning behavior that has been "bootstrapped" with other instruction modes. When teaching concepts by examples, 75% of participants used positive *and* negative examples, while 25% only used positive examples, which were sufficient for the teaching task. This evidence suggests that humans tend to provide exceptions along with rules.

In contrast to the relatively simple object concept teaching, our studies showed that teaching a procedure is non-trivial. For example, when teaching procedure definitions, we found that teachers do not always declare the procedure up front. While 60% of participants declared the procedure before beginning to teach it, 20% of the teachers identified the procedure only after providing a demonstration. The remaining 20% of teachers vacillated between both styles. Furthermore, 41% of our teachers never explicitly defined a procedure, even though teaching at least one procedure was required to complete the teaching task. In our post-study questionnaire, 41% identified the object labeling construct as "easy to use", compared to only 16% for the procedure construct, and 23% identified teaching a procedure as a difficult task. Finally, we observed that in most transcripts, some procedures were taught implicitly. In these cases, the Teacher directed the Student to perform the same sequence of actions repeatedly in different locations of the world but never explicitly declared that a procedure was being taught.

We also split each teaching session into 3 equal time phases and analyzed whether the usage of instruction modes changed over time. Even though a teaching or testing instruction may continue across several phases (such as a procedure demonstration), it was only classified under the time phase in which it was *started*. We found that teaching concepts by example was prevalent throughout the teaching session (61%, 45%, 59%), and 84% of the teachers *began* their session by labeling objects. In contrast, teaching by demonstration (43%, 41%, 64%) and by reinforcement feedback (27%, 36%, 68%) increased in the later phases. We believe this pattern demonstrates a "bootstrapping" technique as most teachers attempted to teach procedures later in the teaching session based on the object labels taught earlier. Moreover, the steady increase of reinforcement feedback over time reflects the effects of testing the Student and providing feedback to fine-tune its behavior in the later phases.

3.2 Teaching and Testing Patterns

Teachers testing their students is an important facet of Teacher-Student interaction. All but 6 of our participants made use of the testing tools at some point during their teaching sessions. Using the 3 temporal phases described above, we observed that while teaching tools were used throughout the teaching session (84%, 68%, 93%), testing tools were most popular in the third phase (41%, 43%, 75%). We also found 4 distinct patterns of teaching and testing employed by our participants. **Type A** teachers always test the Student's comprehension after teaching a concept or procedure and before teaching another new concept. **Type B** teachers loosely interleave teaching and testing, introducing several new concepts to the Student at a time before doing any testing. **Type C** teachers reserve all testing for the end of the session whereas **Type D** teachers do not test at all.

We found that half of our participants fell under Type A, followed by Type B (25%), Type D (14%), and finally, Type C (11%). We hypothesize that Type A teaching is an indication that a teacher is uncertain about how the Student actually learns. We noticed 2 teachers who began the session with Type B but then switched to Type A after the Student failed a test. Furthermore, 4 teachers tested the Student *before* doing any teaching (perhaps in an attempt to understand the Student's base knowledge). Finally, it was common for teachers to give feedback during or immediately following a test protocol, either to express satisfaction or disappointment, or to complement the teaching.

3.3 Teaching Styles

Our transcript analysis also revealed distinct styles of teaching based on the *organization* of lessons. *Structured* teachers (16% of participants) were consistent and methodical in the execution of their instruction commands. They consistently used the interface's object labeling construct to teach object concepts and the procedure demonstration construct to define procedures. These teachers always tested Student's comprehension after teaching a lesson. *Semi-structured* teachers (50%) began with a less structured teaching style but became progressively more structured as the teaching session continued. They made use of the GUI features almost as intended, sometimes with early exploration of usage. *Free style* teachers (34%) were the most difficult to follow, mainly because these teachers made use of GUI features in novel ways. A few of these teachers tested Student's knowledge of world object labels *before* doing any teaching. Four teachers even appeared to use the procedure testing tool to provide further teaching examples of a procedure originally taught via the procedure definition construct.

One novel use of the procedure construct was to use it as a concept labeling device. That is, free-style teachers might define two separate procedures with the same sequence of actions, yet give them different names ("cargo boat" and "fishing boat") in an apparent attempt to teach the labeling distinction through procedure names (25% of participants did so). This stands as a warning to interface designers who might try to tailor an aspect of the GUI to a single mode of instruction – users may find new ways to use UI elements.

Another unexpected usage of the interface was the use of deictic or pointing actions to teach. This often happened in concert with the labeling of concept examples. While structured teachers would fly the plane to an object and then label it using the concept labeling tool (a process that expressly involved clicking on the object), we saw freestyle teachers often using procedure names or other unintended methods to label a concept that was in the *vicinity* of the UAV. The lesson here is that interface designers should be aware that human teachers may expect a certain amount of spatial reasoning performed by the interface or the electronic student on the other side.

4   Conclusions and Discussion

To the best of our knowledge, BLUI's teaching interface is the first to simultaneously support several modes of Teacher-Student interaction over the agent's lifetime: teaching concepts by example, through demonstration and via reinforcement, and testing Student's learning. Looking back at the questions we posed in Section 1, we found that in over half of the teaching sessions, all three modes of instruction were used and the switch between instruction modes usually indicated a "bootstrapping" interplay, such as the use of reinforcement to fine tune behavior previously taught using one of the other instruction modes. Our data suggests that teachers view testing as a a critical part of teaching; we hypothesize that testing helped assure teachers that Student understood what was being taught. Teachers preferred to test the Student intermittently throughout the teaching session rather than doing a monolithic testing episode at the end. The importance of testing in teaching was also observed in our pilot studies, using different teaching tasks [2]. We catalogued several levels of organization that characterized teaching trajectories, and noted that teachers frequently used the GUI in unexpected ways. Finally, while we found that much of the human teaching using BLUI's instruction interface is explicit, the presence of implicit procedure definitions highlights a challenge for ML algorithms, which typically need carefully aligned instructions.

Based on our observations of teaching patterns, we suggest that teaching interfaces for human-robot interaction should (1) allow for fine-grained testing of student's learning, (2) facilitate a bootstrapped teaching style in which concepts or procedures can be taught with one mode and refined with another (such as feedback), (3) allow teachers to provide positive *and* negative teaching examples, and (4) accommodate teachers who may not declare instructional intent in advance.

Our ultimate goal is to build an electronic student that can learn from natural human instruction. This study sought to illuminate how human teachers behave when interacting with intelligent computer systems or robots. The next step is to develop a system which can parse Teacher-Student interactions automatically, identify the boundaries of lessons, feed them to concept (e.g. ILP [4]) or procedure (e.g. planning operator [7]) learners, and then improve upon those learned concepts when feedback is given. However, extracting each teaching episode automatically (without human facilitation) is a non-trivial task, as exemplified by the evidence presented in this study of the different types of teaching-testing patterns and teaching styles naturally used by human teachers.

Acknowledgments. This work was supported by DARPA under contract 27001328 and ONR "Science of Autonomy" under contract N00014-09-1-0658.

References

1. Argall, B., Chernova, S., Veloso, M.M., Browning, B.: A survey of robot learning from demonstration. Robotics and Autonomous Systems 57(5), 469–483 (2009)
2. Kaochar, T., Peralta, R.T., Morrison, C.T., Walsh, T.J., Fasel, I.R., Beyon, S., Tran, A., Wright, J., Cohen, P.R.: Human natural instruction of a simulated electronic student. In: AAAI Spring Symposium (2011)
3. Knox, W.B., Stone, P.: Combining manual feedback with subsequent mdp reward signals for reinforcement learning. In: AAMAS (2010)
4. Natarajan, S., Kunapuli, G., Maclin, R., Page, D., O'Reilly, C., Walker, T., Shavlik, J.: Learning from human teachers: Issues and challenges for ILP in bootstrap learning. In: AAMAS Workshop on Agents Learning Interactively from Human Teachers (2010)
5. Stumpf, S., Rajaram, V., Li, L., Wong, W.-K., Burnett, M., Dietterich, T., Sullivan, E., Herlocker, J.: Interacting meaningfully with machine learning systems: Three experiments. International Journal of Human-Computer Studies 67(8), 639–662 (2009)
6. Thomaz, A.L., Breazeal, C.: Teachable robots: Understanding human teaching behavior to build more effective robot learners. Artificial Intelligence 172(6-7), 716–737 (2008)
7. Walsh, T.J., Subramanian, K., Littman, M.L., Diuk, C.: Generalizing apprenticeship learning across hypothesis classes. In: ICML (2010)

Towards Open Corpus Adaptive Hypermedia: A Study of Novelty Detection Approaches

Yi-ling Lin and Peter Brusilovsky

School of Information Sciences, University of Pittsburgh,
135 North Bellefield Avenue, Pittsburgh, PA 15206, USA
{yil54,peterb}@pitt.edu

Abstract. Classic adaptive hypermedia systems are able to track a user's knowledge of the subject and use it to evaluate the novelty and difficulty of content encountered by the user. Our goal is to implement this functionality in an open corpus context where a domain model is not available nor is the content indexed with domain concepts. We examine methods for novelty measurement based on automatic text analysis. To compare these methods, we use an evaluation approach based on knowledge encapsulated in the structure of a textbook. Our study shows that a knowledge accumulation method adopted from the domain of intelligent tutoring systems offers a more meaningful novelty measurement than methods adapted from the area of personalized information retrieval.

Keywords: Novelty detection, knowledge modeling, personalization.

1 Introduction

The World Wide Web greatly increased the volume and the variety of educational content available to the public. However, the abundance of content makes it difficult for users to find "the right content" that matches their individual goals, interests, and knowledge level. A user may benefit from personalized guidance to help manage and navigate through this abundance of resources. In a number of educational adaptive hypermedia (AH) systems, adaptive navigation support techniques were able to help individual students locate, recognize, and comprehend relevant information, thus increasing learning outcomes and retention [1],[2],[3],[4]. Unfortunately, these systems cannot be directly applied to an open corpus of Web educational content. Existing adaptive navigation support techniques are only able to work within a closed corpus of documents that have been manually structured and indexed with domain concepts and metadata at design time; however, they are impractical for most web-based real world applications.

We believe that the field of educational AH has to undergo the same transformation as the field of information retrieval (IR) did when it moved from manual indexing to automatic indexing procedures. User modeling and adaptation techniques based on manual concept indexing must be augmented or replaced by techniques based on automated text analysis (ATA). This transformation

Joseph A. Konstan et al. (Eds.): UMAP 2011, LNCS 6787, pp. 353–358, 2011.

will make it possible to provide personalized educational guidance for large volumes of online content. Some approaches to building open corpus hypermedia using ATA have been already explored [5]. This study takes another step towards open corpus educational AH by exploring several ATA-based approaches to knowledge-based novelty detection.

2   Novelty Detection for Educational AH

Let us imagine the common situation where students are studying a specific concept in a class. If the topic is one of the main concepts in the class, relevant content can be found in several different textbooks and online sources. Suppose a student has read a textbook section devoted to the target concept and wants more information about it. Ideally, the very next section will offer more information about the concept. The author of this textbook assumes that the new content is suited to the student's already acquired knowledge. However, this assumption doesn't hold if the new content is found in another textbook or on a Web page. While search engines might help the student to find dozens of pages with relevant contents, no search engine can ensure that this content is suitable for the student's knowledge level. Pages that are "just right" (new, and ready to be learned) will be intermixed with multiple pages that present learned information about a concept in a varied way and pages with new content at yet a more complex level than the student is capable of understanding.

Adaptive navigation support in classic educational AH was able to warn the user about "nothing new" and "not ready" pages [4], however, it was based on manual page indexing with concepts. In our research, we attempted to recreate a part of this functionality by developing an ATA-based approach to knowledge-based novelty detection. This approach aims to provide open corpus with an adaptive navigation support which can warn users about pages that might have little or no new content and distinguish them from pages that present new content. The open corpus version of the "not ready" approach is not specifically considered in this paper; however, one can argue that the ability to find pages with a very high level of novelty could be the closest analogy to the "not ready" functionality in classic AH which can warn the student of too advanced content. To achieve the goal we explored three straightforward approaches to novelty: vector space approach, language model approach, and knowledge modeling approach.

Vector Space Model approach is based on the classic IR algebraic model for representing text documents [6] which is commonly used for IR user profiling approaches. Each document is represented as a vector in m-dimensional space using TD-IDF as the weighting scheme. The fundamental intuition of TF-IDF is a) the more frequent the term is, the more indicative the term is of the topic, and b) the less frequent the term is in the corpus, the greater power the term could have to discriminate the importance of the term in the corpus. The document is denoted as a vector $d_i = (w_1(d_i), w_2(d_i), ..w_m(d_i))^t$. To represent a student's knowledge, we used the centroid of documents viewed by the student.

If the student has read $d_1, d_2, ...d_n$, the student knowledge vector could be represented as $d_i = (\sum_{k=1}^n \frac{w_1(d_k)}{n}, \sum_{k=1}^n \frac{w_2(d_k)}{n}, ..., \sum_{k=1}^n \frac{w_m(d_k)}{n})$. In this context, document novelty is a measure of dissimilarity between document vector and student knowledge vector. Since cosine similarity is the standard similarity measure in IR context [7], we define one minus cosine similarity of these vectors as our measure of novelty.

Language Model is a probabilistic distribution that captures the probability of a sequence of features. In modern IR, it has shown promise for identifying relevant documents in different tasks [8],[9],[10]. A natural approach to novelty detection using a language modeling approach is estimating the likelihood that a set of documents viewed by a certain student and an upcoming new document are generated by the same language model. Kullback-Leibler (KL) divergence is a distributional similarity measure to estimate the redundancy of one document d given a set of viewed document. $R(d_t|d_i) = -KL(\theta_{d_t}, \theta_{d_i}) = -\sum_{w_i} p(w_i|\theta_{d_i}) \log(\frac{p(w_i|\theta_{d_i})}{p(w_i|\theta_{d_i})}))$. In the language model approach, a document d is represented by a unigram word distribution θ_d, and it is a multinominal distribution. θ_d can be simply estimated by maximum likelihood estimation (MLE). The problem with using MLE is that it will get a zero probability if a word never occurs in a document d. If a word is in d_t but not in d_i, it will cause $KL(\theta_i|\theta_j) = \infty$. The Dirichlet distribution [10] is a smoothing technique using the conjugate prior for a multinominal distribution. It could be used to adjust the amount of reliance on the words according to the total number of the words. For a Dirichlet distribution with parameter $(\lambda p(w_1), \lambda p(w_2), ...\lambda p(w_m))$. The posterior distribution using Bayesian analysis is $P_\lambda(w_i|d) = tf(w_i, d) + \lambda p(w_i)/\sum_{w_j}(tf(w_j, d) + \lambda p(w_j))$

Knowledge Model approach is our attempt to implement classic knowledge modeling from the domain of intelligent tutoring systems in the open corpus context. This classic approach is based on concept-level or skill-level domain models and uses an overlay model of user knowledge that measures the probability that the user knows a concept or has mastered a skill. For our model, we used the Bush-Mosteller-Atkinson asymptotic modeling approach [11] replacing traditional concept with words extracted by ATA. The knowledge K of each word in a student knowledge vector is: $K_0 = 0, K_{n+1} = K_n + pV \times \frac{W_{i,d_{n+1}}}{\sum_i W_{i,d_{n+1}}}$ where: pV is the speed of knowledge growth for a student (ranged from 0 to 1 and set as an average 0.5 in our experiments). $W_{i,d_{n+1}}$: the weight of word i in document d_{n+1} which is the most recent document. $\sum_i W_{i,d_{n+1}}$: the sum of all word weights in document d_{n+1}. A new document could be represented as a vector: $d_i = (pV \times \frac{W_{1,d_i}}{\sum_i W_{i,d_i}}, pV \times \frac{W_{2,d_i}}{\sum_i W_{i,d_i}}, ...pV \times \frac{W_{m,d_i}}{\sum_i W_{i,d_i}})^t$. This knowledge modeling approach replaces the IR-based centroid model of the vector space approach, retaining cosine approach to novelty calculation.

3   Experimental Methodology

A proper evaluation of a novelty approach is a challenging task that requires a large-scale user study. We believe, however, that a meaningful comparison of

c1. The first document in the introduction
c2. End of introduction
c3. Beginning of the chapter
c4. Beginning of the document
c5. End of the document
c6. End of a chapter
c7. End of a book

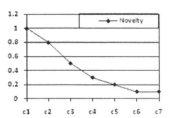

Fig. 1. The novelty trend

novelty approaches can be performed using an expert writer's knowledge encapsulated in the structure of a textbook.

Our idea is based on a previously-mentioned assumption that a good textbook is constructed from sequentially-written chapters where each new subsection has a reasonably stable level of novelty from the perspective of a sequential reader. Consider a subsection in the middle of a chapter (for example, 10.2.1). At the beginning of a book, the subsection should be completely new to the student (highest novelty value). After reading the introduction, the student should have a general idea about book topics, which will reduce the novelty value for the subsection. Likewise, after reading the introduction to chapter 10, the student will have an even better idea of the contents of that chapter which will decrease the novelty value for the remaining documents in the chapter. After reading the probed document (10.2.1), its novelty value should drop to a very low level. After that, the novelty should change very little, although we assume that a minimum novelty remains until the end of the book. Our method simply evaluates how a specific model represents an expected decrease in document novelty by examining several criteria shown in Fig. 1.

4   Evaluation

In our study, we use the textbook, **Interactive System Design**[12], containing 15 chapters, 504 pages, and 399 documents (numbered subsections). We examined the novelty trend for all the documents in each chapter with our three models. A sample of this analysis for three different chapters is shown in Fig. 2. Our assumption was that a better novelty measurement approach should more closely model the expected declining novelty trend. We also assumed that, in a better model, the novelty decrease trajectories of documents in the same chapter should be reasonably similar to each other due to their comparable amount of novelty and position in the book.

We analyze this prospect the novelty trajectories of the vector space model shown in Fig. 2a. The left graph represents the novelty of 18 documents in chapter 3 computed for each checkpoint. As we can see, the trajectories do not match our expectation. The novelty of documents remains relatively high; even after the chapter has been read. Moreover, the expected decrease in novelty

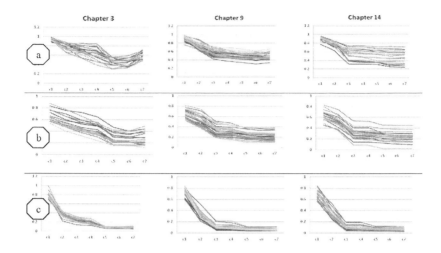

Fig. 2. (a)The novelty trend of vector space model; (b) The novelty trend of language model (c) The novelty trend of knowledge model

clearly changes to a counterintuitive increase after c6, which is observed for all chapters except 13 & 14. In addition, document novelty trajectories greatly differ within the same chapter.

For the language model, in order to make it comparable with other models, the KL values have been normalized by the maximum of the KL results. In our experiment, the larger the number for divergence, the more novel it is. The behavior of this approach (Fig. 2b) is closer to the expected than the previous one. Yet, we still observe unnatural novelty increases and the novelty trajectories in this model are more spread out. We suspect that the model might be more sensitive inorder to predict the probability of each word in the document. It is better at identifying a topic from a document, but not as good in identifying the novelty of the document from a set of documents read by the student.

The knowledge model produces more consistent trajectories than the other two models and the pattern is closer to our expectations (Fig. 2c). The only unexpected trend is a too steep drop at the beginning of the pattern; however, the rate of decrease depends of the learning speed and can be matched to the expected behavior by selecting the proper speed. In the future, we will have further studies on those factors.The results delivered by our evaluation process should not be considered as a proof that the knowledge model provides a reliable mechanism for novelty modeling. The study was designed not to prove the quality of a specific approach (for that we would need real users and a much larger variety of content than sections from the same book), but to forecast which of the three roads is more promising for further work on novelty detection in an education context. Contrary to the current trends in novelty detection, which are solely focused on IR approaches, our study indicates that a combination of IR document processing with knowledge modeling might be more promising.

5 Conclusion

Our paper attempts to contribute to solving the open corpus adaptive hypermedia problem by comparing several novelty measurement approaches based on ATA. Using an original evaluation method based on knowledge encapsulated in a textbook structure, we compared two approaches inspired by classic and modern information retrieval ideas with an approach inspired by intelligent tutoring ideas. Our results indicate that traditional IR modeling approaches that are known to work well for interest modeling might not be appropriate for knowledge modeling and novelty estimation. In contrast, knowledge modeling based on the fusion of IR and intelligent tutoring ideas looks promising and has to be investigated further.

References

1. Brusilovsky, P.: Adaptive Hypermedia. User Modeling and User Adapted Interaction 11(1/2), 87–110 (2001)
2. Brusilovsky, P., Pesin, L.: Adaptive Navigation Support in Educational Hypermedia: An Evaluation of The ISIS-Tutor. Journal of Computing and Information Technology 6(1), 27–38 (1998)
3. Weber, G., Specht, M.: User Modeling and Adaptive Navigation Support in WWW-based Tutoring Systems. In: 6th International Conference on User Modeling, pp. 289–300. Springer, Wien (1997)
4. Brusilovsky, P., Eklund, J.: A Study of User-Model Based Link Annotation in Educational Hypermedia. Journal of University Computer Science 4(4), 429–448 (1998)
5. Brusilovsky, P., Henze, N.: Open Corpus Adaptive Educational Hypermedia. In: Brusilovsky, P., Kobsa, A., Nejdl, W. (eds.) Adaptive Web 2007. LNCS, vol. 4321, pp. 671–696. Springer, Heidelberg (2007)
6. Salton, G., Wong, A., Yang, C.S.: A Vector Space Model for Automatic Indexing. Communications of the ACM 18(11), 613–620 (1975)
7. Jones, W.P., Furnas, G.W.: Pictures of Relevance. Journal of the American Society for Information Science (1987)
8. Kraaij, W., Pohlmann, R., Hiemstra, D.: Twenty-one at TREC-8: Using Language Technology for Information Retrieval. In: 8th Text REtrieval Conference, TREC-8 (1999)
9. Miller, D.R.H., Leek, T., Schwartz, R.: A Hidden Markov Model Information Retrieval System. In: 22th Annual International ACM SIGIR Conference on Research and Development in Information Retrieval, pp. 214–221. ACM, New York (2001)
10. Zhai, C., Lafferty, J.: Model-based Feedback in the Language Modeling Approach to Information Retrieval. In: 10th International Conference on Information and Knowledge Management, pp. 403–410. ACM, New York (2001)
11. Atkinson, R.C., Bower, G.H., Crothers, E.J.: An Introduction to Mathematical Learning Theory. John Wiley & Sons, New York (1965)
12. Newman, W.M., Lamming, M.G.: Interactive System Design. Addison-Wesley, Reading (1995)

4MALITY: Coaching Students with Different Problem-Solving Strategies Using an Online Tutoring System

Leena Razzaq, Robert W. Maloy, Sharon Edwards, David Marshall,
Ivon Arroyo, and Beverly P. Woolf

University of Massachusetts Amherst, 140 Governors Drive, Amherst, MA 01003 USA
{rwm,sedwards}@educ.umass.edu,
{leena,marshall,ivon,bev}@cs.umass.edu

Abstract. 4-coach Mathematics Active Learning Intelligent Tutoring sYstem (4MALITY) is a web-based intelligent tutoring system for 3rd, 4th, and 5th grade students who are learning math content from the state of Massachusetts (USA) required curriculum framework. The goal of 4MALITY is to personalize help for students by offering them problem-solving strategies authored from multiple points of view. Four virtual coaches (Estella Explainer, Chef Math Bear, How-to Hound, and Visual Vicuna) are designed to capture the character and content of these different problem-solving approaches with language, computation, strategy, and visual hints. A preliminary study was run with 102 students in fourth and fifth grade math classrooms over a period of two months. The results showed that the effect of using 4MALITY produced a statistically significant increase in post-test scores. We explored student performance, help-seeking behavior and meta-cognitive strategies by gender and math ability and report these results.

Keywords: personalizing help, intelligent tutoring systems, problem-solving strategies.

1 Introduction

Web-based or virtual tutoring is emerging as a promising educational learning tool in K-12 schools. Teachers can use these systems to individualize or differentiate instruction for students. Students can preview or review material at their own pace. The assessment data generated by virtual tutoring systems provide immediate feedback on student performance. Moreover, studies have found that students using virtual tutors have shown gains in attitudes, confidence, and academic skills [1, 2]. To date, however, fewer research studies have focused on how younger, elementary school-aged children use and learn from virtual tutors.

Our research focuses on two dimensions of how elementary school students engage in solving math word problems: student behavior and student performance. In many American classrooms, math is taught as a whole group activity where concepts are introduced by a teacher and then practiced by students using worksheets, computer games, and other drill and rote learning activities. Students in such learning environments come to assume that being smart in math is a result of working alone to

Joseph A. Konstan et al. (Eds.): UMAP 2011, LNCS 6787, pp. 359–364, 2011.

finish problems quickly (student behavior), and getting a high number of questions correct on a test (student performance). Over time, those youngsters who are able to work quickly and get most questions right adopt a mindset that they are good or skilled at math; those youngsters who get confused by math problems adopt an opposite mindset that they are not good or skilled at math. It has been suggested that the belief that one is naturally not good at math is part of the basis for mathematical learning disabilities (LD) among students who struggle to learn math [3].

Students bring their learned attitudes and behaviors about math with them when they begin using a virtual tutoring system such as 4MALITY [4]. Many assume that the goal is to finish problems quickly whether one understands the mathematical operations or not—a pattern that can be characterized as "guessing and clicking."

However, 4MALITY is designed to function very differently by inviting students to be deliberative and thoughtful, to "work" math word problems by consulting the four coaches and thinking about their various problem solving points of view, watching animations and viewing images, and accessing the definitions of words in an online glossary—a pattern that can be characterized as "thinking and checking." There is evidence that students with LD may especially benefit from coaching of problem-solving strategies [5, 6]. The goal is for students to slow down, spend more time on math problems, consider the possible answer choices, and then choose the solution that makes the most sense of the problem at hand. Ideally, as student behavior changes from "guessing and clicking" to "thinking and checking," student performance will improve and student attitudes about themselves as math learners will become more positive.

The problems in 4MALITY are taken from third, fourth and fifth grade Massachusetts Comprehensive Assessment System (MCAS) math tests. Each question in the system features strategies for solving math problems presented by coaches who offer suggestions from four different perspectives:

- *Estella Explainer* helps children understand the language and meaning of questions.
- *Chef Math Bear* provides computational strategies (addition, subtraction, multiplication and division).

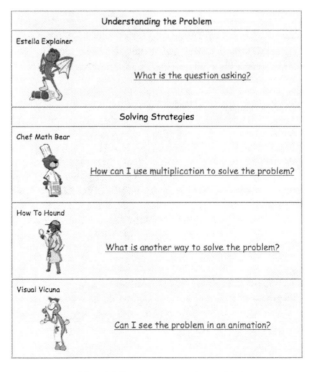

Fig. 1. The 4 coaches of 4MALITY

- *How-to-Hound* presents strategic thinking clues (rounding, estimation, elimination of wrong answers).
- *Visual Vicuna* offers ways to see problems and their solutions in pictures, animations, charts and graphs.

These different perspectives represent different approaches that students can use to understand and solve math problems.

2 Evaluation Design

The goal of this preliminary study of 4MALITY was to learn more about how young students solved math problems with the system and how they used the virtual coaches. Do students learn from using the system? Are there consistent preferences for particular coaches? Does this choice of character help students? Do students who stay with a single coach improve performance more than students who do not?

2.1 Setting and Participants

We used 4MALITY with 102 fourth and fifth grade students in a rural school in western Massachusetts. In 2010 in this school, 69.2% of students received free or reduced lunch, and the school population was 76.2% white, 14.5% Hispanic and 4.1% African American. In the 2010 state math test for 4th grade, the students scored 23% Advanced/Above Proficient, 26% Proficient, 33% Needs Improvement and 18% Warning/Failing. Statewide, 52% of 4th grade students scored in the Needs Improvement or Warning/Failing categories.

Among the students who participated in this study, 11.7% of the students had a learning disability, 13.6% had Title 1 (a federally funded program for economically and educationally disadvantaged students) status, and 39.8% were teacher-rated as below average in math (this includes students with IEPs or Title 1 designation).

4MALITY was explained first to administrators and then to teachers. Teachers agreed to use the system as part of their math instruction for at least six weeks. A computer lab in the school with internet-connected computers was used with the students. Four classrooms of 4th graders used the system during their morning math instruction during regular school hours. Two fifth grade groups used the system during an after school program for extra practice with skills in math. Upon completion of the six weeks, these teachers have requested to continue using the system for another four weeks later in the year.

2.2 Procedures

We created six units of fourth grade math topics and the teachers decided that they would like students to work on the units in this order: 1) Place Value, 2) Combinations, 3) Rounding and Estimation, 4) Totals (adding and subtracting word problems), 5) Charts and Graphs and 6) Multiplication. Each unit consisted of three modules: a pre-test, practice and post-test. Students worked on one unit per week.

The system was introduced to the class by viewing a math MCAS question and showing how each virtual coach helped to solve the question with different strategies.

The students were encouraged to consult the coaches while they were working on the system to become familiar with the different problem-solving strategies and think about their preferred strategy.

Before starting the first unit, students were given a survey. We were most interested in how students responded to the following questions:

- What do you do most often when you are unsure how to solve a math word problem? (Guess the answer, Skip the problem, Try to figure out the answer, or Ask for help)
- What strategy do you use most often to answer math word problems? (Read the questions carefully to know what is being asked, Add, subtract, multiply or divide, Try a new way to find the answer, or Draw a picture or chart)
- Which coach do you think will be most helpful to you in solving math word problems? (Estella Explainer, Chef Math Bear, How-to Hound, or Visual Vicuna)

Variations of these questions were also asked after every unit to see how students' answers changed over the course of using the system.

3   Results

A one-sample t-test was run to determine if the gain from pre- to post-test was significantly different from zero. Table 1 shows that students on average gained significantly from pre- to post-test. In the analyses of individual units, only students who completed the pre- and post-tests and did not get all of the pretest items correct for each unit are included.

Table 1. Students had significant learning gains from pre- to post-test

	Pretest Ave	Post-test Ave	t	df	Sig. (2-tailed)	95% Confidence Interval of the Difference Lower	Upper
Average gain on all units	46.7%	63.1%	7.93	94	.000	12.291	20.502
Place value gain	49.7%	59.7%	2.59	63	.012	2.352	18.342
Combination gain	38.95%	64.5%	5.72	62	.000	17.048	35.386
Rounding gain	30.5%	46.3%	2.58	39	.014	.035	.290
Totals gain	49.1%	59.8%	1.89	34	.068	-.9459	25.230
Charts gain	55.2%	76.6%	5.16	43	.000	12.546	28.666
Multiplication gain	56.9%	71.4%	2.42	20	.025	1.99	26.59

We defined the students who were "struggling with math" as students who had an IEP, Title 1 status or teacher-rated as "below average" in math. We found that these students gained an average of 14% from pre- to post-test [$t(48) = 4.797$, $p < 0.001$]. Although male and female students did not have significantly different pre-test scores [$F(92, 1) = 1.509$, $p = 0.223$], females gained more (mean = 18%) on the post-test than males (mean = 11.25%), [$F(93, 2) = 2.385$, $p = 0.098$].

We were interested in investigating what effect the use of 4MALITY's virtual coaches had in determining outcomes. We looked at the number of hints accessed by students to correlate between the number of hints received and gain in performance. We found that the number of hints accessed did not significantly predict gain score from pre- to post-test. We speculate that students were encouraged to use the hints and used them more or less consistently, and therefore the number of hints seen did not correlate to gain scores. There was however, a positive correlation between the average learning gain for students with LDs and the average time spent per unit, $r = 0.613$, $n = 12$, $p < 0.05$. We speculate that this could mean that LD students spent more time with coaches and propose to look at this more closely in future work.

How did students who preferred one coach compare to students who accessed all of the coaches more uniformly? Students who looked at one coach at least 50% more than any other coach were labeled as "generally one coach," otherwise they were labeled as "generally different coaches." Using average time per unit as a covariate, students who looked at mostly different coaches had higher learning gains than those who stayed mostly with one coach (18.7% vs. 12.1%), but this was not significant [$F(92, 1) = 2.27$, $p = 0.136$]. Female students were more likely to access mostly different coaches than male students [$F(92, 2) = 3.97$, $p = 0.02$].

In addition to performance on the post-test, we were interested in what the students thought about the virtual coaches and their different problem-strategies. Before using the system, the majority of students considered "Reading the question carefully" to be the best strategy. However, the preference for this strategy decreased over time. It appeared that the students' favorite strategy also depended on the current topic.

Although the majority of students thought that "Reading the question carefully" was their best strategy before using the system, they did not choose Estella Explainer as the coach that they thought would be most helpful. Figure 2 shows that we found that the popularity of Visual Vicuna increased over time.

Additionally, we asked students "What do you do most often when you are unsure how to solve a math word problem?" (Guess the answer, Skip the problem, Try to figure out the answer, or Ask for help). "Ask for help" increased steadily throughout use of the system from 12.5% at pre-survey to 72% after the last unit. We find this encouraging, as previous studies have shown that students often exhibit unproductive help-seeking behavior when using learning technologies [7].

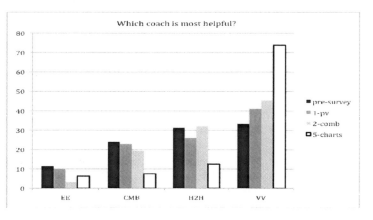

Fig. 2. Preference for the visual coach increased over time

4 Conclusions and Future Work

In this initial study, our goal was to evaluate the impact of 4MALITY, a web-based tutoring system that focuses on problem-solving strategies in order to determine which strategies worked best for individual students. We tested the system with 102 elementary school students over a period of two months. We found a significant mean learning gain of 16.35% from pre- to post-test. Students with LDs or who were below average in math also made significant learning gains. Female students seemed to benefit more than male students. Students who did not stick to one coach had higher learning gains and female students were less likely to stick to one coach. Visual Vicuna was the favorite coach of the majority of the students. This is understandable since Vicuna can be flashy, but we do not know if she was the most effective coach.

Our results encourage us to plan randomized controlled experiments so we can better determine which coaches are benefitting which students. We would like to run studies to compare the effectiveness of each coach for students based on gender and math ability. We also propose running a study to examine further whether females had higher gains because they learned more problem-solving strategies by accessing more coaches. We believe this work will help us to personalize help in 4MALITY.

Acknowledgments. This material is based upon work supported in part by the National Science Foundation (NSF), under Grant #0937060 to the Computing Research Association (CRA) for the CIFellows Project. Any opinions, findings, and conclusions or recommendations expressed in this material are those of the author(s) and do not necessarily reflect the views of the NSF or the CRA.

References

1. Beal, C.R., Walles, R., Arroyo, I., Woolf, B.P.: Online tutoring for math achievement testing: A controlled evaluation. Journal of Interactive Online Learning 6(1), 43–55 (2007)
2. Razzaq, Heffernan, Koedinger, Feng, Nuzzo-Jones, Junker, Macasek, Rasmussen, Turner, Walonoski: Blending Assessment and Instructional Assistance. In: Nedjah, N., de Mourelle, L., Borges, M.N., Almeida, N.N. (eds.) Intelligent Educational Machines, pp. 23–49 (2007)
3. Whitin, P., Whitin, D.J.: Math is language too: Talking and writing in the mathematics classroom. National Council of Teachers of English, Urbana (2000)
4. Maloy, R.W., Edwards, S.A., Anderson, G.: Teaching Math Problem Solving Using a Web-based Tutoring System, Learning Games and Students' Writing. J. of STEM Education 11(1&2), 82–90 (2010)
5. Borkowski, J., Estrada, M.T., Milstead, M., Hale, C.: General Problem-Solving Skills: Relations between Metacognition and Strategic Processing. Learning Disability Quarterly 12(1), 57–70 (1989)
6. Jitendra, A.K.: Teaching students math problem-solving through graphic representations. Teaching Exceptional Children 34(4), 34–38 (2002)
7. Aleven, V., McLaren, B.M., Roll, I., Koedinger, K.R.: Toward tutoring help seeking: Applying cognitive modeling to meta-cognitive skills. In: Lester, J.C., Vicari, R.M., Paraguaçu, F. (eds.) ITS 2004. LNCS, vol. 3220, pp. 227–239. Springer, Heidelberg (2004)

Capitalizing on Uncertainty, Diversity and Change by Online Individualization of Functionality

Reza Razavi

Ambient Activity Systems SARL
Ecostart - centre d'entreprise et d'innovation
Foetz - Luxembourg
razavi@acm.org

Abstract. Uncertainty, diversity and change create endless streams of unexpected new opportunities. To seize those opportunities, new web-based systems are emerging that enforce participative design and empower end-users to take actively part in the creation and maintenance of functionality that fits specific needs and conditions. For example, Yahoo! Pipes is a "participative site" with visual online programming means for defining and readily deploying web-based services that fetch, aggregate and process web feeds. Standard and dedicated engineering tools for developing such web sites are however yet to be invented. This paper describes our software platform for their development by reuse and extension, while meeting the requirements of end-user accessibility, expressivity, interpretability, web compatibility, shareability and traceability as they appear in person-centric areas like Ambient Assisted Living. We allow dynamic and user-driven individualization of functionality by capturing at runtime, and processing complex interaction patterns that involve end-users, their physical environment and software components.

Keywords: Model-based Personalization, Web Technology, User-Generated Services, Adaptive Object-Model, Design Pattern, Framework, Pull Model.

1 Context and Motivations for Participative Web Sites

1.1 The Pull Model for Participative Personalization and Its Wide Applications

In December 2010 and January 2011, David Siegel posted two Open Letters to Apple and Google Executives [1] respectively, where he emphasizes in the following terms the paramount importance of a shift to the "pull" service delivery model [2]:

- *Apple can turn software from a "lobster trap" model into an open ecosystem of services that make everyone both a producer and a consumer, with much less waste.*
- *If you want to beat Facebook, you'll have to empower people to collect and use their own data for themselves, even if that means not sharing it with Google's advertisers. But it's okay, you'll still be able to make lots of money from them by helping them do just that.*

Joseph A. Konstan et al. (Eds.): UMAP 2011, LNCS 6787, pp. 365–376, 2011.
© Springer-Verlag Berlin Heidelberg 2011

These observations are in alignment with the vision developed by the authors of "The Power of Pull" who admit uncertainty, diversity and change as permanent sources of complications, confusions, and challenges, which they also consider as endless streams of unexpected new perspectives, practices, and opportunities, if end-users and their communities are perceived themselves as valuable actors of service innovation and personalization, and empowered to assume their responsibilities. [2]

Application areas of the pull model are quite broad, and include domains where uncertainty, diversity, and change are the rule rather than exception, and where end-user empowerment is as a strategic priority. These include individualized remote monitoring, learning-support services, medical follow-up, and entertainment. Many specific applications are also being revealed by ongoing research in the area of User-Generated Services (see for example [3]).

In the case of ICT-based services to the elderly, it is unconceivable to anticipate all individual needs and rigidly shape a software solution. This is due to the unpredictable and rapid changeability of the elderly conditions throughout the phases of ageing, and the diversity of their cultures, capabilities, attitudes, and values. It is also unconceivable, at least for the years to come, to auto-discover changes in their needs and auto-generate appropriate care processes. Our approach is to empower end-users, typically relatives and professional caregivers, to actively take part in the creation, personalization and validation of ICT-based care processes.

1.2   The Role of Flexible Knowledge Models and Declarative Systems Like AOMs

Furthermore, in his introductory comments on his book "Pull: The Power of the Semantic Web to Transform Your Business" [4], David Siegel summarizes the past, present and particularly future of software in the following way: *"We'll start using flexible knowledge models and declarative systems that use data, rather than encoded processes, to drive business systems. Today's procedure-driven software has already broken (most enterprises spend 80% of their IT budgets on maintenance). Tomorrow's flexible systems will be adaptive – they will respond in real-time to business events and change themselves daily as the business environment changes."* [5]

The fact is that pioneer companies have for some time been *handcrafting* adaptive and user-empowering business applications called Adaptive Object-Models (AOM) [6]. For example, the User-Defined Product (UDP) framework by The Hartford is an AOM that enables insurance managers to dynamically create complex and fully operational insurance policy objects, capable of responding to standard messages like "price" and "print", and make them available to Sales employees without any programming [7]. The UDP framework also keeps a complete history of those adaptations, which is indispensable, for example, for business analysis activities.

Many AOMs have been "mined", and their design patterns documented, typically those for representing as data, rather than code, business objects, their relations and governing rules [8]. Knowledgeable end-users are further provided with graphical interfaces to change that meta-data, which takes effect immediately and promptly adapts the application's behavior to specific needs as they arise.

1.3 AOMs Allowing Personalization by Capturing Online Interaction Patterns

We are particularly interested in web-enabled AOMs, which we will hereafter refer to as "participative sites". These allow participative design and personalization by capturing and processing sophisticated and dynamic interaction patterns that in addition to software components may involve users and their environment. Typically, in Ambient Assisted Living (AAL) applications, individualized care processes may be defined at runtime in terms of which data to collect and sense, how to analyze it, how to predict future trends, how to make and enforce supportive, assistive and predictive decisions, and finally which users to involve.

As an example, a participative AAL site is expected to empower end-users to specify and readily enforce interaction patterns like the following. These respond to the specific needs of Jane, a 75 year-old living alone at home, but supported by her son Joe and assistant Julie: *Measure Jane's weight on a weekly basis, wirelessly, via the smart environment facilities, and if there is a loss of more than one kg per week, then send an email to her doctor Jennifer and also an SMS to Joe. Also, add an information entry to Julie's agenda and Jane's "ambient" 'info board'.*

In previous work [9], we have investigated and prototyped a participative site (at that time called the "uQuery engine") for modeling such interaction patterns. In the absence of standard tools, we report in this paper a software platform designed and implemented to enable the development of participative sites by reuse and extension by regular programmers (and not only by experts in advanced design patterns and tool builders). Sections 2 and 3 describe and illustrate respectively our design goals and approach, while Section 4 summarizes our contributions and work perspectives.

2 Illustration and Design Goals

2.1 Concept Illustration with the Well-Known Yahoo! Pipes

In [9], we have already illustrated the concept of participative site by means of a research prototype that allows quite complex interaction patterns including sensing devices installed in the environment. A less sophisticated but well-known and commercial product is Yahoo! Pipes [10]. This is a web application that enforces participative service delivery by allowing visual programming and online management of interaction patterns among software components that fetch, aggregate and process web feeds. New web-based services are created online by composing software "modules" using a Web 2.0 graphical interface. The available modules belong to the application's "library", where they are grouped into "categories" like "Sources", "User inputs", and "Operators" (left side of Fig. 1).

A typical pipe example is the "eBay Price Watch" by Ed Ho, designed to use eBay's RSS API to find items within a certain price range [11]. The interaction model of this pipe is composed of (1) eight module "instances", that instantiate six modules (namely "Search for", "URL Builder", "Text Input", "Fetch Feed", "Simple Math", and "Filter"), and (2) several data flow links among them (right side of Fig. 1). For example, the result of the "URL Builder" module instance is passed to the "Fetch Feed" module instance, which in turn passes its result to the "Filter" module instance.

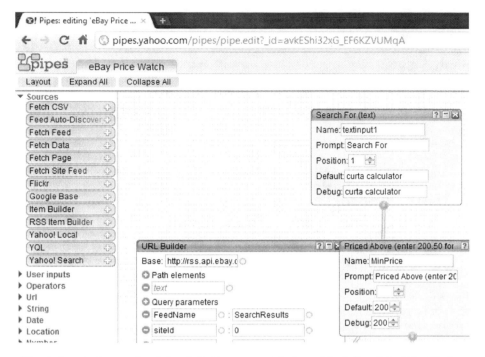

Fig. 1. A typical example of pipe definition – a partial view of the "eBay Price Watch" pipe

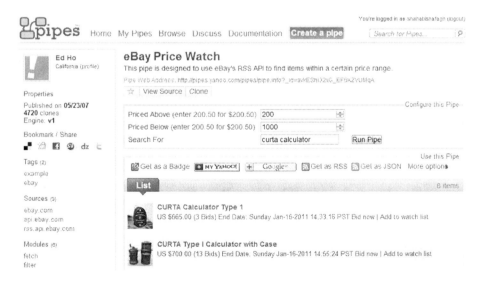

Fig. 2. An execution of the "eBay Price Watch" pipe on Jan. 2011 (partial list of two items)

Fig. 2 provides a partial view (due to space limitations) of the execution results of this pipe, obtained by simply pointing to its URL. The two "Text Input" module instances render input fields for typing the upper and lower values of the searched price range. The "Search for" module instance renders also an input field for typing the search pattern. The other module instances take these values as input, execute behind the scene, and compute the list of rendered items (bottom-right of Fig. 2).

Yahoo! Pipes appears as a successful example of the pull model. Several thousand pipes are currently defined and made available online by the Yahoo! community of pipe creators. It illustrates how the definition and deployment of even complex services may be successfully decentralized and delegated to communities of users.

2.3 Quality Requirements for Interaction Pattern Modeling Languages

A major component of participative sites is their embedded interaction pattern modeling language. So, to be effective, a tool like our software platform for developing participative sites is expected to significantly facilitate the programmers' task of implementing such languages for their specific application domains. The standard technique applied in AOMs like the UDP framework consists in *handcrafting* a class hierarchy following the Interpreter design pattern [12]. However, being based upon real-life industrial application use cases, AAL scenarios, and research prototypes, our platform is designed to allow interaction languages that meet the following goals, and go beyond Yahoo! Pipes facilities as also explained below:

- *Expressivity*: Interaction models must be able to capture complex and realistic automation logic. They must allow arbitrary control structure (iterations, conditionals, and sub-procedure calls), and arbitrary atomic services (for calculation, communication, interaction, search, sensing, etc.). This goes beyond the rather limited set of modules that Yahoo! Pipes provides.
- *End-user accessibility*: The creation of interaction models must be accessible to ordinary end-users (who constitute the large majority of potential participant end-users). For example, in the case of a "pull" service delivery system for the elderly, interaction modeling is expected to be performed by (trained) family members and professional caregivers. This goes beyond Yahoo! Pipes where an examination of the modules and examples provided shows that pipe composition is only accessible to professional programmers.
- *Interpretability*: Interaction models, whether defined by users or auto-generated, must be promptly interpretable, thereby avoiding any specific deployment action and latency related to compile-run cycles, and supporting the immediate effect of end-user models. This is achieved by Yahoo! Pipes, which, however, draws apparently on a representation technique with comparatively more limited capabilities (See the paragraph on "expressivity").
- *Web compatibility*: Interaction models must have transparent access to Internet resources. This enables a more effective support to daily end-user activities and interactions, by providing access to remote and reusable information, processing, and presentation resources. This is also achieved by Yahoo! Pipes, which basically relies on the broad range of widespread Internet standards.
- *Shareability*: Interaction models must be sharable online with other end-users and manageable from everywhere, anytime, like Yahoo! Pipes.
- *Traceability (closed-loop lifecycle management)*: Executions of interaction pattern models must be traced to allow the implementation of history-dependent and context-sensitive analysis and prediction functionality.

The next Section describes how our software platform, called AAS-Platform [13], enables interaction pattern modeling languages that meet these requirements.

3 AAS-Platform Pillars: Purpose-Built Languages and Containers

Mike Shapiro describes "purpose-built" as languages that *"even defy a strict definition worthy of a prescriptive compiler grammarian..."* but still play a key role as part of the development of larger software systems. He observes further that these *"little languages often live in symbiotic partnership with the mainstream development language or with the software system itself. ... The macro language of your favorite spreadsheet is another example: it exists to provide a convenient way to manipulate the user-visible abstractions of the containing software application."* [14]

In the case of Yahoo! Pipes, for example, we consider the pipe visual programming language as a purpose-built, or purpose-specific language for creating and executing pipes (Fig. 1). This is "contained" in a web application that provides additional functionality like saving, organizing, browsing, sharing, and cloning pipes (Fig. 2).

These examples reveal two recurrent aspects in implementing participative sites for pull service delivery: (1) the end-user-oriented interaction modeling language, and (2) its container application. The following two Subsections describe our approach in the design of tool support for each of these aspects in AAS-Platform.

3.1 Implementing Interaction Modeling Languages by Reuse and Extension

Interaction pattern modeling languages are purpose-built in that they provide non-professional programmer end-users with a "convenient way" to manipulate the interaction modeling abstractions of the containing software applications (next Subsection). Domain-specificity is further admitted as key to end-user accessibility and convenient modeling [15], and application domains for pull service delivery are diverse. So, we propose a framework approach [16] to enable application programmers to develop, by reuse and extension, purpose-built interaction pattern modeling languages that meet the requirements stated in the previous Section.

The architectural design principles that govern the implementation of such a framework are described in detail in [17]. To summarize, our tailor-made and graph-based modeling method captures the hierarchical structure of interaction patterns in an executable format. It places semantic-free placeholders for declarations of calls to *atomic services* (as understood in service-oriented computing) in the graph nodes and the declarations of data flows between them on the arcs connecting those nodes. This is different from *activity networks* used in workflow systems, for example, where "activities" (which correspond to atomic services) are directly placed as graph nodes.

We further clearly separate in graph design the following aspects: (1) structure construction from computation description, (2) computation description from execution strategy implementation, (3) structure construction from structure rendering strategy (on graphical user modeling interfaces), and (4) atomic services implementation from their "signature" (annotation mechanism called *contract*).

This separation of different design aspects is reflected in our practice-informed design and implementation as fully-fledged class hierarchies, endowed with extension hooks, for adapting each of those aspects to specific needs by reuse and extension.

AAS-Platform relieves programmers from the burden of designing, implementing, incorporating and maintaining purpose-built interaction modeling languages from scratch. For example, the Yahoo! Pipe language could be implemented by reusing our framework, and "hooking" implementations of their domain-specific "modules" as atomic services like "URL Builder", "Text Input", and "Fetch Feed". Also, the UDP's "Rule" class hierarchy that implements a simple language for computing policy prices could be implemented by "simply" plugging adequate primitives into our framework. Further, online modeling of care interaction patterns like that of Jane (Subsection 1.3) requires primitive services like "weekly do", "select community member", "measure weight", "compare values", "if true then do", "send email to", and "add entry to". Finally, see the next Subsection for an example that parallels the pipe in $2.2.

In addition, AAS-Platform provides a framework for implementing interactive Web 2.0 online modeling interfaces, which it uses itself for implementing a set of "knowledge-level" editors (Tables 1). It comes also with a default runtime engine, and automates history (lifecycle) management, dialog box generation, and persistence by reusing third-party components as explained in [17]. Application programmers may extend and adapt to specific needs the default behavior of these components.

Table 1. Interactive "knowledge-level" user interfaces delivered by AAS-Platform

No.	Title	Description
1	Catalogue of contracts	This catalogue contains the primitive services that end-user service creators may "combine" in order to create their individualized (composite) services online.
2	Catalogue of concepts & instances	This catalogue contains: (a) A short description of each domain concepts that support the system functionality, i.e. is produced and consumed by system operations, and (b) For each domain concept, a list of all its instances, situated in the context of the operation and activity that has created it.
3	Catalogue of activity models & lifecycles	This catalogue provides access to the end-user contributed services, and the results of their execution (life-cycles). Both services and their executions may be organized by means of end-user defined themes ("communication", "shopping"...).

For space limitations, for concrete examples of these interfaces please refer to URLs listed in Table 2. It should be noted that these interfaces adhere to a plug-and-play design approach. They can operate on arbitrary sets of domain concepts and atomic primitives that better match the user service requirements and their mental model.

Table 2. URLs to access the examples of "knowledge-level" interfaces described in Table 1

No.	URL
1	http://www.afacms.com/cats/contracts/
2	http://www.afacms.com/cats/concepts/
3	http://www.afacms.com/cats/activities/

3.2 Illustration

To illustrate the interaction modeling languages allowed by AAS-Platform, while almost fitting to the space limitations of this paper, we have designed a (necessarily rather simple) feed processing example, which is nevertheless quite representative in that (a) it comprises a nontrivial logic including an iteration and hierarchical structure; (b) it invokes interesting Internet-based atomic services comparable to those of Yahoo! Pipes; (c) the atomic services are provided by third parties, and thereby illustrate the openness of our technology. A step-by-step explanation of this example, including execution screenshots, may be found online at www.afacms.com/examples.

We assume an end-user willing to automate a specific feed processing logic as follows: (1) Login to a Twitter account, and (2) While tweets are successful, then (a) fetch the traffic information in South East England from www.highways.gov.uk, and (b) interactively post it to that Twitter account.

Implementing a purpose-built language by AAS-Platform for modeling such interactions implies coding (I) object classes like "Traffic Information" and "Twitter Connection", and (II) atomic services like "Connect to Twitter", and "Read Traffic Info" (in the present case courtesy of Andreas Raab and Nick Ager from Squeak (squeak.org) and Seaside (seaside.st) Communities). Atomic services must further be annotated in a computer-understandable format. For that we propose a "contract" class hierarchy whose instances allow describing the atomic service properties like name, purpose, input data types and output data type. Control structures like "While True" are also implemented as atomic services and "wrapped" with contracts. Some are delivered by AAS-Platform by default (like here "While true"). Otherwise, "hooks" are provided to implement them by reuse and extension.

It should be noted that to better ensure the engagement of end-users and the accessibility of the language, the choice of domain concepts and atomic services must be discussed and co-decided with their representatives. From this perspective, development methodologies like Domain-Driven Design [18] may be of great help.

Once these foundations (concepts and contracts) are in place, programmers are provided with a "distribution builder" that takes some inputs like the target domain name and the server access port, and pre-configures and packages a web application endowed with online interaction pattern modeling facilities ready to deploy (Table 1).

Then, when the application is deployed behind a front-end server, end-users may use the dedicated interactive interface, illustrated in Fig. 3, to compose their interaction patterns and define individualized functionality. Based on our industrial experience, we have preferred a list format, rather than a graph, for rendering models. Graphs tend to become hard to manage when the model grows. Users are also provided with facilities (enactment links and content management [17]) to wrap launch accesses to their services via other web pages.

As illustrated by Fig. 3 and 4 respectively, the logic described earlier in this Subsection may be implemented by two "actions": (1) the "Tweet" action that embodies the logic for reading sequentially the traffic info feed, and interactively sending it to the Twitter account, and (b) the "Main" action that implements the interaction logic over the "Tweet" action, preceded by the login to Twitter operation. The "Tweet" action is considered as being subordinated to the "Main" in that its execution may only be invoked by the latter. They are hence structured hierarchically.

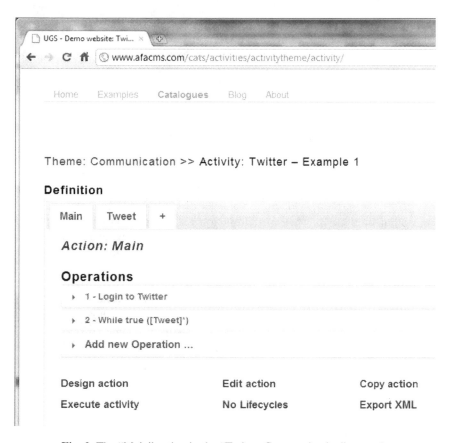

Fig. 3. The "Main" action in the "Twitter Communication" example

Definition

| Main | Tweet | + |

Action: Tweet

Operations

▸ 1 - Latest traffic information for South East England

▸ 2 - Interactive tweeting (1@ Main ', 1) returns: Tweeting result

▸ Add new Operation ...

Fig. 4. The "Tweet" action in the "Twitter Communication" example

The interaction pattern modeling interface (Fig. 3 and 4) allows the creation of arcs between graph nodes by selecting an operation ("instance" of atomic service) like "interactive tweeting", and pressing a link called "define arguments". Consequently, a dialog box is automatically generated, based on the corresponding contract, which contains one selection list per required argument. The items of those lists are also automatically filtered (1) to ensure type compatibility, and (2) to avoid cycles.

3.3 Adaptive Object-Models as Containers for Pull Service Platforms

Now, for putting purpose-built interaction modeling languages in the larger context of their "container" application domain, the Adaptive Object-Model architectural style provides a "natural" medium and disciplined approach. This style provides, by design, "hooks" for purpose-built modeling languages that allow dynamic maintenance and customization of the application's automation services by non-technical end-users themselves. Therefore, AOMs are powerful "uncertainty management" tools.

From this perspective, the Yahoo! Pipes web application may be perceived as a web-based AOM that allows end-users to define and share online their feed processing services with a personalized logic. In the case of UDP framework, Interpreter-based trees are incorporated and "attached" to runtime defined composite insurance policies, specifically their price-related attributes. Those trees of "rule" objects serve as runtime defined interaction patterns for computing policy prices. Also, in the previous Subsection, we described a case based on the AAS-Platform.

4 Summary of Contributions and Outlook

This paper continues previous communications on our practice-informed development platform for pull-oriented software and customized services. [17] It pinpoints how our work relates to the pull model, describes our design goals, recalls our major design decisions, positions our modeling language framework in the larger context of their containers, and illustrates our solution in comparison with a commercial solution.

Pull service delivery models are based on such atypical assumptions, e.g. uncertain and changing needs and decentralized service delivery control, that imply fundamentally different design and implementation principles and tools. The often unstated and unexamined, but quite general assumption in most of today's legacy IT systems and architectures that end-users' needs may be anticipated, specified and "hard-coded" by strictly managed resources does not hold anymore. [2]

Aware of their critical role in cloud-based adaptive services, we have investigated and implemented an industrial-scale software platform as a contribution to the large-scale development of websites like Yahoo! Pipes by regular application developers, where the active and collaborative participation of end-users as partners in the service innovation and delivery processes is supported by design. In other terms, personalization and adaptation, supported by a home-made meta-data data model and related online (content) management facilities, allow collaborative and open development of intuitively limitless individualized services by end-users.

Our platform eases the development of participative sites for professional programmers, by providing a development framework that clearly separates the implementation of the application components (isolated and implemented as atomic services) from that of the flow of control and data among those components (their *connectors*). This is achieved without imposing on programmers the burden of a separate CASE tool. We have, in effect, implemented a platform that seamlessly integrates into standard Smalltalk object-oriented programming languages, systems, and web development frameworks. Smalltalk is selected for necessary reflective features, specifically continuation-passing programming style as described in more details in [17]. We further propose an alternative solution to UML-based CASE tools by supporting software models that are end-user accessible, sharable, and executable.

With AAS-Platform, programmers are equipped and guided for creating web applications that incorporate adaptation "ingredients" (interaction pattern modeling language), while non-professional programmers are provided with interactive Web 2.0 interfaces to define online and enforce customized interaction pattern models on an ad-hoc basis. We provide end-users with the combined benefits of a constrained programming environment for creating productive results, and the power of a full-fledged server side programming platform used to create and maintain those end-user programming tools.

Furthermore, by maintaining an "open interaction pattern model", AAS-Platform-based web applications allow end-users to interact with and modify that model, which is otherwise "hard-coded" by programmers. Every piece of meta-data and data that end-users care about may be accessed via dedicated atomic services and reused when assembling new services, thereby contributing to the "data-driven ecosystems" [1].

We address the issue of very large-scale deployment of these highly dynamic and reflective architectures by a distributed architecture, where the front-end web server (e.g. Apache) spawns a dedicated back-end distribution by analyzing HTTP requests.

All in all, this appears to bring us a major step closer to *"helping them do just that"* while seizing development opportunities offered by uncertainty, diversity and change.

AAS-Platform builds on close to two decades of work on related areas in both industrial and academic environments. It has been validated by means of simple yet representative case studies. We also provide a showcase distribution available online at www.afacms.com (stands for activity *flows as content* management system), which is set up with the goal allowing Internet users to "play" with the technology and to get a feeling of how it allows online creation, documentation, execution, and traceability of individualized interaction patterns. Pre-built examples in areas like communication, shopping, and entertainment are also provided and documented.

Now, we are investigating opportunities for large-scale validation and deployment, including community-based large-scale creation of atomic services, and very-large-scale just-in-time provisioning of personalized services, specifically for the elderly and their formal and informal caregivers. We are, in particular, in the process of finalizing a participative site builder for commercial ambient assisted living care processes, from which the case of Jane (Subsection 1.3) is an example. Further, AAS-Platform is a commercial product whose availability to third parties is subject to bilateral agreements. Finally, we speculate that a combination with other end-user information collection, representation, mining and reasoning techniques will allow self-adaptation and personalization by auto- generation of interaction pattern models.

Acknowledgments. This work has been funded by Ambient Activity Systems SARL, a startup supported by the Luxembourg Ministry of Economy and Foreign Commerce. We would also like to acknowledge the insightful comments by Gul Agha, Christophe Dony, Ralph Johnson, Jean-François Perrot, David Potter, and Joseph Yoder on early versions of this paper, as well as the technical support of Goya Razavi.

References

1. The Power of Pull, http://thepowerofpull.com/pull/blog
2. Hagel III, J., Brown, J.S., Davison, L.: The Power of Pull: How Small Moves, Smartly Made, Can Set Big Things in Motion. Basic Books, New York (2010)
3. Dustdar, S., Hauswirth, M. (Juanjo) Hierro, J.J., Soriano, J., Urmetzer, F., Möller, K., Rivera, I. (eds.): First Workshop on User-generated Services at ICSOC 2009, CEUR-WS, Vol. 540 (2009)
4. Siegel, D.: Pull: The Power of the Semantic Web to Transform Your Business. Penguin Group (December 2009)
5. David Siegel (Pull), http://thepowerofpull.com/what/introduction
6. Yoder, J., Johnson, R.: The adaptive object-model architectural style. In: Bosch, J., Morven Gentleman, W., Hofmeister, C., Kuusela, J. (eds.) Third IEEE/IFIP Conference on Software Architecture. IFIP Conference Proceedings, vol. 224, pp. 3–27. Kluwer, Dordrecht (2002)
7. Johnson, R., Oakes, J.: The User-Defined Product Framework (1998),
   http://st-www.cs.illinois.edu/users/johnson/papers/udp/udp.pdf
8. Adaptive Object-Models, http://adaptiveobjectmodel.com/
9. Razavi, R., Mechitov, K., Agha, G., Perrot, J.-F.: Ambiance: A Mobile Agent Platform for End-User Programmable Ambient Systems. In: Augusto, J.C., Shapiro, D. (eds.) Advances in Ambient Intelligence, Frontiers in Artificial Intelligence and Applications (FAIA), vol. 164. IOS Press, Amsterdam (2007)
10. Yahoo! Pipes, http://pipes.yahoo.com
11. eBay Price Watch,
    http://pipes.yahoo.com/pipes/
    pipe.info?_id=avkEShi32xG_EF6KZVUMqA
12. Gamma, E., Helm, R., Johnson, R., Vlissides, J.: Design Patterns: Elements of Reusable Object-Oriented Software. Addison-Wesley, Reading (1995)
13. AAS-Platform, http://www.aas-platform.com/
14. Shapiro, M.: Purpose-built languages. Commun. ACM 52(4), 36–41 (2009)
15. Nardi, B.: A Small Matter of Programming: Perspectives on End User Computing. MIT Press, Cambridge (1993)
16. Johnson, R., Foote, B.: Designing Reusable Classes. Journal of Object-Oriented Programming 1(2), 22–35 (1988)
17. Razavi, R.: Web Pontoon: A Method for Reflective Web Applications. In: Haupt, M., Hirschfeld, R. (eds.) Selected Papers of the International Workshop on Smalltalk Technologies (IWST 2010), HPI, University of Potsdam (GR), TR, vol. 40, pp. 1–10 (2010)
18. Evans, E.: Domain-Driven Design: Tackling Complexity in the Heart of Software. Addison-Wesley, Reading (2005) ISBN: 0-321-12521-5

Prediction of Socioeconomic Levels Using Cell Phone Records

Victor Soto, Vanessa Frias-Martinez,
Jesus Virseda, and Enrique Frias-Martinez

Telefonica Research, Ronda de la Comunicacion s/n, 28043, Madrid, Spain
{vsoto,vanessa,jvirseda,efm}@tid.es

Abstract. The socioeconomic status of a population or an individual provides an understanding of its access to housing, education, health or basic services like water and electricity. In itself, it is also an indirect indicator of the purchasing power and as such a key element when personalizing the interaction with a customer, especially for marketing campaigns or offers of new products. In this paper we study if the information derived from the aggregated use of cell phone records can be used to identify the socioeconomic levels of a population. We present predictive models constructed with SVMs and Random Forests that use the aggregated behavioral variables of the communication antennas to predict socioeconomic levels. Our results show correct prediction rates of over 80% for an urban population of around 500,000 citizens.

1 Introduction

The Socioeconomic Level (SEL) is an indicator used in the social sciences to characterize an individual or a household economic and social status relative to the rest of the society. It is typically defined as a combination of income related variables, such as salary, wealth and/or education. As such, the socioeconomic status of an individual or a household is also an indication of the purchasing power and the tendency to acquire new goods. The information provided by this variable is very relevant from a commercial perspective, as adapting the interaction between a company and a potential client considering the purchasing power of the client is a key element for the success of the interaction. Also, from a public policy perspective, socioeconomic levels are typically used to implement and evaluate social policies and study their evolution over time. The relevance of the SEL as a factor to explain a variety of human behaviors and social conditions can be widely found in the literature. These studies present the effects that different socioeconomic levels might have in various scenarios like access to health services [1] or public transportation [2].

National statistical institutes provide socioeconomic information, for particular geographical areas, typically stratified into three levels: high socioeconomic level, middle socioeconomic level and low socioeconomic level. Nevertheless, computing these indicators has some limitations: (1) acquiring the data set of socioeconomic levels for a whole country can be extremely expensive; (2) the census

Joseph A. Konstan et al. (Eds.): UMAP 2011, LNCS 6787, pp. 377–388, 2011.
© Springer-Verlag Berlin Heidelberg 2011

and/or the personal interviews needed to calculate SELs are usually done every 5 to 10 years, thus not being able to capture changes in SEL in a timely fashion and (3) although the socioeconomic data for developed economies is reliable, such information in developing economies is not as available and/or reliable because economic activities usually happen in an informal way. As a result, although SELs are key elements for public policy, computing them remains a costly and time consuming procedure.

Due to its ubiquity, cell phones are arising as one of the main sensors of human behavior, and as such, they capture a variety of information regarding mobility, social networks and calling patterns, that might be correlated to socioeconomic levels. In the literature, we can find reports highlighting these relations. For example, [3] and [4] use cell phone records to study the impact of socioeconomic levels in human mobility, concluding that higher socioeconomic levels tend to have a higher degree of mobility. Similarly, authors in [5] study the relation between socioeconomic levels and social network diversity, and indicate that social network diversity seems to be a very strong indicator of the development of large online social communities.

In this paper we evaluate the use of aggregated cell phone data to model and predict the different socioeconomic levels of a population. These socioeconomic prediction models have two potential applications: (1) from a commercial perspective, they can be used to tailor offers and new products to the purchasing power of an individual and (2) from a public policy perspective, they can be used as a complement to traditional techniques for estimating the socioeconomic levels of a population in order to implement public policies and study their impact over time. The application of predictive socioeconomic models solves some of the limitations that traditional techniques to obtain SELs have: they are not based on personal interviews and thus constitute a cost-effective solution.

2   Preliminaries

In order to create models that are able to predict the socioeconomic levels of the population within a geographical area, we propose to use supervised machine learning techniques applied over cell phone records obtained from cell phone networks. First, we give a brief overview about how these networks work.

Cell phone networks are built using a set of base transceiver stations (BTS) that are in charge of communicating cell phone devices with the network. Each BTS tower has a geographical location typically expressed by its latitude and longitude. The area covered by a BTS tower is called a cell. At any given moment, one or more BTSs can give coverage to a cell phone. Whenever an individual makes a phone call, the call is routed through a BTS in the area of coverage. The BTS is assigned depending on the network traffic and on the geographic position of the individual. The geographical area covered by a BTS ranges from less than 1 km^2 in dense urban areas to more than 3 km^2 in rural areas. For simplicity, we assume that the cell of each BTS tower can be approximated with a 2-dimensional non-overlapping region computed using Voronoi tessellation.

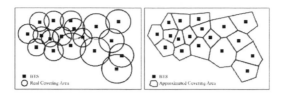

Fig. 1. (Left) Example of a set of BTSs and their coverage and (Right) Approximated coverage obtained applying Voronoi Tessellation

Figure 1(left) shows a set of BTSs with the original coverage of each cell, and Figure 1(right) presents its approximated coverage computed using Voronoi. Our final aim is to predict the socioeconomic level of each cell in the Voronoi tessellation using the aggregated cell phone information of the BTS tower that gives coverage to each area.

CDR (Call Detail Record) databases are generated when a mobile phone connected to the network makes or receives a phone call or uses a service (e.g., SMS, MMS, etc.). In the process, and for invoice purposes, the information regarding the time and the BTS tower where the user was located when the call was initiated is logged, which gives an indication of the geographical position of a user at a given moment in time. Note that no information about the exact position of a user in a cell is known. From all the data contained in a CDR, our study only uses the encrypted originating number, the encrypted destination number, the time and date of the call, the duration of the call, the BTS tower used by the originating cell phone number and the BTS used by the destination phone number when the interaction happened.

In order to generate supervised models for the prediction of socioeconomic levels using cell phone records we need: (1) ground truth data about the socioeconomic levels; and (2) the residence location, expressed as a BTS, of the cell phone users. Given these, we will be able to compute a feature vector –for each BTS– that contains both its socioeconomic level, and the aggregated behavioral, social and mobility characteristics of the individuals that have their residence in the area of coverage of each particular BTS. These feature vectors constitute the traditional machine learning set that will be used to train and test the socioeconomic prediction models. National statistical institutes compute the socioeconomic indicators for specific geographical regions (GR) that they define. However, these GRs do not necessarily match the geographical areas produced by Voronoi tessellation, thus we first need a mechanism that assigns to each Voronoi cell (and to its BTS) a socioeconomic level. On the other hand, given that socioeconomic levels are obtained interviewing people that live within specific GRs, we need to compute the residential BTS of the individuals in our study. For that purpose, we will use an algorithm that can identify the residential BTS of an individual from its calling patterns. The following section gives more details about the data acquisition process and the mechanisms here described necessary to prepare the dataset.

3   Data Acquisition and Pre-Processing

3.1   Cell Phone Traces and Behavioral Variables

For our study, we collected anonymized and encrypted CDR traces from a main city in a Latin-American country over a period of 6 months, from February 2010 to July 2010. The city, which is covered by 920 BTS towers, was specifically selected due to its diversity in socioeconomic levels. From all the individuals in the traces, only users with an average of two daily calls were considered in order to filter those individuals with insufficient information to characterize their patterns. The total number of users considered after filtering was close to 500,000. For each one of these users a total of 279 features modelled from CDR data were computed. The features include information regarding 69 behavioral variables (such as total number of calls or total number of SMSs), 192 social network features (such as in degree and out degree) and 18 mobility variables (such as number of different BTSs used and total distance traveled). Details of the most relevant variables are given in the following sections. In order to identify the residential location of each user, we applied a residential location algorithm that uses the calling patterns to identify which BTS can be defined as home. Details of the algorithm can be found in [6]. With this information, an aggregated set of features is obtained for each BTS as the average of the 279 features for the set of users for whom that BTS is their residence.

3.2   Socioeconomic Levels

The distribution of the socioeconomic levels for the city under study were obtained from the corresponding National Statistical Institute. These values are gathered through national household surveys and give an indication of the social status of a geographical region (GR) relative to the rest of GRs in the country. In our particular case, the National Statistical Institute defines three SELs (A, B, and C), with A being the highest SEL. The SEL value is obtained from the combination of 134 indicators such as the level of studies of the household members, the number of rooms in the house, the number of cell phones, land lines, or computers, combined income, occupation of the members of the household, etc. The SELs are computed for each GR defined by the National Statistical Institute which consists of an area between 1 km^2 and 4 km^2. The city under study is composed of 1,200 geographical regions (GR) as determined by the National Statistical Institute and the SEL distribution is as follows: A levels represent 12% of the GRs, B 59% and C 29%.

3.3   Matching Behavioral Variables with Socioeconomic Levels

The data described in Sections 3.1 and 3.2 provides: (1) aggregated behavioral data for each one of the 920 BTSs that cover the city and (2) a set of 1200 geographical regions (GRs) with its socioeconomic level (A, B or C). In order to create socioeconomic predictive models we need a training set that has, for each BTS, both its cell phone data and its socioeconomic level. However, given

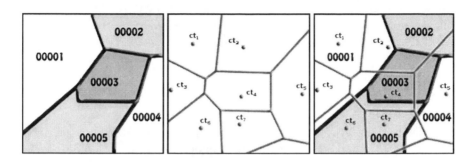

Fig. 2. (Left) Example of Geographical Regions (GR) that have a SEL associated; (Center) The same geographical areas with the BTS towers (coverage approximated with Voronoi tessellation) and (Right) The correspondence between GRs and BTS towers used by a scanning algorithm to assign a SEL to a BTS tower area

that the GRs do not necessarily overlap with the coverage areas, we seek to associate to the area of coverage of each BTS the set of GRs that are totally or partially included in it. Each GR within the BTS area of coverage will have a weight associated to it. The weight represents the percentage of the BTS cell covered by each GR. A graphical example is shown in Figure 2. Figure 2(left) presents the set of GRs (00001 through 0005) defined by the National Statistical Institute. Each GR has an associated SEL value (A, B or C). Figure 2(center) represents, for the same geographical area, the BTS towers (ct1 though ct7) and their cell phone coverage computed with Voronoi tessellation. Finally Figure 2(right) shows the overlap between both representations. This mapping allows to express the area of coverage of each BTS cell (ct) as a function of the GRs as follows:

$$ct_i = w_1 GR_1 + ... + w_n GR_n \qquad (1)$$

where w_1 represents the fraction of GR_1 that covers the coverage area of BTS tower ct_i. Following the example in Figure 2 , ct_1 is completely included in $GR0001$ and as such $n = 1$ and $w_1 = 1$. The same reasoning applies to ct_3. A more common scenario is ct_4, which is partially covered by GR 00003, 00001 and 00005 with $n = 3$ and weights $w_1 = 0.68$, $w_2 = 0.17$ and $w_3 = 0.15$ respectively. The process to compute the mapping between the BTS coverage areas (cts) and the GRs uses a scan line algorithm to obtain the numerical representations of each GR and BTS map [7]. These representations are then used to compute the fractions of the BTS cells covered by each GR. A more detailed description of the algorithm can be found in [6]. Once each BTS tower is represented by a set of GRs and weights, we can associate a SEL value to each BTS. To do so, we first transform the discrete SEL values into a [0-100] range where values in [0-33.3] represent a C SEL, values in [33.4-66.6] a B socioeconomic level and values in [66.7-100] a socioeconomic level A. The final SEL value associated to a BTS can be obtained by computing Formula (1) assuming the central values of the range associated with each SEL: $A = 83.3$, $B = 50$, and $C = 16.6$. Following the previous examples and assuming that the SEL of GRs 00001, 00005 and 00003 are respectively B, B and C, the SEL associated with BTS ct1 and ct3 will be 50, socioeconomic level B, while the SEL associated with BTS ct4 will be 0.68*50+0.17*16.6+0.15*50=44.3, also a B socioeconomic level.

4   Feature Selection

After the initial pre-processing, the training set consists of 920 vectors (one per BTS), each one composed of 279 features (as described in Section 3.1) with its target class, the socioeconomic level. In order to improve the prediction models, we first evaluate the features that are more relevant in our dataset. By boot-strapping the prediction models with vectors of features ordered by relevance, we expect to optimize our classification results. For that purpose, we apply two different feature selection techniques: maxrel and mRMR [8,9]. Maxrel selects the features with the highest relevance REL to the target class, while mRMR selects the features that maximize a heuristic measure of minimal redundancy RED between features and maximal relevance REL of each feature with respect to the target class. This heuristic can be defined in two ways, as a difference (mRMR-MID) and as a quotient (mRMR-MIQ) between the relevance REL and the redundancy RED. The mRMR implementation used is available at `http://penglab.janelia.org/proj/mRMR/`. Both feature selection techniques need all dimensions to be discretized, including the target class. However, the discretization is applied only during the feature selection process. The target class is discretized as explained in the previous section: class C ranges between $0 < SEL \leq 33.3$, class B ranges between $33.3 < SEL \leq 66.7$, and finally class A ranges between $66.7 < SEL \leq 100$. The rest of the features are discretized to three values using the following scheme:

$$x^j \in (-\infty, \mu - \sigma/2) \Rightarrow x^j_{new} = -1 \tag{2}$$
$$x^j \in [\mu - \sigma/2, \mu + \sigma/2] \Rightarrow x^j_{new} = 0 \tag{3}$$
$$x^j \in (\mu + \sigma/2, \infty) \Rightarrow x^j_{new} = +1 \tag{4}$$

4.1   Top Features Selected

The three techniques used for feature selection (maxrel, mRMR-MID and mRMR-MIQ) identify a very similar set of variables as the most relevant ones. In this section we describe the top ten features after averaging their position for the three techniques used. It is important to recall that all features are computed – for each BTS – as the average of the users' features whose residence location is that particular BTS. The most relevant features 1, 2, 7 and 8 correspond to mobility variables; features 3, 5 and 9 are behavioral variables and features 4, 6 and 10 social network variables:

(1) Number of different BTS towers used (weekly): it represents the average number of different BTS towers used by an individual during the chronological period under study.

(2) Diameter of the area of influence(weekly): the area of influence of an individual is defined as the geographical area where a user spends his/her time doing his/her daily activities. It is computed as the maximum distance (in kilometers) between the set of BTS towers used to make/receive calls during the temporal period under study.

(3) Total number of weekly calls: total number of calls that an individual makes and receives every week during the period of study.

(4) Closeness of incoming SMS-contacts in relation to all communications: it is defined as the average geographical distance in kilometers of all the contacts that sent at least one text message to the individual divided by the total geographical distance for SMS, MMS and voice. Low values of this measure mean that the user's text-contacts live closer than his/her voice or MMS contacts.

(5) Percentage of incoming SMSs with respect to all incoming communications: number of received SMSs over all communications (SMS, MMS and voice).

(6) Percentage of SMS-contacts with degree of reciprocity 5: number of contacts that an individual exchanges SMS with and that account to at least five text messages per week over all the individuals' contacts (SMS, MMS and voice) that exchange communications at least five times per week during the period under study.

(7) Radius of gyration: it is defined as the root mean squared distance between the set of BTS towers and its center of masses. Each tower is weighted by the number of calls an individual makes or receives from it during the time period under study. The radius of gyration r_g and the center of masses r_{cm} are computed as:

$$r_g = \sqrt{\frac{1}{n}\sum_{i=1}^{n}(r_i - r_{cm})^2}, \quad (5) \qquad\qquad r_{cm} = \frac{1}{n}\sum_{i=1}^{n}r_i. \quad (6)$$

The radius of gyration can be considered an indirect indication of the distance between home and work (and of the daily commute), given that the towers with the highest weights typically correspond to the towers that give service to the user while at work or at home.

(8) Total distance traveled(weekly): it is defined as the sum of all weekly distances traveled during the time period under study for the individuals whose residence is at that BTS.

(9) Median of total number of calls: the median of the number of calls of all the individual living in the area of coverage of a tower.

(10) Percentage of voice-contacts with degree of reciprocity 2: number of contacts that an individual exchanges voice calls with and that account to at least two calls per week over all the individuals' contacts (SMS, MMS and voice) that exchange calls at least two times per week during the period under study.

Once the features have been ordered according to their relevance, the prediction of socioeconomic levels can be formalized as a classification problem that we solve using SVMs and Random Forest, or as a regression problem which we solve using SVMs.

5   SEL Prediction as a Classification Problem

The classification problem can be formalized as assigning one of the $SEL = \{A, B, C\}$ to a given BTS, and by extension to its area of coverage, based on its aggregated feature vector. Although we have tested several classification methods, we only report the results obtained by SVMs and Random Forests, which yielded the best classification rates. We have tested the classification methods with the feature vectors ordered according to each one of the three feature selection techniques described before in order to understand which one produces better results. On the other hand, we have also tested them on all of its subset vectors from 1 to 279 ordered features so as to determine the number of relevant variables needed for a good prediction rate. In all cases, the BTS dataset with the ordered features and its associated SEL was partitioned for training and testing, containing 2/3 and 1/3 respectively. The classification was implemented using the SVM library libsvm-Java [10] and the Weka Data Mining Software [11] for the Random Forest.

5.1   Support Vector Machines

SVMs have been extensively and successfully used in similar classification problems [12,13]. We have used a Gaussian RBF kernel that is based on two parameters: C and γ. C is a soft-margin parameter that trades off between misclassification error and rigid margins and γ determines the RBF width. For each feature selection order (produced by maxrel, mRMR-MID and mRMR-MIQ), and for each subset of ordered features in $n = \{1, \ldots, 279\}$, we identify the optimum values for (C, γ) as the ones that maximize the accuracy using 5-fold cross-validation over the training set. The search was performed with values of $C \in \{2^{-5}, 2^{-3}, \ldots, 2^{13}, 2^{15}\}$ and of $\gamma \in \{2^{-15}, 2^{-13}, \ldots, 2^{1}, 2^{3}\}$ [14]. Figure 3(left) shows the grid search during the cross-validation stage of one specific feature ordering.

After that, each SVM model is tested using the test set. Figure 3(right) shows the accuracy (Y axis) for each subset of ordered features (X axis) for the three feature selection techniques used. Results for datasets with more than 50 features are not shown, as the classification rate stabilizes. It can be observed that maximum relevance feature selection (maxrel) produces better accuracy results than mRMR-MIQ or mRMR-MID. The best result with maxrel is obtained when using the top 38 features (80% accuracy). A compromise solution would be using the top 17 features, given that we obtain a similar accuracy (79.1%) with considerably fewer variables. The confusion matrices when using 38 and 17 features are:

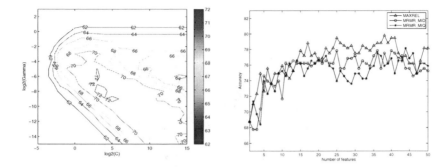

Fig. 3. (Left) Example of the identification of the optimum C and γ values when using mRMR-MIQ and the 38 most relevant features, and (Right) Correct classification rate (Y axis) for the most relevant subsets of $n = 1,...,50$ ordered features when using maxrel, mRMR-MID and mRMR-MIQ

$$P^{38}_{maxrel} = \begin{pmatrix} 0.67\ 0.33\ 0.00 \\ 0.09\ 0.87\ 0.04 \\ 0.02\ 0.30\ 0.68 \end{pmatrix}, P^{17}_{maxrel} = \begin{pmatrix} 0.67\ 0.33\ 0.00 \\ 0.08\ 0.88\ 0.04 \\ 0.02\ 0.38\ 0.61 \end{pmatrix} \qquad (7)$$

An interesting fact that can be observed across all confusion matrices is that if SELs A or C are misclassified, they are misclassified as B, reflecting the implicit order between the three SELs. This implies that when a classification error occurs, the closest SEL to the real one is selected, thus limiting the impact of the incorrect classification in the analysis.

5.2   Random Forest

Random Forest is an ensemble classifier in which two basic ideas are used: bootstrap sampling and random feature selection [15,16]. Basically, Random Forest takes a bootstrap sample as the training set and the complementary as the testing set. During the training of the tree, each node and its split is calculated using only m randomly selected features, $m << M$ where M is the dimension of the feature space. We build Random Forest models with t trees where $t = \{10,\ldots,100\}$ for each subset of ordered features in $M = \{1,\ldots,279\}$, and for each feature selection technique used. Depending on the size of the subset M, $m = \log_2(M + 1)$ random features were considered in each split. Figure 4(left) shows the classification accuracy (Z axis) depending on the size of the forest generated (Y axis) when considering subsets of up to 50 ordered features produced by maxrel. Larger subsets did not improve classification rates. Figure 4(right) shows the maximum accuracy for each subset of features across all values of t (number of trees). We observe that the three feature selection methods reach very similar rates. The best classification rate is achieved by the mRMR-MIQ (82.4%) when using 38 features (and 44 random trees). The mRMR-MID method reaches 80.7% with 28 trees and 41 features and maxrel yields an accuracy of 80.4% with 33 features and 83 trees.

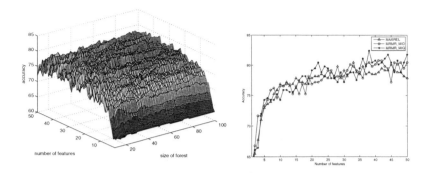

Fig. 4. (Left) Accuracy of the random trees generated for the feature subsets of up to 50 variables produced by maxrel, and (Right) Maximum accuracy obtained for each subset of features produced by each feature selection technique

The confusion matrix of mRMR-MIQ with 38 features 8 (and most of the confusion matrices obtained) indicate that the classifier has the desirable effect of predicting the adjoining class when a classification error is made.

$$P^{38}_{mRMR-MIQ} = \begin{pmatrix} 0.77 & 0.23 & 0.00 \\ 0.07 & 0.90 & 0.03 \\ 0.02 & 0.34 & 0.64 \end{pmatrix} \tag{8}$$

6   SEL Prediction as a Regression Problem

Regression techniques approximate a numerical target function by minimizing a loss function on a training set. The literature reports some cases in which the use of regression instead of classification methods improved the final prediction rates [17]. Thus, given that socioeconomic levels can be expressed as numeric intervals, we explore the computation of socioeconomic prediction models using regression. Support Vector Regression (SVR) Machines [18] are based on similar principles as SVMs for classification: the dataset is mapped to a higher dimension feature space using a nonlinear mapping and linear regression is performed in that space. An important difference between SVMs and SVRs is a loss function that defines a tube of radius ϵ around the predicted curve. Samples lying within this ϵ-tube are ignored and the model is built taking into account the remaining training dataset. The ϵ parameter needs to be determined beforehand.

Following a similar approach to Section 5.1, we use 5-fold cross validation to select the parameters (C, γ, ϵ) that minimize the mean squared error for each subset of ordered features in $M = \{1, \ldots, 279\}$ produced by each feature selection method. We then measure the accuracy of the SVRs against the test set. Figure 5(left) shows the root mean square error (Y axis) for each subset of features

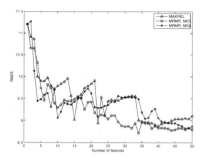 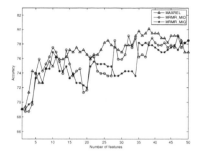

Fig. 5. (Left) Root mean squared error for each subset of features and each feature selection mechanism, and (Right) Accuracy of SEL prediction for each subset of features and each feature selection mechanism when discretizing regression results

(X axis) and each feature selection technique. In this case, mRMR-MID usually obtains the best results, with an RMSE in the range (8.5, 11.5). However, our main interest lies not so much in the numerical socioeconomic value ([0-100]), but in the SEL class associated to that number *i.e.,* in identifying whether SEL is A, B or C. Figure 5(right) shows the accuracy results after discretizing the results of the regression from the range [0-100] onto classes {A,B,C}. Not surprisingly, the best accuracy (80.13%) is achieved when using the 38-feature subset produced by maxrel, although smaller subsets reach similar results. In our particular case, there is not a relevant improvement in the prediction accuracy when using regression as a proxy for classification. However, the use of SEL expressed numerically ([0-100]) instead of through labels, might provide more meaningful information.

7   Conclusions

The identification of socioeconomic levels is a key element for both commercial and public policy applications. Traditional approaches based on interviews are costly both in terms of money and time. Thus, it becomes relevant to find complementary sources of information. Because cell phones are ubiquitously used, they have become one of the main sensors of human behaviors, and as such, they open the door to be used as proxies to study socioeconomic indicators. In this paper we have presented the use of the information collected from cell phone infrastructures to automatically assign a socioeconomic level to the area of coverage of each BTS tower using classification and regression. Each BTS tower was characterized by the aggregated behavioral, social network and mobility variables of the users whose residence lies within the BTS coverage area. Our results indicate that call data records can be used for the identification of SELs, achieving a correct classification rate over 80% using only 38 features.

References

1. Propper, C., Diamiano, M., Leckie, G., Dixon, J.: Impact of patients' socioeconomic status on the distance travelled for hospital admission in the english national health service. Journal Health Serv. Res. Policy 12(3), 153–159 (2007)
2. Carlsson-Kanyama, A., Liden, A.: Travel patterns and environmental effects now and in the future: implications of differences in energy consumption among socio-economic groups. Ecological Economics 30(3), 405–417 (1999)
3. Rubio, A., Frias-Martinez, V., Frias-Martinez, E., Oliver, N.: Human mobility in advanced and developing economies: A comparative analysis. In: AAAI Spring Symposia Artificial Intelligence for Development, AI-D, Stanford, USA (2010)
4. Frias-Martinez, V., Virseda, J., Frias-Martinez, E.: Socio-economic levels and human mobility. In: Qual Meets Quant Workshop - QMQ 2010 at the Int. Conf. on Information & Communication Technologies and Development, ICTD (2010)
5. Eagle, N.: Network diversity and economic development. Science 328(5981) (2010)
6. Frias-Martinez, V., Virseda, J., Rubio, A., Frias, E.: Towards large scale technology impact analyses: Automatic residential localization from mobile phone-call data. In: Int. Conf. on Inf. & Comm. Technologies and Development (ICTD), UK (2010)
7. Lane, M., Carpenter, L., Whitted, T., Blinn, J.: Scan line methods for displaying parametrically defined surfaces. Communications ACM 23(1) (1980)
8. Peng, H., Long, F., Ding, C.: Feature selection based on mutual information: criteria of max-dependency, max-relevance, and min-redundancy. IEEE Transactions on Pattern Analysis and Machine Intelligence 27, 1226–1238 (2005)
9. Ding, C.H.Q., Peng, H.: Minimum redundancy feature selection from microarray gene expression data. J. Bioinformatics and Comp. Biol. 3(2), 185–206 (2005)
10. Chang, C.C., Lin, C.J.: LIBSVM: a library for support vector machines (2001), Software available at http://www.csie.ntu.edu.tw/~cjlin/libsvm
11. Hall, M., Frank, E., Holmes, G., Pfahringer, B., Witten, I.H.: The weka data mining software: an update. SIGKDD Explor. Newsl. 11, 10–18 (2009)
12. Burbidge, R., Buxton, B.: An introduction to support vector machines for data mining. Technical report, Computer Science Department, UCL (2001)
13. Frias-martinez, E., Chen, S.Y., Liu, X.: Survey of data mining approaches to user modeling for adaptive hypermedia. IEEE Transactions on Systems, Man and Cybernetics, Part C: Applications and Reviews 36(6), 734–749 (2006)
14. Hsu, C.W., Chang, C.C., Lin, C.J.: A practical guide to support vector classification. Technical report, Department of Computer Science, Taiwan Univ. (2003)
15. Ho, T.K.: The random subspace method for constructing decision forests. IEEE Trans. Pattern Anal. Mach. Intell. 20(8), 832–844 (1998)
16. Breiman, L.: Random forests. Machine Learning 45, 5–32 (2001)
17. Frias-Martinez, E., Chen, S., Liu, X.: Automatic cognitive style identification of digital library users for personalization. Journal of the American Society for Information Science and Technology 58(2), 237–251 (2007)
18. Drucker, H., Burges, C.J.C., Kaufman, L., Smola, A.J., Vapnik, V.: Support vector regression machines. In: NIPS, pp. 155–161 (1996)

User Perceptions of Adaptivity in an Interactive Narrative

Karen Tanenbaum, Marek Hatala, and Joshua Tanenbaum

School of Interactive Arts + Technology,
Simon Fraser University
250-13450 102 Avenue
Surrey, BC, V3T0A3 Canada
{ktanenba,mhatala,joshuat}@sfu.ca

Abstract. We present results from a user study of the Reading Glove version 2.0, a combination wearable and tabletop interactive narrative system. The system was designed to study user perceptions of adaptivity. The system's reasoning engine guides users through the story using three different recommendation modes: random recommendations, story content-based recommendations, and user model based recommendations. We look at the differences in user behaviour and experience across the three recommendation systems, using information from system logs and user surveys and interviews.

Keywords: Adaptivity, User Modeling, Expert Systems, Interactive Narrative.

1   Introduction

This paper presents the results of a study using the Reading Glove, an adaptive narrative system with a combination wearable and tabletop interface. The goal of this research is to turn a critical eye on the notion of adaptivity, specifically within the realm of tangible and ubiquitous systems. In educational and workplace applications, adaptivity is typically task-oriented and aimed at helping users achieve a particular learning or productivity related goal. This means that the adaptive mechanisms can be much more explicit, intervening directly with the user to offer them assistance or advice. In ubiquitous environments, however, the nature of the interaction with technology shifts. Computational elements are embedded in the environment or in smaller, handheld devices. Users may not be paying explicit attention to the system, and the activities taking place are less task-oriented. Some of the most common uses of adaptivity in ubiquitous spaces are for leisure activities, such as museum guide systems that combine entertainment with education, or domestic systems that automate or anticipate common user behaviours. Since users of these systems are less focused on interacting with the technology itself, the goal of the system is to unobtrusively monitor the users and adapt itself to suit them in some way. The novelty of this kind of interaction is a significant issue in constructing adaptive components that work as intended [1]. In adaptive systems outside of the home, such as in museums and other educational settings, this novelty extends not just to the method of interaction but also the frequency of use. Most of the time, these systems

Joseph A. Konstan et al. (Eds.): UMAP 2011, LNCS 6787, pp. 389–400, 2011.
© Springer-Verlag Berlin Heidelberg 2011

will be "single use", with each person interacting with the system being a new user who needs to learn the interaction paradigm quickly. Unlike domestic or personal systems that have time to learn about their users gradually, ubiquitous public systems have a much more limited window in which to deploy effective adaptation.

The study presented here was designed not to test a particular hypothesis or evaluate the performance of a specific algorithm, but rather to explore the nature of the user experience of adaptivity in this kind of one-time or infrequent use system. We were not concerned whether the adaptive system was "useful" or "effective" in an objective sense, but rather in seeing what kind of sense the users made of the system and of the different forms of adaptive behaviour displayed by the system. We believe this kind of exploratory and subjective experience-oriented research is necessary for truly understanding how and why to design adaptive systems of this nature.

2 Previous Work

2.1 Perception of Adaptivity and Novelty

There are a handful of studies which have taken a similar approach to investigating the user experience of novel systems. Williams et al. focus specifically on the nature of space in intelligent and augmented environments, looking at how people understand ubiquitous computing as a "spatially situated phenomenon" [2]. They created an installation called SignalPlay, which involved a series of large, moveable props which each had a different effect on the soundscape of the room. Visitors to the space had to experiment with the objects in order to understand how they worked; no explicit instruction was given. From observing visitor interactions with the props, the authors identified three modes of object interaction used when learning how to control and interpret new interaction mechanisms: 1) iconic, where they interact in ways suggested by what the props represented; 2) intrinsic, where they interact based on physical characteristics of the objects; 3) instrumental, where they interact based on the effect it has on the system [2].

On a simpler scale, Svanaes and Verplank approach this issue from a different direction with a study of the naturally arising metaphors and mental models that people create when playing with a set of interactive tiles [3]. The authors observed that participants spontaneously made use of five fundamental metaphors: Cartesian space, state space, linear time, relational metaphors (human relations), and paranormal phenomena. Each of these reflects a different mental model that the users were applying to learn how to interact with the system. Understanding these mental models can suggest different ways of designing a tangible interface to leverage the intuitive use of that model, or perhaps to explicitly design against it if the model leads to inappropriate intuitions about how the system works. Both of these studies show how a rich, qualitative-focused investigation of how people interact with computational systems can result in insight into the nature of these technology-enhanced experiences and how to design them.

2.2 Interactive Narrative and Recommender Systems

Most work on intelligent narrative systems centers around how to adapt the story and environment to choices made by the interactor, i.e. how to restructure the plot so that story coherence is maintained or how to create non-player characters that can interact with the player in a life-like manner [4]. In the Reading Glove system, the narrative and the environment are fixed. The interactor selects what order the story is heard in, but cannot fundamentally change what happens. The reasoning engine that drives the guidance system on the tabletop thus functions essentially as a knowledge-based recommender, helping the "reader" move through the story in a coherent manner. As a result, the intelligence techniques used in the system are most similar to those used in recommender systems in educational and informational applications, where the goal is to present a static body of content to the user in an intelligent and dynamic manner based on her choices and actions [5-7].

3 The Reading Glove System

The current Reading Glove system is version 2.0 of an earlier iteration of the project. The first version, discussed in [8-9], consisted of a glove-based reader and a set of tagged objects used to access a non-linear story. The current version adds an intelligent recommender system and tabletop display (See figure 1). These additions assist interactors in navigating the narrative while also allowing us to study user perceptions of adaptivity. This paper is the first to discuss results from this iteration.

Fig. 1. The objects on the tabletop (left) and a reader using the system (right)

3.1 The Reading Experience

Interaction with the Reading Glove system is straightforward. The "reader" puts on a soft fabric glove and begins by picking up one of the objects sitting on a tabletop. This tabletop displays pictures of each object arranged in a rectangle (see figure 3 below). When the palm of the glove registers the tag on the object, a segment of recorded audio narration is played back over the speakers. Several seconds before the clip ends, the tabletop display delivers a set of recommendations on which object to pick up next by enlarging and brightening photos of the recommended objects. The reader can choose to follow the on-screen advice or not. Each object has two clips of audio narration associated with it, so the reader must engage with each object multiple times to uncover all the story fragments.

The story embedded in the Reading Glove system was developed based on the objects, which were picked to fit a certain historical aesthetic. Other aspects of this aesthetic are echoed in the background image of the tabletop display and in the table itself. The plot of the story revolves around a British spy operating in French-occupied Algiers around the turn of the 20th century. The narrative traces the spy's discovery that his cover has been blown and his unraveling of how this came about. The uncovering of facts in the narrative mimics the uncovering of story fragments that the readers perform with the objects. Thus the puzzle-like nature of the story and the interaction support and reinforce each other. The story can also be experienced in a small group, with one person wearing the glove and the others assisting in untangling the narrative and selecting the next objects to engage with.

3.2 The Glove and Objects

The central component of the system is the Reading Glove itself, a soft fabric glove containing an Arduino Lilypad microcontroller, an Innovations ID-12 RFID reader, and an Xbee Series 2 wireless radio. Interactors pick up objects associated with the story, each of which has been tagged with an RFID chip. When the RFID reader in the palm of the glove detects a tag, the tag ID is communicated wirelessly via the Xbee radio to a second Xbee unit connected to the serial port of a laptop. The serial data is read into a java program in Eclipse which processes the tag activation and triggers the audio playback of a specific "lexia": a pre-recorded story fragment associated with the object.

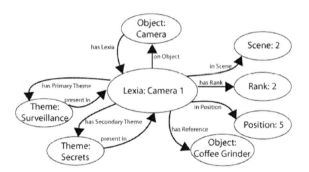

Fig. 2. The structure of the ontology for one lexia

3.3 The Table and Reasoning Engine

In addition to generating audio feedback, picking up an object also triggers the reasoning engine to generate a set of recommendations that will be shown to the interactor when the audio clip nears its completion. The reasoning engine is a rule-based expert system written in the Jess language. The reasoning component relies on an OWL (Web Ontology Language) ontology that encodes semantic knowledge about the story content. A rule-based expert system was used because this type of artificial intelligence mostly closely mimics the behaviour of a human expert, in our case the interactive story writer, as suggested by [10]. The rules can be hand-crafted based on expert knowledge and thus do not rely on a large corpus of data from which to generate models or rankings.

Ontology. The ontology has 5 classes and 11 object properties that link classes together in a directional relationship. The object and lexia classes have a reciprocal relationship, with each item in the object class (e.g. the physical object Telegraph Key) linking to two entities in the lexia class (e.g. the sound files Telegraph Key 1 and Telegraph Key 2) and each lexia connecting back to the object. See figure 2 for an example of a specific lexia in the ontology, Camera 1, on the object Camera. The lexia class also has a set of non-reciprocal object properties connecting each sound file to different pieces of information. The "hasRank" property indicates how important the lexia is to the overall narrative, as determined by us as the story authors. Rank varies from 1 to 9, with 1 being the most important. The "inScene" property indicates what scene each lexia was part of; there were 4 scenes determined by changes in the location of the narrative. The "hasReference" property was only active for some lexia, those which contained a direct reference to another object within the text of the audio clip. For example, the camera1 lexia includes the sentence "I made certain to lose myself in the chaotic traffic of one of the city's open air markets before stopping to inspect the coffee grinder.", so in the ontology the lexia is linked to the coffee grinder object. Finally, each lexia is associated with 2-3 themes present in the story, such as "surveillance" or "disguise". This relationship was also represented reciprocally between the lexia and theme classes with the properties "hasPrimaryTheme" and "hasSecondaryTheme" connecting lexia to themes and "presentIn" connecting theme to lexia. All of the relationships in the ontology were asserted as facts in the JESS rule base at the start of each system run. For the implementation details on working with ontologies in Jess see [11].

Fig. 3. The tabletop screen in neutral (left) and recommender (right) states

Recommendations. The Jess rules use this knowledge base to recommend a set of three objects that will be most likely to advance the interactor's understanding of the story. Thus the recommender system acts as a kind of "expert storyteller", leading the reader through the narrative. The recommendations appear on the table several seconds before the end of the lexia. This delay is intended to focus attention on the story and objects rather than the display, encouraging the user to listen to the full lexia rather than just skip ahead. During most of the lexia playback, all 10 objects are visible on the screen in small, semi-transparent boxes. When the recommendation system kicks in, the pictures of the recommended objects grow in size and become fully opaque (See figure 3). The display remains in this state until another object is picked up, at which point in reverts to the neutral state.

3.4 Recommender Types

Three separate versions of the recommender were developed: a story content recommender, a user model recommender, and a random recommender.

Story Content Recommender. The story content recommender uses encoded knowledge about the narrative to recommend three objects that will be most likely to continue the story in a coherent and helpful way. The interactor can choose any object to start the story, after which the recommendation system begins to assist based on their ongoing choices. Each of the three recommended objects are chosen based on a different set of criteria: Theme, Importance, or Position. The last lexia chosen by the interactor is used as a "seed" to the recommendation system, generating a set of weights that rank all other available "candidate" lexia. The highest ranked candidate after all the weights are calculated is the one recommended for each criterion.

Theme. The Theme criterion uses the ontology-encoded themes of the seed to evaluate the candidates based on how closely their themes matched. Each lexia has two themes, primary and secondary. The weighting of the candidates is based on whether both the theme and the theme type match the seed. Table 1 gives the weights for ranking seed and candidate themes. If the seed lexia text contains a direct reference to the object of the candidate lexia, this contributes an additional 50 points. After all the weights are calculated and summed together, the candidate with the highest sum is designated the Theme recommendation. Again, for implementation details of applying our weighting scheme using rules we refer the reader to [11].

Table 1. Weightings for matching themes

Seed \ Candidate	Primary Theme	Secondary Theme
Primary Theme	50	20
Secondary Theme	30	40

Position. The Position criterion looks at the chronological order of the lexia and favors candidates that would either move the story forward or fill in the backstory. The highest weights are given to candidates that are 1-4 positions past the seed, while medium weights are given to candidates positioned prior to the seed location, and low weights are given to candidates 5 or more ahead of the seed. So if the seed lexia is in position 5, the candidates in positions 6 would have a weighting of 50, 7-9 would be weighted 30, 1-4 would be weighted 20 and 10-20 would be unweighted. This prioritizes continuity of the story and deprioritizes leaping ahead to the end of the narrative. The candidate with the highest weight at the end of this calculation would be designated the Position recommendation.

Importance. The importance criterion looks at what the most important pieces of the story are and favors recommending the most crucial information. The importance weights combine information about what scene the fragment is in and what the overall rank of each lexia within the scene is. Candidate lexia in the same scene as the seed lexia are given a weight of 50 while candidates from different scenes are unweighted. Next, importance weightings are assigned based on rank, with rank 1 = 45, 2 = 40, 3 = 35, and so on down to rank 9 = 5. The ranks of both of the lexia on an object were summed together with the scene weighting for each candidate lexia. This mechanism was necessary in order to uncover lexia on objects that had not yet been interacted with. For example, an object might have a lexia with rank 8 as the initial state and a lexia with rank 2 as the secondary state. Although the second lexia is very important, if the first lexia is never listened to, the other one will never become available. Summing the importance for both lexia on the object allowed unimportant lexia to be recommended in order to get access to the more important pieces also on the same object. The scene and rank weights were summed and the candidate with the highest sum would be designated the Importance Recommendation.

After all these calculations are completed, the recommendations generated by each of the criteria are presented to the user on the tabletop. Each recommendation has a subtly colored border indicating which criterion it represents, with blue for theme, green for position, and red for importance.

User Model. The user model recommender is built on top of the story content recommender, adding additional weights based on the specific actions the user takes with the system. It promotes lexia that have not yet been listened to by adding weights to the candidate calculations described above. The user model also tracks which of the recommendation streams are followed if the user selects from one of the three highlighted objects. If the user consistently follows one recommendation criterion over the others, the user model component will begin to push that recommendation to the user earlier, before the other two.

Random. The random recommender is simple and straightforward: three objects are selected at random from the set of available objects using a random number generator in Processing, and are presented to the user via the tabletop display. The colored borders around the pictures are maintained, but are essentially meaningless.

4   User Studies

We designed our user study to investigate the following questions using the Reading Glove system:

1. How do interactors respond to the adaptive system?
2. How do the responses differ across the different types of adaptivity?

Our goal was to explore the user response to adaptivity rather than to evaluate the strict effectiveness of the adaptive mechanisms. We were interested in how the users made sense of a system that responded to them in intelligent or intelligent-seeming ways when they were not given any explicit information about what the system would be reacting to.

4.1   Study Protocol

In the fall of 2010 we conducted a mixed-methods user study with 30 participants in roughly one hour long sessions. We collected a wide variety of data, including pre- and post-interaction surveys, a post-interaction interview, video of the participants using the system, and log data generated by the system itself. Participants were randomly assigned to one of three conditions, corresponding to the three versions of the system described above. They were given a brief tutorial on how to use the glove by interacting with a set of training objects, and then engaged with the full system. They were not told which condition they were in, and the only description they were given of what the system did was as follows: "You will be interacting with this collection of objects. Interact with them until you feel like you understand the story. The images on the screen can help guide you through the story. You are free to handle, play with, and move the objects around as much as you like. You may take as long as you like. Let us know when you are ready to stop."

4.2 Participant Demographics

Of the 30 participants we ran in the study, we had 19 men and 11 women. Ages ranged between 23 to 55 years old, with the median at 31 years. All were graduate level students, 20 working on their Masters degrees and 10 working on PhDs. Most were from media and technology oriented programs. Participants were asked to self-rank themselves on their English fluency, with 18 reporting to be native speakers, 7 reporting as fluent speakers and 5 as advanced speakers. All participants were administered a listening comprehension test at the start of the session as well, to check for English comprehension issues, and all passed.

5 Results and Discussion

To begin to answer our research questions, we looked at descriptive and correlational statistics drawn from the system logs, questionnaires, and interviews. Portions of the interview data were coded in order to generate ratings for how well participants understood the story.

5.1 Basic Response to the System

At the very end of the user study session, we asked participants to fill out a short Likert-style survey consisting of 8 questions. The questions were paired as negative and positive versions of 4 basic concepts, with participants asked to rate them on a 5-point scale consisting of "Strongly Disagree", "Disagree", "Undecided", "Agree", "Strongly Agree" and "No Answer". The pairs were presented in a jumbled order to the participant, but are listed here by concept for ease of reading.

- Ease of Use: The system was easy to use; The system was hard to use
- Enjoyment: The system was enjoyable to use; The system was confusing to use
- Story: The actions I took didn't influence the story; My actions changed the story
- Experience Again: I would not be interested in experiencing another story like this; I would like to experience another story this way

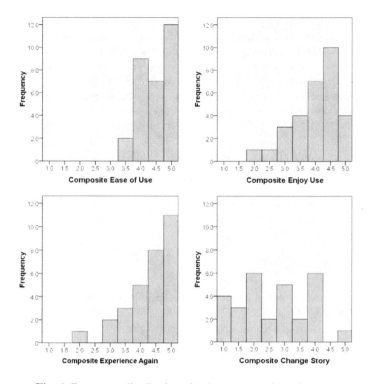

Fig. 4. Frequency distributions for the post-questionnaire items

The charts in figure 4 show the composite participant responses on the post-questionnaire, with "Strongly Disagree" coded as 1 and "Strongly Agree" as 5. Responses from the paired questions were combined to yield a composite measure. The second version of the question was subtracted from 6 (i.e. a score of "5" became a score of "1") and then the responses were summed and divided by 2. The scores on "Ease of Use" (mean 4.483), "Enjoyment of Use" (mean 4.017) and "Experience Again" (mean 4.317) were consistently high enough that we feel safe in concluding that there were no serious usability issues that were affecting the way participants engaged with the system. The most variable results come from the question regarding whether or not they perceived the story as changing as a result of their actions (mean 2.638). A full discussion of these results addresses separate research questions regarding the interpretation of interactive narrative experiences, and is outside the scope of this paper. No significant correlations were found between the condition that the participant was in versus the ratings they gave the system in the post-questionnaire.

In the post-interaction interview, we asked participants to articulate their understanding of how the system worked. There were three main questions which elicited responses about the adaptive component:

1. Can you describe in your own words how the system worked?
2. What did you think was going on with the pictures of the objects on the screen?
3. How did you decide which object to pick up next?

Nearly all of the participants explicitly stated in the interview that they believed the system was responding intelligently to their actions by highlighting particular elements on the screen, but none of them had any confident guesses about how the system was making the decisions. The most common guess was that the system recommended the chronologically next item; some participants also speculated that it recommended objects that hadn't been picked up yet. One participant described their experience as follows: "So for the first half I picked objects up in sequence according to what was highlighted...The one time I did it out of sequence I got something out of sequence and so it was a little confusing. So there was sort of good bread crumbs there that when I didn't follow them, you know, broke the story a little bit." Similarly, another participant said the recommendation system "was helpful I think in sort of helping me move through the story: when I sort of went away from that I found the story got a little more broken apart and all over the place." We were surprised to find that almost no one recognized that the three recommendations could be distinguished from each other by their colored border; it's possible that the color tints were too subtle. Most people selected from amongst the three recommended objects based on whim or personal attraction to a particular object. One of the participants in the random condition volunteered that sometimes the recommendations "didn't really make sense", but when asked later what he thought the system was doing with the enlarged pictures on the screen claimed that there "I think there's some sort of really complicated algorithm in the background that's figuring out what to display." These statements suggest that participants are strongly inclined to believe that the system is smart—possibly even smarter than them—in that they assume they would not be able to guess at the complexity underlying the system behaviour.

5.2 Response to Different Forms of Adaptivity

After investigating the overall response to the adaptive system, we focused on the research questions stated above and studied the difference between the versions. We wanted to see if there were patterns in participant behaviour that indicated an unconscious reaction to the nature of the intelligence underlying the system, even if they could not articulate that understanding when questioned. We began by examining descriptive statistics based on the data in the system logs, which included elements like how many distinct lexia each person listened to, how many times they followed a recommendation, and how much overall time they spent interacting with the system.

One thing that we noticed early on was that one of our 30 cases was an outlier in almost every metric collected. Because this participant's numbers were so far outside the cluster of everyone else, we chose to discard that data rather than allow it to skew the results. It seemed clear that this person interacted with the system in a very different way than the rest of the participants. If we had a larger sample, it might be possible to identify whether this represents a particular subset of the population who consistently responds in a particular way, but in the absence of more data we cannot tell what is going on.

While examining the descriptive statistics and graphs of the data collected, we noticed that on two key behavioral factors, the participants in the random condition appeared to be on the low end of the scale compared to the participants in the two intelligent conditions (see figure 5). These were "Average Listens per Lexia" and "Total Lexia Activated", measures that are related to each other. Both of them give an indication of how much of the story was listened to. Since there were 20 lexia, participants who listened to fewer than 20 total lexia obviously did not hear everything. Average listens gives a similar indication of the saturation of the reading, with a score of 1 indicating that they listened to each lexia once, higher numbers showing that they listened to some of the lexia repeatedly, and lower numbers indicating that they did not hear every piece of the story.

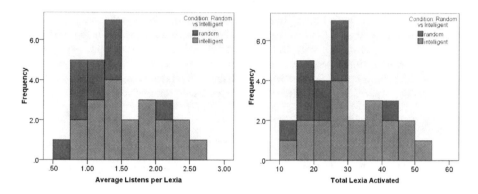

Fig. 5. Frequency distributions for two behavioural measures separated by condition (random = blue, intelligent = green)

We ran an ANOVA on these two factors to see if the apparent correlation between condition and behaviour was significant. There was a significant effect of condition on the number of lexia interacted with: $F(1, 27) = 4.736$, $p<.05$, $w = .33$ as well as a significant effect of condition on average number of listens per lexia, $F(1, 27) = 5.838$, $p<.05$, $w = .38$. What is particularly interesting about this result is that we also ran an ANOVA on amount of time spent with the system, and failed to find a significant correlation between time spent and condition. So it was not simply that the interactors in the intelligent condition spent more time with the system, but rather that they listened to more lexia repeatedly within the time that they spent. This points to a deeper and more dedicated engagement with the system that is driven by the adaptivity.

6 Conclusions and Future Work

We have described a tangible interactive narrative system that uses intelligent techniques to recommend paths through the story space. We presented a user study where participants were exposed to one of three different recommender systems to explore the user experience of adaptive systems. We have shown that users are unlikely to be able to articulate their understanding of the intelligence of the system, but that this doesn't mean they don't respond to it at some level. Statistical results regarding behaviour with the system suggest a deeper level of engagement as a result of the adaptive behaviour.

Acknowledgments. We gratefully acknowledge that this project was funded by the PLAYPR group of the GRAND NCE and NSERC Discovery Grants Program.

References

1. Edwards, W.K., Grinter, R.E.: At Home with Ubiquitous Computing: Seven Challenges. In: Abowd, G.D., Brumitt, B., Shafer, S.A.N. (eds.) UbiComp 2001. LNCS, vol. 2201, pp. 256–272. Springer, Heidelberg (2001)
2. Williams, A., Kabisch, E., Dourish, P.: From Interaction to Participation: Configuring Space through Embodied Interaction. In: Beigl, M., Intille, S.S., Rekimoto, J., Tokuda, H. (eds.) UbiComp 2005. LNCS, vol. 3660, pp. 287–304. Springer, Heidelberg (2005)
3. Svanaes, D., Verplank, W.: In Search of Metaphors for Tangible User Interfaces. Designing Augmented Reality Environments, Elsinore, Denmark (2000)
4. Thue, D., Bulitko, V., Spetch, M., Wasylishen, E.: Interactive Storytelling: A Player Modelling Approach. In: Artificial Intelligence and Interactive Digital Entertainment Conference (AIIDE), Stanford, CA, pp. 43–48 (2007)
5. Damiano, R., Gena, C., Lombardo, V., Nunnari, F., Pizzo, A.: A stroll with Carletto: adaptation in drama-based tours with virtual characters. User Modeling and User Adaptive Interaction 18, 417–453 (2008)
6. Hatala, M., Wakkary, R.: Ontology-Based User Modeling in an Augmented Audio Reality System for Museums. User Modeling and User Adaptive Interaction 15, 339–380 (2005)
7. Hatala, M., Tanenbaum, K., Wakkary, R., Muise, K., Mohabbati, B., Corness, G., Budd, J., Loughin, T.: Experience Structuring Factors Affecting Learning in Family Visits to Museums. In: Cress, U., Dimitrova, V., Specht, M. (eds.) EC-TEL 2009. LNCS, vol. 5794, pp. 37–51. Springer, Heidelberg (2009)
8. Tanenbaum, K., Tanenbaum, J., Antle, A., Seif El-Nasr, M., Hatala, M.: Experiencing the Reading Glove. In: Tangible, Embodied and Embedded Interaction. ACM Press, Madeira (2011)
9. Tanenbaum, J., Tanenbaum, K., Antle, A.: The Reading Glove: Designing Interactions for Object-Based Tangible Storytelling. In: Augmented Human, pp. 132–140. ACM Press, Megeve (2010)
10. Darlington, K.: The Essence of Expert Systems. Prenctice Hall, Harlow (2000)
11. Hatala, M., Wakkary, R., Kalantari, L.: Ontologies and Rules in Support of Real-time Ubiquitous Application. Journal of Web Semantics 3(1), 5–22 (2005)

Performance Prediction in Recommender Systems

Alejandro Bellogín

Universidad Autónoma de Madrid, Escuela Politécnica Superior
Calle Francisco Tomás y Valiente 11, 28049 Madrid, Spain
alejandro.bellogin@uam.es

Abstract. Research on Recommender Systems has barely explored the issue of adapting a recommendation strategy to the user's information available at a certain time. In this thesis, we introduce a component that allows building dynamic recommendation strategies, by reformulating the performance prediction problem in the area of Information Retrieval to that of recommender systems. More specifically, we investigate a number of adaptations of the query clarity predictor in order to infer the ambiguity in user and item profiles. The properties of each predictor are empirically studied by, first, checking the correlation of the predictor output with a performance measure, and second, by incorporating a performance predictor into a recommender system to produce a dynamic strategy. Depending on how the predictor is integrated with the system, we explore two different applications: dynamic user neighbour weighting and hybrid recommendation. The performance of such dynamic strategies is examined and compared with that of static ones.

Keywords: recommender systems, performance prediction, query clarity, personalisation, user modelling.

1 Introduction

The aim of Recommender Systems (RS) is to help users to cope with information overload by suggesting "interesting" items from huge databases or catalogues. Three types of recommender systems are commonly recognised, based on how item suggestions are made [1]: content-based filtering (CBF), collaborative filtering (CF), and hybrid filtering (HF). CBF recommends the user items similar to the ones she preferred in the past, CF recommends the user items that people (called neighbours in the literature) with similar tastes and preferences liked in the past, and HF combines content-based and collaborative filtering approaches. In this context, although many alternatives are possible, the most common form of ground evidence of user preferences, upon which recommendations are generated, consists of explicit numeric ratings for individual items.

In the RS research area, a barely explored issue –as a problem to be addressed by systematic approaches– is how to dynamically adapt a recommendation strategy to the user's preference information available at a certain time. Let us consider the following two examples: neighbourhood building in CF, and ensemble recommenders, as a special case of HF. In both cases, most of existing recommendation approaches are

Joseph A. Konstan et al. (Eds.): UMAP 2011, LNCS 6787, pp. 401–404, 2011.
© Springer-Verlag Berlin Heidelberg 2011

not adaptive in the sense that every user is considered equally, from the system viewpoint. In user-based CF [1], the user's neighbours are only weighted according to the similarity between the user and each neighbour, not considering global characteristics of each neighbour that would make them less appropriate, such as their confidence or trustworthiness [7]. In ensemble recommenders, on the other hand, the weighting factor which aggregates the outputs from individual recommenders is usually the same for every user and item, again, not taking into account inherent properties of the different users and items.

In this thesis, we aim at addressing the following research question: **how to dynamically adapt a recommendation strategy to the available user's information?** For such purpose, we investigate the adaptation of Information Retrieval (IR) performance prediction techniques to RS, where performance prediction refers to the estimation of the performance of an IR system in response to a specific query [5]. More specifically, we draw from the notion of *query clarity* [4] as a basis for finding suitable predictors. In essence, query clarity captures the lack of ambiguity in a query, by computing the distance between the language models induced by the query and the collection. In analogy to query clarity, we hypothesise that the amount of uncertainty involved in user and item data (reflecting ambiguity in the users' tastes, and popularity patterns in the items) may correlate with the accuracy of a system's recommendations. We believe this uncertainty can be captured as the clarity of users or items by performing a reformulation of query clarity. Thus, we could introduce a performance predictor in a recommender system to produce an adaptive recommendation strategy. In this way, we would build dynamic neighbourhoods and ensemble recommenders by exploiting user or item clarity values. Moreover, our approach allows for an interpretation of the weights given to the user, in contrast to other works in the literature [3, 6]. This is possible since these weights are closely related with her ambiguity in the system, which would provide for further explanation to the user about her current performance in the system and how she could improve it.

2 Performance Prediction in Recommender Systems

The main goal of this thesis can be summarised as predicting the best way for combining the available information from a recommender system in a user-basis, such as deciding the user's weight in a hybrid recommender and when building her neighbourhood in a CF approach. For this purpose, we first need to capture the ambiguity in user's tastes, and then introduce it within the recommendation process to build an adaptive strategy.

Starting problem

Our main problem is that of considering the ambiguity in a user's tastes, so that, depending on this prediction, we may adapt the recommendation strategy. For instance, let us suppose a movie recommendation situation, where user tastes are represented by rating-movie pairs, and ratings are in a 1-5 scale. Then, let us assume user U with the following tastes: (*Matrix*, 5), (*Star Wars*, 2), (*Titanic*, 1), (*Pretty Woman*, 4). Moreover, let the community be defined as follows (*Matrix*, 4), (*Star Wars*, 5), (*Titanic*, 2), (*Pretty Woman*, 1). Then, it seems user U is an ambiguous user because she rates those movies very differently, such as *Matrix* and *Star Wars*, which are movies with tastes commonly shared by the community. Moreover, this user is not only difficult to be recommended from the system point of view, but if we use her as a neighbour in a CF recommender, the performance would probably degrade because, in user-based CF, items liked by neighbours would be recommended. In this situation, if a profile only partially matches the user U's profile, she could receive unexpected suggestions, e.g., the system may recommend *Pretty Woman* if *Titanic* is low rated and *Matrix* is highly rated.

In this context, we then should solve the following problems: 1) define a proper ambiguity predictor, 2) check its predictive power, and 3) evaluate whether the use of the predictor improve the final performance or not. In the next section, we introduce the solutions being developed for the problems described above.

Proposed Solution
We state that estimating the user's ambiguity by predicting her performance (in IR terms) could bring relevant contributions to the Recommender Systems community and be used to address the problems mentioned above.

In particular, we have revised the research literature on performance prediction in IR, and adapted some of its more prominent models, such as query clarity [4], for recommendation. In this way, we have defined *user clarity* as follows: clarity$(u) = \sum_{x \in X} p(x|u) \log p(x|u)/p_c(x)$, where x denotes items, users, or ratings. We assume different probability models, for instance, we may have the probability space X defined as the space of all possible rating values, then we can estimate $p_c(r)$ and $p(r|u)$ using uniform probabilities, or other distribution estimations [8] (more details in [2]).

Once a user performance predictor has been defined, we need to confirm that it has some predictive power. Thus, the first goal is to find strong correlation between the envisioned predictor and a performance metric, which depends on the final application. In this context, Pearson and Spearman correlation coefficients are the most common sources of evidence. Then, also depending on the application, we would incorporate the predictor into the recommendation process in different ways.

Our research, so far, has demonstrated that when a predictor obtains strong (or positive enough) correlation with respect to a performance metric, a significant improvement is obtained when the predictor is introduced into the recommendation process for building an adaptive strategy. For instance, in [2] we describe how a predictor can be used for dynamic neighbour weighting. In this situation, we obtained an improvement of over 5% with respect to the baseline, which in this experiment was the standard (static) CF algorithm. It is worth noticing our method outperformed the baseline, even though Pearson's correlation between the predictor and the performance metric was not very large, obtaining correlation values between 0.15 and 0.20.

Moreover, latest experiments shown consistent results for different ensemble recommenders, such as combination of CBF and CF recommenders, and different types of CF algorithms (user- and item-based). In these cases, Pearson's correlation between our clarity-based predictors and the performance metric hovered around 0.3 and 0.46, and the improvements over the baseline –in this case, a fixed hybrid recommender with the same weight for all the users– were between 3 and 12%.

The obtained results confirm that performance prediction is also possible in recommendation. Two applications have been proposed: dynamic user neighbour weighting and dynamic hybrid recommendation. In both situations, adaptive strategies outperformed non-adaptive ones.

3 Conclusions and Future Work

The main contribution of our work is the idea of inferring the user's performance within a recommender system in order to use it for building adaptive recommendation strategies, such as boosting those neighbours which are predicted to perform better, and weighting differently users or items in ensemble recommenders. Preliminary obtained results are promising and encouraging, showing that our approach is useful, improving the performance of state-of-the-art algorithms.

The main focus of our research concerns the definition of user performance predictors, as well as different applications where it can be used. In this line, this thesis needs to a) find a theoretical background about why some predictors work better than others, i.e., have stronger correlations; and b) explore other input sources apart from ratings. Regarding the first aspect, there are open issues that need further investigation, like for example analysing why some recommenders are more inclined to correlate stronger with respect to different formulations of the same predictor than others. In order to explore other input sources, the next step will be to obtain more heterogeneous datasets where not only ratings, but implicit feedback, time and social relations are available. Furthermore, new performance predictors using this data should be defined and evaluated accordingly.

Acknowledgments. This work was supported by the Spanish Ministry of Science and Innovation (TIN2008-06566-C04-02) and Dirección General de Universidades e Investigación de la Comunidad de Madrid and Universidad Autónoma de Madrid (CCG10-UAM/TIC-5877).

References

1. Adomavicius, G., Tuzhilin, A.: Toward the Next Generation of Recommender Systems: A Survey of the State-of-the-art and Possible Extensions. IEEE Transactions on Knowledge and Data Engineering 17(6), 734–749 (2005)
2. Bellogín, A., Castells, P.: A Performance Prediction Approach to Enhance Collaborative Filtering Performance. In: Gurrin, C., He, Y., Kazai, G., Kruschwitz, U., Little, S., Roelleke, T., Rüger, S., van Rijsbergen, K. (eds.) ECIR 2010. LNCS, vol. 5993, pp. 382–393. Springer, Heidelberg (2010)
3. Claypool, M., Gokhale, A., Miranda, T., Murnikov, P., Netes, D., Sartin, M.: Combining Content-Based and Collaborative Filters in an Online Newspaper. In: ACM SIGIR 1999 Workshop on Recommender Systems: Algorithms and Applications (1999)
4. Cronen-Townsend, S., Zhou, Y., Croft, B.W.: Predicting Query Performance. In: 25th International ACM SIGIR Conference on Research and Development in Information Retrieval (SIGIR 2002), pp. 299–306. ACM Press, New York (2002)
5. Hauff, C.: Predicting the Effectiveness of Queries and Retrieval Systems. PhD thesis, University of Twente, Enschede (2010)
6. Lathia, N., Hailes, S., Capra, L.: Temporal Collaborative Filtering with Adaptive Neighbourhoods. In: 32nd International ACM SIGIR Conference on Research and Development in Information Retrieval (SIGIR 2009), pp. 796–797. ACM Press, New York (2009)
7. O'Donovan, J., Smyth, B.: Trust in Recommender Systems. In: 10th International Conference on Intelligent User Interfaces (IUI 2005), pp. 167–174. ACM Press, New York (2005)
8. Wang, J., de Vries, A.P., Reinders, M.J.T.: Unified relevance models for rating prediction in collaborative filtering. ACM Trans. Inf. Syst. 26(3), 1–42 (2008)

Multi-perspective Context Modelling to Augment Adaptation in Simulated Learning Environments

Dimoklis Despotakis

School of Computing, University of Leeds, West Yorkshire,
Leeds LS2 9JT, United Kingdom
scdd@leeds.ac.uk

1 Research Problem

Simulated environments, where learners are involved in simulated situations that resemble actual activities, gain a growing popularity in professional training, and provide powerful experiential learning tools for developing soft skills in ill-defined domains[1]. Adaptation and personalization will play a key role in these environments[2]. To be effective, training environments for adults should offer learning experiences *directly relevant to the real world job context* and *align with the learner's needs in practice* [3]. In contrast, simulated environments embed predefined interactive scenarios with fixed parameters, whereas real world activities are affected by dynamic conditions and complex situations, hard to capture in the simulated world.

On the other hand, there is a vast amount of user contributed social content about real world activity (e.g. user comments or stories) which represents different viewpoints and contexts. This abundance of user generated digital content provides useful traces that can *"tell"* what happens in the real world. The **key challenge** is:

> *Can digital traces from the social web be used to construct a model of the real-world activity and how can this model improve adaptation in simulated learning environments?*

This PhD project addresses the above challenge within the context of interpersonal communication, considering *job interview training* as the activity **use case** and utilizing *user comments on job interview videos* as digital traces of real world experiences. Based on this, the following **research questions** are addressed:

- **RQ1:** *How to develop an elicitation mechanism to derive an extended context model that will enable intelligent augmentation of digital records of job activities taking into account different user perspectives?*
- **RQ2:** *How to use the extended context model to retrieve content given a particular simulated setting, including user activity, simulated context, and user perspective?*

To address these questions, a **Context-rich Activity Modelling (CRAM)** framework is being developed to (a) derive a multi-perspective activity model from user comments, (b) augment job activity videos with semantics, and (c) retrieve content related to simulated scenarios.

Joseph A. Konstan et al. (Eds.): UMAP 2011, LNCS 6787, pp. 405–408, 2011.
© Springer-Verlag Berlin Heidelberg 2011

2 Related Work and Main Contribution

Intelligent environments for experiential workplace learning have been in the focus of research in technology-enhanced learning. APOSDLE [4] promotes self-regulated learning by capturing job-related experiences into job-related (task) objects, focusing on computer-based tasks. MATURE [5] aims at capturing organizational knowledge from experiences, considering broad job activities, while AWESOME [6] deals with capturing student experiences in academic writing. KP-LAB [7] used records of job-related activities to create pedagogical scenarios for experiential learning where people work in groups and reflect on job activities. We aim to distinguish from these projects in four points: include multi-perceptiveness (i.e. individual knowledge views) in the activity model; advance the knowledge elicitation process by implementing methods to provide user-awareness of context and related activities; provide more expressive models to augment digital content; and test the smart CRAM objects in simulated settings for learning.

The user modelling community is starting to look at utilizing **'real-world' work context** models to improve adaptation, e.g. [8] presents an approach to exploit context for adaptive notifications in collaborative environments. Our research contributes to this stream by developing a 'real-world' context model for adaptive learning using social content as the main source. This makes a contribution to a recent trend in using digital traces from social content to derive user profiles [9]. Instead of explicit user profiling, we will provide a mechanism for deriving an extended context model which preserves different perspective on an activity, and can be used to improve adaptation, as well as a source for clustering and profiling users. Similarly to[10] we focus on awareness and recognition of social signals to empower adaptation, but we are applying it to job interviews where diverse interpretations should be catered for.

3 Proposed Solution

A conceptual framework for contextual knowledge capturing and retrieval, which consists of three layers, as shown in Figure 1, is proposed. The **Acquisition Layer** deals with the development of a model to capture multi-perspective knowledge of job-related activities. This utilizes digital records of a specific **Activity** (e.g. job interview **videos**) and user input (e.g. comments/stories about interviews) to capture personal experiences and descriptions of the activity presented in the digital content. This will enable us to extract a **Context-rich Activity Model (CRAM)** in the **Modelling Layer**. The **Application Layer** will provide a retrieval mechanism to map contextual representation of digital content to representation of a specific simulated context and suggest relevant digital content.

Context Dimensions. To define context, the definition from [11] has been followed referring to information which characterizes an entity involved in a system. Here, *system* refers to the training activity, e.g. the job interview. *Entities* are people involved in the activity, e.g. interviewer and interviewee, which are characterized by the social signals they use[12]. Context is grouped into two categories: *internal* that is related to the video activity and *external*, which is related to the individual's personal

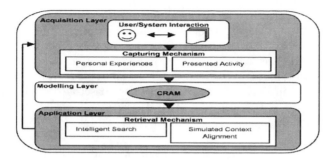

Fig. 1. Conceptual framework for capturing multi-perspective knowledge of job-related activities and individual experiences

experience and perspective. The retrieval mechanism includes: (a) *Multi-perspective Context Aggregation*, which concerns the micro-level representation. CRAM will include aggregation algorithms which pull relevant context dimensions that correspond to the simulated context of the query; (b) *Multi-perspective Activity Integration* which concerns the macro-level representation, i.e. the activity structure. This includes the merging of perspectives according to time and semantics.

4   Progress to Date and Future Work

A **baseline social system** for collecting user comments has been developed. This provides a YouTube-like interface where users watch videos of job interviews and provide comments in structure-free textual format on parts of the video. A pilot study with five users has been conducted to **collect initial user input**, consisting of 39 user comments with internal and external context about the behaviour of both the interviewee or the interviewer. The comments have been analysed using **ontology based information extraction** with existing taxonomies (WordNet Affect, GUMO, and SUMO) and Antelope as text mining framework[1]. Initial findings showed that comments can be linked to main concepts from the ontologies (e.g. emotion categories mentioned by users). For the perspectives, there is an indication that people pick different social signals (e.g. hand motions or facial expressions), identify different time frames in the videos. These perspectives are not contradicting but rather complimenting one another.

The **immediate future work** includes the **first experimental study** which is being organized at the moment. It follows the pilot experiment, and includes a questionnaire to measure user's previous experience and perspective on the job interview process and the first iteration of the activity capturing mechanism. The questionnaire will used to extract profiling statements which will be correlated with the qualitative analysis of user comments. This will provide validation of the activity modelling mechanism and will indicate the dimensions of user perspectives.

---

[1] Proxem. *Antelope NLP Framework*. Available from:
www.proxem.com/Default.aspx?tabid=119.

The **follow-up work** will improve the modelling mechanism using heuristics from social scientists to indicate important concepts and strategies to exploit inside the information extraction mechanism. A richer context model will be derived and related to simulated context. This will be conducted within one of the use cases of the ImReal EU project (www.imreal-project.eu), which aims at developing simulated environments for Immersive Reflective Experience-based Adaptive Learning. The evaluation study will examine the Multi-perspective Context Aggregation and Activity Integration mechanisms.

Acknowledgement. The research leading to these results has received funding from the European Union Seventh Framework Programme (FP7/2007-2013) under the ImREAL project, ICT 257831.

References

1. Mitrovic, A., Weerasinghe, A.: Revisiting Ill-Definedness and the Consequences for ITSs. In: Proceeding of AIED 2009, pp. 375–382. IOS Press, Amsterdam (2009)
2. Gaffney, C., et al.: A survey of soft skill simulation authoring tools. In: Proceedings of the 19th ACM Conference on Hypertext and Hypermedia, pp. 181–186 (2008)
3. Knowles, M.: The modern practice of adult education: From pedagogy to andragogy. Follett, Chicago (1980)
4. Ley, T., Kump, B., Gerdenitsch, C.: Scaffolding self-directed learning with personalized learning goal recommendations. In: De Bra, P., Kobsa, A., Chin, D., et al. (eds.) UMAP 2010. LNCS, vol. 6075, pp. 75–86. Springer, Heidelberg (2010)
5. Weber, N., et al.: Knowledge Maturing in the Semantic MediaWiki: A Design Study in Career Guidance. In: Proceedings of ECTEL 2009, pp. 700–705. Springer, Heidelberg (2009)
6. Bajanki, S., et al.: Use of Semantics to Build an Academic Writing Community Environment. In: Proceeding of AIED 2009, pp. 357–364. IOS Press, Amsterdam (2009)
7. Markkanen, H., et al.: Knowledge Practices Laboratory (KP-Lab) Overview (2008)
8. Ardissono, L., et al.: Managing Context-Dependent Workspace Awareness in an e-Collaboration Environment. In: Proceedings of Web Intelligence and Intelligent Agent Technology 2009, pp. 42–45. IEEE Computer Society, Los Alamitos (2009)
9. Leonardi, E., et al.: A flexible rule-based method for interlinking, integrating, and enriching user data. In: Proceedings of the 10th International Conference on Web Engineering, pp. 322–336. Springer, Vienna (2010)
10. Dim, E., Kuflik, T.: Social signal processing: detecting small group interaction in leisure activity. In: Proceeding of the 14th International Conference on Intelligent User Interfaces, pp. 309–312. ACM, Hong Kong (2010)
11. Dey, A.: Understanding and Using Context. Personal Ubiquitous Computing 5(1), 4–7 (2001)
12. Vinciarelli, A., et al.: Social signal processing: Survey of an emerging domain. Image Vision Comput. 27(12), 1743–1759 (2009)

Situation Awareness in Neurosurgery: A User Modeling Approach

Shahram Eivazi

School of Computing, University of Eastern Finland, Lansikatu 15,
P.O. Box 111, FIN-80101, Joensuu, Finland
seivazi@cs.joensuu.fi

Abstract. Situation awareness is a perception of the available information, events, resources, and environment within a given time and space. Humans have limited abilities to obtain and maintain situation awareness, as they need to carefully orchestrate the available resources. A failure to maintain situation awareness may lead to serious errors in human behavior. Investigation of the situation awareness of neurosurgeons using cognitive architectures is a new and exciting application of computational user modeling. Accurately modeling of the surgeons' behavior and their mental states while they perform operations using miniature instruments and movements require various implicit measures of the surgeons' behavior. The user modeling community has been searching for such data sources in other domains and have indicated that eye-tracking, as a non-invasive methodology, can be used to enrich the user models and increase their quality. In this research I will 1) investigate what are the constituents of situation awareness during neurosurgery, 2) how eye-tracking methodologies fit to created suitable user models of situation awareness, and 3) how data should be processed, and what features of eye-tracking data work best. We propose to use eye tracking techniques to develop a comprehensive computational model of the surgeons' behavior. The model will be further interpreted, to understand how information, events, and surgeons' actions will impact neurosurgery operations.

Keywords: User modeling, Eye-tracking, Machine learning, neurosurgery.

1 Introduction and Related Work

In neurosurgery, the surgeon conducts operations using miniature movements and instruments. The process requires concentration and any distraction may have serious consequences. For example, manually repositioning the microscope, in order to obtain a new view on the brain or modifying the parameters and settings of the device, can be distractive during the surgery. The distractions might impact the surgeons' goals and objectives, both at the time that surgeons make a decision or in the near future. An accurate measure of situation awareness (SA) is essential in such a task, where neurosurgeons' decisions may lead to serious consequences. Situation awareness has been defined as "the knowledge, cognition and anticipation of events, factors and variables affecting the safe, expedient and effective conduct of the mission." as cited by [1]. SA is an internal process occurring inside the mind and requires a high level

Joseph A. Konstan et al. (Eds.): UMAP 2011, LNCS 6787, pp. 409–413, 2011.

cognitive function [2]. The cognitive model of SA already exists but from practical point of view the predictive accuracy of any model depends on the way a user state is measured.

Higher level cognitive states are rarely observable. A number of verbal protocol and eye-tacking techniques have been used for capturing the cognitive states in various experiments (e.g. [3, 4]). Loboda & Brusilovsky [5] used eye tracking to prove that adaptive applications were more engaging for students, than non-adaptive applications. Both think aloud and eye tracking methods have been indicated as measurement techniques that often are used to show operator situation awareness during the task performance [6]. Salmon et al. [6] reported that information from eye trackers have been employed in SA assessment exercises within numerous studies. As the accuracy of eye trackers improves, it is increasingly bing applied to domain such as, medical research, usability and user modeling. For example, radiology image perception [7], surgical eye control [8, 9], eye-controlled microscope for surgical applications [10], and finding differences between medical specialties (e.g. differences between experts and novices) [11, 12]. We propose the use of computational theories with the purpose of inferring and reasoning about the current situation of the neurosurgeons. We elaborate on the cognitive architectural model that enables the system to predict cognitive states autonomously according to the neurosurgeons' behavior model.

2   Research Questions and Proposed Approach

The project goals are: 1) to develop a relevant model of the neurosurgeons situation awareness supported by a cognitive architecture, 2) search for underlying eye movement features, and 3) develop a method to improve the performance of probabilistic a users' behavior model within a real time assessment tool. This quest involves examining neurosurgeons' behaviors under a variety of conditions. We aim to answer following research questions:

1. *What are the ways to develop a comprehensive computational model of a surgeons' behavior?* Today's there are various cognitive mechanisms that explain situation awareness [13]. The largest constraint for investigating situation awareness of neurosurgeons is the lack of a model that shows what the neurosurgeons are seeing and doing. We are looking for a simplified version of a cognitive architecture. For example, one can suggest the reusing of the ACT-R model fragments in the context of neurosurgery.

2. *What are the ways of embedding eye-tracking technology into modern neurosurgical microscopes?* We initially plan to integrate a binocular eye tracker within a neurosurgical microscope. We propose to use a similar method as Charlier et al. [10] presented for running an eye-controlled microscope for surgical applications. However the focus will be on the recording eye movements from neurosurgeons.

3. *Can we improve the accuracy of the model using eye movement patterns?* Analysis of the relations between eye movements and human cognition has indeed proved to be fruitful in different domains, such as reading comprehension, visual search, selective attention, and studies of visual working memory [14]. There are numerous studies

which show that the eye movements during the observation of complex visual stimuli are regular and systematic [15, 16]. Muldner et al. [17] investigated the relations between eye tracking information and information on the relevant student states in a user modeling experiment. They focused on the relation between pupil size and the effect of reasoning. They found that the larger pupil size is related to the more constructive reasoning events in the current state.

4. *Can we improve the accuracy of the model using a modern machine learning technique?* User modeling has been extensively investigated in machine learning domain. Machine learning techniques could provide a comprehensible recognition or unambiguous interpretation of the users' behavior. We aimed to generate a function that can find patterns between input features (e.g. eye movements) and user current state.

3   Preliminary Results and Future Work

So far we have worked on the second research question which relates to integrating an eye tracker within a microscope. Moreover we began to answer a fundamental question: is eye tracking a help technique to infer user states of interest and expertise. An eye tracking experiment was conducted to find a prediction model related to user's cognitive states [18, 19]. These studies reported on a data collected from human subjects while solving puzzles on a computer under a "think-aloud" protocol. Using a well-known machine learning algorithm called Support Vector Machine (SVM), the eye-tracking data is used as a regressor to predict 1) high level cognitive states among five categories of the think-aloud utterances and 2) distinguish between novice and expert users. User's expertise was categorized into one of three discrete classes (high, medium and low) based on problem solving performance. This prediction was approximately 67% in defining the levels of expertise for unknown participants. Cognitive states were also categorized into one of five discrete classes (Planning, Intention, Cognition, Evaluation, and Concurrent move) and the prediction was achieved approximately 53% for known cognitive states.

In the intermediate future we are planning to present the improved results from our latest experiment [19]. We develop the computational method used before to improve prediction accuracy significantly. Moreover we begin answering the fundamental questions which have began to address by examining the size of the sampling window and overlap of feature extraction for modeling high-level cognitive states.

Predicting cognitive state from eye movement is an important problem, and work in this area would certainly be helpful for modeling user's behavior. The next step of our work is to reuse the current computational model while recording eye movement of neurosurgeons. We consider the constituents of situation awareness during neurosurgery. A possible outcome of this research could be a model which can be used for training novices when a failure to maintain situation awareness by novices may lead to serious errors in neurosurgery. Moreover one can build a tool that dynamically captures situation awareness of neurosurgeons and responds appropriately to their user states.

The work proposed here so far shows that modeling users' behavior from eye movement is possible. We would like to receive advices and possible problems with our proposed research directions.

References

1. Salmon, P.M., Stanton, N., Walker, G.H.: Distributed Situation Awareness: Theory, Measurement and Application to Teamwork. Ashgate Publishing (2009)
2. Wilson, G.F.: Strategies for Psychophysiological Assessment of Situation Awareness, ch. 8, pp. 175–189. CRC Press, Boca Raton (2007)
3. Ericsson, K.A.: Protocol analysis and verbal reports on thinking. Department of Psychology at Florida State University, Tech. Rep. (2002),
   http://www.psy.fsu.edu/faculty/ericsson/ericsson.proto.thnk.html
4. Anderson, J.R., Gluck, K.A.: What role do cognitive architectures play in intelligent tutoring systems?, ch. 8, pp. 227–263. Erlbaum, Mahwah (2001)
5. Loboda, T.D., Brusilovsky, P.: User-adaptive explanatory program visualization: evaluation and insights from eye movements. User Modeling and User-Adapted Interaction 20, 191–226 (2010)
6. Salmon, P., Stanton, N., Walker, G., Green, D.: Situation awareness measurement: A review of applicability for c4i environments. Applied Ergonomics 37, 225–238 (2006)
7. Krupinski, E.A.: The importance of perception research in medical imaging. Radiation Medicine 18, 329–334 (2000)
8. Tchalenko, J., Dempere-Marco, L., Hu, G.Y.X.P.: Quantitative analysis of eye control in surgical skill assessment. In: 11th European Conference on Eye Movements (2001)
9. Yang, G.-Z., Mylonas, G., Kwok, K.-W., Chung, A.: Perceptual docking for robotic control. In: Takeyoshi Dohi, I.S., Liao, H. (eds.) Medical Imaging and Augmented Reality, 4th International Workshop. Springer, Heidelberg (2008)
10. Charlier, J., Sourdille, P., Behague, M., Buquet, C.: Eye-controlled microscope for surgical applications. Developments in Ophthalmology 22, 154–158 (1991)
11. Law, B., Atkins, M.S., Kirkpatrick, A.E., Fraser, S., Lomax, A.J.: Eye gaze patterns differentiate novice and experts in a virtual laparoscopic surgery training environment. In: Proceedings of the 2004 Symposium on Eye Tracking Research & Applications (2004)
12. Tien, G., Atkins, M.S., Zheng, B., Swindells, C.: Measuring situation awareness of surgeons in laparoscopic training. In: Proceedings of the 2010 Symposium on Eye-Tracking Research 38; Applications (2010)
13. Baumann, M.R., Krems, J.F.: A comprehension based cognitive model of situation awareness. In: ICDHM 2009: Proceedings of the 2nd International Conference on Digital Human Modeling: Held as Part of HCI International 2009 (2009)
14. Kaller, C.P., Rahm, B., Bolkenius, K., Unterrainer, J.M.: Eye movements and visuospatial problem solving: Identifying separable phases of complex cognition. Psychophysiology 46, 818–830 (2009)
15. Just, M.A., Carpenter, P.A.: Eye fixations and cognitive processes. Cognitive Psychology 8, 441–480 (1976)
16. Velichkovsky, B.M., Rothert, A., Kopf, M., Dornhöfer, S.M., Joos, M.: Towards an express-diagnostics for level of processing and hazard perception. Transportation Research Part F: Traffic Psychology and Behaviour 5, 145–156 (2002)

17. Muldner, K., Christopherson, R., Atkinson, R., Burleson, W.: Investigating the utility of eye-tracking information on affect and reasoning for user modeling. In: Houben, G.-J., McCalla, G., Pianesi, F., Zancanaro, M. (eds.) UMAP 2009. LNCS, vol. 5535, pp. 138–149. Springer, Heidelberg (2009)
18. Eivazi, S., Bednarik, R.: Inferring problem solving strategies using eye-tracking: System description and evaluation. In: Proceedings of the 10th Koli Calling International Conference on Computing Education Research (2010)
19. Eivazi, S., Bednarik, R.: Predicting problem-solving behaviour and expertise levels from visual attention data. In: To appear in the 2nd Workshop on the Eye Gaze in Intelligent Human Machine Interaction (2011)

Adaptive Active Learning in Recommender Systems

Mehdi Elahi

Faculty of Computer Science, Free University of Bozen - Bolzano
39100, Bolzano, Italy
mehdi.elahi@stud-inf.unibz.it

Abstract. Recommender Systems (RSs) generate personalized suggestions to users for items that may be interesting for them. Many RSs use the Collaborative Filtering (CF) technique, where the system gathers some information about the users by eliciting their ratings for items. To do so, the system may actively choose the items to present to the users to rate. This proactive approach is called Active Learning (AL), since the system actively search for relevant data before building any predictive model of the user interests. But, since not all the ratings will improve the accuracy in the same way, finding the best items to query the users for their ratings is challenging. In this work, we address this problem by reviewing some AL techniques and discussing their performance on the base of the experiments we made.

1 Introduction

Nowadays, people are used to get recommendations from others by words, reference letters, media reports, or travel guides. RSs enhance this social process while people are exploring and searching for available items to find the most interesting products. RSs suggest to users items that are judged to be desirable based on the users' preferences [1] [3] [7]. In collaborative-based RSs the users express their preferences by ratings the items they have experienced before, and then the RS finds the most like-minded users by comparing the ratings of the target user with those of all the users, and recommends to the target user the items that similar users favored [3] [4]. The more ratings are given by the users the better the accuracy of CF becomes. However, not all of the ratings bring equivalent information about the user's tastes. The main goal of AL in CF is to achieve higher accuracy with fewer preferences (ratings) acquired from the users [2]. The accuracy improvement should be measured together with an estimation of its relative cost. In other words, one has to take into account the trade-off between the price of acquiring some information from the users, as they are not typically interested to provide such information, and the benefit coming from exploiting such information. This is why it is important to have a strategy to choose the least in number and the most informative instances to train the system. In the other words, in CF an AL *strategy* is a precise procedure for selecting which items to present to the user for rating elicitation. There are distinctive strategies proposed so far each of which considering the problem of AL with different perspective.

Joseph A. Konstan et al. (Eds.): UMAP 2011, LNCS 6787, pp. 414–417, 2011.

2 Preliminary Results

The main topic of this paper is concerned with "Adaptive AL". In order to tackle the adaptation issue in AL, as a preliminary step, one has to assess the behavior of simpler non-adaptive AL strategies in RSs to determine if they are performing distinctively during the process of rating elicitation. To do so, we conducted several experiments considering several AL strategies using two popular datasets: Movielens and Netflix. We adopted an offline setup where a ready-to-use dataset was exploited to simulate the process of the dataset growth. The dataset is split randomly into three subsets: *Known*, *Unknown*, and *Test*. The *Known* set is simulating the known preferences of the users that the system has already gathered initially (without AL), assuming that the users have provided them in the starting process (e.g. signing up). The *Unknown* set corresponds to the part of the dataset that is supposed to be unknown to the system but known to the user, i.e., the information that can be elicited from the users. Hence, during the active learning progress, some ratings are requested to the user and if these are part of the *Unknown* set then they are removed from the *Unknown* set and added to *Known* set. This can be considered similar to rating elicitation in an online system as the AL component identifies the items whose rating should be asked to a user and then the rating is added to the *Known* set if it is present in the *Unknown* set. The *Test* subset is used for cross-validation of the results.

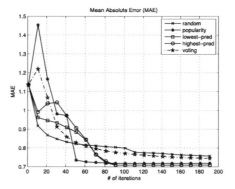

Fig. 1. MAE over the time (Netflix dataset)

We evaluated several strategies, with different features. However, due to the lack of space here we illustrate only some of them, i.e., those showing the main characteristics of the full set of strategies that we consider. The first is *popularity*, a strategy that selects most popular items. Then, *highest-predicted* apply a state of the art collaborative filtering algorithm (Factor Model) to compute rating predictions for all the items and then the items with the highest predicted ratings are selected. *Lowest-predicted* apply the same CF algorithm to compute the rating prediction for all the items, but then the items with lowest predicted ratings are selected. *Voting* strategy, a novel approach that we introduced, employs a committee of strategies which vote for some of the available items and then the most voted items are selected.

Finally, the *random* strategy selects items randomly, and represents a baseline for comparison. Fig.1 shows the result of the conducted experiments depicting the MAE of different strategies over the time (iterations), so as at each iteration, each user is requested to rate 10 items. Every line in the figure denotes a different AL strategy. As it can be seen, there are some monotonic (highest-predicted and popularity) and non-monotonic (lowest-predicted and random) strategies, i.e., in the monotonic strategies the error is always decreasing as new ratings are acquired in the *Known* set, whereas in the non-monotonic ones at certain points the error increases and then tends to decrease till the end of the experiment. First of all, this result implies that acquiring more data is not always leading to the improvement of the system. This is the fact that was predicted in [3] but not observed before. There can be different reasons behind this phenomenon. In the popularity strategy (non-monotonic strategy) users typical like popular items and therefore their high ratings push the predictive model to predict for the other items ratings higher than their true value. This phenomenon is called *prefix-bias* [3]. Additionally a particular behavior is observed for voting strategy, presenting an average performance of the combined strategies. For this strategy, the combination of the strategies may effectively modify the characteristics of the voting strategy and result in different behavior, which is important to beer in mind when defining the strategy. Nevertheless, in our experiments we have observed that the voting approach has the better overall performance, especially when the quality of the recommendation is evaluated with Normalized Discounted Cumulative Gain (NDCG), i.e., a measure of the goodness of the ranking produced by the recommender system [6].

3   Current and Future Works

Using a single strategy to actively learning the users' preferences is not always the best approach. One alternative is to create a model, which can adapt itself to the different cases, e.g. different users or stages of the system data set (e.g., cold start vs. maintenance). We called this problem *adaptive AL* where the learner selects the best strategy from a number of candidate simpler strategies, which may better suited to different situations [1]. The problem is that in the real case scenario the performances of the all strategies are not available or may be very expensive to estimate. Hence, in order to identify which one may suit better for the current situation, it is therefore important to define a way to measure the differences of the possible situations. For instance, as some initial experiments suggest, the average size of the user profiles currently stored in the system could be used as a switching condition. Then, according to this measure one can try to implement methods for selecting one among the possible strategies. One alternative approach is to consider the change (gradient) of the target metric that is to be optimized (e.g., MAE). In each stage of the system the target metric is computed for all the competing strategies. Then the strategy with the best trend is selected. The main difficulty in this case is how to evaluate several strategies at a certain point in time. This could be done by branching the system in several competing systems acquiring their ratings with the different competing strategies: on different micro slots of time or segments of users. Another approach can be based on some heuristic knowledge. For example, it is clear that highest-predicted strategy will try to add ratings with highest value. Then if the system were biased toward the popular items (which are typically rated high by the users), this strategy would not be a good option to switch. Another important issue in AL is related to the personalization of the item selection strategy so that one particular strategy may better suit a specific type of user profile. For example, strategy A can result in better performance for user u while strategy B performing finer for user v. An adaptive strategy then would assign and personalize the strategy A for user u and strategy B for user v, respectively. This scenario can happen when there is little number of ratings elicited for a particular user, and the user profile is poor; then the prediction may be difficult and the error would be high. In this case, one strategy can select better items to instantly recover the prediction error. However, when the user profile is enriched by eliciting sufficient amount of preferences, another strategy can select better items to ask from the user. This issue is more crucial in a large scale RS where the data space has a high heterogeneity, i.e., there are entirely different user profiles (size). In such a case the AL system may face problems handling all users with a single strategy. In Amazon.com, which is a typical RS, there are different types of customers with different purchase pattern. Therefore, assigning local models for a certain region of the input may be a better choice producing a better global outcome.

4 Conclusion

Active Learning for RSs is still a new research area and many open issues for this area of research remain. An important notion that has not been explored so far is related to the concept of adaptive strategies. Such strategies are implemented as a sequence of simpler strategies each of which working differently and more suited to the particular state of the system at a certain point in time. The open concern in this discussion is the problem of identifying the best strategy in each particular situation in order to choose the appropriate strategy better adapted with regards to and different goals (error reduction, coverage improvement, etc.).

References

1. Rubens, N., Kaplan, D., Sugiyama, M.: Active learning in recommender systems. In: Ricci, F., Rokach, L., Shapira, B. (eds.) Recommender Systems Handbook. Springer, Heidelberg (2011)
2. Settles, B.: Active Learning Literature Survey, Computer Sciences Technical Report, University of Wisconsin–Madison, Updated on: January 26 (2010)
3. Rashid, A.M., Albert, I., Cosley, D., Lam, S.K., McNee, S.M., Konstan, J.A., Riedl, J.: Getting to Know You: Learning New User Preferences in Recommender Systems. In: IUI 2002, San Francisco, California, USA, January 13-16 (2002)
4. Adomavicius, G., Tuzhilin, A.: Toward the Next Generation of Recommender Systems: A Survey of the State-of-the-Art and Possible Extensions. IEEE Computer Society, Los Alamitos (2005)
5. Carenini, G., Smith, J., Poole, D.: Towards more Conversational and Collaborative Recommender Systems. In: IUI 2003, Miami, Florida, USA, January 12-15 (2003)
6. Manning, C.: Introduction to Information Retrieval. Cambridge University Press, Cambridge
7. Su, X., Khoshgoftaar, T.M.: A Survey of Collaborative Filtering Techniques. In: Advances in Artificial Intelligence. Hindawi Publishing Corporation (2009)

Extending Sound Sample Descriptions through the Extraction of Community Knowledge

Frederic Font and Xavier Serra

Music Technology Group, Universitat Pompeu Fabra
Roc Boronat, 138, 08018 Barcelona, Spain
{frederic.font,xavier.serra}@upf.edu

Abstract. Sound and music online services driven by communities of users are filled with large amounts of user-created content that has to be properly described. In these services, typical sound and music modeling is performed using either content-based or context-based strategies, but no special emphasis is given to the extraction of knowledge from the community. We outline a research plan in the context of Freesound.org and propose ideas about how audio clip sharing sites could adapt and take advantage of particular user communities to improve the descriptions of their content.

Keywords: sound and music computing, online communities, folksonomies, emergent semantics, freesound.

1 Introduction and Related Work

The proliferation of domain specific online services with social networking capabilities has created new ways of sharing information items such as pictures, videos and audio recordings. These services are typically filled with content contributed by communities of users with very different motivations and interests, generating large amounts of information that has to be properly described. Examples of this kind of services are Flickr (photo sharing), YouTube (video sharing), SoundCloud (music sharing) and Freesound (audio clip sharing)[1].

Traditional approaches of information modeling in sound and music online services are either focused on content-based or context-based techniques. Freesound is a collaborative database of contributed audio samples that uses content-based analysis - via manual tagging or sound waveform analysis - to perform queries and similarity search among audio files. On the other side, music services like Last.fm or Spotify[2] use context-based collaborative filtering techniques for their recommendation systems. In this case, explicit feedback provided by users in the form of comments, ratings or annotations is being analyzed, but also implicit information that can be extracted from their habits - such as the most common

---

[1] www.flickr.com, www.youtube.com, www.soundcloud.com, www.freesound.org
[2] www.last.fm, www.spotify.com

Joseph A. Konstan et al. (Eds.): UMAP 2011, LNCS 6787, pp. 418–421, 2011.

listened artists - can be considered, allowing the creation of user models for a personalized recommendation. Current research trends are proposing combinations of both content-based and context-based analysis to perform those tasks.

There has been extensive research on the analysis, modeling and knowledge extraction from communities of users. Some studies have performed group modeling through the aggregation of individual user profiles with the purpose of improving TV content recommendations [6,9]. Other papers have proposed community models to study users behavior (*e.g.* to analyze document sharing patterns among an online community of researchers [5]). In the context of the semantic web, the trend of *emergent semantics* proposes the analysis of online communities for the extraction of ontologies that structure the concepts and terms of a particular domain [1]. Peter Mika [7] demonstrates ontology emergence through the analysis of tag folksonomies in a social bookmarking tool. Community knowledge extraction has been also investigated in [3], where the folksonomy of tags in Flickr is categorized using the concepts of a collaboratively built ontology with the purpose of improving tag-based recommendations. Similar ideas have been studied for music annotation and retrieval purposes [2,10], but none of them gives a special emphasis to community-based approaches for the description of sound and music.

There is a need to move the emphasis of sound and music information modeling *from audio* - namely sound files - *to user* - people that use sound and music services - *to community* - understanding sounds and users as members of common particular contexts -, and be able to integrate and take advantage of all them. This does not only mean to perform better analysis of community knowledge, but also to use this knowledge for the adaptation of the technology to the particular needs of user communities in order to improve the "quality" of the information we can gather from them. In our thesis, we will address this problem aiming to propose community-based methods for the description of sound samples in Freesound.

2   Freesound and Its Community

Freesound.org is a collaborative sound database where people from different disciplines share recorded sound samples under an open Creative Commons license[3]. It was started in 2005 and it is being further developed within our research group. Nowadays, there are 1.8 million registered users that have uploaded more than 100.000 sound samples (although only 1.5% of the users have uploaded at least one sample), and there is a rate of 30.000 unique visits per day. Registered users can provide information through comments and ratings on sounds (average of 0.5 comments and 5.5 ratings per sound), forum posts (already more than 25.000) or sound tags (with more than 26.000 different concepts used, average of 6.24 tags per sound). The search process is either based on raw tags attached to sound samples (without any post-processing for "cleaning" or classifying these tags) or in acoustic audio similarity (using automatic feature extraction). Freesound does

---

[3] www.creativecommons.org/licenses/sampling+/1.0

not support the explicit grouping of users into communities, nevertheless it has been observed that different implicit communities exist related to the interests of users [8]. As a consequence, Freesound turns out to be a highly heterogeneous database in types of sounds, their descriptions and user interests. This makes Freesound interesting as a framework for researching community-based approaches of improving sound descriptions.

3   Research Challenges and Work Plan

In our current approach for addressing the problem of improving sound sample descriptions using community knowledge, we can identify two research challenges: *i)* how can we better analyze and gather knowledge from the community? and *ii)* how can we improve sound descriptions using this knowledge? A work plan for addressing these challenges is now described.

As a first step, we will focus in one of the implicit communities of interest found in Freesound [8]. Applying the Actor-Concept-Instance model described in [7], we expect to come upon a lightweight ontology emerging from the community and resembling the most important used tags - and their relations - for the description of sounds. We have already tried to apply this model to the whole database of Freesound and we have seen that, although many interesting semantic relations between tags arise (*e.g.* the connection of the tag *drums* with *snare, hi-hat, percussion...*), we obtain a huge cloud of small clusters that does not bring much information as a whole. We expect to get more interesting results by just considering sounds and users belonging to a particular community of Freesound.

Our next step will be to "post-process" tag descriptions based on the previously obtained ontology and other ontologies such as WordNet[4] (a lexical database that relates English terms in sets of cognitive concepts). Similarly to what is done in [2,3], the idea is to map existing tags to concepts of the ontology and get more insight in their meaning. Then, we can extend the description with related and complementary tags (*e.g.* extending the tag *guitar* with the tag *musical-instrument*). We will carry on user-based evaluation to asses the expected improvement of sound descriptions.

We will then investigate how can we influence users behavior in describing sounds with the re-design of some Freesound functionalities, thus shaping the information we gather from the community. As an example, the system could recommend tags based on the relevant concepts identified for the particular community (similarly to [4]). In that way, when tagging sound samples of recorded musical instruments, the interface could recommend the use of tags describing important perceptual qualities such as *key* or *pitch*. Again, we will carry on user testing to evaluate the improvement of the descriptions.

Later stages of our research will include the extension of the work done to include other communities of Freesound and the evaluation of the overall impact of the new functionalities. For that purpose, we plan to build a community model

---

[4] http://wordnet.princeton.edu

(similarly to [5]) to quantify the activity with respect to a number of previously decided key aspects (*e.g.* sound sample sharing, users collaboration in sound description, reuse of existing tags...).

4 Conclusions

With our thesis we expect to develop methodologies to better analyze and extract knowledge from communities of users. Although we are particularly focused in the case of sound sample descriptions, we believe that our work will be of relevance to other types of media. Furthermore, by implementing those methods in Freesound, we expect to drive the site into a more dynamic, rich and creative platform for users, and a more valuable source of information for researchers.

Acknowledgments. This work is partially supported under BES-2010-037309 FPI grant from the Spanish Ministry of Science and Innovation for the TIN2009-14247-C02-01 DRIMS project.

References

1. Aberer, K., et al.: Emergent Semantics Principles and Issues. In: Proc. of the International Conference on Database Systems for Advanced Applications, pp. 25–38 (2004)
2. Cano, P., et al.: Knowledge and Content-based Audio Retrieval Using WordNet. In: Proc. of the International Conference on E-business and Telecommunication Networks, pp. 301–308 (2004)
3. Cantador, I., Konstas, I., Jose, J.M.: Categorising Social Tags to Improve Folksonomy-based Recommendations. Web Semantics: Science, Services and Agents on the World Wide Web 9(1), 1–15 (2011)
4. Jäschke, R., Marinho, L., Hotho, A., Schmidt-Thieme, L., Stumme, G.: Tag recommendations in folksonomies. In: Kok, J.N., Koronacki, J., Lopez de Mantaras, R., Matwin, S., Mladenič, D., Skowron, A. (eds.) PKDD 2007. LNCS (LNAI), vol. 4702, pp. 506–514. Springer, Heidelberg (2007)
5. Kleanthous, S., Dimitrova, V.: Analyzing Community Knowledge Sharing Behavior. In: De Bra, P., Kobsa, A., Chin, D. (eds.) UMAP 2010. LNCS, vol. 6075, pp. 231–242. Springer, Heidelberg (2010)
6. Masthoff, J.: Group Modeling: Selecting a Sequence of Television Items to Suit a Group of Viewers. User Modeling and User-Adapted Interaction 14(1), 37–85 (2004)
7. Mika, P.: Ontologies are Us: A Unified Model of Social Networks and Semantics. Web Semantics: Science, Services and Agents on the World Wide Web 5(1), 5–15 (2007)
8. Roma, G., Herrera, P.: Community Structure in Audio Clip Sharing. In: Proc. of the International Conference on Intelligent Networking and Collaborative Systems, pp. 200–205 (2010)
9. Senot, C., Kostadinov, D., Bouzid, M., Picault, J., Aghasaryan, A., Bernier, C.: Analysis of Strategies for Building Group Profiles. In: De Bra, P., Kobsa, A., Chin, D. (eds.) UMAP 2010. LNCS, vol. 6075, pp. 40–51. Springer, Heidelberg (2010)
10. Wang, J., Chen, X., Hu, Y., Feng, T.: Predicting High-level Music Semantics using Social Tags via Ontology-based Reasoning. In: Proc. of the International Conference on Music Information Retrieval, pp. 405–410 (2010)

Monitoring Contributions Online: A Reputation System to Model Expertise in Online Communities

Thieme Hennis

Jaffalaan 5, 2628 BX, Delft, the Netherlands
T.A.Hennis@tudelft.nl

Abstract. This document contains a brief description of my PhD research, with problem definition, contribution to the field of reputation systems and user modeling, and proposed solution. The proposed method and algorithm enable evaluation of contributions in online knowledge-based communities. The innovation in the approach is the use of authority and specifying reputation on the keyword-level.

Keywords: reputation, user-modeling, motivation, transitivity, context.

1 Problem Statement

The decentralized nature of many online communities implies that voluntary contributions of its members are required to make it sustainable. Motivating members to contribute is a significant challenge [14]. Another major challenge in online communities concerns managing the quality of contributions [1]. Reputation systems address both challenges simultaneously. Reputation is information used to make a value judgment about an object or person [5]. Reputation systems have the objective to increase the reliability and performance of electronic communities [16]. They utilize the history of past interactions (log files, ratings) to provide information about abilities and dispositions. An expectation that people will consider one another's past constrains and motivates behavior in the present [15]. Also, people have strong inclination to participate and contribute in online communities if they perceive that it enhances their professional reputations [13,18]. As more and more activities take place on the web [3], we are better able to use logs about behavior and interactions to develop personalized learning paths and match people with content or other people [4], or evaluate the value of an object or person [12]. This also calls for standardization of online reputation, because that would increase reusability of reputation profiles across communities. Especially in knowledge-based communities, with a range of expertise domains, inferring reputation from online interactions is a major challenge [19]. Because people are continuously creating new knowledge, an explicit a-priori representation of information is not possible [9,20]. Rather than providing a 'global' trust value [7,10,11], reputation systems for knowledge-based communities must address the dynamic nature of shared information. In other words, reputation cannot be reused without relevant contextual information. The objective of a reputation system for knowledge-based communities should be to specifically

Joseph A. Konstan et al. (Eds.): UMAP 2011, LNCS 6787, pp. 422–425, 2011.
© Springer-Verlag Berlin Heidelberg 2011

model the value (in terms of expertise or competencies) of an individual based on his/her shared and created knowledge. Thus, in order to make reputation usable and increase transitivity it must integrate a means of incorporating context.

How can we design a reputation system that models value of contributions and contributors linked to specified objectives?

In addition, rewards and objectives differ across communities, so such a system must be configurable according to the specific community context and objectives.

How can we use reputation to achieve specified objectives (participation, contributions, reading, etc.) within online communities?

2 Contributions to the Field

We have seen that in order to model the expertise or value of individuals in knowledge-based environments, it is required to incorporate context. Reputation has dynamic properties, and reputation attribution takes place in communication processes. In this process, both the "reputed agent" and the "reputing agent" should be considered, and the relevant context factors [17]. I want to contribute to the field of online communities with an innovative approach that supports the analysis of interactions to model the dynamic value of users and objects. The model is flexible, so it can be reconfigured based on community context, and the configuration of weights allows for evaluating different incentives and scenarios. Another challenge I would like to address is that of reusability. There are significant advantages when reputation can be understood and reused across communities, especially when we consider the growing importance of online reputation in the exchange of labor and knowledge in companies and on the market [6,18]. There is a need for support in the design of value or reputation systems that sustain decentralized management and exchange of reputation information across community boundaries.

3 Proposed Solution

Based on literature review and an analysis of several popular reputation systems, we developed an initial method and algorithm [8]. The model we propose decomposes a reputation statement on a keyword-level: for each reputation statement, we detect the relevant keywords affiliated with the object being evaluated/rated, and create a separate claim for each of the keywords, allowing weights for each claims to be different. In a more human way of explaining: If a professor in economics and a PhD in software architectures evaluate the scalability of a proposed software architecture, the PhD is probably better able to judge about it than the professor. This difference in subject-authority is integrated in the model because reputation value is defined per keyword. With regard to software related topics, the PhD's reputation will be higher than the economics professor, even though the professor's overall reputation score will probably be higher. Hence, the programmer has a higher authority, which counts as weight. We describe reputation as a set of keywords with values in order to enable analysis, filtering and matching, and search. The example in Fig. 1 shows how a source object s_i rates a target object t_j. This initiates the generation of separate claims for each of the *affiliated keywords* (belonging to the target object) and retrieves the reputation of the *source object* for each of the affiliated keywords (authority). In this case, the target object is a paper about 'Skin Diseases, Hart Diseases, etc. (see Fig. 1). The mathematical representation of a single claim is then the multiplication of (i) Affiliated keyword weight, (ii) Target weight, (iii) Claim weight, (iv) Claim value (3/5), and (v) Source weight (which is based on the source reputation or authority about the keyword). As we describe above, we introduce several other weights that may influence reputation. As such, it may be used as a model to investigate contextual factors and rewards in the process of knowledge-sharing, i.e. the influence of adaptive rewards [2].

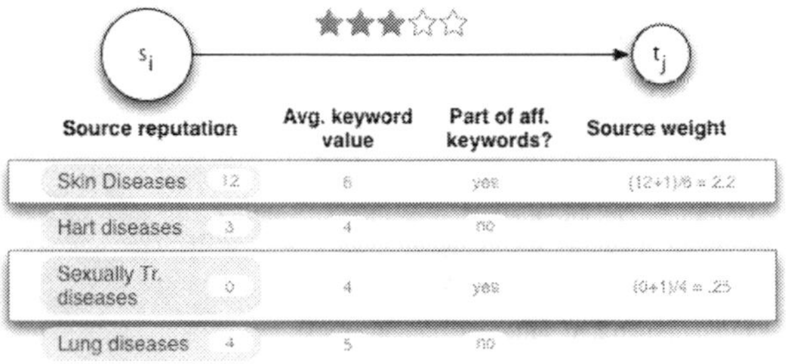

Source reputation		Avg. keyword value	Part of aff. keywords?	Source weight
Skin Diseases	12	6	yes	(12+1)/6 = 2.2
Hart diseases	3	4	no	
Sexually Tr. diseases	0	4	yes	(0+1)/4 = .25
Lung diseases	4	5	no	

Fig. 1. The example shows how source reputation values are transformed into weights to be used as an input for separate claims

In addition to the reputation model, we propose a stepwise approach to configure the proposed model to suit the specific context of the community. These steps include the definition of all relevant, measurable, and meaningful contribution types (called target objects) and possible (implicit and explicit) reputation statements by source objects. These target objects and reputation statements must be ranked according to their importance and expressiveness, which results in relative weights for target object and reputations statement types. For example, rating a document is more expressive than counting the number of readers. The weights can also be defined in a function, i.e. a function that relates the weight of a target object with the number of readers, or the weight of the source object with cognitive centrality [12]. Also, as keywords are the basic constituents of reputation, there needs to be a way to contextualize target objects using keywords (i.e. through tagging or content analysis).

4 Future Work

Future work will focus on the testing and improving the proposed method and algorithms using real case studies. Specifically, we will look at the ability of the system to model expertise in large distributed knowledge-based environments, such as forums. Evaluation addresses motivation of reputed individuals and change in behavior. If calibrated well, the model could be used to detect patterns in activity and knowledge generation among users (i.e. [12]), and test different strategies to improve knowledge-sharing behavior. In addition we will look at gaming strategies and standardization with regards to reputation calculation to improve reusability across and beyond communities through mapping and inference.

References

1. Agichtein, E., et al.: Finding high-quality content in social media. In: Proceedings of the International Conference on Web Search and Web Data Mining, WSDM 2008, p. 183 (2008)
2. Cheng, R., Vassileva, J.: Design and evaluation of an adaptive incentive mechanism for sustained educational online communities. User Modeling and User-Adapted Interaction 16(3-4), 321–348 (2006)
3. Davidson, C.N., Goldberg, D.T.: The future of learning institutions in a digital age. The MIT Press, Cambridge (2009)
4. Drachsler, H., et al.: Personal recommender systems for learners in lifelong learning networks: the requirements, techniques and model. International Journal of Learning Technology 3(4), 404–423 (2008)
5. Farmer, F.R., Glass, B.: Building Web Reputation Systems. O'Reilly Media, Sebastopol (2010)
6. Gal-Oz, N., et al.: Cross-Community Reputation: Policies and alternatives. In: IADIS Int. Conf. on Web Based Communities (WBC 2008), pp. 197–201 (2008)
7. Golbeck, J., Hendler, J.: Accuracy of Metrics for Inferring Trust and Reputation in Semantic Web-based Social Networks. LNCS (2004)
8. Hennis, T., et al.: Reputation in peer-based learning environments (in print). In: Santos, O.C., Boticario, J.G. (eds.) Educational Recommender Systems and Technologies, IGI (2011)
9. Huizing, A.: The value of a rose: rising above objectivism and subjectivism. Working Papers on Information Systems 7(11), 25 (2007)
10. Jøsang, A.: Trust and reputation systems. In: Aldini, R., Gorrieri, R. (eds.) Foundations of Security Analysis and Design, vol. 2006, pp. 209–245. Springer, Heidelberg (2007)
11. Kamvar, S.D., et al.: The Eigentrust algorithm for reputation management in P2P networks. In: WWW 2003, pp. 640–651. ACM Press, New York (2003)
12. Kleanthous, S., Dimitrova, V.: Analyzing community knowledge sharing behavior. In: De Bra, P., Kobsa, A., Chin, D. (eds.) UMAP 2010. LNCS, vol. 6075, pp. 231–242. Springer, Heidelberg (2010)
13. McLure-Wasko, M., Faraj, S.: Why Should I Share? Examining Social Capital and Knowledge Contribution in Electronic Networks of Practice. MIS Quarterly 29(1) (2005)
14. Moore, T.D., Serva, M.A.: Understanding member motivation for contributing to different types of virtual communities: a proposed framework. In: Proceedings of the 2007 ACM SIGMIS CPR Conference on Computer Personnel Research: The Global Information Technology Workforce, pp. 153–158. ACM, New York (2007)
15. Resnick, P., et al.: Reputation Systems. Communications of the ACM 43(12), 45–48 (2000)
16. Sabater, J., Sierra, C.: Review on Computational Trust and Reputation Models. Artificial Intelligence Review 24(1), 33–60 (2005)
17. Squazzoni, F.: Review of Reputation in Artificial Societies: Social Beliefs for Social Order, http://jasss.soc.surrey.ac.uk/7/3/reviews/squazzoni.html
18. Tuomi, I.: Learning in the Age of Networked Intelligence. European Journal of Education 42(2), 235–254 (2007)
19. Vu, L.-H., et al.: Synergies of Different Reputation Systems: Challenges and Opportunities. In: 2009 World Congress on Privacy, Security, Trust and the Management of e-Business, pp. 218–226. IEEE Computer Society, Saint John (2009)
20. Vygotsky, L.S.: Mind in society: The development of higher psychological processes. Harvard University Press, Cambridge (1978)

Student Procedural Knowledge Inference through Item Response Theory

Manuel Hernando

Dpto. Lenguajes y Ciencias de la Computación.
Universidad de Málaga. Bulevar Louis Pasteur, 35,
Campus de Teatinos, 29071 Málaga, Spain.
mhernando@lcc.uma.es

Abstract. This paper describes our research lines that focus on modeling and inferring student procedural knowledge in Intelligent Tutoring Systems. Our proposal is to apply Item Response Theory, a well-founded theory for declarative knowledge assessment, to infer procedural knowledge in problem solving environments. Therefore, we treat the problems as tests and the steps of problem solving as options (or choices) in a question. An important feature of our system is that it is not only based on an expert analysis, but also on data-driven techniques so that it can collect the largest amount of students' problem solving strategies as possible.

Keywords: Student modeling, procedural knowledge, Item Response Theory.

1 Introduction

The way learners acquire and improve their knowledge has changed over the last 30 years with the arrival of new technologies. Nowadays, teachers can combine their methods of teaching with computer-aided methods derived from Artificial Intelligence and psychological research in the field of education which are more effective than just the traditional methods[5]. These systems are able to guide students' instructional processes in order to improve students' knowledge. To this end, they maintain a student model which represents the student knowledge in a given domain. Building this student model by interpreting a student's actions is a critical problem in this field. For instance, in problem solving environments, student models should be updated with the actions provided by the student while solving a problem, and through these actions the student knowledge should be inferred and the next most suitable pedagogical action should be recommended.

In literature, we can find several strategies to represent student models such as overlay modeling where the student knowledge is a subset of the expert knowledge; differential modeling where the student model is represented by missing conception which is the difference between the expert knowledge and the student knowledge; perturbation modeling which is similar to overlay model but adding the knowledge that the student has, but which is wrong(bugs); and constraint-based modeling where there is a set of constraints that students cannot violate and the student model is the list of constraints that he/she has violated.

Joseph A. Konstan et al. (Eds.): UMAP 2011, LNCS 6787, pp. 426–429, 2011.

In this paper, we propose at echnique to infer the student procedural knowledge by using the Item Response Theory, a well-founded theory conventionally used to infer student declarative knowledge. Next section is devoted to the state of the art of procedural knowledge inference strategies. Section 3 describes our proposal and Section 4 current research lines.

2   State of the Art

During the last decades, Intelligent Tutoring Systems(ITS) have played a relevant role in research of Artificial Intelligence, Cognitive Science, and Education. Early theories, such as ACT Theory[2], assume the procedural-declarative distinction. Declarative knowledge in a given domain is the integrated knowledge of important principles that can be flexibly applied to new tasks[12],whereas procedural knowledge is a type of strategy that involves step-by-step actions for solving problems[4]. Procedural-declarative distinction is already one of the main points in ITS research. Systems used to assess student knowledge are usually based on this distinction.

Cognitive Tutors [1] are a family of ITS based on ACT Theory. In these tutors, procedural knowledge is improved by model tracing [3] and assessed by knowledge tracing [1]. Model tracing is a paradigm that uses a set of correct and incorrect rules for performing a certain skill. Knowledge tracing is a student modeling technique. While the student solves some kind of problem, the tutor uses a Bayesian procedure to estimate the probability that the student has learned each of the rules in the cognitive model. Thus, knowledge tracing can be used to predict post-test performance. The probability that a student will solve each exercise correctly can be accurately derived from the probability that student has learned each of the necessary rules.

Andes is an ITS developed for Newtonian physics[6]. Andes student model uses Bayesian networks to do long-term knowledge assessment, plan recognition and prediction of students' actions during problem solving. In terms of procedural knowledge assessment, Bayesian networks are used to estimate student knowledge and they are updated at each step of problem solving. However, updating Bayesian networks is in the worst case NP-hard, so their response time could be extremely large.

The best-known strategy for declarative knowledge asessment is testing. Perhaps the most popular and well-founded strategy for knowledge inference in testing systems is the Item Response Theory (IRT)[8]. IRT is based on two principles: (a) results obtained by a student in a test could be explained by a set of factors (such as the knowledge level) that are not observable; (b) the performance of a student with a certain knowledge level answering an item can be probabilistically predicted and modeled by means of certain functions called characteristic curves. There are hundreds of IRT-based models, and different classification criteria for them. One of them describe how the models update the estimated student knowledge in terms of his/her response. Thereby, IRT-based models can be[10]:

Dichotomous models: Only two possible scores are considered, i.e. either correct or incorrect. A characteristic curve is enough to model each item. This curve expresses the probability that a student with a certain knowledge level will answer the item correctly.

Polytomous models: The former family of models does not make any distinction in terms of the answer selected by the student. No partial credit is given. This means information loss. However, in this family of models each possible answer has an operating characteristic curve [7], which expresses the probability that a student with a certain knowledge level will select this answer [9]. These models are therefore more informative than the former ones[8].

3   The Proposal

The main objective of this work involves the assessment of the student procedural knowledge using an IRT-based polytomous model. Our hypothesis is that by understanding problem solving as a test, procedural steps in problems could be understood as choices in test questions, therefore in our model, each step in problem solving has an operating characteristic function associated. As polytomous items in IRT could have as choices as necessary, each problem state could have as later steps as needed. The student model could be updated during problem solving using these operating characteristic functions.

Problems are modeled internally as directed graphs where vertexes are states of problem solving, and edges are the different steps followed to navigate between states. In each graph, the correct path to reach the solution state and other paths that represent different wrong paths usually taken by students are included. As in polytomous IRT, not all wrong paths are equally incorrect, there are different degrees of incorrectness(e.g. adding fractions multiplying denominators instead of calculating the least common denominator is less incorrect than adding them by adding both the numerators and denominators).

Problems' graphs are not designed by a domain expert, but they should be generated by data-driven procedures analyzing students' responses at each problem state. In order to build each problem graph, the teacher specify the ideal solution of the problem and then the graph will be updated from students' interactions. Using these data-driven procedures, we could also determine the difficulty, discrimination and guessing factors of each operating characteristic function. Thus, we try to limit human influence in tutor construction. Using data-driven techniques to build problem graph allows the ITS to use both the teacher's ideal solution and other non-incorrect solutions inferred from students' responses.

We have tested our proposal through a virtual evaluation. To this end, we have developed a simulator which includes virtual problems and virtual students. Virtual problems are modeled by directed graphs which represent the set of problem states and actions, and virtual students as an entity with a prior real knowledge level that determines their behavior while solving a problem.

Virtual students solve the problem by navigating the graph according to their real knowledge level and then the simulator tries to estimate their level using our proposal.

4   Current Research Lines

We are currently implementing a web-based problem solving platform called Dedalo which uses this proposal. Our goal is to evaluate this model with real students in a real learning environment. We are also exploring different data mining strategies(i.e. sequence patterns and association rules[11]) to feed the problems' graphs with student's problem solving strategies in order to dynamically model the space of all possible student actions in the graph.

Acknowledgements. This work is financed by the Andalusian Regional Ministry ofScience,Innovation andEnterprise(P09-TIC-5105).

References

1. Anderson, J.R., Corbett, A.T., Koedinger, K.R., Pelletier, R.: Cognitive Tutors: Lessons learned. The Journal of the Learning Sciences 4(2), 167–207 (1995)
2. Anderson, J.R.: The architecture of cognition. Harvard University Press, Cambridge (1983)
3. Anderson, J.R., Boyle, C.F., Corbett, A.T., Lewis, M.W.: Cognitive modeling and intelligent tutoring. Artif. Intell., 7–49 (1990)
4. Bisanz, J., LeFevre, J.: Strategic and nonstrategic processing in the development of mathematical cognition. In: Bjorklund, D. (ed.) Children's Strategies: Contemporary Views of Cognitive Development, pp. 213–244. Lawrence Erlbaum Associates, Inc., Hillsdale (1990)
5. Bloom, B.S.: The search for methods of group instruction as effective as one-to-one tutoring. Educational Leadership 13(8), 4–17 (1984)
6. Conati, C., Gertner, A.S., Vanlehn, K., Druzdzel, M.J.: On-line student modeling for coached problem solving using bayesian networks, pp. 231–242. Springer, Heidelberg (1997)
7. Dodd, B.G., Ayala, R.J.D., Koch, W.R.: Computerized adaptive testing with polytomous items. Applied Psychological Measurement (19), 5–22 (1995)
8. Embretson, S.E., Reise, S.P.: Item response theory for psychologists, 1st edn. Lawrence Erlbaum, Mahwah (2000)
9. Guzmán, E., Conejo, R.: A model for student knowledge diagnosis through adaptive testing. In: Lester, J.C., Vicari, R.M., Paraguaçu, F. (eds.) ITS 2004. LNCS, vol. 3220, pp. 12–21. Springer, Heidelberg (2004)
10. Guzmán, E., Conejo, R., Pérez-de-la Cruz, J.L.: Adaptive testing for hierarchical student models. User Modeling and User-Adapted Interaction 17(1-2), 119–157 (2007)
11. Nkambou, R., Mephu Nguifo, E., Couturier, O., Fournier-Viger, P.: Problem-solving knowledge mining from users' actions in an intelligent tutoring system. In: Bozapalidis, S., Rahonis, G. (eds.) CAI 2007. LNCS, vol. 4728, pp. 393–404. Springer, Heidelberg (2007)
12. Rittle-Johnson, B., Koedinger, K.R.: Designing Knowledge Scaffolds to Support Mathematical Problem Solving, ch. 23(3), pp. 313–349. Routledge, New York (2005)

Differences on How People Organize and Think about Personal Information

Matjaž Kljun

Infolab21, School of Computing and Communications,
Lancaster University, Lancaster, LA1 4WA, United Kingdom
m.kljun@lancaster.ac.uk
http://scc.lancs.ac.uk/

Abstract. Personal information management (PIM) is a study on how people handle personal information to support their needs and tasks. In the last decade a lot of studies focused on how people acquire, organize, maintain and retrieve information from their information spaces. Results have led to many research prototypes that tried to either augment present tools or integrate these collections within entirely new designs. However, not much has changed in the present tools, and hierarchies still prevail as the storage foundation. Our research aims at understanding the difference between how people organize their information in various applications and physical space and how they actually think of this information in relation to tasks they have to accomplish. We carried out a preliminary study and are currently finishing another study which both show that there is a difference on how information is organized in formal structures on computers and physical spaces and how it is thought of in users' heads. These findings have motivated the design of an application that tries to mimic the latter and adapts to current computer activities.

Keywords: personal information management, task, information collection, mental links.

1   Introduction

PIM studies vary from the usage of office space for managing information [10] [13], to computer documents [11][7], email [6] and web bookmarks management [1]. Some studies covered several types and studied how fragmented information is managed across tools [3] and even devices [12]. Many research prototypes addressed the issues found in mentioned studies with spatial management, piles, different visualizations, context awareness, tagging and agents to improve and ease management practices of users. Some prototypes also addressed the fragmentation problem using either existing applications and embed other information types (such us Taskmaster) or work above them as another layer (such us WorkspaceMirror), while others introduce new interfaces with mixing several information types (such us Haystack).

There have also been a lot of studies on how users perform tasks, such as how interruptions are affecting the task's completion, which noted that users have

Joseph A. Konstan et al. (Eds.): UMAP 2011, LNCS 6787, pp. 430–433, 2011.

most problems returning to long lasting tasks [5]. Several suggested solutions also tried to bring together information that is task related [8][2]. Some solutions even bend towards helping users to complete their tasks with suggesting future possible actions [4].

However none of the mentioned studies and prototypes focused on understanding the difference between how people organize their information in personal information collections (PICs) in software applications and tools, and how they manage information in their heads when they have a task to complete (which we are calling Task Information Collection). The aim of our study is to understand the difference between the two collections, how the gap between them can be bridged and if it has to be bridged at all.

2   Research Goals

People need information to complete their tasks and they acquire information by different tools and means. We named all information relating to a task a TIC (Task Information Collection). Our studies showed that TICs are partly supported by tools (desks, file cabinets, clips), software applications (divided by information types), web space and are also partly held in our heads. Although there is a need to integrate information of various types and formats, it was still not studied what is the best way and to what extent users want to integrate their information in support of tasks. Our research goals are to understand:

- How users think of their information that relates to a task at hand and how they manage TICs in their heads over time.
- How and if TICs changes are related to how information is acquired (created, found, given), its importance, duration of a task, etc.
- How TICs overlap and how information in PICs is reused in various TICs.
- How to preserve some of the TICs for users and for how long or if they need to be preserved at all.

Answering these questions will help us understand the difference and relations between the two collections and their changing over time. The results will be used to build the prototype application to support the management of TICs in relation to information scattered over several applications and WWW.

3   Progress To Date

Theoretical Research and User Studies
In our preliminary study we studied some PIM practices of 7 undergraduate students that signed up and volunteered to enter data each day for a month in an anonymous questionnaire [9]. The main questions of the study were: (1) which information items participants regarded as important after each day, (2) how much time they spent on creating (editing), finding or reading these items, (3) which of these items participants considered linked to other items.

We found (1) that more than half of information regarded as important was created, (2) that level of importance dropped quickly for most information items, (3) that users linked information in their heads regardless of the application used to manage it and (4) that mental links to information items not regarded as important were also maintained. These results led to our present longitudinal study which aims to understand how people talk about their tasks and information related to these tasks. In semi-structured interviews we ask participants (all PhD students) about most important tasks they had to work on in the last two weeks. They give us a tour of information related to a task on their computers and desks and draw how all presented information is related to a task. The results show that TICs are formed by information of various types and formats and they overlap as well. Most of also TICs take a form of a mind map. This results are the base for our TICs management research prototype.

Prototype Design and Implementation

Several PIM prototypes tried to guess and present related information to currently used documents to boost productivity. However, we think that giving users some control over structuring related information can result in significant improvements to adapting the environment to a current task. We are currently implementing the research prototype called *Task Information Map*. It allows users to define tasks and subtasks to which they can drag digital documents, folders, URLs and to some extent email from their existing applications. It also allows to rate importance of information items through time. Results of our current study show that TICs mostly take form of a mind map where items are individual documents and PICs, and these often take part in several tasks. The prototype builds a map and finds overlaps between tasks, it allows users to navigate their information through their tasks and vice versa.

Giving users the possibility to easily create mental maps of related information, allowing the computer to understand TICs (information relations, information overlap, subjective importance of information, task duration, etc.) and connect these information with automatically gathered data (how much time information item are worked on, how often, which information is used together, etc.) are in our opinion the key factors to successfully adapting the environment, based on currently used information. The prototype development is in its initial phase and as such has not been tested. Nevertheless, the prototype sketches received encouraging feedback. After completing the prototype we plan to extensively evaluate it in participants' working environments.

4   Key Contributions

This research aims to understand how the organization of information in the physical and digital worlds differs from mental organization of information related to tasks users need to complete. We hope that this contribution will affect future designs of software applications addressing the information fragmentation problem and ease management of personal information.

Acknowledgements. I would like to thank my advisor, Dr. Alan Dix, for insightful discussions, advice and support.

References

1. Abrams, D., Baecker, R.: How people use www bookmarks. In: CHI 1997: CHI 1997 Extended Abstracts on Human Factors in Computing Systems, pp. 341–342. ACM, New York (1997)
2. Bergman, O., Beyth-Marom, R., Nachmias, R.: The user-subjective approach to personal information management systems design: Evidence and implementations. J. Am. Soc. Inf. Sci. Technol. 59(2), 235–246 (2008)
3. Boardman, R., Spence, R., Sasse, M.: Too many hierarchies? The daily struggle for control of the workspace. In: Proc. HCI International 2003, Citeseer (2003)
4. Catarci, T., Dix, A., Katifori, A., Lepouras, G., Poggi, A.: Task-Centred Information Management. In: Thanos, C., Borri, F., Candela, L. (eds.) Digital Libraries: Research and Development. LNCS, vol. 4877, pp. 197–206. Springer, Heidelberg (2007)
5. Czerwinski, M., Horvitz, E., Wilhite, S.: A diary study of task switching and interruptions. In: CHI 2004: Proceedings of the SIGCHI Conference on Human Factors in Computing Systems, pp. 175–182. ACM, New York (2004)
6. Fisher, D., Brush, A.J., Gleave, E., Smith, M.A.: Revisiting Whittaker & Sidner's "email overload" ten years later. In: CSCW 2006: Proceedings of the 2006 20th Anniversary Conference on Computer Supported Cooperative Work, pp. 309–312. ACM, New York (2006)
7. Jones, W., Phuwanartnurak, A.J., Gill, R., Bruce, H.: Don't take my folders away!: organizing personal information to get things done. In: CHI 2005: CHI 2005 Extended Abstracts on Human Factors in Computing Systems, pp. 1505–1508. ACM, New York (2005)
8. Kaptelinin, V.: Umea: translating interaction histories into project contexts. In: CHI 2003: Proceedings of the SIGCHI Conference on Human Factors in Computing Systems, pp. 353–360. ACM, New York (2003)
9. Kljun, M., Dix, A., Solina, F.: A study of a crosstool information usage on personal computers: how users mentally link information relating to a task but residing in different applications and how importance and type of acquisition affect this (November 2009), http://eprints.lancs.ac.uk/33816/
10. Malone, T.W.: How do people organize their desks?: Implications for the design of office information systems. ACM Trans. Inf. Syst. 1(1), 99–112 (1983)
11. Ravasio, P., Schr, S.G., Krueger, H.: In pursuit of desktop evolution: User problems and practices with modern desktop systems. ACM Trans. Comput.-Hum. Interact. 11(2), 156–180 (2004)
12. Tungare, M.: Pérez-Qui nones, M.A.: Mental workload in multi-device personal in- formation management. In: PIM Workshop 2009, Vancouver, BC, Canada, November 7-9 (2009)
13. Whittaker, S., Hirschberg, J.: The character, value, and management of personal paper archives. ACM Trans. Comput.-Hum. Interact. 8(2), 150–170 (2001)

Towards Contextual Search: Social Networks, Short Contexts and Multiple Personas

Tomáš Kramár

Institute of Informatics and Software Engineering, Faculty of Informatics and
Information Technologies, Slovak University of Technology,
Ilkovičova 3, 842 16 Bratislava, Slovakia
kramar@fiit.stuba.sk

Abstract. In this paper we present an approach to contextual search, based on
the automatically extracted metadata from visited documents. User model
represents user's interests as a combination of tags, keywords and named
entities. Such user model is further enhanced by automatically detected
communities of similar users, based on the similarities of their models. The user
may belong to multiple communities, each representing one of her possibly
many personas – roles or stereotypes, facets of her interests. We discuss further
possibilities of using this model to bring more fine-grained contextualization
and search improvement by using short contexts.

Keywords: personalized search, search context, personas, social networks.

1 Introduction and Related Work

Traditional, fulltext-only search is often incapable of handling user queries
satisfactorily and has been gradually shifting towards becoming more personalized.
Traditional search engines have no way of knowing the meaning the user is looking
for; they treat all documents the same, looking for the textual matches and ordering
the resulting documents by a ranking function. As the consequence, the search results
contain a mixed set of documents, covering all possible meanings of the word and the
disambiguation is left to the user alone.

This problem is well researched and has been addressed in many ways. The
solution usually boils down to building a user model, which captures user's interests,
which can later be used to personalize the search. The interests are often modeled
using the tags [5] and other metadata extracted from visited pages [12]. In [3], authors
propose a method for building an interest-based user model based on the ODP
taxonomy and the Topic-Driven Random Surfer Model. The user model is a weighted
vector representing user's interests in 16 top-level ODP categories. This vector is then
used in Topic-sensitive PageRank algorithm [2] to favor documents with topics
matching user's interests. Similarly, a method described in [4] builds the user's interest
model (context) from his interaction with the browser and influences the final
ranking. Many times, some kind of social structures [6] are used to enrich the user
model with data from similar users, sharing the same interests.

Many of the existing methods focus only on re-ranking the standard results – they
do not solve the problem of actually getting the results into the list. This is usually

Joseph A. Konstan et al. (Eds.): UMAP 2011, LNCS 6787, pp. 434–437, 2011.

solved with query expansion [1], which is often based on static information which does not accurately capture user's interest. We believe that query refinement could achieve deeper level of personalization by also analyzing the documents and behavior of similar users. We propose a method which extends and combines social networks and query refinement methods. We link the users in a social network not only by analyzing URLs of the visited pages, but also by analyzing the content features of these pages. We later use these features to capture user's current interest when she is searching, and also to provide the basis for our query refinement methods. This approach can better capture the users' dynamics and shifts in interests.

Moreover, one of the most serious drawbacks of current research is that it focuses on user as a stable, monolithic entity. Once the interest-based user model is built, it is used for search personalization in every context. There are though many situations, where the user is exploring the area beyond her usual field of interest (imagine a biologist buying a new Jaguar car). This is the area where most of the existing solutions fail, as they are unable to detect and use the short-term context to provide accurate search results. In [7], the authors show that short-term context is important and that best results are achieved by using a combination of short and long-term context. This work is however focused only on the idea of short-context and does not attempt to intelligently detect context switching – only a simple time-based method is used. Similarly, the user usually has many personas – social roles or characters – one might be a biologist but also a car enthusiast, interchanging these roles. A monolithic user model may be easily confused and it would clearly be advantageous to build and use a separate user model for each persona.

2   Metadata Based Interest Modeling with Multiple Personas

User's interests are usually modeled from a limited set of data of her activity. The number of actions carried by the user and the actions available to the search engine for analysis is disproportional. To gain a better insight into users' interests, we have developed a tool which allows us to monitor the users' activity on the whole Web – a personalized proxy server platform [9,11]. All traffic is directed through the proxy, which has access to request and response data. The process is described in Fig. 1.

Based on the automatically extracted metadata (tags, keywords, ODP categories, named entities) from the visited documents, we build an interest-based user model [8]. The model is a hypergraph, where vertices represent documents, their terms, and accesses to these documents. The user model is further enhanced by data from similar users. First, we build a social network, where the users are linked by their similarity. We consider two users similar if they visited the same document, or the intersection of their metadata is not empty.

The relations in the social network are weighted, based on the quantification of above conditions. The resulting social network represents users, linked by their interests. One user may be connected to other user only by a subset of her interests. Next, we detect communities of similar users by running a spreading activation algorithm on the underlying social network, building a community of similar users for each user. Each user may end up in multiple communities, each one representing one of her possible personas. We refer to the user's model, the related communities and models of the related users as the enhanced user model.

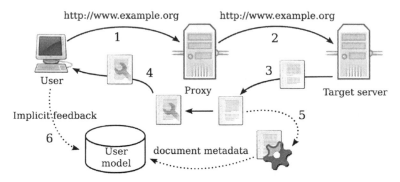

Fig. 1. User modeling process. First the user's requests (1) is routed through the proxy which requests the document (2). The response (3) is extended with a tracking JavaScript and sent back to the client (4). The processes depicted by a dashed line happen asynchronously. The document is processed and relevant metadata are extracted (5). The tracking JavaScript reports implicit feedback indicators (6), which influence weights of metadata in the user model.

When the user enters query into the search engine, we use the enhanced user model to expand the query and include additional keywords, which help to provide search results more narrowed to the user's interests. To obtain the additional keywords, we analyze the enhanced user model and search for reformulation patterns in historical queries. Similarly to this, we search for frequent co-occurrences – metadata in the enhanced user model, which occur frequently together with the keywords from the current query. We conducted an experiment with real users [10], using the same enhanced proxy platform. We hooked our method into one of the major search engines. The expanded queries were shown together with the top four results for these queries. The results were clearly separated from the original search results. We found out that nearly 70% of these recommendations were clicked, and furthermore, when looking at the implicit feedback indicators, mainly time spent on page that the recommended results were perceived twice more useful than the standard results.

3   Research Focus and Future Work

In our work we focus on modeling user interests with various automatically extracted document metadata and combining the created user models based on the similarity of user interests. The enhanced user models, which are a combination of metadata based interests, communities of similar users and the interests of similar users provide more data for the personalization, leading to more accurate search results.

We see the limitations of current contextual search in its long-termness. The user model is built from all available data, combining all user interests into one model. This brings difficulties, when the user is trying to search for something beyond her usual area of interest or when she is switching between multiple personas.

To deal with the problem of long-term user model, we propose to use a short-term context, built only with data from the current search session, enhanced with user models of users with similar interests, based on the short-term interests. This approach would have the advantage of the rich, enhanced user model, but would not contain the damaging long-term interests. The main challenge in this area is finding the moment of context switch, based on the vectors of document metadata. We also have to deal with parallel browsing sessions by maintaining a stack of short contexts.

To deal with the problem of multiple personas, we propose a layered, contextual user model, where each interest is constrained with its context – time, date, location or other available sources. When the user model is about to be used to provide search context, it would be possible to only consider those layers, which match the given constraints. Also, the created social network should be layered and when enhancing the user model, only some layers should be used.

Acknowledgement. This work was partially supported by the grants VG1/0675/11, KEGA 028-025STU-4/10, APVV-0208-10 and it is the partial result of the Research & Development Operational Programme for the project Support of Center of Excellence for Smart Technologies, Systems and Services II, ITMS 26240120029, co-funded by the ERDF.

References

1. Anagnostopoulos, L., Becchetti, C.: Castillo, and A. Gionis, An optimization framework for query recommendation. In: Web Search and Web Data Mining, pp. 161–170 (2010)
2. Haveliwala, T.H.: Topic-sensitive PageRank. In: Proc. of Int. Conf. on World Wide Web (WWW 2002), pp. 517–526. ACM, New York (2002)
3. Qiu, F., Cho, J.: Automatic identification of user interest for personalized search. In: Proc. of Int. World Wide Web Conference (WWW 2006), pp. 727–736 (2006)
4. Xiang, et al.: Context-aware ranking in web search. In: Proc. of Int. ACM SIGIR Conf. on Research and Development in Information Retrieval, pp. 451–458. ACM, New York (2010)
5. Wetzker, R., Zimmermann, C., Bauckhage, C., Albayrak, S.: I tag, you tag: translating tags for advanced user models. In: Web Search and Web Data Mining, pp. 71–80 (2010)
6. Teevan, J., Morris, M.R., Bush, S.: Discovering and using groups to improve personalized search. In: Web Search and Web Data Mining, pp. 15–24 (2009)
7. White, R., Bennett, P., Dumais, S.: Predicting short-term interests using activity-based search context. In: Information and Knowledge Management, pp. 1009–1018. ACM, New York (2010)
8. Kramár, T., Barla, M., Bieliková, M.: Disambiguating search by leveraging a social context based on the stream of user's activity. In: De Bra, P., Kobsa, A., Chin, D. (eds.) UMAP 2010. LNCS, vol. 6075, pp. 387–392. Springer, Heidelberg (2010)
9. Kramár, T., Barla, M., Bieliková, M.: Adapive proxy server: Operation and experiences after one year. In: Proc. of the 5th Workshop on Intelligent and Knowledge Oriented Technologies (WIKT 2010), Equilibria, pp. 48–51 (2010)
10. Kramár, T., Barla, M., Bieliková, M.: Open-web User Modeling. In: Proc. of Znalosti 2011, pp. 112–123 (2011)
11. Barla, M., Bieliková, M.: Ordinary Web Pages as a Source for Metadata Acquisition for Open Corpus User Modeling. In: Proc. of WWW/Internet, pp. 227–233. IADIS Press (2010)
12. Holub, M., Bieliková, M.: Behavior Based Adaptive Navigation Support. In: Proc. of the Workshop on the Practical Use of Recommender Systems, Algorithms and Technologies (PRSAT 2010). CEUR, vol. 676, pp. 47–50 (2010)

Using Folksonomies for Building User Interest Profile

Harshit Kumar and Hong-Gee Kim

BIKE Lab, Seoul National University, Yeong-gun, Jong-ro, Seoul, South Korea

Abstract. This work exploits folksonomy for building User Interest Profile (UIP) based on user's search history. UIP is an indispensable source of knowledge which can be exploited by intelligent systems for query recommendation, personalized search, and web search result ranking etc. A UIP consist of a clustered list of concepts and their weights. We show how to design, implement, and visualize such a system, in practice, which aids in finding interesting relationships between concepts and detect outliers, if any. The experiment reveals that UIP not only captures user interests but also its context and results are very promising.

Keywords: User Profiling, Folksonomy, Clustering.

1 Introduction

The basic research problem, addressed in this paper, is building a User Interest Profile which models user interests. Given a list of clicked URLs, interesting research problems are: How to summarize it as a list of concepts, How to eliminate noise, and How to cluster concepts? To summarize a URL, one of the solutions is employing NLP. This often results in a lot of insignificant terms. Moreover, computing such a list of terms using NLP has high time complexity. An interesting solution proposed by researchers is using folksonomy like del.icio.us[1]. Social services like del.icio.us has an incredible source of information - it has a list of tagged URLs; such a list of tags is comprehensive and thus enabled to disambiguate different meanings associated with a concept (i.e. semantics, disambiguate polysemy, synonyms, and context). We believe that tags associated with a URL can be modeled as concepts. Moreover, to make these concepts more meaningful i.e. to associate context with them, the related concepts should be clustered together. A final list of clustered tags with weights is called as UIP. We use Pajek to visualize the UIP which uncovers interesting facts for ex: outliers, related terms, and contextual terms.

Automatic construction of user profile usually deals with the observation of user browsing behavior. Kelly and Teevan [2] reviewed several possible approaches for inferring user preferences. Agichtein et al.[3] organized user interests as a set of features. Teevan et al.[4] and Chirita et al.[5] uses user's desktop to estimate their interests and used that to construct his/her profile. A major limitation of these approaches is that there can be a lot of terms on user's desktop, which can make a user profile noisy or misleading. Following, the existing work

Joseph A. Konstan et al. (Eds.): UMAP 2011, LNCS 6787, pp. 438–441, 2011.

that uses folksonomy[1,6,7] in IR domain, their limitation and how our system improvises over them is discussed. **Limitation 1**: A resource like URL is tagged by users. But since, users don't tag resources religiously; it may be possible that a particular URL receive higher weights while others don't. The existing work does not take into account the biasness of tagging by users. To alleviate such biasness, we propose to normalize the tag weights. **Limitation 2**: The existing work assumes that a user has a delicious account. We don't make such assumption. We observe and analyze user search behavior to construct his profile. Thus our system is applicable to all the users. **Limitation 3**: After collecting group of terms, such a group is termed as a user profile; User profile is further used to re-rank search results by calculating cosine similarity of a given query term with all the terms in the user profile. This approach is a good solution however there is still some scope of improvement as later we will show in our experiment section that clustering the terms indeed makes the UIP more meaningful.

2 Modeling User Interest Profile

Using delicious API, input as a clicked URL, the output received is a list of tags and their respective tag frequencies. In this work, tags included in the UIP are referred to as terms or concepts. Our system extracts the top three tags and as explained above, to remove biasness, tag weights are normalized using the following equation: $ntw_i = \frac{tw_i}{\sum_k tw_k}$. The weight of repeated terms is accumulated and further they are arranged in decreasing order of term weights. We observed during computation of term similarity matrix that the terms with lower weight have very low similarity with other terms. This means that, if the system does not discard terms, they will later be classified as outliers by clustering algorithm. Therefore, in the initial stages of computation, we delete lower weight terms up to a threshold k to reduce the time complexity of calculating the similarity matrix, clustering algorithm, and visualization algorithm.

In order to cluster terms, we first compute the term-term similarity matrix using Normalized Google Distance (NGD). The NGD computes similarity between two terms t_1 and t_2, $NGD(t_1, t_2) = \frac{max\{logf(t_1), logf(t_2)\} - logf(t_1, t_2)}{logN - min\{logf(t_1), logf(t_2)\}}$, based on information distance and Kolmogorov complexity. The variables $f(t_1)$, $f(t_2)$, $f(t_1, t_2)$ are number of search results for term t_1, t_2, and t_1 and t_2 respectively. Given the term-term similarity matrix, the system put it to cluster terms into contextually similar related terms using hierarchical agglomerative clustering (HAC). At the outset, HAC treat each term as a singleton cluster and then successively merge pair of clusters until all clusters have been merged into a single cluster that contain all the terms. This gives a hierarchical view of the clusters represented as a dendrogram. There are four key pieces of information that one can observe in a dendrogram: *weight* gives the rough percentage of all terms that fall into one cluster, *compactness* measures the similarity between terms in a cluster, *distinctness* is the measure of difference between neighboring clusters, and *leaf* shows the outliers i.e. those terms that don't fall into any hierarchy are grounded as outliers.

auction dogs college myspace nyc religion politics free search airlines
ipod government video books lessonplans bills news jazz howto history
tv library yoga garden mixtapes resources publishers science medical
bank coffee shopping forum songs rap education wireless oberlin music
torrent reference school lword ancient social youtube forums spanish
activism celebrities health hiphop language television translation recipes
lyrics starbucks networking dictionary tech research thinkquest thesaurus
directory radio finance shop phone travel atlanta skin lesbian coupons
schools pets cheerleading reviews cheer videos comparison encyclopedia
food la movies mp3 blog magazine banking dermatology soaps film
university deals daily entertainment database egypt amazon neworleans

Fig. 1. Extracted concepts, from user search history, using delicious API

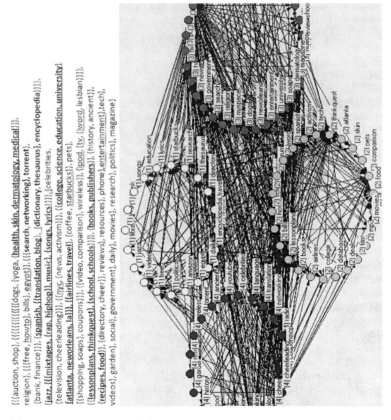

Fig. 2. (a) Clustered concepts (b)A snapshot of visualization of concepts and their association

3   Results

To evaluate the effectiveness of the proposed UIP, we used AOL Query log [14] which has 657,426 unique user Ids, and 10,154,742 unique queries over a period of 3 months. We use Pajek for visualization of UIP and developed our own implementation of Hierarchical Clustering Algorithm for clustering concepts. To verify our work, we show results for one user who has anonId 1812207. Due to space limitations, we can not report results for other users who showed similar behavior. The user 1812207 issued 271 distinct queries which resulted in 675 clicked URLs, out of which 198 were not tagged in Delicious. This means approx 25% of URLs were not tagged on delicious. The total number of extracted terms, with their weights amounts to 263, which after applying the threshold of 1.0 reduced to 100. We observed similar results with other users i.e. applying threshold of 1.0 reduces the number of terms by almost 50%. On careful examination of terms and their associated weights in Fig. 1, it is imperative that the user preferences are: medical, music, food, education, etc. On further investigation, one can also judge the context of the aforementioned user preferences: dermatology as medical, rap and hiphop as music, science as education. There are also indications of some light interests like books, spanish language, and travelling. This manual observation can be inferred and processed by machines using clustering, shown in Fig.2. One such cluster is $\{health, skin, dermatology, and medical\}$ which disambiguates the use of term health and medical. Similarly cluster, $\{jazz, rap, hiphop\}$, disambiguate the context of term music. The cluster, $\{college, science, educaiton\}$, disambiguates user's litereary interests. The weight assigned to a cluster is accumulation of weight of terms or concepts contained in a cluster. Such a UIP is an important source of information which if utilized intelligently can be effectively used for query suggestion, query classification, web page recommendation, search engine personalization, and web search result ranking. Fig. 2(b) depicts a different visualization i.e. network connection between terms as inter partition and intra partition. The terms in partition 4 (higher weights) have less interaction with each other as these are high level concepts. These terms have high degree of connection with partitions that have terms of lower weights. Moreover, terms in lower level partitions have moderate interactions with each other.

References

1. Noll, M.G., Meinel, C.: Web search personalization via social bookmarking and tagging. In: Aberer, K., Choi, K.-S., Noy, N., Allemang, D., Lee, K.-I., Nixon, L.J.B., Golbeck, J., Mika, P., Maynard, D., Mizoguchi, R., Schreiber, G., Cudré-Mauroux, P. (eds.) ASWC 2007 and ISWC 2007. LNCS, vol. 4825, pp. 367–380. Springer, Heidelberg (2007)
2. Kelly, D., Teevan, J.: Implicit feedback for inferring user preference: A bibliography. In: SIGIR, pp. 18–28 (2003)
3. Agichtein, E., Brill, E., Dumais, S., Ragno, R.: Learning user interaction models for predicting web search result preferences. In: SIGIR, pp. 3–10 (2006)
4. Teevan, J., Dumais, S.T., Horvitz, E.: Personalizing search via automated analysis of interests and activities. In: SIGIR, pp. 449–456 (2005)
5. Chirita, P.A., Firan, C., Nejdl, W.: Summarizing local context to personalize global web search. In: CIKM, pp. 287–296. Springer, Heidelberg (2006)
6. Vallet, D., Cantador, I., Jose, J.M.: Personalizing web search with folksonomy-based user and document profiles. In: Gurrin, C., He, Y., Kazai, G., Kruschwitz, U., Little, S., Roelleke, T., Rüger, S., van Rijsbergen, K. (eds.) ECIR 2010. LNCS, vol. 5993, pp. 420–431. Springer, Heidelberg (2010)
7. Xu, S., Bao, S., Fei, B., Su, Z., Yu, Y.: Exploring folksonomy for personalized search. In: SIGIR, pp. 155–162 (2008)

Designing Trustworthy Adaptation on Public Displays

Ekaterina Kurdyukova

University of Augsburg, Universitaetsstr. 6a, 86159 Augsburg, Germany
Katja.Kurdyukova@informatik.uni-augsburg.de

Abstract. Adaptation on public displays brings certain advantages and risks. Due to the implicit nature of adaptation, the users often miss the causality behind the adaptive behavior. Moreover, a high degree of autonomy in adaptive displays may leave the users with the feeling of control loss. Limited amount of transparency and controllability leads to the loss of user trust. As a result, the users feel insecure, frustrated, and are likely to abandon the system. The research goal of this work is to optimize the system actions in a ubiquitous display environment, in order make adaptation design transparent, controllable, and thus trustworthy. By means of a decision-theoretic approach the user trust can be assessed in different trust-critical contexts. The contexts describe the changes in the environment that call for adaptation: privacy of content, social setting, and accuracy of knowledge. The generated decisions enable the system to maintain trust and keep interaction comfortable.

Keywords: Adaptation, public displays, trust.

1 Motivation

Adaptive ubiquitous displays come with a lot of benefits, but also lots of risks. On the one hand, adaptation can simplify the access to the needed data and make interaction more efficient. On the other hand, automatic adaptation can cause frustrations and the loss of trust. If the users cannot trace the rationales behind the adaptation process, or don't have leverages to control the adaptation, they end up confused, insecure, and feeling control loss [1]. As a result, their trust is diminished and they are likely to abandon the system.

In order to avoid such an outcome, design solutions should be found to maintain trust in critical situations. The following typical trust-critical contexts call for adaptation on public displays:

- *Privacy of Content*: The public setting with the possibility to expose personalized information to surrounding people inevitably raises privacy issues [2] (see Fig. 1).
- *Social Setting*: The high dynamics of public environments require the systems to constantly adapt to the new situation. Due to the complexity of the adaptation mechanism, the users can be irritated and perceive the system as unpredictable.
- *Accuracy of Knowledge*: The content on public displays is often based on sensor data, such as e.g. location data or user activity data. The loss of the data due to unstable transmission technologies or incompleteness of available data can seriously affect user trust, since the system is no longer perceived as reliable and secure.

Joseph A. Konstan et al. (Eds.): UMAP 2011, LNCS 6787, pp. 442–445, 2011.

The research challenge therefore is to find the adaptation strategy and design that supports user trust in the described critical situations.

Fig. 1. Public setting calls for adaptation of the display to protect private data

Research on trustworthy design indicates *transparency* and *controllability* as the main aspects supporting user trust. Glass and colleagues emphasized the importance of transparency and control in the design of trustable agents [1]. Graham and Cheverst studied interaction paradigms that maintain trust in mobile guides [3]. The authors identified that the lack of transparency and control potentially diminishes user trust. Cheverst and colleagues designed a system that dynamically adjusts to a learnt user model [4]. The authors emphasize the importance of sufficient transparency and comprehensibility of the system and the need to control the existing user model. Bellotti and Edwards [5] as well as Lim and Dey [6] claim that intelligibility significantly improves user trust in context-aware systems. If private data is involved in the adaptation, transparency and control gain even a greater importance. Langheinrich claims that ubiquitous systems should explicitly inform users of aspects that relate to their privacy [7]. The users should be empowered to cancel unauthorized actions.

Despite the evident importance of transparency and controllability, no research has been done so far to investigate the guidelines for trustworthy adaptation on public displays, i.e. *how* and *to which extent* transparency and control should be provided. An extreme level of transparency or controllability can significantly burden the interaction and cause unacceptable distractions. Therefore, the research should strive for a design trade-off that affords high level of user trust, but keeps interaction comfortable.

2 Research Goal and Approach

The research goal of this work comprises the optimization of the system actions to reflect adaptation in trustworthy and comfortable way. We apply a decision-theoretic approach to model user trust in critical contexts. The basic idea of the approach is to define factors that impact the user's feeling of trust and to investigate how these factors can be influenced by particular system actions. The current state of the environment can be captured by the combination of context variables: *Privacy of Content*, *Social Setting*, and *Accuracy of Knowledge*. Different *System Actions* model adaptive reaction of the system with varying levels of *Transparency* and *Controllability*. To take a decision, the system evaluates the resulting user *Trust* and *Comfort of Use* of all possible options and chooses the option with the highest values.

The decision-making process should address the following questions:

- **How to design presentation and interaction of trustworthy adaptation?** Which presentation and techniques are appropriate for various critical situations?
- **How much transparency and control do the users need?** Which level of transparency suffices to notify the users about the performed adaptation? Which leverages the users need to control the adaptation behavior?
- **Which factors influence the user choice of adaptation design?** How the surrounding context influences the choice of adaptation design? (e.g. relationships between the users, privacy level and the type of the displayed data)

3 Research Progress and Future Plan

As a test bed for our research, we employ two adaptive display systems. The first system, called Friend Finder runs on the University's public displays. It visualizes the user's social network overlaid over an interactive campus map. The second system, called Arrow Navigator supports outdoor navigation with a GPS-enables mobile device coupled with a mobile projector.

The experiments so far have been done with Friend Finder, exploring trust-critical situations triggered by privacy issues and dynamic social setting. The user-centered design informed the privacy protecting adaptation mechanism [8] and the choice of system actions that support trust in multi-display environment [9]. Friend Finder reacts to the presence of people around the display by masking the private pictures and moving them to an assisting mobile device. The adaptation is performed automatically based on the real context. The camera integrated into the large display runs the face detection; the microphone performs noise level recognition. The mobile interface allows the users to manually correct the performed automatic adaptation any time, using the mobile interface. The evaluations showed that such ubiquitous control was appreciated by the users. In adaptive systems reacting on social context, the users do need a leverage to control the adaptation, since the decision to protect the data is usually based on personal relationships with observers.

As the next step, we are going to take a deeper insight into the relationship-based adaptation, exploring the impact of privacy context combined with the social setting. Then, the multi-user mode of Friend Finder will be investigated to understand how to optimize system actions to present the dynamic content adaptation in trustworthy way. Finally, the second show case application, Arrow Navigator, will be used to explore trust issues in the context of accuracy of knowledge.

The guidelines derived from the experiments will be used to automate the system adaptation based on the incoming context.

4 Conclusion

Ubiquitous display environments require a high degree of flexibility due to the changing social context, the necessity to protect private data, and the need to adjust presentation of available inaccurate data. In order to support user trust in such environments, the system should be able to evaluate the consequences of its actions. By means of a decision-theoretic approach, we assess the impact of system actions on user trust in critical contexts. The resulting decisions inform the design of adaptive display systems that delivers an optimized trade-off between user trust and perceived comfort of use.

Acknowledgements. This research is partly sponsored by OC-Trust (FOR 1085) of the German research foundation (DFG).

References

1. Glass, A., McGuinness, D.L.: Wolverton. M.: Toward establishing trust in adaptive agents. In: Proceedings of the International Conference on Intelligent User Interfaces, IUI 2008, pp. 227–236. ACM Press, New York (2008)
2. Roecker, C., Hinske, S., Magerkurth, C.: Intelligent privacy support for large public displays. In: Proceedings of the International Conference on Human-Computer Interaction HCI International 2007, pp. 198–207. Springer, Heidelberg (2007)
3. Graham, C., Cheverst, K.: Guides, locals, chaperones, buddies and captains: managing trust through interaction paradigms. In: 3rd Workshop 'HCI on Mobile Guides' at the International Symposium on Human Computer Interaction with Mobile Devices and Services, pp. 227–236. ACM Press, New York (2004)
4. Cheverst, K., Byun, H.E., Fitton, D., Sas, C., Kray, C., Villar, N.: Exploring Issues of User Model Transparency and Proactive Behaviour in an Office Environment Control System. User Modeling and User-Adapted Interaction 15(3-4), 235–273 (2005)
5. Bellotti, V., Edwards, W.K.: Intelligibility and accountability: human considerations in context-aware systems. Human-Computer Interaction 16(2), 193–212 (2001)
6. Lim, B.Y., Dey, A.K.: Toolkit to Support Intelligibility in Context-Aware Applications. In: Proceedings of the International Conference on Ubiquitous Computing, UbiComp 2010, pp. 13–22. Springer, London (2010)
7. Langheinrich, M.: A Privacy Awareness System for Ubiquitous Computing Environments. In: Borriello, G., Holmquist, L.E. (eds.) UbiComp 2002. LNCS, vol. 2498, pp. 237–245. Springer, Heidelberg (2002)
8. Kurdyukova, E., André, E., Leichtenstern, K.: Trust-centered Design for Multi-Display Applications. In: Proceedings of the 8th International Conference on Advances in Mobile Computing & Multimedia, MoMM 2010 (2010)
9. Kurdyukova, E., André, E., Leichtenstern, K.: A Decision-Theoretic Approach to maintain Trust in Ubiquitous Display Environments. International Journal of Computing 9(3), 220–227 (2010)

Using Adaptive Empathic Responses to Improve Long-Term Interaction with Social Robots

Iolanda Leite

INESC-ID, Instituto Superior Técnico,
Taguspark, Porto Salvo, Portugal
iolanda.leite@ist.utl.pt

Abstract. The goal of this research is to investigate the effects of empathy and adaptive behaviour in long-term interaction between social robots and users. To address this issue, we propose an action selection mechanism that will allow a social robot to chose adaptive empathic responses, in the attempt to keep users engaged over several interactions.

Keywords: social robots, affective user modeling, empathy, adaptive feedback.

1   Introduction and Research Questions

For robots to become part of our lives, they should be able to communicate with people in similar ways people interact with each other [2]. This requires not only the ability to convey verbal and non-verbal behaviours, but to do so at the appropriate timing and in response to an action or expression perceived from the user. There are still many open challenges when developing robots and virtual agents for long-term social interaction, in particular the role that affect plays is still not clear. The ability to understand and respond appropriately to the affective states of others is commonly designated as empathy [6]. Empathic virtual agents have been widely studied in a variety of contexts, and the results suggest that the presence of empathic behaviours positively affects users' opinion of those agents [1]. Pedagogical agents that model and respond to user's affect have also been employed successfully in intelligent learning environments [11]. In the field of social robotics, the first empathy studies also are starting to appear [5]. However, these findings were obtained in studies where subjects interacted with these agents for a short period of time. Further research is needed to ensure that these results still apply in long-term interaction, as users' opinion is likely to change.

The goal of this research is to study the role of empathy in social robot companions. In particular, our aim is to investigate the effects of adaptive empathic behaviour in the relationship established between the robot and the user. Most of the existing pedagogical agents that model and respond to user's affect are based either in stereotypes (derived from cognitive or psychological theories) or on machine learning techniques that determine the "optimal" intervention for

Joseph A. Konstan et al. (Eds.): UMAP 2011, LNCS 6787, pp. 446–449, 2011.

each case [3]. This means that the agent displays the same behaviour whenever the user is experiencing an affective state, without knowing if such response is actually effective for that user, or if it is just making the user feel more frustrated. However, as suggested by Rich [10], "often individual users vary so much that a model of a canonical user is insufficient", especially if the user will spend a lot of time interacting with the system. As our goal is to build an artificial robot companion for long-term interaction, the robot should be capable of adapting its affective behaviour to the behaviour of a particular user. We aim to achieve this goal by addressing the following research questions: *What is the role of empathy and adaptive behaviour when developing social robots for long-term interaction? How the robot's empathic behaviour influences the relationship established between the user and the robot?* We defend the hypothesis that if the robot adapts its behaviour by selecting the most effective empathic responses for a particular user, users will be more willing to interact with the robot and, consequently, their relationship may improve.

2   Progress to Date

Our application scenario consists of a Philips' iCat robot that plays chess with children using an electronic chessboard. The iCat provides feedback on the moves that children play by conveying facial expressions determined by its affective state. A previous study showed that the affective behaviour expressed by the iCat increased children's perception of the game [7]. With the approach proposed in this paper, we aim to improve this scenario by endowing the robot with adaptive empathic capabilities. Most of the efforts so far have been dedicated to preliminary experiments that will serve as basis for the research challenges that we aim to address. To date, two studies in different directions have been completed.

The first experiment investigated the changes in children's perception of a social robot after several interactions. In this study [8], we analysed the same group of children playing an entire chess game with the iCat over five sessions (once a week). Children filled in a social presence questionnaire both in the first and last week of interaction. The results suggest that social presence decreased over time, especially in terms of perceived affective and behavioural interdependence (the extent to which users believe that the behaviour and affective state of the robot is influenced by their own behaviour and affective state). The outcomes of this experiment strengthen our hypothesis that the ability to understand and respond to user's affect is crucial for long-term interaction.

In the second experiment [9], we evaluated the influence of empathic behaviours on user's perception of a social robot. For this study, a slight variation of our application scenario was implemented, where the iCat observes and comments a chess match between two human players. The robot exhibits empathic behaviours towards one of the players and neutral comments to the other player, through facial expressions and verbal comments. The results of this study suggest that players towards whom the iCat displayed empathic behaviour perceived the robot as friendlier.

3   Proposed Solution

To address the questions presented above, we need to create a model of the user that contains: (1) a prediction of the current user's affective state and (2) a dynamic representation of the user's preferences in terms of empathic strategies employed by the robot. The first step, a multimodal system for predicting some of the user's affective states, is currently being developed in the context a research project[1]. The affective states that this system is able to predict in real time are user's *engagement* and user's *valence of feeling* (positive or negative). The focus of this proposal is on the second part, which deals with selecting the empathic responses that are most effective to keep the user in a positive affective state.

We intend to adapt the robot's empathic behaviour as follows. During the game, after every user's move, the robot updates its affective state and the user model component updates the user's affective state. Then, taking into account its affective state, the user's affective state and the previous user reactions to certain empathic behaviours, the robot selects an empathic response. A while after the robot's action, the affect detection system updates the user model about the new affective state of the user. This new affective state serves as feedback to update the user's preferences in terms of empathic responses. As an example, consider a situation where the user is experiencing a negative feeling for loosing an importance piece in the game and the iCat responds with an encouraging utterance. If the user's valence changes from negative to positive, then utterances containing encouraging behaviours will become part of the user's preferences in that particular situation. As the same users are expected to interact with the robot for several games, the preferences for a particular user are updated even over different interaction sessions. To dynamically learn patterns associated to a particular user, we are considering to use Reinforcement Learning, as it was successfully employed before to induce pedagogical strategies without requiring a large training corpus [3]. Several empathic and pro-social strategies existing in the literature are being considered for implementation in the robot's behaviour [4], for example: facial expressions (e.g., mimicking the user's affective state or suppressing strong positive emotions that might offend the user), empathic utterances to encourage and motivate the player, and game related strategies (for example, propose a new game or suggest a good move for the user to play).

4   Future Work

We are currently implementing the action selection mechanism that will allow the iCat to provide empathic feedback on the children's moves. Among the list of possible empathic strategies for a particular situation, at this stage the robot is randomly choosing one. We will perform a long-term experiment with this model to evaluate if the presence of empathic behaviour influences participants' perception of the robot after several interactions. After that, we intend to improve the user model by implementing the adaptive feedback mechanism described

---

[1] http://lirec.eu/

earlier, so that the robot is able to choose the most effective strategy for a particular user rather than a random one. With this new model, we plan to conduct another long-term experiment and compare the results obtained from the two experiments. Measures such as social presence and perceived friendship are being considered for this study.

Acknowledgements. This research was supported by EU 7th Framework Program (FP7/2007-2013) under grant agreement n° 215554 and a PhD scholarship (SFRHBD/41358/2007) granted by FCT.

References

1. Brave, S., Nass, C., Hutchinson, K.: Computers that care: investigating the effects of orientation of emotion exhibited by an embodied computer agent. International Journal of Human-Computer Studies 62(2), 161–178 (2005)
2. Breazeal, C.: Role of expressive behaviour for robots that learn from people. Phil. Trans. R. Soc. B: Biological Sciences 364(1535), 3527–3538 (2009)
3. Chi, M., VanLehn, K., Litman, D.J., Jordan, P.W.: Inducing effective pedagogical strategies using learning context features. In: De Bra, P., Kobsa, A., Chin, D. (eds.) UMAP 2010. LNCS, vol. 6075, pp. 147–158. Springer, Heidelberg (2010)
4. Cooper, B., Brna, P., Martins, A.: Effective affective in intelligent systems: Building on evidence of empathy in teaching and learning. In: Paiva, A.C.R. (ed.) IWAI 1999. LNCS, vol. 1814, pp. 21–34. Springer, Heidelberg (2000)
5. Cramer, H., Goddijn, J., Wielinga, B., Evers, V.: Effects of (in) accurate empathy and situational valence on attitudes towards robots. In: Proceedings of the 5th ACM/IEEE Conference on HRI, pp. 141–142. ACM, New York (2010)
6. Hoffman, M.L.: Empathy and moral development: Implications for caring and justice. Cambridge University Press, Cambridge (2001)
7. Leite, I., Martinho, C., Pereira, A., Paiva, A.: iCat: an affective game buddy based on anticipatory mechanisms. In: Proceedings of AAMAS 2008. IFAAMAS, pp. 1229–1232 (2008)
8. Leite, I., Martinho, C., Pereira, A., Paiva, A.: As Time goes by: Long-term evaluation of social presence in robotic companions. In: Proceedings of RO-MAN 2009, pp. 669–674. IEEE, Los Alamitos (2009)
9. Leite, I., Mascarenhas, S., Pereira, A., Martinho, C., Prada, R., Paiva, A.: "Why can't we be friends?" an empathic game companion for long-term interaction. In: Safonova, A. (ed.) IVA 2010. LNCS, vol. 6356, pp. 315–321. Springer, Heidelberg (2010)
10. Rich, E.: Users are individuals: individualizing user models. International Journal of Man-machine Studies 18(3), 199–214 (1983)
11. Woolf, B., Burleson, W., Arroyo, I., Dragon, T., Cooper, D., Picard, R.: Affect-aware tutors: recognising and responding to student affect. International Journal of Learning Technology 4(3), 129–164 (2009)

A User Modeling Approach to Support Knowledge Work in Socio-computational Systems

Karin Schoefegger

Knowledge Management Institute
Graz University of Technology, Inffeldgasse 21a, 8010 Graz Austria
k.schoefegger@tugraz.at

Abstract. The rise of socio-computational systems such as collaborative tagging systems, which rely heavily on user-generated content and social interactions, changed our way to learn and work. This work aims to explore the potentials of those systems for supporting knowledge work in organizational and scientific domains. Therefore, a user modeling approach will be developed which enables personalized services to shape the content towards individual information needs of novice, advanced and experienced knowledge workers. The novelty of this approach is a modeling strategy which combines user modeling characteristics from distinct research areas, the emergent properties of the socio-computational environment as well as non-invasive knowledge diagnosis methods based on the user's past interaction with the system.

Keywords: User modeling, emergent semantics, work-integrated learning, personalized services, collaborative tagging systems, knowledge work.

1   Introduction

Innovations in social and semantic technologies are bringing people and computers together in new powerful ways, enabling them to generate, aggregate and share information in social environments which demonstrates collective intelligence that was previously not achievable by neither people or computers alone. A prominent example of those socio-computational systems are social (semantic) tagging systems to collaboratively collect, share and structure and (re-)find resources like web pages or research papers. This new kind of systems does not only influence our way to learn and work but also give rise to new challenges: The individual knowledge workers, e.g. in the organizational or scientific domain face difficulties to handle the continuous growth, the complexity and trustworthiness of the user-generated content for identifying suitable and relevant information to satisfy personal information needs. Personalized search and recommendation services can shape the user-generated content towards individual information needs, based on their topics of interest and previous knowledge to provide personalized access to the content and through that, help to overcome the rising challenges.

Joseph A. Konstan et al. (Eds.): UMAP 2011, LNCS 6787, pp. 450–453, 2011.

2   User Modeling for Knowledge Work

The quality of personalized services to foster knowledge work through for example personalized search or recommendation services depends heavily on the system's knowledge about each individual user. Imagine for example a researcher who has a seemingly novel idea for a new research proposal outside her area of expertise and wants to find the most relevant publications about this topic. This person has different information needs compared to a researcher familiar with the area who simply wants to stay up to date about the topic.

The informal and self-directed nature of knowledge work creates special requirements for personalized services [7] such as personalized search or recommendations of relevant information sources: Firstly, it needs a representation of the users (a user model) not only in terms of their topics of interests but also based on corresponding skills or knowledge as one of the main aspects for providing personalization in work-integrated learning; Secondly, this should happen in a non-invasive way as explicit testing is not an option in an informal and self-directed setting. Traditional approaches have been developed in two main areas: Web personalization (e.g. personalized search [8]) happens on emergent knowledge domains and often implicit. Personalization in the context of e-learning incorporates knowledge diagnosis but often operates on static knowledge domains [1]. A non-invasive user modeling approach for static knowledge domains has been presented in [7], which is based on the idea of 'knowledge indicating' events (KIE) which indicate that a user has knowledge about a certain topic or a certain skill. E.g. 'being asked for help about a certain topic' versus 'to ask for help about a certain topic' are contrary actions performed by persons supposed to be knowledgeable versus being a novice in a specific topic. Recently, some approaches for expertise ranking have been developed in collaborative tagging systems for spam detection and knowledge exploration but do not include individual knowledge levels ([2], [3]). Thus, the existing approaches and methods are not directly applicable to build personalized, intelligent services in socio-computational systems used by knowledge workers in their everyday work practices.

This work will target the following two main research questions to develop an appropriate user modeling approach for knowledge work in organizational and scientific domains:

- *Given an emergent semantic structure as an underlying domain model, e.g. in social tagging systems, and the historical interaction data of a user, how can we identify the topics a user is dealing with or interested in to build and maintain the corresponding user model?*
- *Given the historical interaction data (event history) of a user (community), how can we infer the knowledge levels for different topics the individual knowledge worker is dealing with or interested in to enable non-invasive knowledge diagnosis?*

3   Proposed Approach and Preliminary Results

To construct a user model based on emergent semantics, we need to infer the current topics a user is interested in. To avoid commonly known problems tags exhibit (e.g. hypernyms or synonyms [4]), we will apply a tag clustering method (e.g. [10]) to derive tag clusters representing a topic/concept in the emergent domain ontology. We will also utilize more formal domain knowledge (e.g. through DBPedia or social semantic bookmarking) to support tag clustering. Events performed on each of the terms within a cluster will be considered as being performed on the same topic. Finally, a user event within the system is modeled as $\langle u, r, e, e_t, dt \rangle$, based on five different entities: a user u, a resource r, an event type e, an event topic e_t and a timestamp. This allows us to generate a network-theoretic model of user events, usable for statistical and network-theoretic analysis and data mining.

To address the second research question, we will evaluate and apply theoretical approaches of human learning processes to model the knowledge levels of single users for different topics to adequately realize a mapping between the 'real' knowledge of the users and knowledge levels as implemented in the system. This mapping will be based on past user interactions with the system, e.g. the generality of search queries entered or tag annotations made. Information needs but also the behavior of individuals differ significantly for novices and experts when using a system or performing a tasks, based on their different background knowledge, thus an interest based user model approach alone is not sufficient. For example, [5] observed different exploratory search behaviors between novices and experts, in collaborative tagging systems and in traditional search engines.

As a first step we conducted a small-scale study with students using a social semantic bookmarking system for collecting and sharing information sources [9]. The research questions was whether they would start performing more sophisticated activities (KIE) throughout their learning trajectory from novices to advanced or even experts within a limited domain. Results did not show a clear correspondance between the 'real' learning process of the users/students and individual activities within the system. This indicate that besides the dimension of the kind of activities, external information is needed in combination with the KIE approach. For further studies, semantics as an additional dimension will be taken into consideration, this includes the analysis of the kind and granularity of tags (as in [6]) or search keywords used (as in [5]).

4   Discussion and Future Plans

The first empirical results are limited to a small-scale study, thus in future, we will expand our analysis to a larger amount of data from organizational (developed at our institution) as well as social academic reference management systems (e.g. Mendeley.com), both based on social and semantic web technologies. Events in the log data from both systems range from user searches or tagging activities to more general interaction patterns such as opening documents or adding a document to a collection of documents.

Analyzing the corresponding event patterns from log data will not only allow us to identify topics of interests and corresponding knowledge levels but also to detect topic drifts over time for improving personalized services such as search rankings based on the user's knowledge or recommendation of knowledgeable people or relevant information sources.

Acknowledgments. This work has been partially funded by the European Commission as part of the FP7 Marie Curie IAPP project TEAM (grant no. 251514) and as part of the MATURE IP (grant no. 216346) within the 7th Framework Programme of IST.

References

1. Brusilovsky, P., Sosnovsky, S., Yudelson, M.: Adaptive Hypermedia Services for E-Learning. In: Workshop on Applying Adaptive Hypermedia Techniques to Service Oriented Environments at the Third International Conference on Adaptive Hypermedia and Adaptive Web Based Systems, pp. 470–479 (2004)
2. Budura, A., Bourges-Waldegg, D., Riordan, J.: Deriving Expertise Profiles from Tags. In: CSE 2009: Proceedings of the 2009 International Conference on Computational Science and Engineering, pp. 34–41. IEEE Computer Society, Washington, DC (2009)
3. Fu, W.-T., Dong, W.: Facilitating Knowledge Exploration in Folksonomies: Expertise Ranking by Link and Semantic Structures. IEEE, Los Alamitos (2010)
4. Golder, S.A., Huberman, B.A.: The Structure of Collaborative Tagging Systems. Journal of Information Science (2006)
5. Kang, R., Fu, W.-T., Kannampallil, T.G.: Exploiting knowledge-in-the-head and knowledge-in-the-social-web: effects of domain expertise on exploratory search in individual and social search environments. In: Mynatt, E.D., Schoner, D., Fitzpatrick, G., Hudson, S.E., Edwards, K., Rodden, T. (eds.) CHI, pp. 393–402. ACM, New York (2010)
6. Ley, T., Seitlinger, P.: A Cognitive Perspective on Emergent Semantics in Collaborative Tagging: The Basic Level Effect. In: Proceedings of International Workshop on Adaptation in Social and Semantic Web (SAS-WEB 2010), pp. 1–10 (2010)
7. Lindstaedt, S.N., Beham, G., Kump, B., Ley, T.: Getting to Know Your User – Unobtrusive User Model Maintenance within Work-Integrated Learning Environments. In: Cress, U., Dimitrova, V., Specht, M. (eds.) EC-TEL 2009. LNCS, vol. 5794, pp. 73–87. Springer, Heidelberg (2009)
8. Micarelli, A., Gasparetti, F., Sciarrone, F., Gauch, S.: Personalized Search on the World Wide Web. In: Brusilovsky, P., Kobsa, A., Nejdl, W. (eds.) Adaptive Web 2007. LNCS, vol. 4321, pp. 195–230. Springer, Heidelberg (2007)
9. Schoefegger, K., Seitlinger, P., Ley, T.: Towards a user model for personalized recommendations in work-integrated learning: A report on an experimental study with a collaborative tagging system. In: Proceedings of the 1st Workshop on Recommender Systems for Technology Enhanced Learning (RecSysTEL 2010), vol. 1, pp. 2829–2838. Procedia Computer Science (2010)
10. Tomuro, N., Shepitsen, A.: Personalized Search in Folksonomies with Ontological User Profiles. In: Proceedings of the International Joint Conference Intelligent Information Systems, pp. 1–14 (2009)

Modeling Individuals with Learning Disabilities to Personalize a Pictogram-Based Instant Messaging Service

Pere Tuset-Peiró

Secció de Projectes de Transferència, TecnoCampus Mataró-Maresme
Av. Ernest Lluch, 32. 08302 Mataró - Spain
ptuset@tecnocampus.cat

Abstract. Individuals with learning disabilities are excluded from the information and knowledge society because information present in such media, as well as software that enables access to it, does not meet their communication and accessibility requirements. To improve this situation, we have developed and evaluated an Instant Messaging (IM) service and client based on a pictographic communication system, and with a user interface designed taking into account their accessibility requirements. But the evaluation with individuals with learning disabilities has pointed out the need to take into account the great communications and computer skills diversity, even in groups with similar disability levels. Therefore, in this paper we present our plans to model the communication and accessibility requirements of individuals with learning disabilities in order to develop a mechanism to automatically personalize the IM client user interface and adapt it to their needs.

Keywords: Learning disabilities, Pictographic Communication System, Instant Messaging services, User modeling, Interface personalization.

1 Introduction

Individuals with learning disabilities are excluded from the information and knowledge society as many of its services, e.g. the web or electronic mail, do not meet their user requirements [1]. On the one hand, access to information and communications in the Internet are based on text, which is not suitable considering the language limitations posed by their condition. On the other hand, individuals with learning disabilities have trouble understanding abstract concepts and making generalization between different contexts, which limits the user interface suitability of mainstream software, e.g. web browsers. This situation limits autonomy and increases isolation, which causes their social and digital exclusion.

One alternative to overcome this exclusion situation is to adapt or develop new software to access Internet services that takes these requirements into account. For instance, user interfaces that use complex metaphors should be avoided as they may cause cognitive overload to the user. But adapting the software user interface is not enough, especially considering the communication requirements of individuals with learning disabilities. Therefore, Augmentative and Alternative Communication (AAC) [2], such as pictographic communication systems, need to be introduced in the

Joseph A. Konstan et al. (Eds.): UMAP 2011, LNCS 6787, pp. 454–457, 2011.
© Springer-Verlag Berlin Heidelberg 2011

software as a replacement for written language. Up to today, different proposals have been made in this direction. For instance, the World Wide Augmentative and Alternative Communication (WWAAC) project [3] developed a pictogram-based web browser for individuals with learning disabilities, whereas the Mejla Pictogram [4] is a pictogram-based electronic mail client for individuals with learning disabilities.

But there are some information society services that have not yet been adapted or created with support for individuals with learning disabilities. One of these cases are Instant Messaging (IM) services [5], which are designed to enable users to communicate with their relatives and acquaintances by means of exchanging near real-time presence information and text-based messages through the Internet. In this direction, we have developed an IM service [6] based on a pictographic communication system and an IM client that takes into account the user interface accessibility requirements of individuals with learning disabilities. Nevertheless, considering the great diversity of individuals with such disabilities, there is a need for personalization of the user interface to provide a valid alternative for a larger portion of the population [7]. But designing a user interface for individuals with learning disabilities is a difficult task, mainly due to the lack of suitable design guidelines.

2   Adapting an Instant Messaging Service to Individuals with Learning Disabilities

To develop the pictogram-based IM service and client and evaluate how individuals with learning disabilities use it to communicate we have used a User Centered Design (UCD) methodology based on three well-known and widely-used software development techniques: ethnography, semi-structured interviews and user sessions.

First of all we have used ethnography to understand the context in which the pictogram-based IM service and client will be used. For that purpose we have collaborated with Fundació El Maresme, a non-profit organization that promotes the social integration of individuals with learning disabilities. Specifically, two groups of individuals with learning disabilities, as well as a pedagogue and two social educators, have participated throughout the development and evaluation process. In second place, considering the communication limitations of individuals with learning disabilities [8], we have conducted semi-structured interviews with the pedagogues and social educators. From applying these first two techniques we have obtained the requirements of individuals with learning disabilities regarding communication and user interface design. On the one hand, we have replaced written communication with a pictographic communication system to suit their communication requirements. On the other hand, we have properly adapted the user interface of the IM client to suit their accessibility requirements. Last but not least, we have organized fortnightly one-hour long sessions with two groups of users, as well as the pedagogues and social educators, to check that the IM service and client are compliant with their requirements. These sessions have enabled us to become directly involved with individuals with learning disabilities and observe how they interact with the IM client user interface to communicate using pictograms.

The results of our research confirm that all the users that have participated in evaluating the IM service have been able to communicate using pictograms.

Nevertheless, our observations also show that, even in groups of individuals that have a similar level of learning disabilities, there is a huge diversity in pictographic system communication skills and their ability to interact with the user interface of the IM client. Thus, there is a need for personalization and adaptation of the IM client user interface to better suit their individual accessibility requirements.

3   Modeling Individuals with Learning Disabilities to Personalize the Instant Messaging Client User Interface

Considering the huge diversity of individuals with learning disabilities previously described, it seems necessary to develop mechanisms that enable personalizing the IM client user interface. The ultimate goal of this approach is to better adapt the IM client to the accessibility requirements of individuals with learning disabilities.

The first step towards personalizing the IM client user interface is to model the requirements of different individuals with learning disabilities. For instance, during the evaluation we have observed that there are individuals with learning disabilities that are able to read textual messages, whereas others are unable. With this approach, different generic profiles that contain the basic requirements of the user interface can be defined. As an example, a user profile may determine that the user requires textual representation of the different user interface elements, i.e. the pictograms, in order to ease the communication and promote his/her learning process.

Once the generic user profiles have been defined, a syntax to describe the user interface requirements of such profiles needs to be created. The syntax to describe user profiles has to fulfill two basic requirements. On the one hand, it shall be able to describe all the elements of the user interface that may require personalization and which types of personalization allow. On the other hand, the syntax must enable a quick processing by software, as it will have to be processed each time the IM client is started. In order to define the syntax, we plan to use eXtensible Markup Language (XML), which offers both language flexibility and ease for machine interpretation.

Finally, after the generic user profiles and the syntax to describe user interface requirements have been defined, individuals need to be classified into the generic user profiles and a module capable of adapting the IM client user interface according to the requirements specified in the profile needs to be developed.

4   Conclusions and Planned Work

Up to today, the main contribution of our work has been the design and evaluation of an IM service and client that are adapted to individuals with learning disabilities. On the one hand, the IM service replaces written communications with a pictographic communications system. On the other hand, the user interface of the IM client takes into account the accessibility requirements of the target collective. These requirements have been obtained through applying a UCD methodology based on ethnography, semi-structured interviews and user sessions. To our knowledge, this is the first IM service and client with such characteristics and the evaluation has demonstrated that it enables individuals with learning disabilities to communicate with their relatives and acquaintances over the Internet.

Nevertheless, the evaluation process has also revealed that there is work that remains to be done in order to better suit the requirements of individuals with learning disabilities and understand how they communicate using pictograms. On the one hand, the diversity in communication skills, even in groups with similar learning disability levels, have raised a question regarding the need to provide proper adaptation mechanisms to personalize the user interface of the IM client. In this direction, we are working towards defining generic user profiles and a syntax to describe user interfaces that will be used to automatically personalize the IM client user interface according to their requirements. On the other hand, the interactivity aspects related to pictogram communications noticed during the evaluation sessions have raised the necessity to further investigate how individuals with learning disabilities communicate using pictograms. In this sense, we are working to implement a logging system that enables us to capture information about how users interact with the IM client user interface to communicate in a real world environment.

Finally, from the experience obtained through developing and evaluating an IM service and client that suits their communication and accessibility requirements, we plan to create guidelines to help practitioners develop software to make other Internet services accessible for individuals with cognitive disabilities. Ultimately, these guidelines will contribute to approach information and communication technologies to individuals with learning disabilities, thus reducing the impact of the digital divide.

References

1. Glinert, E., York, B.: Computers and People with Disabilities. ACM Transactions on Accessible Computing 1(2), 1–7 (2008)
2. Glennen, S., DeCoste, D.: Handbook of Augmentative and Alternative Communication. Singular Publishing Group, San Diego (1998)
3. Poulson, D., Nicolle, C.: Making the Internet accessible for people with cognitive and communication impairments. Universal Access Information Society 3(1), 48–56 (2004)
4. Zarin, R.: Mejla Pictogram 2.0: e-mail made easy. Technical report. Ümea Institute of Design and Swedish Institute for Special Education Needs (January 2009)
5. Jennings, R., Nahum, E., Olshefski, D., Saha, D., Shae, Z., Waters, C.: A Study of Internet Instant Messaging and Chat Protocols. IEEE Network, 16–21 (July/August 2006)
6. Tuset, P., Barberán, P., Janer, L., Delgado, S., Buscà, E., Vilà, N.: Messenger Visual: A pictogram-based IM service to improve communications among disabled people. In: NordiCHI 2010: 6th Nordic Conference on Human-Computer Interaction, pp. 797–800 (October 2010)
7. Fischer, G.: User Modeling in Human–Computer Interaction. User Modeling and User-Adapted Interaction 11(1-2), 65–86 (2001)
8. Lepistö, A., Ovaska, S.: Usability evaluation involving participants with cognitive disabilities. In: NordiCHI 2004: 3rd Nordic Conference on Human-Computer Interaction, pp. 305–308 (October 2004)
9. Chin, D.N.: Empirical Evaluation of User Models and User-Adapted Systems. User Modeling and User-Adapted Interaction 11, 181–194 (2001)

FamCHAI:
An Adaptive Calendar Dialogue System

Ramin Yaghoubzadeh

Sociable Agents Group, CITEC, Bielefeld University
PO box 10 01 31, 33501 Bielefeld, Germany
ryaghoub@techfak.uni-bielefeld.de

Abstract. The dissertation project *FamCHAI* aims at creating a 'calendar companion' system in the form of a bidirectionally natural-language interactive scene with a virtual agent, and exploring the effects of adaptation of the agent to specific users both in terms of the support given (i.e. giving options the user likes) and in communication (i.e. presentation in a form the user prefers, and learning their idiosyncrasies for better understanding). Harnessing these models, interactions will grow steadily more effective, comfortable and natural for users.

Keywords: Scheduling, Dialogue Models, Adaptivity in Conversation.

1 Introduction

Repeated conversation and cooperation change the interpersonal relationship in human dyads in characteristic ways. Increased familiarity with the needs of others facilitates effective accommodation. Verbal communication tends to display better flow of conversational turns, less social "embellishment" of possibly unpleasant topics, a tendency towards simpler grammatical structures, and discussion of more topics while interweaving personal information (self-disclosures). Unfamiliar dyads tend to obscure personal intentions and employ mitigation using *distance, deference* or *camaraderie* stratagems [7].

Lee [4], analyzing the Map Task Corpus, characterized communicative differences between strangers vs. friends: unfamiliar dyads tended to use more query/response pairs, more explicit feedback, and more explicit signals for readiness. Cassell et al. [2] experimentally identified improved coordination of dialogue turns and reduced superficial positivity in dyads with repeated interaction.

Regarding the aspect of cooperative task-solving, repeated interaction has the property of increasing overall performance (e.g. time for correct solution). This effect can often be attributed to a familiarization of the participants with the task, yet it has been shown [3] that this effect is not wholly dependent on the task itself: fast improvement is also observable when the tasks across sessions are completely unrelated. Therefore, the improvement must be also explained by a familiarization effect within the human dyad, by building up a model of the communicative behavior of the other, and a notion of their general knowledge and capabilities.

Joseph A. Konstan et al. (Eds.): UMAP 2011, LNCS 6787, pp. 458–461, 2011.

2   Scheduling Dialogue Scenario

Consider the relationship between secretary (S) and his or her 'client' (hence-forth termed the 'user' (U), from an artificial-agent-centered perspective). When talking about U's schedule, both parties have some common ground: knowledge about the current schedule, and at least some contextual knowledge, such as inherent time constraints and a-priori importance of events. When the two are familiar with each other, they will also exhibit some of the conversational features detailed above. Moreover, S has a better knowledge about the nature of U's personal appointments: some are regular, some have clearly differing priorities, some types are liked and others disliked. The secretary might know some of this by simply having observed the same schedule operations repeatedly, and some by experiencing the user's state while talking (possibly during small-talk). Both parties can have intentions or knowledge about modifications to the schedule, which prior to the interaction need not be in a synchronized state. Miscommunication and erroneous recording of entries can moreover lead to later inconsistencies; their resolution also forms part of discussions about the schedule.

We have currently successfully finished recordings for an explorative study aimed at obtaining a corpus of human dyads solving the same calendar issues in free dialogue. The subjects, one playing the role of secretary, and the other the user, talked about the user's fictive two-week schedule. Each role had its own set of desired modifications or updated states of schedule items (adding, canceling, moving, etc.), designed to include various types of purpose-built collisions, and events with well-known priority differences. Sixteen dyads participated, half had no prior acquaintace, and the other half were well-acquainted. Five of the zero-acquaintance dyads agreed to participate a second time with a new calendar, whereby rapid effects on the interpersonal relationship with their effect on the next dialogue can be explored. The study yielded five hours of dialogue about scheduling, containing different conflict resolutions, various ways of communicating the same modifications, and statements of priority and valence towards schedule items. Since the recording phase has only recently ended, in-depth analysis of the data is still pending, and no quantifying statement is made here.

The next step will be the annotation of the corpus, using the technique described by DeVault and colleagues [1], on a word-by-word and dialogue-act basis. The ontology of intentions and dialogue acts contains prototypes relevant to the exchange of facts, to the internal states of the parties, and to the appraisal of individual items. The annotation will also indicate differences in *valence* (e.g. of "ok, great!" vs. "well, ok..."), *priority* and application of mitigating stratagems.

3   Calendar Companion Dialogue System

After the development of the dialogue infrastructure IPAACA [6], development for FamCHAI continues on a dialogue system with an emotionally expressive artificial agent as the secretary (Fig. 1), enabling users to negotiate schedules using natural language, as an interesting and controllable domain to explore familiarity

Fig. 1. ECA *Billie* as a calendar companion

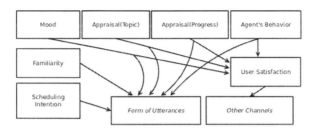

Fig. 2. Causal model for the form of generated utterances

effects on conversation. The repertoire obtained from the first study will be used as an uncertain intention–behavior mapping for the agent. The model will enable both clarifying paraphrase and alignment to the user. Features identified as characteristic for unfamiliar or familiar dyads can be used to estimate observed utterances, and also used in production, corresponding to the development of familiarity inside the dyad.

Factors influencing dialogue. Figure 2 shows a tentative causal model influencing the selection and embellishment of utterances made by the user. Based on the model, there is an opportunity of inversely determining likely states for the variables from observations using Bayes' theorem. The *mood*, having an extended baseline effect, can be estimated using the mean of observed affective states over time. *Progress appraisal*, indicative of perceived flow in an effective conversation, could be estimated using the number of turns per topic. *Topic appraisal* can be estimated with prior knowledge about the user's past appraisal of similar situations, or utterances expressing valence. *Behavior of the Agent* is the only remaining factor. When the others can be ruled out as an explanation, the agent can assume that its way of saying things has caused any observed changes. *User Satisfaction* can be estimated independently – lower-level acoustical features (pitch, speed) and facial expressions can be indicative of the user's affective state – a focus of recent work, and deployable in our lab. When uncertain, the agent could ask explicitly to pinpoint the source of the change.

Building and applying knowledge. Preference learning for schedules is the focus of recent work (e.g. [5]), merging instances of appointments into hypothesized preferences – their extraction from conversational *episodes* is a required step for FamCHAI as well. The episodes are enriched with affective information gathered from the various channels, which facilitates estimation of the expected user state when similar situations arise. Using such uncertain preferences, the agent can take the initiative and make sensible suggestions. Uncertainty about the validity of a preference leads to more effort verbalizing the rationale for its use, repeatedly accepted preferences decrease in the need for justification. Once the agent gains experience with the way a user expresses themselves, it can use the resulting personalized communicative model. With a notion about the user's expected appraisal of situations, the agent could observe the effects of its 'way of saying things' on the user's satisfaction, and attribute any deterioration to its selected behavior, allowing to explore the repertoire for more familiar ways to express an intention, as long as the user is not being imposed upon.

The vision for FamCHAI is a calendar companion agent which can foster a working relationship with a human user, make suitable suggestions, detailing its rationale when required, and detect the user's likes or dislikes in dialogue. The system would actively try to use language deemed more familiar by the user, reducing distance while being able to detect when it went too far.

Acknowledgements. This research is supported by the Deutsche Forschungs-gemeinschaft (DFG) in the Center of Excellence in Cognitive Interaction Technology (CITEC).

References

1. DeVault, D., David Traum, D., Artstein, R.: Making grammar-based generation easier to deploy in dialogue systems. In: 9th SIGdial Workshop on Discourse and Dialogue (SIGdial 2008), Ohio (2008)
2. Cassell, J., Gill, A.J., Tepper, P.A.: Coordination in conversation and rapport. In: Proceedings of the ACL Workshop on Embodied Natural Language, Prague, CZ, pp. 40–50 (2007)
3. Harrison, D.A., Mohammed, S., McGrath, J.E., Florey, A.T., Vanderstoep, S.: Time matters in team task performance: Effects of member familiarity, entrainment, and task discontinuity on speed and quality. Personnel Psychology 56, 633–669 (2003)
4. Lee, A.: The effect of familiarity on knowledge synchronisation. In: AISB 2005 Proceedings of the Joint Symposium on Virtual Social Agents, Hatfield, UK, pp. 185–190 (2005)
5. Oh, J., Smith, S.F.: Learning user preferences in distributed calendar scheduling. In: Burke, E.K., Trick, M.A. (eds.) PATAT 2004. LNCS, vol. 3616, pp. 3–16. Springer, Heidelberg (2005)
6. Schlangen, D., Baumann, T., Buschmeier, H., Buß, O., Kopp, S., Skantze, G., Yaghoubzadeh, R.: Middleware for incremental processing in conversational agents. In: Short Paper Proceedings of the SIGdial 2010 Conference, Tokyo (2010)
7. Tannen, D.: Conversational style: Analyzing talk among friends. Ablex, Norwood (1984)

Author Index